Manua

Of

Forensic Odontology

A Publication of

ASFO

American Society of Forensic Odontology

Edited by

Edward E. Herschaft
Marden E. Alder
David K. Ord
Raymond D. Rawson
E. Steven Smith

Fourth Edition

First Edition edited by Seigel and Sperber, 1980
Forensic Odontology Workbook

Second Edition edited by Averill, 1991
Manual of Forensic Odontology

Third Edition edited by Bowers and Bell, 1995
Manual of Forensic Odontology
ISBN 0-9650223-5-8.
ISBN 978-0-9650223-5-4

Third Revised Edition edited by Bowers and Bell, 1997
Manual of Forensic Odontology
ISBN 0-9650223-4-X.
ISBN 978-0-9650223-4-7

Fourth Edition edited by Herschaft, Alder, Ord, Rawson, Smith, 2006
Manual of Forensic Odontology
ISBN 0-9650223-6-6
ISBN 978-0-9650223-6-1

Library of Congress Control Number:

Authors can be reached for assistance or information by contacting ASFO Website:
http://www.asfo.org

CONTRIBUTORS

Marden E. Alder, DDS, MS, DABFO
Susan G.S. Anderson, DMD
Douglas M. Arendt, DDS, MS, v
David C. Averill, DDS, DABFO
Robert E. Barsley, DDS, JD, DABFO
Gary L. Bell, DDS, DABFO
Gary M. Berman, DDS, DABFO
Mark L. Bernstein, DDS, DABFO
Hugh E. Berryman, Ph.D.
C. Michael Bowers, DDS, JD, DABFO
Ashley Bradford, BA, MAR
Mary A. Bush, DDS
Peter J. Bush, BS.
Bryan Chrz, DDS, DABFO
J. Curtis Dailey, DDS, DABFO
Robert A. Danforth, DDS
Sheila M. Dashkow, DDS
Thomas J. David, DDS, DABFO
Stacey Davis, FBI/CJIS Management Analyst
Richard L. Dickens, DDS, PhD
Joseph A. Dizinno, DDS
Robert B. J. Dorion, DDS, DABFO
Scott R. Firestone, DDS
Adam J. Freeman, DDS
Tadao Furue, BA *
Ingrid Gill, JD
Gregory S. Golden, DDS, DABFO
Arthur D. Goldman, DDS, DABFO *
Bernard L. Harmeling, DMD, DABFO *
Edward F. Harris, PhD
Arnold Hermanson, DDS
Edward E. Herschaft, DDS, MA, DABFO
Jeremy A. Herschaft, JD, LLM
Mitchell M. Holland, PhD
L. Thomas Johnson, DDS, DABFO
Gene A. Jones, DDS, MSD
Jane A. Kaminski, DDS
Isaac Kaplan, DDS
John P. Kenney, DDS, MS, DABFO
Thomas C. Krauss, DDS, Diplomate Emeritus ABFO *
Cathy A. Law, DDS, DABFO
Elisabeth Latner, Constable (Hamilton, Ontario)
Philip J. Levine, DDS, MA, MS, MSM, DABFO
William R. Maples, PhD, DABFA *
Curtis A. Mertz, DDS, DABFO *
John D. McDowell, DDS, MS, DABFO
James B. McGivney, DMD, DABFO
Raymond G. Miller, DDS
Harry H. Mincer, DDS, MS, PhD, DABFO
Gene L. Mrava, BSME, MS

PAST PRESIDENTS
AMERICAN SOCIETY OF FORENSIC ODONTOLOGY

2006 - 2007 Douglas M. Arendt, DDS, MS, DABFO
2005 - 2006 David W. Johnson, DDS, DABFO
2004 - 2005 J. Curtis Dailey, DDS, DABFO
2003 - 2004 Gary M. Berman, DDS, DABFO
2002 - 2003 Marden E. Alder, DDS, MS, DABFO
2001 - 2002 Jeffrey R. Burkes, DDS, DABFO
2000 - 2001 Philip J. Levine, DDS, DABFO
1999 - 2000 David Sweet, DMD, PhD, DABFO
1998 - 1999 Richard H. Fixott, DDS, DABFO
1997 - 1998 John D. McDowell, DDS, MS, ABFO
1996 - 1997 William M. Morlang, DDS, ABFO
1995 - 1996 David C. Averill, DDS, DABFO
1994 - 1995 Robert E. Barsley, DDS, JD, DABFO
1993 - 1994 Peter F. Hampl, DDS, DABFO
1992 - 1993 E. Steven Smith, DDS **
1991 - **1992** George Burgman, DDS **
1990 - 1991 Frank A. Morgan, DDS, DABFO
1989 - 1990 Edward E. Herschaft, DDS, MA, DABFO
1988 - 1989 Wilbur B. Richie, DDS, DABFO **
1987 - 1988 James A. Cottone, DDS, MS, DABFO
1986 - 1987 Haskell Askin, DDS, DABFO
1985 - 1986 Norman D. Sperber, DDS, DABFO
1984 - 1985 Thomas C. Krauss, DDS, Diplomate Emeritus ABFO **
1983 - 1984 Gerald M. Reynolds, DDS, DABFO
1980 - 1983 Edwin E. Andrews, DMD, MEd, DABFO
1979 - 1980 George Morgan, DDS
1978 - 1979 Paul G. Stimson, DDS, MS, DABFO
1977 - 1978 Edward V. Comulada, DDS, DABFO **
1976 - 1977 Curtis A. Mertz, DDS, DABFO **
1974 - 1976 Lester L. Luntz, DDS, DABFO **
1971 - 1974 Robert Boyers, DDS, LTC, DC **

*** Deceased*

FORWARD

It is an honor to serve as president of the American Society of Forensic Odontology and as the individual invited to write the forward for the 4th edition of the *ASFO Manual of Forensic Odontology*. Numerous superb individuals have served the organization in a variety of capacities including president, officers, members of the board of governors and project leaders. All would be equally deserving of the opportunity to write the foreword. However, as fate would have it, it is my turn to further serve the *team* by writing this introduction.

This task is especially personal for me since the first meeting of the ASFO took place at the Armed Forces Institute of Pathology where I spent part of my residency and my final tour while on active duty with the United States Navy. As I reflect on my own career I am extremely thankful that I had the opportunity to professionally interact with many of the founding fathers (see history of ASFO) as a fledgling in forensics. I strongly encourage the reader to thank those founding members still with us for their trailblazing, and, in your own way honor those past with a moment of silent prayer. Their sacrifice and forward thinking set the framework on which additional forensic professionals have contributed to the community as well. So, as you learn and study the Manual, think about what you might do to further strengthen the profession, the organization and the science.

The ASFO is approaching its 37th anniversary and this text exemplifies the strength and maturity of the organization. We can be very proud of the great strides in membership growth, organizational competency, stellar on-line capabilities, quarterly newsletter publication, superb annual continuing education programs and now the 4th edition of the *ASFO Manual of Forensic Odontology*. Since the inception of this ASFO sponsored forensic resource in 1980, it has matured from a workbook to an evidence based scientific publication. The goal of the 4th edition of the Manual is to provide a ready to use, up-to-date reference source for both the novice and experienced forensic scientist.

September 11th was a tragic moment in our country's history. It will be remembered forever! Its aftermath, however, has helped us shape many new forensic protocols. These new paradigms are reflected in this text as well as in global mass fatality organization protocols. They are exemplified by new approaches in technology recently seen in deployable disaster response teams i.e., DMORT, local teams and by the Department of Defense (DoD) 21st century, state of the art, mortuary complex at Dover (Delaware) Air Force Base.

As president of the ASFO I most heartily congratulate and thank the editor in chief, editors and chapter authors for a job well done, *Bravo Zulu*.

Douglas M. Arendt, DDS, MS, DABFO
President – ASFO (2006-2007)

PREFACE

Forensic odontology can be considered the study of oral and paraoral structures and devices and their relationship to questions of law. Thus, this discipline represents the practice of dentistry in a way that would be helpful in the legal setting. The complexity of criminal and civil cases within the judicial system that require forensic expertise demands that when dental evidence is a component of the forensic data, it be collected, analyzed and presented in a scientific manner by trained forensic odontologists.

There are well established procedures related to the practice of forensic dentistry. However, there should always be a healthy respect and understanding that this is a developing science. As the twenty-first century began, dental science experienced rapidly changing methods of practice with innovations in computer technology, development of new dental materials and concepts related to record management, retrieval and storage. As part of this dynamic change, forensic dentistry is also evolving into a more sophisticated and complex field.

It is the purpose of the American Society of Forensic Odontology to promote the development and competence of dentists involved in this specialized area of dentistry. The 4th edition of the *ASFO Manual of Forensic Odontology* is a resource sponsored by the Society in this endeavor. It is important to realize that the ideas and techniques contained within this document are the opinions of the individual authors. Guidelines, standards, or policies which have been adopted by certain forensic organizations are specifically delineated.

The discipline of forensic odontology has continued to evolve since the publication of the 3rd edition of the *ASFO Manual of Forensic Odontology*. In the current publication, the editors have endeavored to present the latest technological and evidence based forensic methodology that is supported by scientific practice. In this regard, material concerning the following topics have been updated or added:

- Health Insurance Portability and Accessibility Act (HIPAA) regulations affecting forensic dental practice and procedures

- Updated ABFO Guidelines

- Digital radiographic and photographic information

- Computer assisted record management

- Multiple fatality incident preparedness and DMORT in a post 9/11, tsunami and Hurricane Katrina world.

Please consider this manual as an overview of the field of forensic dentistry. Dentists active in casework, research and education in the discipline have contributed significantly to the scientific literature. These efforts have developed a body of *evidence based knowledge* concerning forensic dental history, individual and multiple fatality identification, bite mark analysis, human abuse recognition, dental litigation, DNA analysis, photographic and radiographic techniques, management of dental records and forensic dental involvement within local, state and federal mass disaster forensic teams.

This material can only be partially presented in the 4th edition of the *ASFO Manual of Forensic Odontology*. This text is designed to be a basic workbook and procedural guide to the numerous tasks performed in the execution of forensic dental casework. Additionally, it is a reference guide to forensic resources available to both the practitioner new to the field and the experienced forensic dentist.

Serious students of the subject should use this book to grasp the challenges of the varied and changing forensic science of forensic odontology and be enticed by this effort to pursue further knowledge of the discipline. To assist the reader in understanding the outcomes desired by reading respective sections of the text, we have added *outcome assessments* (learning objectives) for each chapter. These appear at the end of each chapter and reflect the didactic, psychomotor and affective skills required to perform the tasks demanded of a forensic dentist. Additionally, a color atlas of typical examples of forensic dental evidence and case-based material is included as a resource.

Finally, a caveat is given to all who read this text and practice forensic dentistry. The conclusions and opinions of every practitioner are critical to the overall fairness and justice that affects the lives of real people. Following the Hippocratic Oath, the health care practitioner promises to do no harm to those who seek help and the forensic practitioner takes the added burden that their opinions will be accurate and correct or others will surely be harmed. In the forensic odontologist's deliberations, there should never be a sense of shame or failure if one has to follow the example of the Federal Bureau of Investigation and report that "there is insufficient information for a determination."

There is no room for personal opinion based on emotion, instinct, prejudice, subjectivity or anything less than careful scientifically based study. Accepted techniques and procedures should be used for all opinions and those techniques should be exercised in such a way as to demonstrate careful competency.

It is important to continue the process of developing new techniques and procedures. However, proven techniques founded on evidence based science should always be the primary basis of our opinions. New techniques can be validated concurrently. It is recommended that the practicing forensic dentist maintain a standard policy to perform casework and case presentations by employing at least two standard techniques. Additionally, one developing technique can be added if appropriate to the situation.

A person's freedom or life should never be jeopardized by sloppy or inexpert forensic dental casework or opinions. There is a high standard demanded for the practitioner in forensic dentistry. One way to maintain that high standard is through mentoring or sharing one's work product with at least one other competent practitioner for review.

It is often appropriate to include students and always appropriate to include less experienced dentists in mentoring experiences and casework by experienced forensic odontologists. These individuals should not make the decisions and should be considered participants to learn and advance their abilities and provide insight through inquiry. All practicing forensic dentists have had to learn through participation in field work and our discipline should stand out for sharing and cooperative advancement.

The justice system in the United States is based on an adversarial approach to the resolution of legal questions brought before the courts. Competitive criticism among the forensic experts called to assist in this arena can not and should not be tolerated. Disagreement and difference of opinion, yes! Competitive criticism of colleagues and peers, however, is unbecoming and detrimental to the overall credibility of the discipline of forensic dentistry.

We hope and trust that you find this manual helpful in your endeavors to understand the discipline of forensic odontology and function effectively as a scientifically founded, ethical and eager participant in the field.

Edward E. Herschaft, BA, DDS, MA
Marden E. Alder DDS, MS
David K. Ord, BS, DDS
Raymond D. Rawson, BS, DDS, MA
E. Steven Smith, BS, DDS
September, 2006

ACKNOWLEDGEMENTS TO THE FOURTH EDITION

The editors wish to acknowledge the support and understanding of our families, and peers. The effort to produce this textbook required many sacrifices from the former and selfless willingness to share knowledge from the latter. Their help provided the environment necessary to complete this project. They are examples of the loved ones and colleagues who enable all of us to provide assistance to the community of man by the practice of our discipline of dental science.

Our thanks to all those who have contributed to this book with their knowledge, experience and patience. They have thereby helped us make this endeavor possible. The first three editions of the *ASFO Manual of Forensic Odontology* were the stepping stones for this current effort. We acknowledge the foundation that these works provided the current editors as we endeavored to maintain their ability to disseminate the most current evidence based information in the field of forensic odontology.

Special appreciation is directed to the text's peer review committees led by Drs. Iain Pretty and David R. Senn and to the efforts of Dr. Katherine M. Howard, Dr. Nikki R. Norton, and Ms. Nipa Patel in formulating and standardizing the reference sections of the text.

Drs. Raymond J. Johansen and C. Michael Bowers are acknowledged for providing an electronic version of their text *Digital Analysis of Bite Mark Evidence Using Adobe Photoshop* as a supplement to the 4th edition of the ASFO Manual of Forensic Odontology. This material can be accessed through a secured area of the ASFO web site for those individuals who have obtained a copy of the 4th edition of this Manual.

We would like to acknowledge the American Board of Forensic Odontology for providing the editors with current guidelines for various procedures in forensic odontology. These guidelines have been established by the working groups of the ABFO and are continually monitored and updated as *evidence based* information concerning respective procedures becomes available.

Everyone involved in this project deserves equal credit and appreciation for their contributions which were often acquired under duress during dangerous, emotional, traumatic and stressful situations involving terrorist acts, natural disasters or tragedies resulting from human error or criminal activity.
EEH, MEA, DKO, RDR, ESS

HISTORY OF THE ASFO

The embryonic seeds of the American Society of Forensic Odontology (ASFO) were planted in 1962, in Washington, D.C. It was there that the Armed Forces Institute of Pathology (AFIP) gave its first course in Forensic Odontology. The course was attended by 45 people, 36 from the Armed Forces, and 9 civilians. The dental presenters at this course were Albert Dahlberg, Louis Hansen, John Salley, Viken Sassouni, and David Scott. The presenters at future AFIP courses (the next was in 1970) were the eventual founding members of the AFSO; Robert Boyers, Edward Comulada, Lowell Levine, Lester Luntz, Curtis Mertz and Paul Stimson.

In 1969, the dental members of the American Academy of Forensic Sciences (AAFS) were approached by Cyril H. Wecht, M.D., J.D. and Arthur Schatz, J.D., President-Elect and Secretary-Treasurer of the AAFS, respectively. Louis Hansen, Lester Luntz, and David Scott were already dental members of the General Section of the AAFS. By the latter part of 1970, Dr. Luntz had recruited the other required members to form the Odontology Section. He became the section's first representative to the Academy's Executive Committee. The other existing sections at that time were: Criminalistics, Jurisprudence, Pathology & Biology, Psychiatry, Questioned Documents, Toxicology, and General.

The ASFO was also initiated in 1970, based on the ideas and leadership of Robert Boyers, Chief of Oral Pathology at the AFIP. He felt that since only dentists actively engaged in forensic dentistry and associated with some type of law enforcement agency were eligible for membership in the Odontology Section of the AAFS, others interested in the discipline would be ineligible for formal affiliation in the Forensic Academy. The ASFO was developed to permit anyone with an interest in forensic odontology to meet and further their knowledge of this dental field. Thus, the organization's goal is to provide entry level dentists in this discipline an opportunity to receive training and interaction with experienced members. In addition to the founding members mentioned earlier, George Green, George Ward, and Edward Woolridge were also charter members of the ASFO.

Initially, the ASFO had no President. The first officers were Drs. Robert Boyers, Secretary-Treasurer, Edward Comulada, Corresponding Secretary, and George Green, Curtis Mertz, and Lester Luntz representing the Board of Governors. Robert Boyers was later elected as the first President of the organization in 1971.

Since 1970, the Society has met annually. The initial meetings were held during the AFIP Forensic Odontology course and many of the attendees joined the Society. Other independent annual meetings were held in Chicago, Oklahoma City, and New York City. It soon became difficult for members to attend the ASFO Annual meetings in these different locations, so it was decided to convene during the AAFS Annual Meeting.

The first joint meeting was held at the Statler Hilton Hotel in Washington, D.C. in February, 1976 and the second in St. Louis, Missouri in 1978. The ASFO did not meet with the AAFS jointly again until 1983 in Cincinnati, Ohio. The two organizations have held concurrent meetings since 1983 and the ASFO membership has grown steadily over these years. In 1974, there were 171 members. By 1976 the membership grew to 215. At the 1994 Annual Meeting in San Antonio, Texas, membership reached 411. By 2006, the ASFO had grown to the largest forensic dental organization in the world with over 1000 members representing 26 countries.

The ASFO has come a long way in the last 36 years, and its current leadership and membership look forward to making additional contributions to the discipline of forensic odontology as the American Society of Forensic Odontology advances to the half century mark.

Membership dues were initially ten dollars annually which included a subscription to the International Journal of Forensic Odontology. In 1971, the ASFO produced its own Forensic Odontology Newsletter, written by Robert Boyers. Dr. George Furst became the editor of the Newsletter in 1984 and continued in this position until 1997 when Susan Rivera held the post. Dr. Rivera became Executive Director of the ASFO in 2000. In 2005, Howard Cooper assumed the editorship of the Newsletter and Ben Gibson became the Executive Director. The Newsletter is published three times a year. The ASFO Forensic Odontology Workbook was written and compiled by Drs. Robert Siegel and Norman Sperber in 1980. Many members of the Society contributed to this and subsequent editions which have been published as the ASFO Manual of Forensic Odontology. The second and third editions were edited by Dr. David Averill (1991) and Drs. C. Michael Bowers and Gary Bell (1995, 1997 revised) respectively. The second edition sold over 750 copies and the third editions approximately 2000.

DEDICATION

This book is dedicated to the memory of the victims of catastrophic natural and human events and their families for which the knowledge and services of forensic dentists has helped to bring closure and peace.

CONTENTS

Editors   iii
Contributors   iv

Past Presidents of the American Society of Forensic Odontology   v
Forward   vi
Preface   vi
Acknowledgements   ix

History of the American Society of Forensic Odontology   ix

Chapters

1   Introduction to Forensic Odontology   1
    Starting a Career as a Forensic Dentist   1

2   Human Identification   7
    Introduction   7
    Personal Recognition and Personal Effects   9
      Facial Superimposition   9
      Facial Reconstruction   12
        General Technique   12
    Fingerprinting   13
    Dental Identification   16
      General Dental Participation   16
        Records Availability   17
      Providing Permanent Identification for Your Patients   18
      Recognizing and Reporting Suspected Cases of Abuse and Neglect 19
      Participating in DMORT or State Identification Teams   19
      Response to Bioterrorism and Emergency Medical Care   19
      Forensic Imaging Techniques   20
        Photography   20
        Radiography   20
        Scanning Electron Microscopy and X-ray Spectroscopy 25
      Antemortem Considerations   26
        Sources for Antemortem Information   27
        Charting, Retention of Records and Data Bases   27
        The Clinical Record   29
        Undocumented Individuals   32
      Post Mortem Considerations   32
        The Oral Autopsy   32
        Children   32
        Partial Decomposition and Trauma   38
        Incineration   44
        The Burning Process   45
        Burning and Dental Evidence   47
        Skeletonized and Partial Remains   48
      Comparison Considerations and Issues   51
      Age Estimation   53
        Purpose, Value, and Limitations of Age Estimation   55
        Dental Age Estimation   55
        Formation and Growth of Teeth   55
        Eruption of Deciduous and Permanent Teeth   55
        Progressive Changes in Developing Teeth   56
        Histologic Changes in Teeth   57

Biochemical Changes in Teeth	57
Other Methods	58
Living Individuals	58
Deceased Individuals	60
Summary	60
Anthropology	62
Occupation	65
Medical Conditions and Treatments	66
Medical Conditions with Oral Hard Tissue Manifestations	66
Habits and Addictions	67
Abnormalities of Tooth Formation and Eruption	70
Place of Residence	70
Sex Determination	72
Ethnicity	73
Genetic (DNA) Comparison	74
Chemical Composition of DNA	75
Mitochondrial DNA (mtDNA)	77
Methods of DNA Analysis	84
Responsibilities of the Odontologist	86
Establishing Rapport with the Laboratory	86
Management of the Evidence	87
DNA from Oral Tissues	87
Reporting Results	89
Salivary DNA Recovered From Human Bite Marks	89
3 Multiple Fatality Incident Management, and Bioterrorism Issues	103
Introduction	103
Problems Associated with Identification in a Multiple Fatality Incident	106
National Dental Image Repository (NDIR)	106
Organization and Planning for Emergency Management	108
The National Response Plan	108
The National Incident Management System	109
Incident Command System (ICS)	109
Communication and Information Management	112
Preparedness	112
Joint Information System (JIS)	112
NIMS Integration Center (NIC)	112
NRP Maintenance	112
Formation of a Dental Identification Team	112
Team Administration and Maintenance Information	115
Notification of Team Existence and Logistical Issues	115
Team Organization	117
The Post Mortem Section	117
The Radiography and Photography Section	118
The Antemortem Section	119
The Comparison Section	127
Computer System	128
Compensation	129
DMORT and DMAT	130
History of DMORT	130
Disaster Mortuary Operational Team (DMORT)	131
Organizational Structure of DMORT	131
Composition of DMORT Strike Teams	133
Interaction with Local Authorities	135
Deployment of DMORT Personnel	137

Command Structure of DMORT 137
Technical Needs of the Dental Section 141
Dental Section Protocols 145
Assessment of DMORT Dental Response Following Hurricane Katrina 148
Development of Protocols for Use in Future Multiple Fatality Incidents 149
Planned Deployment of Personnel – Problems Encountered 151
Planned Procurement of Necessary Equipment and Supplies 151
Long Term Planning 152
Disaster Medical Assistance Team (DMAT) 152
Bioterrorism and Weapons of Mass Destruction 153
Background Information 154
Bioterrorism and Biological Weapons 154
History of Bioterrorism 154
Weapons Agents Used by Terrorists 155
Identification of Bioterrorism Threats 158
Detection of Bioterrorism Agent Threat 159
Detection of Biological Agents 159
Laboratory Response Network (LRN) 159
Historical and Practical Examples 160
Technology Advances in Identification Issues since September 11, 2001 160
Historical Perspective 160
Transition 161
Accomplishing Transition Goals 162
Protocols Developed and Implemented 162
Lessons Learned 163

4 Bite Mark Analysis 168
Introduction and History 168
Dr. Jonathan Taft and Other Significant Early Cases 169
State of the Science 170
Recognition of Bite Marks 170
General Considerations 179
Victim Examination and Evidence Collection 182
Non-Invasive Analysis 182
Two-Dimensional Evidence 182
Three-Dimensional Evidence 186
Invasive Analyses 189
Tissue Incision 189
Tissue Excision 189
Tissue Sampling 191
Histological Evaluation 191
Transillumination 194
Suspect Examination and Evidence Collection 194
Two-Dimensional Evidence 195
Photography 195
Buccal Swabs 196
Three-Dimensional Evidence 196
Bite Mark Impressions 196
Analysis and Comparison of the Evidence 198
Description of the Injury 199
Description of the Dentition 201
Comparison of the Dentition to the Injury 201
Metric Analysis 201
Overlay Comparison 203
Specialized Procedures 204

Scanning Electron Microscopy (SEM)   204
    Future Directions   206

5 Human Abuse and Neglect   210
    Overview of Human Abuse   210
    Information Concerning Abusers   211
    Child Abuse/Neglect   211
    Risk Factors   214
    Signs and Symptoms Associated with the Various Types of Child Abuse   215
            Physical Abuse   215
            Sexual Abuse   219
            Emotional Maltreatment   221
            Neglective Abuse   223
        Munchausen by Proxy Syndrome (MBPS)   224
        Diagnosis of Child Abuse   224
    Dental Implications of Child Abuse/Neglect   225
    Intimate Partner Violence (IPV)   225
        Dental Implications of IPV   227
    Elder Abuse   227
        Dental Implications of Elder Abuse   234
    Abuse of the Disabled   235
    Examination and Documentation of Suspected Inflicted Trauma   236
    Intervention   237
    Protective Custody Issues   238
        Resources   238
        The PANDA Program   240
    Conclusion   241

6 Technological Aides in Forensic Odontology: 244
    Introduction   244
    Film Based Photography   244
        Basic Principles   244
            Optical Physics   244
            Exposure   248
            Equipment for Forensic Dentistry – Film Based   248
    Digital Based Photography   252
        Basic Digital Protocol   253
        Standard Photography Views   255
            Identification Cases   255
            Bite Mark Cases   256
        Advanced Photographic Techniques   262
        The Electromagnetic Spectrum and Photography   263
        Alternate Light Imaging (ALI/Fluorescent Photography)   263
        ALI Protocol   264
        Reflective (Long Wavelength) Ultraviolet Photography (UVA)   267
            Ultraviolet Photography Protocol   268
        Infrared Photography (IR)   270
            Infrared Protocol   270
    Radiology   271
        Digital Radiology (DR)   271
            Basic Terminology Associated with Electronic Imaging   272
            Advantages of DR Technology   274
            Disadvantages of DR Technology   275
            Legal Ramifications of DR Technology   276
            DR Technology/Radiographic Film Comparison   276

Application of DR in Forensic Dental Identification Cases 277
The Future Role of DR Technology in Dental Identification Settings 278
Hand Held Portable X-Ray Generators 279
Cone-Beam Computed Tomography (CBCT) 282
CBCT Role in Forensic Odontology 283
Scanning Electron Microscopy with X-ray Spectroscopy (SEM/EDS) 284
Introduction 284
SEM Imaging Concepts 284
Energy Dispersive X-Ray Spectroscopy (EDS) 285
Sample Preparation for SEM 285
Distinguishing Tooth Structure from Bone and Other Materials 285
Evidence of Restorative Procedures 287
Analysis of Restorative Materials 288
Bite Mark Analysis and Evidence from Skin Using SEM 293
Materials & Methods 294
Exemplar Analyses 295
Interpretation of Analyses 295
Conclusion 296
X-Ray Fluorescence (XRF) 296
Computer Software and Hardware 302
Historical Programs 303
WinID 303
Other Software Programs 305
Adobe Photoshop 306
MideoSystems: CASEWORKS 306
CASEWORKS and Bite Mark Identification 308
New Output Technology 309
Conclusion 310

7 Dental Jurisprudence: 314
The Admissibility of Scientific and Non-Scientific Evidence in Court 314
Rules of Evidence 315
The Odontologist's Role as an Expert Witness 318
Pre-Trial Preparation 320
Evidence Management 321
The Trial 325
Qualifying the Expert Witness 325
General Comments Regarding Testimony 326
Direct Examination 327
Cross Examination 328
Malpractice: Professional Liability Issues 330
Legal Background 331
Standard of Care Issues 333
Malpractice 334
Plaintiff Review 336
Personal Injury Cases 337
Ethical Considerations 339
Professional Ethics 339
Attorney's Ethics in Dealing with Experts 341
The Expert's Ethical Obligations 341
Absolute Immunity – The Rationale 342
Expert Witness Immunity Relative to Dental Testimony 342
A Perspective 344
HIPAA Regulations – Applications to Forensic Odontology 344
Voluntary Observance of the Privacy Rule 347
The Privacy Rule - Key Terms 347

Appendices:

A: The Scientific Method and Forensic Odontology   354

B: Representative Acceptable Courses in Forensic Odontology   359

C: ABFO Guidelines   360

D: Charts on Facial Tissue Depth for Reconstruction   361

E: Resources to Assist in Forensic Identification   366

F: Tooth Conversion Tables   371

G: Information for DMORT Membership   374

H: Tasks Related to WIN ID Comparison Procedures   375

I : Court Rulings of 1st and 4th Amendments and the Patriots Act   383

J: Abuse and Neglect Protocols   384

K: Case Presentation of a Dog Bite Homicide   388

L: Bite Mark Cases of Note   390

Index   399

CHAPTER 1

INTRODUCTION TO FORENSIC ODONTOLOGY

As one gets older one sees many more paths that could be taken. Artists sense within their own work that kind of swelling of possibilities, which may seem a freedom or a confusion.

Jasper Johns, Jr., abstract expressionist American artist, born, May 15, 1930

STARTING A CAREER AS A FORENSIC DENTIST

The field of forensic dentistry or forensic odontology is that area of dentistry concerned with the correct management, examination, evaluation and presentation of dental evidence in criminal or civil legal proceedings. This discipline of dentistry has existed for many years and practiced by a small number of dedicated clinicians. Within the last twenty years, the idea of becoming involved in the legal aspects of dentistry has become popular among an increasing number of practicing dentists. This is due, in part, to an increasing awareness by both professionals and the lay public of the role that forensic science and forensic dentistry play in the resolution of criminal and civil legal issues. This is best exemplified by noting the membership of the organization sponsoring this manual. The American Society of Forensic Dentistry (ASFO) currently exceeds 1000 members. There were thirty members when ASFO was founded in 1970.

Despite the growing interest in this discipline and the fact that formal education in forensic odontology has existed for over a 100 years and forensic dental training is an integral component of undergraduate dental education in many countries, it is still not a required subject in many dental schools in the United States. Even in Europe where a survey of five university dental programs revealed the development of detailed curricula in forensic odontology, coverage of recent advances in forensic science was found to be lacking. In those institutions which currently provide forensic dental education it is essential that instruction be undertaken by qualified forensic odontologists.

The initial interest in getting involved in this field must be tempered with an understanding of the accompanying responsibilities. The results of a forensic dentist's decisions effect lives. The ramifications of an inaccurate or personally biased opinion can be extensive and immutable. The majority of ASFO members are practicing dentists. Much of their clinical experience and performance is within the confines of a dental office. This manner of practice produces dentists who are self sufficient and generally independent of one another. Routine peer review is an extremely rare event.

In contrast, forensic activity is performed in an arena in which everything that is stated, performed and documented is subject to review. The idea of forensic dentistry being a scientific community is both a legalistic and actual fact. The decisions dentists make in criminal and civil investigation are transmitted within the judicial and professional systems far beyond the dental office. The dentist involved in this discipline, whether neophyte or sage veteran, must establish the scientific basis of his or her decisions when testifying in court as a forensic expert. The reliability of the scientific, evidence based opinion of the forensic expert, founded on the principles of the scientfic method is paramount. (**Appendix A**) Therefore, personal experience and training as well as independent verification from forensic colleagues is expected.

The forensic newcomer has a challenge and "How do I get started?" is the common query. The dentist, newly exposed to the forensic aspects of the profession, should join the organizations dedicated to education, research and fellowship within the forensic dental community. Developing friendships with seasoned forensic dentists will result in mentoring opportunities that foster a team approach to problem solving.

Many dentists, untrained in the forensic discipline, have performed admirably using their basic dental training when called upon to help in a forensic case. Much more education is required, however, to become qualified as a forensic dental expert. Given the current interest in the field, the aspiring dentist should obtain information on accredited forensic courses that will develop one's necessary skills (**Appendix B**). One's focus, however, should not be limited to just the dental aspects of forensic science. Dentistry is a specialty of the forensic community and overlaps with many of the other disciplines that comprise forensic science. These include physical anthropology, pathology, forensic psychiatry, jurisprudence, criminology, engineering and toxicology among others. The American Academy of Forensic Sciences (AAFS) supports this concept by example. Its membership structure is divided into ten forensic discipline based sections, including forensic odontology.

The most obvious place to begin a career in forensic dentistry is to contact a local law enforcement agency. Most contributors to this manual are affiliated with their county medical examiner's or coroner's office or some other state or regional legal entity. Some states have regional or statewide forensic investigative departments exemplified by the Georgia Bureau of Investigation (GBI) and South Carolina Law Enforcement Division (SLED). Since most jurisdictions already have a dentist as a consultant, one's initial phone call or visit will probably be directed to that individual as a point of contact.

Larger jurisdictions have a complete forensic dental team, coordinated by a chief-of-service. It is likely that, annually, this individual receives numerous requests to help out from dentists or dental auxiliaries. Don't be discouraged if you are met with a certain amount of red tape. Persevere in your efforts to become affiliated while realizing that the number of cases requiring dental expertise in the department will vary among jurisdictions. Metropolitan districts can have 20 to 30 cases a month whereas rural areas may experience only half a dozen per year.

Create a curriculum vitae, defining all pertinent areas of training and experience. Mail it in whether neophyte or sage veteran, advance of your initial interview to the appropriate contact person in the department in which you are seeking an affiliation. Enclose a picture and a business card. You want to stand out from the crowd and present a professional approach. Ask to receive a tour of the agency's facility. A prearranged appointment time is best. Be punctual and prepared to view the internal workings of a death investigation department. If inexperienced, one needs to determine your tolerance of the realities of forensic science. Everyone in the field understands that new people go through an initial break-in period. Do not be reluctant to ask questions.

Be flexible and work at understanding the existing system within your area. Realize that as a forensic dentist your responsibility is to the chief forensic pathologist or the county coroner depending upon the structure of the department in your state. Most appointments as a forensic dentist are at the pleasure of these individuals. Make an effort to meet them since they are highly trained and can be of tremendous assistance in mentoring your career. The chief-of-service, pathologist and/or coroner will be encouraged to retain your services if you have already begun specialized training in the field. The opportunity for on the job training can be a slow process in some areas.

As more experience is gained in the field, prepare a business card and stationery representing your forensic endeavors. Expand your curriculum vitae to include a specific forensic section without embellishment or exaggeration of your qualifications. To do so will prove disastrous and forever destroy credibility as a consultant and courtroom expert. Integrity, honesty, ethical values and professionalism, in addition to one's knowledge base of forensic dental procedures and policies, are the foundations that establish a practitioner as a forensic dentist.

Other agencies that may require the services of a forensic dentist and can be resources for contact and affiliation include:

Police agencies are involved in gathering dental evidence when crime scene investigators need assistance developing a case which may require identification of a missing individual or includes a tooth fragment or tooth mark on skin or an inanimate object. Contact local police departments and specifically talk to crime scene analysts or investigation bureau detectives.

Child protective service agencies require the availability of a trained forensic dentist. Their activities are independent of the coroner's or medical examiner's offices because the victims they represent may not be decedents. Develop contacts that will introduce you to child protective service investigators and additionally, advocates for battered women and their organizations and shelters.

District attorneys, public defenders, and civil attorneys are resources for involvement as a forensic dental consultant or expert witness. Review past cases involving dental evidence and inform appropriate officials of your interest.

Joining the AAFS and the ASFO will establish your commitment and enthusiasm for the discipline of forensic dentistry. The former organization has eleven sections representing the major sub-disciplines of forensic science. There are over 5000 members of the AAFS in the United States and abroad. Each year, the February meeting of the AAFS is held in a different region of the United States. The majority of active forensic dentists belong to the Odontology Section of the AAFS. Currently, there are 424 members of the Section.

Membership levels vary from Student to Fellow and advancement within the organization is based on research, case work and contributions to the knowledge base of forensic odontology. The AAFS membership includes distinguished experts from various fields. It publishes the Journal of Forensic Sciences six times a year and its membership directory is a valuable aid to the dentist starting in this discipline. The AAFS Newsletter includes a calendar of multi-

disciplinary training programs and meetings.

The ASFO has its annual meeting in conjunction with the AAFS. This organization's goal is to provide entry level dentists and others interested in this discipline an opportunity to receive training and interaction with its more experienced members. The one day annual meeting consists of presentations on topics specifically targeted to aspiring odontologists. The quarterly ASFO Newsletter contains articles and commentary on diverse subjects in the field and social information on members, their activities, and approved training programs. Additionally, this publication contains a current listing of scientific articles published in numerous peer reviewed journals. Both the AAFS and ASFO provide seed grants for worthy start-up research projects in the field of forensic dentistry.

Currently, there are no full time training programs available in the United States for postdoctoral degrees in forensic dentistry. A week long training program in forensic odontology is offered by the Armed Forces Institute of Pathology, Washington, D.C. An extensive course on various aspects of forensic dentistry is offered bi-annually by the Southwest Symposium on Forensic Dentistry. This is sponsored by the University of Texas Health Sciences Center Dental School in San Antonio, which has also initiated a program whereby practicing dentists who want more comprehensive information and practical experience in forensic dentistry than is feasible during the symposium can participate in a one-year fellowship in this discipline. Refer to **Appendix B** for further details and contact information.

McGill University offers a certificate program in forensic dentistry since 2004. It comprises 24 weeks of theory and assignments taken on the web, in addition to two weeks of hands on practice in identification and bite mark evidence at the Laboratoire de Sciences Judiciaires et de Médecine Légale in Montreal. The latter is believed to be the first forensic laboratory under legislative authority in North America. Refer to **Appendix B** for further details and contact information.

Other continuing education courses and workshops have been offered by local, regional and national components of the American Dental Association and the American Academies of Oral and Maxillofacial Pathology and Oral Medicine. International meetings, symposia and conferences dealing with forensic dental issues have been held in the United Kingdom, Australia and Southeast Asia.

The Bureau of Legal Dentistry (BOLD) is a forensic odontology laboratory at the University of British Columbia in Vancouver. This Canadian laboratory is dedicated to full-time forensic dental research and graduate teaching. The faculty and staff at BOLD apply modern forensic techniques and laboratory analysis to dental evidence to assist in the resolution of legal issues. BOLD is a resource for practicing forensic odontologists and other forensic scientists who deal with teeth, bones, saliva, DNA and dental records (**Appendix B**).

The Laboratory for Forensic Odontology Research (LFOR) was established in 2006 at the State University of New York (SUNY) at Buffalo, School of Dental Medicine. The LFOR faculty is actively engaged in forensic odontology research and associated fields (forensic anthropology, chemistry and geology). Educational activities consist of a senior selective course for dental students and courses which fulfill continuing dental education requirements. Student internships and research projects are mentored by the LFOR faculty. The mission of the organization is to advance research methodology and techniques in forensic research and to educate and disseminate knowledge in this field. The LFOR program also has access to facilities available at SUNY at Buffalo, including the South Campus Instrumentation Center in the School of Dental Medicine and the Gross Anatomy Cadaver Donation Program in the Medical School.

After gaining some experience with involvement in forensic dental cases, the individual maturing in this discipline can develop slide, Microsoft PowerPoint and lecture presentations concerning the subject. Newcomers can purchase a slide collection from the American Board of Forensic Odontology (ABFO). Dental and law enforcement groups are always interested in providing good speakers the opportunity to present to their constituents. These groups need to have regular continuing education. Information related to the forensic dentist's role as a facilitator in legal problems involving identification, bite mark analysis, mass disaster identification and problems of human abuse are always well received.

One's first forensic case is often referred by a local agency. The excitement of becoming part of an actual investigation, however, can be fraught with hidden dangers. The dentist involved in a forensic setting must clearly understand that he or she is not an advocate for the agency or the individual that engages their services. The dentist's quest should be to accurately evaluate and render an opinion that is free from personal bias or agendas. It is normal to want to make the case for the law enforcement or prosecutorial agency that has requested your expertise. The caveat in this situation is to remain neutral. Any true professional understands this role. Do not permit local friendships to influence judgment.

Often the forensic dentist's opinion is demanded long before the entire dental investigation has been completed. Resist the urge to answer to this request. Defer a response until there is certainty that the opinion to be offered is based on all of the material required to make a scientific determination of the facts. Do not hesitate to consult a more experienced forensic dental mentor, colleague or Diplomate of the ABFO.

The ABFO certifies individuals who have reached a specified level of experience and training. Application for certification is voluntary and applicants are granted Diplomate status after successful application, review of case documentation, personal references, and completion of a three day didactic and practical examination. One hundred and thirty three dentists in the United States, Canada and Europe have attained Diplomate status in the ABFO. Of these, 90 are currently affiliated with a legal agency and/or are active in case work and consulting.

This ABFO, as well as forensic specialty boards in the other disciplines of forensic science, is sponsored by the Forensic Sciences Foundation of the AAFS. These discipline based boards were initiated in 1972 when the Law Enforcement Assistance Administration (LEAA) Act offered grant funding to the AAFS to organize boards of certification in the various disciplines represented in the Academy. Each discipline has a set of guidelines established to enhance educational requirements, experience and credibility in the various areas they represent. These guidelines are targeted to individuals within disciplines that evaluate and analyze a variety of evidentiary material for law enforcement and issues involving the court systems.

The Odontology Section of the AAFS was formed in 1970. By 1974, "The Mason White Papers" had been presented to the Academy dealing with certification of forensic scientists. Deliberations concerning the Academy's possible role in the certification program had been discussed yearly since the mid-1950s. An ad hoc certification committee headed by Dr. Dubois was formed after the presentation of the Mason Papers. Its report was provided to the AAFS Fellows in 1975 and the Forensic Sciences Foundation acquired a federal grant to study forensic sciences certification. From this study, the following certifying boards were founded:

- American Board of Forensic Anthropology

- American Board of Forensic Document Examiners

- American Board of Forensic Odontology

- American Board of Pathology/Biology

- American Board of Forensic Psychiatry and Neurology

- American Board of Forensic Toxicology

Additional certifying boards have also been created since the establishment of the original five. These include:

- American Board of Medicolegal Death Investigators

- American Board of Criminalistics

Criteria were formulated for Diplomate status in each of the specialty boards. Drs. Lowell Levine, Lester Luntz, and Edward Woolridge were instrumental and active in the early discussions concerning the establishment of these criteria for odontology. Governance issues and the various board functions associated with the formation of the ABFO were also addressed.

The odontology criteria included dental examinations and identification cases, verification of experience, work history in a forensic environment and letters of recommendation that would verify the experience and background of the various candidates. The guidelines required that an examination should be given to the candidates.

The original group of dental candidates who met the initial requirements for certification by the ABFO were: Edward D. Woolridge (1), Richard R. Souviron (2), Curtis A. Mertz (3), Arthur D. Goldman (4), Gerald L. Vale (5), Stanley M. Schwartz (6), Lowell J. Levine (7), Robert B. J. Dorion (8), Paul G. Stimson (9), David B. Scott (10), Manuel M. Maslansky (11), George T. Ward (12), and John P. Williams (13). The certification numbers of these charter diplomates of the ABFO are indicated.

Each of these candidates was asked to submit a series of questions concerning forensic odontology. This provided the bank of questions from which the first written examination was derived. Upon completion of the development of the question bank, each candidate was asked to answer the questions and critique the examination.

Thus, each of the candidates was grandfathered by the board while still having the opportunity to take the written examination that would be given to subsequent candidates the following year. A practical examination was then arranged and given for the first time in the Miami-Dade County Medical Examiners Office in 1978. The first board certificates were awarded on February 18, 1976 at the AAFS meeting in Atlanta, Georgia.

Presently, the ABFO maintains a bank of test questions related to all aspects of the specialty. The written examination of the ABFO can be administered electronically at any testing center capable of meeting the security provisions. In this way, a candidate can take the examination near his or her home and after successful passage be allowed to take the practical and oral portion of the examination. Additionally, the certification committee of the ABFO has entertained a suggestion to administer the oral and practical portion of the examination in conjunction with future annual meetings of the AAFS.

ABFO diplomates meet annually, concurrent with the AAFS scientific session. Pursuing advanced training and experience in forensic dentistry is a major commitment to those involved in this discipline. Therefore, activities at the annual meetings of the AAFS and the ASFO include workshops, table clinics and reports of research projects. In addition to these activities, the ABFO meetings are involved in the development of professional guidelines and standards for the practice of forensic odontology.

For most in this field, financial rewards are minimal while the personal rewards are many. Everyone involved in the discipline of forensic dentistry believes that by doing their best, based on scientific principles and by maintaining high professional standards they are helping to make the world a better place in which to live.

EDUCATIONAL OUTCOMES

By completing this chapter and **Appendix A** the reader will:
- Define scientific method, bias, scientific peer review, evidence based science, junk science.
- Describe the process of the scientific method.
- Appreciate how the scientific method is used in the practice of forensic odontology.
- Define forensic odontology.
- Develop a foundational knowledge of the processes involved in becoming active and affiliated in this discipline.
- Know the principal scientific forensic organizations which dentists can join for educational, research, interdisciplinary dialogue and certification opportunities.
- Identify resources for advanced education in this discipline.

CONTRIBUTORS

C. Michael Bowers, DDS, JD, DABFO
Mary A. Bush, DDS
Peter J. Bush, BS
Robert B.J. Dorion, DDS, DABFO
Edward E. Herschaft, DDS, MA, DABFO
John D. McDowell, DDS, MS, DABFO
Paul G. Stimson, DDS, MS, DABFO
Edward D. Woolridge, Jr., DDS, DABFO

REFERENCES

Starting a Career as a Forensic Dentist

Acharya AB (2006). Teaching forensic odontology: an opinion on its content and format. Eur J Dent Educ 10:137-41.

Bowers CM (1997). Introduction to Forensic Odontology. In: Manual of Forensic Odontology, 3rd ed. C Bowers and G Bell editors. Ontario: Manticore Publishers, pp. 1-3.

Field K (1998). History of AAFS, 1948-1998. Philadelphia: ASTM.

Herschaft EE (2002). Forensic Dentistry. In: Oral and Maxillofacial Pathology, 2nd ed. BW Neville editor. Philadelphia: W. B. Saunders, pp. 763-783.

Herschaft EE, Rasmussen RH (1978). The teaching of forensic dentistry: a status report. J Dent Educ 42:532-6.

CHAPTER 2

HUMAN IDENTIFICATION

"A complete life may be one ending in so full an identification with the oneself that there is no self left to die."
Bernard Berenson – American art critic (1865-1959)

Introduction

Discovery of an unidentified body requires a significant effort on the part of public authorities to reach a resolution. It is important for the family and other loved ones to come to an understanding and proof of the loss of someone important in their life. It is fundamental to our society based on law to have scientific proof before death certificates can be issued, insurance payments assigned, public benefits allowed, or estate and marital issue resolution.

The key statement here is proof not opinion. There needs to be a high degree of scientific certainty related to the determination of identity of remains. Tragic errors are not common in forensic dentistry, but there are dramatic examples of misidentification. Each case is important and has significant ramifications if manipulated or misunderstood.

The process of identification and the specific method used depends somewhat upon the circumstances. If a sudden death of a known individual occurs, it is common to depend upon personal recognition for identification. Thus, a parent will commonly identify their son or daughter as the victim of an accident or overdose.

It is difficult to precisely determine the number of misidentifications caused by personal recognition, but it has been estimated that as many as 30 percent of identifications by this method are in error. That error can be caused by the emotion of difficult circumstances. There are cases of purposeful misrepresentation of the identity as well as simple mistakes and it is always best to have a scientific confirmation to anyone's statement of identity.

It is always important to remember the basic principles of identification:

- The identification of victims must be accurate, and based on scientific principles.

- It takes training, organization and experience to identify victims accurately

- The difficulty of identification increases exponentially with the number of victims.

The process of identification should start with gaining as much information as possible about the person represented as *unknown remains*. Age, gender, stature, race, and medical history are issues with which the forensic dentist and physical anthropologist can assist. Fingerprints and DNA determination are known to be reliable and will be discussed in detail.

The thorough evaluation of the human dentition of an unidentified person could be accurately referred to as an oral autopsy. Complete dental identification involves processing antemortem and post mortem information, doing a comparison of the information, forming an opinion and preparing a report of the findings. It must be emphasized that, when dealing with the post mortem dental evidence the forensic dentist must secure the proper authority to collect and process the dental evidence. A coroner or medical examiner must give permission for the dentist to view, chart, photograph, videotape, or surgically remove the jaw segments. It may also be necessary to gain access to the oral cavity with incisions just as the physician medical examiner who evaluates internal organs. Failure to gain such approval may place the dentist at risk for legal action.

The American Board of Forensic Odontology Body Identification Guidelines should be followed in all forensic dental identification cases and can be found at www.abfo.org and in **Appendix C**. These guidelines provide an excellent source of information for novice and expert alike in the collection and preservation of post mortem dental evidence, sources of antemortem data, protocols for the comparison of antemortem and post mortem evidence, and categories and terminology for body identification.

Radiography is certainly an essential diagnostic tool, but ultimately, the visual and photographic inspection of the condition of the dentition is basic and fundamental. Every attempt should be made to protect the viewable condition of the face, and there are methods to facilitate that visual inspection. Mouth props, bite blocks and retractors are useful and intraoral probes and lenses have been described and used to good effect. In some cases the resection of jaws is well justified and there are approaches other than the standard incision at the corner of the mouth that can protect the facial architecture for potential viewing for family or funeral services.

The condition of every tooth should be recorded. Missing teeth should be noted and where possible, antemortem or post mortem changes indicated. We have found that once the oral autopsy is concluded, it is difficult to reacquire the victim remains to verify information. It is always best to thoroughly record the evidence at the time of examination and to depend upon that information to guide the search for identity. This situation is particularly critical in the mass disaster setting, because of the difficulty associated with multiple handling of the remains.

A standard chart should be completely filled out for every unidentified set of remains. When dental records come into the examiners control, they should be translated to that standard chart format so that errors in charting can be minimized. The various methods of charting are a constant source of irritation and error and can greatly complicate the process of identification.

Ultimately, the comparison of radiographic features represents a gold standard for identification, but the use of chart recordings is most often the screening method that leads to that final comparison. Standardization of charting is very important to accurate identification by dental experts. Harvey described the history and development of dental charting in his textbook, *Dental Identification and Forensic Odontology*. In 1861 Zsigmondy modified an old system and developed the quadrant notation also known as the Palmer system. This method is still used today in the United Kingdom, parts of the United States of America and Japan.

By 1891 Haderup used the + and − sign to precede the tooth number for upper or lower arch. The upper right central incisor is represented by the symbol 1 + and the upper left central incisor would then be represented as + 1. This was useful for the typewriter and teletype. A number of Scandinavian and other European countries adapted to this method.

The Universal System was basically developed when Parreidt abandoned quadrants in 1882. Although not used universally, despite its name, it is taught in many dental schools in the U. S., Canada, and the United Kingdom. It is time for the adoption of a universal system and it is amazing that there are still U.S. dental schools teaching different systems.

It is also time for an easily accessed central repository for dental and other information for all missing persons. The U. S. Department of Justice publishes the National Incidence Studies of Missing, Abducted, Runaway, and Throwaway Children (NISMART2) at http://www.missingkids.com/en_US/documents/nismart2_overview.pdf.

Additionally, the National Dental Image Repository (NDIR) provides an image repository for law enforcement agencies in the United States that wish to post supplemental dental images related to National Crime Information Center (NCIC) Missing, Unidentified, and Wanted Person records in a Web environment (**refer to Chapter 3, Multiple Fatality Incident, Dental**

Identification And Bioterrorism Issues). This allows for easier access and retrieval of the information by qualified individuals performing dental comparisons.

In 1999 it was estimated that there were 1,315,600 missing children in the United States. The actual reported missing children reached 797,500 for a rate of 11.4 per 1000. Compared to a sexually transmitted rate of 9 per 1000 we are truly seeing an issue of epidemic proportions. A common system of charting would certainly help in the resolution of this deplorable situation.

Personal Recognition and Personal Effects

The medical examiner/coroner will allow a viewing of remains when that is possible. It

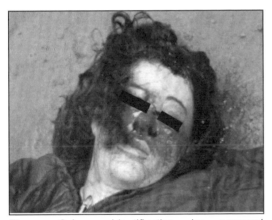

Figure 2-1: Identification by personal recognition

Figure 2-2: Identification by personal effects

accomplishes several things. First, the parent or other loved one is able to process the fact of death and although difficult, it is probably helpful in the overall process of closure. Secondly, it may provide an indication of the true identity of the individual. It does not provide a scientific proof of identity in most cases, but is extensively used and often accepted without question.

Official pictures such as those found on passports or other identity papers can be compared to the remains, but this method must be considered subjective (**Figure 2-1**). Fortunately, there is often a fingerprint record related to official identification papers and that allows for a scientific demonstration of identity.

Identification based on the comparison of dental characteristics, medical radiographic characteristics or fingerprint features are the norm in the United States. These methods are scientific in nature and all insure a positive identification. Personal effects such as clothing, jewelry and wallets have been used to establish human identifications (**Figure 2-2**). The use of personal effects is not a scientific method of establishing identification. There is always the worry that personal effects known to belong to one person may be maliciously placed on another unidentifiable human being in an effort to collect insurance money or for some other criminal reason. It is also very common for individuals to share personal items with others, so it is not unusual to find items of clothing or jewelry providing a misdirection in the identification process. It is also not unusual to find purposeful identity theft or alias use as part of criminal behavior.

Facial Superimposition

At times, the Medical Examiner or Coroner is faced with the task of establishing an identification for an individual for whom no medical, dental or fingerprint records can be located. If a photograph of the putative victim can be obtained, it may be possible to establish identification through a technique known as photographic superimposition. When using photographic superimposition, it is important to remember that a full face smiling antemortem photograph

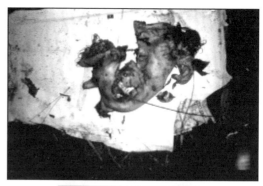
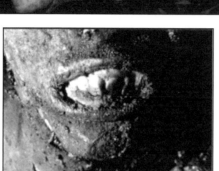
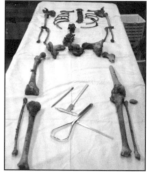

Figure 2-3: Occasionally, viewing is not possible due to burning, trauma or skeletonization.

must be available. If teeth are not visible, do not proceed with the techniques as there will be no scientific basis for any conclusions.

The antemortem photograph is studied. The position of the head in relation to the camera is noted. The position in relation to the camera involves rotations about any of three axes. The axes as shown in **Figure 2-4**, are anterior-posterior (AP), vertical (head to foot) and transverse (ear to ear).

A skull bowl is used to hold the skull. The skull is placed in the bowl upside down. This is later remedied by simply turning the skull photograph to the proper orientation. Small balls of soft wax are used to hold the skull firmly in place inside the bowl. Three pieces of masking tape are placed on the skull away from the facial area. Marks are placed on the masking tape so that the skull may be repositioned in the bowl in this same orientation, if necessary. The bowl holding the skull is placed on a lazy Susan bracket. The diameter of the circular opening in the lazy Susan bracket is slightly less than the diameter of the skull bowl. As the bowl is slid in the bracket, as shown in **Figure**

2-5, the skull can be positioned about the A-P and transverse axis. The lazy Susan bracket itself allows rotation about the vertical axis.

The skull is now oriented to attempt to obtain the best possible match of the position of the face in the photograph. This is done by eye. This initial position is recorded. Two marks, one more positive than the initial position and the other more negative, are placed along each of the three axes. One specific location on each of the three axes of the position of the face portrayed in the antemortem photograph.

A total of 27 photographs will be exposed. The combination of three marks on each of three axes taken three at a time (3x3x3) is 27 positions. The skull positioning device is correctly illuminated for photography. A neutral background such as a sheet of matte cardboard is placed in back of the skull. The camera is placed at a reproducible distance and height from the positioning device. An exposure meter or other method is used to determine the correct exposure factors, i.e. exposure time and f-stop. Starting at the first position on each of the axes, a photograph is taken.

Photographs are taken at all 27 possible positions. Each photograph has a unique orientation, slightly different from all others. The 27 negatives should be contact printed. The best match is selected from the contact prints. The corresponding negative is then enlarged to life size. Measurements taken from the skull give information to allow the skull photograph to be enlarged to life size. The mesiodistal dimension of several teeth taken as a group is one of the easiest to measure dimensions that can be used to enlarge the photograph to life size.

Attention is now turned to the antemortem photograph. If possible, the original negative is obtained. If this is not possible, the antemortem photograph is photographed to yield a negative. The negative will be blown up to life size. Note the teeth that are visible on the antemortem photograph. Measure these same teeth on the skull. Use this dimension to enlarge the antemortem negative to life size. The negative is placed In an enlarger. The enlarger may have to be turned so that is projects on the wall, to accommodate the amount of enlargement.

Kodak Fine Grain Release Positive Film is exposed on the enlarger.

Release positive is a transparent plastic type of film that can be exposed on an enlarger; the resulting print is a transparency suitable for superimposition. The two life size photographs necessary for the superimposition are now ready. The life size photograph of the skull is secured on a flat surface. The transparency with the life size print of the antemortem photograph is now placed on top of the post mortem film. The transparency is now precisely positioned to allow maximum overlap of similar anatomical features.

The experience and judgment of the forensic dentist is now used. Points of comparison in a photographic superimposition are rarely as significant as even one amalgam restoration in a regular dental identification. The concordance of the following features is noted: outline of the skull compared to the soft tissue outline of the face, nasal aperture to nose, orbit to eye, brow ridges to eyebrows and forehead, zygomatic process to cheek bone support, and most important, exact

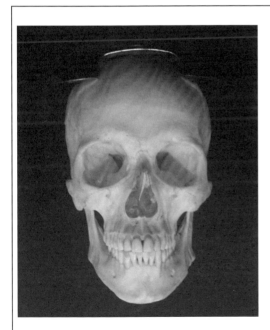

Figure 2-4: The axes and points established for later comparison

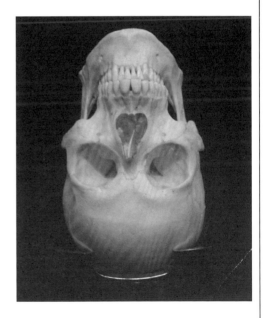

Figure 2-5: Skull placed in bowl on lazy Susan.

superimposition of the teeth in both size and angular position.

Gross discrepancies between the two films will serve to rule out the individual as the deceased. If the discrepancies are minor, there may have been an error in selection of the proper photograph of the skull. Another skull photograph may be selected, enlarged and printed, and then superimposed. In offering an opinion in this type of identification, the forensic odontologist must be very careful. When all anatomical details match, but no other detail rich feature is found, the choice of a *consistent with* opinion is most appropriate.

The presence of a detail rich feature such as brow furrow, skeletal trauma or obvious skeletal disfigurement may allow the forensic investigator to give the opinion of positive identification by the superimposition of skeletal and photographic images. For courtroom testimony, the properly oriented antemortem and skull life size photographs can be mounted side by side. Two video cameras are then placed at identical distances from the photographs and focused, one on each photograph. A stereo optic camera set up is then hooked up between the cameras and the photographs are then superimposed over each other and videotaped at this same time.

If there are problems with the antemortem photographs (blurring, fading, over or underexposure, etc.) it is possible to recover lost detail or sharpen unclear detail using computer enhancements of the photographs. There are many such techniques, but E.I. DuPont Co. in Delaware has the equipment and techniques to attempt to enhance otherwise unacceptable photographs. It is desirable to gain experience in facial superimposition when there are other scientific methods of identification available.

Facial Reconstruction

Facial reconstruction is another useful method of indicating possible identity. The basic process is illustrated in the following figures and the workup must be considered subjective. There has been extensive work to establish the normal soft tissue thickness at various anatomic points on the skull. These thickness values are known for different race types, both sexes and various age ranges, but they must be considered average values statistically.

The skull can provide useful information regarding the sex, age and racial type of the unknown individual. DNA evidence can now confirm this information so that the facial reconstruction is as accurate as possible. Once this basic information is ascertained the process of facial reconstruction illustrated in **Figures 2-7** through **2-11** can be undertaken. Essentially, standard points are located on the skull and depth markers are attached to the skull at each of these points. Charts published in the anthropologic forensic literature and provided in **Appendix D** of this text are used to determine tissue depths on the skull based on age, sex and racial characteristics observed.

There are various ways of reproducing the skull, so that the reconstruction can be accomplished on material other than the skull. Three dimensional imaging or various impression techniques can be used to protect the original skeletal evidence. The various accepted anatomic points can then be marked with erasure material or clay of the average thickness for that individual anatomic point. The tissue between those points is then built up until the face takes shape. The most subjective aspect of the whole process relates to the eyes, nose, lips, ears, and hairline and style. Once the reconstruction is finished it can be photographed and published in an effort to gain attention.

If an identity is unknown and skeletal material is present, then a facial reconstruction will possibly allow for a public recognition of a missing person. More scientific methods can then be used to provide a positive identification.

General Technique

All materials are laid out on a table where they can be undisturbed until finished. Forensic dentists would be well advised to try several reconstructions to gain appreciation for the possibilities and difficulties of this important technique.

Fingerprinting

It has been recognized since antiquity that the ridge patterns of the fingers and palms of the hands are unique and that no two individuals, including identical twins, have the same arrangement of loops, arches and whorls. This individuality and uniqueness of fingerprints permitted their use in governmental papers and contracts in ancient China, the Levant and the West to finalize these documents. It was not until 1880, however, that the Scottish physician Henry Faulds published an article in Nature describing a scientific method using printer's ink for recovering a fingerprint for identification.

After Faulds' first fingerprint identification this science evolved rapidly as others began using the ridge patterns on the fingers and palms for scientific identification in cases involving civil and criminal legal issues. By

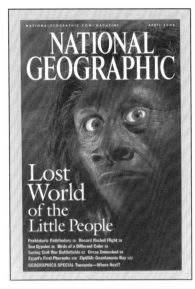

Figure 2-6: Popular use of facial reconstruction is very common today.

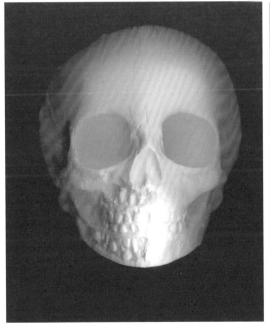
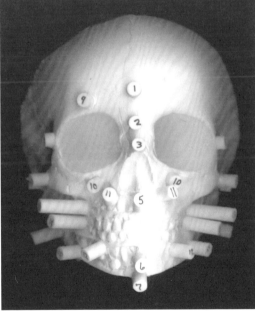

Figure 2-7: Starting with the replica skull of a child, the general process of sticking thickness measures (rubber erasure material) in place are shown.

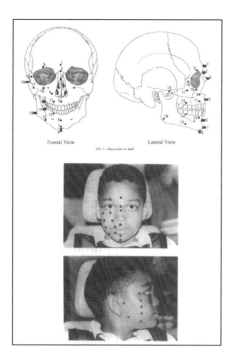

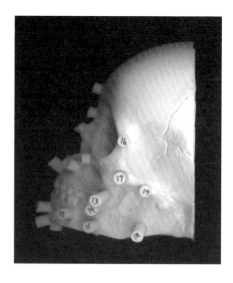

Figure 2-8: Demonstrates the use of one approach to find the exact depth measurements for each facial point. "In Vivo Facial Tissue Depth measurements for Children and Adults," by Manhein, MH, et al.

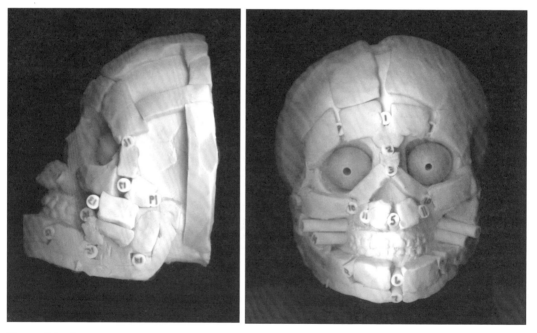

Figure 2-9: Continuing the process of adding clay to join each depth measurement guide until the face takes shape.

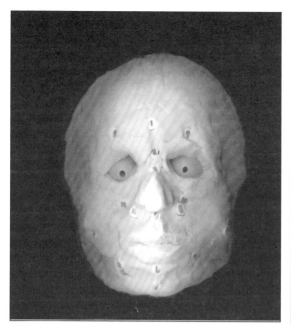 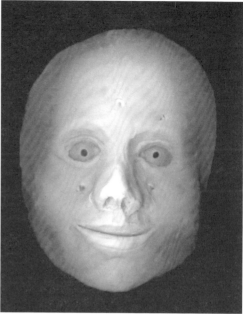

Figure 2-10: Illustration of the process of adding clay until the general facial contours are finished. The difficult decisions are regarding the expression wanted, e.g., closed lips, smile, frown, or sneer.

Computerized
Reconstruction of a
Neanderthal Child's Skull
and Face

THIS COMPUTERIZED RECONSTRUCTION of a
Neanderthal child's skull and face was
generated by computer scientists at the
University of Zurich by using computer
graphics newly developed for this
purpose. AFP-JIJI PHOTO

Figure 2-11: The final result will certainly depend upon the skill and experience of the reconstruction artist. When finished, the creation can be scanned or photographed for public display and/or publication.

1892, the British anthropologist, Sir Francis Galton established that fingerprints were not only unique and individual but permanent. His calculations determined that the probability of two different individuals having the same fingerprint were 1 to 64 billion.

Galton is credited with defining the identifying characteristics of fingerprints. These *Galton* *details* were modified by Sir Edward Henry in 1901 and remain the basis for the Henry Classification System which is still used for the non-computerized classification of fingerprints in English speaking countries.

The use of fingerprints in the United States began in 1902 when the New York Civil Service Commission fingerprinted job applicants.

Identification of criminals also began in New York the following year when the State prison system commenced the routine practice of fingerprinting its prison population.

Throughout the 20th century the science of fingerprinting became firmly established and recognized not only as a means of resolving issues of identification in criminal and civil legal settings but for its uses in military identification as well. Repositories of fingerprint information were created, managed and shared among legal agencies through data bases established by the FBI Identification Division and such foreign agencies as INTERPOL.

In 1999, the Integrated Automated Fingerprint Identification System (IAFIS) was established by the FBI, Criminal Justice Information Services (CJIS) Division. This system permits fingerprint information to be matched through automated computer searches which have the ability to rapidly scan all fingerprint records in the files for a match (**Figure 2-12**). Once the proper information is acquired, it can then be electronically transmitted to the requesting agency. As of this printing of the ASFO Manual of Forensic Odontology, the IAFIS system is the largest repository of fingerprint information in the world with over 47 million subjects in the Criminal Master File.

There are other sources of fingerprint information and some states keep their own files of non-criminals. Nevada takes fingerprints on all workers in the gaming industry and the Bureau of Alcohol Tobacco and Firearms records fingerprints on licensed firearm dealers and owners of Class III and IV weapons.

The system, which is in service 365 days a year, incorporates the fingerprint information with corresponding criminal history information which has been submitted voluntarily by state, local, and federal law enforcement agencies. It has been instrumental in helping police and civil agencies resolve questions of identification involving missing individuals, amnesiacs, homicides, robberies, mass disasters and other criminal and civil issues.

The IAFIS services provided law enforcement includes the following areas:

-Ten-Print Based Fingerprint Identification Services:

- Criminal Ten-Print Fingerprint Submission

- Civil Ten-Print Fingerprint Submission

- Latent Fingerprint Services

- Subject Search and Criminal History Services

- Document and Imaging Services

- Document.

- Fingerprint Image Services

- Photo

- Remote Ten-Print and Latent Fingerprint Search Services

Many medical examiners have access to digital fingerprint recording equipment and crime laboratories in most jurisdictions have access to cabinets and equipment that can recover fingerprints from inanimate objects. (**Figure 2-13**)

Although the unique, individual and permanent features ascribed to fingerprints by Galton make them tremendously advantageous as an identification tool, there are some disadvantages to having this method as the sole means of identification. In the forensic setting, a body may be discovered in a decomposing, burned or skeletonized status. Thus, fingerprint retrieval from the epidermal soft tissues for comparison in the IAFIS or any other data base would be precluded.

Dental Identification

General Dental Participation

There are many ways in which the private practicing dentist and his or her team members can be active participants in forensic dentistry within the framework of their own dental practice. Recognizing and reporting the signs

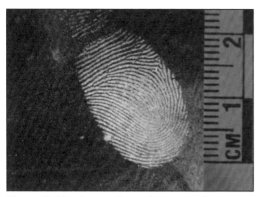

Figure 2-12: Comparison of the basic fingerprint is considered a very trusted and scientific method of identification.

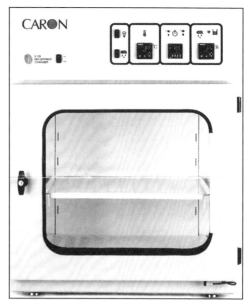

Figure 2-13: One of the many types of fingerprint recovery cabinets on the market. It is commonly used with cyanoacrylate vapor to develop the print.

and symptoms of human abuse may prevent further injury and initiate resolution of the problem. The opportunity to provide complete records from one's practice that provide sufficient antemortem information to permit identification is a rewarding experience even if the clinician has not personally conducted the comparison of those records with the post mortem dental material.

Basic, comprehensive, well organized body identification guidelines have been developed by the American Board of Forensic Odontology (ABFO) at www.abfo.org, and in **Appendix C**. They outline the procedures, equipment and materials necessary to identify unknown human remains by the teeth. They should be followed in all dental identification cases. These guidelines provide an excellent source of information for novice and expert forensic odontologists concerning the collection and preservation of post mortem dental evidence, sources of antemortem data, methods for the comparison of antemortem and post mortem evidence, and terminology used in the reporting of results, opinions and conclusions related to human identification by the dentition. The material provided in the following sections is a narrative intended to emphasize the importance of following the ABFO Guidelines when called to identify a victim by their teeth and paradental structures.

Records Availability

It is important to keep good dental records

primarily because they are an essential part of high quality patient care. Accurate recording of the patient's original condition, the treatment rendered and problems encountered will be of great assistance in evaluating and correctly treating any future problems that may arise. And these same records may become the practitioner's most valuable defensive weapon if a professional liability claim should occur. In addition, these records may be of great value if the patient is involved in an automobile accident, or becomes a victim of violent crime and requires identification. The anguish of family members will be greatly curtailed, and practical concerns such as settling the estate can be handled much more expeditiously if identification can be accomplished promptly.

Records should be appropriately complete, including proper charting and radiographic examination when the patient is first seen, and at subsequent recall visits. Because of their importance, radiographs should be of good diagnostic quality and charts should be legible. When forwarded for forensic purposes, it is preferred that the original records are provided, with the dental office retaining good quality copies. However, if duplicates are forwarded for forensic purposes, the dentist should personally ascertain that they are of good quality, and that duplicated radiographs are marked *Right* and *Left* for orientation.

Both the radiographs and the patient's chart should be forwarded, since the chart often records treatment that was provided after the radiographs were taken. If the chart is not sent, the forensic investigator may lack important information. For example, in the absence of the chart, the investigator may be completely unaware that the patient had all of his or her teeth removed after the radiographs were taken.

If intraoral photographs are available, they should also be forwarded. Other patient records may also be of great value, such as diagnostic models or work models, old dentures, bleach trays, etc. However, these items may be somewhat inconvenient to pack and ship and they may not be needed. In such a case it would be wise to promptly provide the radiographs, chart, and photographs (if available), and include a conspicuous note naming the additional materials that are available if needed.

Dentists should be aware that state laws often describe in detail the right of investigating agencies to obtain health records when they are needed as part of an official investigation. In California, for example, Civil Code Section 15.10 provides that a health care provider "shall disclose medical information" if the disclosure is compelled in various ways. This includes a search warrant issued to a law enforcement agency. Disclosure may also be compelled by a coroner, when requested for the purpose of identifying the decedent or next of kin, or when investigating deaths or other specified matters within the coroner's jurisdiction.

Other pertinent statutes include Sec. 14206 of the Penal Code. This section authorizes law enforcement agencies when dealing, for example, with an adult who has been missing for thirty days, to issue a written declaration stating that an active investigation is being conducted and that medical and dental radiographs are necessary for this purpose. This signed declaration gives the dentist, police or other agency sufficient authority for the dentist, physician or medical facility to release the missing person's dental or skeletal radiographs.

Providing Permanent Identification for Your Patients

The dental office can provide an important service to the patient and to the community by providing the patient with a durable form of personal identification. For example, placing identifying information such as the patient's name, initials, or social security number on the patient's complete denture may result in recovery of a denture lost in a nursing facility or in a hospital operating room. The identifying information would also establish identify if the patient becomes the victim of an accident, crime, or mass fatality incident. This would greatly assist the patient's family with their need for emotional closure, and the equally pressing practical and financial problems often related to the death of a family member. In a number of states, placement of identifying information in complete dentures is mandated in the state dental practice act (e.g. Sec. 1706 of California's Business and Professions Code).

Over the years, other forms of identification have become available. One such example was the micro-chip, containing identifying information that could be bonded to a strategically placed tooth. At this writing, there is considerable interest in a system known as Toothprints, primarily intended to assist in identification of children. Briefly, teeth are imprinted into a thermoplastic wafer. Properly preserved, the imprint is intended to be a useful means for dental identification, as well as a source for DNA comparison and a means of providing a scent for use by tracking dogs.

On September 8, 2004, the American Board of Forensic Odontology commented on the dental identification aspect of the system. The Board applauded the efforts and intent of the developers of the system, but expressed the view that it is presently of limited use in establishing identification through dental means. In the absence of an organized database of dental characteristics, the Board's position is that conventional dental records, such as dental radiographs would provide more useful information in many cases.

Recognizing, Documenting and Reporting Suspected Cases of Abuse and Neglect

The importance of the dental team's role in recognizing, documenting and reporting suspected cases of abuse and neglect cannot be overemphasized. Because 65 percent of all physical child abuse and 75 percent of all physical domestic violence results in injuries to the head, neck, and/or mouth, the dental professional is often the first person to render treatment to abuse victims. This provides us with the opportunity to interrupt the chain of events that threatens the life and well being of the victim. By learning the signs and symptoms of abuse, knowing how to document what is seen, and by fulfilling our legal duty to report suspected cases of abuse, the dental professional may help to mend a family in distress or save the life of a helpless child or adult. This topic is treated in more detail in **Chapter 5 - Human Abuse**.

Participating in DMORT or State Identification Teams

Disaster Mortuary Operational Response Team (DMORT) is a federally funded organization consisting of civilian volunteers in the forensic specialties, including dentistry. It is currently a part of the Department of Homeland Security. When a coroner's office asks for help in dealing with a disaster that overwhelms the resources of the local death investigation agency, DMORT may deploy a team or teams of its members to assist. The team members become federal employees when activated. Membership in DMORT provides private practicing dentists with the opportunity to obtain training and forensic experience, while still continuing their private practice. However, the number of DMORT positions is limited, and vacancies are not always immediately available.

In some states dental identification teams also exist at the state level to assist local coroners when needed. California, for example, has the California Dental Identification Team (CALDIT), which will function as part of the Coroners Mutual Aid Program. This team is composed of dentists who are affiliated with local death investigation offices and are experienced in the investigation of mass fatality incidents.

Nevada set up a state dental identification team funded through the Department of Emergency Management (FEMA). It maintains equipment palletized and housed at the coroner's office in Las Vegas, but is a state-wide resource and available to FEMA.

Response to Bioterrorism, and the Provision of Emergency Health Care

The events of September 11, 2001, followed by the October anthrax contamination of the United States mail, forcefully demonstrated that our nation is vulnerable to major acts of terrorism, including those involving biologic agents. Organized dentistry has proposed that our profession join in the ongoing efforts to:

- Develop an effective response to acts of bioterrorism.

- Fully utilize the knowledge and skills of health care workers in a major disaster in order to assist medical workers in providing care for the injured.

Efforts are underway to develop legislation authorizing dentists, in a federally declared emergency, to perform various procedures that are normally outside of the dental practice acts. There are related efforts to provide appropriate immunity from legal liability for these actions. Action is also being taken to develop an emergency system of registration in advance of need to identify those individuals who have taken the necessary training and are qualified to serve as voluntary workers in a major emergency.

As these programs are developing, dentists are encouraged to use existing resources to improve their knowledge and skills in emergency medicine. For example, courses are now available in emergency medical care for dentists in the armed forces, and are beginning to also become available in the private sector. Related training can also be taken at institutions that offer paramedic training programs, as well as shorter courses offered by the Red Cross. Courses dealing with emerging medical diseases and bioterrorism are available in continuing education programs offered at dental schools and dental society educational programs. Dentists who avail themselves of these educational opportunities will gain knowledge that may ultimately benefit patients in the office, family members at home, and may also benefit the community at large.

Forensic Imaging Techniques

Photography

Photography is used by the forensic dentist to document clinical findings in identification, person abuse and bite mark cases. The well-made photograph surpasses, but does not replace, written or verbal descriptions or sketches because photographs are more accurate, graphic, objective and verifiable. Photographs capture perishable or transient evidence. They allow case reconstruction for investigators and assist in illustrating findings to jurors and colleagues. They provide the technically accurate working materials in bite mark analysis. Photography can also be used to discover unsuspected findings by extending the range of human visibility, employing such techniques as microphotography, infrared and ultraviolet photography.

As with all scientific and evidence photography, the objective is to standardize a technique to produce consistent and accurate results. Artistic composition is sacrificed in favor of sharp, well exposed, labeled images that provide a true and accurate representation of what was observed by the investigator. To affect this result, the forensic dentist must have background knowledge of photographic theory and must be accomplished in the use of his or her equipment. As is the nature of forensic dentistry, the photographer and the equipment must be constantly in a ready state for instant implementation.

Luntz cites three reasons why the forensic dentist must be photographically self-reliant:

- Police may not be available to make needed photographs

- Police may not be trained or equipped to make close-up photographs

- Chain of evidence is shorter

Additionally, an illustration composed directly by the forensic dentist renders a more accurate interpretation of the dental findings than one produced by an intermediary instructed to take the picture. Therefore, photography, which is merely an adjunct in most fields of dentistry, is absolutely integral to the practice of forensic odontology. Further, detailed discussion of this topic is found in **Chapter 6 -Technological Aides in Forensic Odontology.**

Radiography

Dental radiography is of prime importance in the identification of human remains. The comparison of high quality antemortem and post mortem radiographs whether film-based or digital provides a multitude of maxillofacial, tooth and dental restorative characteristics distinguishable to an individual which may be observed and compared. Radiographic images are objective and much less susceptible to human error when compared to written dental charts and records. In fact, it is common procedure for the dental images in a forensic case to serve as the *gold standard* whenever there is a discrepancy or suspected error in the patient's antemortem written record or charting, and in the miscoded post mortem record.

Most forensic odontologists will agree that it is often the case that a single dental radiographic image can lead to a positive dental identification. This, however, requires radiographic images of high quality. This chapter will concentrate on the aspects of dental radiology most often encountered in human identification and mass disaster scenarios.

Imaging Fundamentals and X-Ray Machine Variables

The fundamentals of exposing, processing and interpreting dental radiographs are the same when used for forensic purposes as in the private practice of dentistry with a few notable exceptions. They also hold true whether the image has been captured via dental film or with more recent digital imaging systems. There are five system variables which affect the resultant radiographic image: mA, kVp, exposure time, aluminum filtration and distance from the object. The quality of an image is normally assessed by evaluating its having the proper density (overall blackness), contrast (comparison of blacks, whites and grays) and sharpness. **Table 2-1** below shows the relationships of the variables and their effects on the resultant image.

As can be seen in the table above, all five variables affect image density with filtration and aluminum filtration having a negative or decreasing effect. Increased kVp and filtration are the only variables which affect image contrast by producing an increase in shades of gray (low visual contrast) as the two are increased. Image sharpness is affected only

with changes in distance with the sharpest image and least magnification produced by a long target-to-film distance and a short object-to film distance.

To summarize, mA and exposure time should be used to determine the amount of image density and can be used interchangeably. Therefore, halving the mA gives the same exact image density results as halving the exposure time and vice versa. The use of kVp to determine image density is discouraged because the preferred high image contrast - mostly blacks and whites - will be lost as kVp is increased.

Forensic Imaging Technique, Receiving Medium and Beam/Object Orientation

The objective of exposing post mortem dental radiographs is to ultimately compare those radiographic images to antemortem images of known individuals. Post mortem beam/receiver (receiver meaning film or digital systems) geometry should be similar to that used when the individual's antemortem images were created in order for the tooth structures and dental restorations to be visually comparable.

In general, the imaging plane should be parallel to the long axis of the teeth and the beam should *always* be directed perpendicular to the imaging plane and aligned with the tooth embrasures as shown in **Figure 2-14.** However, to duplicate the angulation of most antemortem images, increased vertical

Variable	Density	Contrast Scale	Sharpness
mA	X	----	---
kVp	X	more shades of gray	----
Exposure Time	X	---	---
Aluminum Filter	X	more shades of gray	---
Distance	X	---	X

Table 2-1: The relationship of variables to the end image.

angulation should be used when creating maxillary periapical radiographs and little or no downward vertical when creating bitewings. Since the most common antemortem radiographic image is the bitewing projection, any post mortem radiographic survey should include a bitewing projection. Again, the most important aspect of alignment geometry is to keep the beam perpendicular to the plane of the receiver regardless of the receiver's angle relative to the teeth.

A common pitfall often occurs when exposing small fragments of human dental remains involving improper alignment of the dental specimen and the image medium by placing the receiver buccal to the surface of the fragment with the beam originating from the lingual. This results in an image which appears to have been taken on the opposite side of the arch when film is mounted or viewed in the normal manner. Additionally, when using a digital receiver, there is no *herringbone* pattern to indicate that the image was taken backwards. This may be avoided by always insuring that the location of the receiver and beam direction relative to the specimen simulates the normal alignment in living individuals.

It is suggested that when using radiograhic film, double film packs be used to take post mortem radiographs. Thus, the odontologist can retain one set of radiographs for his or her records even if one set is retained as evidence by the court. Periapical, bitewing and occlusal films are also commonly used to reproduce the types of radiographic images in the antemortem record. Lateral plate films of various sizes (5x7 and 8x10 inch) and panoramic radiographs may also be of use when dealing with burn victims. With the permission of the medical examine/coroner the entire skull may be disarticulated and radiographed *in toto* so as not to disrupt the incinerated dentition.

Positioning aids for stabilizing dental remains to be radiographed and insuring that the *imaging plane is parallel to the long axis of the teeth and the beam is directed perpendicular to the imaging plane and aligned with the tooth embrasures may include:*

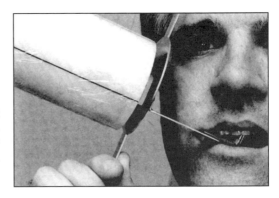

Figure 2-14: Illustration of basic radiographic technique.

- Pedestal or jig (autopsy neck rest)

- Modeling clay

- Wet paper towels

- String or wax

When attempting to radiograph resected jaws, one should position the articulated or masticated jaws on the positioning aide at the beam source (tube) height. Secure the film to the teeth using clay or wax and expose for either bitewing or periapical views using exposure principles discussed previously. When the jaws are not to be removed a combination periapical /bitewing view can be obtained by making an incision in the tissue medial to the inferior border of the mandible and sliding and securing an occlusal film along the lingual surfaces of the teeth.

Skeletonized remains, jaw fragments and avulsed teeth can be radiographed by stabilizing the osseous and dental fragments on a periapical or occlusal film. When the masticatory muscles are in rigor a lateral plate film can be aligned and exposed so that the beam source is projecting a lateral jaw exposure.

In panoramic radiography the beam direction is effectively opposite from intraoral radiography that is from lingual toward buccal or facial with the beam passing through all of the intervening structures of the head and neck. Efforts should be made to radiograph the post mortem specimen with panoramic radiography. However, with badly fragmented and/or missing parts, this may not be feasible. Consequently, when attempting to emulate antemortem panoramic views with post mortem intraoral radiography it may be helpful to reverse the beam direction by placing the film or sensor on the buccal or facial and directing the beam from the lingual. This is especially true if you are using anatomical rather than restorative features for the comparison.

Exposure Energy With Forensic Specimens

Exposure energy sufficient to obtain images of proper density is often greatly reduced in forensic specimen due to the lack of normal tissue overlying the dental structures. Accordingly, either the exposure time or mA setting should be reduced by one-third in most cases and by as much as one-half in skeletonized and burned remains to avoid images that are overly dark.

Film Processing

Film processing procedures and machine maintenance is often overlooked when conducting forensic analysis, particularly in mass disaster settings where a certain amount of chaos and urgency may be a factor. Indeed, due to the serious medico-legal issues involved in the usual forensic case, this can be a critical mistake with severe consequences even beyond that of the normal dental private practice setting.

Proper use of fresh chemicals and following the manufacturers' recommended processing steps will help ensure images of high quality that will remain so over great lengths of time. Shortcuts such as using higher processing temperatures with shorter developing time or an inadequate film wash such as with the cheaper processing units will result in failure and discoloration of the image over time. The *endodontic setting* of many film processors can also create films which are not of sufficient archival quality. This error is particularly serious in that it is immediately apparent and

may only be observable over a certain period of time.

Another common mistake involves outdated daylight loaders in which the colored filter is inadequate to prevent film fog with many of today's faster film speeds. The color filter should be a dark, ruby-red and should not be used directly under fluorescent lighting in order to avoid film fog. Additionally, remember that time is an important factor with daylight loaders. Film left unwrapped for lengthy time periods within a daylight loader may become fogged. It is also essential that images be mounted and labeled as soon as the series comes out of the dental film processor to eliminate an incorrectly labeled film series which would very lead to misidentifications.

Forensic Image Comparison and *Image Viewing Conditions*

Even with the highest degree of image quality, detailed dental structures cannot be clearly observed when films are held up to ceiling lights and open windows for viewing. Post mortem and antemortem image comparison should be done under proper viewing conditions, particularly when the dental findings are small and bone structures, pulp chambers and root patterns must be seen and compared. This requires a properly sized or masked X-ray view box in a room with subdued background lighting. Images compared on computer monitors should also be done in subdued lighting and the eyes should be adjusted to the subdued lighting.

Issues with Duplicated Radiographs

Most dentists in the United States orient dental films on the view box and in film mounts with the orientation dimple of the film facing upward; away from the view box surface. This establishes the orientation of the film series as if the viewer is facing the patient.

However, a very common concern in forensic dentistry is the improper orientation of duplicate antemortem radiographs where the dimple of the original film can be seen, but not felt. Even if it is assumed or proven that the duplicating film was oriented properly during duplication, it is possible that the original films were placed dimple down at that time. This will confuse the issue of the patient's right from left.

The most reliable method of determining if the dimple is or was up at the time of duplication is to consider the location of the dimple relative to the corners of the individual films themselves. Whenever the dimple is placed upward on a film, its location will always be in the lower right or upper left corner of the film when it is oriented horizontally. The dimple location in the opposite corners indicates a dimple down orientation. Is so, the duplicate should then simply be flipped and/or rotated until the dimples of the films are seen in the corners indicated above. This will assure a dimple up orientation and the films can then be properly compared.

Digital Radiography

Digital radiology in dentistry is now an accepted method of obtaining radiographic images. The reality of near instant image viewing gives digital technology a real advantage over the use of film. The image quality is equal to or better when using line pair density for comparison. The ability of digital images to be enhanced to optimize contrast and density often eliminates the need for numerous re-takes. Also, the fact that developing systems are eliminated greatly simplifies the process of producing the image. Digital radiography, however, cannot overcome poor angulation techniques. All digital systems require a good working knowledge of receptor and beam positioning principles to produce images of diagnostic quality.

The digital sensor replaces the traditional film pack commonly used in dentistry. There are angulation devices to assist in positioning the sensors for proper placement. Three types of sensor systems are in use today which may or may not be connected to the computer with a wire. The first two are the Charged-Coupled Device (CCD) and the Complementary Metal Oxide Semiconductor sensor (CMOS). These allow each image to be loaded directly into the computer as the images are taken providing for immediate viewing. Wireless sensors use various wireless systems to connect with the computer and also enable immediate viewing. These systems are being continually improved to address electric interference and distance to receiver issues. Direct systems utilize either a CMOS or CCD sensor. There are advantages to both and individual research is needed to determine which will work best in different situations.

The third type of sensor employs an indirect system using phosphor plate or Photo-Stimulated Phosphor technology (PSP). This system uses an energized plate to transfer images from the patient to a plate-scanning device. These screens are reusable and can be cut to any size desired. If used in a panoramic machine, the intensifying screens are removed from the cassette and replaced with the phosphor plate. After exposure, the scanner then *reads* the plate and sends a digital image to the computer. Most scanners then erase the screen to prepare it for the next exposure. With some systems, this process takes about three minutes which is the equivalent time required to develop conventional radiographs.

The advantage of phosphor technology is that the plates are almost identical to films and require no operator adaptation or learning curve when it is substituted for film. At this writing, phosphor plates may be reversed in their holders, thus creating confusion when electronic mounting is employed. Small metal indicators may be attached to a corner of the plate to ensure proper placement was employed. The scanners require no chemicals and thus eliminate the environmental impact of the wastes film processing produces. The images can be imported directly into WinID or viewed in any Dicom-3 compliant software. PSP technology does not have the same time advantage as other digital formats.

Due in part to efficiency, digital radiography has proven to be an extremely valuable and time-saving tool for the forensic odontologist. In mass fatality incidents with large numbers of victims, digital radiography with new portable hand-held x-ray generators have become the state of the art (**Figure 2-15**). Integrating scanned antemortem radiographs and digital post mortem images with a computerized identification program such as WinID allows the odontology section of morgue operations to become a completely paperless environment. Dental comparisons can begin immediately at the completion of each post mortem examination.

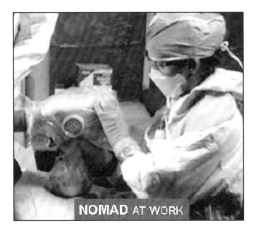

Figure 2-15 Hand held dental x-ray unit in use.

Digital radiography is an accepted method of obtaining images from a subject. It is a new tool to add to the armamentarium of the forensic odontologist. It can be used to augment conventional radiography or stand alone as the designated system. Digital systems still require the knowledge of beam angulation and sensor positioning to create diagnostic quality images.

Enhanced diagnostic capability is an additional benefit that digital radiography offers. The brightness and contrast of the image can be altered by the computer to a limited degree. Images that are slightly too dark or light can be enhanced to the ideal. Magnification also improves the diagnostic value of the image. When comparing additional morphology in antemortem and post mortem, such as bone trabeculae, magnifying the image images is especially helpful.

Because forensic situations and applications are prone to be scrutinized by third parties, chain of custody and storage of unaltered images in a permanent format must be considered an essential part of digital radiography.

Radiation Safety

Radiation safety is and should always be a concern when exposing dental radiographic images. Although no damage will be imposed to the post mortem specimen, scatter radiation from the exposure of that specimen will always be a factor. Any exposure of x-radiation should be considered harmful, even if the effects are small. Safety issues are undoubtedly magnified in mass disaster settings where numerous persons may be working at or near the area of exposure.

The most important safety procedures for operators in that setting are sensitive image receptors and distance. New digital sensors are considerably more sensitive than film and thus, reduce back scatter. Those exposing images should never hold the film or receiver in place during exposure. Also, all personnel should avoid being in the pathway of the beam and be at least six feet away from the source of the scatter (the object being irradiated). If that is not possible, then a lead-lined barrier or an operator lead apron must be used. This is particularly important with the advent of the recently developed and utilized hand-held x-ray beam generators where the operator is close to the subject and cannot always be behind the scatter shield due to the subject being in the supine position.

It is common radiation safety-sense that any effort that reduces the total ionizing energy of the exposure to the forensic specimen such as fast films and digital imaging receivers, also delivers that same amount of radiation dose reduction to the operators involved.

Scanning Electron Microscopy and Energy Dispersive X-ray Spectroscopy

When presented with a challenging case, it is important for the forensic odontologist to be aware of the scientific resources that are available and how they can aid in resolution of the case. A valuable technique which may provide considerable information is Scanning Electron Microscopy with Energy Dispersive X-ray Spectroscopy (SEM/EDS). Possibly the largest hindrance to maximizing utilization of this tool is lack of awareness of the information it can provide and the ways in which it can be used. The basic use of the SEM is described here and more detail is presented in **Chapter 6 -Technological Aides in Forensic Odontology.**

The principal areas of forensic identification investigation in which SEM/EDS are useful include: recognition and differentiation of tooth structure from other materials, verification of the use of specific restorative procedures and identification of inorganic restorative materials. This information is potentially important in identification of human remains. The techniques are applicable to decomposed, disarticulated and incinerated individuals. In the latter, they may offer the forensic odontologist a last line of approach to retrieve evidence.

The ability to analyze microscopic samples means that this technique can provide results from trace amounts of evidence. SEM has also been utilized in bite mark analysis, and there is some new potential for this technique in examination of the transfer of microscopic patterns from fabric to skin (**Chapter 4 - Bite Mark Analysis** and **Chapter 6 - Technological Aides in Forensic Odontology**).

Overview

SEM/EDS are a well established combination of instrumental techniques which gives information about the microstructure and inorganic elemental composition of a sample. SEM facilities may be found in crime laboratories and in every major university. For those unfamiliar with SEM/EDS, there is typically a specialist who can assist in specimen preparation and selection of analysis conditions

The result of analysis will be an image showing microstructural features or chemical phase distribution in the sample. Simultaneous elemental analysis (EDS) can also be performed producing an x-ray spectrum that may be considered a fingerprint of the major elements present in the sample. This elemental analysis can return quantitative results under the correct conditions.

Antemortem Considerations

Upon completing the post mortem examination, the next step is to identify a population of missing persons that may provide the identity of the decedent. Under most circumstances, the forensic odontologist will not be the investigator responsible for collecting missing person lists. The agency in charge of the identification will usually already have possible missing persons that they suspect may match the identity of the decedent.

Having a suspected missing person, the investigator will have solicited a dental record (or records if there are multiple possibilities) from the suspected decedent's dentist. There are often many clues associated with the decedent that may render a possible identity. These could include a wallet or driver's license, clothing, jewelry, other personal effects, and medical and dental information.

If there are no clues regarding the identity of the victim, the forensic odontologist should assist law enforcement in entering all post mortem findings into a central clearinghouse for matching missing or unidentified persons. This central clearinghouse is usually the Federal Bureau of Investigation (FBI) National Crime Information Center (NCIC). The problem existing today is that all missing person information is not recorded in the NCIC. Many jurisdictions are hampered by the lack of professional staff or budgets to allow for expert help. It is well recognized that many individuals go unidentified in the United States and there is a pressing need for a workable central information center.

All information that has been collected about a victim should be entered onto an input form and keyed into the NCIC computer in Washington, D.C. The computer can then begin a nationwide search for possible decedent matches that can be sent back to the investigator. The investigator can then use these lists to attempt identification. The address and phone number of the NCIC are listed later in this chapter. It should be noted that the NCIC computer does not have the capability of identifying possible decedents based solely on dental information and this is a situation that must be addressed. Many other physical descriptors are needed to generate possible matches.

When a possible identity for the victim is established, an antemortem dental record of the suspected victim is obtained by the investigators. This record is then given to the forensic odontologist for use in attempting identification. It is extremely important for the forensic odontologist to take the entire antemortem record and completely review all contents before attempting to put together an antemortem record for a comparison.

Many times there are pieces of dental information buried in the record that can be overlooked by the forensic odontologist who only reviews the radiographs. The accuracy of the dental charting should be verified with the radiographs and vice versa. Phone conversation with the treating dentist is sometimes useful. Notations concerning photographs, dental models and dental prosthetics should be explored in detail.

All possible antemortem dental information must first be collected and analyzed. Then an attempt to prepare an antemortem dental chart can be undertaken. The Antemortem Dental Record should include the information in **Table 2-2**:

Also included should be the written records of dental procedures, all dental radiographs, study models, and photographs.

Sources for Antemortem Information

Antemortem data may be defined as dental radiographs, written records, models and photographs. Original radiographs should be obtained if possible. Care must be exercised with original records to be absolutely certain that they are not damaged or lost. Again, the discovery and collection of antemortem records is ordinarily the responsibility of the investigative agency that has access to missing persons reports at the local, state or national level. However, the forensic odontologist may recognize additional characteristics (e.g., prior orthodontic treatment) beyond the general description which could be helpful in establishing a possible source of information. **Appendix E** lists a variety of resource agencies and/or individuals that might provide assistance in locating records.

Charting, Retention of Records and Data Bases

Universal standards for dental charting will ease the burden of identifications in mass disasters, missing persons, or unidentified bodies nationwide by providing the forensic odontologist with antemortem charts that can be readily interpreted and easily entered into the WinID computer program. Forensic odontologists must lead the way by setting the example for general dentists.

Any forensic odontologist who has made a dental identification or worked a disaster is familiar with the difficulties of reading and interpreting antemortem dental records from the general dentist or specialist. Often dentists have their own shorthand and charting techniques, which vary from area to area, dentist to dentist, and even country to country. This presents a major problem for odontologists when trying to compare antemortem and post mortem records.

Dental schools teach that the standard for recording information on patients in a dental office should be a complete charting of the head and neck, extraoral, intraoral, and dental regions. Included in this is charting of all present restorations and caries, and a full mouth set of radiographs. Unfortunately, many dentists do not completely chart patients for a baseline. Many only record the dental work needed to be done and chart the work completed.

Incomplete charting provides little or no information for the odontologist to use in comparison. This travesty is a disservice to families of deceased or missing loved ones. Only complete head and neck, extraoral, intraoral, dental and radiographic recording in the chart can provide an adequate baseline from which a comparison can be made.

Name, address and sex of the patient	Partial and full removable prostheses:

Name and address of the dentist providing the record	Type of denture base
	      Metal/acrylic
	      Shade, mold, plastic vs. porcelain

Social Security Number	denture teeth
Date of birth	Existing caries
All existing teeth:	Root canal therapy:

Erupted
    Unerupted impacted
    Supernumerary
	Type of filling material
	    Retrofill procedures
	    Apicoectomy

All missing teeth	Tooth positions:
All existing restorations:	Faciolingual versions Rotations

Amalgams
    Nonprecious metaV metals
    Fixed prostheses
    Implants
    Non-metallic acrylics:
	Intrusion
	    Extrusion
	    Diastemas
	
	Atypical crowns

Composites
      Porcelain
	Peg shaped laterals
	    Fusion/gemination
	    Enamel pearls
	    Supernumerary cusps

	Exostoses, tori
	Periodontal conditions

Table 2-2: Antemortem dental record information.

It is critical for forensic dentists to set the example to initiate universal charting standards and complete charting procedures. Using charting designations based upon the WinID computer program standardizes records making interpreting and translating these records into the WinID program antemortem chart significantly easier and faster.

The WinID program has been used to facilitate identifications in the following mass fatality incidents.

- Commuter plane crash, Guam, 1996

- Korean Air disaster, Guam, 1997

- Amtrak train wreck, Bourbonnais, Illinois, 1999

- Air Egypt crash, Rhode Island, 1999

- Alaska Air disaster, Ventura, California, 2000

- World Trade Center terrorist attack, New York, 2001

It was reported that WinID was also used in Madrid on March 11, 2004 (known as 3/11) and in Bali in the aftermath of the terrorist bombing in 2002. **Chapter 3 - Multiple Fatality Incident, Dental Identification and Bioterrorism Issues** provides specific examples of multiple identification following dramatic events.

WinID is available in several languages, including English, Spanish, French and German. An improved French and Italian version are expected soon. The charting's simplicity makes it attractive for use by general dentists, and its ease makes it straightforward to incorporate into the dental record.

The WinID Antemortem Chart provides odontograms and a descriptors list of primary and secondary codes for charting the oral cavity. The new NCIC dental codes (NCIC2000) are a subset of the WinID codes. Included on the page is personal and radiographic information. Using this chart can assist the dentist in assuring that the chart is complete and conforming to universal standards.

When a dentist conscientiously charts a code for every tooth area using WinID codes, minutes if not hours can be shaved from the time it takes the forensic odontologist to translate this information into the computer program. For instance, if a dentist charts teeth #17, 18 and 22 as EXT, CR and *nothing*, respectively, the odontologist has to interpret and translate those designations into the WinID codes before entering it into the antemortem chart. However, if the dentist codes them X, MODFL/GCR, and V respectively, the codes can be immediately transferred to the chart.

Disasters and increasing numbers of missing or unidentified persons occur at an alarming rate. The ease and speed with facilitation of the process by which an odontologist can make identification is related to the ability to read and interpret antemortem records provided by the treating dentist. Establishing a universal dental charting standard based upon the computer program WinID dental records maintained in general practices provides the forensic odontologist with records that can be quickly and easily added to the WinID database for comparison with post mortem data. Forensic dentists must set the example by implementing these standards into their own offices and encouraging dentists who are not forensically trained to do likewise.

The Clinical Record

Primarily, the dental record must comply with the rules and regulations of the Dental State Board of Examiners in each state. A complete record must accurately reflect the treatment provided to the patient. It is not limited to the following but should include:

- Patient's demographic information including name, address, sex, date of birth, phone numbers (including home cellular and business), social security number, martial status, emergency, contact information, personal referal information, insurance information and financial data concerning billing of the patient or third party payer

- Past medical information which is regularly updated to provide a current list of diseases, allergies, medications including dosage and/or a copy of prescriptions, over-the-counter (OTC) and herbal preparations and treating physicians

- Chief complaint including duration and symptoms

- Past dental history includes previous treatments, types of appliances (retainers, night guards, dentures), dental hygiene compliance

- Clinical examination and charting of hard and soft tissues of the head and neck including pre and post treatment intraoral and facial photographs.

- Radiographs of diagnostic quality

- A treatment record including consent and dates of therapy, materials used, special recommendations or referrals for treatment or consultation by specialists including those refused by the patient.

Records may be written or maintained using computer software programs established for this purpose. Regardless of whether records are kept through a paper or electronic system, the dental practitioner must follow the recommendation of jurisdictional licensing boards related to their generation and maintenance. In some states, patient records, including all radiographs, must be maintained for at least seven years from the date of last entry. In others the standard is five years.

In the case of minors, the federal government in the United States requires that records be retained until the patient would have reached the age of majority (twenty-one years of age). Many forensic dentists have employed records older than the standard for identification purposes. Diagnostic study casts must be kept for three years from the date made.

A patient or authorized representative may present the dentist with a written request for a legible copy of their record. This would include duplicates of casts and copies of their radiographs. This material should to be provided within fourteen days of the request. In a forensic situation requiring recovery of antemortem dental records, these may be furnished by the patient or authorized representative, or a dentist that the patient chooses. The dentist may charge a reasonable fee for reproducing records.

If a dentist is directed to submit records by the Board of Dentistry, police agency or Office of the Attorney General, they should be originals and unedited. The dentist should retain good quality copies. If duplicate records are forwarded for forensic purposes, the dentist should personally ascertain that they are of diagnostic quality and that duplicated radiographs are marked *Right* and *Left* for orientation. All clinical notes must be legible and understandable. *Great care must be exercised in carefully reproducing accurate records.* The cost of producing such records is borne by the doctor. In a mass disaster situation or crime scene incident it would not be reasonable to expect that the records would be returned to the submitting dentist. Therefore, a legible copy should always be maintained in the files.

When requested, it is important to forward both the radiographs and the patient's chart, since the latter often indicates treatment that was provided after the radiographs were taken. If the chart is not sent, the forensic investigator may lack important information such as the fact that the patient had all of his or her teeth removed since the radiographs were taken. If intraoral photographs are available, they should also be labeled and forwarded.

Other patient records may also be of great value, including by not limited to diagnostic or working casts, old dentures and bleaching trays. However, these items may be somewhat inconvenient to pack and ship and they may not be needed initially. In such cases it would be wise to promptly provide the patient's radiographs, chart, and photographs and include a detailed note identifying the additional materials that are available upon request.

Dentists should be aware that state laws often describe in detail the right of investigating agencies to obtain health records when they are needed as part of an official investigation. In California, for example, Civil Code Section 15.10 provides that a health care provider "shall disclose medical information" if the disclosure is compelled in various ways including:

- A search warrant issued to a law enforcement agency

- A coroner, when requested for the purpose of identifying the decedent or next of kin

- Investigation of deaths or other specified matters within the coroner's jurisdiction.

Another pertinent statute in California is Sec. 14206 of the Penal Code which authorizes law enforcement agencies to issue a written declaration stating that an active investigation is being conducted, and that medical and dental radiographs are necessary when dealing, for example, with an adult who has been missing for thirty days. This signed declaration gives the police or other agency sufficient authority to impel the dentist, physician or medical facility to release the missing person's dental or skeletal radiographs.

Following are suggestions and requirements to facilitate the process of providing the authorities with a dental record. The records should include:
- Proper patient dental charting
- Radiographs
- Casts
- Laboratory prescriptions
- Insurance records
- Any other information that would aid in determining a person's dental identification.

Legible dental charting should note which tooth numbering system is used. Understandable and acceptable abbreviations and medical and dental terminology should be used in charting and recording of treatment notes. Include additional patient information or unusual dental treatment provided, such as, dental implants, removable appliances, intraoral tattoos and other soft tissue anomalies. Specifically, the written record should provide information about the dental treatment before and after submitted radiographs were taken. Materials used and/or surfaces restored, as well as any other identifying features are also important to note. An onlay might include the following tooth surfaces: MOD, MODB, MODL or MODBL. It could be made of gold, porcelain or composite material. Since it is often difficult from a radiograph to determine whether restorations include buccal and lingual surfaces the caveat to submit written records is reinforced.

Medical information concerning the patient is important to include. In a recent case, the dentist provided a medical history stating the need for premedication for a hip replacement. This information allowed for a positive identification to be made since manufacturers place serial numbers on implants which will aid in identification. It is also important to include

a list of any specialists that the patient may have been referred to and their addresses and phone numbers. They may be able to provide additional radiographs and clinical information to supplement the patient's record.

Dental radiographs are essential to the forensic dentist when attempting to make a positive identification. A current, properly exposed full mouth series which exhibits an accurate image of the patient's dentition and supporting structures is often the most informative. Panoramic, cephalometric, bitewing and occlusal radiographs are also helpful if a full series is not available.

These radiographs permit the odontologist to make comparisons of restorations, root form or position, crown shape, location and position of impacted teeth and sinus and orbital patterns. All antemortem radiographs should be properly labeled with the patient's full name and date and the dentist's name, address, and phone number. Digital radiographs should be printed on high quality paper for the best definition and properly labeled *Right* and *Left*. Any duplicate films should be so labeled.

Original records should not be released to family members of a victim. This may violate the Health Insurance Portability and Accessibility (HIPAA) regulations in the United States which are intended to insure one's right to privacy concerning medical records. Additionally, dental and medical records have been misplaced or lost by grieving family members. This can seriously hinder the investigative process.

Records should be provided to the appropriate law enforcement or investigating agency involved (**Chapter 7 - Jurisprudence**). When submitting original records or radiographs, the dentist should keep a legible and diagnostic copy should a backup be necessary. A receipt must be obtained for any item given to the authorities to allow for a chain of evidence continuity.

The dental practitioner with no specific forensic training who maintains accurate, legible, thorough records can make the difference in affecting an identification that returns a loved one to their family and provides much needed closure in a tragedy.

Undocumented Individuals

The global market has changed the level and intensity of visitation to the United States and other countries. It is not unusual to find communities with thirty percent of the population having permanent residence in another country. In America, states located adjacent to the northern and southern borders certainly have a high influx of foreign workers and other visitors.

Interior cities like Las Vegas, however, with a yearly visitor rate of 45 million people, may have more than 100 thousand foreign nationals in the community on any particular day. Many of these visitors may be undocumented and this becomes a significant problem when an individual is reported missing or injury and death from natural or man made disasters occur. This situation was reinforced by the failure to identify some victims of the World Trade Center terrorist attack because they were undocumented citizens and their antemortem records were not submitted for comparison.

It is important to have well trained and prepared teams with experience in working with national and international authorities for identification purposes. Following the tsunami disaster in the Indian Ocean, international teams were mobilized from Europe, Asia and the Americas to identify and repatriate foreign victims and assist local authorities in identification of the victims among their populations.

Post Mortem Considerations

The Oral Autopsy

To avoid creating bias, some forensic odontologists suggest restricting the amount of information available to them concerning the circumstances surrounding the death of the decedent. These minimalists request only the most basic information including, but not limited to, mode and manner of death, sex of decedent, time of death, the putative identity and the availability of possible antemortem dental records. Others, however, are of the opinion that the more knowledge they have concerning the circumstances of a case the better they can prepare the dental aspects of the situation.

When no dental restorations are present the forensic odontologist increasingly relies on anatomical landmarks and tooth and bone anatomy to arrive at identification. Teeth may be missing because of extraction in an antemortem setting. This type of tooth loss will be manifested by alveolar ridges and sockets with rounded, smooth edges and surfaces. Conversely perimortem or post mortem tooth loss will present with sharp alveolar ridges associated with the missing tooth socket. If the victim's remains are exposed to environmental factors for extended periods, the status of the dentition and mandibular and maxillary bone may also be affected.

Table 2-3a-c contains examples of objective findings the forensic odontologist should evaluate and eventually compare between the antemortem and post mortem records. While these are not intended to be all inclusive, they can serve as a checklist and demonstrate the range of findings that may be observed:

Children

On occasion the forensic odontologist may be called upon to perform identification on a child or adolescent. The ABFO Body Identification Guidelines (BIG) certainly apply when working with children (**Appendix C**) Special challenges may present themselves to the odontologist unaccustomed to working with deciduous and/or mixed dentition. This section will offer some suggestions when working with the developing dentition.

Special Concerns When Identifying Children

Due to the emphasis on preventive dentistry and the utilization of fluorides it is becoming more common for children to reach adulthood caries free and therefore, with no restorations.

Some children have never been to a dentist and therefore no antemortem dental records exist. The young person's mouth is dynamic and constantly undergoing change as teeth are developing, erupting and exfoliating.

For these reasons antemortem radiographs taken one or more years prior to a juvenile's death may be difficult for the odontologist to use or interpret. Certain dental sealants, and preventive resin and composite restorations are often difficult to detect clinically and radiographically. Children who have seen a dentist and needed no treatment may have little information recorded in their dental record that is of use to the odontologist.

The majority of dentists who treat children are conservative when exposing them to dental radiation. Radiographs may not be taken of some children until the age of five years or later. Orthodontic care is currently available to many children with the result that many adolescents attain a *normal* Class I occlusion after correction of unusual or individual malocclusion characteristics. Orthodontists usually maintain significant, detailed records including sequential casts and cephalometric radiographs that are useful for antemortem comparison.

There are many different tooth identification systems in use. Most dentists in the United States use the Universal Numbering System which encodes the deciduous teeth with letters from **A** to **T**. **A** is the maxillary right second primary molar and **T** the mandibular right second primary molar. Some dentists, including many orthodontists, continue to use the Palmer Notation System which also uses letters. In this system, **A** represents the maxillary and mandibular central incisors and **E** for the second primary molars in both arches. The odontologist may also be confronted with a dental record which uses the Federation Dentaire International System (FDI) system of nomenclature. Refer to the tooth conversion tables printed in **Appendix F** for a list of the different charting systems that are in use.

Always perform a complete dental examination of the remains. Record the presence or absence of teeth, both deciduous and permanent, including the partial eruptions of teeth. Note any retained primary teeth. Make note of any dental sealants on specific teeth and note as to whether it is a clear, white, tinted or tooth-colored sealant. Be specific as to the type of material and location, size and shape of any dental restorations. Indicate any restorations which appear to have been lost. This is a common occurrence with primary teeth.

Be observant of enamel irregularities such as fluorosis, hypoplastic or hypocalcified enamel and other abnormal colorations of the enamel. Note the presence of dental caries. Be specific concerning the size of carious lesions. A *sticky occlusal pit* may not have been charted as caries by the child's dentist. Be aware that in some children's mouths dental caries can progress very rapidly. An interproximal lesion on a deciduous molar on a current bitewing radiograph may appear as a clean, non-carious surface on a bitewing film taken only 6-12 months earlier.

Indicate the type of occlusion. Be specific about types of cross-bites or the presence and location of the malposed tooth or teeth. Record the presence and degree of interdental spacing, both in the deciduous and permanent dentition. Note any incisal or occlusal wear. Bruxism in the deciduous dentition is very common and unless significant wear is noted in the antemortem record, the finding of moderate wear with the primary teeth should not influence the identification process. Less commonly seen findings in children's mouths that are also important would include:

- Primary hypodontia (congenital absence of primary teeth)

- Fused primary teeth

- Gemination of primary teeth

- Supernumerary primary teeth

- Mesiodens (usually a *ullet-shaped* small tooth observed radiographically above the root apices of the maxillary primary central incisors)

TEETH	STATUS	DESCRIPTOR
Present	Erupted Unerupted Impacted	
Missing	Congenitally missing Antemortem loss Post mortem loss	Healed extraction Recent extraction
Type	Permanent Deciduous Mixed dentition Retained primary Supernumerary	
Position	Normal Malposed	Faciolingual version Rotated Super erupted Infraerupted Diastemas Occlusal discrepancies
Crown morphology	Size and shape Enamel thickness Contact points Cementoenamel junction location Racial variations	Shovel shaped incisors Carabelli cusp
Crown pathology	Caries Attrition Abrasion Erosion Atypical variations	Peg laterals Fusion Gemination Enamel pearls Multiple cusps
Root morphology	Size Shape Number Divergence of roots	
Root pathology	Dilaceration Fracture Hypercementosis External / internal resorption Hemisections	
Pulp chamber / root canal morphology	Size, shape, number Secondary dentin	

Table 2-3a: Objective dental and paraoral findings – Teeth (continued next page)

TEETH	STATUS	DESCRIPTOR
Pulp chamber / root canal pathology	Pulp stones Dystrophic calcification Root canal therapy Retrofill procedures Internal resorption Apicoectomy	Gutta percha Silver points Endodontic paste
Periapical pathology	Abscess Granuloma Cyst Cemental dysplasia Condensing osteitis / enostosis	

Dental restorations	Metallic restorations:
	    Non-full coverage
	
	    Full coverage
	
	Non-Metallic restorations:
	    Non-full coverage
	
	    Full coverage
	Dental implants
	Maryland bridges
	Partial / complete removable prostheses
		Amalgam
		Gold inlays / onlays
		Pins
		
		Cast crowns
		Veneers
		Porcelain fused to metal crowns
		
		Acrylics
		Silicates
		Composites
		Bonded restorations
		Porcelain laminates
		
		Non-metallic full crowns

Table 2-3a: Objective dental and paraoral findings – Teeth

- Pegged maxillary permanent lateral incisors (may be noted on radiographs prior to eruption)

- Congenital absence of permanent teeth. Maxillary lateral incisors and mandibular 2nd premolars are commonly absent radiographically.

- Transposition of permanent teeth and rotational positions of permanent teeth should be noted. Occasionally a maxillary premolar may be rotated 180 degrees.

When attempting to determine a dental identification on a child the odontologist may be faced with the situation that the antemortem and/or post mortem dental evidence available may not be sufficient to reach a positive identification. This may be associated with the following factors:

- There may be no restorations or sealants present

- The dentition may appear quite normal

Gingivae and Periodontium	STATUS	DESCRIPTOR
Gingival morphology & pathology	Contour	Gingival recession :
		Focal
		Diffuse
		Enlargements
		Interproximal craters
	Color	
		Inflammatory red changes
		Physiologic/pathologic
		pigmentations
	Plaque and concretions	
		Oral hygiene status
		Stains
		Calculus
Periodontal ligament morphology & pathology	Thickness Widening Lateral periodontal cyst	Diffused systemic sclerosis
Alveolar process and lamina dura	Crestal bone	Height Contour Density
	Interradicular alveolar bone Exostoses, tori Pattern of lamina dura	Thickness Loss Increased density
	Periodontal bone loss	Horizontal Vertical
	Trabecular bone pattern	Osteoporosis Radiodensities
	Residual root fragments Metallic fragments	

Table 2-3b: Objective dental and paraoral findings – Gingivae and periodontium

- There may be no antemortem dental radiographs

- There may be no orthodontics involved.

What does the odontologist do in these situations? If there are antemortem radiographs available, they may only reflect the status of the individual's mouth at a much younger age, prior to all the permanent teeth erupting. Observe the sizes and shapes of the permanent crowns, numbers and anatomy of the roots of the permanent teeth and relationships and positions of adjacent teeth.

Remember that permanent teeth can shift positions as the young mouth matures. There is often a mesial shift of the permanent first molar following the normal exfoliation of the primary second molar. This type of shift must be recognized when comparing antemortem and post mortem radiographs taken many years apart.

If no antemortem radiographs are available, check for the existence of any skull radiographs that may have been taken for head trauma. Contact the child's physician, local hospital and treating dentist checking all records very carefully. The dentist may have charted one of the dental anomalies listed above or

Anatomic Features	Status	DESCRIPTOR
Maxillary sinuses -	Size Shape Retention cysts Foreign bodies Oral-antral fistula Relationship to adjacent teeth	
Anterior nasal spine	Median palatal suture	
Incisive canal	Size Shape Cyst	
Pterygoid hamulus	Size Shape Fracture	
Mandibular canal Mental foramen	Diameter Bifurcated canal Relationship to adjacent teeth	
Coronoid / condylar processes	Size Shape	
Temporomandibular joint	Size Shape Hypertrophy Atrophy Ankylosis Fracture Arthritic changes	
Other pathologic processes	Developmental cysts Hemorrhagic bone cysts Salivary gland depression Reactive / neoplastic lesions, Metabolic bone disease Other disorders	Radiolucencies/ Radiopacities: Focal Diffuse Orthognathic surgery Other osseous surgery Trauma evidence: Wire sutures Surgical pins

Table 2-3c: Objective dental and paraoral findings – Anatomic features

mentioned a particular malocclusion. If no antemortem dental records are available, contact the family for photographs of the child showing the anterior teeth. Parents often take many pictures of their children and school photographs can be obtained.

It can be significant to look for comparisons in interdental spacing or crowding in the dentition. The majority of young children do not have primary interdental spacing. Parents can be asked about any known dental characteristics of their child, such as significant overbite or overjet, trauma to the anterior teeth resulting in premature loss or discoloration, or chipping of an anterior tooth.

The child's physician may also have notes in the record concerning the mouth including the presence of bottle caries or some other untreated dental condition. If the odontologist is not experienced with the primary or mixed dentition, it is strongly recommended that he or she seek consultation with an experienced pediatric dentist. Perhaps consultation with an orthodontist might also be advisable. The odontologist may realize that a positive dental identification cannot be made when a child or adolescent is involved. They may then be asked to give dental age estimation.

Partial Decomposition and Trauma

The victim of trauma will have suffered a violent death and will usually have significant physical injuries to preclude visual identification or personal recognition by a family member. With the authorization of the medical examiner or coroner these types of remains can be analyzed in such a manner that will maximize visualization of orofacial structures. Under most circumstances the disarticulation and removal of the maxilla and mandible can be performed to present their best possible view for recording and documenting the dental structures for comparison with antemortem records.

The remains of a victim of drowning may be viewable or decomposed. The temperature and length of time spent in the aquatic environment creates this variability among cases. Cold water victims may appear as severely bloated and basically well preserved, while remains from warm or hot water environments are often badly bloated and decomposed. In the case of an unburied victim, decomposition of the body by intestinal bacterial flora, insect larval action and temperature from the time of death until discovery increases the probability that the remains will not be viewable for identification purposes.

Advanced decomposition of a decedent often results from exposure to relatively high environmental temperature and humidity. Better preserved remains will usually be observed in colder environments. The ultimate result of decomposition is the skeletonization of the remains. These will be devoid of most soft tissues. In this state, care must be taken to insure that dental structures are not dislodged or lost. As soft tissue, the periodontal ligament will have decomposed and the teeth can unexpectedly fall out of their respective sockets in the dental arches. Feral, scavenging animals may also contribute to the post mortem loss of teeth and crime scene investigators should insure that these structures are located and recovered from the site.

Drs. Law and Bowers modified and employed a technique developed by Dr. Brion Smith in which dental impression material enhanced with a radiopaque substance was injected into the root sockets of maxillary teeth lost at or around the time of death. A comparison of antemortem and post mortem radiographs from the same areas of the mouth were used to determine if root morphology of the teeth could be reproduced after post mortem dental loss.

It had been determined anthropologically that the remains used in this case were most likely those of a Caucasian or Hispanic adult female. Although post mortem radiographs of the skull had been taken previously they revealed no distinguishing dental features and no dental identification of the decedent was made initially. In 1994 the maxilla was re-radiographed after cleaning the skull of debris with water and a soft toothbrush and reproducing the missing facial walls of alveoli by adding radiolucent dental material called Adaptol (Jelenko Dental Health Products) to these areas.

This material is softened in hot water and molded into the desired shape. By replacing facial alveolar walls injectable impression material containing an opaque substance could be held within the confines of the alveolar dental socket. Remaining alveolar areas were sealed with up to five layers of Duro Super Glue (Loctite Corp). This cyanoacrylate was applied with a fine paintbrush and allowed to thoroughly dry between coats. Multiple coats were needed in most areas because the cortical bone of the maxilla was missing and remaining bone was extremely porous.

The injectable impression material employed is commonly used for making crown and bridge impressions of teeth. This is a Type 11, silicone based dental material called Cuttersil Light by Miles, Inc. The impression material, combined with 98 precent barium sulfate powder (proprietary), was mixed per manufacturer's instructions. The amount of powder used was one teaspoon to three inches of impression material. This was injected into the socket areas with a dental syringe.

Radiographs of the maxillary alveolar areas were taken after the impression material set. Special care was taken to angulate the film so that the radiographs were oriented to maximize the mesiodistal width of the socket. This avoided introducing any error from the placement of the reconstructed facial aspect of the sockets. The radiographs were exposed using both large and small periapical dental films with a General Electric dental x-ray unit at 15 mA, 70 kVp for 1/5 seconds. The resulting radiographs showed dental detail not previously seen in the original panoramic or periapical radiographs. The fused roots of teeth #2 and #15 became visible. In addition, the morphology of the apices of teeth #12 and #13 was clearly shown. These post mortem radiographs have been compared to antemortem radiographs made available by the California State Department of Justice.

Post mortem status of a victim may include a combination of several of the categories described above. There are special requirements for the preservation of the dentition and related structures in these cases. This requires that the forensic dental examiner exercise diligence in the examination of the remains to avoid overlooking, losing or destroying dental evidence.

Record management is an important part of forensic dentistry and the forensic dentist is well advised to keep accurate records. This process should begin with the phone call from the coroner, medical examiner or their authorized representative requesting assistance in identification.

A check list for inclusion in the documentation of case information could include:

- Case Number

- Date and Time

- Jurisdiction and/or agency requesting the odontologist's services

- Contacting agent for the jurisdiction

- Authorization to process the remains

- Location where examination is performed

- Body Type - including estimated age, sex, and race

-Type of Remains: burned, dismembered, decomposed, skeletonized

- Description of Dental Remains

- Putative Identification

Depending on the condition of the decedent, the exact procedures used for the identification may vary. The following outline details possible techniques a forensic dentist may employ in processing a dental identification.

I. Visually Identifiable Body (**Figure2-16**):

  A. Photographs
  B. Radiographs
  C. Dental charting

D. Dental impressions and cast construction (if indicated)

E. Preservation of oral structures (if indicated)

II. Decomposed/Incinerated/Traumatized Body (**Figure 2-17**):

A. Photographs
B. Radiographs
C. Dental charting
D. Stabilization and/or preservation of remains (if indicated)

Figure 2-16: Visually identifiable remains.

III. Skeletonized Remains (**Figure 2-18**):

A. Photographs
B. Radiographs
C. Dental charting
D. Jaw artiulation and occlusal analysis
E. Preservation of remains (if indicated)

The post mortem dental examination will require having access to basic equipment and supplies. Most of this equipment may be available in the morgue. The odontologist should maintain a *go kit* to insure access to an armamentarium suitable for making a forensic dental identification. It is important to know in advance what equipment is available and what equipment may be needed. The shelf life of all supplies should be monitored and maintained in a current status. Possible items for inclusion in a *go kit* could include:

- Personal protective devices (PPDs)

- Disposable gowns, latex and nitrile gloves, eye protection, face masks

- Peroxide, disclosing solution, bleach, hair spray or spray varnish, cyanoacrylate. (used to stabilize fragile tissues)

- Radiographic film in various sizes and speeds

- Flashlight or other external light source

- SLR and/or digital camera, flash attachment, color and black and white film, cheek retractors and mouth mirrors, video camera

Figure 2-17: Visually unidentifiable remains.

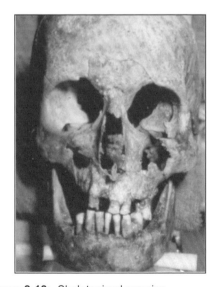

Figure 2-18: Skeletonized remains.

- Pens, pencils (red and black), post mortem dental charts

- Basic instruments: mouth mirrors, cotton pliers, mouth props, explorers, periodontal probes, tooth brushes

- Disposables: cotton rolls and gauze, tongue blades and cotton swabs

Charting of the dental structures is done after appropriate photographs, slides and videotapes are completed. The Universal Tooth Numbering System should be used.

As was done during the antemortem information retrieval, representative dental charting should evaluate (**Figure 2-19):**

- All existing dentition / missing dentition and restorations including:

  - Types of restorative materials and surfaces restored

  - Evaluation of periodontal status, calculus and staining

  - Tipped, rotated, impacted or partially erupted teeth

  - Determination of post mortem loss of teeth

- Fixed, removable and implanted prosthetic restorations

- Identifying marks on any removable prostheses

- Occlusal relationships

- Unique characteristics within and between the dental arches such as tori and supernumerary teeth

- Unique individual tooth characteristics

- Soft tissue pathology

Radiographic interpretation of post mortem radiographs should include:

- Presence of endodontic therapy, restoration, implants

- Unique presentation of normal structures:

  - Dilacerated roots, root morphology

  - Pulp stones, pulpal anatomy

  - Trabecular patterns, enostoses, exostoses

  - Sinus morphology

Photographic and videotape review should also be of an evidentiary quality and maintained through chain of evidence protocols (**Figure 2-20**).

Dental impressions should be taken and casts constructed when indicated. Soft tissue abnormalities would be such an indication. When taking impression and constructing casts adhere to the following procedures:

- Use an ADA approved silicone impression material

- Pour casts in dental stone *not* plaster using manufacturer approved water/powder ratios and setting times

- Pour two sets of casts for each impression maintaining one in an unaltered state

- Label each set with date, forensic dentist's name, case number and victim's name

- Label to maintain the chain of evidence

- Keep the impression materials in their trays and with the casts for future use

After the post mortem examination is completed and all dental evidence defined, it is important to transfer the findings to an appropriate post mortem dental form. Many such forms have been developed by forensic dentists over the years. An appropriate form would include space to account for all post mortem dental findings and allow easy comparison with a corresponding antemortem record.

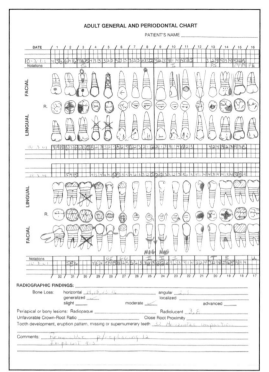

Figure 2-19: Representative dental charting

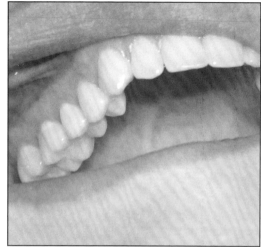

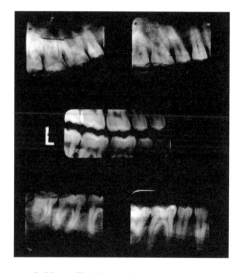

Figure 2-20: Radiographic and photographic documentation.

To provide full access to dental structures, techniques in resection or dissection may be necessary. Confirm that proper written authority has been obtained prior to beginning dissection or resection of any human remains. OSHA guidelines regarding blood borne pathogens and handling infectious diseased specimens should always be followed when handling any human remains. It is best to assume all decedents' remains are potentially infectious or bio-hazardous. Proper use of PPDs including gloves, gowns, masks and eye protection is always indicated when performing forensic dental evaluation of post mortem material.

When working on viewable, identifiable bodies, restricted opening due to rigor requires the utilization of methods to access the oral structures. The dentition can be accessed by intraoral incision of the masticatory muscles, with or without fracturing of the condyles. Additionally, rigor may be broken with bilateral leverage on the jaws in the retromolar pad area. One could also wait until the rigor subsides. Mandibular dissection with or without mandibular resection may also be accomplished in order to examine the oral structures.

Removal of the tongue and/or larynx at autopsy may facilitate the visual examination of the teeth and placement of intraoral films. Any tissues removed should either be retained by the pathologist or replaced with the body. Jaw resection facilitates dental charting and photographic and radiographic examinations when dealing with decomposed, incinerated or traumatized bodies. Careful dissection of the incinerated head, in particular, is required to preserve fragile tooth structures and jaws.

Radiographs should be made prior to manipulation of badly burned fragments. Mechanical or chemical stabilization of such tissues should be instituted where necessary. With skeletonized remains, it is usually not necessary to resect the jaws. The mandible will usually separate from the base of the skull and a full visualization of the oral structures will be present.

Listed below are several techniques for exposing the dental structures for examination and recording dental evidence. Often, the condition of the remains will dictate the technique or techniques that will be necessary. Combinations of techniques may also be used. None of these procedures should be performed without proper, documented authorization. Additionally, with proper authorization, body parts may be resected, preserved and sent to other facilities for additional examination and testing. If the remains are to be cremated and the body is still unidentified, preservation of the oral structures is strongly indicated.

- ***Extraoral Incisions*** (facial dissection) – Extend bilateral incisions from the oral commissures to the body of the rarmus on a line parallel with the plane of occlusion, through the masseter to bone. Reflect the soft tissue for access and examination.

- ***Inframandibular Incision*** - Incise the skin inferior and medial to the mandible in a direction from the ear across the midline to the opposite ear. Reflect the tissue superiorly over the body of the mandible to expose the oral structures. This technique can be used for a viewable victim.

- ***Jaw Resection*** - After the skin and tissues have been exposed and denuded, it is possible to remove the jaws. Reflect all soft tissue, including muscle and oral mucosa to expose bone. Use a Stryker autopsy saw to make a cut on the ascending ramous of the mandible **(Figure 2-21)**. Be careful to avoid the third molar area. The mandible will be freed from the skull except for the

soft tissue attachments of the tongue and floor of the mouth. These can be dissected with an autopsy knife. The maxilla can be removed, if necessary, by making an incision in the most superior portion of the maxilla with the Stryker saw blade angled superiorly, again avoiding any impacted third molars.

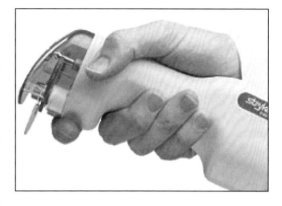

Figure 2-21: The Stryker Saw with resected jaws.

Start in the most posterior-superior part on one side of the maxilla and continue across the midline to the ending spot on the opposite side. Be careful not to cut off root tips of the teeth. Cutting off root tips will easily occur if the cuts are not positioned superiorly enough. This is especially true in the anterior region. After completing the cut, place a flat chisel or osteotome in the cut and pry down on the maxilla. This will free the maxilla from the base of the skull. The pharyngeal tissues can now be dissected with a knife or surgical scissors to free the maxilla completely.

If a Stryker autopsy saw is not available, a mallet and chisel, a piano wire saw or pruning shears make suitable alternatives. The location of the cuts is the same. Again, care must be exercised to avoid bisecting the root tips with any of these techniques. Dental hard structures such as teeth and resected or fragmented jaw segments can be preserved in either ten percent formalin or embalming fluid. They must be placed in sealed and properly labeled containers. The label must be such that it cannot be smeared, removed or fade over time. It must include the case number, date and examiner bearing the responsibility for storing the specimen.

- Preservation – Although most autopsy facilities under a medical examiner or coroner's jurisdiction will preserve and store soft tissues in ten percent formalin or embalming fluid, these fluids will cause desiccation and shrinkage distortion of the tissues. Pigmentations or blood by-products within or under the epidermis or mucosal surface may be dissolved as well in these solutions. Depending on the environment, some pathologists simply freeze the soft tissue specimens. There are other solutions that can be used which cause less distortional change in soft tissues. Two such mixtures include:

- Two parts five percent acetic acid, four parts formaldehyde and four parts water. Place tissue in solution, then remove and wrap in towel of solution and store in a labeled zipper freezer bag and freeze.

- Campden Solution - a fruit preservative available from a local chemist. Place tissue in the solution, remove and wrap in towel soaked in solution, place in a labeled zipper freezer bag and freeze.

Incineration

Verification of identity of burn victims can certainly be some of the more challenging case work for the forensic dentist. As a result of high heat, teeth and supporting bony structures become brittle, dehydrated and fragile. With dehydration and the ensuing shrinkage, teeth can loosen from the bony sockets. Unrestored enamel and dentin can separate. Teeth with restorations fracture and lose their filling materials and those materials can distort. All these changes leave the forensic odontologist with an assortment

of pieces of dental evidence to examine and evaluate without the benefit of all the orienting features of the oral cavity upon which to rely.

The burning of hard and soft tissue can be the result of direct contact with open flames or the exposure to high heat. Both will result in various degrees of burning. Physicians classify these various levels of burning into four categories or degrees:

- First Degree Burns: These injuries are superficial. No blisters develop and the area is swollen, red and painful.

- Second Degree Burns: Some or most of the epidermis is destroyed in these injuries. Blistering does occur and scarring sometimes results.

- Third Degree Burns: Both the epidermis and dermis are destroyed. Pain is often absent due to destruction of nerve endings and scarring always occurs.

- Fourth Degree Burns: Charring occurs with total destruction of skin and underlying tissue. It is at this stage that the forensic odontologist begins to encounter some difficulties in the examination of the oral cavity. With the charring of soft tissue comes muscle contraction. The same effect which causes the pugilistic positioning of the upper and lower limbs causes such contraction of facial muscles to make opening into the oral cavity by normal means impossible. In these cases, the masseter muscle must be dissected away to expose the ascending rami. The rami are then bisected bilaterally to allow the mandible to drop open after relaxing incisions are made in other intraoral muscles.

The forensic odontologist can now gain access to the teeth and supporting tissues. Often the posterior teeth have been completely protected by the presence of the soft tissue and are left unaffected by the heat. Thus, examination and comparisons of antemortem radiographs with post mortem records usually can be accomplished rather easily. Alternatively, the anterior teeth are often directly exposed to heat or flames and are usually affected more quickly and severely, leaving minimal dental evidence for comparison.

- Fifth Degree Burns or cremated remains (sometimes referred to as *cremains*): At the extreme, a normal adult body is reduced to two to three pounds of desiccated bone with no remaining soft tissue. This process takes approximately one and one-half hours at controlled and constant temperatures of 870 degrees to 980 degrees C. In frail elderly adults or infants and young children, the reduction may occur much more rapidly due to the decreased calcification of hard tissue and its decreased density and mass.

The heat of the fire alone does not turn the bones into ash. Most cremated skeletal remains are recognizable (**Figure 2-22** and **23**). An anthropologist will still be able to look at the bones and determine sex and estimate age. Cremated bones are very fragile and will crumble easily. Extreme care must be taken when handling them.

In commercial cremation, it is a second step, called *processing*, which obliterates all recognizable fragments and produces the familiar ash like cremated remains. In processing, the skeletal remains are placed in a large machine and ground for 30 to 60 seconds (**Figure 2-23**). Under less controlled conditions (i.e. non-commercial cremations), the reduction of mass is likely to be less complete leaving more recognizable and larger fragments of teeth, bone and restorations which may be used for identification purposes..

The Burning Process

There are two processes which have been identified in the burning of all organic and inorganic material. These two processes are *combustion* and *pyrolysis*. Combustion is the chemical process which occurs when combustible material and oxygen are brought together above the point of ignition. *Pyrolysis*

Figure 2-22: Skull fragments and teeth recovered from a cremated individual 1010 degrees C for 2.5 hours. The skull is clearly identifiable after a typical fire.

is defined as the resulting decomposition of organic compounds when these compounds are exposed to very high heat.

The severity of the burn depends on two variables related to heat. These include the heat's intensity and duration and these variables may themselves be influenced by factors such as chemical accelerants, insulators of varying types, location of the fire or radiating heat source, and accessibility to oxygen supplies.

In typical house fires, temperatures seldom reach 650 degrees C whereas chemical fires can quickly reach temperatures exceeding several thousand degrees centigrade. House fires depend upon the supply of chemicals or fuel and may continue for hours. They generally have slowly rising temperatures until the flash-over point is reached. Then the fire spreads rapidly to adjacent areas, reaching its highest

Richards assessed and documented the destruction of an adult body at temperatures held constant at 680° C. The pyrolytic changes on body conditions as a function of time were noted as follows:

- After 10 minutes, the arms are badly charred.

- After 14 minutes, the legs are badly charred as well.

- After 15 minutes, bones are visible in the face and arms.

- After 20 minutes, the skull and ribs a r e exposed.

- After 30 minutes, the bones of the upper and lower legs are exposed.

Figure 2-23: Skeletal remains following cremation, but before pulverizing.

temperature relative to the amount of fuel and oxygen available. With the use of accelerants, this normal pattern is modified, prolonged and intensified. Victims of this latter type of fire are more likely to be categorized as a fourth or fifth degree burn victim.

He also suggests that if the order of destruction is different or the destruction appears to be much quicker than that noted above, the investigator should expect either a very severe localized fire or a fire that was somehow assisted by use of an accelerant

The forensic dentist should expect to see a victim with fourth degree burning over the entire body with contraction of muscles due to the extreme heat. This results in several characteristic appearances of fourth degree burning including a pugilistic attitude or pose. The flexor muscles have a greater mass of muscle fiber which will usually cause the arms and legs to bend and rotate into a flexed position when denaturing of muscle protein occurs in burns of this degree. This denaturing of muscle protein may be powerful enough to break long bones in victims of this degree of burning.

The fists are clenched and this characteristic in burn victims is sometimes sufficient to protect the finger pads from destruction so that identification may be made by fingerprints. The tongue will often protrude due to contraction of facial and neck muscles. Substantial skin splitting will be noted and the build-up of steam from the boiling of internal fluids results in the rupture of the cranial vault and abdomen

If extreme temperatures persist, the body is submitted to progressive desiccation and finally carbonization. Crystals of bone actually will fuse and this results in shrinkage. The ultimate result of these processes is a fifth degree burn victim.

Bones undergo color changes as they burn. They change from their normal creamy white color to black as the organic materials carbonize. As the organic materials continue to burn, the black fades to dark gray, light gray and finally to chalky white. At this stage the bones are said to be *calcined*. *Calcined* bones have no organic material remaining.

Additionally, cremated bone color gives a clue to the status of bones in the pre-burned state since there are differences between dried or fresh boney material. Some environmental conditions during the burning may also be related to color changes. Color is a good predictor of the presence of the collagen content of the bone and this may be useful in determining possible fragments to be selected for DNA testing.

Texture of the bone also changes when it is burned. Burned bones have a different surface appearance based on the thickness of the bone. Those with a thin surface produce a curved, crescent shape pattern. Color and texture changes occur in predictable ways and can be used to determine the conditions of the fire.

Hard tissue shrinkage is another phenomenon associated with burning. A shrinkage factor of one to two percent in bone exposed to temperatures below 770 dregees C has been reported. Other studies indicate a maximum of five percent shrinkage of bone exposed to high temperatures. This shrinkage is also determined by the amount of tissue covering the bones. If a body is skeletonized prior to incineration, it will shrink less than a body that is still covered by flesh. Most studies describe 20 to 25 percent shrinkage in an intact, flesh-covered body that has been cremated.

Burning and Dental Evidence

Unprotected natural teeth can be turned to ash at 540 to 650 degrees C. In most badly burned victims (fourth and fifth degrees burn cases) a carbonization of the crowns of the anterior teeth occurs. These teeth are virtually unprotected while the posterior teeth, insulated by layers of skin, muscle and fatty tissue, remain unscathed and readily available for identification comparisons.

Other materials used in dental restorations have varying melting points as indicated:

- **Porcelain** can resist temperatures in excess of 1100^0 C. Porcelain fused to metal restorations have a fusion temperature between 1150^0 and 1450^0 C.

- **Amalgam** is composed of silver, copper, tin, mercury (45% of the total composition) and sometimes zinc. Mercury evaporates at 100^0 C with the loss of the entire restoration occurring at 500^0 and 1000^0 C. The remaining elements experience phase changes as the mercury is evaporated. These elements will recombine as the material cools and this alters the appearance of the amalgam material.

- **Gold alloy restorations** have a fusion temperature which varies with the amount of precious metal present. All gold alloys melt between 870^0 and 1070^0 C. At lower temperatures oxidation of various alloy components can cause the surface color to blacken.

- **Base metal alloys** found in partial dentures melt between 1275 and 1500 degrees C; however the surface of the metal will tarnish around 900 degrees C after 1.5 hours exposure.

- **Acrylic** components of a denture are destroyed at temperatures below 540

- **Composite materials** exposed to temperatures of 101 degrees C for 2.5 hours show some color change but the shape and size of the composite restoration remains virtually unaltered. The inorganic composition (filler particles) remains unaltered. This permits the resins to be named by brand or brand groups. Depending on the brand, some resins fracture easily and crumble while others remain almost intact.

Most dental restorations will survive extreme fires even though the teeth may fragment or shrink. In addition, the amount of destruction of dental materials can assist in revealing the temperatures involved in the fire. If a fire has been hot and prolonged enough to eliminate the soft tissue insulation of the posterior teeth, the usual evidence found at the scene is fragmented. The evidence will include enamel crowns separated from the dentin and root structure that may still be retained within the bony structure of the maxilla or mandible. Apparently the insulating factors of the bone and relative temperature gradients between infra-bony and extra-bony structures cause tooth fractures at the height of the ridge to occur.

Even with enamel disruption or anatomical crown loss in a burn situation much dental information is still available in the root morphology, bone trabeculation and interradicular bone patterns observed radiographically. Intact anatomical crowns can be identified with their universal tooth number and assumed to be unrestored teeth. This can be surmised because the existence of a restoration establishes inherent fracture lines within the enamel and dentin. Restorative materials have an expansion rate that differs from human dentin and enamel and under high heat tooth fracturing will be produced.

Knowledge of normal mandibular and maxillary bony anatomy can prove to be invaluable. In addition to comparing bone trabeculation and root morphology, other stable characteristics, such as the location and morphology of the mandibular canal, the mental foramen, the sinuses, the zygomatic process and the hamular notch configuration can be helpful in making identification of a burn victim from your realm of possibilities.

Skeletonized and Partial Remains

With the steady increase in the number of identification cases involving severely fragmented, dismembered, or skeletonized remains, forensic teams are finding that successful resolution may often depend upon radiographic comparisons involving small amounts of post mortem material. Frequently, the quality of antemortem radiographs, against which a comparison must be made, is compromised. This may be due to the submission of less than archival quality radiographic images that have aged or been inadequately developed or fixed during processing. Improper storage with subsequent damage from mold, mildew or heat also contributes to the problem.

While various disciplines of forensic science may routinely utilize radiographic comparison, forensic odontologists handle the vast majority of cases involving such comparisons. Therefore, it is not uncommon from among this group to hear the lament, "If only we had better radiographs with which to work!" The members of the forensic odontology section at the U.S. Army Central Identification Laboratory, Hawaii (CILHI), are no exception in this regard. Part of the mission of the CILHI is the identification of remains from World War II, the Korean War, and the Vietnam War. The last U.S. serviceman listed as missing during the Vietnam War was lost in 1973. Therefore, the most current radiographs available to the CILHI forensic odontologist are 33 years old, and many radiographs used for comparison date back to the mid-to-late 1950's.

It is to be expected then that the CILHI forensic team would encounter radiographs of compromised quality with greater frequency than other forensic units. By necessity, they must employ some innovative techniques to glean the maximum amount of available information from poor quality radiographs. One such technique employs a simple photographic darkroom procedure. During identification efforts at CILHI it is often necessary to compare post mortem radiographs with full-mouth series of antemortem periapical radiographs in extremely poor condition. The surface layers of individual antemortem radiographs are often in various stages of peeling and severely corrugated. When placed on a radiographic view box and viewed with reduced room light the interpretive value is extremely low and of no diagnostic value in these situations.

When placed on a view box in the darkroom and extraneous light eliminated, the same radiographs yield sufficient information to allow a successful antemortem to post mortem radiographic comparison. The results of an identification process are only as good as the supporting documentation Thus, it is necessary to produce a high quality representation of the darkroom observations. Simple duplication of the original radiographs using a Rinn model 72- 1200 x-ray duplicator and Kodak X-Omat duplicating film processed with GBX chemicals, results in the duplication of most flaws. The following photographic steps produced the superior result:

Mount the frame of radiographs on the darkroom view box.

- Mask all areas of extraneous light emitted from the view box.

- Place the masked view box horizontally on the base of a copy stand.

- Photograph the frame of radiographs using a Polaroid MP 4 format camera (4 inch x 5 inch negative) mounted to the copy stand and Kodak Royal Pan (4141) film. Stop down the lens to *f*-16 and expose for one second. These exposure settings may vary with other equipment. Therefore spot metering is recommended as well as bracketing the exposure, when first utilizing this technique.

- Routine processing of the exposed film suggested by the manufacturer is performed to produce the negative and print. A #4 contrast filter is employed to make the final print.

This uncomplicated and easily reproducible technique for obtaining high quality and diagnostic photographic images from damaged and seemingly useless radiographs is intended as a guideline only. The choice of photographic equipment, film and exposure settings is limited only by the imagination of those who would utilize this technique. The results will prove that the effort is worth the minimal amount of time and expense required. Eventually, every forensic scientist who relies on radiographic comparison for identification will open an antemortem radiographic envelope with great expectations, only to be severely disappointed by the contents. With this photographic technique identifications can be made that would not have otherwise been possible.

A variety of other techniques can be used to improve radiographs that are too dark or light for optimal forensic interpretation or for use as courtroom exhibits. A number of chemical methods for intensifying or lightening films are available. Dark radiographs may be lightened by chemically removing some of the silver that forms the image. Similarly, light films may be intensified by binding another visible substance to the silver.

Some of the disadvantages of chemical techniques are that special reagents, some of which are toxic or otherwise hazardous, are required, and that the original evidentiary film will be altered. Alternatively, with some chemical methods there is the advantage that the action may be watched and stopped when the desired intensity is attained. In some reactions the chemicals may be applied only to a specific area of the radiograph for selective local alteration.

An advantage of this method is that the original film will not be altered. However, a darkroom, and special film and equipment are required and the process cannot be watched and controlled as with chemical methods. Kodak X-Omat Duplicating Film is specially made for this purpose. It is available in several sizes with 50 to 150 sheets per package. In the darkroom simply place the defective film (or set of films) over a sheet (or part of a sheet) of duplicating film and expose to ultraviolet light. Two FI5T8BLB fluorescent lamps are an excellent exposure source. Approximate exposure time is worked out by trial and error.

Since the radiograph to be duplicated must be held in close contact with the emulsion side of the duplicating film to prevent blurring, a covering sheet of glass or a photographic printing frame obtained from a photography supply house is useful. Also, several types of contact printers specially made for duplicating radiographs are commercially available. Some of these products, which have built-in light sources, are marketed by Rinn Corp., Lester A. Dine, Inc., Ada Products, and Star X-Ray Co.

Duplicating film is direct-reversal film and longer exposure time will produce a lighter duplicate while shorter exposure will result in a darker image. Therefore, a dark film can be corrected by increasing exposure, and if the density of the radiograph is too low, exposure should be decreased. Duplicating film is developed exactly like regular dental radiographic film; e.g., in an automatic film processor. The procedure may be repeated until a duplicate of desired density is obtained. A recent innovation is periapical-size duplicating film (Kodak X-Omat Cat. No.1586460). This film has a raised dot near one corner like that on radiographic film. During duplication, the dot on the duplicating film is matched to that on the original so that the marker for *Left* or *Right* is maintained.

Some films are so light that detail on duplicates made from them cannot be brought to a satisfactory level. Sometimes viewing such a radiograph upon which a very light duplicate has been superimposed will result in an interpretable image. Similarly, a film that is too dark even for duplication may sometimes be made usable by removing the emulsion from one surface. Soak the film in water for a few hours, place it on a soft towel to prevent damage to the opposite side and rub the emulsion off with a wet, light duty, plastic scouring pad (e.g. Scotch-Brite , 3M, St. Paul, MN 55144). Rinse the film and allow it to dry. The surface will be slightly scratched but still suitable for interpretation on a view box or for duplication.

Defective radiographs can also be duplicated and enhanced by using a photographic camera setup with commercial slide or print film, either color or black-and-white. Changing transmitted light intensity from a view box, altering exposure time or lens opening, or using different speed films can be used to correct the density of the duplicate. Kodak Rapid Process Copy Film is a 35 mm direct reversal film which will make duplicate slides from original radiograph. It is designed for automated processing, but can also be developed manually.

A 35 mm slide duplicator such as a Honeywell Repronar or a Bowens Illumitran is a very useful device for 1-to-1 duplication of periapical-size radiographs onto color or monochromatic film. Many commercial photography laboratories can produce acceptably dense duplicates of radiographs by standard photographic methods. This technology is constantly changing and the forensic odontologist is advised to keep abreast of current methodology, equipment and materials.

A number of electronic techniques can be used to salvage the image on improperly exposed or incorrectly processed radiographs. Electronic images, unlike standard radiographs, are not generally recorded on film. They are usually recorded on electronic tape or discs, and can be viewed on a monitor screen or printed on paper. One system uses a real-time analog enhancer. This is basically a television camera connected to a viewing monitor with electronic controls for changing contrast and brightness. More sophisticated methods use computer generated digital image processing which can enhance the observer's ability to detect and quantify subtle differences in hard tissues.

Many types of computer hardware and software for image enhancement are now available. The efficacy of a given system depends in large part on its resolution capability which unfortunately is largely a function of its cost. Whether a forensic expert uses a digitizing method to enhance radiographic images depends on availability of equipment and expertise. For several reasons, not the least of which is the potential for reducing radiation dosage to the patient, it appears that direct digitizing of images is becoming standard radiographic procedure in dental schools clinics and offices.

Comparison Considerations and Issues

Previous discussion has focused on retrieval and documentation of antemortem and post mortem dental records. That information must now be compared employing techniques that have been established to facilitate this process and insure that errors are not made that may result in misidentification.

It is extremely important to remain objective when making identification. Objectivity may be made more difficult because of apparent discrepancies caused by the submission of poor quality antemortem or post mortem dental information. Additionally, external pressures to reach a conclusion concerning the identity of the decedent can be initiated by the victim's family, law enforcement, the press/media and/or representatives of an airline or other corporate entity.

Using forms provided by the coroner/medical examiner or other suitable paper or electronic source, transfer all dental findings obtained from the review of antemortem dental material provided and post mortem dental examinations performed to the appropriate record. Include notations for all thirty-two permanent teeth and/or twenty deciduous teeth using consistent tooth numbering schemes and charting of restorations, extractions, endodontic therapy, etc. Thus, when the comparison between the two records is performed, it will be a comparison of *apples to apples.*

After the findings have been transferred to the charts a second forensic odontologist should verify the charting. There should be concurrence between the two comparisons. This is especially important when there are multiple decedents or if the forensic odontologist has been working on the case(s) for an extended period of time.

Compare the antemortem and post mortem radiographs tooth by tooth including all findings listed previously. If the antemortem and post mortem radiographs were exposed at similar angulations, it may be possible to superimpose one on the other to help with the comparison. If the superimposition shows a match, this will help determine a positive identification. Radiographic projections useful for comparison include:

- Periapical
- Bitewing

- Occlusal
- Panoramic

- Lateral jaw
- Lateral skull

- Anterior-Posterior skull
- Temporomandibular joint (TMJ)

Antemortem study casts can be used for direct comparison with the decedent's jaws. Compare each tooth for coronal anatomical similarities, including cusps, marginal ridges, transverse ridges, grooves, and fossae. Allow for differences between antemortem and post mortem teeth related to time. If there is an extended period of time between the construction of the study cast and date of death there can be differences in wear facets, restorations, and the number and position of the teeth present.

Antemortem photographs can be compared to the decedent. Since photos usually only show the anterior teeth, the forensic odontologist may only be able to compare the anterior teeth for positioning, shapes, fractures, missing teeth, or any unusual anatomy.

Antemortem and post mortem charts and radiographs should be placed side by side and a comparison made tooth by tooth and point by point. Below are guidelines to help the forensic odontologist analyze the findings of the comparison. Look for similarities and/or discrepancies. Similarities are all points that match. Discrepancies are those that do not.

Discrepancies can sometimes be explained. If a tooth is present in the antemortem record and missing in the post mortem it could have been extracted after the antemortem records, radiographs, or study models were obtained. This type of discrepancy does not necessarily preclude the positive identification if other points including anatomical structures and landmarks are comparable.

Additionally, caries observed on an antemortem radiograph may lead to the possibility of changes in a post mortem radiograph reflected as endodontic therapy, restoration, or extraction of the same tooth. Even when a tooth is lost after death from activity of scavenging animals, desiccation or incineration, if the discrepancy can be explained, identification may be possible. When all available information matches, even with minimal antemortem material available, attempts to obtain additional antemortem information should be made to achieve a positive identification.

Look for the mold numbers on the backs of the teeth when evaluating dentures. One can remove the teeth from the acrylic and see the mold numbers on the back if they have not been ground (Figure 2-24). Shades of teeth may also been compared. If the dentist has been careful and noted the shades and molds that were used in the record, it can be a great help in identifying a denture wearer. Sometimes even a single periapical radiograph, if laden with many restorations, bases, root canal fillings and many unusual configurations in these various restorations, can give the forensic dentist many concordant points for identification.

Observe unusual dental findings, both visually and radiographically. Anatomic anomalies should also be looked for, such as inverted tooth buds, impacted teeth, malformed teeth, etc. These can be unique features that may help in identification. Recent surgical wounds and healing sockets can also be helpful. When the comparison procedure has been completed, the report is composed. Be sure that the report is as complete as possible, understandable (especially to a non-dentist) and to the point. Be sure to include the following information:

- Medical examiner/coroner number

- Place of examination and comparison

- Date of examination and comparison

- Forensic dentist's name, address, title, phone and fax numbers

- Tentative name of deceased (if known)

- Antemortem and post mortem charting

- Text report covering all of the points that matched if a positive identification, or the inconsistencies and impossibilities if there is no match

- Name, address, telephone and fax numbers of the dentist from whom the antemortem records were obtained

- Conclusion

- Signature

Duplicate the report and keep a copy. One may want to hand write any unusual circumstances concerning the case on the copy that will allow recall of significant details of the case. It is not unusual to have a lapse of months or years between the identification and a legal proceeding, such as a deposition or trial. The forensic odontologist will be expected to recall, with much detail, the evidence and conclusions surrounding the case. These extra notes on the personal copy of the report of the forensic odontologist will greatly assist the recall efforts.

The results of a comparison between antemortem and post mortem dental information leads to one of the following conclusions:

- **Exclusion** - the antemortem and post mortem data are clearly not comparable and do not match. One unexplainable discrepancy, such as a restoration observed in the antemortem data base and a virgin tooth observed in the post mortem material, rules out identification. If the discrepancies are unexplainable, not dentally possible and error has been ruled out, then exclusion is the resulting conclusion of the comparison. Preliminary identification by exclusion may be an accepted technique in certain circumstances. These include separation of multiple decedents by age, race or sex.

- **Positive Identification** - antemortem and post mortem data match in sufficient detail to establish that they are from the same individual. In addition, there are no irreconcilable discrepancies.

- **Possible Identification** - antemortem and post mortem data have consistent features. However, poor quality of either the post mortem or antemortem information through fragmentation, incineration or tooth loss, or incomplete dental records, precludes the possibility to positively establish dental identification. There may still be no unexplainable discrepancies.

- **Insufficient Evidence** - the available information is insufficient to form the basis for a conclusion.

Many beginning forensic odontologists feel the need to have a conclusive opinion in every case they review. It is extremely important not to overstate the findings and attempt to render an opinion not based solely on the scientific facts. If there is not enough information to render a definitive opinion, do not be afraid to state just that. The examining dentist may be under intense pressure to render an opinion about the identity of the decedent. Stick to the scientific facts and tell the investigator that there is not enough information to render a definitive opinion. Forensic odontologists have their integrity and the scientific facts of the evidence. Do not be put in a position to compromise either one.

Age Estimation

Tooth development and the sequence of eruption have been used extensively as a method of aging. The permanent dentition commences mineralization just before birth and is completed by 20 to 25 years of age. There have been three important charts produced from dental surveys of cross sections of the population to demonstrate the progressive states of dental development for each year of age.

The most used ageing chart based on the dentition was developed by Schour and Massler. It consists of a series of drawings illustrating 21 chronological stages of tooth eruption and maturation (**Chart 2-1**). The major problem associated with the Schour and Massler chart is the limited sample size. This is a result of the development of the chart based on jaw sections from only 30 American children. Moorees, Fanning and Hunt published a chart based upon a radiographic survey of 380 American school children that provides more information on the individual stages of development than other charts. There is some difficulty in radiographic interpretation of the posterior teeth which limits the usefulness of this chart to < 15 years of age.

Gustafson and many others have added to the reliability of dental age determination techniques depending upon development and eruption. The Gustafson method of age determination assesses the progression of wear and age changes in the teeth. There are six pathologic conditions that can be considered for any tooth. Each condition by itself is considered unreliable. However, assessed together for age estimation they result in a 95 percent confidence limit of +/- 14 years.

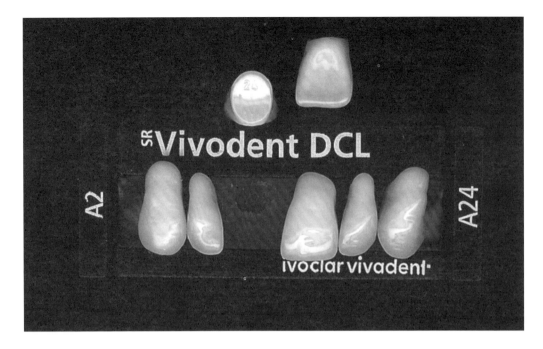

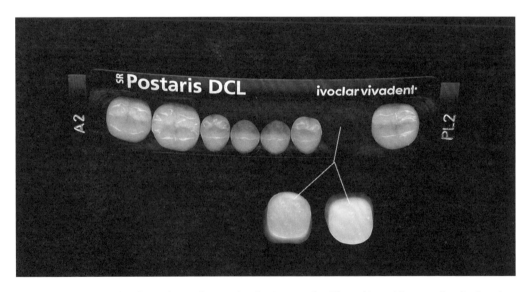

Figure 2-24: An example of anterior and posterior denture teeth with mold markings on the denture base surface.

Current methods of age estimation can predict an individual's age to within +/- ten percent for ninety-five percent of the population <18 years of age. By the end of the period of tooth formation (20-22 years of age) the methods employing the stages of tooth development as ageing landmarks are no longer applicable. It is important for the forensic dentist interested in age determination to become familiar with each of these methods. By using the various methods and undergoing constant self evaluation one will be able to develop a working knowledge of age estimation that is evidence based.

Purpose, Value, and Limitations of Age Estimation

Age estimation is useful in forensic investigations to aid in the process of identifying unknown victims. The estimation of age at death is a starting point for narrowing the search for possible matching data retrieved from local, regional, and national missing person lists. Age estimation may also be useful in limited population fatality incidents and in clustered victim cases when ages of the victims vary and other identifying information is unavailable. Additionally, age estimation is commonly used in many countries to assist immigration authorities or other law enforcement officials in deciding whether refugees or illegal immigrants have reached that designated age that separates a juvenile from an adult. This may be especially important in cases involving protection of unaccompanied minors.

In immature individuals, age estimation can be performed with relative accuracy using morphological (developmental) methods. This is primarily possible because a number of age-dependent features involving the dental and skeletal system can be evaluated. Toward the end of skeletal growth and development, only a few age-dependent features remain to be used for age estimation by morphological methods. These include evaluation of the development of the bones of the wrist and hand, clavicles, ribs, cervical vertebrae and third molar teeth. Consequently, there is generally a decrease in accuracy of age estimation near and after the end of the growth period. In adulthood, the discriminatory potential of most morphological methods is poor. For this age group a biochemical method based on analysis of metabolically stable tissue offers the most accurate results.

The following discussion is limited to consideration of dental age estimation techniques. In practical case work all available methods for estimating age should be considered and the most appropriate ones applied. The most accurate age estimates for a specific case will result when multiple techniques are employed. Individual techniques that look at multiple variables are generally more useful that those that consider only one. Anthropologists are experienced in estimating age from skeletal features. A combination of anthropological, medical, and dental techniques will likely give the most accurate results for a specific case.

Dental Age Estimation

Current dental age estimation techniques are based on age-related changes in teeth that can generally be divided into three categories with subcategories:

- Formation and growth of teeth

- Progressive changes in forming and developing teeth
- Eruption of teeth

- Post-formation changes in teeth

- Gross anatomical changes in teeth
- Histological changes in teeth

- Biochemical changes in teeth

The techniques can be additionally classified by their utility and complexity. Some are useful in both living and deceased individuals. Others are more exclusively appropriate for the former or latter situation. Some techniques may require extraction and sectioning of teeth while others use radiographic analyses or visual external examination only or combinations of several approaches. The particular technique most suitable is dependant upon the specific circumstances.

Formation and Growth of Teeth

Eruption of Deciduous and Permanent Teeth

Generally, techniques based upon eruption schedules are the least accurate methods. After 1944 almost every dental school and dental office in the United States had a copy of an eruption schedule that depicted the developing teeth at different ages from five months *in utero* to adulthood. Although later independent studies show that the actual ranges can be as much as +/- 5 years this chart represented the most common dental age estimation method used by non-forensic professionals for many years. A recent method has been suggested that again analyzes eruption and tooth bud formation.

Progressive Changes in Developing Teeth

Several techniques analyze the progressive changes in developing teeth for estimating age. In 1963 Moorees, Fanning, and Hunt published a very detailed study of the development of teeth. The technique employs a visual guide to establishing the level of crown and root development for ten permanent teeth for both sexes (**Chart 2-2**).

The method then uses an uncomplicated scale for mean age estimation base upon analysis of the development of each examined tooth's crown, root, and apex. The scale notes one and two standard deviation ranges for each (**Chart 2-3**). The technique is useful for estimation of ages from birth to the early twenties. Although this early study was limited to 99 subjects it remains a very useful and widely used tool.

Data Shown for Third Molars

In 1993 Mincer, Harris, and Berryman reported on the use of the development of molars (especially third molars) as a means of estimating age for individuals in the middle to late teens. This method uses Demirjian type development stages and is widely used in the United States to assist Immigration and Customs Enforcement agents to estimate ages in illegal immigrant cases. In these cases the important legal question remains, "Has this individual reached his or her 18th birthday?" The technique offers empirical probability percentages that the subject has attained that milestone.

The method has limitations and large standard deviations due principally to the high variability in the development of the third molar. Nevertheless age estimation based on third molar development has been shown to be reliable in independent

studies and currently is the only developmental method available for use in this age group. A modified chart developed by Kasper combines the original Demirjian letter designations and molar development line drawings with radiographic examples (**Chart 2-4**). Insufficient population studies for specific groups have been completed and published for this technique.

Post-formation Changes in Teeth and the Gross Changes in Teeth after Eruption

The techniques that look at gross changes in teeth after eruption are appropriately most often used to estimate age in adults. These methods examine one or a combination of the following features:

- Incisal or occlusal attrition
- Periodontal status
- Apical root resorption
- Ratio of pulp size to tooth size
- Dentin color
- Secondary dentin apposition
- Cementum apposition
- Dentin transparency

In 1950 Gustafson published his seminal report describing a technique for estimating the age at death through quantitative analysis of macrostructural and histological changes in teeth. The procedure is based on six age-related changes which are assigned a score on an ascending scale of 0 to 3 depending on the degree of change (**Figure 2-25**). This method then applies linear regression statistical analysis to the results to determine age based on the total score.

Subsequent projects have amplified and attempted to improve Gustafson's technique, suggest new methodology and apply the original methods to special situations. A study by Burns and Maples improved on the Gustafson dentin aging technique by using a much larger sample size (355 teeth from 267 individuals compared to Gustafson's use of 41 teeth). In Maples opinion acceptable results could be obtained by using just two variables of the Gustafson regression line - secondary dentin formation and root translucency.

By 1995, Kvall and others had described a method that allows age estimation based upon morphological measurements of the features of individual teeth. Other studies have reported unsatisfactory results and although the Kvall method is less discriminatory than those, it has the important advantage of being non-invasive and non-destructive because it does not require extraction of teeth. The Kvall method employs regression analysis of all data with age as the dependent variable (**Figure 2-27**). The measurements include comparisons of pulp and root length, pulp and tooth length, tooth and root length, and pulp and root widths at three defined levels.

Vandevoort et al, in 2004, reported a morphometric method pilot study using microfocused computed tomography (CT) to compare pulp-tooth ratios in the determination of age. In the same year Cameriere and others proposed a method using pulp-tooth ratios of second molars for aging purposes.

Histological Changes in Teeth

Three histological features are included in Gustafson's 1950 list (**Figure 2-26**):

-Progressive increase in the transparency of dentin

-Secondary dentin formation

-Apposition of cementum.

These features have been studied by subsequent investigators of age estimation. A simplified technique that evaluates just periodontal status and root transparency has been recommended. Early reports that transparent dentin development required a vital pulp have been disproved. Kvall and Solheim describe a non-destructive method that is based in part on histological features. It now appears that endodontically restored teeth have the same or greater rate of transparent dentin formation as vital teeth. Pretty reports acceptable clinical forensic utility when root transparency alone is considered.

Biochemical Changes in Teeth

Amino Acid Racemization. In nature, amino acids are synthesized as levorotary or L-isomers. Spontaneous conversion by a process known as racemization slowly converts the L-form of amino acids into a mixture of L and D-forms. These stereoisomers are detectable mirror image enantiomers. It is well known that an age-dependent racemization occurs in various human and animal tissues. These tissues include tooth enamel and dentin, the white matter of the brain (but not the grey matter), the lens of the eye, the aorta, cartilage, skin, and bone.

It is possible to calculate the ratio of the L and D-forms in long-lived proteins that are metabolically stable. Based on accuracy of estimated age, simplicity of the method, time required, and reproducibility, tooth dentin is considered one of the best target tissues for age estimation by detection of aspartic acid enantiomers. The conversion rate is temperature dependent and increases with increased temperature indicating that the environmental temperature in the post mortem interval may be important. Assuming a normal body temperature and non-extreme post mortem environment it is possible to estimate the age of the individual from the tissue amino acid examined. Among the amino acids tested aspartic acid appears to give the most reliable results although serine and glutamic acid from dental collagen have also been examined.

If used to determine age of a deceased individual, investigators must consider the post mortem environment from which the body was recovered since the D/L conversion rate may be influenced by elevated temperature. One study claims the method is useful even in burned bodies. This method offers the potential for the most accurate age estimation with the smallest ranges for all age groups. Some researchers claim accurate age estimation ranges of +/- 3-4 years. The technique requires relatively complex chromatography capability. Gas chromatography (GC) has been most often used but there have been recent experiments using high performance liquid chromatography (HPLC) coupled with detection of fluorescence.

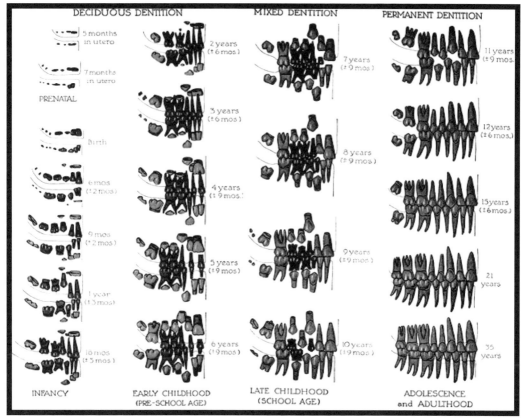

Chart 2-1: Development of the dentition. (From Massler and Shour)

Other Methods

Worldwide interest in age estimation from teeth has generated studies of alternate methods. Studies have described techniques using analysis of dental pulp DNA to evaluate age related human telomere shortening. Others have measured and graded attrition rates in permanent molars in Northeastern China populations. The method or methods that are appropriate for a specific case vary. The capabilities and resources of investigators may differ and guidelines for choosing the methods or procedures with the most potential for successful age determination in each case have been determined.

Living Individuals

Techniques for aging living individuals that apply radiological assessment are most applicable. In children up to the age of puberty those techniques using dental development are preferable to those using eruption schedules. From puberty to the time that growth and development have ceased around age twenty-one the most useful dental techniques involve analyzing the development of the teeth including the third molar. It is well known that the third molar development varies more than that of any other tooth but it remains the only tooth still developing in the target group.

There is a need for more population studies for specific geographic and ethnic groups. For adults after the age of twenty-one the applicable dental techniques are those that look at gross, histological, and biochemical changes to teeth. In living adults these are limited to the radiological and visual examination techniques unless a valid clinical reason for removing all or part of a tooth exists.

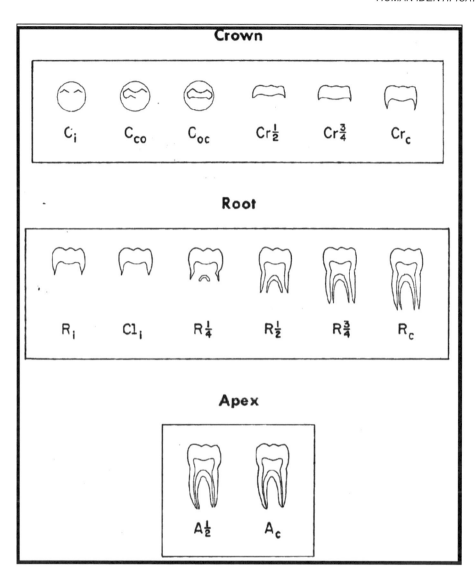

Chart 2-2: The development of crown and root according to Moorees and Fanning.

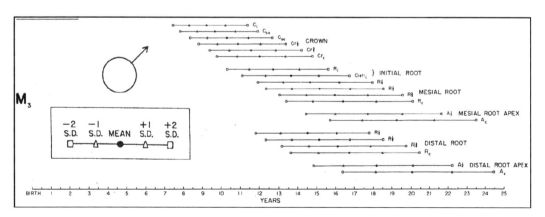

Chart 2-3: The Moorees and Fanning chart for developing age by plotting the development of three teeth.

A		Cusp tips are mineralized but have not yet coalesced.	E
B		Mineralized cusps are united so the mature coronal morphology is well-defined	F
C		The crown is about ¾ formed; the pulp chamber is evident and dentinal deposition is occurring.	G
D		Crown formation is complete to the dentino enamel junction. The pulp chamber has trapezoidal form.	H

E			Formation of the inter-radicular bifurcation has begun. Root length is less than the crown length.
F			Root length is at least as great as crown length. Roots have funnel-shaped endings.
G			Root walls are parallel, but apices remain open.
H			Apical ends of the roots are completely closed, and the periodontal membrane has a uniform width around the root.

Chart 2-4: The development of third molars according to Kasper.

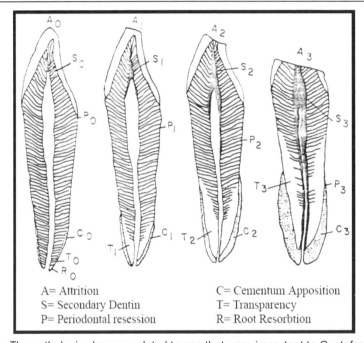

A= Attrition
S= Secondary Dentin
P= Periodontal resession
C= Cementum Apposition
T= Transparency
R= Root Resorbtion

Figure 2-25: The pathologic changes related to age that were important to Gustafson.

In those cases aspartic acid racemization analysis may be performed.

Deceased Individuals

The same radiographic and visual procedures used for living individuals can be used for decedents. However, with coroner's or medical examiner's permission and authorization teeth can be removed for age estimation studies. All of the methods that consider post-formation changes in teeth can be used. Although much work remains to be done in validating the value of determining the ratios of amino acid racemization this method is the most promising currently available for improving age estimation results in all age groups.

Summary

The use of human teeth for the estimation of age is well established. Numerous studies have demonstrated varying accuracy, reliability, and precision among the various techniques available for age estimation. Reproducible and reliable results are possible when the appropriate techniques for a given situation are properly applied and understood. In 2003, Soomer et al stated that, "Forensic odontologists should evaluate each age estimation case and, in addition to their visual age assessment, choose one or more methods that would best serve their particular case, keeping in mind that accuracy and precision are the main requirements." It has been concluded that, "An important aspect in dental age estimation is that the investigator should apply a number of different techniques available and perform repetitive measurements and calculations in order to improve reproducibility and reliability of the age estimation."

Table 2-4 lists the dental techniques that are considered most helpful for specific cases. When possible, more than one dental technique or a combination of dental and skeletal techniques should be used. Research into age estimation is ongoing. Forensic dentists performing age estimation must continually monitor the scientific journals and presentations that report new developments and validate or challenge existing techniques.

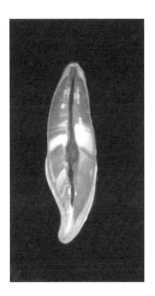 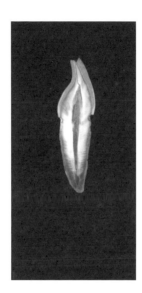 

Figure 2-26: Case files showing young, mid, and older tooth examples of thin section prepared for Gustafson aging.

Linear regression, confidence levels, and standard deviations are statistical measurements that relate to means for the population studied. Specific individuals within a population may live at either end of the range or fall outside the range. Error exists in every system of age estimation. The research and population data available to date is not adequate to allow precise age estimation results for every case. Age estimation reports should clearly convey that data reported represents mean ages based on features studied for a specific population. They should include realistic ranges based on statistical principles. Specific case work requires combining dental, medical, and anthropological methods to arrive at the most accurate conclusions possible.

Tooth Mineralization Standards for Blacks and Whites from the Midsouth United States

Dental age is one of just a few measures of physiologic development that is uniformly applicable from infancy through late adolescence. This contrasts with the use of tooth eruption alone and is more broadly applicable than the onset of secondary sexual characteristics in determining sub-adult age. Moreover, dental development appears to be well buffered, being comparatively unaffected by nutritional, endocrine and other factors impacting the tempo of an individual's progress toward maturity. The present study was undertaken to provide sex-specific standards for Blacks and a regionally and economically comparable series of Whites.

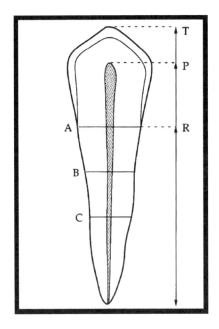

Figure 2-27: The proper classification of the progressive increase in transparency of dentin, secondary dentin formation, and apposition of cementum as studied by Kvaal, Kolltveit, Thomsen, and Solheim

Several prior studies, primarily focusing on tooth eruption, indicate that commonly applied standards based on Whites can markedly underestimate the chronological age of American Blacks.

Estimating the Child's Age by the Dentition

When the odontologist is asked to give an estimation of age of a young individual they might first consider going to one of the available tooth formation charts. Consultation with an experienced pediatric dentist and/ or orthodontist is highly recommended. There can be extreme variations in the development, exfoliation and eruption of children's teeth. Infants may be born with erupted teeth, eighteen month old children may have no teeth yet erupted and four year old children may present with fully erupted permanent teeth. An eight year old may present with no primary teeth yet exfoliated or at the other extreme have twenty-eight fully erupted permanent teeth. All of these

situations have occurred in children with normal medical histories.

The development and eruption of third molars have been considered in helping determine an individual's age. caution must be exercised when analyzing third molars for age determination since there are reports of fourteen year old children with four fully erupted third molars. It is important to consult a good tooth eruption/development chart. Consultation with a dentist experienced in growth and development is advised to obtain a dental age range in a specific case. The odontologist should avoid giving a specific estimated age.

Anthropology

Seventy years ago physical anthropologists were aware of reliable indicators of age associated with various skeletal components. Age at time of death during the pre-adult years is adequately determined by studying the centers of ossification, epiphyseal unions, development of the teeth, and eruption sequence of the dentition.

Forensic dentists tend to rely upon tooth development and eruption sequence, but they should be aware that radiographic studies of the hand and wrist are considered by many to be the most useful method for determining the developmental status of children. In health, the development of a child proceeds harmoniously in all systems. The dentition would be expected to develop at a similar pace to the skeleton. To the extent that it shows detectable evidences of progressive maturation, any organ system could be used for determining the developmental status of an organism as a whole.

The skeleton may have a number of advantages for the study of age or maturation and it may be useful for the forensic dentist to gain more information in this regard. The changes associated with progressive maturity are readily visible through radiographic analysis. Those changes occur in an orderly sequence, cover the entire period from birth to adulthood and permit the direct comparison among children without regard to genetic or other differences in body size.

There has been thorough study of the growth and development of children three to fourteen years of age and the use of radiographic analyses of the hand and wrist are very common although complex and associated with problems. It is estimated that by the 11th prenatal week in humans there are 806 centers of bone growth. This is reduced to 450 at birth. Further combinations of the centers through growth and development reduce the total to 206 bones in the adult skeleton. This represents a reduction of 600 centers of bone growth from birth to adulthood.

The large number of centers of bone growth can yield a tremendous variability if care is not exercised in finding the central tendency or average for each stage of bone development. Increasing age leads to more bone variability and more difficult determination of the average. It is suggested that accurate age determination from bone is limited above 23 years of age. Illness, trauma and extremes in diet also have an effect upon developing bone and may extend the upper limit to thirty years of age.

The use of the unique features of the human dentition to aid in personal identification is well accepted within the forensic field. Indeed, despite advances in DNA and other identification methodologies, comparative dental identifications still play a major role in identifying the victims of violence, disaster or other misfortune. The classic comparative dental identification employs the use of post mortem and antemortem dental records (principally written notes and radiographs) to determine similarities and exclude discrepancies. In many cases the tentative identification of the individual is unknown and therefore antemortem records cannot be located.

In such a situation a dental profile of the individual is developed to aid the search for the individual's identity. With such a profile a forensic odontologist can identify and report indicators for age at time of death, race (within the four major ethnic groups) and sex. In addition to these parameters the forensic dentist may be able to give more insight into the individual's identity. Additional personal information can be derived from the teeth of the decedent which may assist in their ultimate identification by placing them in a distinguishing subpopulation.

Post mortem dental profiles are employed when the tentative identity of an individual is not available and therefore antemortem records cannot be sourced. Such situations are not uncommon when remains are skeletal, grossly decomposed or are found naked in locations unrelated to their place of residence. The purpose of the post mortem profile is to provide information for investigators that will restrict the search to a smaller population of individuals. For example, by profiling the sex of the individual, fifty precent of the possible population can be excluded. Forensic odontologists can usually determine the sex, race (within the four major races), and age (at time of death) from careful study of the teeth, their anatomical arrangement and the skull's osteologic features.

In addition to the parameters described above odontologists may be able to provide information concerning the habits or addictions of an individual, their occupation, likely place of residence, medical history and socio-economic status. These additional dental findings are discussed so that dentists and non-dental forensic experts alike are cognizant of these various aspects of the dentition that may assist in a post mortem profile.

It is important to note that additional dental findings are merely indicators. Few of them offer definitive proof of identity. However, faced with the alternative any information that may help in the search for identity is likely to be useful. Those features associated with osseous and dental hard tissues will be emphasized since the condition and status of most remains requiring profiling of additional dental findings negates the use of soft tissue indicators. Remember, however, that soft tissue features such as tattoos birth marks

Recommended Dental Age Estimation Procedures

Status	Examination Type	Specific Techniques or Methods
Children (Birth to Puberty)		
Living	Non-Extraction (Radiographs)	Moorees, Fanning, and Hunt
	Shed Tooth-Biochemical*	Aspartic Acid Racemization
Deceased	Non-Extraction (Radiographs)	Moorees, Fanning, and Hunt
	Extracted Tooth-Biochemical	Aspartic Acid Racemization
Adolescents (Puberty to Approximately Age 21)		
Living	Radiographs-Developmental	Mincer et al and Moorees et al
	Extracted Tooth-Biochemical*	Aspartic Acid Racemization
Deceased	Radiographs-Developmental	Mincer et al and Moorees et al
	Extracted Tooth-Biochemical	Aspartic Acid Racemization
Adults		
Living	Radiographs/Morphological	Kvaal and Solheim (dental radiographs)
	Extracted Tooth-Biochemical*	Aspartic Acid Racemization
Deceased	Post-Formation Changes	Johanson Sectioning
	Post-Formation Changes	Lamendin et al
	Post Formation Changes	Bang and Ramm
	Biochemical	Aspartic Acid Racemization
Special Situations		
Immigration/Legal Adulthood (18th anniversary of birth)		
Living	Radiographs-Developmental	Mincer, Harris, and Berryman
Anthropological/Historical Collections		
Skeletal	Non-Destructive	Kvall/Solheim Intact Methods

* With appropriate standard of care considerations.
Table 2-4: Different methods of age estimation and their possible application.

and scars are also often useful in forensic identifications.

The parameters that will be discussed relating to additional dental findings include:

  - Occupation

  - Medical conditions and treatments

  - Medical conditions with oral hard tissue manifestations

  - Habits and addictions

- Abnormalities of tooth formation and eruption

- Place of residence

- Sex determination

- Ethnicity

By the very nature of these topics the following discussion is not meant to be all inclusive and the reader is referred to Neville et al's text, *Oral and Maxillofacial Pathology*, 2nd edition, Philadelphia: W. B. Saunders, 2002 for further insight.

Occupation

Knowledge of an individual's occupation can assist forensic investigators in locating antemortem records by narrowing the search and targeting appropriate work environments. The use of occupational health schemes to locate antemortem dental or medical records may also assist in the identification task. The list of occupational situations affecting the teeth includes some of the more common dental diseases or conditions (**Table 2-5**).

Most occupational diseases result in the loss of dental hard tissues or in staining of dental structures. The loss of tooth integrity caused by occupational etiology is associated with four situations represented by abrasion, attrition, erosion and caries. Individuals working within dusty or particulate environments will frequently exhibit abrasion of their dental hard tissues. This is caused by the grinding of teeth onto hard, roughened particles within the mouth and is therefore a mechanical process. Such abrasion is most commonly seen on the occlusal, incisal and facial surfaces of the teeth.

Employees of flour mills, grain elevators, quarries and cement factories may, in the absence of proper precautionary measures, exhibit such loss of tooth substance. Such wear may eventually lead to the exposure of dentin and ultimately the pulp complex.

Treatments include the provision of adhesive gold onlays or resin-bonded tooth colored restorative materials. While it would be impossible to identify the actual particulate causing the abrasion the location of a factory or mill of this type in the area of body discovery may assist in the ultimate recovery of antemortem information and records to accomplish identification.

Erosion is the dissolution of enamel or dentin by acidic conditions. Workers in acidic environments including battery factories, chemical plants producing acid products or even wineries may exhibit dental erosion. Individuals in this group can be distinguished from other erosive causes by the location of the erosion on the labial or buccal surfaces of the teeth.

This often indicates an extrinsic source for the acid. Intrinsic acid sources, such as purging in the bulimic patient, will typically produce erosion on the palatal surfaces. **Figure 2-29b** illustrates an example of labial erosion on the maxillary central incisors. Dental treatment for such erosion will typically involve restoring the lost tissue with tooth colored restorations, porcelain crowns or veneers.

Dental caries on the facial surfaces of anterior teeth can be an occupational hazard for those individuals working in the confectionery trade or similar professions. The anterior teeth are dusted with sugar that is metabolized by acidogenic bacteria causing dissolution of tooth enamel. Without provision of facemasks and good oral hygiene rampant caries can occur. Such patterns of caries are rare in the adult population and could represent an important occupational indicator. Carious lesions are likely to be restored with resin-bonded tooth colored restorations.

Extrinsic staining of teeth is a feature of a number of different occupations, especially those in the metal working industry. **Table 2-5** details the appearance of the stains. An interesting appearance is that of dental fluorosis – which may appear in its mildest form as white spots or brown discoloration in the severest cases (**Figure 2-29d**). This is a typical feature of the superphosphate fertilizer industry and is particularly acute in individuals who began working in the industry at a young age. Fluorosis has also been detected in cryolite workers and also in those living in close proximity to cryolite factories. Dental fluorosis may be treated by restorative options similar to those for erosion or by gentle acid abrasion to remove the outer layers of enamel. Levels of fluoride can be determined following enamel biopsy and chemical analysis by typically using a fluoride probe.

Occupational patterns of tooth wear occur frequently in professions where items may be held between the teeth leaving the hands free. These findings are observed in carpet layers, seamstresses, carpenters and electricians. The latter often use their teeth to strip electrical wires (**Figure 2-29a** and **c**). Some musicians including wind instrument players can have characteristics wear patterns. The patterns of tooth wear in these individuals are often highly characteristic. Since they are functional they are rarely treated unless painful. Detailed characterization of dental wear patterns can be elucidated using scanning electron microscopy.

Currently, individuals employed in certain aspects of the music industry, members of gangs, those involved in the sale of narcotics or who are pimps may have unique dental prostheses inserted. These are referred to as *grills* because they resemble the metal accoutrements that were common on American automobiles in the 1950's. These *grills* are often studded with jewels and are made of gold or white metal and cover the anterior teeth in the maxilla and mandible (**Figure 2-28**).

Medical Conditions and Treatments

Knowledge of an individual's health status can be an important clue in the determination of identity and can provide another valuable variable to narrow the search for antemortem records. Medical records can be searched using keywords relating to a particular disorder or treatment and when combined with other defining characteristics may enable investigators to provide a tentative identification. Conditions that have a genetic component can be traced using family histories which may provide a useful insight to an individual's identity.

The multitude of obscure diseases that can present intra-orally can be narrowed when considering those which impact upon the dental hard tissues. It is likely that, in a post mortem dental profile, it is these tissues that will form the basis of the odontologist's examination.

Medical Conditions with Oral Hard Tissue Manifestations

Numerous medical conditions can cause dental erosion. Unlike occupational erosions described previously these lesions tends to occur on palatal and lingual surfaces of teeth because they are associated with systemic intrinsic sources for the erosive agent. Any condition that causes a prolonged acidic assault on the teeth will cause erosion. Differentiating among the various causes cannot be accomplished by appearance alone. Factors such as age and sex of the individual must be taken into account. A range of gastrointestinal conditions including hiatal hernia, intestinal ulcers and gastro-esophageal reflux disease (GERD) can also cause erosion of the palatal surfaces of maxillary teeth and lingual surfaces of the mandibular (**Figure 2-30c**).

Individuals with eating disorders such as anorexia, bulimia and rumination also suffer from dental erosion because of self-induced vomiting. These disorders are most common among adolescent females but there is an increasing expression of eating disorders in teenage males. Rumination is an eating disorder in which the stomach contents are voluntarily regurgitated and then either re-swallowed or expelled. Chronic alcoholics frequently vomit and therefore present with similar patterns of dental erosion. Such individuals can normally by distinguished by their poor oral care, which is in contrast to the patients with eating disorders for whom erosion is often the only dental pathology.

Several medical conditions can cause unique discoloration of the dental hard tissues. Neonatal jaundice causes a green or yellowish brown stain of the teeth. This intrinsic stain caused by bile pigments deposited in the developing enamel and dentin can be associated with disturbances of enamel development. The staining is often treated in childhood by composite restorations or porcelain veneers.

Congenital porphyria is a rare condition, which results from an error in porphryin metabolism. This defect leads to a hemolytic anemia, photosensitivity (and blistering of exposed skin) and red-brown pigmentation of teeth (and bones). The dental aspects of the condition are likely to be addressed in childhood although the staining may be visible on untreated non-aesthetic surfaces.

Syphilis, while easily treated with antibiotics is enjoying resurgence in the western world. Congenital syphilis presents orally as misshapen molars (Mulberry molars) and incisors (Hutchinson's incisors). The disease is caused by the transmission of the causative organism (*Treponema pallidum*) from the mother to fetus. The appearance of the condition is more apparent in the deciduous than permanent dentition (**Figure 2-30d**).

With the exception of iatrogenic medical or dental damage to teeth, systemic conditions with hard tissue presentations in the oral cavity are all associated with staining of the dentition. Iron supplementation for the treatment of anemia can cause a surface deposition resulting in a black or brown staining of the teeth. It should be noted that iron supplements may be taken without prescription and therefore may not be documented in medical records.

Minocycline and the popular mouthwash chlorhexidine cause a brown/black staining on all surfaces of the teeth by precipitating dietary chromogens. Such stains can be difficult to remove and may be associated with poor oral hygiene or periodontal disease. One of the most profound stains is that caused by tetracycline. Because of its association with staining of the dentition its use in individuals with developing teeth or in females who are pregnant has been banned in Europe and North America. The long term use of this antibiotic is common in the treatment of acne.

Tetracycline is deposited in developing hard tissues and causes bands of stain in teeth which may fluoresce. Such bands can be used to determine when the tetracycline was administered. Tetracycline staining can be seen in children and adults (**Figures 2-30a** and **b**). The staining is most frequently hidden using bleaching techniques, porcelain crowns or veneers (**Figure 2-30b**).

Habits and Addictions

A number of lifestyle habits and addictions have an effect on the dental tissues. This can be useful in the search for an individual. For example, information indicating that the decedent was a pipe smoker can facilitate the antemortem record search and prompt individuals to come forward with additional comparative material . Common habits, such as tea and coffee drinking cause extrinsic stains. Due to the high incidence of their consumption in the population, their use as identifying features may be insignificant.

Other habits may offer more useful indicators for investigators. As mentioned previously, a history of pipe smoking may be instructive. Habitually, pipe smokers place the pipe stem in the same location and over time create a unique wear pattern in this area. Pipe smoking is also associated with the usual nicotine stains and a range of soft tissue appearances which are beyond the scope of this text. The ability to instruct a forensic artist to include a pipe on, say, the left hand side, may greatly increase the chances of recognition by a friend or relative (**Figure 2-31c**). The recognition of smoking stains can also be of use in the placement of a cigarette in an artist's impression (**Figure 2-31b**).

Betel nut chewing produces an unusual stain and is more normally seen in individuals from India, Pakistan and Bangladesh. The quid is usually placed on one side of the mouth, and this is normally the same on each occasion that the betel is placed in the mouth. This habit produces a unilateral brown staining of the buccal surfaces of the teeth typically 1 mm above the gingival margin (**Figure 2-31a**). It may be possible to use laboratory techniques to analyze the stain and more objectively determine its source. The betel quid is shown in **Figure 2-32**.

Recreational use of more addictive drugs can also be detected by examination of the teeth. Cocaine is often tested or taken by rubbing into the maxillary premolar area of the gingivae. Frequently cut with sugar, this can cause localized caries in the area in addition to severe gingival recession. Often, this pattern of decay and/or periodontal disease occurs in the absence of other decay or periodontal disease.

The use of methamphetamines or Ecstasy (3,

Figure 2-28: Examples of dental *grill* restorations

4 methylenedioxy-methamphetamine) among younger individuals is increasing due partly to its association with the dance culture in both the United States and the United Kingdom.

Dental effects described as *meth mouth* have been reported in chronic consumers of these drugs This is related to the clenching of teeth resulting in occlusal wear. Individuals

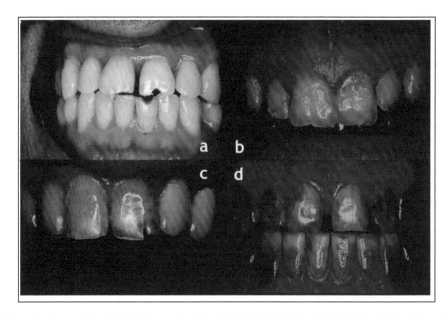

Figure 2-29 a-d: Occupational situations affecting the teeth (a) This individual exhibits characteristic notching of the mandibular and maxillary left central incisors associated with electrical wire stripping. The individual has worked as an electrician for many years (b) Labial erosion characteristic of the type seen among workers in acidic environments (c) A notch caused by the holding of pins between the teeth, this individual was a seamstress (d) a severe case of dental fluorosis of the type seen among workers in the superphosphate industries

OCCUPATION	DENTAL APPEARANCE	CAUSE
Miners Cement and sand workers Grinders Stone cutters Saw mill workers Flour mill workers	Generalized abrasion	Abrasive dust formation and collection on the occlusal surfaces on the teeth
Sugar refiners Bakers Candy makers	Caries on the labial and buccal surfaces of the teeth	Sugar dust deposits, and stagnates, on the labial surfaces of the teeth.
Metal workers: Copper Nickel Iron Tin	Green staining of dentition Green staining of dentition Fine black lines on teeth Yellow staining of teeth	Inhalation of dust Inhalation of metal fumes leads to deposition of tin sulfide
Chemical workers: Citric acid, tartaric acid, hydrochloric acid, sulfuric acid, other acids	Smooth polished eroded surfaces	Decalcification of enamel and dentine, due to exposure to fumes. Main effect to labial surfaces. Mastication and tooth brushing lead to loss of tooth substance
Superphosphate industry production of phosphorus and hydrogen peroxide	Fluorosis	Fluorine compounds used in this industry have a direct effect on ameloblasts, especially in younger workers.
Battery factory worker	Yellow, gold-brown staining of labial surfaces of teeth and erosion of incisors	Cadmium exposure causes the extrinsic staining while the battery acids are responsible for the erosion.
Shoe makers Upholsterers Glass blowers Dress designers Seamstresses Electricians	Abrasion – single of multiple groves found on incisors	Holding nails, takes, needles etc, between their teeth.
Wine tasters	Erosion, mainly on the labiocervical surfaces on maxillary incisors and canines	Wine tasting on a daily basis with at least 20 wines tasted per day. Wine pH varies from 3.0 to 3.6 typically

Table 2-5: Occupational situations affecting the teeth.

who use Ecstasy frequently dehydrate and the current recommendation among users is that copious liquids be consumed during the *trip*. These are often sugary carbonated drinks and therefore an increased caries risk with associated abrasion and erosion of the teeth can be seen. The symbiotic relationship of an acidic environment with tooth grinding increases the loss of tooth structure and therefore profound wear can be seen in these young individuals.

Heroin users often exhibit severe oral neglect, and while this is not a unique finding (alcoholics may exhibit the same pattern) the age of the individuals is often a defining characteristic. Heroin abusers who are in treatment programs are frequently prescribed methadone that is often delivered in a syrup form with elevated sugar content. With the associated poor oral hygiene of these individuals, an increased caries rate can be seen. All of the previous factors may be of confirmatory use in identifications.

Abnormalities of Tooth Formation and Eruption

There are a range of rare developmental conditions that affect the developing dentition leading to distinctive hard tissue appearances. These are listed and described in **Table 2-8** and illustrated in **Figure 2-33**. The incidence and prevalence levels are low for each condition and therefore they present useful identifying features for investigators. Many are associated with severe systemic syndromes and diseases and it is likely that extensive medical and dental records (often in specialist practices) will be available for identification of individuals with these problems. The uniqueness of physical and dental appearances in these individuals is easily recognizable to witnesses, relatives and family members. Since many of these conditions have a genetic basis, a family history may also be available.

Supernumerary teeth (**Figure 2-40c**) and hypodontia are among the commonest of dental developmental disorders. A mesiodens (supernumerary tooth in the maxillary midline) has been used in the identification of an individual with no dental restorations. Severe forms of hypodontia are found in individuals with Down syndrome and ectodermal dysplasia along with associated physical characteristics.

Abnormalities of tooth size (macrodontia as seen in **Figure 2-40d** and microdontia) are rare although so called *peg laterals* are common. Enamel hypoplasia can range from small white spots visible on the teeth to extensive enamel pitting (**Figure 2-33b**). This condition may be iatrogenically associated with early loss by extraction of the deciduous predecessors. Additionally, it may be related to the patient having a concurrent high fever systemic disease at an age of tooth development. Therefore, its occurrence may be noted in the treating dentist's records.

The genetic conditions of enamel and dentin malformation exhibit a range of presentations. Most always require the care of a dental specialist. These conditions are referred to as amelogenesis imperfecta and dentinogenesis imperfecta, respectfully (**Figure 2-33a**) (**Figure 2-33c**). Many individuals with these defects of enamel or dentin will be treated with full or partial prostheses from an early age.

Place of Residence

Possible indications of an individual's residence may be associated with and/or based on the dental techniques used and quality of treatment and dental materials employed to restore the dentition. Assuming that individuals have the majority of their dental treatment performed in their country of residence, the dentistry observed may indicate nation or region of origin in a forensic identification scenario. Although it is unlikely that a particular country can be identified geographical areas in which particular dental procedures are performed may be recognized.

Dental techniques and the materials available to perform them vary widely, and are usually influenced by the affluence of the country in which these procedures are performed. Dental training is also highly variable and in many countries there is little or no formal dental education. To illustrate the previous comments two examples are described.

Dentistry observed in the former Soviet Union can often be categorized by the use of non-precious metal faced with acrylic rather than porcelain crowns. Non-precious metals are often used in the anterior portion of the dental arch and the quality of the restorations is often less than that observed in Western Europe. It must be noted that these are generalizations and with the increased wealth in the former Soviet Republics, an accompanying increase

in health care quality should be anticipated. The illustrations serve as examples of typical Soviet restorative dental therapy. Should such treatments be observed, it is highly unlikely that they would have been performed in Western Europe and more likely to have been placed in the former Soviet region (**Figures 2-34a** *and* **2-34d**).

An example of Asian dental therapy is illustrated in **Figure 2-34b**. The treatment uses only two natural teeth (canines) to provide support for extensive fixed prosthetic dental therapy. The fixed prosthesis is acrylic

MEDICAL CONDITION	APPEARANCE	CAUSE
Conditions and diseases		
Hiatal Hernia Gastric ulcer Gastroesophageal reflux disease (GERD)	Marked erosion of the palatal surfaces of the maxillary incisors and premolars	Regurgitation or vomiting of gastric contents. Gastric acid has a pH below 3
Anorexia nervosa Anorexia athletica Bulimia nervosa Rumination Chronic alcohol abuse	As above	Induced vomiting of stomach contents
Neonatal jaundice	Green to yellowish-brown discoloration of the teeth Enamel hypoplasia may also occur	Most frequently associated with rhesus incompatibility.
Congenital porphyria	Affected teeth show a pink-brown discoloration that fluoresces red under UV light	Autosomal recessive inheritance. Circulating porphyrins in the blood are deposited in the dental hard tissues.
Congenital syphilis	Hutchinson's incisors and Mulberry molars – distinctive shaped teeth.	Transmission of *Treponema pallidum* from an infected mother.
Drugs used in treatments		
Iron supplements	Black staining of teeth	Surface deposition following oral courses
Minocycline Chlorhexidine	Brown/black staining	Precipitation of dietary chromogens
Tetracycline	Yellow/brown bands becoming darker following exposure to light	Systemic administration during the period of tooth development. Deposition occurs in dentine along incremental growth lines

Table 2-6: The effect of medical conditions and drugs on the dentition.

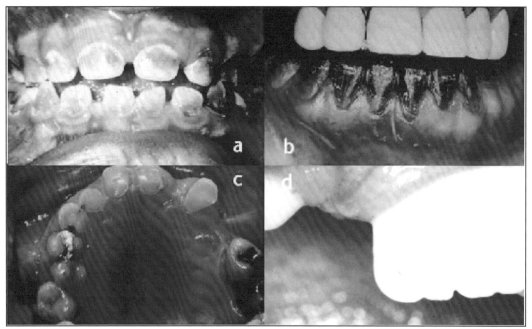

Figure 2-30: Medical conditions and treatments (a) pediatric tetracycline staining (b) severe adult tetracycline – note that the upper incisors have been treated by the provision of (poor) porcelain crowns (c) an example of intrinsic erosion – note that the anterior teeth have lost almost all of their clinical crowns (d) an example of a Hutchinson's incisor in a case of congenital syphilis.

with wooden components and an underlying metal framework. In Western Europe and the Americas more likely approaches to treatment would have been a removable denture, over-denture or implant supported prosthesis. The teeth in **Figure 2-34c** also demonstrate severe fluorosis in an individual from China. Fluorosis such as this suggests that the individual has lived in an area with over 3ppm fluoride in the drinking water. This is common in areas of China and Africa and may be of use in determining country or region of origin.

These examples serve to illustrate that dental treatments can be possible indicators of place of residence. Unusual restorative techniques may alert the investigator to the possibility that the individual may originate from, or have spent time, in a foreign country. It is important to remember that good and poor quality dental therapy can be provided in any country. However, unusual or gross departures from the norm should always be considered as potentially significant.

Sex Determination

Several authors have examined the ability to determine gender using odontometric analyses. Rao et al used the mandibular canine index to determine sex although others have issued a caution in using this technique. Another study, using dental casts of children, showed that the teeth, and in particular the canines, were larger in males than females, and suggested this method for determining gender in children whose secondary sexual characteristics had not developed.

Many believe that measurements of tooth size or assessment of morphology are insufficiently accurate for forensic identification, particularly in light of more objective methods. One such method is a microscopic technique in which the pulp tissue is examined for Barr bodies (present only in females). This technique has been shown to be of value in burnt and mummified remains and is highly accurate. The second method is based upon PCR analysis of DNA sourced from the dental

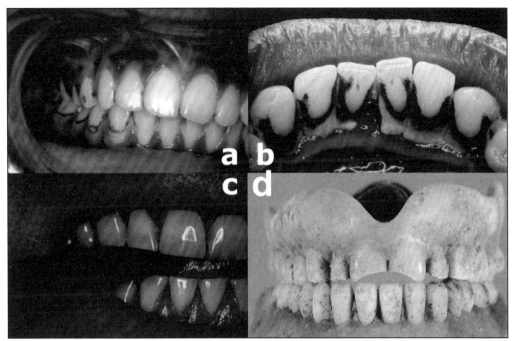

Figure 2- 31a-d: Lifestyle habits (a) Classic example of unilateral betel nut stain, also known as smokeless tobacco (b) lingual stain and associated poor oral hygiene in a heavy cigarette smoker (c) pattern of anterior wear associated with habitual pipe smoker – the wear is unilateral (d) denture wearer who smoked a pipe; the habitual placement has led to characteristic wear on the maxillary central incisors

pulp. After recovery, the pulp is subsequently subjected to analysis of the amelogenin gene for sex determination. While not unique to DNA obtained from dental pulp, the teeth often remain the only source for DNA following incineration or other post mortem events.

Figures 2-35 through **2-37** illustrate the osseous sex differences associated with the mastoid process, gonial flair and robust brow ridges of the male skull regardless of race.

Ethnicity

There are a number of dental features that can be employed to determine an individual's ethnicity. This analysis is best performed in consultation with and assistance of a forensic anthropologist. Odontologists can usually place an individual within one of the three main ethnic groups - Mongoloid, Negroid or Caucasoid. Many of the dental features of ethnic groups are related to morphological findings and therefore any examination must be careful and methodical. Odontologists

should be aware that the process of tooth restoration can mask such features since many are perceived as unaesthetic. Examples include diastemas and peg shaped lateral incisors.

Some non-morphological features of ethnicity have been described previously in the text. For example, the presence of betel quid staining will suggest that the individual is of Indian descent since this practice is rare in the West. Similarly, high levels of fluorosis in certain ethnic groups may be of assistance in identification. **Table 2-9** describes the principal anthropologic indicators of ethnicity and some of these are demonstrated in **Figure 2-38** and **2-39.**

Shovel shaped incisors are one of the commonest dental features used to determine ethnicity. Classically associated with the Mongoloid ethnic group which includes most Asians and Native Americans, its incidence can be as high as 89 percednt in these populations (**Figure 2-40a**). It is rare in non-Mongoloid

Figure 2-32: The composition of a betel quid. (a) leaf of the betel (Piper betel), (b) sliced areca nut, one of the major constituents of betel quid (paan) that can also be chewed on its own, still resulting in the classic stain, (c) sweeteners are added to children's paan (d) once the ingredients have been placed, including lime, the leaf is folded and can be placed for chewing or to suck.

individuals. A good indicator for Caucasoid ethnicity is the presence of Carabelli's cusp – an additional cusp on the first maxillary molar (**Figure 2-40b**). It is present in approximately 80 percent of Caucasians and is almost always absent in non-white individuals. The cusp can be either positive or negative in appearance, i.e. a depression rather than a more classic cuspal profile.

Occlusal enamel pearls are a strong ethnic indicator for Mongoloid or Inuit origin although they are much rarer than the shoveling and Carabelli traits. Such abnormalities are often lost to the forensic odontologist through either the processes of wear or treatment. The use of numerous ethnic indicators such as orbital morphology, zygomatic prominence and the variations within the dentition always leads to a more accurate assessment of ethnic origin. The expertise of forensic anthropologists should not be neglected and should always be sought in cases where the ethnicity is ambiguous.

Genetic (DNA) Comparison

The maxillofacial complex and all forensic evidence derived from its structures are within the purview of the forensic odontologist to evaluate. Traditionally, forensic dental record comparison has been used for human identification in cases where destruction of bodily tissues or prolonged exposure to the environment has made other means of identification impractical.

DNA contained in teeth, oral soft tissues and saliva can be extracted and typed. Therefore, it is prudent for the forensic odontologist to become familiar with the fundamentals for obtaining and analyzing DNA from the oral tissues. It is not necessary for the odontologist to achieve academic equivalency with the molecular biologist in the evaluation of DNA extracted from oral tissues. However, the forensic dentist is best qualified to determine how dental evidence is managed

HABIT	APPEARANCE	CAUSE
Coffee, tea, red wine drinkers	Brown/black staining on labial, lingual and palatal surfaces	Extrinsic staining
Pipe smoking	Unusual patterns of tooth wear in addition to staining.	Wear
Painting (canvas)	Unusual patterns of erosion especially on the buccal surfaces	'Gauche' in paint is acidic, and transferred to mouth as brushes are often placed intra-orally
Betel nut use	Staining on buccal surfaces, usually unilateral	Extrinsic staining
Alcoholism	Tooth erosion	Two-fold – the acidity of the alcoholic drink and acid-reflux because alcohol is a gastric irritant
Cocaine	Localized and severe dental caries, particularly in the maxillary premolar region	Testing the purity of cocaine by rubbing it into the gums. Cocaine is often mixed with sugar.
Amphetamines (Ecstasy)	Occlusal wear of molar teeth and acid erosion	Clenching of teeth plus consumption of carbonated drinks during the 'trip'
Heroin	High caries rate and severe periodontal disease	Oral neglect
Methadone syrup	Rampant caries	Methadone is often delivered as a sugary syrup with adheres to teeth tenaciously

Table 2-7: The effects of habits and addictions on the dentition.

and to supervise the proper evaluation of all components of that evidence.

The following review of DNA structure and an explanation of some common terms associated with DNA analysis are presented to prepare the reader for the description of current methods of DNA analysis. The potential role of the odontologist in managing DNA evidence and a brief review of some innovative research conducted with salivary DNA and bite mark material is also included for review. A list of cases involving the typing of DNA from oral sources is intended to provide relevant examples in which the odontologist played an important role in the analysis of DNA.

Chemical Composition of DNA

Polysaccharides, proteins, and nucleic acids are the three fundamental macromolecules in cells. Polysaccharides are composed of linked sugars and generally serve as a stored energy source, whereas proteins are made up of various combinations of amino acids and are involved in structural, regulatory, and enzymatic roles.

It is the two nucleic acids, deoxyribonucleic acid (DNA) and ribonucleic acid (RNA), however, that provides the genetic recipe by which all other activities are directed. DNA is a polymer(s) composed of four different nucleotides and whose polymorphic sequence accounts for the genetic diversity of all living

ABNORMALITY	DESCRIPTION	PREVALENCE
Supernumerary teeth	Most common in the premaxilla. 75% do not erupt (visible on post mortem radiographs). May be conical, tuberculate (multi-cusped), supplemental or odontoma-like.	1.5 – 3.5% M:F 2:1
Hypodontia	Missing teeth. Effects, in descending order of frequency, mandibular and maxillary 3rd molars, mandibular 2nd molars, maxillary lateral incisors, and 2nd premolars. Severe hypodontia is associated with Down Syndrome and ectodermal dysplasia	3.5 – 6.5% M:F 1:4
Macrodontia & Microdontia	Abnormality of tooth size, microdontia mainly effects the maxillary lateral incisors – *peg laterals* Strongly associated with hypodontia	1.1% (Macro) Overall occurrence 2.5%
Fluorosis	Enamel defects caused by high levels of fluoride. >1ppm. Mildest form presents as white flecks or diffuse cloudiness, severest exhibits brown patches with surface enamel pitting	More common in areas of high natural fluoridated water, i.e. Africa, India and the Middle East. Can also be caused by inappropriate fluoride therapies and dentifrice ingestion by children. See also occupational.
Hypoplasia	Enamel defects – usually caused by premature loss of deciduous teeth – can be an indicator of neglect, poor oral care or high fever disease during tooth development	
Amelogenesis imperfecta	Genetic defect with various presentations, either hypoplastic or hypocalcified	Family history good predictor – genetic basis
Dentinogenesis imperfecta	Translucent grey teeth – shell teeth may be present	Uncommon – genetic association – family history

Table 2-8: Abnormalities of tooth formation and eruption

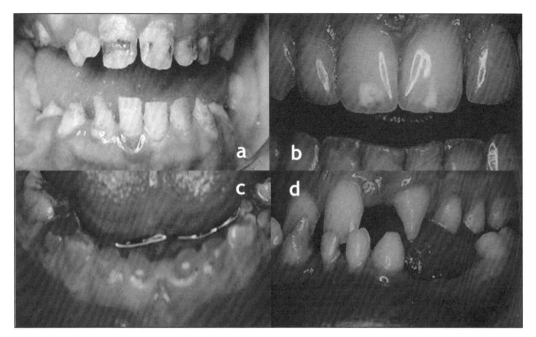

Figure 2-33: Developmental conditions (a) amelogenesis imperfecta (b) hypoplastic enamel presenting as white spots on the maxillary central incisors (c) severe Dentinogenesis imperfecta with shell teeth (d) hypodontia in a case of ectodermal dysplasia.

things. Each of the four nucleotides constituting DNA (thymine, cytosine, adenine and guanine) consists of a sugar (deoxyribose), a phosphate group and a nitrogen-containing base (**Figure 2-41**).

The nucleotides form a continuous strand with the adjacent sugars bound by the intervening phosphate group. The phosphodiester linkage always occurs between the 3' carbon of one sugar and the 5' carbon of the adjacent nucleotide giving the molecule polarity or direction (**Figure 2-42**). By convention, the sequence of DNA is discussed in the 5' to 3' direction. In its natural form, single strands of DNA are cross linked by hydrogen bonds occurring between the nitrogen bases of paired strands (**Figure 2-43**). This configuration results in a *railroad track* of double-stranded DNA that twists to form the well recognized double helix.

The pairing of bases between the two strands is very specific with hydrogen bonds occurring only between adenine and thymine, and between guanine and cytosine. With one strand running in the 5' to 3' direction and the perfectly matched, yet opposite strand running in the 3' to 5' direction, the strands are said to be anti-parallel and complementary.

Mitochondrial DNA (mtDNA)

Mitochondrial DNA differs from nuclear or chromosomal DNA in a number of ways that make it an attractive alternative for forensic analysis. Unlike nuclear DNA, mitochondrial DNA is distributed throughout the cytoplasm of cells. As its name suggests, mtDNA is confined to the mitochondria or *power house* of the cell. This component of the cell is responsible for the synthesis of adenosine triphosphate (ATP). Whereas nuclear DNA is double-stranded and linear, mitochondrial DNA is double-stranded and circular.

The mtDNA contains only 16,569 base pairs that code for two ribosomal RNAs (rRNA), 22 transfer RNAs (tRNA) and 13 proteins. (Nuclear DNA is huge by comparison with 6 x l09 base pairs.) The two strands of the mtDNA molecule are designated light (L-strand) and heavy (H-strand), based upon buoyant

ABNORMALITY	DESCRIPTION	ETHNICITY?
Incisors: Chisel / Blade	Smooth palatal surfaces with little or no expansion of the proximal margins, small cingulum, rarely a cingulum pit	Black & Caucasian
Shovel-shaped incisors:	Varying degrees of lingual edge thickening giving rise to shovel appearance	Mongoloid
Premolar: Occlusal enamel tubercle / pearl	A nodule of enamel on the occlusal surface, often with a pulp horn extension; normally lost early in life; can also be present at furcations	Mongoloid
Maxillary molar Carabelli cusp	Of varying size, this additional cusp can be seen on the mesiopalatal aspect of the first maxillary molar	Caucasoid
Mandibular molars: Supernumerary distolingual root	Third root present on the distal aspect of lower molars	Mongoloid, Inuit, Native American
Fourth molars: more frequent less frequent	Additional molar distal to the third molar	Negroid
Macrodonts	Typically of central incisors	Caucasoid

Table 2-9: Dental indicators of ethnicity.

density. By convention, base pairs of the mtDNA molecule are numbered in a clockwise direction starting at its origin of replication (D loop or control region). The control region contains hypervariable segments (highly diverse) and is the area around which most forensic work has centered.

Of particular forensic significance is the hereditary character of mtDNA. Chromosomal DNA is inherited from both the mother and father, whereas mtDNA is strictly maternally inherited. This means there is no mixing of sequence types from one generation to the next so that distant maternal relatives should have the identical mtDNA sequence. Thus, when identifying a set of human remains, if close relatives are not available, distant maternal relatives can be used as a reference source to support identification.

Furthermore, there are hundreds of copies of mtDNA in each cell compared to two copies of chromosomal DNA. Even cells without a nucleus, red blood cells found in whole blood or urine, for example, will have 3' end mitochondria. In many forensic cases, limited quantities of DNA are recovered from the evidentiary material (i.e., skeletal remains and hair shafts). Therefore, mtDNA testing may be successful when nuclear DNA testing fails.

The following terms are frequently encountered when actively engaged in the analysis of DNA. Procedural nomenclature and specific commercial product names will differ according to the laboratory. The reader is encouraged to add to this glossary as his or her experience grows or as interaction with a particular laboratory necessitates.

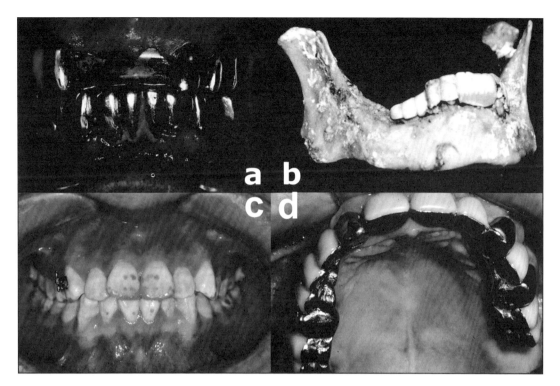

Figure 2-34a-d: Likely country of residence (a) example of Ukraine dental work (b) example of Chinese dental treatment, (c) individual from China with grade 4 (TF) Fluorosis, (d) example of Russian dental treatment.

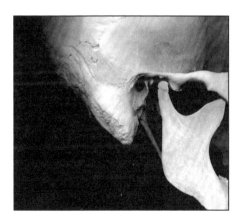
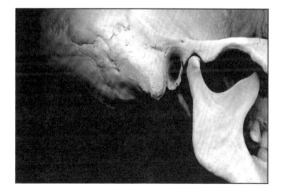

Figure 2-35: Comparison of the larger male mastoid process for an indication of the sex of an individual.

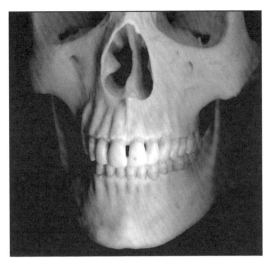
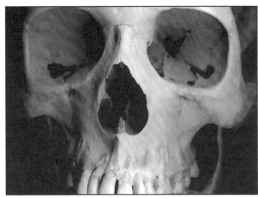

Figure 2-36: Comparison of the gonial flair of the mandible. The greater flair seen on the left is considered a male trait.

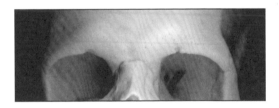
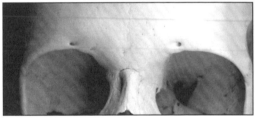

Figure 2-37: The more robust brow ridges are usually seen in males.

Allele - one of two or more contrasting genes on the same locus in homologuous chromosomes Represents VNTR on a specific chromosome. Since autosomal chromosomes are paired, all alleles except the majority of those located on the sex chromosomes are represented twice. If the alleles are the same the individual is said to homozygous for that locus. If different alleles occupy the locus, the individual is heterozygous.

AmpFLP - amplified fragment length polymorphism evaluates STR and LTR loci using the PCR.

Autoradiograph - radiograhic film placed in contact with membrane lifted from an electrophoretic gel, permitting the radioisotope tags to produce light areas on the film. The brightness of the spot is proportional to the quantity of labeled DNA and the location on the membrane corresponds to the molecular weight of the fragment.

Chromosome - a structure (usually paired) that contains linear threads of DNA which transmit genetic information. The human nucleus normally contains 46 chromosomes consisting of 22 pairs of autosomes and either XX (female) or XY (male) sex chromosomes.

Core repeat - a small segment of DNA which is repeated to yield a VNTR.

Degradation of DNA - disruption of the molecule. Usually caused by strand breakage, damage to the bases or by cross-linking of

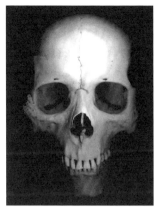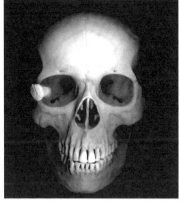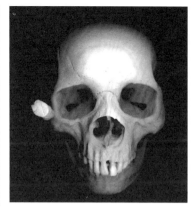

Figure 2-38: A comparison of the general racial features of the skeletal face. Caucasian – left; Oriental – middle; African - right.

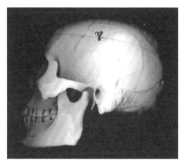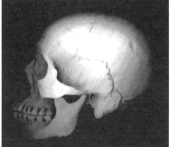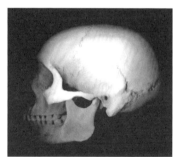

Figure 2-39: The lateral view of the same race types seen above

bases to each other or to protein. Fragmentation of DNA is usually caused by environmental conditions such as endonuclease activity and excessive shearing forces. Severe degradation may result in segments too small to contain any polymorphic sequences necessary for individualization.

Electrophoretic gel - a colloid placed in an electric field that serves as a sieve to separate DNA fragments of various sizes. Smaller pieces generally move quicker (further) than large pieces.

Evidence specimen - source of DNA to be identified, such as a tooth from unknown human remains or semen removed from rape victim (unknown source).

Fluorophors - chemical tags that fluoresce

at different wavelengths and provide the sequencing instrument with a means of distinguishing between nucleotides and, therefore, reading the DNA sequence 3' 5'

Gene - functional unit of heredity that occupies a specific location (locus) on a chromosome and consists of a discreet segment of DNA containing the correct base sequence to code for a series of amino acids needed to form a specific peptide.

Length specific typing - analysis based upon the number o base pairs within a specific section of a DNA molecule, which translates to size or length differences.

Locus - a specific position on a chromosome. The plural form is loci.

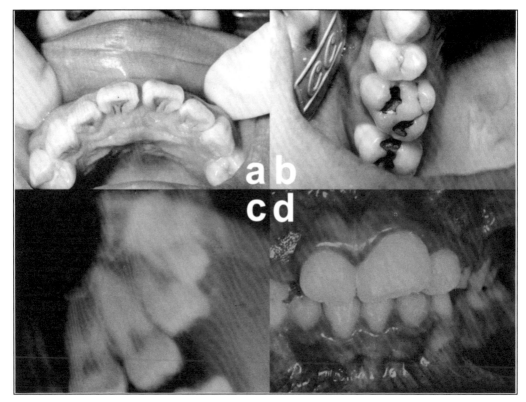

Figure 2-40: Dental ethnicity indicators. (a) shovel shaped incisors strongly associated with a Mongoloid ethnicity, (b) cusp of Carabelli found commonly in Caucasoids, (c) supplemental molars (9's) in the maxillary arch most commonly seen in Negroid individuals, (d) macrodont of the upper left central incisor most commonly seen in Caucasoids but not as strongly associated as the Carabelli trait

Microsatellite - short tandem repeats (STR)

Minisatellite - long tandem repeats (LTR)

Oligonucleotides - small pieces of DNA that will bind exclusively with a complementary section of the DNA genome. When tagged with a fluorescent or radioactive marker, oligonucleotides can be used as a probe to highlight specific sequences of DNA.

PAGE - polyacrylamide gel electrophoresis. A similar process to argarose gel electrophoresis but the polyacrylamide provides better resolution.

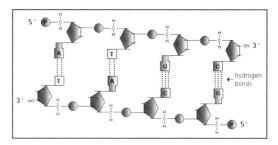

Figure 2-41: The structure of a deoxy-nucleotide as it appears in DNA. The deoxy refers to the absence of an oxygen atom at the number 2 carbon of the sugar. Linkage to adjacent nucleotides will occur via phosphodiester bonds (phosphate group) attached to carbons 3 and 5. Variability in the structure of the four different nitrogen bases (thymine, cytosine, adenine, guanine) provide for sequence variation.

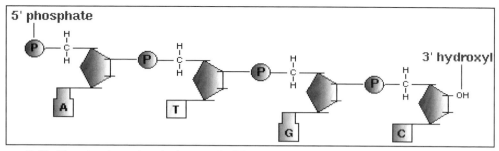

Figure 2-42: The structure of a single strand of DNA is pictured, showing the phosphodiester bonds between adjacent 3' and 5' carbons. (Variability in the bases is not illustrated here.)

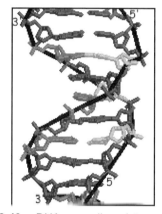

Figure 2-43: DNA normally exists as a double stranded molecule with the two strands bound by weak hydrogen bonds between the specifically paired base groups (i.e. adenine only pairs with thymine and guanine only pairs with cytosine).

PCR - polymerase chain reaction. A laboratory technique in which a target section of DNA is duplicated. In this manner, a few copies of a specific DNA sequence can be amplified into millions of copies sufficient for *analysis*

Polymorphism – region of genetic variability serving as a basis for distinction between individuals. Some sequences are highly variable (rare) and others are less so.

Purification of DNA - cleansing of DNA to remove inhibitors of PCR or restriction enzyme activity. Purification is usually conducted by:

- Lysis of cellular membrane

- Removal of protein

- And one of the following:

-Precipitation of DNA from solution by ethanol,

- Dialysis of DNA solution with large quantities of buffer

- Ultrafiltration.

Quality of DNA - determination of the intactness of the DNA strands and the purity of the sample relative to the amount of protein or phenol contamination.

Quantity of DNA - determination of amount of DNA in the sample. Results are usually recorded as nanograms (ng) or micrograms (ug) per millileter (mL).

Radioisotope - an unstable isotope that decays to a stable state by emitting radiation which will show up on x-ray film. Radioisotopes may be used to tag DNA to help determine DNA quantity or the location of DNA bands after electrophoresis and Southern blotting.

Reference specimen - source of DNA to which the evidence specimen will be compared, such as blood sample from parents of a missing child or blood sample from a suspected rapist (known source).

Restriction enzymes - an endonuclease used as *biological scissors* that hydrolyzes double stranded DNA at specific sites, resulting in DNA fragments of various sizes.

RFLP - restriction fragment length polymorphism analysis uses endonucleases to cut the DNA at specific locations, resulting in fragments of different lengths.

Sequence-specific typing - analysis based upon the order in which different base pairs are linked within a specific section of a DNA molecule TE buffer - solution used to stabilize DNA following purification

VNTR - variable number tandem repeats are short segments of DNA which are repeated in tandem. The number of repeat units will differ between individuals

Methods of DNA Analysis

Forensic scientists have a number of DNA testing methods to choose from when answering questions such as, "Did this semen stain come from the accused rapist?" Or, "Can we identify this set of human remains as John Doe?" These testing methods will reveal either sequence-specific or length-specific variations in DNA.

The choice of which method or methods to use will depend on the quality and quantity of the DNA removed from the evidence specimen and the reference source available at the time of analysis. Prior to testing, review of the evidence and references may dictate the type of testing to be performed. Through this type of pre-testing triage, the success of the analysis and the speed of completing the testing will be greatly enhanced.

When a biological specimen (semen, blood, saliva, tooth, etc.) is recovered for forensic analysis, the DNA profile from this specimen can be directly compared to a suspect's or victim's DNA profile. The most widely used procedure to accomplish this is the RFLP method. The ability to differentiate between individuals using RFLP analysis was first described in 1980. The application of RFLP testing to obtain a conviction in a criminal investigation began in the United States in 1986 (State of Florida v. Tommie Lee Andrews, tried in 1987). To date, RFLP testing has been successfully performed in thousands of forensic cases.

RFLP analysis involves the following procedures:

- Removal and purification of DNA from the source material

- Cutting of the purified DNA into thousands of fragments using restriction enzymes (*biological scissors*)

- Separation of the fragments in a sieving matrix (gel) according to size

- Transfer of all DNA fragments in the gel to a nylon membrane

- Detection of specific DNA fragments using oligonucleotides labeled with radioisotopes (small pieces of. radioactive DNA).

The labeled oligonucleotide will recognize one pair among the thousands of DNA fragments immobilized on the membrane. The size of these fragments (2,000-10,000 nucleotide base pairs) will vary from one individual to the next based on a VNTR found within each fragment. By looking at a series of different VNTR locations (loci), a DNA profile is generated.

A match of the suspect and evidence DNA profiles at four or more of these VNTR loci will infer identification of the perpetrator. The RFLP method can also be used to identify the parent of a child, or the victim of a crime or disaster. Unfortunately, RFLP analysis requires large quantities of high molecular weight DNA. DNA degradation, insufficient quantities of DNA (less than 100 nanograms), or both could result in an incomplete RFLP profile. Consequently, approximately 20 percent of forensic investigations involving RFLP analysis are unsuccessful; this percentage is even high for the identification of cadaver tissue.

With the development of the PCR in 1985 fragmented and minute quantities of DNA can be analyzed. During the PCR, copies of a specific location (locus) are made using the same basic DNA replication machinery that a cell uses prior to mitosis. The ensuing amplification results in millions of copies of the original locus. Consequently, PCR amplification allows for analysis of DNA quantities as low as 100 picograms and below. Given this elevated level of sensitivity, analysis of DNA from a stamp that has been licked by an embezzler, or from the rim of a baseball cap left at the scene of a crime by a thief, or from skeletal remains from the Vietnam War, has become more common.

In order to address the problems associated with DNA degradation, PCR methods have focused on smaller VNTR loci. Microsatellite and minisatellites VNTR loci, ranging from 100 to 1500 nucleotide base pairs in length have been evaluated for forensic purpose. The microsatellite loci, or STRs, are 100 to 350 base pairs in length with a core repeat unit of 2 to 5 base pairs. The minisatellite loci, or LTRs, range in length from 400 to 1500 base pairs with a core repeat unit of 16 to 70 base pairs.

The evaluation of STR and LTR loci using the PCR is referred to as AmpFLP analysis. The PCR products generated during AmpFLP analysis can be separated using conventional PAGE methods. Following or during the PAGE detection of DNA fragments can be achieved using non-isotopic (non-radioactive) methods, such as silver staining and fluorescence. Discontinuous vertical PAGE and silver stain detection is being used routinely in a number of forensic laboratories.

Fluorescence-based detection methods are an attractive alternative to conventional silver staining methods for many reasons. Multiple fluorophors allow for internal lane standards and for multiplexing many STR or LTR systems together in the same lane (each locus is labeled with a different colored fluorophor). Fluorescently labeled DNA fragments are detected in real time using laser technologies. Thus, no further steps are required following electrophoresis to visualize the alleles (different sized fragments at the same locus).

Finally, data analysis is computerized, eliminating the need for additional imaging systems. The Applied Biosystems 373A DNA Sequencer has been adopted by a number of laboratories to analyze STR and LTR loci for case work. Using either detection method, evaluation of 4 to 8 AmpFLP loci will provide a power of discrimination approaching that of RFLP analysis.

The PCR has also been utilized to help determine sequence specific differences at various genetic loci. The AmplitypeO HLA DQ alpha and PolyMarker (PM) typing kits manufactured by Perkin Elmer are used for PCR based analyses. There are six different loci which are analyzed between the two kits. These are listed in order of decreasing size:

- Human leukocyte antigen DQalpha locus for the HLA DQ alpha kit

- Low density lipoprotein receptor (LDLR)

- Lycophorin A (GYPA)

- Hemoglobin G gammaglobin (HBGG)

- D7S8

- Group specific component (GC) loci for the PM kit

Typing of all six loci is performed by incubating the PCR products with a membrane strip (one strip for HLA DQ and one for PolyMarker).

Small oligonucleotides are immobilized onto the strip. The oligonucleotides are specific for sequence differences in the PCR product. Therefore, only PCR product which is a perfect match will bind to the membrane. Specifically bound PCR product is detected using a bound enzyme conjugate and the conversion of a colorless substrate to a colored precipitate. The combination of colored spots on the two membranes results in a genetic profile. The combined power of discrimination for these six loci is 2 or more orders of magnitude lower than RFLP or AmpFLP testing. Regardless, the AmplitypeO kits are simple, efficient and an excellent method for moderate level DNA typing.

Another method of sequence-specific DNA typing is the direct, full-length sequence analysis of PCR product. The only example of this type of analysis used in forensics is mitochondrial DNA testing. The control region of the mtDNA genome is the most polymorphic, evolving 5 to 10 times faster than single copy nuclear markers. Therefore, this is the target for the majority of mtDNA analyses. Portions of the control region are amplified using the PCR, and the primary sequence of the PCR product is determined.

Sequence analysis is performed using conventional or automated methods of the Sanger sequencing technique. The mtDNA sequence generated from a maternal relative can then be compared directly to the sequence obtained from human remains in order to identify the remains. Similarly, the mtDNA sequence generated from biological evidence can be compared directly to the sequence obtained from a suspect in order to imply association of the suspect to a crime.

Mitochondrial DNA sequence analysis is moderately informative. While the mtDNA control region is highly informative, the probabilities of individual polymorphisms cannot be multiplied together as they are linked. Thus, the discriminatory power of mtDNA testing is better than many single locus nuclear tests, but less informative than the combined Amplitypem kits and multi-locus RFLP or AmpFLP testing. Using the methods described above, DNA testing can be a powerful method of human identification. When performing DNA testing on forensic evidence, first determine what question is being asked.

"Could the biological specimen found at the scene of a crime have come from the suspect or victim?"

When this is the question, any of the methods could provide useful information. Following extraction of DNA from the specimen, determine the quantity and quality of the DNA. If greater than 50 nanograms of high molecular weight DNA is present, RFLP testing can be performed. If degradation has occurred, as is commonly found in cadaver tissue, AmplitypeR HLA DQalpha and PolyMarker and/or AmpFLP testing can be performed. If extensive degradation and/or limited quantities of DNA were recovered, mtDNA testing may be the only viable alternative.

"Who is this individual?"

When this is the question, the reference source may dictate the type of testing to be performed. If immediate relatives, mother, father, spouse, and/or children are available, nuclear methods can be used. When close relatives are unavailable, or when the quantity and/or quality of the DNA extract is poor, mtDNA sequence analysis of maternal relatives can be performed. By being prepared to answer questions of identity that may arise during a forensic investigation, DNA analysis can, and will be an important tool for establishing the identity of a suspect, victim or parent.

Responsibilities of the Odontologist

Establishing Rapport with the Laboratory

Some odontologists may be intimidated by the DNA laboratory environment. However, the reader is encouraged to contact the nearest DNA laboratory to become familiar with the contact individuals and DNA procedures before a dental case arises. Most laboratories will welcome the opportunity to discuss their capabilities, techniques and experiences.

Once rapport is established, and time allows, you may want to observe certain procedures or participate in hands-on testing if circumstances permit. Collaboration in a well thought-out, yet simple scientific investigation can be an excellent basis for establishing a relationship with a laboratory. A research protocol can be quite simple and the results need not be earth-shattering, but both parties will benefit from the interaction. Clarification of the odontologist's and laboratory's roles can be addressed during this time as well, should an actual dental DNA case arise.

Management of the Evidence

The odontologist should be consulted on all matters of dental and salivary evidence. To what degree the odontologist participates is based upon his or her relationship with the medical examiner, law enforcement personnel, and the laboratory. Dental evidence may be recovered by an investigator at the crime scene or removed directly from human remains by the odontologist.

Regardless of when the tooth or salivary sample is submitted to the laboratory and who performs the initial recovery, the odontologist must be allowed to examine the evidence thoroughly and document the circumstances under which it was obtained. Normally, documentation should include photographs and/or radiographs, where appropriate. These may be supplemented by sketches and a thorough written description of the evidence and immediate environment from which the evidence was removed. Besides the usual description of the location and identifying features of the evidence, temperature, humidity and potential sources of contamination should be noted as well. Two examples illustrating variables are seen in the case files at the end of this chapter.

The most frequent contaminating material will be blood or saliva but may include bacterial sources such as feces, decaying tissue, vomit, or animal hair. These contaminants may act as inhibitors to procedural steps such as restriction enzyme activity and PCR but may also represent unintended sources of DNA as well. All material should be labeled and managed according to the local procedures for maintaining the chain of custody. To be useful for forensic analysis, DNA must be relatively undamaged.

Generally, DNA is a hardy molecule, but there are specific environmental conditions that put its forensic usefulness at risk. DNA may become denatured (unwound) at high temperatures or extremes in pH (pH less than 4 or greater than 13 are not desirable). Denatured DNA poses no problem when PCR is used, but can prohibit the use of RFLP. Wet or humid surroundings foster degradation (breaking apart) by nucleases, and exposure to ultraviolet light or other radiation can cause damage to the DNA molecule as well. Specimens are ideally preserved in a freezer at -20 degrees C or in a cool, dry environment until freezer storage is accessible.

DNA from Oral Tissues

Soft tissue (gingivae, tongue, follicular tissue, blood clot) and salivary evidence can be transported to the laboratory after complete documentation. However, in cases where DNA is to be extracted from dental hard tissue, the odontologist may be asked for an opinion concerning how best to access the DNA. Because teeth possess identification value beyond that of DNA analysis alone (radiographic, ultrastructural and biochemical studies), the tooth should not be arbitrarily destroyed. If other studies are to be conducted, such decisions must occur before the tooth is manipulated.

First, consider the nature of the case. If the hard tissue is to be retained for further analysis, then a conservative technique is mandatory. However, if documentation is complete and no further need of the intact tooth is anticipated, a more aggressive technique can be employed. Generally, the most DNA-rich site will be the dental pulp which is enclosed by the coronal pulp chamber, root canals, and accessory canals. Some DNA may be recovered from the dentin or cementum but none should be expected within the enamel. Molar teeth are generally better protected due to their location and tend to have larger pulp chambers, if not deeply restored.

If several teeth are available, the molars are probably the best place to start and if more than one tooth can be sampled (and there is no doubt that they are from the same individual), chances of recovering sufficient DNA for analysis will be increased. All procedures should be conducted under sterile conditions to protect the evidence from contamination and the operator from infection. Gloves, mask, eye protection and a clean working environment are mandatory, and a biological exhaust hood is desirable. Such facilities may be located at the genetic testing laboratory.

Performing the sampling in the laboratory that will subsequently do the analysis eliminates the need to shuttle evidence between offices. With that in mind, the following guidelines for obtaining dental DNA are offered:

- Determine if there is any soft tissue or blood adherent to the tooth that should be sampled. If so, remove this material and place it in a separate container, such as a sterile 1.5 rnL polypropylene tube or glass vial. If analysis is to take place within a few hours, label and store at 4 degrees C, otherwise freeze at -20 degrees C until ready for analysis. The time and conditions under which dental pulp retains its integrity and provides forensically significant DNA is not yet well established. It is recommended to examine the outer surface of the tooth and if severe pulpal desiccation is suspected, proceed to step 4. If soft tissue and blood are not to be sampled, continue to step 2.

- Debride the tooth of any plaque or calculus with a curette and wash thoroughly with hydrogen peroxide followed by ethanol. This reduces contamination by extrinsic sources of DNA and degradation by bacterial nucleases. Cleaning efforts can be less vigorous in areas of open root tips or deep caries so as not to force chemicals into the pulp chamber. Thoroughly rinse the tooth in sterile deionized water.

- If the tooth is intact (unrestored, non-carious, unbroken) and is believed to have been removed from the alveolus recently, a conventional endodontic access and instrumentation can be conducted. The problems associated with this technique are limited access and violation of the occlusal surface along with any occlusal restorations and distinct occlusal morphology. If these are not concerns, then this familiar, relatively conservative procedure may provide sufficient pulp issue to perform DNA typing. If the tooth is not intact (fractured, large restorations, severely carious, or extensively desiccated), proceed to step 4.

- Sectioning the tooth is the next most aggressive procedure and permits greater access to the pulp chamber. Some authors have documented consistent success with longitudinal sectioning of the tooth while others have advocated a transverse sectioning technique. It is more important to have a clear plan and rationale for the method used than to maintain strict adherence to a single approach. Establishing a plane through the longitudinal (vertical) axis of the tooth provides the maximum access to the entire pulp chamber and still preserves the basic anatomical form of the tooth for future radiographic or morphologic investigation. Disadvantages of the longitudinal approach are that it may be slightly more difficult to perform and some features of the coronal anatomy may be altered.

- A transverse (horizontal) section through the cervical portion of the tooth is easy to perform, does not violate coronal restorations, and generally maintains the basic anatomical form. However, the horizontal section will probably not provide as much direct access to the root canals as the vertical section. Either a chisel or rotary instrument (bur or disk) may be used to section the tooth. Potential risks are that a chisel is likely to fragment a severely dried specimen and the rotary instrument may create heat that could theoretically damage the DNA.

Once the tooth is opened, the walls of the pulp chamber can be curetted or instrumented with a slow-speed rotary bur. Pulp tissue and powder can be collected over a wide-mouthed sterile container. In dried specimens, the pulp may be mummified, parchment-like, or consist of wispy strands of tissue contracted against the chamber wall. After instrumentation, the chamber is best irrigated with TE buffer. Subsequent ultra filtration of the liquid at the laboratory will remove the cellular material needed for analysis.

As described in step 1, if analysis is to take place within a few hours, label and store the specimen at 4 degrees C. If analysis is delayed, freeze at -20 degrees C. Specimens being transferred from a remote location to the laboratory should be kept as cold as possible. Packing the specimen in dry ice is recommended. The remaining tooth should be kept at -20 degrees C even after the pulp is removed because additional efforts to retrieve DNA may be necessary at a later time.

As a last resort, crushing the tooth may necessary. This is the simplest, yet most irreversible of all methods. It does, however, provide for complete sampling of the tooth and may be the best approach when the condition of the tooth is so poor that all other manipulative techniques will cause disintegration anyway. However, consider the following compromise if conservation of the crown is still important to the case:

- Section the tooth horizontally at the cervix. The upper one-half, containing the coronal pulp chamber, is thoroughly instrumented to remove pulp tissue and some dentin. The residual shell of enamel which is unlikely to contain DNA is put aside for its potential morphologic and radiographic value. The lower one-half, consisting of the roots, is instrumented and subsequently crushed under sterile conditions. The entire specimen is stored for analysis as previously described.

Reporting Results

Regardless of what procedures have been performed, if the odontologist has been consulted in any manner, he should provide a full report to the evidence contributor. His report should address only those procedures that he performed and the findings he obtained. The report should be written in clear and concise layman's terms so that the reader can easily understand the dental results. Unless the odontologist is also an expert in DNA analysis, all DNA testing procedures and interpretations should be reported and testified to by the DNA examiner alone.

Salivary DNA Recovered From Human Bite Marks

Human saliva has been shown to be an excellent source of high molecular weight DNA. Saliva recovered from material at crime scenes has been successfully isolated, analyzed and compared to reference sources obtained from suspects. For example, DNA has been isolated from saliva found on clothing, cigarette butts, postage stamps and envelope flaps. Simultaneous with these successful case findings has been the advancement of alternate light technology which permits investigators to identify the location of body fluids, such as saliva, blood and semen left on the skin of a victim or other objects at a crime scene. Preliminary research has been conducted regarding the recovery and analysis of salivary DNA deposited on a victim's skin in association with a bite mark. Some conclusions are worth mentioning:

- Validation studies have confirmed that human saliva is indeed a useful source of forensic DNA evidence. Some samples have yielded as much as 15 ng/mL of DNA.

- In the case of a deceased victim, forensically significant DNA appears to be stable and may be recovered up to 48-60 hours after deposition on the skin, depending upon environmental influences. After this period, products of tissue breakdown, appear to contaminate the skin surface and degrade the DNA.

- In the case of a living victim, the saliva is often washed away by the victim or emergency room personnel. However, in the absence of washing or otherwise disturbing the site, the DNA in dried saliva may be retrievable for up to 72 hours.

- Contamination of the saliva with other DNA is a potential problem. The victim's blood or sloughed skin cells are the most frequent source of this contamination. Control samples from the victim are necessary to establish his or her DNA profile to guard against this possibility.

- In contrast to the single, moist swab recommended for recovery of saliva for ABO blood group typing, a double swab technique for salivary DNA has been recommended. An initial (moist) swabbing loosens the dehydrated oral cells adherent to the victim's skin, but does not completely remove them. The second (dry) swab collects the loosened cells more effectively. The following specific steps are suggested:

- Dip a sterile cotton swab into distilled sterile water until the tip is completely wet.

- With the plane of the skin positioned parallel to the supporting surface, roll the swab over the area of the bite, attempting to thoroughly wash the site and collect saliva onto the swab

- Set this first swab aside to completely air dry

- Use a second dry sterile cotton swab to wipe the area   and absorb the moisture which remains on the skin (deposited by the first swabbing)

- After air drying (minimum 30 minutes) both swabs can be placed together for:

- Immediate analysis

- Immediate freezing at -20°C or lower

- Temporary storage   in a porous container such as a paper evidence envelopefor transfer to a freezer or laboratory.

EDUCATIONAL OUTCOMES

By completing this chapter the reader will:

- Build a foundational knowledge of the legal and humanitarian requirements for positive identification of decedents in criminal and civil cases.

- Describe the relationship of the forensic odontologist to the various legal agencies involved in the determination of a decedent's or missing person's identity.

- Know the advantages and disadvantages of each of the methods of post mortem identification.

- Identify resources for potential retrieval of antemortem dental records.

- Understand the principles of dental record management required to provide sufficient antemortem information for identification.

- Understand the principles of radiographic, photographic and scanning electron micrographic technology in the resolution of forensic dental identification problems.

- Describe the methods used in determination of an individual's age by the dentition.

- Recognize the social and physical anthropologic criteria for age, race and sex determination and dental markers associated with habits, addictions and place of origin.

- Build a foundational knowledge of the procedures and protocols required to compare antemortem and post mortem dental records in a forensic setting.

- Critically evaluate relevant forensic dental scientific literature based on an understanding of evidence based concepts.

CONTRIBUTORS

Susan G.S. Anderson, DMD
Mark L. Bernstein, DDS, DABFO
Hugh E. Berryman, Ph.D.
C. Michael Bowers, DDS, JD, DABFO
Mary A. Bush, DDS
Peter J. Bush, BS
Jon Curtis Dailey, DDS, DABFO
Sheila M. Dashkow, DDS
Richard L. Dickens, DDS, PhD
Joseph A. Dizinno, DDS
Tadao Furue, BA*
Arthur D. Goldman, DDS, DABFO
Gregory S. Golden, DDS, DABFO
Bernard L. Harmeling, DMD, DABFO*
Edward F. Harris, PhD

Edward E. Herschaft, DDS, MA, DABFO
Mitchell M. Holland, PhD
Gene A. Jones, DDS, MSD
Isaac Kaplan, DDS
Cathy A. Law, DDS, DABFO
James McGivney, DDS, DABFO
William R. Maples, PhD, DABFA*
Raymond G. Miller, DDS
Harry H. Mincer, DDS, MS, PhD, DABFO
Ann L. Norrlander, DDS, DABFO
David K. Ord, DDS
Diane T. Penola, RDH, BS, MA
Iain A. Pretty, BDS (Hons), MSc, PhD, MFDS
 RCS(Ed)
Raymond D. Rawson, DDS, MA, DABFO
David R. Senn, DDS, DABFO
Harvey A. Silverstein, DDS, DABFO
Brion C. Smith, DDS, DABFO
Duane Spencer DDS, DABFO
David. Sweet, DMD, PhD, DABFO
Warren Tewes, DDS, MS, DABFO
Gerald L. Vale, DDS, MPH, JD
Richard A. Weems, DMD, MS, DABFO
Franklin D. Wright, DMD, DABFO

*Deceased

REFERENCES

Personal Recognition

Manhein MH, Listi GA, Barsley RE, Musselman R, Barrow NE, Ubelaker DH (2000). In vivo facial tissue depth measurements for children and adults. J Forensic Sci 45:48-60.

Fingerprinting

Beavan, Colin. Fingerprints: The Origins of Crime Detection and the Murder Case That Launched Forensic Science. Hyperion, 2001.

Camenson, Biythe. Opportunities in Forensic Science Careers.Contemporary Books, 2001.

Campbell, Andrea. Forensic Science: Evidence, Clues, and Investigation. Chelsea House, 1999.

Coppock, Craig A. Contrast: An Investigator's Basic Reference Guide to Fingerprint Identification Concepts. Charles C. Thomas, 2001.

Evans, Colin. The Casebook of Forensic Detection: How ScienceSolved 100 of the World's Most Baffling Crimes. John Wiley and Sons, 1998.

Inman, Keith, and Norah Rudin. Principles and Practice of Criminalistics: The Profession of Forensic Science. CRC Press, 2000.

Jones, Charlotte Foltz. Fingerprints and Talking Bones: How Real-Life Crimes Are Solved. Yearling Books, 1999.

Jones, Gary W. Introduction to Fingerprint Comparison. Staggs, 2000.

Parker, Janice. Forgeries, Fingerprints, and Forensics: Crime. Raintree/Steck Vaughn, 2000.

Rainis, Kenneth G. Crime-Solving Science Projects: Forensic Science Experiments. Enslow, 2000.

Ramsland, Katherine M. The. Forensic Science of C.S.I. Boulevard, 2001.

Dental Identification

American Board of Forensic Odontology (1994). Body identification guidelines. J Am Dent Assoc 125:1244-6.

http://www.abfo.org. American Board of Forensic Odontology. Promotion of the Use of a Thermoplastic Material to Aid in the Identification of Human Remains.

Anderson GS, McGiveny J Universal standards for charting in the dental office using winid.

Dashkow S, Forensic Record Keeping, Personal communication.

http://www.dmort.org. Disaster Mortuary Response Teams.

Mathe G, (2005). Personal communication.

Ortiz A (1987). Dental Records- A Tool in Forensic Dentistry. Annual World Dental Congress.

Shanel-Hogan K, Family Violence is a Social and Healthcare Issue Professionals Against Violence, Personal communication.

Woelfel JB, Permar D (1984). Dental anatomy: its correlation with dental health service. 3rd ed. Philadelphia: Lea & Febiger.

Photography

http://www.linear-systems.com.

http://forensicpf.com.

http://www.laboratorytalk.com/news/ocu/ocu101.html.

http://www.photo.net/learn/optics/edscott/ir000010.htm.

http://www.tomar.com.

http://www.theiai.org/guidelines/swigt/index.php.

David TJ, Sobel MN (1994). Recapturing a five-month-old bite mark by means of reflective ultraviolet photography. J Forensic Sci 39:1560-7.

Eastman Kodak Co. Ultraviolet & Fluorescence Photography M-27: 1972.

Forensics RC, Personal communication.

FujiFilm (2006). S3 IR Professional camera brochure: FujiFilm North America.

Golden G (1994). Use of Alternate Light Source Illumination in Bite Mark Photography. J Forensic Sci 39.

Golden G, Wright FD (2005). Photography. In: Bitemark evidence. RBJ Dorion editor. New York: Marcel Dekker, pp. xix, 629 p.

Krauss TC (1993). Forensic evidence documentation using reflecive ultraviolet photography. Photo Electronic Imaging.

Krauss TC, Warlen SC (1985). Technical Note. J Forensic Sci 30:262-268.

Luntz LL, Luntz P (1973). Handbook for dental identification; techniques in forensic dentistry, by Lester L. Luntz and Phyllys Luntz Philadelphia,: Lippincott.

Menzel ER, Duff JM (1979). Laser detection of latent fingerprints--treatment with fluorescers. J Forensic Sci 24:96-100.

People v Castro. 96-03434

Quain B (2000). Pro-sumer Power!: International Network Training Institute.

Sharf S, Gabbay R, Brown S (1997). Infrared Luminescence of Indented Writing as Evidence of Document Alteration. J Forensic Sci 42.

Stoilovic M (1991). Detection of semen and blood stains using polilight as a light source. Forensic Sci Int 51:289-96.

Stokes GG (1853). On the Change of Refrangibility of Light. Philosophical Transactions of the Royal Society of London:385-396.

Vandenberg N, van Oorschot RA (2006). The use of Polilight in the detection of seminal fluid, saliva, and bloodstains and comparison with conventional chemical-based screening tests. J Forensic Sci 51:361-70.

West M, Barsley R (1995). Ultraviolet Forensic Photography ASFO Manual of Forensic Odontology.

Williams RA (1988). Reflective Ultraviolet Photography in Dermatological Research. Journal of Biological Photography 56.

Wright FD, Golden G (1997). Forensic Photogtaphy. In: Forensic dentistry. PG Stimson and CA Mertz editors. Boca Raton, Fla.: CRC Press, pp. xvi, 301 p.

Scanning Electron Microscopy

Basu S, Millette JR (1986). Electron microscopy in forensic, occupational, and environmental health sciences New York: Plenum Press.

Bush MA, Bush PJ, Miller RG (2006). Detection and classification of composite resins in incinerated teeth for forensic purposes. J Forensic Sci 51:636-42.

Carr RF, Barsley RE, Davenport WD, Jr. (1986). Postmortem examination of incinerated teeth with the scanning electron microscope. J Forensic Sci 31:307-11.

David TJ (1986). Adjunctive use of scanning electron microscopy in bite mark analysis: a three-dimensional study. J Forensic Sci 31:1126-34.

David TJ (1987). The use of scanning electron microscopy in bite mark analysis. In: Electron Microscopy in Forensic, Occupational, and Environmental Health Sciences. S Basu and JR Millette editors: Springer, pp. 294.

Fairgrieve SI (1994). SEM analysis of incinerated teeth as an aid to positive identification. J Forensic Sci 39:557-65.

Jakobsen J, Holmen L, Fredebo L, Sejrsen B (1995). Scanning electron microscopy, a useful tool in forensic dental work. J Forensic Odontostomatol 13:36-40.

Merlati G, Danesino P, Savio C, Fassina G, Osculati A, Menghini P (2002). Observations on dental prostheses and restorations subjected to high temperatures: experimental studies to aid identification processes. J Forensic Odontostomatol 20:17-24.

Merlati G, Savio C, Danesino P, Fassina G, Menghini P (2004). Further study of restored and un-restored teeth subjected to high temperatures. J Forensic Odontostomatol 22:34-9.

Muller M, Berytrand MF, Quatrehomme G, Bolla M, Rocca JP (1998). Macroscopic and microscopic aspects of incinerated teeth. J Forensic Odontostomatol 16:1-7.

Rawson RB, Starich GH, Rawson RD (2000). Scanning electron microscopic analysis of skin resolution as an aid in identifying trauma in forensic investigations. J Forensic Sci 45:1023-7.

Robinson FG, Rueggeberg FA, Lockwood PE (1998). Thermal stability of direct dental esthetic restorative materials at elevated temperatures. J Forensic Sci 43:1163-7.

Rossouw RJ, Grobler SR, Phillips VM, Van W Kotze TJ (1999). The effects of extreme temperatures on composite, compomer and ionomer restorations. J Forensic Odontostomatol 17:1-4.

Smith BC (1990). A preliminary report: proximal facet analysis and the recovery of trace restorative materials from unrestored teeth. J Forensic Sci 35:873-80.

State of Minnesota v Donald Blom. 682 N.W. 2d 578

Suzuki K, Hanaoka Y, Minaguchi K, Inoue M, Suzuki H (1991). [Positive identification of dental porcelain in a case of murder]. Nippon Hoigaku Zasshi 45:330-40.

Ubelaker DH, Ward DC, Braz VS, Stewart J (2002). The use of SEM/EDS analysis to distinguish dental and osseus tissue from other materials. J Forensic Sci 47:940-3.

Wilson DF, Massey W (1987). Scanning electron microscopy of incinerated teeth. Am J Forensic Med Pathol 8:32-8.

Wilson GS, Cruickshanks-Boyd DW (1982). Analysis of dental materials as an aid to identification in aircraft accidents. Aviat Space Environ Med 53:326-31.

Antemortem Considerations

Age determination from the teeth (1974). In: Forensic dentistry. JM Cameron and BG Sims editors. Edinburgh: Churchill Livingstone, pp. ix, 158 p.

American Board of Forensic Odontology (1994). Body identification guidelines. J Am Dent Assoc 125:1244-6, 1248, 1250 passim.

Clements EM, Davies-Thomas E, Pickett KG (1953). Order of eruption of the permanent human dentition. Br Med J 1:1425-7.

Clements EM, Davies-Thomas E, Pickett KG (1957). Age at which the deciduous teeth are shed. Br Med J:1508-10.

Clements EM, Davies-Thomas E, Pickett KG (1957). Time of eruption of permanent teeth in British children at independent, rural, and urban schools. Br Med J:1511-3.

Dickens RL, Kaplan I (1986). Intensifying a processed dental radiograph. Gen Dent 34:140-3.

Eastman Kodak Co. Kodak X-Omat Duplicating, Publication 03-8. Rochester, NY: Kodak Eastman Co.

Eastman Kodak Co. Film Technique Guide. Rochester, NY: Eastman Kodak Co.

Eastman Kodak Co. Kodak Rapid Process Copy Film, Publication M3-1. Rochester, NY: Kodak Eastman Co.

Fanning EA (1961). A Longitudinal Study of Tooth Formation and Root Resorption. Dental Journal 57:202.

Francis CC (1939). The Apperance of Centers of Ossification from Six to Fifteen Years. American Journal of Physical Anthropology 27:127-138.

Francis CC, Werle PP, Behm A (1939). The Apperance of Centers of Ossification from Birth to Five Years. American Journal of Physical Anthropology 24:273-299.

Fujita M, Kodera Y, Ogawa M, Wada T, Doi K (1988). Digital image processing of periapical radiographs. Oral Surg Oral Med Oral Pathol 65:490-4.

Greulich WW, Pyle SI (1957). Radiographic atlas of skeletal development of the hand and wrist. 2d ed. Stanford, Calif. Stanford Univ. Press.

Gustafson G (1950). Age determination on teeth. J Am Dent Assoc 41:45-54.

Johanson A (1971). Age Determination From Human Teeth. Odontologisk Revy 22:21.

Kaplan I, Dickens RL (1985). Improving the diagnostic quality of radiographs by reduction. Gen Dent 33:140-3.

Kraus BS (1957). Calcification of the Human Deciduous Teeth. J Am Dent Assoc 59:245-260.

Krogman WM (1953). The Skeleton in Forensic Medicine. Graduate Medicine 42 Section 2 and 3:17.

Langland OE, Sippy FH, Langlais RP (1984). Textbook of dental radiology. 2nd ed. Springfield: Thomas.

Nolla C (1957). The Development of the Permanent Teeth. Journal of Dentistry for Children 27:254

Ortiz A (1987). Dental Records- A Tool in Forensic Dentistry. Annual World Dental Congress.

Schour I, Massler M (1939). The Development of the Human Dentition. J Am Dent Assoc 28:1153.

Snodgrasse RM, Dreizen S, Currie C, Parker GS, Spies TD (1955). The association between anomalous ossification centers in the hand skeleton, nutritional status and rate of skeletal maturation in children five to fourteen years of age. Am J Roentgenol Radium Ther Nucl Med 74:1037-48.

Van Dis ML, Beck FM, Miles DA (1989). Video enhancement of dental radiographic films. Oral Surg Oral Med Oral Pathol 68:226-31.

Wenzel A (1994). Sensor noise in direct digital imaging (the RadioVisioGraphy, Sens-a-Ray, and Visualix/Vixa systems) evaluated by subtraction radiography. Oral Surg Oral Med Oral Pathol 77:70-4.

Woelfel JB, Permar D (1984). Dental anatomy: its correlation with dental health service. 3rd ed. Philadelphia: Lea & Febiger.

Post Mortem Considerations

Abbott WE, Davis JH (1956). The pathology of thermal burns-changing concepts; a review of the literature since 1945. Surgery 40:788-806.

Addy M, Moran J, Newcombe R, Warren P (1995). The comparative tea staining potential of phenolic, chlorhexidine and anti-adhesive mouthrinses. J Clin Periodontol 22:923-8.

American Board of Forensic Odontology (1994). Body identification guidelines J Am Dent Assoc 125:1244-6, 1248, 1250 passim.

Andersen L, Juhl M, Solheim T, Borrman H (1995). Odontological identification of fire victims--potentialities and limitations. Int J Legal Med 107:229-34.

Bachanek T, Chalas R, Pawlowicz A, Tarezydto B (1999). Exposure to flour dust and the level of abrasion of hard tooth tissues among the workers of flour mills. Ann Agric Environ Med 6:147-9.

Bailit HL (1975). Dental variation among populations. An anthropologic view. Dent Clin North Am 19:125-39.

Bartlett DW, Evans DF, Anggiansah A, Smith BG (2000). The role of the esophagus in dental erosion. Oral Surg Oral Med Oral Pathol Oral Radiol Endod 89:312-5.

Bartlett DW, Evans DF, Smith BG (1996). The relationship between gastro-oesophageal reflux disease and dental erosion. J Oral Rehabil 23:289-97.

Bartlett DW, Smith BG (1994). The dental impact of eating disorders. Dent Update 21:404-7.

Bohnert M, Rost T, Pollak S (1998). The degree of destruction of human bodies in relation to the duration of the fire. Forensic Sci Int 95:11-21.

Botha CT (1986). The dental identification of fire victims. J Forensic Odontostomatol 4:67-75.

Bradtmiller B, Buikstra JE (1984). Effects of burning on human bone microstructure: a preliminary study. J Forensic Sci 29:535-40.

Bucolo DL (1987). Special treatment planning for musicians. Dentistry 7:28-30.

Buikstra JE, Swegle M, Bonnischen R, Sorg MH (1989). Bone Modificiation: Bone Modification due to burning: Experimental Evidence.

Bush MA, Bush PJ, Miller RG (2006). Detection and classification of composite resins in incinerated teeth for forensic purposes. J Forensic Sci 51:636-42.

Caro I (1980). Discoloration of the teeth related to minocycline therapy for acne. J Am Acad Dermatol 3:317-8.

Centers for Disease Control and Prevention. Outbreak of syphilis among men who have sex with men--southern California, 2000. (2001). Journal of American Medical Association 285:1285-7.

Centers for Disease Control and Prevention. Primary and secondary syphilis--United States, 1999. (2001). Journal of American Medical Association 285:1284-5.

Chaudhry SI, Harris JL, Challacombe SJ (1997). Dental erosion in a wine merchant: an occupational hazard? Br Dent J 182:226-8.

Clark DH (1992). Practical forensic odontology London: Wright.

DeVore DT (1977). Radiology and photography in forensic dentistry. Dent Clin North Am 21:69-83.

Dodd MA, Dole EJ, Troutman WG, Bennahum DA (1998). Minocycline-associated tooth staining. Ann Pharmacother 32:887-9.

Donachie MA, Walls AW (1995). Assessment of tooth wear in an ageing population. J Dent 23:157-64.

Duffy JB, Waterfield JD, Skinner MF (1991). Isolation of tooth pulp cells for sex chromatin studies in experimental dehydrated and cremated remains. Forensic Sci Int 49:127-41.

Eccles JD (1979). Dental erosion of nonindustrial origin. A clinical survey and classification. J Prosthet Dent 42:649-53.

Edlund JF (1997). Fire Victims. In: Forensic Pathology: A Handbook for Pathologists. RS Fisher and CS Petty editors: US Department of Justice.

Fayle SA, Pollard MA (1994). Congenital erythropoietic porphyria--oral manifestations and dental treatment in childhood: a case report. Quintessence Int 25:551-4.

Ferguson MM, Dunbar RJ, Smith JA, Wall JG (1996). Enamel erosion related to winemaking. Occup Med (Lond) 46:159-62.

Fiedler RS, Reichl RB (2000). Combined professional and home care nightguard bleaching of tetracycline-stained teeth. Gen Dent 48:257-61.

Florescu M (1972). [Dental lesions in workers from the sulfuric acid industry]. Stomatologia (Bucur) 19:395-403.

Frencken JE, Rugarabamu P, Amuli JA, Mulder J, Lihepa A (1989). Oral health status of employees in sugar and sisal estates in Tanzania. Afr Dent J 3:9-16.

Gamble J, Jones W, Hancock J, Meckstroth RL (1984). Epidemiological-environmental study of lead acid battery workers. III. Chronic effects of sulfuric acid on the respiratory system and teeth. Environ Res 35:30-52.

Gill GW, Reichs KJ (1998). Craniofacial Criteria in the Skeletal Attribution of Race Forensic osteology : advances in the identification of human remains. 2nd ed. Springfield, Ill., U.S.A.: Charles C. Thomas.

Grahnen H, Sjolin S, Stenstrom A (1974). Mineralization defects of primary teeth in children born pre-term. Scand J Dent Res 82:396-400.

Grandjean P (1982). Occupational fluorosis through 50 years: clinical and epidemiological experiences. Am J Ind Med 3:227-36.

Gray A, Ferguson MM, Wall JG (1998). Wine tasting and dental erosion. Case report. Aust Dent J 43:32-4.

Gupta BN (1990). Occupational diseases of teeth. J Soc Occup Med 40:149-52.

Haller E (1992). Eating disorders. A review and update. West J Med 157:658-62.

Hanihara K (1967). Racial characteristics in the dentition. J Dent Res 46:923-6.

Harris CK, Warnakulasuriya KA, Johnson NW, Gelbier S, Peters TJ (1996). Oral health in alcohol misusers. Community Dent Health 13:199-203.

Hede B (1996). Determinants of oral health in a group of Danish alcoholics. Eur J Oral Sci 104:403-8.

Herbert FL, Delcambre TJ (1987). Unusual case of green teeth resulting from neonatal hyperbilirubinemia. ASDC J Dent Child 54:54-6.

Hermann B (1977). On Histological Investigations of Cremated Human Remains. Journal of Human Evolution 6:101-103.

Hinkes MJ, Gill GW, Rhine S (1990). Shovel-shaped Incisors in Human Identification Skeletal Attribution of Race: Methods for Forensic Anthropology: Maxwell Museum of Anthropology.

Human Dentition in Biological Perspective (1969). In: Dental Anatomy and Occlusion. BS Kraus, L Abrams and RE Jordan editors. Baltimore: Williams & Wilkins, pp. xvi, 317 p.

Jailwala JA, Shaker R (2000). Oral and pharyngeal complications of gastroesophageal reflux disease: globus, dental erosions, and chronic sinusitis. J Clin Gastroenterol 30:S35-8.

Kashyap AS, Sharma HS (1999). Discolouration of permanent teeth and enamel hypoplasia due to tetracycline. Postgrad Med J 75:772.

Kieser JA, Groeneveld HT (1989). The unreliability of sex allocation based on human odontometric data. J Forensic Odontostomatol 7:1-12.

Lasker GW, Lee MMC (1957). Racial Traits in the Human Teeth. Journal of Forensic Sciences 2:401-419.

Law CA, Bowers CM (1996). Radiographic reconstruction of root morphology in skeletonized remains: a case study. J Forensic Sci 41:514-7.

Lund H, Mornstad H (1999). Gender determination by odontometrics in a Swedish population. J Forensic Odontostomatol 17:30-4.

Maples WR, Browning M (1994). Dead men do tell tales: the strange and fascinating cases of a forensic anthropologist. 1st ed. New York: Doubleday.

Merlati G, Savlo C, Danesino P, Fassina G, Menghini P (2004). Further study of restored and un-restored teeth subjected to high temperatures. J Forensic Odontostomatol 22:34-9.

Meurman JH, Toskala J, Nuutinen P, Klemetti E (1994). Oral and dental manifestations in gastroesophageal reflux disease. Oral Surg Oral Med Oral Pathol 78:583-9.

Muller M, Lupi-Pegurier L, Quatrehomme G, Bolla M (2001). Odontometrical method useful in determining gender and dental alignment. Forensic Sci Int 121:194-7.

Namdar F, Atasu M (1999). Macrodontia in association with a contrasting character microdontia. J Clin Pediatr Dent 23:271-4.

Nordbo H, Eriksen HM, Rolla G, Attramadal A, Solheim H (1982). Iron staining of the acquired enamel pellicle after exposure to tannic acid or chlorhexidine: preliminary report. Scand J Dent Res 90:117-23.

Novacek G, Plachetzky U, Potzi R, Lentner S, Slavicek R, Gangl A, Ferenci P (1995). Dental and periodontal disease in patients with cirrhosis--role of etiology of liver disease. J Hepatol 22:576-82.

Petersen PE, Gormsen C (1991). Oral conditions among German battery factory workers. Community Dent Oral Epidemiol 19:104-6.

Pindborg JJ (1982). Aetiology of developmental enamel defects not related to fluorosis. Int Dent J 32:123-34.

Poorman J (1986). Fire, Death and the Medico-Legal Investigation. Science Digest January-June.

Pretty IA, Sweet D (2001). A look at forensic dentistry--Part 1: The role of teeth in the determination of human identity. Br Dent J 190:359-66.

Rao NG, Pai ML, Rao NN, Rao TSK (1986). Mandibular Canines in Establishing Sex Identity. Journal of the Indian Academy of Forensic Medicine 18:5-12.

Rasmussen P (1999). Severe hypodontia: diversities in manifestations. J Clin Pediatr Dent 23:179-88.

Richards NF (1977). Fire investigation--destruction of corpses. Med Sci Law 17:79-82.

Robb ND, Cruwys E, Smith BG (1991). Regurgitation erosion as a possible cause of tooth wear in ancient British populations. Arch Oral Biol 36:595-602.

Roberts MW, Tylenda CA (1989). Dental aspects of anorexia and bulimia nervosa. Pediatrician 16:178-84.

Robertsson S, Mohlin B (2000). The congenitally missing upper lateral incisor. A retrospective study of orthodontic space closure versus restorative treatment. Eur J Orthod 22:697-710.

Rogers SL (1988). The Testimony of Teeth: C.C. Thomas

Rudowski W, National Library of Medicine (U.S.). Special Foreign Currency Program. (1976). Causes of Death after Burns, in Burn therapy and research Baltimore: Johns Hopkins Univ. Press.

Rytomaa I, Jarvinen V, Kanerva R, Heinonen OP (1998). Bulimia and tooth erosion. Acta Odontol Scand 56:36-40.

Sauer NJ (1992). Forensic anthropology and the concept of race: if races don't exist, why are forensic anthropologists so good at identifying them? Soc Sci Med 34:107-11.

Scheutzel P (1996). Etiology of dental erosion--intrinsic factors. Eur J Oral Sci 104:178-90.

Schroeder PL, Filler SJ, Ramirez B, Lazarchik DA, Vaezi MF, Richter JE (1995). Dental erosion and acid reflux disease. Ann Intern Med 122:809-15.

Smith BC (1992). Reconstruction of root morphology in skeletonized remains with postmortem dental loss. J Forensic Sci 37:176-84.

Smith BG, Robb ND (1989). Dental erosion in patients with chronic alcoholism. J Dent 17:219-21.

Spitz WU (1973). Thermal Injuries. In: Medicolegal investigation of death; guidelines for the application of pathology to crime investigation. WU Spitz and RS Fisher editors. Springfield, Ill.: Thomas, pp. xvii, 536 p.

Stevens PJ (1977). Identification of Bodies from Fires. Medical SciLaw 17:95.

Tedeschi CG (1977). Systemic and Localized Hyperthermia Injury. In: Forensic medicine : a study in trauma and environmental hazards. LG Tedeschi, WG Eckert and CG Tedeschi editors. Philadelphia: Saunders.

Thesleff I (2000). Genetic basis of tooth development and dental defects. Acta Odontol Scand 58:191-4.

Tuominen M, Tuominen R (1991). Tooth surface loss among people exposed to cement and stone dust in the work environment in Tanzania. Community Dent Health 8:233-8.

Tuominen M, Tuominen R (1992). Tooth surface loss and associated factors among factory workers in Finland and Tanzania. Community Dent Health 9:143-50.

Tuominen ML, Tuominen RJ, Fubusa F, Mgalula N (1991). Tooth surface loss and exposure to organic and inorganic acid fumes in workplace air. Community Dent Oral Epidemiol 19:217-20.

Variations and Anomalies (1952). In: Dental anatomy, including anatomy of the head and neck. M Diamond editor. New York: Macmillan, pp. xii, 471 p.

Walker PL, Miller KP (2005). Time, Temperature, and Oxygen Availability: an Experimental Study of the Effects of Environmental Conditions on the Color and Organic Content of Cremated Bones. American Journal of Physical Anthropology 126 Supplement 40.

Weedn VW (1998). Postmortem identifications of remains. Clin Lab Med 18:115-37.

Whittaker DK, MacDonald DG (1989). A colour atlas of forensic dentistry London, England: Wolfe Medical Publications.

Williams WP, Becker LH (2000). Amelogenesis imperfecta: functional and esthetic restoration of a severely compromised dentition. Quintessence Int 31:397-403.

Zero DT (1996). Etiology of dental erosion--extrinsic factors. Eur J Oral Sci 104:162-77.

Comparison Considerations and Issues
Age Estimation

Arany S, Ohtani S, Yoshioka N, Gonmori K (2004). Age estimation from aspartic acid racemization of root dentin by internal standard method. Forensic Sci Int 141:127-30.

Bang G, Ramm E (1970). Determination of age in humans from root dentin transparency. Acta Odontol Scand 28:3-35.

Benesova T, Ales H, Pilin A, Votruba J, Flieger M (2004). A modified HPLC method for the determination of aspartic acid racemization in collagen from human dentin and its comparison with GC. J Sep Sci 27:330-4.

Black GV (1924). A work on special dental pathology devoted to the diseases and treatment of the investing tissues of teeth and the dental pulp including the sequelae of the death of the pulp; also, systemic effects of mouth infections, oral prophylaxis and mouth hygiene. 3d ed. Chicago,: Medico-Dental Pub. Co.

Burns KR, Maples WR (1976). Estimation of age from individual adult teeth. J Forensic Sci 21:343-56.

Cameriere R, Ferrante L, Cingolani M (2004). Variations in pulp/tooth area ratio as an indicator of age: a preliminary study. J Forensic Sci 49:317-9.

Cameriere R, Ferrante L, Cingolani M (2004). Precision and reliability of pulp/tooth area ratio (RA) of second molar as indicator of adult age. J Forensic Sci 49:1319-23.

Carolan VA, Gardner ML, Lucy D, Pollard AM (1997). Some considerations regarding the use of amino acid racemization in human dentine as an indicator of age at death. J Forensic Sci 42:10-6.

Chagula WK (1960). The age at eruption of third permanent molars in male East Africans. Am J Phys Anthropol 18:77-82.

Cloos PA, Jensen AL (2000). Age-related de-phosphorylation of proteins in dentin: a biological tool for assessment of protein age. Biogerontology 1:341-56.

Costa RJ (1968). Age Determination of Human Remains. In: Dating and Age Determination of Biological Materials. Angel and Zimmerman editors. London: Croom Helm Ltd.

Demirjian A, Goldstein H, Tanner JM (1973). A new system of dental age assessment. Hum Biol 45:211-27.

Fanning EA (1962). Third Molar Emergence in Bostonians. American Journal of Physical Anthropology 20:339-345.

Foti B, Lalys L, Adalian P, Giustiniani J, Maczel M, Signoli M, Dutour O, Leonetti G (2003). New forensic approach to age determination in children based on tooth eruption. Forensic Sci Int 132:49-56.

Furuhata T, Yamamoto K (1967). Forensic odontology Springfield, Ill.,: Thomas.

Garn SM, Lewis AB, Blizzard RM (1965). Endocrine Factors in Dental Development. J Dent Res 44: SUPPL:243-58.

Garn SM, Lewis AB, Koski K, Polacheck DL (1958). The sex difference in tooth calcification. J Dent Res 37:561-7.

Gleiser I, Hunt EE, Jr. (1955). The permanent mandibular first molar: its calcification, eruption and decay. Am J Phys Anthropol 13:253-83.

Gunst K, Mesotten K, Carbonez A, Willems G (2003). Third molar root development in relation to chronological age: a large sample sized retrospective study. Forensic Sci Int 136:52-7.

Gustafson G (1950). Age determination on teeth. J Am Dent Assoc 41:45-54.

Gustafson G, Koch G (1974). Age estimation up to 16 years of age based on dental development. Odontol Revy 25:297-306.

Hagg U, Matsson L (1985). Dental maturity as an indicator of chronological age: the accuracy and precision of three methods. Eur J Orthod 7:25-34.

Helfman PM, Bada JL (1976). Aspartic acid racemisation in dentine as a measure of ageing. Nature 262:279-81.

Helfman PM, Bada JL, Shou MY (1977). Considerations on the role of aspartic acid racemization in the aging process. Gerontology 23:419-25.

Johanson G (1971). Age determination from teeth. Odontology Revy 22:1-126.

Kasper K, Senn D (2004). Reliability of Third Molar Development on a North Texas Hispanic Population: A Comparison Study for Age Estimation. American Academy of Forensic Sciences.

Krogman WM (1962). The human skeleton in forensic medicine Springfield, Ill.: Thomas.

Kvaal S, Solheim T (1994). A non-destructive dental method for age estimation. J Forensic Odontostomatol 12:6-11.

Kvaal SI, Kolltveit KM, Thomsen IO, Solheim T (1995). Age estimation of adults from dental radiographs. Forensic Sci Int 74:175-85.

Kvaal SI, Sellevold BJ, Solheim T (1994). A comparison of different non-destructive methods of age estimation in skeletal material. International Journal of Osteoarchaeology 4:363-370.

Kvaal SI, Solheim T (1995). Incremental lines in human dental cementum in relation to age. Eur J Oral Sci 103:225-30.

Lamendin H, Baccino E, Humbert JF, Tavernier JC, Nossintchouk RM, Zerilli A (1992). A simple technique for age estimation in adult corpses: the two criteria dental method. J Forensic Sci 37:1373-9.

Li C, Ji G (1995). Age estimation from the permanent molar in northeast China by the method of average stage of attrition. Forensic Sci Int 75:189-96.

Loevy HT (1983). Maturation of permanent teeth in Black and Latino children. Acta Odontol Pediatr 4:59-62.

Lucy D, Pollard AM (1995). Further comments on the estimation of error associated with the Gustafson dental age estimation method. J Forensic Sci 40:222-7.

Maples WR (1978). An improved technique using dental histology for estimation of adult age. J Forensic Sci 23:764-70.

Maples WR, Rice PM (1979). Some difficulties in the Gustafson dental age estimations. J Forensic Sci 24:168-72.

Martin-de las Heras S, Valenzuela A, Bellini R, Salas C, Rubino M, Garcia JA (2003). Objective measurement of dental color for age estimation by spectroradiometry. Forensic Sci Int 132:57-62.

Massler M, Schour I (1946). The Appositional Life Span of the Enamel and Dentine Forming Cells. Journal of Dental Research 25:145.

Massler M, Schour I (1947). The Appositional Life Span of the Enamel and Dentine Forming Cells. Journal of Dental Research 26:427-431.

Mincer HH, Harris EF, Berryman HE (1993). The A.B.F.O. study of third molar development and its use as an estimator of chronological age. J Forensic Sci 38:379-90.

Moorrees CF, Fanning EA, Hunt EE, Jr. (1963). Age Variation of Formation Stages for Ten Permanent Teeth. J Dent Res 42:1490-502.

Moorrees CF, Fanning EA, Hunt EE, Jr. (1963). Formation and Resorption of Three Deciduous Teeth in Children. Am J Phys Anthropol 21:205-13.

Nichols R, Townsend E, Malina R (1983). Development of Permanent Dentition in Mexican American Children. American Journal of Physical Anthropology 60:232.

Ogino T, Ogino H (1988). Application to forensic odontology of aspartic acid racemization in unerupted and supernumerary teeth. J Dent Res 67:1319-22.

Ogino T, Ogino H, Nagy B (1985). Application of aspartic acid racemization to forensic odontology: post mortem designation of age at death. Forensic Sci Int 29:259-67.

Ohtani S (1994). Age estimation by aspartic acid racemization in dentin of deciduous teeth. Forensic Sci Int 68:77-82.

Ohtani S (1995). Estimation of age from the teeth of unidentified corpses using the amino acid racemization method with reference to actual cases. Am J Forensic Med Pathol 16:238-42.

Ohtani S, Abe I, Yamamoto T (2005). An application of D- and L-aspartic acid mixtures as standard specimens for the chronological age estimation. J Forensic Sci 50:1298-302.

Ohtani S, Ito R, Arany S, Yamamoto T (2005). Racemization in enamel among different types of teeth from the same individual. Int J Legal Med 119:66-9.

Ohtani S, Ito R, Yamamoto T (2003). Differences in the D/L aspartic acid ratios in dentin among different types of teeth from the same individual and estimated age. Int J Legal Med 117:149-52.

Ohtani S, Kato S, Sugeno H (1996). Changes in D-aspartic acid in human deciduous teeth with age from 1-20 years. Growth Dev Aging 60:1-6.

Ohtani S, Yamada Y, Yamamoto I (1997). Age estimation from racemization rate using heated teeth. J Forensic Odontostomatol 15:9-12.

Ohtani S, Yamamoto K (1987). [Age estimation using the racemization of aspartic acid on human dentin]. Nippon Hoigaku Zasshi 41:181-90.

Ohtani S, Yamamoto K (1991). Age estimation using the racemization of amino acid in human dentin. J Forensic Sci 36:792-800.

Ohtani S, Yamamoto K (1992). Estimation of age from a tooth by means of racemization of an amino acid, especially aspartic acid--comparison of enamel and dentin. J Forensic Sci 37:1061-7.

Ohtani S, Yamamoto T (2005). Strategy for the estimation of chronological age using the aspartic acid racemization method with special reference to coefficient of correlation between D/L ratios and ages. J Forensic Sci 50:1020-7.

Prapanpoch S, Dove SB, Cottone JA (1992). Morphometric analysis of the dental pulp chamber as a method of age determination in humans. Am J Forensic Med Pathol 13:50-5.

Pretty IA (2003). The use of dental aging techniques in forensic odontological practice. J Forensic Sci 48:1127-32.

Ritz-Timme S, Schutz HW, Waite ER, Collins MJ (1999). "Improvement" of age estimation using amino acid racemization in a case of pink teeth. Am J Forensic Med Pathol 20:216-7.

Ritz S, Schutz HW, Peper C (1993). Postmortem estimation of age at death based on aspartic acid racemization in dentin: its applicability for root dentin. Int J Legal Med 105:289-93.

Ritz S, Schutz HW, Schwarzer B (1990). The extent of aspartic acid racemization in dentin: a possible method for a more accurate determination of age at death? Z Rechtsmed 103:457-62.

Schour I, Massler M (1931). Studies in Tooth Development: The Growth Pattern of Human Teeth. Journal of the American Dental Association 27:1918-1931.

Schour I, Massler M (1940). Studies in Tooth Development: The Growth Pattern of the Human Teeth Part 1. Journal of the American Dental Association 27:1778-1793.

Smith H (1991). Standards of Human Tooth Formation and Dental Age Assessement: Wiley-Liss Inc.

Solari AC, Abramovitch K (2002). The accuracy and precision of third molar development as an indicator of chronological age in Hispanics. J Forensic Sci 47:531-5.

Solheim T (1993). A new method for dental age estimation in adults. Forensic Sci Int 59:137-47.

Solheim T, Sundnes PK (1980). Dental age estimation of Norwegian adults--a comparison of different methods. Forensic Sci Int 16:7-17.

Soomer H, Ranta H, Lincoln MJ, Penttila A, Leibur E (2003). Reliability and validity of eight dental age estimation methods for adults. J Forensic Sci 48:149-52.

Takasaki T, Tsuji A, Ikeda N, Ohishi M (2003). Age estimation in dental pulp DNA based on human telomere shortening. Int J Legal Med 117:232-4.

Tanner JM (1962). Growth at adolescence; with a general consideration of the effects of hereditary and environmental factors upon growth and maturation from birth to maturity. 2d ed. Oxford,: Blackwell Scientific Publications.

Thomas GJ, Whittaker DK, Embery G (1994). A comparative study of translucent apical dentine in vital and non-vital human teeth. Arch Oral Biol 39:29-34.

Ubelaker D (1991). Human Skeletal Remains Washington D.C.: Taraxacum Press.

Valenzuela A, Martin-De Las Heras S, Mandojana JM, De Dios Luna J, Valenzuela M, Villanueva E (2002). Multiple regression models for age estimation by assessment of morphologic dental changes according to teeth source. Am J Forensic Med Pathol 23:386-9.

Vandevoort FM, Bergmans L, Van Cleynenbreugel J, Bielen DJ, Lambrechts P, Wevers M, Peirs A, Willems G (2004). Age calculation using X-ray microfocus computed tomographical scanning of teeth: a pilot study. J Forensic Sci 49:787-90.

Voors AW (1973). Can Dental Development be Used for Assessing Age in Underdeveloped Communities? Journal of Tropocal Pediatrics and Environmental Child Health 19:242.

Willems G (2001). A Review of the Most Commonly Used Dental Age Estimation Techniques. Journal of Forensic Odonto-Stomatology 19:9-17.

Willems G, Moulin-Romsee C, Solheim T (2002). Non-destructive dental-age calculation methods in adults: intra- and inter-observer effects. Forensic Sci Int 126:221-6.

Willems G, Van Olmen A, Spiessens B, Carels C (2001). Dental age estimation in Belgian children: Demirjian's technique revisited. J Forensic Sci 46:893-5.

Yekkala R, Meers C, Van Schepdael A, Hoogmartens J, Lambrichts I, Willems G (2006). Racemization of aspartic acid from human dentin in the estimation of chronological age. Forensic Sci Int 159 Suppl 1:S89-94.

Anthropology

Kharat DU, Saini TS, Mokeem S (1990). Shovel-shaped incisors and associated invagination in some Asian and African populations. J Dent 18:216-20.

Genetic (DNA) Comparison

Alberts B, Bray D, Lewis J, Raff M, Roberts K (1989). Molecular biology of the cell. 2nd ed. New York: Garland Pub.

Avitabile M, Dell'Osso G, Rasa R, Tripi F, Campagna NE, Magri GA, Sciacca G, Rasa A (1993). [DNA extraction from hard dental tissues]. Minerva Stomatol 42:15-8.

Berlin YA, Kazazian HH, Jr. (1992). Rapid preparation of genomic DNA from dried blood and saliva spots for polymerase chain reaction. Hum Mutat 1:260-1.

Boerwinkle E, Xiong WJ, Fourest E, Chan L (1989). Rapid typing of tandemly repeated hypervariable loci by the polymerase chain reaction: application to the apolipoprotein B 3' hypervariable region. Proc Natl Acad Sci U S A 86:212-6.

Botstein D, White RL, Skolnick M, Davis RW (1980). Construction of a genetic linkage map in man using restriction fragment length polymorphisms. Am J Hum Genet 32:314-31.

Budowle B, Chakraborty R, Giusti AM, Eisenberg AJ, Allen RC (1991). Analysis of the VNTR locus D1S80 by the PCR followed by high-resolution PAGE. Am J Hum Genet 48:137-44.

Cam RL, Stoneking M, Wilson AC (1987). Mitochondrial DNA and Human Evolution. Nature 325:1-36.

Dange AH, Malvankar AG, Madiwale MS (1978). [Determination of the sex origin of teeth]. Arch Kriminol 162:115-9.

De Leo D, Tagliaro F (1990). [The identification of esterase D isoenzyme (EsD) phenotypes in the dental pulp by isoelectric focusing]. Minerva Stomatol 39:435-8.

Duffy JB, Waterfield JD, Skinner MF (1991). Isolation of tooth pulp cells for sex chromatin studies in experimental dehydrated and cremated remains. Forensic Sci Int 49:127-41.

Edwards A, Civitello A, Hammond HA, Caskey CT (1991). DNA typing and genetic mapping with trimeric and tetrameric tandem repeats. Am J Hum Genet 49:746-56.

Edwards A, Hammond HA, Jin L, Caskey CT, Chakraborty R (1992). Genetic variation at five trimeric and tetrameric tandem repeat loci in four human population groups. Genomics 12:241-53.

Eriksen B, Svensmark O (1993). DNA-profiling of stains in criminal cases: analysis of measurement errors and band-shift. Discussion of match criteria. Forensic Sci Int 61:21-34.

Fahy JV, Steiger DJ, Liu J, Basbaum CB, Finkbeiner WE, Boushey HA (1993). Markers of mucus secretion and DNA levels in induced sputum from asthmatic and from healthy subjects. Am Rev Respir Dis 147:1132-7.

Fregeau CJ, Fourney RM (1993). DNA typing with fluorescently tagged short tandem repeats: a sensitive and accurate approach to human identification. Biotechniques 15:100-19.

Giles RE, Blanc H, Cann HM, Wallace DC (1980). Maternal inheritance of human mitochondrial DNA. Proc Natl Acad Sci U S A 77:6715-9.

Gaytmenn R, Sweet DJ (2003). Forensic DNA from various regions of human teeth. J Forensic Sci 48:622-25.

Gill P, Ivanov PL, Kimpton C, Piercy R, Benson N, Tully G, Evett I, Hagelberg E, Sullivan K (1994). Identification of the remains of the Romanov family by DNA analysis. Nat Genet 6:130-5.

Ginther C, Issel-Tarver L, King MC (1992). Identifying individuals by sequencing mitochondrial DNA from teeth. Nat Genet 2:135-8.

Haertig A, Krainic K, Vaillant JM, Derobert L (1980). [Medicolegal identification : teeth and blood groups (author's transl)]. Rev Stomatol Chir Maxillofac 81:361-3.

Hanni C, Laudet V, Sakka M, Begue A, Stehelin D (1990). [Amplification of mitochondrial DNA fragments from ancient human teeth and bones]. C R Acad Sci III 310:365-70.

Henke J, Bauer L (1980). [The detection of Gm and Km factors in the dental pulp of humans (author's transl)]. Z Rechtsmed 85:149-52.

Henke J, Bauer L, Schweitzer H (1982). [Detection of Gm, Km, and EsD phenotypes in the dental pulp of human cadavers]. Z Rechtsmed 88:271-6.
Higginson AG, Hill IR (1980). Blood group determination from teeth. Aviat Space Environ Med 51:1026-9.

Hochmeister MN, Budowle B, Jung J, Borer UV, Comey CT, Dirnhofer R (1991). PCR-based typing of DNA extracted from cigarette butts. Int J Legal Med 104:229-33.

Holland MM, Fisher DL, Lee DA, Bryson CK, Weedn VW (1993). Short tandem repeat loci: application to forensic and human remains identification. Exs 67:267-74.

Holland MM, Fisher DL, Mitchell LG, Rodriquez WC, Canik JJ, Merril CR, Weedn VW (1993). Mitochondrial DNA sequence analysis of human skeletal remains: identification of remains from the Vietnam War. J Forensic Sci 38:542-53.

Honda K, Harihara S, Nakamura T, Hirai M, Misawa S (1990). [Sex identification by analysis of DNA extracted from hard tissues]. Nippon Hoigaku Zasshi 44:293-301.

Horn GT, Richards B, Klinger KW (1989). Amplification of a highly polymorphic VNTR segment by the polymerase chain reaction. Nucleic Acids Res 17:2140.

Ishizu H (1993). [Sex identification of forensic biological materials]. Nippon Hoigaku Zasshi 47:423-34.

Kasai K, Nakamura Y, White R (1990). Amplification of a variable number of tandem repeats (VNTR) locus (pMCT118) by the polymerase chain reaction (PCR) and its application to forensic science. J Forensic Sci 35:1196-200.

Kauffman DL, Keller PJ, Bennick A, Blum M (1993). Alignment of amino acid and DNA sequences of human proline-rich proteins. Crit Rev Oral Biol Med 4:287-92.

Khan R (1989). Chemistry and Genome Organization for the Forensic Scientist. International Symposium of the Forensic Aspects of DNA Analysis.

Kido A, Kimura Y, Oya M (1993). Transferrin subtyping in dental pulps. J Forensic Sci 38:1063-7.

Kido A, Komatsu N, Ose Y, Oya M (1987). alpha-L-fucosidase phenotyping in human tissues, dental pulps and hair roots. Forensic Sci Int 33:53-9.

Kido A, Komatsu N, Oya M, Sekiyama S (1989). Simultaneous determination of FUC and PGM1 by isoelectric focusing. Med Sci Law 29:311-4.

Kimpton CP, Gill P, Walton A, Urquhart A, Millican ES, Adams M (1993). Automated DNA profiling employing multiplex amplification of short tandem repeat loci. PCR Methods Appl 3:13-22.

Komatsu N, Kido A, Kimura Y, Oya M (1990). PGD phenotyping in bloodstains, organ tissues, dental pulps and hair roots by isoelectric focusing. Forensic Sci Int 48:185-94.

Korszun AK, Causton BE, Lincoln PJ (1978). Thermostability of ABO(H) blood-group antigens in human teeth. Forensic Sci 11:231-9.

Lawton ME, Stringer P, Churton M (1989). DNA Profiles from Dental Pulp. International Symposium on the Forensic Aspects of DNA Analysis.

Lopez-Abadia I, Ruiz de la Cuesta JM (1993). A simplified method for phenotyping alpha-2-HS-glycoprotein. J Forensic Sci 38:1183-6.

Marcucci M, Bandettini MV, Caverni G, Gabriele M, Ghio G, Giari A (1987). [Analysis of A and B antigens in dental tissue (method: absorption-elution)]. Mondo Odontostomatol 29:45-8.

Morse DR (1991). Age-related changes of the dental pulp complex and their relationship to systemic aging. Oral Surg Oral Med Oral Pathol 72:721-45.

Ohhashi A, Aoki T, Matsugo S, Simasaki C (1993). [PCR-based typing of human buccal cell's DNA extracted from whole saliva and saliva stains]. Nippon Hoigaku Zasshi 47:108-18.

Paabo S, Gifford JA, Wilson AC (1988). Mitochondrial DNA sequences from a 7000-year old brain. Nucleic Acids Res 16:9775-87.

Petersen N, Heide KG (1974). [Demonstration of genetic markers in dental pulp]. Arch Kriminol 153:106-10.

Potsch L, Meyer U, Rothschild S, Schneider PM, Rittner C (1992). Application of DNA techniques for identification using human dental pulp as a source of DNA. Int J Legal Med 105:139-43.

Presley LA, Baumstark AL, Dixon A, et. al (1993). The Use of Polymerase Chain Reaction (PCR) HLA-DQalpha Typing in Forensic Casework. American Academy of Forensic Sciences 45th Annual Meeting, Boston, MA.

Robin ED, Wong R (1988). Mitochondrial DNA molecules and virtual number of mitochondria per cell in mammalian cells. J Cell Physiol 136:507-13.

Saiki RK, Scharf S, Faloona F, Mullis KB, Horn GT, Erlich HA, Arnheim N (1985). Enzymatic amplification of beta-globin genomic sequences and restriction site analysis for diagnosis of sickle cell anemia. Science 230:1350-4.

Saiki RK, Walsh PS, Levenson CH, Erlich HA (1989). Genetic analysis of amplified DNA with immobilized sequence-specific oligonucleotide probes. Proc Natl Acad Sci U S A 86:6230-4.

Sanger F, Nicklen S, Coulson AR (1977). DNA sequencing with chain-terminating inhibitors. Proc Natl Acad Sci U S A 74:5463-7.

Schmechta H, Portsmann T (1978). [Sex identification of a single tooth: fluorescent microscope detection of y-chromosome in the necrotic dental pulp (author's transl)]. Zahn Mund Kieferheilkd Zentralbl 66:249-52.

Schwartz TR, Schwartz EA, Mieszerski L, McNally L, Kobilinsky L (1991). Characterization of deoxyribonucleic acid (DNA) obtained from teeth subjected to various environmental conditions. J Forensic Sci 36:979-90.

Smeets B, van de Voorde H, Hooft P (1991). ABO bloodgrouping on tooth material. Forensic Sci Int 50:277-84.

Smith BC, Fisher DL, Weedn VW, Warnock GR, Holland MM (1993). A systematic approach to the sampling of dental DNA. J Forensic Sci 38:1194-209.

Southern EM (1992). Detection of specific sequences among DNA fragments separated by gel electrophoresis. Biotechnology 24:122-39.

Stoneking M, Hedgecock D, Higuchi RG, Vigilant L, Erlich HA (1991). Population variation of human mtDNA control region sequences detected by enzymatic amplification and sequence-specific oligonucleotide probes. Am J Hum Genet 48:370-82.

Suenaga S (1980). [On the sex determination of human teeth (author's transl)]. Igaku Kenkyu 50:65-72.

Suyama H, Ohya I, Fukae T, Imai T (1976). Identification of blood groups and isoenzymic phenotypes from blood stains, heart blood and nervous tissues after transfusion. Forensic Sci 8:277-80.

Sweet DJ, Hildebrand DP (1998). Recovery of DNA from human teeth by cryogenic grinding. J Forensic Sci 43:1199-1202.

Sweet DJ, Hildebrand DP (1999). Saliva from cheese bite yields DNA profile of burglar. Int J Legal Med 112:201-03.

Sweet DJ, Hildebrand DP, Phillips D (1999). Identification of a skeleton using DNA from teeth and Pap smear. J Forensic Sci 44:630-33.

Sweet DJ, Lorente JA, Lorente M, Valenzuela A, Villanueva E (1997). An improved method to recover saliva from human skin: the double swab technique. J Forensic Sci 42:320-22.

Sweet DJ, Lorente JA, Lorente M, Valenzuela A, Villanueva E (1996). Forensic identification using DNA recovered from saliva on human skin. Adv Forensic Haemogenet 6:325-27.

Sweet DJ, Lorente JA, Lorente M, Valenzuela A, Villanueva E (1997). PCR-based typing of DNA from saliva recovered from human skin. J Forensic Sci 42:447-51.

Sweet DJ, Lorente M, Lorente JA (1994). PCR-based typing of DNA from saliva recovered from human skin. J Can Soc Forensic Sci 27:238.

Sweet DJ, Shutler GG (1999).Analysis of salivary DNA evidence from a bite mark on a submerged body. J Forensic Sci 44:1069-72.

Sweet DJ, Sweet CH (1995). DNA analysis of dental pulp to link incinerated remains of homicide victim to crime scene. J Forensic Sci 40:310-4.

Turowska B, Trela F (1977). Studies on the isoenzymes PGM, ADA and AK in human teeth. Forensic Sci 9:45-7.

Walsh DJ, Corey AC, Cotton RW, Forman L, Herrin GL, Jr., Word CJ, Garner DD (1992). Isolation of deoxyribonucleic acid (DNA) from saliva and forensic science samples containing saliva. J Forensic Sci 37:387-95.

Weber JL, May PE (1989). Abundant class of human DNA polymorphisms which can be typed using the polymerase chain reaction. Am J Hum Genet 44:388-96.

Whittaker DK, Rothwell TJ (1984). Phosphoglucomutase isoenzymes in human teeth. Forensic Sci Int 24:219-23.

Yamada Y, Yamamoto K, Yoshii T, Ishiyama I (1989). Analysis of DNA from tooth and application to forensic dental medicine. Nippon Hoigaku Zasshi 43:420-3.

Yamamoto K (1992). [Molecular biological studies on teeth inquests]. Nippon Hoigaku Zasshi 46:349-55.

Yokoi T, Aoki Y, Sagisaka K (1989). Human identification and sex determination of dental pulp, bone marrow and blood stains with a recombinant DNA probe. Z Rechtsmed 102:323-30.

CHAPTER 3

MULTIPLE FATALITY INCIDENT, DENTAL IDENTIFICATION AND BIOTERRORISM ISSUES

"It gives me great pleasure to greet all those gathered in Chicago for the (first) <u>Dentistry's Role and Responsibility in Multiple Fatality Incident Identification Symposium</u> sponsored by the American Dental Association, the American Board of Forensic Odontology and Northwestern University.

In bringing together experts to discuss the latest problems and findings in the field of dental forensics, this symposium will improve our ability to identify the victims of crimes and disasters. Your efforts will not only help solve crimes, but also help mitigate suffering and uncertainty on the part of the bereaved.

I commend those who have worked so hard to make this event possible and send you all my best wishes for a successful and informative conference. God bless you."

Ronald Reagan,
President of the United States of America
1988

Figure 3-1: President Ronald Reagan

Introduction

The world has changed significantly since President Reagan's congratulatory statement was read to the participants of the 1988 Multiple Fatality Incident Identification Symposium (MFI) at the American Dental Association Headquarters in Chicago. Although dental expertise had been used in contemporary MFI settings such as the Tenerife, Canary Islands and San Diego airline multiple fatality incidents, Jonestown, Guyana massacre, Mount St. Helens volcano eruption, Las Vegas MGM Grand Hotel fire and the Marine Barracks terrorist attack in Beirut, Lebanon the deployment of federally deputized teams

of private dental practitioners and other health care professionals in response to multiple fatality incident emergencies was not yet in practice at that time (**Figures 3-1 to 3-10**).

The new millennium has brought acts of internal and international terrorism to the American homeland, Europe, Africa, the Middle East and Southeast Asia. Recent natural multiple fatality incidents of apocalyptic dimensions in the Indian Ocean and gulf coast of the United States and the threat of bioterrorism internationally have added to the need to provide teams of experts to recover and identify the remains of victims. Preparations have been initiated worldwide

Figure 3-2: Air disaster at Tenerife, Canary Islands.

Figure 3-3: Jonestown, Guyana massacre

Figure 3-4: Destruction in Afghanistan.

Figure 3-5: Mount St. Helens volcano eruption

Figure 3-6: Las Vegas MGM Grand Hotel fire

Figure 3-7: Fireball of a nuclear detonation.

Figure 3-8: Marine Barracks terrorist attack in Beirut, Lebanon.

Figure 3-9: International threat of bioterrorism.

Figure 3-10: Views of the air disaster at Sioux City, Iowa

to defend against these and other situations resulting in disruption of governmental and civic infrastructure, mass injury and death. These efforts have evolved into the creation of trained multiple fatality incident preparedness teams in many countries around the world.

Additionally, the problems associated with identification of thousands of missing individuals, unidentified remains and wanted persons is, in a sense, an extended multiple fatality incident of international importance. In the United States this situation is being addressed by creation an image repository of dental information for law enforcement agencies that wish to post supplemental dental images related to National Crime Information Center (NCIC) Missing, Unidentified, and Wanted Person records in a Web environment.

Forensic odontologists can be a vital resource in the mitigation of the aftermath of a mass-fatality incident, natural multiple fatality incident , act of bioterrorism or identification of a cold case missing individual. However, they seldom understand how their individual participation interfaces in the overall response scenario. Among Hawaiian dentists surveyed concerning their level of preparedness for responding to bioterrorism, results indicated that there was a low prevalence of prior training. This fact, in conjunction with a high willingness to provide assistance in the event of a bioterrorism attack required the need for additional bioterrorism preparedness training among dentists. Illinois has passed public health legislation which authorizes the Illinois Medical Emergency Response Team (IMERT) to provide for modification(s) to the scope of dental and dental hygiene practice in the state to allow for a Dental Emergency Responder (DER). Within the scope of dental and dental hygiene practice in an emergency the IMERT DER is authorized to provide the following services and is indemnified while serving in this capacity:

- Basic triaged care

- Airway care (including intubations)

- Inoculation care

- Drug dispensing (during bioterrorism acts or pandemic multiple fatality incidents)

- Walking well care

American Dental Association recommendations that provide for expanded duties for oral health care providers in syndrome surveillance, inoculation and drug dispensation during multiple fatality incident s are consistent with the role that is filled by the IMERT DER in Illinois.

Often, the organizational structure, chain-of-command protocols, acronyms used by governmental agencies and procedures for interfacing with various governmental and law enforcement entities requires that the forensic dentist participating in a multiple fatality incident incident be cognizant of the functions of other participants and agencies outside of his or her role within the spectrum of the incident. To this end, an overview of the legislation in the United States, which defines the roles of various governmental agencies in multiple fatality incident situations and identification of missing, unidentified and wanted individuals, is presented with the understanding that similar protocols and organizations have been established internationally.

Problems Associated with Identification of Missing, Unidentified, and Wanted Persons - an Extended Multiple Fatality Incident

Unfortunately, all missing person information is not recorded in the NCIC Missing, Unidentified, and Wanted Persons database. Many legal agencies are hampered by the lack of professional staff or budgets to allow for expert help in the interpretation of dental information for comparison. It is well recognized that many individuals go unidentified in the United States and there is a pressing need for a workable central information center. All information that has been collected about a victim should be entered onto an input form and keyed into the NCIC computer in Washington, D.C. The computer can then begin a nationwide search for possible decedent matches that can be sent back to the investigator. The investigator can then use these lists to attempt identification. It should be noted that the NCIC computer does not have the capability of identifying possible decedents based solely on dental information and this is a situation that must be addressed. Many other physical descriptors are needed to generate possible matches.

National Dental Image Repository (NDIR)

To help resolve some if the concerns addressed above the NDIR has been established. It provides an image repository for law enforcement agencies that wish to post supplemental dental images related to National Crime Information Center (NCIC) regarding Missing, Unidentified, and Wanted Person records in a Web environment. This permits easier access and retrieval of the information by qualified individuals performing dental comparisons. Participation is voluntary. The NDIR is purely an additional tool for agencies to use in attempting to more easily identify missing, unidentified, and wanted persons.

The NDIR website can be found on Law Enforcement Online (LEO) at http://cgate. leo.gov. This website provides the law enforcement, criminal justice, and public safety communities a secure *anytime and anywhere* national and international method of electronic communication, education, and information sharing. An authorized password is required to enter the LEO website which provides a state of the art secure common communications link to all levels of law enforcement, criminal justice, and public safety by supporting broad, *immediate* dissemination and exchange of information.

LEO is accessed through the Internet using a dial-up connection like America Online (AOL), Microsoft Network (MSN), or any other Internet service provider, DSL, Cable Modem or LAN connection with Internet access. The LEO network system is only available to persons duly employed by a law enforcement, criminal justice or public safety agency/department and whose position requires secure communication with other agencies. Persons interested in obtaining a LEO account must complete an application by sending an e-mail to agmu@leo.gov. Users generally receive their username and password in approximately three weeks, along with instructions on how to access LEO.

The NDIR website provides specific technical instructions for scanning and submitting digital images to the NDIR. To access the NDIR, click on the following from the LEO homepage: LEOSIGS; All LEOSIGS; CJIS; Programs; National Dental Image Repository.

Agencies convert information to electronic format according to the specifications on the web site and e-mail the information to Information includes:

- Missing, Wanted, or Unidentified Submission Form

- Digitized copy of the NCIC Record

- Digitized copy of the Dental Condition Worksheet

- Digitized copy of the Dental Report Form

- Digitized copies of the available radiographs and miscellaneous digital scans used for identification purposes

Upon receipt by the Federal Bureau of Investigation's (FBI) Criminal Justice Information Services (CJIS) Division, a member of the NDIR Review Panel will be contacted to review the dental record. Agencies have the option of declining to have their records reviewed by a member of the NDIR Review Panel. This must indicated upon submission of the Material. The NDIR Review Panel is comprised of ABFO diplomates, or dentists who have the recommendation of an ABFO odontologist. The latter must have specialized training in the proper coding of NCIC dental records and the comparison/identification of dental records. Additionally, they must have volunteered to participate in the project.

A member of the NDIR Review Panel is e-mailed all the information to review the dental coding and determine if the coding is correct. If they agree with the coding, they advise the CJIS Division via e-mail, and the information is posted to the NDIR. If the NDIR Review Panel member determines the NCIC dental record is improperly coded, they will notify the FBI and the submitting agency in an attempt to correct inaccuracies. The information will be returned to the submitting agency for correction and re-submission. NDIR Review Panel members will be contacted on a rotational basis to review the dental coding of records submitted to the NDIR. Review Panel members must be available to review the record and provide comment in less than 72 hours.

Once a record packet is reviewed and approved by the NDIR Review Panel member, or submitted with a request to waive the review by a Review Panel member, it will be posted by the NCIC Number in an electronic folder under the Missing and Wanted Person area or the unidentified area of the NDIR on LEO. The information will be listed in numerical order. Each record will contain a copy of each piece of information in the original format as well as a zip file containing all the documentation to allow for the easy download of all the information.

When a record is cleared from the NCIC, the information will be removed from the NDIR and placed in an archive file at the CJIS Division. The NDIR will also house data collection guides and forms related to NCIC Missing, Unidentified and Wanted person entries, a place for frequently asked questions and eventually training information.

A registry of forensic odontologists available for consultation by law enforcement agencies will also be included.

More information regarding the NDIR can be obtained by contacting Mrs. Stacey C. Davis, FBI-CJIS Division, at phone number: (304) 625-2618 or email: stdavis@leo.gov

Organization and Planning for Emergency Management

The National Response Plan

The National Response Plan (NRP) has been developed to provide a comprehensive, risk-based, and all-hazards approach to emergency management. The NRP establishes guidelines to manage domestic response due to radiological, technical, natural, or terrorist incidents.

The primary strategic goal of emergency response is life safety. Tactics to decrease loss of life and to limit casualties are of supreme importance. Incident stabilization and the ability to protect property and the environment are also considered important aspects in an emergency response algorithm. The NRP cites twelve Emergency Services Functions (ESFs) and the agencies charged with performing

ESF	LEAD AGENCY	ROLE
1 Transportation	U.S. Dept. Of Transportation	Transport resources, restore Roads
2 Communications	U.S. Office of Science/ Tech Policy	Provide and Restore Communications in Response
3 Public Works Engineering	Department of Defense & Army Corps of Engineers	Restore Utilities, Barricades
4 Firefighting	U.S. Dept. Of Agriculture U.S. Forest Service	Mainly wildfire management
5 Information & Planning	FEMA	Collect, collate information
6 Mass Care	American Red Cross	Basic needs(shelter, food, and first aid)
7 Resource Support	U.S. General Services Administration	Logistical Operations
8 Health & Medical Services	U.S. Dept. of Health and Human Services/ Public Health Service/ DHS	Medical and Mortuary Services-DMAT/DMORT/ MMRS
9 Urban Search & Rescue	FEMA	Search and Rescue ops
10 Hazardous Materials	U.S. Environmental Protection Agency	Aid Local & State Hazmat Response
11 Food	Department of Agriculture	Transport/Allocation of Foodstuffs to Disaster Site
12 Energy	Department of Energy	Aid in energy infrastructure

Table 3-1: Emergency Services Functions (ESFs) of the National Response Plan

these tasks when a response is required (**Table: 3-1**).

On June 6, 1995 PDD-39 *United States Policy on Counterterrorism* identified the FBI as the lead agency for crisis management and FEMA as the lead agency for consequence management in a multiple fatality incident situation. The former addresses the law enforcement aspects of an incident in order to neutralize, apprehend, and prosecute perpetrators. In a multiple fatality incident situation, the latter is designed to alleviate damage, loss, hardship and to protect the public health. Traditionally, the role of the forensic odontologist falls under ESF #8 with the primary goal to recover and identify victims. The threat of a future biological terrorist incident may lead to an expanding role of forensic dentists in the areas of bioterrorism syndrome surveillance and perhaps mass immunization facilitators.

The National Incident Management System

The National Incident Management System (NIMS) was developed as a result of the terrorist attacks of September 11, 2001. It is part of the law signed by President George W. Bush in 2003 which created Homeland Security Presidential Directive (HSPD) - 5. The overall objective of NIMS is to coordinate governmental agencies, non-governmental organizations (NGOs), and the private sector to resolve incidents of national significance.

Full compliance for local, state, and federal agencies was required by 2005. Compliance with NIMS is a requirement to be integrated into the National Response Plan (NRP). Essential to NIMS strategy is that it is applicable across all jurisdictions and disciples and is organized to include the following components:

- NIMS Concepts and Components:

 - Incident Command System (ICS)

 - Communication and Information Management

- Preparedness

- Joint Information System (JIS)

- NIMS Integration Center (NIC)

- NRP Maintenance

Incident Command System (ICS)

The concept of ICS originated in the Firefighting Resources of California Organized for Potential Emergency (FIRESCOPE). The 1970's saw unprecedented loss of life due to differing command modules used in the mitigation of California wildfires. Following after-action evaluations ICS was developed to reduce human and property losses. OSHA regulations 29 CFR 1910.120 mandates the use of the Incident Command System for all hazardous material responses. In addition, EPA regulation 40 CFR 311.1 requires these standards to be adhered to when an individual state does not have a dedicated state plan under Section18 of 1970 OSHA Act. ICS concepts and design have been established to provide consistency of operational design in the following areas:

- **Common Terminology** -
There is use of Standard English throughout the commandstructure to describe actions and response. Clarity is essential so there is no use of "10" codes.

- **Organizational Best Practices** -
All personnel, equipment and other resources are allocated to the fullest extent to support the resolution of the incident.

- **Span of Control** - In order to effectively manage the incident a limit must be placed as to how many individuals one oversees. Manageable span of control is three to seven with a supervisor ratio of one to five. If these numbers are exceeded then the organizational structure must be adjusted.

- **Accountability** – Requires observation of a consistent chain of command with a known line authority.

- **Organizational Facilities** – An infrastructural design of a multiple fatality incident site includes:

  - Incident Command Post - Area for command to oversee the sight. This is most often designated by a green light/flag to distinguish it from other *flashing lights* on the scene.

  - Base - Area where logistics is based.- this is often at the Incident Command Post Camp where resources are kept to support operations

  - Staging Area – Location where personnel and equipment are held prior to receiving their assignments.

  - Helibase/Helispot - Locations where air operations are conducted.

- **Use of Incident Action Plan -** This plan is used over the 12 hour operational period and outlines the overall objectives, plans and procedures of the response.

- **Flexible and Expandable -** Ability to conform the use of ICS to all types and sizes of situations. This can be expanded or contracted as situations dictates.

- **Position Titles -** Incident Commander (IC) - One individual who is in charge. There is one IC per incident. He or she can be relieved at an end of an operational period. These titles are used at the scene only. They do not reflect the day-to-day position an individual holds.

- **Unified Command -** Command structure where the IC is in command of the scene although multiple agencies may be involved in a coordinated response. An Area Command is used when operations are done on site as in the case of multiple incidents or a public health emergency.

- **Integrated Communications -** Ability to transfer information throughout the response effort is based on the concept of communications interoperability. The overall goals of the Incident Command System are open communication, mutual trust, and constructive conflict resolution. ICS allows expansion of staffing into two distinct groups:

  - Command Staff

  - General Staff

Command Staff

The Incident Commander (IC) position is filled at every response. The IC is responsible for all actions from initial scene evaluation through demobilization and development of the Incident Action Plan (IAP). The IC delegates authority allocates resources and assigns personnel into needed staff positions. As an incident evolves, the IC may be replaced due to situational or jurisdictional changes.

The Public Information Officer (PIO) is responsible for providing information to all stakeholders, the general public, and the media. Media relations are under direct control of the PIO and are released only under their authorization.

The Safety Officer (SO) has the overall responsibility for the development of site safety plans. Their duty is to ensure the safety of the working environment through the use of personal protection equipment (PPE) and OSHA compliance and accountability. The SO is the only individual on site other than the IC who can halt operations if safety issues become a concern.

The Liaison Officer (LO) has the crucial responsibility for maintaining a flow of information via communication between agencies during a multi-agency response. The LO is responsible for contact between the different groups involved in a response. If complexity of the situation dictates a larger response then additional expansion of the ICS may be necessary.

General Staff

Management functions are part of the General

Staff's duties. The four sections that comprise the General Staff are:

- Operations

- Planning

- Logistics

- Finance and Administration.

Operations Section

The Operations Section has the duty for the specific actions or tactics that need to be carried out to achieve the strategic goals that are found in the Incident Action Plan. The Operations Section Chief is responsible for all resources that are part of field operations. If necessary, the Operations Section can be further subdivided into Divisions and Groups. The former separates operations by geographic location and the latter by function. Both are led by a Supervisor.

When manageable span of control is exceeded in either a Division or Group they can be divided further into Branches. Each Branch is managed by a Director and these units are most often used in large, multi-agency responses because of the number of functional groups required for incident stabilization and resolution.

Other resources that are found in the Operations Section include single resources, task forces, and strike teams. An example of a single resource would be the availability of one helicopter for aerial damage assessment or body recovery. A task force is a team of mixed resources under one team leader. A strike team consists of the same kind and type of members under the supervision of a team leader.

Planning Section

The Planning Section is responsible for the collection and dissemination of information related to the Incident Action Plan (IAP). This document is concerned with what tasks need to be accomplished, who accomplishes those tasks, how communication occurs and resolution of procedural issues necessary to carry out the action. The Planning Section documents the situation as it develops from inception to demobilization. Corrective Action Plans (CAPs) are developed following post-incident debriefing of the participants to address and evaluate the "lessons learned" during the deployment. The Planning Section may be further subdivided into the following units:

- Resource Unit - monitors all available personnel and equipment.

- Situation Unit - alters the IAP if the scene changes.

- Documentation Unit - is responsible for paperwork and photo-documentation of the scene.

- Demobilization Unit - is responsible f o r the winding down and release of resources as the incident stabilizes. Specific Technical Specialists (STSs) can also be found in this section.

Logistics Section

The Logistics Section is responsible for the services and support for incident resolution. Logistics' aim is to procure, allocate, and maintain personnel, equipment, food, and transportation. It is necessary for the Logistics Section to obtain resources by *size, amount, location* needed, duration of the operation (*time*), and *type* of response. Thus, this process is referred to as SALTT.

Finance and Administration Section

Finance and Administration monitors and tracks all costs related to an incident. Cost analysis, contract negotiation, and compensation for worker injury or property damage is documented. It is crucial in a large response to a multiple fatality incident that accurate records are kept for reimbursement. This section may be further subdivided into Procurement, Time, Cost, and Compensation Units.

Communication and Information Management

Standard requirements for communications are dictated under NIMS. Past experience has shown that the most crucial aspect of any response has been clear communications. Coordinated response has been hindered by a lack of interoperability of communication systems. The solution to this has been the acceptance of the 800 Megahertz radio system. Communications and development of support technologies is also encouraged.

Preparedness

NIMS encourages a continuous cycle of planning, training, and exercising. After-action evaluations have consistently shown that individuals respond the way that they train. Hazard mitigation strategies for public infrastructure and the population of a threat area are to be developed to lessen the vulnerability of local jurisdictions to a known threat or hazard. Where there is no vulnerability the significance of a hazard is diminished to private citizens and their surroundings. Mitigation efforts may be found in uniform building codes, flood plain management, or property relocation or acquisition. The goal of preparedness is to reduce or eliminate human and property vulnerability.

Joint Information System (JIS)

The Joint Information Center (JIC) is a central location where public information about an ongoing emergency is shared. Within the JIC different agencies will have their PIOs involved in the coordination of information release. The PIO of each agency retains their independence but coordinate to express a unified message. The messages issued may be about evacuation, shelter-in-place, re-entry, or recovery concerns.

NIMS Integration Center (NIC)

The purpose of the NIC is to develop national standards for personnel and equipment to be used in the National Response Plan. All governmental, voluntary agencies, and tribal communities must adhere to these standards for training, certification, and credentialing. Personnel must be trained to a minimum level of knowledge and skill to affect a coordinated response. Mutual Aid Agreements become more effective when personnel and equipment are standardized. The NIC is involved in the review of specific training and acceptable courses to maintain credentialing and certification. Resource management and inventory control as well as standards aid in a multi-agency response.

NRP Maintenance

The National Response Plan provides a framework to mitigate a natural multiple fatality incident or terrorist act. Education and preparedness for all responders is necessary in order for recovery to take place. Thus, former guidelines concerning education and preparedness are now required by law. The NRP was designed by local, state, federal, and tribal organizations to stabilize an emergency incident. The final component of NIMS is the ongoing development and maintenance of the NRP.

Formation of a Dental Identification Team

With an increasingly mobile population, the potential for transportation accidents is always present. OSHA regulations have lowered the occurrence of industrial to a multiple fatality incident in the United States however, they still occur in this country and abroad. Although the impact of natural multiple fatality incident s may be greatest in densely populated areas, no region is exempt. Additionally, there is a global concern about acts of terrorism and bioterrorism. Recent incidents directed at the transit systems in Madrid, Tokyo, and London reinforces the need for preparedness in light of the probability of future attacks.

Despite the federal approach now taken in the United States and other countries to centralize the response to assist the injured and recover and identify the dead in a multiple fatality incident situation, individual states and local jurisdictions may still maintain teams of trained dentists mandated to function in these situations. This is especially important in underserved areas where regional multiple fatality incident teams have proven to be valuable resources in the event of a multiple fatality incident . California, Nevada, Michigan, South Carolina and other states have established such teams. With the creation of the NRP it is important for organizers of these teams to understand and work within the parameters of the NRP guidelines.

Additionally, it must be remembered that although many multiple fatality incident situations require mobilization of highly sophisticated teams with computer capabilities, cutting edge equipment and highly trained personnel; smaller scale multiple fatality incident incidents may only require local or regional expertise that may not have the opportunity or the budget to use more than traditional means of dental comparison. Thus, despite the emphasis on the DMORT system a discussion of the protocols for establishing a local or regional Dental Identification Team is also presented.

Preparation and training prior to a multiple fatality incident has been stressed and this often requires development of a forensic dental identification team sponsored or established by the state or local dental association, the Medical Examiner/Coroner's office within the jurisdiction or legislation dealing with multiple fatality incident preparedness. State dental associations often have resources not otherwise available to small local societies. In addition, the endorsement of a professional organization lends credibility to a newly organized dental multiple fatality incident team.

Prior to the establishment of a state or regional dental multiple fatality incident team the following questions should be addressed to insure that the expertise of those involved will be utilized:

-Is this resource already available in your state or district?

-Is the coroner or medical examiner receptive to the idea of having a dental identification team available?

-What is the probability of the team being used in a multiple fatality incident setting?

-What are the region's vulnerabilities? These may include the presence of airports and other centralized public transportation hubs, high rise buildings, stadiums, high density residential areas, dams, mines, factories, refineries, fuel pipe lines and public utilities. Environmental dangers should also be assessed.

Local emergency planning and civil defense agencies and airline multiple fatality incident plan coordinators should be consulted to ascertain what resources already exist to incorporate a dental multiple fatality incident team into emergency preparedness infrastructure. Establish an operational plan for the team by answering the following questions:

- Will the team serve a metropolitan area, county or region of a state or district?

- What local resources are available to enable team formation?

- Are trained and experienced leaders and team members available? Should board certified experts be called upon, or are dentists with little or no training in forensic dental identification fully capable? Occasionally, dentists who are perceived as *trained* in forensic dentistry by credentialed through attendance at short continuing education courses in forensic dentistry/dental identification are called upon to identify the victims of tragedy. More formal training can be accomplished through regional or local governmental agencies, coroner and medical examiner seminars, state government emergency training programs, airport fire and rescue training programs, the Armed Forces Institute of Pathology (AFIP) annual course in forensic dentistry, workshops sponsored by the American Board of

Forensic Odontology (ABFO), annual meetings of the odontology section of the American Academy of Forensic Sciences (AAFS), the American Society of Forensic Odontology (ASFO), British Association of Forensic Odontology (BAFO), International Organization for Forensic Odonto-Stomatology (IOFOS), and other international forensic organizations.

- Are the team members considered volunteers or temporary employees?

- Are team members protected by worker's compensation and liability insurance?

- Who is responsible for OSHA regulations covering the team?

A written participation agreement with team members should be established. Develop a similar agreement outlining the specific duties and responsibilities of the team with its authorizing agency. This precludes any misunderstandings related to staffing, deployment policies and logistical issues.

Since a multiple fatality incident identification team will hopefully not be frequently utilized in the real time setting, maintaining the interest and readiness of its members is an important consideration. Periodic training meetings with interesting presentations on all facets of multiple fatality incident response are recommended to keep interest and moral of the team at a readiness level. Topics of interest can be provided by groups other than dental resources. These may include airport fire and rescue service, airline multiple fatality incident response coordinators, emergency government administrators, civil defense and volunteer services agencies and medical examiner/coroner personnel.

Attempts should also be made to interest local dentists in participating. Solicit community support for the educational and service roles of the dental multiple fatality incident response team through the provision of equipment, supplies and/or sponsorship. Contact agencies may include coroner/medical examiner offices, state/local dental societies and state/local emergency management agencies.

A team leader should be selected according to his or her knowledge and experience in the field of multiple fatality incident identification. Consideration should be given for the team leader to reside in the area of the state most vulnerable to the possibility of a multiple fatality incident. Additional team leaders may be indicated in larger states with multiple threat areas and high population density. During a multiple fatality incident situation, however, only one designated team leader should be in command of the dental unit. The team leader should be actively involved as a forensic odontologist and be affiliated major forensic dental associations.

It is beneficial for the team leader to have a close working relationship with the medical examiner/coroner of the jurisdiction. Their agency will direct the operations associated with body recovery and identification in a multiple fatality incident and the dental identification team will work under its authority. It is the responsibility of the team leader to meet with other emergency service agencies to help develop the multiple fatality incident plan as it relates to the dental identification. The team leader must designate a replacement in their absence and notify the appropriate agencies of this individual's role.

Annually, the team leader should conduct a seminar and/or mock multiple fatality incident exercise to update team members regarding forensic activity of the team and other organizations throughout the country. The team leader must be prepared to commit to mobilize the state team when called upon. This is a seven day a week, twenty-four hour per day commitment. The dental multiple fatality incident identification team can be divided into two principal groups. These include *Go Team* and *Support Team* members (**Figures 3-11 through 3-14**).

- *Go Team* – this term is often given to smaller units within the statewide or local team which are comprised of participants who can serve in leadership roles. Members should be selected in consultation with the team leader and should have previous experience in forensic dentistry. If possible, they should have current affiliation with a medical examiner/coroner's office. Each member must make a commitment to remain for an entire multiple fatality incident situation or until relieved by order of the team leader. Ideally, each member should have experience in all facets of the identification process. *Go Team* members will act as section leaders and must be proficient in their assigned tasks. Ten dentists are the appropriate complement for a state wide *Go Team*. This assures that at least five members will respond to a given situation.

- ***Support Team*** - The *Go Team* is supplemented by other dentists and auxiliaries as indicated by the severity of the multiple fatality incident . These participants are *Support Team* members and are individuals who have an interest in forensic identification and are willing to assist should a multiple fatality incident occur in their area. It is important that a variety of dental and non-dental personnel be included on the *Support Team,* including administrative personnel.

In the event of a multiple fatality incident many talents are required to allow the forensic dental identification team to perform at maximum efficiency. Identification cards must be issued to all team members. *Go Team* members should have no expiration date. All others should be reissued every three years. The ID cards should have a photograph, descriptive information about the team member including weight, height, hair and eye color, date of birth and an area for the member's signature. The team leader and the dental association representative should also sign the team member's identification card. Identification cards allow authorized team members unimpeded access to the multiple fatality incident site.

Team Administration and Maintenance Information

The administration and maintenance of team

information should be handled by the state or local dental association, in conjunction with the team leader. This information should include profiles on all team members and the experience of each team member in actual and mock situations. Team responsibility should be divided into regions, and team members assigned to individual regional teams according to their location. This expedites the mobilization of the team when a multiple fatality incident situation occurs.

Demographic data concerning team members should be electronically generated and stored allowing the team leader easy access to members of the multiple fatality incident team. The roster should include: name, address, home/office telephone numbers and county and team region. A roster of this nature makes it easier to call on team members from any particular area of the state or region.

Team members should sign a disclaimer releasing the particular agency or association of any damages or liability related to the service of the dental multiple fatality incident team member. They should also inform their malpractice insurance carrier of their involvement in forensic aspects of dental practice.

Notification of Team Existence and Logistical Issues

Following the formation of the Forensic Dental Identification Team, all county medical examiners/ coroners and state police posts should be notified of the existence of the team and instructed concerning whom to contact should they need its services **(Figure 3-15).** Dental suppliers should be informed of the team's existence and arrangements for commitment of supplies needed by the team in the event of a multiple fatality incident situation should be established.

When notified of the need for deployment of the team, the state/local dental association or the team leader can activate the team by the following methods:

Figure 3-11: The Nevada Identification team preparing for National Guard transportation for an exercise.

Figure 3-14: The tired ID Team on thereturn flight after a 12 hour day 450 miles from home.

Figure 3-12: Members of the Nevada and Utah Identification Teams on the C130 Flight

Figure 3-13: The quickly assembled headquarters for the Nevada Identification Team is a component of the palletized cache of equipment.

- When the team leader has been advised of all the facts, the team leader notifies the *Go Team* and the executive office of the state/local association. Team members should be instructed not to call the team leader, state/local association, or medical examiner/coroner as it creates confusion and slows the efficiency of the operation. A predetermined phone chain is activated by the team members.

- The requirements for and deployment of additional personnel should be reevaluated after the *Go Team* meets at the multiple fatality incident site. The team leader decides which individuals from the *Support Team* will be called depending on the location and magnitude of the multiple fatality incident

Mass multiple fatality incident situations are trying times, both physically and mentally. Previous knowledge and understanding of the emotional status of team members in stressful situations will help to make the difficult tasks performed by a forensic odontologist run smoothly. Professional psychological and emotional support in debriefing sessions is advisable at the conclusion of a deployment to insure that these needs of team members are met.

When meeting with the medical examiner/coroner, the team leader should suggest the use of dental personnel in the field during the recovery operation. Ideally, a dentist with experience in a multiple fatality incident situation should be assigned to each of the body recovery teams. Dentists are attuned to look for small jaw fragments, teeth, restorations and appliances and it is difficult to train lay-personnel to recover these small objects under such trying circumstances.

A group of dentists with equipment such

O: All County Medical Examiners/Coroners, Department of Public Health, Department of the State Police, State Medical Society

The (state) Dental Association is proud to announce the formation of a statewide forensic dental identification team. This team was formed to be ready in the event of a multiple fatality incident. All members of the team have received training in the field of dental forensics. Should the need arise for action by the dental forensic team, please contact (team leaders name), team leader at (leader's office & home telephone numbers)

If the team leader is not available please contact (representative at state association), at the (state association name) Central Office at (telephone number). We will coordinate the efforts of the other team members to have them in place as soon as possible. If you would like more information on our dental forensic identification team, or if you have any questions, please contact me.

Sincerely,

Figure 3-15. Example of a letter notifying agencies of the formation of a dental identification team.

as rakes, shovels and sifting devices can scan the multiple fatality incident site each day following other recovery efforts. This is especially critical when large objects such as the tail section or wing of an airplane have been removed from the site. Many dental fragments which help in the identifying process are found during these excursions. It is beneficial from a psychological standpoint to have only those team members who express an interest, carry out the field operation. Team members should be rotated to allow all those interested in having this opportunity to work in this segment of the identification process.

It is important to keep a log of which team members are in the field or assigned to the morgue facility. This can be accomplished with a sign-in/out sheet to keep track of team member's assignments. This form should include the participant's name, date and times of arrival and departure. The section in which the individual is working and supervisor's approval should also be included.

Team Organization

The dental multiple fatality incident team is divided into the following sections for efficient utilization of personnel and the information

- The Post Mortem Section

- The Radiography and Photography Section

- The Antemortem Section

- The Comparison Section

The Post Mortem Section

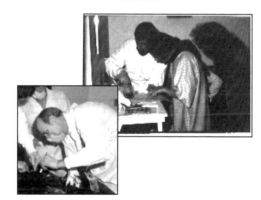

Figure 3-16: Members of the Post Mortem Section performing an oral autopsy on a victim of the MGM Grand Fire.

Figure 3-17: ID team members recording information from the oral autopsy on standard forms developed by the Armed Forces Institute of Pathology.

Personnel

A Section Leader with at least three teams of three members each is recommended for the charting of post mortem dental material. The team can be comprised of three dentists or two dentists and one auxiliary. A section leader should be present at all times. If it is necessary for the section leader to leave the area, a person should be designated as temporary leader.

Working Area

The working area should have good lighting, comfortable chairs and adequate tables. An adequate water supply should be readily available to wash and clean specimens. It is important to clean specimens in a container or bucket so that loose teeth are not lost down the drain.

Responsibilities and Functions

The post mortem section has the responsibility of examining and charting all post mortem (dental) body parts (**Figure 3-16**). It is recommended that at least two dentists work on a specimen. This dramatically reduces the chance for errors. Along with the team leader and post mortem section leader, the determination of the necessity to resect the maxilla and mandible of the victims is presented to the medical examiner/coroner. In severe bum cases, it may be helpful to keep the maxilla in situ to prevent the anterior teeth from fracturing.

The use of transillumination and/or a dye placed on the teeth are helpful tools in the recognition of composite resin restoration both in the anterior and posterior areas. Arrangements for this type of equipment and/or materials should be made in advance. Each specimen is charted on a Post Mortem Record sheet **(Figure 3-17)** by at least two (and preferably three) individuals working together. One individual (a dentist) examines the specimen and a second (a dentist) verifies the information that is placed on the record sheet by a dentist, hygienist, or student.

All fragments and resected maxillae and mandibles will be labeled and placed in containers. A flow sheet will trace the movement through the section to the radiograph and photography section, final completion of the post mortem packet and then placement of the specimen in the refrigerator truck for storage.

The Radiography and Photography Section

Personnel

The Radiography and Photography Section is made up of a section leader and alternate with at least one additional dentist and one auxiliary.

Working Area

The X-ray units should be placed to minimize radiation to surrounding areas. Many states have requirements for the placement and operation of x-ray units. These requirements should be known prior to the multiple fatality incident event and taken into consideration whether a temporary or permanent morgue is being established. Adequate tables, chairs and electrical outlets for radiographic and developer equipment are necessary. Special dark room and plumbing arrangements may be necessary depending on the type of equipment that is used for developing radiographs.

Materials and Equipment

A portable x-ray unit(s) is necessary for the functioning of this section (**Figure 3-18**). The number of units is dependent: on the size of the multiple fatality incident ; the number of members in this section and their availability; and, the availability of the radiographic equipment. Proper radiation shielding aprons for members of this section are important. This also includes shielding such as moveable radiation shields to protect other members of the response team. State regulations should be reviewed to insure that the equipment set up conforms to regulations established for the protection of the identification team members. Automatic developing machines should be available at the morgue site. Daylight type loaders are preferred as this eliminates the necessity for a dark room.

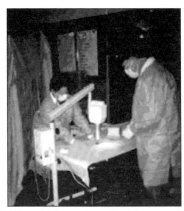

Figure 3-18: Radiography of jaw fragments using portable X-ray equipment.

- Anterior view - maxilla and mandible

- Lateral - right and left

- Occlusal view - maxilla and mandible

- Additional fragments - individual teeth

A Polaroid system is ideal for use in this section because of the immediate availability of the photographs. For photographic documentation of the team and its functions a 35mm camera can be used. Only the person appointed by the team leader as official photographer of the dental team should be allowed to photograph the proceedings.

Responsibilities and Functions

The Antemortem Section

This section works closely with the post mortem section. After the radiographs and photographs are completed on a specimen, the section leader meets with the post mortem section leader to complete the post mortem record of the specimen by supplementing the visual examination post mortem chart with all the information derived by the radiographs. The team leader meets periodically with these two section leaders to verify the completion of the charts, approve them and transfer them to the comparison section. Each specimen has both bitewing and periapical radiographs, if possible. (Care must be made to establish the facial/labial versus lingual especially in the fragmented jaws). All radiographs should be mounted and labeled in the radiology section. Additionally, the specimen containers should be marked to indicate that they have been in the radiology section.

Figure 3-19: Antemortem Section personnel

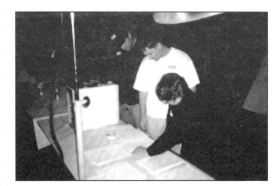

Figure 3-20: Members of the Antemortem Section recording information on potential victims as it arrives.

Photographs are a valuable aid in the identification of a victim when dental antemortem radiographs are not available. The cameras used by this section may also be used by the medical examiner/coroner to document physical findings such as tattoos, scars, moles, etc., found on some of the victims. A close-up type camera system should be utilized whenever possible. The following photographs should be taken:

Figure 3-21: Ivan Futrell of the FBI sending and receiving information regarding fingerprints.

Personnel

The antemortem section is made up of a section leader and his/her alternate with at least three teams of three members each (consisting of at least two dentists with either an auxiliary or student as the third member). The antemortem section leader should be present at all times. If it is necessary for the section leader to leave the area, a person should be designated as temporary section leader.

Working Area

Telephones should be set up close to the antemortem section for both incoming and outgoing calls. A fax machine should also be readily available. The antemortem section requires good lighting and enough outlets for an adequate amount of x-ray view boxes. Comfortable chairs and tables with adequate space are necessary. When setting up this section a separate area for cataloging incoming antemortem information should be considered (**Figures 3-20 and 3-21**).

Materials and Equipment

This section will be supplied with antemortem charts, master charting procedures and tables of various domestic and foreign charting methods. The following is a list of materials needed for the antemortem section:

- Antemortem Charting Forms

- Charting Diagram Explanation Keys

- Pencils, Colored Markers (waterproof, non-smearing)

- Legal Size File Folders with Tabs (hanging type, 2 or 4 colors)

- Racks or Cabinets for Files

- Charting Conversion Tables (Foreign and domestic, **Tables 3-2, 3-3a and 3-3b**)

- Colored Tape

- Radiographic View Boxes

- Tables and Comfortable Chairs

Responsibilities and Functions

The antemortem section leader and alternate leader must be able to respond immediately when called. The section members must be able to respond within twelve hours after notification. The antemortem section will record and catalog all antemortem records received at the multiple fatality incident site. Members of this section will interpret antemortem records received and place all information on common forms for manual and/or computer comparison.

During the time of the interpretation of the records they also convert all charts to the universal charting system. Upon completion of the interpretation and charting on the common form the section leader reviews the record for accuracy and completeness. Following the review by the section leader the antemortem record is sent to the comparison section. File folders should be labeled with the name of each known or suspected casualty. Use colored file folders or strips of colored tape on folders to separate adult males and adult females and children with mixed and primary dentition. There are six sets of files that should be maintained:

- Records Requested - An early attempt should be made to determine ages of casualties, particularly children and infants. This information should be recorded in each individual's record. This

	Upper Right					Upper Left				
	2M	1M	C	I2	I1	I1	I2	C	1M	2M
Universal	A	B	C	D	E	F	G	H	I	J
Palmer	E+	D+	C+	B+	A+	+A	+B	+C	+D	+E
FDI	55	54	53	52	51	61	62	63	64	65
Hareup	05+	04+	03+	02+	01+	+01	+02	+03	+04	+05
Other	V	IV	III	II	I	I	II	III	IV	V
Other	5D	4D	3D	2D	1D	1D	2D	3D	4D	5D
Other	d5	d4	d3	d2	d1	d1	d2	d3	d4	d5
Other	5m	4m	3m	2m	1m	1m	2m	3m	4m	5m
Other	A	B	C	D	E	E	D	C	B	A
Other	dm2	dm1	dc	di2	di1	di1	di2	dc	dm1	dm2
FDI Modified	55	54	53	52	51	61	62	63	64	65

	Lower Right					Lower Left				
	2M	1M	C	I2	I1	I1	I2	C	1M	2M
Universal	T	S	R	Q	P	O	N	M	L	K
Palmer	E-	D-	C-	B-	A-	-A	-B	-C	-D	-E
FDI	85	84	83	82	81	71	72	73	74	75
Hareup	05-	04-	03-	02-	01-	-01	-02	-03	-04	-05
Other	V	IV	III	II	I	I	II	III	IV	V
Other	5D	4D	3D	2D	1D	1D	2D	3D	4D	5D
Other	d5	d4	d3	d2	d1	d1	d2	d3	d4	d5
Other	5m	4m	3m	2m	1m	1m	2m	3m	4m	5m
Other	A	B	C	D	E	E	D	C	B	A
Other	dm2	dm1	dc	di2	di1	di1	di2	dc	dm1	dm2
FDI Modified	75	74	73	72	71	81	82	83	84	85

Table 3-2: Dental Nomenclature Conversion Table: Deciduous Teeth. Compiled by Dr. Robert Dorion

will expedite record keeping and avoid requests for nonexistent dental records on small children.

- Records Received - to be charted.

- Incomplete Records – additional information requested by section leader.

- Antemortem Chart File - file males and females and children with mixed primary dentition separately.

	Upper Right								Upper Left							
	3M	2M	1M	2P	1P	C	I2	I1	I1	I2	C	1P	2P	1M	2M	3M
Other	UR8	UR7	UR6	UR5	UR4	UR3	UR2	UR1	UL1	UL2	UL3	UL4	UL5	UL6	UL7	UL8
Hareup	8+	7+	6+	5+	4+	3+	2+	1+	+1	+2	+3	+4	+5	+6	+7	+8
Palmer	8⌋	7⌋	6⌋	5⌋	4⌋	3⌋	2⌋	1⌋	⌊1	⌊2	⌊3	⌊4	⌊5	⌊6	⌊7	⌊8
Universal	1	2	3	4	5	6	7	8	9	10	11	12	13	14	15	16
FDI	18	17	16	15	14	13	12	11	21	22	23	24	25	26	27	28
Bosworth	8	7	6	5	4	3	2	1	1	2	3	4	5	6	7	8
Lowlands	M3	M2	M1	P2	P1	C	I2	I1	I1	I2	C	P1	P2	M1	M2	M3
Europe	D8	D7	D6	D5	D4	D3	D2	D1	G1	G2	G3	G4	G5	G6	G7	G8
Holland	sdM3	sdM2	sdM3	sdP2	sdP1	sdC	sdI2	sdI1	sgI1	sgI2	sgC	sgP1	sgP2	sgM1	sgM2	sgM3
FDI Modified	18	17	16	15	14	13	12	11	21	22	23	24	25	26	27	28
Other	16	15	14	13	12	11	10	9	8	7	6	5	4	3	2	1

Table 3-3a: Dental Nomenclature Conversion Table: Permanent Teeth

	Lower Right								Lower Left							
	3M	2M	1M	2P	1P	C	I2	I1	I1	I2	C	1P	2P	1M	2M	3M
Other	LR8	LR7	LR6	LR5	LR4	LR3	LR2	LR1	LL1	LL2	LL3	LL4	LL5	LL6	LL7	LL8
Hareup	8-	7-	6-	5-	4-	3-	2-	1-	-1	-2	-3	-4	-5	-6	-7	-8
Palmer	8⌉	7⌉	6⌉	5⌉	4⌉	3⌉	2⌉	1⌉	⌈1	⌈2	⌈3	⌈4	⌈5	⌈6	⌈7	⌈8
Universal	32	31	30	29	28	27	26	25	24	23	22	21	20	19	18	17
FDI	48	47	46	45	44	43	42	41	31	32	33	34	35	36	37	38
Bosworth	H	G	F	E	D	C	B	A	A	B	C	D	E	F	G	H
Lowlands	M3	M2	M1	P2	P1	C	I2	I1	I1	I2	C	P1	P2	M1	M2	M3
Europe	d8	d7	d6	d5	d4	d3	d2	d1	g1	g2	g3	g4	g5	g6	g7	g8
Holland	diM3	diM2	diM3	diP2	diP1	diC	diI2	diI1	giI1	giI2	giC	giP1	giP2	giM1	giM2	giM3
FDI Modified	38	37	36	35	34	33	32	31	41	42	43	44	45	46	47	48
Other	32	31	30	29	28	27	26	25	24	23	22	21	20	19	18	17

Table 3-3b: Dental Nomenclature Conversion Table: Permanent Teeth

- Post mortem Chart File - (from post mortem section) – identified by body or body part number. File known males and females and children with mixed primary dentition separately.

- Casualties Identified – combine antemortem and post mortem records into one folder identified by name.

The team leader or antemortem section leader should request antemortem dental records on all known or suspected casualties (**Figure 3-22**). As dental records are received for each decedent, the antemortem section leader should record the receipt and a description of exactly what was received. (Medical records should be transferred to the appropriate section, but a record of their receipt should be maintained.) This information should be recorded on a master list maintained by the section leader and on an individual sheet placed with the record in the individually labeled file folder.

Each record is charted on an Antemortem Record Sheet by at least two (and preferably three) individuals working together. One individual (a dentist) reads the record, and the second (a dentist, a hygienist, or a dental assistant) charts using the guidelines set for charting. If the recording team consists of three individuals, the third individual (a dentist) verifies the information and the recording accuracy of the others. If the recording team consists of only two individuals, each must verify the other's interpretation or recording. At least one dentist in each team should be a general practitioner who is aware of the variety of restorative materials and is familiar with the diversity of appliances and techniques utilized in dentistry.

Prior to being replaced in the files each charted record should be double-checked and initialed by the antemortem section leader (or designee) to verify accuracy and completeness and to determine if additional information should be requested. The antemortem record is then transferred to a rack for records which are incomplete (additional information requested by the section leader) or the antemortem chart file.

Dear Doctor
As you may be aware, your patient, was a possible victim of the disaster that occurred
As team leader of the Dental Association Forensic Dental Identification team, I am requesting all dental records you may have available for this individual. Any charts, radiographs, photographs and/or diagnostic models you can provide would be helpful. If possible, original records should be sent. We will be happy to return the records to you after the identification process is completed.
Sincerely,
Team Leader
Please return this form with the records you supply.

I am supplying the following records:
- -
These records are Original Copies (please clarify any unusual abbreviations, numbering system, etc.)
Patient's Name:
Treating Dentist's Name
Address
City, State, Zip
Telephone
I would like these records returned to me: Yes   No

Figure 3-22: Example of letter requesting dental information from a victim's dentist

Only records which are transferred to the antemortem chart file by the antemortem section leader should be entered into the computer (if available). It is important to establish a librarian to be responsible for filing and keeping completed antemortem and post mortem records intact. It is this individual with the assistance of auxiliary personnel who will catalogue and control access to the records. The librarian is directly responsible to the antemortem section leader and must know the location of all completed antemortem and post mortem records.

When post mortem records arrive for comparison, the librarian assumes responsibility for their location as well. This is accomplished through the maintenance of a log sheet indicating who has each record after it is recorded as received by the antemortem section leader. This log sheet allows the team leader to know where, when, and who, has a particular record. Study models or similar records that cannot be filed should be maintained in a separate laceration with a note in the individual's file indicating the location of these records and their source. Confidentiality dictates that access to records is limited to those individuals responsible for recording the data and dentists who are involved in comparison of antemortem and post mortem records for dental identification.

All dentists submitting antemortem records are assured that if records are submitted they will be returned. This requires an accurate audit of the dental record's contents and who supplied them. Because of time and the need for additional facilities during a multiple fatality incident , record providers are instructed that records will be duplicated and returned within one month after the project's completion. The return of the records is the responsibility of the dental team leader and/or the medical examiner/coroner or other official responsible for the identification of casualties.

Guidelines for charting consistency are essential for ease of comparing antemortem and post mortem records. All information that can be obtained regarding the status of every tooth should be recorded. This applies to antemortem records as well as post mortem examinations. Additionally, any information related to spacing, rotations, occlusion, etc. should be indicated since it may be important in identification. Information related to orthodontic appliances or prostheses should be recorded if available. A composite antemortem record is a written description, or graphic recording, of all existing dental work in an individual's mouth up to the time of death as ascertained from all available dental charts and radiographs. This is compiled in a historically sequential fashion beginning with the first entry in the records through the most recent entry prior to death.

It must be understood that there always exists the possibility the victim may have had dental therapy completed that does not appear within the available antemortem dental documents. As a result, any seemingly insignificant discrepancy between antemortem and post mortem information must be explainable or no identification will be possible. An example of an explainable discrepancy is the situation in which a tooth has a small single surface restoration according to the antemortem data yet is found to have a large multiple surface restoration post mortem. It is quite possible in this example that the individual had the larger restoration placed by another dentist from whom records could not be obtained or the existence of such records was unknown to the authorities. When the odontologist is comparing antemortem and post mortem dental information it is impossible for restorations to become smaller in the latter examination of tooth surfaces or radiographs. Thus, such discrepancies in the comparison must always be considered a mismatch.

Table 3-4 summarizes the number of errors created in a study of thirty-two composite antemortem records prepared by inexperienced dentists during an actual multiple fatality incident identification effort. This study was conducted at the conclusion of the multiple fatality incident operation with the purpose of documenting the errors made and determining their significance. After the original composite antemortem records were reviewed, the numbers and types of errors were tabulated. It became apparent from the errors seen that the severity of those errors could be categorized fairly succinctly. Thirty-two composite antemortem records were divided into two categories based upon the degree of difficulty in their preparation:

- **Complex Record** - A complex record is comprised of an extensive number of narrative entries concerning various types of restorative procedures performed on numerous teeth over a long period of time. Many entries may be repetitive procedures, for example numerous re-restorations of a tooth, added *patch* restorations, or replacement of a restoration with one incorporating more surfaces and/or different materials.

- **Simple Records** - A simple record is most easily defined as all other records.

The types of errors observed were subdivided into three categories based upon their severity in relation to any untoward effect they might have in an identification process. The definitions of errors included the following:

- **Critical Errors** – Those which could prevent a set of dental remains from being identified, result in an individual being mistakenly excluded, or lead to a misidentification, in inexperienced hands. Examples of such errors encountered with the records from this multiple fatality incident were:

- **CE Type 1** - Listing a tooth as missing when present. The severity of such an error is lessened when considering third molar/wisdom teeth. Such a charting error is undoubtedly the most commonly encountered in all of dentistry, and is universally known to dental practitioners. Therefore, third molars are not considered in the critical error category.

- **CE Type 2** - Adding a surface(s) to a restoration or incorrectly listing the surfaces restored for a tooth. Each tooth has five designated surfaces: mesial, distal, lingual, facial (buccal) and occlusal (incisal). In dental notation these are abbreviated by using the first letter of each surface: M, D, L, F or B, 0 or I.

- **CE Type 3** - Listing a tooth as restored when it is not.

- **CE Type 4** - Missing some unusual or unique feature or pathologic entity such as failure to note the presence of a supernumerary tooth, apicoectomy or pathologic bony defect.

- **CE Type 5** – Failure to include multiple restorative procedures for the same tooth (e.g. root canal therapy, post-and-core restoration and a fixed prosthesis).

- **Moderate Errors** – Those that should not lead to a misidentification, or prevent identification from occurring. This type of error simply creates more work for an already overtaxed forensic odontology staff. Valuable time is often wasted in the resolution of differences noted between dental remains and inaccurate antemortem composite records. These types of errors might be best described as nuisance errors. Examples include:

ME Type I - Omitting a restored surface (e.g. calling an MOD-Amalgam a DO-Amalgam)

ME Type 2 – Noting a tooth as un-restored when it has a restoration

- **Minor Errors** – Do not affect the identification effort but are indicative of less than perfect record preparation and ineffective quality control. Examples include:

MNR Type 1 - Omitting additional restorations of similar surfaces (e.g. a molar has more than one 0-Amalgam or more than one F-Amalgam and the record only indicates one 0-Amalgam or one F-Amalgam).

MNR Type 2 - Third molars are recorded as missing when they are present or recorded as present when they are missing. The insignificance of MNR Type 2 was discussed under CE Type 1 errors.

Among the thirty-two records examined only eleven were error free. While the sample size for Critical Errors in both Complex Records and Simple Records was too small to allow statistical analysis, the majority of errors were either CE Type 2 or CE Type 3 classifications. Since the restoration of teeth is the predominant component of dental practice procedures, such findings are not surprising.

The results observed for Moderate Errors for both Simple and Complex record types were statistically significant and analyzed using a Chi-square test. The results obtained were as follows:

- Complex Records, Moderate Errors: $X^2 = 12.1$, p = .001

- Simple Records, Moderate Errors: $X^2 = 8.33$, p = .004

The significance factor (p value) is quite high for both record types. There were no Complex Records prepared without errors. Only eleven of twenty-six Simple Records (42 percent) were error free. This study is the first to attempt to define antemortem dental records by preparation difficulty, and indicate, define, document and tabulate error types in those records. While a computer data base was not utilized during the multiple fatality incident in this discussion, in order to appreciate the possible ramifications of the data obtained it is imperative to appreciate the role of data automation in dental remains identification and the relationship between the accuracy of input data and the eventual results obtained from computerized sorting of that data.

It has become standard practice to utilize computer software as an integral part of the forensic odontology section for multiple fatality incidents involving large numbers of remains. This culminated in the post Katrina DMORT exercise in which computers were used exclusively in the creation of composite antemortem records for comparison with post mortem computer charts and radiographs.

Availability of records may necessitate utilizing those which are old and possibly out of date. Care must be taken to record dates where applicable, i.e. obtained from old radiographs or records without recent information. Photographs revealing teeth may sometimes be useful, particularly if dental information is insufficient. Both an anatomically accurate diagrammatic representation and a written description should be recorded for each tooth for which there is information.

The variety of charting symbols, numbering systems, and record designations employed by dentists makes it imperative that care be taken to accurately interpret information recorded on the antemortem dental chart. A key to symbol and abbreviations used in a chart should be requested with the records. If the recording team cannot interpret the record, it should be referred to the antemortem section leader or team leader, who may need to contact the dentist supplying the records for assistance in interpretation. Financial records of the putative decedent may be useful in determining whether or not a procedure has been performed.

The method of mounting of radiographs may differ among the various areas of the United States as well internationally and by experience in one's dental training. Thus, it is essential that confirmation of *Right* and *Left* be accurately determined. If a copy of radiographs is provided rather than originals, the provider should indicate *Right* and *Left* for each radiograph.

Special attention should be made by the dental team to recheck if a duplicate has been sent (i.e. periapical #2 duplicate radiographic film may resemble original radiographs). The attending family dentist should be contacted to verify the correct chart entry if discrepancies arise regarding orientation of the antemortem radiographs, including but not limited to Right and Left orientation, tooth surfaces restored and variations in tooth numbering.

Radiographs should be remounted for consistency when comparison is made between antemortem and post mortem records. A chart should be provided which demonstrates examples for recording types of restorations, missing teeth, extraction's, impactions, etc. Copies of this or comparable charting diagrams should be available for reference by both the antemortem and post mortem recording teams.

The Comparison Section

Figure 3-23: Members of the comparison section at work with computers and the older method of wall charts.

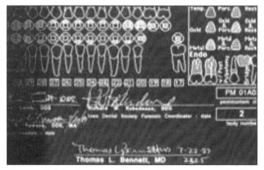

Figure 3-24: A copy of the final signed identification of one multiple fatality incident victim.

Personnel

The comparison section should consist of team members from both antemortem and post mortem sections, with additional support members when necessary.

Working Area

Telephones should be setup for both incoming and outgoing calls. As with the other sections the comparison section also needs good lighting and enough outlets for an adequate amount of x-ray view boxes. Comfortable chairs and adequate table space for both manual and computer comparison procedures are necessary (**Figure 3-23**).

Responsibilities and Functions

Utilizing information available from both the antemortem and post mortem records through manual and/ or computer techniques, records and radiographs are compared so that a proper identification can be established (**Figures 3-24 and 3-25**). After the completion of antemortem and post mortem files the task of comparison for identification begins. If available and the dental staff are well trained in their use, computers can greatly simplify this procedure (**Figure 3-26**). The filed records can be pulled when the computer suggests a possible identification for verification. Remember, however, that computers do not identify victims through dental means, trained odontologists do.

If computers are not available, completed antemortem records can be spread on a table and post mortem records compared individually for possible identifications. If records have been separated according to sex and age, comparing males with females is avoided and reduces the time involved. When possible identification is obtained, all available information is evaluated to verify the identification. This information is placed in the file bearing the decedent's name along with the combined antemortem and post mortem records.

Identified casualties should be filed in a separate section. Dental identification information is then conveyed to the dental team leader. The final process is again reviewed by the team leader and/or the antemortem or post mortem section leader in the former's absence. The positive identification is then communicated to the medical examiner/coroner by the dental

The Crash
of
United Airlines
Flight 232
DC10-10
Sioux City, Iowa
July 19, 1989

Victim Identification Report

Prepared for:

Thomas L. Bennett, MD
Iowa State Medical Examiner

by:
E. Steven Smith, DDS   Raymon D. Rawson, DDS, MA   Forrest A. Lorz, BSEE

Figure 3-25: The first page in the final report of the Sioux City air disaster.

Figure 3-26: The computer station for final comparison and identity determination.

team leader. This report should include a description of how the identification was made.

Prior to final verification of the identification of human remains in a mass fatality incident, the forensic odontologist should cross reference the dental evidence with data obtained by experts in other forensic disciplines including fingerprint records, pathology reports, anthropologic information and analysis of DNA from the victim. If available on site at a Mass Fatality Incident (MFI), utilization of the Victim Identification Profile (VIP) software program may be a very efficient option for obtaining the cross-referenced forensic information previously described

Computer System

The use of computerization to assist in the comparison of post mortem and antemortem records has become an important part of the multiple fatality incident protocol. The computer assists the odontologist in the

elimination of certain records; making the process of comparison more efficient. The system utilized should be efficient, easy to learn, and should generate a final product that can be understood by non-trained individuals. It is important to remember that the purpose of any computer system used to facilitate the antemortem/ post mortem record comparison process is not to make identifications, but merely to increase the efficiency of the investigative team. Commonly used computer programs available to assist in the identification procedure include:

- CAPMI- 4 Computer Assisted Post Mortem Identification) software program

- AFIP The system is precise and capable of eliminating between 92 percent and 99.9 percent of unmatchable antemortem records sorted against post mortem records.

- WinID3- www.winid.com/index.htm. This dental computer system matches missing persons to unidentified human remains by using dental and anthropometric characteristics to rank possible matches. Information about restored dental surfaces, physical descriptors, and pathological and anthropologic findings can be entered into the WinID database. The WinID software stores data in a Microsoft Access Database providing extensive data filtering and data sorting capabilities.

Both programs allow the investigator to limit the scope of the investigation to a small percentage of the total number of antemortem records. Since all of the data from the composite antemortem record of each putative victim is compared to the post mortem dental information obtained from all decedents' records there are only three possible results for each tooth from such comparisons:

- Match - the status of the tooth is the same between records.

- Possible Match - the post mortem status could have evolved since the antemortem status.

- Mismatch - There is no possible match.

These programs are capable of taking a minimal amount of information from incomplete dental remains and narrowing the search field. This makes computer assistance in identification such a valuable tool for the forensic dentistry section in a multiple fatality incident exercise. However, there is a caveat that needs to be remembered when using any data base program. Their capabilities are susceptible to error if the quality of the input data is poor. The axiom *garbage in - garbage out* could not be more appropriately applied than with computer identification programs in forensic dental multiple fatality incident scenarios.

The dental team is part of a large, integral multiple fatality incident plan. This plan is usually maintained and reviewed periodically by the Emergency Management Services of a particular county, municipality, or state. It is imperative that a representative (team leader) of the forensic dental team be invited to participate in these planning sessions. During these planning sessions, such procedures as fire response, crowd control, security, body recovery, morgue setup and supply, food provision for staff and responsibilities and functions of funeral directors, pathologist, odontologists, anthropologists, fingerprint experts, psychologists and clergy are discussed. For a successful operation during a multiple fatality incident, each division must work as a team and rely on other sections to also perform their tasks in a team setting.

Efficiency is sacrificed when divisions overlap and duplicate their duties. The forensic dental identification team has an important role that is both physically and mentally trying. Don't contribute to errors by getting involved in the responsibilities of other disciplines.

Following deployment, debriefing meetings should be held with the entire team and with individual participants. A mental health specialist should be available during these sessions to help with problems associated with post traumatic stress and mental fatigue among team members. Each team member is an individual and responds differently to the emotional trauma experienced in a multiple fatality incident deployment. The use of training sessions at the morgue or through presentations of previous multiple fatality incident situations will help team members. However, no one is completely prepared psychologically for what will be encountered at a multiple fatality incident site. Even though multiple fatality incident s may be similar, each one is unique and the more prepared individuals are before the multiple fatality incident occurs, the easier it will be for the team during the most trying times once activated.

Compensation:

As dentists, we have a moral responsibility to ourselves and our community when asked to help in a multiple fatality incident situation. It is extremely difficult to put a *dollar value* on time spent for such a humanitarian effort. However, team leaders must be prepared to respond to the question of compensating the members of their dental identification team. Since multiple fatality incident workers such as police, firepersons, funeral directors, medical examiners, etc. are paid - must the dental team be composed of volunteers? Dental expertise is needed and as recognized professionals dentists and auxiliary staff should not feel that they must volunteer their services. However, oral health providers must be realistic in the amount of compensation they are likely to receive for their efforts. Each multiple fatality incident and assimilated multiple fatality incident team is different and Individual situations must be evaluated regarding the value to place on the identification task.

The following guidelines may help address questions concerning the appropriateness and amount of compensation:

- Is the team composed of members who have private practices or are they affiliated with a university, federal or state agency?

- What is the team member's role during the identification process (i.e., team leader, section leader, team member, auxiliary or student)?

- Is compensation based on an hourly or daily rate?

Many protocols have emerged concerning the issue of compensation. Some odontologists have been compensated based on a fee per case basis that corresponds to the normal and customary fee received from that jurisdiction for any other identification case. Some feel that compensation to team members should be by their job description (i.e., team leader, section leader, alternate section leader, dental personnel, dental auxiliary (assistant, hygienist), students, etc.). Others believe that compensation should be calculated on a daily basis. Whatever the means of compensation it should be remembered that all team members have volunteered. Therefore, any compensation received will be minimal compared to the time deployed and out-of-office time expended.

Dental team members must be aware that a multiple fatality incident is a sensitive situation that presents trying times to the families of the victims. The media can present additional pressure to team members to disclose what is being done and who has been identified. It is advised that no dental identification team members talk with representatives of the media. If a situation arises, the team leader should speak for the dental team. Typically, the medical examiner/coroner or media spokesperson from these offices will be the media contact person for the identification effort.

DMORT and DMAT

History of DMORT

At 9 PM on October 20, 1978, the U.S. Coast Guard ship Cuyahoga was struck by the Argentine coal freighter Santa Cruz II. The Coast Guard ship sank within minutes in 58 feet of water with the loss of eleven men. As a partial result of this accident the Coast Guard instituted more stringent certifications and controls. This multi-casualty and multi-fatality incident and others that had occurred prompted Coast Guard officials to recognize the need for specially trained groups to respond in emergency situations. The concentration of families of the victims and emotional involvements generated by the accident created an adverse climate which potentially disrupted continuity of operations. Additionally, morale of surviving Coast Guard personnel became compromised.

Based on this incident the Coast Guard established a Casualty Assistance Response Team (CART) which was approved and implemented in April, 1979. This plan outlined the various specialties and personnel and the federal and service organizations from which they could be mobilized in the event of a multiple fatality incident situation. The Navy was requested to assist despite problems created by the fact that the Coast Guard was administered by the Department of Transportation and the Navy and other military service by the Department of Defense. A memorandum of understanding outlining how the service would cooperate in the event of a multiple fatality incident or emergency was initiated by the Navy.

In July, 1983, Dr. C. Everett Koop, the United States Surgeon General, requested a plan for a dental forensic team to be used in multiple fatality incidents. Dr. Robert Mecklinberg, chief dental officer of the U.S. Public Health Service (USPHS) received this request and Dr. E. D. Woolridge was chosen to serve as project officer with the charge of writing a policy position paper with recommendations concerning the advantages and disadvantages of establishing a forensic dental capability within the USPHS. The initial component of this plan was submitted in December, 1983.

By 1989 the USPHS requested a plan for the organization of a forensic dental team for mass casualty multiple fatality incident s. A committee consisting of E. D. Woolridge, chairperson, Norman Clark, project officer and Donald Schnieder began working on this project while conferring with ABFO and AAFS members who were consultants. These contributors included Drs. William Eckert, Director and Milton Helpern International Center for the Forensic Sciences, Wichita State University and Dr. Richard Froede, Chief Medical Examiner, Armed Forces Institute of Pathology (AFIP) and twelve of the founding diplomates of the ABFO.

The completed plan for the organization of a forensic dental team for mass casualty multiple fatality incident s was submitted on September 30, 1989 and approved the following month. This document was used to develop a memorandum of understanding between the USPS and the AFIP. It has been implemented on various occasions. Some Public Health dentists and oral and maxillofacial pathologists from the AFIP have been deployed as forensic dental multiple fatality incident team members to various aircraft accidents involving military planes. They have also assisted in the turret explosion multiple fatality incident on the battleship Iowa.

Concurrent to the actions described above, in the early 1980's a committee was formed within the National Funeral Director Association (NFDA) to address multiple fatality incident situations and more specifically mass fatalities. Members of this particular group had had difficulties in past cases due to a lack of standardization. Each multiple fatality incident scenario was handled differently depending on location and whether local and/or federal assistance was provided. Initial interest in this committee was mortuary profession. These funeral directors soon discovered that the task was just too immense for one group to handle and others with vested interests in multiple fatality incident issues became part of the group.

A nonprofit volunteer organization was formed which was open to all forensic practitioners. The purpose of this group was to create a national level response protocol for all related and interested professions. This group formed and purchased the equipment and supplies for the first portable morgue unit in the country. There are now two operational units located in Rockville, Maryland and Sacramento, California and a third unit is proposed for Dallas, Texas. Units have been on missions in Illinois, Indiana, Guam, Michigan and Texas.

Once this group of volunteers had formed, the federal government became vitally interested in it. After a series of aircraft and similar multiple fatality incident s the families who had lost loved ones felt that the treatment they had received was less than adequate. They demanded and received a response from Congress which passed the Family Assistance Act in October of 1996. This legislation required all American based airlines (and later all airlines operating in the US) to have plans in place to assist families in case of an accident. This has led to the development and staffing of the Family Assistance Center in DMORT operations.

Multiple Fatality Incident Mortuary Operational Team (DMORT)

Organizational Structure of DMORT

DMORT was initially formed under the Department of Health and Human Services (DHHS). In 2003, administrative responsibility for DMORT was transferred to the Department of Homeland Security where it is one of three components of the National Disaster Medical System (NDMS). As of January, 2007 administration of DMORT will be returned to DHHS. The other components of NDMS are Disaster Medical Assistance Teams (DMAT) and Veterinary Medical Assistance Teams (VMAT). The NDMS is part of Federal Emergency Management Agency (FEMA), As previously noted, the National Response Plan charges the NDMS with responsibility to provide victim identification and mortuary services in a multiple fatality incident situation. This is designated under the ESF #8 directive and accomplished by establishing Disaster Mortuary Operational Response Teams (DMORTs).

Among those responsible for the development of the USPHS plan for the organization of a forensic dental multiple fatality incident team, some are of the opinion that this project may have facilitated the bureaucratic processes involved in the formation of DMORT. As previously discussed, planning was already in place for a Public Health Dental Multiple Fatality Incident Team. The late Tom Shepardson and others were able to take some of these USPHS documents and use them as a starting point in the development of DMORT. This has resulted in the creation of a highly effective DMORT program which is capable of deployment to any location in the world at a moment's notice.

In support of the DMORT program, two Multiple fatality incident Portable Morgue Units (DPMUs) are maintained by the Department of Homeland Security (DHS) and Federal Emergency Management Agency (FEMA) Response Divisions. These are staged at FEMA Logistics Centers, in Rockville, MD and San Jose, CA and are depositories of equipment and supplies for deployment to a multiple fatality incident site. Each DPMU contains a complete morgue with designated workstations for each processing element and prepackaged equipment and supplies.

The ten regional DMORT teams are organized throughout the United States corresponding to the ten regional divisions of FEMA. Each team is independent within NDMS and works under local jurisdictional authorities such as coroner/ medical examiners and law enforcement and emergency managers (**Figure 3-27**). Each team includes a Regional Commander, Deputy Commander, Administrative Officer and Training Officer.

DMORTs provide technical assistance and personnel to these agencies to facilitate

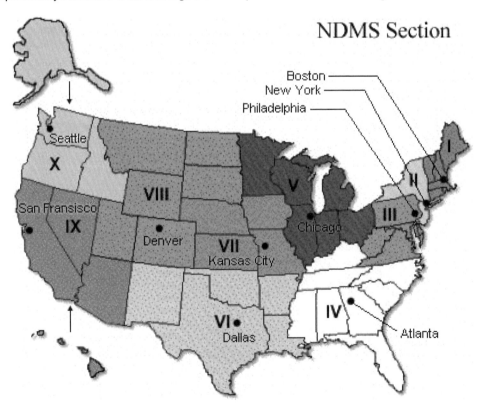

Figure 3-27: Ten regional divisions of FEMA and the national organization of DMORT

recovery, identification and processing of deceased victims and provide logistical support through the deployment of temporary morgue facilities. One or more of the teams may be activated when a multiple fatality incident occurs. Each is composed of a number of forensic specialists who are private citizens having expertise in the following disciplines (**Figure 3-28**). The reader is referred to **Appendix G** for information concerning membership:

- Funeral directors/embalmers
- Medical examiners

- Coroners
- Forensic pathologists

- Forensic anthropologists
- Fingerprint specialists

- Forensic odontologists
- Dental auxiliaries

- X-ray technicians
- Forensic photographers

- DNA specialists

Additionally, essential support personnel (ESP) are a component of each team and include:

- Computer specialists
- Mental health specialists

- Medical records technicians
- Medical records transcriptionists

- Investigative personnel
- Security personnel

- Evidence specialists
- Administrative support staff

- Heavy equipment operators
- Facility maintenance personnel

Team members must maintain appropriate certifications and licensure within their discipline. When activated, the member's licensure and certification is recognized by all

Figure 3-28 : Members of the various disciplines of a DMORT Response Team, Kirksville, Missouri, 2004

States. DMORT members are compensated for their duty time by the Federal government as temporary Federal employees.

The initial DMORT deployment occurred in 1993 with the cemetery desecration caused by the floods in Hardin, Missouri. Other notable deployments were the Murrah Federal Building explosion in Oklahoma City in 1995, the Korean Airline crash on Guam in 1997, 9/11 terrorist events in 2001 in New York City, the search and recovery of the shuttle Columbia in Texas and Louisiana in 2003 and most recently as part of the federal multiple fatality incident response for the recovery and identification of Hurricane Katrina victims in 2005. DMORT has continued to experience tremendous growth since the early 1990s to the current group of over 1200 trained personnel who are capable of responding promptly to a national multiple fatality incident.

Composition of DMORT Strike Teams

The DMORT Strike Teams are deployed as an initial response at a multiple fatality incident site. They are intended to provide an assessment of the comprehensive personnel needs of the Regional Team(s). Strike Teams are composed of a Mortuary Officer, Dentist, Dental Assistant, Fingerprint Specialist and Family Assistance Specialist. Deployment of adequate personnel is dependent on an accurate assessment by the Strike Team of the essential needs of the Team.

The following discussion describes the role

Figure 3-29: Views of the destruction caused by Katrina. All basic infrastructure was damaged, and essential public services were non-existent.

of DMORT dental personnel in the recovery and identification of Hurricane Katrina victims. It provides a chronology of the storm, epidemiologic information concerning the magnitude of the multiple fatality incident in infrastructural and human terms and describes real time experiences of DMORT strike team and DMORT team members in the field. Suggestions are offered for the development of improved protocols for use in future multiple fatality incident s based on the *evidence based knowledge* acquired concerning the logistical, technical and personnel problems encountered by those DMORT members deployed in the Katrina multiple fatality incident .

Interaction with Local Authorities

By the time Hurricane Katrina had swept through the Gulf area, it was the most destructive multiple fatality incident in U.S. history. "The overall area of destruction wrought by Hurricane Katrina, which was both a large and powerful hurricane as well as a catastrophic flood, vastly exceeded that of any other major multiple fatality incident , such as the Chicago Fire of 1871, the San Francisco Earthquake and Fire of 1906, and Hurricane Andrew in 1992." The destruction caused by Hurricane Katrina involved the states of Florida, Alabama, Mississippi, and Louisiana. Nearly 93,000 square miles were involved, across 138 parishes and counties (**Figure 3-29**). The Florida landfall in the Broward-Dade county area resulted in more than a dozen deaths. Upon impact in the Gulf coastal area, Katrina had storm surges that crested up to twenty-seven feet high resulting in overwhelming destruction to businesses, homes, and property for many miles inland.

"This storm surge overwhelmed levees all along the lowest reaches of the Mississippi River and the edges of Lake Pontchartrain. The consequences for New Orleans, which sits primarily below sea level, were dire. Significant levee failures occurred on the 17th Street Canal, the Industrial Canal, and the London Avenue Canal. Approximately eighty percent of the city was flooded. Even beyond New Orleans, Katrina's span of

destruction was widespread. Indeed, one of the gravest challenges presented by this particular multiple fatality incident was the vast geographic distribution of the damage. Towns and cities, small and large, were destroyed or heavily damaged along the Gulf Coast and miles inland. From Morgan City, Louisiana, to Biloxi, Mississippi, to Mobile, Alabama, Hurricane Katrina's wind, rain, and storm surge demolished homes and businesses. Large parts of the coastal areas of these States were devastated."

The loss of life from Hurricane Katrina is estimated at 1,300 people. The majority of the fatalities (estimated at 80 percent), came from the New Orleans metropolitan area. However, the Mississippi areas which took the brunt of the storm surge and wind of Katrina suffered with 231 fatalities. Many of the dead were elderly or infirmed. The special needs of these citizens were often not met. In Louisiana, approximately seventy-one percent of the victims were older than sixty, and forty seven percent of those were over seventy five. At least sixty eight were found in nursing homes, some of whom were allegedly abandoned by their caretakers. Of the total known fatalities, almost two hundred unclaimed bodies remain at the Victim Identification Center in Carville, Louisiana. Although these are horrifying statistics, as of February 17, 2006, there were still 2,096 people from the Gulf Coast area reported missing.

Hurricane Katrina began on August 23, 2005 as Tropical Depression Twelve having formed over the Bahamas. On August 24, 2005 this tropical depression strengthened into a tropical storm and was named Katrina. During the day of August 25th, this storm continued to gain strength and as it approached the coast of Florida, it was upgraded to a Category 1 hurricane. Katrina made landfall in the Broward – Miami Dade counties at 6:30pm and cut a path of destruction across the Florida peninsula. Katrina entered the Gulf of Mexico on August 26, 2005 as a tropical storm and continued to move to the west.

The warm waters of the Gulf of Mexico allowed Katrina to intensify into a Category 2 hurricane. At this time projections were made that Katrina

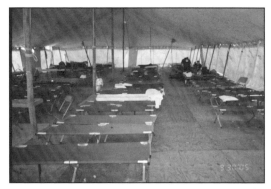

Figure 3-30: Deployment of the Nevada-1 DMAT team which parallels the DMORT facilities, organization and command structure.

would make landfall just east of New Orleans as a Category 4 or 5 Hurricane. Due to Hurricane Katrina's continuing intensification and this projected landfall, Louisiana Governor Kathleen Blanco and Mississippi Governor Haley Barbour declared states of emergency for their respective States. On August 27, 2005 Hurricane Katrina strengthened to a Category 3 storm and nearly doubled in size over the course of the day. On the morning of August 27th, forty-eight hours before Hurricane Katrina's second landfall, FEMA headquarters commenced Level 1 operations and began activating the National Multiple fatality incident Medical System (NDMS),

Multiple fatality incident Medical Assistance Teams (DMATs), Multiple Fatality Incident Mortuary Operations Response Teams (DMORT) and Urban Search and Rescue (US&R) were mobilized. (**Figure 3-30**) That evening, President Bush signed a Federal emergency declaration for the State of Louisiana following a request from Governor Blanco earlier that day. The President

issued additional emergency declarations for Mississippi and Alabama the following day after requests from the governors of those States. On August 27th Hurricane Katrina developed from a Category 4 to a Category 5 storm and became increasingly large.

"Hurricane Katrina made landfall as a powerful Category 3 storm at 6:10 am CDT on Monday, August 29th in Plaquemines Parish, Louisiana. The massive storm continued to move north, rolling over portions of the Louisiana coast before its eye came ashore near the mouth of the Pearl River in Mississippi. At the time, Hurricane Katrina had sustained winds over 115 mph and reported gusts as high as 130 mph. The storm rapidly lost strength as it pushed inland through southern and central Mississippi and by 1:00 pm CDT, it had weakened to a Category 1 hurricane. Six hours later, as it passed northwest of Meridian, Mississippi, and was further downgraded to a tropical storm."

Under the National Response Plan all mortuary affairs are generally a state and local responsibility with the DMORT teams operating under this local leadership. DMORT 1, DMORT 2, DMORT 4, DMORT 5 and DMORT Family Assistance Center (east) along with one DPMU were deployed to the Gulfport – Biloxi Municipal Airport. DMORT 6, DMORT 7, DMORT 8, DMORT WMD, and DMORT Family Assistance Center (west), along with one DPMU, were deployed to St. Gabriel, Louisiana. In Mississippi, Harrison County Coroner Gary Hargrove was the primary coroner working with the DMORT East location and serving as the liaison with the other county coroners in Mississippi. In Louisiana, the DMORT West location worked under the direction of Dr. Louis Cataldie who was appointed by the State of Louisiana from the Baton Rouge Medical Examiner's office.

Deployment of DMORT Personnel

Command Structure of DMORT

DMORT is one of three divisions of the National Multiple fatality incident Medical System (NDMS). As a component of FEMA the director of NDMS reports to the head of the former agency. FEMA in turn is part of the Department of Homeland Security, a Cabinet level agency currently lead by Secretary Michael Chertoff. As a member of the President's Cabinet, Secretary Chertoff reports to and is directly commanded by the President of the United States. Therefore, the President provides direction to the Secretary who passes his orders on to the FEMA Director. In turn, the director of FEMA instructs the NDMS director as to the appropriate response from that agency concerning deployment of DMORT and DMAT units.

Subsequently, NDMS approves deployment of DMORT personnel when deemed necessary. Each DMORT team is independent in the NDMS system and is under the direction of a Regional Commander. Control of operations at a multiple fatality incident site is determined by the location of the multiple fatality incident. The Regional Commander where an incident occurs is in command of the operation. All DMORT personnel report to the Commander under the Incident Command System (ICS) in accordance with the National Incident Management System (NIMS).

Control of Deployment to Multiple Fatality incident Sites

As a program of the Department of Homeland Security, DMORT responds **ONLY** when requested. DMORT services may be requested by any municipality in need of such assistance. This request must come through departmental channels to a local Emergency Management Agency (EMA). The Regional Commander makes the decisions concerning how each mission will operate including the number and type of personnel that are to be deployed. All those deployed from a team must have the authorization of the Team Commander (Regional Commander) prior to deployment. In addition, deployment of personnel from one team to another must also have approval of the appropriate Regional Commander. On a daily basis, the Team Commander is assisted by the Deputy Commanders and Administrative Officers of each Region. In the Katrina deployment the following command structure was employed:

- **DMORT East – Gulfport, Mississippi**

   Control of DMORT East operations were directed by Region IV Commander Cotton Howell. This decision was based on the fact that Mississippi is part of DMORT Region IV(AL,FL,GA,KY,MS,NC,SC,TN)

- **DMORT West – St. Gabriel, Louisiana**

   Control of DMORT West operations were directed by Region VI Commander Todd Ellis. This decision was based on the fact that Louisiana is part of DMORT Region VI (AR, LA, NM, OK and TX)

Coordination of Personnel Needs with On Site Demands

Prior to Katrina, the State of Louisiana did not have any state-wide official serving in the role of state medical examiner. Additionally, there was no official with jurisdiction over the sixty-four elected parish coroners. Therefore, coordination in the face of a multiple fatality incident such as Katrina (especially when complicated three weeks later by hurricane Rita) was non-existent. DMORT had to deal with each parish as an independent entity. Historically, the Orleans Parish Coroner's Office has handled autopsies for the neighboring parish of St. Bernard at the facility in downtown New Orleans. That facility was completely destroyed and flooded by fifteen feet of water for nearly a month. All supplies and equipment were lost. Many employees were unable to return to work. This included several staff pathologists formerly employed by the LSU Medical Center who also staffed the post mortem facility.

With a population 425,000, neighboring Jefferson Parish historically provided autopsy service for Plaquemines Parish in the modern Jefferson Forensic Center. This facility suffered virtually no damage in the storms. Plaquemines parish sustained substantial damage from storm surge, flooding, and wind. St. Bernard Parish suffered virtually 100 percent devastation from storm surge as well as the aftereffects of flood and wind damage. An unknown, but expected to be significant number of dead, were located in each of the four parishes.

Within two days after the storm, DMORT had secured an approximate ten acre site in St. Gabriel, Louisiana about sixty miles northwest of New Orleans for use as a temporary morgue facility. The site contained a closed elementary school campus (then currently in partial use as the municipal offices of the town of St. Gabriel) and abutted a warehouse of over 100,000 square feet with a loading dock and parking area. Temporary food service and sanitary facilities were brought in through cooperation with the US Forest Service and tents were erected to supplement the sleeping quarters carved from the classrooms and cafeteria of the school. The gymnasium was used as a warehouse for FEMA supplies.

The Orleans Parish Coroners Office requested

to join in the DMORT effort and was allowed to establish a temporary morgue facility within the DMORT morgue. This facility eventually processed human remains that were not classified as flood victims including deaths prior to Katrina that had not been autopsied, deaths post-Katrina that were not storm related, and autopsies in which a medico-legal opinion was felt to be needed (hospital and long term care facility fatalities). The Jefferson Parish Coroner (and therefore the Plaquemines Parish Coroner) declined to participate in the DMORT operation.

Human remains recovered in Jefferson and Plaquemines parishes were handled through the Jefferson facility. A decision was made at the state level to engage a commercial multiple fatality incident services company to recover any human remains found in the remaining parishes for transport to DMORT. Through an Executive Order, the Governor of Louisiana appointed a former coroner of East Baton Rouge Parish as the State Medical Examiner for Multiple fatality incidents. This individual would serve as the liaison between FEMA, the State of Louisiana and the local coroners.

The preliminary estimates of deaths in Louisiana ranged from a few thousand to over 60,000 as suggested by a mock hurricane multiple fatality incident scenario practiced in New Orleans in the summer of 2004. Based on those estimates, a decision was made to staff the morgue on a 24 hour basis with a goal of processing 144 sets of remains in each 24 hour period as soon as the DPMU was unpacked and made serviceable. In the case of the dental unit, this required staffing of 27 individual dentists which was more than double the number of dental members of DMORT Region VI. Even with three examination stations functioning, this level of output would also exceed by a large margin the dental output in any previous multiple fatality incident .

Despite these concerns, The Region VI DMORT dental unit felt comfortable in accepting the challenge because this would be the first time that an all digital dental forensic identification effort and use of battery-powered x-ray generators would be employed. These hand-held devices coupled with a newly refined digital dental radiograph capture program in conjunction with WinID identification computer software was thought to make the team equal to the task.

Initially, the three examination stations were linked together in a LAN whose server was contained in the dental morgue station. Eventually, the post mortem and antemortem dental sections would operate through a LAN whose server would be housed in the facility-wide IT office. Employing a digital, paperless dental identification model requires that the data collected must be stored in a fashion that is accessible to all potential users of the data. Therefore, all of the photographs, radiographs, and dental information flowing from each dental station and each set of remains was stored only on the server. Ultimately, the dental server (or system server) would also contain the antemortem dental information, the personal effects photographs, the digital full-body radiographs, and the VIP database.

It was the initial task of the dental team's IT expert to make certain that the LAN functioned, that all data was regularly backed-up and that the dental data could be transferred to any other server as needed as the multiple fatality incident IT effort matured. The initial server for the dental section was a mid 1990s Pentium II laptop. Because *modern* operating systems such as MS Windows XP cannot serve as a server, the older laptop with Windows 2000 was pressed into service.

At least during the initial stages of the Katrina DMORT exercise, the shift team leader had to work closely with the IT expert to schedule on-going data back-ups. This became quite involved because the demand on the laptop required that it function beyond its design capability and back-up was slow. Additionally, each of the three dental teams performing the post mortem examinations had to have completed a case prior to starting a new one before any back-up could be initiated. With no paper back-up extant, the computer data represented the entire work product of the shift. Because the morgue was operating on generator power with attendant power fluctuations, frequent back-up was required.

Initially, the problems faced by the dental teams were limited to computer issues. These were partially resolved when a member of the team was able to arrange a donation of desktop servers and back-up drives from his local computer supplier in Omaha, Nebraska. The Dell Corporation also donated a desktop unit for use in the dental section. These donations greatly reduced the amount of time needed for back-up and were much more robust in the processing and storage of dental data.

Throughout the deployment there were additional morgue-wide problems that required resolution. Some of these included the following:

- The full body radiograph system did not function as expected

- The FBI fingerprint team became a bottleneck point in the flow of remains through the morgue

- The morgue temperatures reached over 100 degrees F during the afternoons on several days requiring that the facility be closed

-There were occasional shortages of personal protective equipment

- It was simply not possible to operate two 12 hour shifts due to the heat and noise which made day-sleeping impossible. There was no ability to house individuals off-site because of the infrastructural damage to the community in which the morgue was located. The morgue's operation was switched to a single twelve hour shift basis. The two 13 person dental teams adapted by having each shift work a four-hour rotation (6:00 am to 10:00 am and 1:00 pm to 4:00 pm). Both teams worked together from 4:00 pm until the day's schedule was completed **(Figure 3-31).**

Figure 3-31: DMORT Post Mortem Dental Identi-fication Teams in St. Gabriel Morgue Louisiana, 2005.

- As the biweekly rotation of new members continued, the dental team was reduced to approximately fourteen members.

On the busiest day, the entire morgue including the dental section processed 78 sets of remains in approximately ten hours exceeding the goal of 72 cases every twelve hours. The specific membership and designated tasks of post mortem dental team members is discussed in the *Post Mortem Section*.

Planning for Long Term Disaster Recovery

During the first weeks of the exercise it was decided that a more permanent facility, designed to accomplish the required tasks, would be necessary. Prior to September 30th an order was placed for a morgue facility to be constructed at Carville, Louisiana on the east bank of the Mississippi River about eight miles south of the St. Gabriel facility (**Figure 3-32**). That facility was occupied before Thanksgiving. Built on 32 acres, the compound included:

- Secure storage for scores of semi-trailers storing human remains and coffin remains

- Six fifty-person dormitories with overflow sleeping for 250

- A spacious morgue facility with:

- Work stations for each discipline

- An administrative complex housing office space for each discipline

- Supply warehouse

- Common area for relaxation and meetings

- Exercise facility

- Food service facility

This facility was occupied until Day 167 following the storm in mid-February 2006. During that time at both facilities 856 remains of flood victims and 414 displaced casket remains were examined by the dental team. Approximately 327 antemortem dental records were received. Since the closing of the Carville facility twenty-five additional sets of human remains have been processed in the Orleans Parish Coroner's Office. There are still over 200 individuals listed as missing who had residences within the major flood zone of Orleans Parish.

The number of dental identifications forthcoming from the efforts of the DMORT dental teams deployed during this multiple fatality incident bears some comment. Approximately 150 identifications were credited to the dental team. Most consisted of the *standard* dental identification whereby the antemortem record and the post mortem finding were compared and determined to have

Figure 3-32: Permanent Morgue Facility in Carville, LA. (2006)

a common origin. However, several of these were somewhat less traditional due in part to the feature of this multiple fatality incident that had the greatest impact on the identification effort overall - *the lack of antemortem material to which comparisons could be made.*

The flooding in the metropolitan New Orleans area covered over 100 square miles for up to thirty days. More that 140,000 housing units were flooded, and an estimated 300,000+ automobiles alone were destroyed. Dental and medical offices as well as hospital record departments lost all of their records. This was further complicated by the dispersion of the survivors and evacuees to all corners of America. The evacuees included the very dentists and physicians whose records were being sought by the DMORT teams. The communication infrastructure in South Louisiana was similarly destroyed making contact with and between evacuees difficult at best.

After prodding by members of the dental team shortly after the initial deployment, FEMA hired a local dentist from New Orleans. This individual was tasked with retrieving dental records from flooded offices. This retrieval process included both individual records of persons known or suspected to be missing and entire record banks from offices where the structure in which they were housed was deemed at risk. An estimated 200,000 records were gathered and stored at the Carville facility. Many, if not most, of these were illegible and the radiographs were unreadable because of water damage from the flooding. Despite these hardships, the dental teams were able to help confirm or contribute to the identification of many individuals by simply confirming that someone had (or did not have) dentures; had a particular missing, discolored, or broken tooth; had an uneven smile line; had a diastema or other oral feature that could be confirmed or denied by relatives or associates.

Technical Needs of the Dental Section

Introduction

Technology has touched the forensic community and carried it into a new century. Computer programs, computer hardware and new innovations are continually emerging. All statements herein are made with the technology available at the time of response to Hurricane Katrina. . With this understanding, a current assessment of technology available to forensic odontologists will be reviewed.

Computer Hardware for a Mass Fatality Incident

The decision as to what is appropriate for each incident rests mainly on the estimated number of fatalities. A basic network along with antemortem and post mortem stations will be outlined. This basic network can be expanded to create a system adequate for the needs of any size operation. Resources in the system can be re-allocated as the operation matures to reflect the dynamic changes of the operation. As an example, post mortem workstations can be changed to antemortem workstations for more comparison teams as post mortem operations wind down. The versatility of these systems makes them very responsive to need. The paperless operation also protects case integrity and prevents loss of evidence or misfiling of traditional information in folder systems.

The heart of a network is the server. The server is a dedicated computer that connects all the workstations together and stores all of the data involved with an operation. A server network allows each workstation to access information on a real time basis. Therefore, once new data has been entered, it is available to all members of the network immediately. Microsoft Server software or compatible software is the recommended operating system for the server. Microsoft Server 2003 was used for the Katrina Operation. This type of software allows the administrator to assign permissions for access and control the flow of information as well as troubleshooting for network difficulties.

The server can reside anywhere there is ample space, but locating a server in the post mortem area would expose it to a potentially damaging environment. Whether the network is connected by cabling or a wireless connection is the decision of the administrator. In past experience, ease of cabling and security of the data makes the cabled system favored over the wireless system at the current time and was used for Katrina.

The hard drive size for the server should be as large as possible. With digital images and charting the data files can become quite large, for instance Katrina's dental data base was twenty-five gigabytes. Newer servers are now rated in terrabytes (1 terrabyte = 1024 gigabytes). This larger size server would be recommended for a major incident. Backup systems should be chosen by the administrator during the creation of the network. Rather than include a complete section on backups in this discussion it will suffice to state emphatically that it is necessary to provide for adequate backups for all stored data. The RAID 5 server used for Katina was a redundant drive system that continually backed up data on multiple drives.

A post mortem computer workstation consists of:

- A computer (laptop or desktop)

- A digital sensor to capture radiographs

- A radiation source

- A printer to allow printing of any necessary documents at the station.

These workstations are placed in a very demanding environment and the equipment must be protected from fluids and contamination. The size of the viewing screen should be adequate to facilitate viewing by all post mortem team members. Wired sensors (Dexis) performed well in past operations and were used for Katrina. They provided instant results on the computer screen for radiographic review and interpretation. Recently, a new hand-held, battery powered radiation

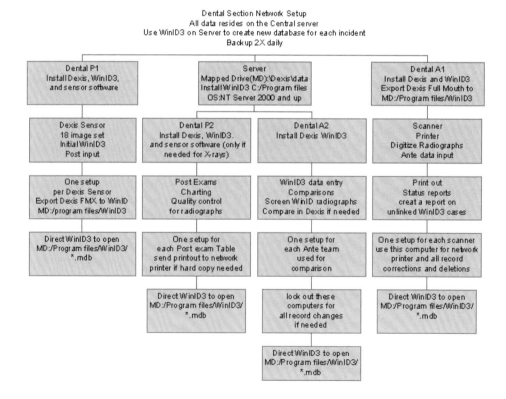

Figure 3-33: Organization of the dental section.

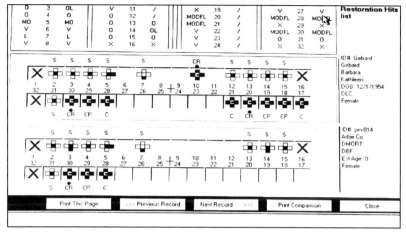

Figure 3-34: WinID Antemortem and Post Mortem Odontograms.

generator (Aribex Nomad) was added to the post mortem cache. This radiation source requires no stand and no power cable to interfere with sensor exposure.

During Katina, it was found that the post mortem team can process each victim in less than 30 minutes. To estimate the number of stations needed to process a known or estimated number of victims, one needs to decide the number of victims to be processed per shift and simply do the math. Once this victim data is entered into the system using the WinID victim identification software, it is ready to be searched by antemortem teams for identification possibilities.

The antemortem workstation consists of:

- A computer (laptop or desktop)

- Quiet secure work area

- Scanner with dental transparency unit to capture images and radiographs from antemortem records

- Any other items useful in interpreting antemortem records including camera, magnifying glass, scratch paper, etc.

The antemortem section has the most difficult job in the identification process. It must acquire antemortem dental records on all victims, verify chain of evidence on these records, and convert the myriad of charting and notation systems into the one composite antemortem record scheme accepted for the operation. It is very important to do all antemortem data input with a team of at least two experienced members. This allows checks and balances to always be in place and greatly reduces errors in dental charting.

The initial entry point for a new record is the scanning station. The initial entry should establish a correct and unique antemortem case number. The antemortem radiographs are scanned into the digital record which allows the original radiographs to be sealed and stored to prevent films from being lost or misplaced. The records can then be translated into the composite antemortem record system used for the current operation. The translated record can then be entered into WinID. The number of scanning stations can be adjusted for total number of cases to be entered. Experience indicates these should be limited to the most experienced team members and the fewest number of stations to accomplish the task.

All other antemortem workstations are for comparisons of post mortem cases against antemortem cases to complete the identification process. These comparison workstations do not need a scanner and are used for limited data entry. A simple chart (**Figure 3-33**) can be used to explain the network system. The chart can be changed to reflect the needs of the operation.

Computer Software for a Mass Fatality Incident

The comparison software used for the Katrina operation was WinID, developed by Dr. James McGivney. WinID is a MS Windows based program written in Visual Basic using MS Access for the database. The software allows for creation of multiple databases that can be used on different operations. It creates an antemortem and post mortem set of records that records tooth information and stores a radiographic image for screening choices during comparison. WinID uses an algorithm to intuitively compare antemortem and post mortem features allowing for normal and expected differences between the two. WinID then generates a *Best Match* screen that ranks possible records to either the antemortem or the post mortem target record. (**Figure 3-34**). This worked well with conventional radiographs, but created a need to scan all radiographs and use an additional graphics program create the screen image for the comparison window.

In 2003 Dr. McGivney teamed with the Dexis Corporation to create a bridge between WinID and the digital radiography program developed for use with the Dexis digital radiography sensor. This allowed for either scanning of antemortem radiographs or acquiring post mortem radiographs directly from the source and creating digital images which are immediately viewable and can be enhanced to maximize diagnostic quality. The Dexis software then automatically creates the screening image to be exported back to WinID for use during comparisons.

The *Dexis* button on WinID screen takes the user back to the fully functional Dexis program and the case radiographs for viewing. In essence, this creates a totally paperless environment. This system was used during the response to Hurricane Katrina. The software package of WinID /Dexis worked well and provided for not only viewing of radiographs for antemortem and post mortem cases, but also color images of pertinent identifying features. This system allowed dental team members to open antemortem records once and then file them in a secure area after they were transformed into digital images.

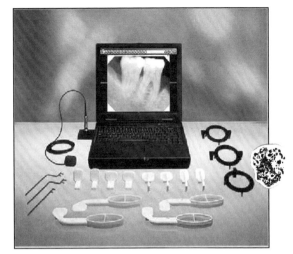

Figure 3-35: The Dexis digital radiography system

Radiography Equipment for a Mass Fatality Incident

The Dexis digital radiography system was used in the Hurricane Katina response. The software bridge with WinID makes it the system of choice for forensic odontology applications. The CCD (Charged Coupled Device) Sensor is a wired sensor that connects a computer through a PCMCIA slot adaptor (**Figure 3-35**). This system is *hot bootable* and can be switched between computers as needed. A full set of positioning tools allows the sensor to be placed in the most optimal position for diagnostic radiographs. The software can be programmed to automatically take the sequence of radiographs selected by the Dental Section Chief of the operation. During Katrina a standard eighteen film survey was used.

The Dexis program senses radiation and moves to the next area to be radiographed with no manual command. On the antemortem side of the program Dexis allows scanning of a full mouth set of radiographs as a single image and automatically separates individual images for the operator position on the screen. Digital photographs can also be taken and stored in the Dexis case folder. Once the full survey is acquired, the case is reviewed and charted in WinID. At this point the case is finished and ready for comparison to antemortem records.

Digital radiography eliminates the need for film developers and chemicals at the field operation site.

The radiation source used in response to Hurricane Katrina was a new hand-held battery operated device created by the Aribex Corporation and marketed as the Nomad (**Figure 3-36**).

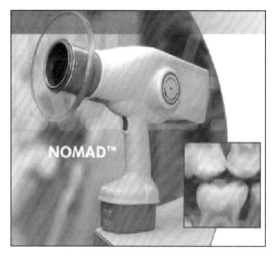

Figure 3-36:   The Nomad hand-held radiation source

The Nomad is approved for human use in dental offices and requires no additional shielding for the operator. The complete operator's manual and specifications are available online at the company's website. The Nomad allows easy access to victims and specimens in limited space. With the elimination of bulky overhead supports, which are required for conventional radiation heads, even more room is available for positioning team members around the examination area. The battery life is adequate for over 300 exposures. With the charger and extra battery, radiographic examinations can run on a continuous 24 hour rotation with only stops to replace the battery (30 seconds).

In reviewing the Katrina Operation, it can be said that by combining WinID and Dexis into a digital radiographic and comparison software package and using the hand-held Nomad radiography unit, the process of post mortem examination and documentation has become a paperless process. The efficiency of the system means that rather than a post mortem process taking over an hour, it now has become a much shorter process yielding a product equal to conventionally acquired evidence.

Dental Section Protocols

Antemortem Section

In Gulfport, Mississippi the DMORT morgue facility was accepting and processing the deceased, utilizing generators for electricity. The infrastructure of the area was not operational - no electricity, phone service, or water. However, there was sporadic cell phone service. DMORT was provided with a communications truck that utilized satellite technology to provide telephone and internet communications. The dental antemortem section decided to be proactive rather than wait for the return of electricity and phone service.

Due to the destruction of utilities, dental offices in the area were not operational. In addition, numerous dental offices had been destroyed by the storm surge of Hurricane Katrina. Therefore, the dental antemortem section of DMORT East established an e-mail address to facilitate communications with the surrounding community. This communications link was particularly important for local dentists who had no phone or mail service.

The section received (via e-mail) a list from the Mississippi State Board of Dentistry of all the dentists in the affected area along with their contact information. In addition, the dental section contacted the local VA Hospital, Dental School as well as all public health dental clinics as a source of possible dental records. During the first week after the multiple fatality incident the dental antemortem section wrote a letter to the affected dentists in the Mississippi area requesting their assistance. The purpose for the presence of DMORT was explained along with an appeal to provide *original* radiographs and charts if requested. This was considered an introductory letter to the dentists and a second written request was sent when an actual patient's record was needed.

Although no mail was being delivered at the time, these introductory letters were addressed and mailed to all the local dentists. Eventually, the dentists would receive their mail and it was believed that the local dentists wanted to be of assistance, but felt hampered by their inability to communicate with the DMORT dental team. This letter provided a means to both explain the DMORT presence and also provide contact information.

DMORT dentists also went personally to the various dental offices to evaluate their status for availability of dental records and deliver a copy of the introductory letter. This was often simply taped to the front door of the office. This facilitated early contact with the local dentists. The dental offices were in various states of disrepair, ranging from only wind damage to complete destruction. Contact was also attempted with two different local dental laboratories by personally visiting their locations. One of these facilities was open and provided valuable information regarding the status of area dental offices and when the practitioners were hoping to return to work.

The antemortem records system was designed and implemented before any antemortem records were received. This included a means to track the antemortem record, it's entry into WinID 3, and the scanning of the antemortem radiographs. This organization allowed for an easy transition from dentists processing post mortem victims into antemortem record workup and entry into WIND 3. E-mail communication was critical in the early stages of this multiple fatality incident before phone service was predictable. It enabled information to be sent easily to the DMORT teams from other parts of the state and country.

If a dental office was destroyed which housed a putative victim's records, other means were necessary to attempt reconstruction of their antemortem dental information. Numerous local employers provided the names of their dental insurance companies. These insurance companies provided the DMORT teams with lists of claims paid by the company during the past few years. In some cases family photographs also provide valuable information regarding the anterior teeth of the victims.

Post Mortem Section

Dental multiple fatality incident victim identification has long been a part of local, regional, and national multiple fatality incident response. DMORT is fortunate to have many dental team members with experience in prior responses whether with DMORT or other agencies. Many DMORT dental team members have been trained at regional and national training sessions. Consequently the design and implementation of a dental post mortem examination area is not unknown territory to these individuals. The field locations of the DMORT, regional or local multiple fatality incident teams are always challenging and during Katrina both morgues were initially assembled in warehouses and required ingenuity and hard work to establish. In Mississippi one post mortem dental station was utilized and in Louisiana, where initial estimates of fatalities were very high, a three dental examination station dental section was created.

DMORT leadership in St. Gabriel had asked for a morgue that could handle approximately 150 cases per day over a twenty four hour period. As previously noted, the decision was made to make the dental post mortem section fully digital and paperless.

The post mortem dental team consisted of two 13 person shifts of forensic dentists, each deployed for twelve hours in the morgue. Initially, there was no need for any dentists in the antemortem or comparison sections. Each shift was managed by a post mortem dental shift leader who had overall responsibility for the operation for each 12 hour shift and could step into any of the other positions to be described when necessary. This individual also interfaced with the other disciplines in the morgue, and ruled on any issues requiring decisions within the dental team.

Each shift had nine dentists assigned to one of three teams (one for each dental station in the morgue). A three person team worked at each post mortem station. Two individuals worked directly with the victim and examined, charted and obtain radiographs. The third team member was the computer operator. As can be expected in highly charged environments like a multiple fatality incident morgue, the positions of each team member quickly became designated by the nicknames of *cutter*, *shooter* and *geek (aka #1, #2 or #3 position)*. The responsibilities of these individuals are delineated below:

- **The *Cutter (*Number One slot**) - was the prosector and initially the leader of each three person dental station. From the head of the gurney they would set the pace, access the oral cavity, hold and position the digital x-ray sensor, and make the assessment of dental findings (restorations, missing teeth, etc.).

- **The *Shooter* (Number Two slot)** - was responsible for holding and positioning the Aribex Nomad portable x-ray generator and triggering it when required from the proper side of the gurney. This individual was also responsible for assuring that the dental findings announced by the *cutter* were accurate and agreed upon.

- **The *Geek* (Number Three slot)** - sat at the laptop computer to operate the software for the digital radiograph capture and entered the dental findings into WinID. This individual was kept *clean* in order to not contaminate the computer terminal. His/her responsibilities included entering charting into the computer, verifying correct radiograph positioning and imaging, controlling the flow of the procedure on each victim. comparing the visual dental findings with the radiographic dental findings to determine if disagreements could be resolved and no findings went overlooked. The *geek* was also ultimately responsible for confirming that the post mortem case ID number of the remains was unique and correct and properly entered into the dental system

(When this information was presented at the AAFS meeting in 2005, it was further suggested during discussion that the post mortem dental shift leader should be designated the **Pit Boss** in future deployments of the DMORT dental team.)

There were two photographers per shift whose responsibilities included floating between different autopsy tables to obtain digital photographs of victims and their teeth and handling the digital photography for all three stations. One served as the chief photographer and the other as their assistant. The chief photographer was also kept *clean* and the assistant handled all of the duties involving contact with the post mortem remains. The assistant was trained to become the next chief as the bi-weekly rotations of dental personnel continued. The assistant photographer also served as a roving *gopher* to handle re-supply issues and step into a gurney-side position when breaks were needed.

One individual was tasked as the Information Technology (IT) or *network* expert. The IT expert dealt with hardware and software problems and later alternated in that role between the morgue and the antemortem/comparison section that was connected to the morgue by a wired network.

As operations evolved the protocols for each team member were modified to improve efficiency. It became clear that the *geek* controlled the flow and set the pace at each station. They were responsible for assuring that accurate demographic, radiographic and dental data was recorded. Concurrently, the *cutter* and *shooter* co-operated in performing the examination. During radiographic procedures they moved around the gurney while protecting the digital sensor cable during radiographic exposure. The *cutter* placed the digital sensor and helped the *shooter* guide the Nomad prior to requesting the exposure. The *geek* requested the next exposure or a re-take.

The fluid motion of the three person team continued until each radiographic survey was completed. The *shooter* checked the *cutter* as they called out information during charting.

Simultaneously, the *geek* confirmed charting information from the digital radiograph before making the WinID entry. This step alone saved valuable time and allowed for more accurate examination since there was no requirement to wait 15-30 minutes for the radiographs to be developed and mounted. Before releasing the remains the *geek* called out the information recorded and the *cutter* and *shooter* confirmed the information recorded by direct re-examination.

Comparison Section

All of the tasks described in **Appendix H** were performed to acquire data that permitted dental team members using WinID3 software to compare post mortem and antemortem information in an effort to determine identity of the victim. The WinID User Manual gives basic instructions for using the software. Becoming proficient with comparisons requires practice and experience and DMORT dental team members received primary training including a PowerPoint presentation that illustrated step-by-step WinID instruction. Excerpts from that presentation are included in **Appendix H.**

Assessment of DMORT Dental Response Following Hurricane Katrina

An objective analysis of the response by DMORT to the Gulf Coast revealed the following positive aspects of the operation:

- DMORT was very well prepared for the rapid notification and deployment of dental personnel. The southeast regional team for example, was operating under a system in which 25-member monthly strike teams of various skill sets were identified several weeks in advance. Those individuals were made aware of their commitments in advance and could request substitutions should they not be able to serve for that particular month. These teams were posted on a web-based system known as the *event tracker*. DMORT teams were deployed and staged at different locations in Alabama, Tennessee and Texas even before Katrina made landfall and were on site very shortly after the storm system had passed.

- Acquisition of DMORT's digital dental data-gathering systems permitted both the East and West dental morgue operations to be conducted in a paperless environment. This included digital X-ray sensors, digital dental charting and digital photography. These systems allowed the insertion of data into the WinID dental matching program in a direct and immediate manner. Antemortem operators were soon able to view all information regarding the victim's dental findings at the touch of a laptop keyboard.

- New hand-held and battery operated radiographic tube head systems were online prior to the deployment. The overall success of the system stemmed from the superior equipment selected DMORT and also many hours of training on this equipment at regional and national meetings and practical workshops prior to the event. Slight modification in the teams' post mortem member assignments and protocols were quickly made by the section leaders early in the operation in order to maximize the effectiveness of this new equipment.

- DMORT dental members' flexibility and *team approach* also contributed to the team's overall success. Dental team members routinely submitted to the task at hand by undertaking jobs assigned by their section leaders even if the particular task seemed outside the range of their training and abilities. Dental team members served as morgue body trackers, manned security gates, sanitized the morgue floors or cleaned and dried muddy dental records that had been submerged underwater. Many members came into the process with forensic credentials qualifying them as team leaders. Yet, they served under others with a cooperative and collegial attitude. The operation would have most likely failed without those who sacrificed their egos to ensure that the job was completed properly.

There were problems identified during the

deployment although most were dealt with quickly by the DMORT Incident Command System. An objective analysis of the response by DMORT to the Gulf Coast multiple fatality incident revealed the following negative aspects of the operation:

- The principal problem involved deployment strategies early in the multiple fatality incident . Individual D M O R T regions deployed more dental personnel than were actually needed in the early stages. However, much of this was due to the wide-spread destruction of the involved area's infrastructure. Many of the victims' dental records were destroyed by the storm, and those that were not were slow in arriving to the DMORT Antemortem Dental Section. With no antemortem records and difficult body retrieval conditions, two to three times more dental personnel were on site than were needed for the first two or three weeks. This could also have created further problems in manpower shortages had the operation continued longer than it did.

Other lessons learned by trial and error led to the following list of recommendations submitted by numerous DMORT team members through debriefings:

- Deploy members via a strategic plan based on input from dental section leaders.

- Deploy members in a more precise manner based on individual skills (particularly computer skills)

- Overlap members who are deployed and those demobilizing by at least one full working day for training purposes.

- Develop onsite training or walk through practice sessions prior to morgue operations for less experienced members.

- Protocols must be followed routinely unless there are revisions made by the dental section leader.

- Photographic protocols should be robust and are as important as radiographs in some cases.

- With new digital systems, high-speed real-time backup systems and daily quality assurance is a must.

- Wireless networks should not be used due to the large size of the image files.

- There should be routine formal interaction between individuals collecting family-assistance victim information and the dental team.

- The Comments Section of WinID should be used more often to integrate additional dental information into the record.

Development of Protocols for Use in Future Multiple fatality incidents

Since September 11, 2001 much work has been done to plan for future multiple fatality incident s by those who are responsible for victim identification. Most notably, a committee consisting of individuals from the NDMS, DMORT and the National Transportation Safety Board (NTSB) have worked to develop a standard operating procedure (SOP) for joint operations involving transportation accidents. Some of the items in the SOP are specific to transportation incidents. However, most are applicable to any incident involving multiple fatalities. The document is titled *DMORT Standard Operating Procedure for National Transportation Safety Board Activations* and is available in its entirety on both NTSB and DMORT websites. This document serves as a template for developing specific protocols for future multiple fatality incident responses.

The 2005 hurricanes Katrina and Rita assaulted the southern United States before these SOPs were available. The days of confusion and disorganization that always accompany multiple fatality incident s of large magnitude were exacerbated by the lack of a coherent coordinated plan of operation. When its services are requested, DMORT is charged with identifying the dead and operates under the Incident Command System. That system was generally followed for these incidents. Because DMORT lacked a single national leader at the time of the Katrina/Rita experience, the effectiveness of the Incident Command System was compromised.

The ten DMORT regions are led by regional *commanders.* This organization works and the *commanders* generally co-operate and co-ordinate the efforts of their teams. However, regional autonomy and eagerness to help contributed to specific examples of uncoordinated, independent actions that disregarded planning and need. Despite the initial chaos, through dedication, resourcefulness, and determination team members in both Mississippi and Louisiana were able to make significant contributions to the task of victim identification. This was accomplished although there were difficult working conditions and widespread destruction of the community infrastructure in which antemortem medical and dental records were maintained.

Paul Sledzik of the National Transportation Safety Board was not involved with the Katrina/Rita response but he very accurately and elegantly describes how responders are able to work amid chaos. "In my experience, effective responders create order in a small circle around themselves. They focus on those things they can directly impact. Within these circles of calm, decisions are made to bring order. These decisions are based on a combination of:

- a set of broadly applicable tools based on experience

- an intuitive feeling of what to do

- an ability to remove/detach themselves mentally from the chaos

- an ability to envision the successful conclusion to the response

- a guiding principle of trying to do things right

Thus, when teams of effective responders come together there are intersections of circles of controlled chaos. This creates a ripple effect that calms the chaos and moves the response forward."

A White House Report entitled *Katrina-Lessons Learned - What Went Right?,* stated that DMORT performed well in response to the Katrina crisis. Although dedication and resourcefulness can encourage those circles of order in the midst of chaos and eventually result in success, good leadership, prior planning, meaningful training and preparation are needed to work efficiently and minimize the problems and frustration associated with multiple fatality incident response. With this in mind newer protocols that enable effective dental response to multiple fatality incident s are necessary.

Protocols developed from *evidence based* experience and planning are necessary instruments for efficient operation. The principal characteristic of operational protocols should be flexibility. They allow for more efficient operation of each element of the response and provide a basis for continuity and consistency in situations where the leadership and personnel are periodically changing.

Failure to follow protocols inevitably causes delay, confusion, errors, and the necessity to repeat difficult work already completed. That any protocol can be modified or changed to meet the needs of the current situation is undeniable but unilateral modifications of protocols by individuals who may have a narrow view of the overall operation or who overestimate their knowledge and ability have also caused concerns. For this reason protocols should be amended only with the agreement of the permanent and current dental leadership of the team.

Planned Deployment of Personnel – Problems Encountered

Specifically needed for future multiple fatality incidents is a rational program for planned deployment. One of the most troubling problems encountered in the dental section during the Katrina and Rita responses in Louisiana and Mississippi was the lack of a coherent, logical plan for deployment of dental team members. Early in the operation dental team members were deployed in large numbers to both Mississippi and Louisiana. After three weeks of operation 108 dental team members had been deployed. This represented approximately half of the 225 total available dental team members nationwide

Among those deployed 60 were sent to Mississippi. This site processed fewer than 250 total fatalities while in operation. Conversely, the 48 dental team members deployed to Louisiana would handle more that 1000 cases. In the Louisiana morgue these Individuals were deployed before an antemortem record management facility was even established. So many dental personnel were in Mississippi that leaders employed two hour per day shifts just to keep everyone involved. In both scenarios more dental personnel were deployed than were needed before infrastructure and resources were in place to efficiently use their skills.

As the operation developed and facilities and systems were in place, DHS, FEMA and NDMS officials seemed unable to understand that most DMORT dentists had busy private practices that depended on their presence for survival. The two week absence of the dentist during DMORT mobilization created patient care and financial hardships for the dentist's practice. Very few dentists can be absent from their practices for two weeks twice in a three month period without dire consequences. Logical attempts to require shorter deployment periods for these key personnel were met with resistance, disdain, and ultimately dismissal by government officials.

Requests for changes in deployment protocol from the dental leadership at the morgue sites in Mississippi and Louisiana were largely ignored. A protocol recommended by DMORT Dental leaders on September 28, 2005 would have allowed for one week absences from practices and if required, redeployment of trained, experienced dental team members. The protocol was considered but rejected or overlooked by the Washington based official making deployment decisions.

Planned Procurement of Necessary Equipment and Supplies

Pre-Katrina requests for necessary dental section equipment were modest and for the most part more modestly supplied. It was assumed from claims made that the Multiple fatality incident Portable Morgue Units, DPMU-East and DPMU-West dental caches were supplied and consistent. This assumption was based on lessons taught during pre-Katrina training. During training, portions of the DPMU-East had been employed but not replenished. Thus, only limited portions of the DPMU East dental cache were useable during the initial phases of the real time exercise.

When the dental cache of DPMU-West was opened in St. Gabriel, Louisiana it contained almost nothing that would be useful. There were ample boxes of **expired** dental radiographic film and **expired** x-ray developer and fixer and a minimally operable x-ray generator, and *almost nothing else.* This lack of useable equipment resulted in the acquisition of very expensive items through flurries of semi-coordinated purchasing and chaotic delivery exercises. Three DMORT dentists spent one entire day away from the morgue to collect needed and valuable equipment from a university campus, police station, courier warehouses and the parking garage of a downtown hotel in Baton Rouge. This equipment had been in Baton Rouge for days but no one knew its destination. This cannot be considered the most efficient and cost effective method of procuring equipment and supplies for the DPMUs.

Ultimately the dental morgues at St. Gabriel and Carville were very well equipped to handle the task using all three stations. The dental morgue in Mississippi appropriately operated with the equipment and supplies needed for one station. There should now be ample high quality dental equipment and unexpired supplies to equip the two DPMUs following the termination of the Katrina deployment. A protocol to insure that this equipment is tested and maintained periodically to assure that it is ready for the next multiple fatality incident must be developed. Both the DPMU-East and DPMU-West should be identically equipped and inventoried regularly for completeness of supplies and equipment. Both DPMU dental caches should be alternately used for the periodic training needed to keep DMORT Dental personnel prepared.

Long Term Planning

Long term planning impacts the quality of the response to complex events. Multiple fatality incident s are certainly complex events and the cost of responding to those events can be optimized by planning. Deployment of personnel and equipment procurement are just two of many facets of planning, but these two were principal problem issues during the response to Katrina. Hopefully the next multiple fatality incident will not occur before these issues are addressed.

Multiple Fatality Incident Medical Assistance Team (DMAT)

Figure 3-37: The arm patch for the Nevada-1 DMAT Team.

The NDMS fosters the development of Multiple fatality incident Medical Assistance Teams (DMATs) in managing the federal medical response to major emergencies and federally declared multiple fatality incidents. A DMAT is a group of professional and paraprofessional medical personnel supported by logistical and administrative staff whose purpose is to provide medical and emotional care during a multiple fatality incident. A fully organized DMAT is capable of running a ten bed mobile hospital with all of its triage, diagnostic and treatment capabilities. Forensic dentists are certainly qualified to join these teams and have been welcomed. Dentists are assigned to a rapid-response element within a DMAT to supplement local medical /dental care until other federal or contract resources can be mobilized or the situation is resolved.

DMATs deploy to multiple fatality incident sites with sufficient supplies and equipment to sustain themselves for a period of 72 hours while providing medical care at a fixed or temporary medical care site. In mass casualty incidents their responsibilities may include triaging patients, providing high-quality medical care despite an austere environment and preparing patients for evacuation and transport. In other situations, DMATs may serve to augment over-loaded local health care facilities and staff. If multiple fatality incident victims are evacuated to a different locale to receive definitive medical care, DMATs may be activated to support patient reception and disposition of patients to hospitals. DMATs can also be assigned to provide medical supervision and health monitoring of the DMORTs deployed in the field.

DMAT members are required to maintain appropriate certifications and licensure within their discipline. When members are activated for training purposes or for an actual emergency situation, they are paid as part-time Federal employees and are covered under the Federal Employees Compensation Act, the Federal Tort Claims Act (malpractice assistance) and the Uniformed Services Employment and employment Rights Act to protect their normal employment when they return home. Current licenses and certifications for members deployed in a

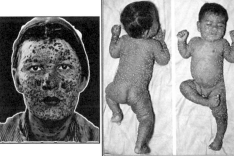

Figure 3-38: CDC pictures of smallpox in various individuals.

DMAT exercise are recognized and accepted by all state jurisdictions within the United States.

Members are required to attend regularly scheduled training meetings in their local area. Medical training is not required for all positions on a DMAT. Many logistical and administrative positions are also available. Uniforms and immunizations are provided to all deploying members of a DMAT. Additionally, team members may be individually deployed and assigned to another DMAT to augment and/or relieve its staff members. DMATs are assigned a quarterly rotation to be *on-call* to respond to

multiple fatality incidents. The duration of a deployment is usually two weeks.

Bioterrorism and Weapons of Mass Destruction

Terrorism has been defined as premeditated, politically or religiously motivated use of violence perpetrated against noncombatant targets by sub-national groups or clandestine agents that is usually intended to coerce or influence an audience.

Since the wake-up call of September 11, 2001 the dental profession has recognized that in addition to its role in the resolution of traditional forensic dental issues it can provide health care workers to triage and assist the injured and other victims of bioterrorism and chemical terrorism acts. In the United States, the Nevada State Board of Dentistry and those of other states now require mandatory continuing education [Nevada (NRS631.342 Regulations concerning CE)].

- This legislation states that dentists must complete a course of instruction, within two years after initial licensure, relating to the medical consequences of an act of terrorism that involves the use of a weapon of mass destruction. The course must provide at least four hours of instruction that includes the following subjects:

- An overview of acts of terrorism and weapons of mass destruction

- Personal protective equipment required for acts of terrorism

- Common symptoms and methods of treatment associated with exposure to or injuries caused by, chemical, biological, radioactive and nuclear agents

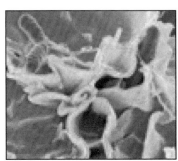

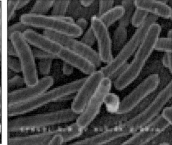

Figure 3-39: Examples of Salmonella, Y. pestis (plague), and E. coli pathogens from the CDC.

Figure 3-40: Anthrax bacillus and an example of a dermal lesion.

-*Syndromic surveillance* and r e p o r t i n g procedures for acts of terrorism that involve biological agents

-An overview of the information available on, and the use of, the CDC Health Alert Network.

Background Information

The basis for the following material was presented as a bioterrorism -multiple fatality incident seminar by Ingrid Gill, JD at the 58th Annual Meeting of the AAFS in February, 2006. This seminar included discussion of joint law enforcement and public health issues, criminal prosecutions of bioterrorism suspects and concerns for balancing the rights of the accused and national security Additional information has been added by the editors.

Bioterrorism and Biological Weapons

History of Bioterrorism

General George Washington's private correspondences released from the archives of the US government in 2006 revealed that he was concerned that the British might have plotted to spread smallpox among the colonial troops and citizens during the American Revolution. Indeed, this was not beyond the ken of others who settled the North American continent as they passed this particular biological agent to the Native Americans in the nineteenth century. Since the end of World War I international conventions held in Geneva, concerning the use of these agents by warring governments has reduced the threat of this kind of warfare. However, the government of Iraq under Saddam Hussein was not averse to using chemicals against ethnic factions (Kurds) among its own citizenry in the latter part of the twentieth century.

The threat of chemical and biological warfare from non-governmental sources or radical fringe groups with political, religious or anarchist agendas has loomed over global society since the end of World War II. In 1970 chemical and biological warfare agents were confiscated from the terrorist group known as the Weather Underground which intended to place them in urban water supplies. Eight microbial pathogens including those that cause typhoid fever, diphtheria, dysentery, and meningitis among others were intended for similar use by an organization calling itself RISE in 1972.

By 1984, *Salmonella* had been used to contaminate salad bars in Dalles, Oregon leaving over 751 sick and in 1991 Ricin was intended for use by the Minnesota Patriots Council until the group was arrested by the FBI. In Japan the doomsday religious cult Aum Shinrikyo released sarin nerve gas into the Tokyo subway in 1995 killing twelve. NATO has designated sarin as GB (O-Isopropyl methylphosphonofluoridate) an extremely toxic substance whose sole application is as a nerve agent. This chemical weapon is classified as a weapon of mass destruction by the United Nations according to UN Resolution 687. Its production and stockpiling was outlawed by the Chemical Weapons Convention of 1993. Throughout September and October 2001, *Bacillus anthracis* was sent through the U.S. mail in Florida and on October 15th of that year an envelope containing weapons grade *B. anthracis* was sent in through the United States Postal Service to the Hart Senate Building in Washington, DC.

Tucker noted that terrorist incidents and hoaxes involving toxic or infectious agents have been on the rise and the preferred choice of target has also changed over time. In an analysis of 135 terrorist incidents for which the target was known he identified two types of targets that have increased in frequency. These include general civilian population targets where the apparent intent is to cause indiscriminate casualties and targeted symbolic buildings or organizations.

Since 1990 the principal motivation for the use of chemical, biological, radiological or nuclear materials by terrorist organizations is the promotion of nationalist or separatist objectives. Retaliation or revenge taking for a real or perceived injury, protestation of government policies and defense of animal rights are also among the most common reasons for terrorist groups to use these agents.

In the United States, the Patriot Act of 2001, Title 18 U.S.C. 175 (b) provides for arrest, prosecution and fines and/or imprisonment of up to ten years for individuals convicted of knowingly possessing a biological agent, toxin, or delivery system which cannot be "justified by a prophylactic, protective, bona fide research, or other peaceful purpose." Title 18 U.S.C. Sec. 2332(a) of the same Act states that any threatened use of a disease causing organism directed at humans, animals or plants is a crime, regardless of whether the perpetrator actually possesses a disease causing agent. Further provisions under Public Law No. 107-40, Sec. 2 (a) 115 Stat 224 authorize the President of the United States to use military force against "the nations, organizations or persons he determines planned, authorized, committed, or aided the terrorist attacks or harbored such organizational persons."

Court rulings concerning Constitutional violations of the First, Fourth Amendment have been handed down since the inception of the Patriot Act of 2001. These challenges primarily relate to issues concerning the balancing of the rights of the accused against National security. Principal decisions are listed in **Appendix I**.

Weapons Agents Used by Terrorists

The following materials have been used as weapons of chemical or biological warfare:

- Chemical Agents

- Radiological Agents

- Explosive and Incendiary Devices

- Biological Agents (Poor Man's Nuke)

There are specific and well developed treatments for most agents, but identification team members must be aware of the significant personal risk of operating around these substances. Most will linger on clothes and human remains and rubber gloves may not be an adequate barrier. Any oral autopsy of the known chemical, radiological or biological victim should only be performed when antidotes/treatments and trained personnel are present and available and with the latest protective equipment. Identification is important, but not the primary concern when unknown agents are suspected.

Chemical agents include substances developed for non terrorist purposes by companies supplying organic and inorganic chemistry, and specific agents developed for use as weapons. Gasoline, propane and many other petrochemicals can be misused by small groups interest in anarchy. The usual and well known weapons substances are:

- Nerve Agents   Sarin, VX
- Blood Agents   Cyanide
- Choking Agents   Phosgene, Chlorine
- Blister Agents   Mustard, Lewisite
- Riot Control   Mace, Pepper Spray, Tear Gas

- Vomiting Agents
- Incapacitating Agents
- Ammonia
- Arsine

Signs and symptoms of chemical exposure are varied, may mimic biological infection and may include those conditions indicated in **Table3-4**.

Signs and Symptoms	Agent
Nausea / vomiting, cholinergic effects	mustard gas
Decreased WBC, RBC, platelets	mustard gas
Erythema, small vesicles that later coalesce blisters/ bulla	mustard gas
Epistaxis, sore throat, hacking cough, hoarseness, dyspnea, productive cough	mustard gas
Mild-severe conjunctivitis, eyelid inflammation damage, blepharospasm, corneal roughening, corneal opacification, ulceration, and/or perforation	mustard gas
Eye irritation, tearing, feeling of pain and sense of fullness in the nose and sinuses, severe headache, burning throat, tightness and pain in the chest, violent coughing and sneezing, nausea, and vomiting	vomiting agents
Severe irritation to eyes, skin, airways immediately after exposure, vesicant effects similar to mustard, no bone marrow effects	lewisite

Signs and Symptoms	Agent
Blepharospasm, tearing, redness, nasal discharge, sneezing, burning, cough, SOB, chest tightness, wheezing, skin burning, erythema, anxiety induced tachycardia hypertension	riot control / tear agents
Sunburn-like skin lesions	radiation exposure
Burning eyes, tearing, pain, corneal injury, lens injury, cough, SOB, chest pain, wheezing, laryngitis, hypoxia, chemical pneumonia, hemorrhage, pain, blisters, deep burns, severe mouth pain, cough, abdominal pain, nausea / vomiting, edema lips, mouth, esophageal stricture, perforation	ammonia

Table 3-4: The Signs and Symptoms of Various Weapons Agents

Differential diagnoses include:

- Tularemia
- Botulism
- Staphylococcus Enterotoxin B
- Mustard
- Lewisite
- Riot Control Agents
- Ammonia
- Intestinal anthrax
- Intestinal tularemia
- Typhoid tularemia
- Hantavirus
- Viral Encephalitis
- Staphylococcal Enter. B
- Mustard
- Ammonia
- Vomiting Agents

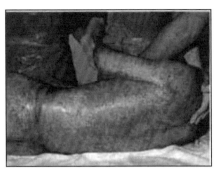 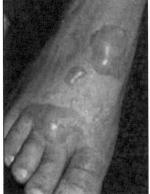 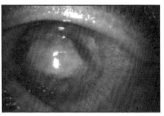

Figure 3-41: Examples of exposure to mustard gas.

Biologic agents include those of bacterial, viral or rickettsial origin and biological toxins. These agents are potentially contagious and it is often difficult to contain and track the attack when they are used. They are easily concealed and almost impossible to detect until employed. Lethal doses vary among the agents employed. Additionally, their victims may have delayed appearance of symptoms. The danger posed by delayed symptoms in victims of biological warfare is that if contagious biological agents are exposed to the general population carriers of the infection will disperse it from the attack site before the existence of a biological weapon attack has been realized. Conversely, an opportunity posed by delayed symptoms is that detection of a biological attack provides an opportunity for containment and treatment efforts that may prevent the onset of the disease or reduce its effects.

Characteristically, bacterial agents have a long shelf life and low biological decay as aerosols. In spore form they are more resistant to cold, heat, drying, chemicals, and radiation than the bacterium itself. The following bacterial agents are the most commonly employed as biological weapons:

Anthrax
Brucellosis
Cholera
Diphtheria
Escherichia coli serotype
Glanders

Melioidosis
Plague (Bubonic and Pneumonic)
Tularemia
Typhoid Fever

Viral agents, being the simplest type of microorganisms, require living hosts for replication. As biological agents they are attractive because they do not respond to antibiotics. Because their incubation periods are longer than bacterial agents incapacitation of victims may be delayed, complicating the identification of an outbreak. Agents in this category include:

Congo-Crimean Hemorrhagic Fever Virus
Dengue Fever Virus
Ebola Virus
Junin Virus
Marburg Virus
Rift Valley Fever Virus
Smallpox
Venezuelan Equine Encephalitis
Yellow Fever Virus

Rickettsiae are obligate intracellular bacteria that are intermediate in size between most bacteria and viruses. They are susceptible to a broad spectrum of antibiotics and are usually spread through bites by infected insects. These agents include:

Endemic Typhus
Epidemic Typhus
Q Fever
Rocky Mountain Spotted Fever

Biological toxins are poisons produced by living organisms. These can be genetically altered and/or synthetically manufactured into weapons grade concentrations:

Botulinum Toxin
Ricin (Isolated from Castor Beans)
Saxitoxin
Staphylococcal enterotoxin B
Tricothecence mycotoxins

Identification of Bioterrorism Threats

Identification of threats of bioterrorism requires coordination between law enforcement and public health investigative agencies. The methodologies used by these to groups, however, often are based on contrasting styles and different objectives when processing a terrorism crime scene and/or investigating a potential biological attack. This can often lead to breakdown in communication between them when investigating the causes of a biological outbreak associated with an act of bioterrorism.

Law enforcement investigations are deductive in nature. Witnesses and potential suspects are interviewed, leads are developed and pursued and all available evidence is collected, identified, and tracked. The suspected perpetrator(s) is identified, arrested, and prosecuted if evidence is adequate. The ultimate goal of this approach is to gather evidence that will meet constitutional standards and withstand legal challenges to obtain a conviction. Law enforcement officials are concerned with confidentiality to protect informants, witnesses and to preserve the integrity of the case for the prosecution.

Public health investigators take an inductive approach to understanding why a biological pathogen causes an outbreak. They conduct interviews, collect data and develop hypotheses to explain transmission. Epidemiological and laboratory studies are conducted to test these hypotheses and if the studies confirm them, prevention and control

Flu-like symptoms	Skin Lesions	Abdominal pain	Eye symptoms	Swollen Glands
Anthrax	Anthrax	Intestinal	Tularemia	Tularemia
Smallpox	Tularemia	anthrax	Botulism	Glanders
Rash may be	Glanders	Intestinal	Staphylococcus	Plague
absent early	Plague	tularemia	Enterotoxin B	
Plague	Smallpox	Typhoidal	Mustard	
Tularemia	Typhus Fever	tularemia	Lewisite	
Viral	Mustard	Hantavirus	Riot Control	
Hemorrhagic	Riot Control	Viral	Agents	
fever	Ammonia	Encephalitis	Ammonia	
Brucellosis	Radiation	Staphylococcus		
Nipah Virus	Exposure	Enter. B		
Typhus Fever		Mustard		
Melioidosis		Ammonia		
Glanders		Vomiting Agents		
Q fever				
Viral				
Encephalitis				
Ricin				
Staphylococcus				
Enterotoxin B				
Hantavirus				
Psittacosis				

Table 3–5: Reviews the symptoms associated with biologic agents that should arouse suspicion of a potential bioterrorism event.

strategies are developed, implemented, and evaluated. All work is held to the standard of scientific peer review, generally through presentation of data at scientific meetings and publication in scientific journals. Patient's records are confidential, therefore not subject to discovery in a court proceeding. Thus, the policy considerations of public health officials are confidentiality to protect sensitive patient medical information, and monitor and control capabilities to contain infectious disease outbreaks.

Current public health detection methodology is based on *syndromic surveillance* principals that detect the early manifestations of illnesses occurring during a bioterrorism related epidemic. The principals include a broad spectrum of activities utilizing information technology to track data that can *red flag* a bioterrorism related disease. Through an enhanced surveillance project the CDC works with hospitals and information system contractors using *syndromic surveillance* to monitor hospital ER visit data, physician office data, 911 calls, school and business absenteeism and over the counter drug sales.

The goal of *syndromic surveillance* is the early diagnosis of the initial stages of disease. Information technology allows for early detection of bioterrorism related diseases through the extraction, processing and analysis of clinical data listed in **Table 3-5.** The effectiveness of early detection of *syndromic surveillance* is often dependent on the size of outbreak.

Detection of Bioterrorism Agent Threat

The FBI's Weapons of Mass Destruction Operations Unit (WMDOU), in conjunction with other federal agencies conducts a threat/credibility assessment to determine if there is an intentional criminal act present. During 2001 anthrax field investigations, FBI investigators and epidemiologists were paired during interviews with possible case patients and exposed persons permitting the collection, processing and sharing of pertinent information to identify the source of the infection and the perpetrator. When

joint investigations by the CDC and FBI are conducted the following legal and medical questions arise which may conflict:

- Are both agencies' interviews of patients subject to discovery in a criminal proceeding?

- Was there a doctor/patient relationship established when a citizen is interviewed by a public health official? If so, is it waived by the presence of the FBI?

- Do certain public health confidentiality laws apply to the interviews conducted by the CDC?

Detection of Biological Agents

On scene detection, identification and assessment (DIDA) of biological agents is the capability to quickly detect, locate, characterize and assess a potential or ongoing terrorist attack. Biological detection systems are currently in the research and early development stages. The paucity of biological field detection equipment can be understood by remembering that detection of biological agents requires high sensitivity due to the very low dose of biological agent required to cause infection and spread disease. A high degree of selectivity is also required because of the scope of the large and diverse biological background material in the environment. Additionally, biological agents are more complex molecules than chemical molecules.

Currently, some commercially available devices have limited usefulness in identifying biological warfare agents. They respond to only a limited number of agents and are generally high cost items, however. It is strongly recommended that first responders be cautious when considering the purchase of any device that claims to detect biological warfare agents.

Laboratory Response Network (LRN)

The LRN was established in accordance with Presidential Decision Directive 39 and is a collaborative effort of the CDC, FBI and Association of Public Health Laboratories. The network became operational August, 1999 and is a multilevel system connecting local and state public health laboratories with the advanced capacity of public health and military laboratories. Clinical specimens are referred to the LRN facilities from local and state public health laboratories for identification of potential covert bioterrorism attacks.

"LRN is the result of predicting the need for validated tests that would be consistent with evidentiary requirements." "A uniform set of laboratory protocols, based on established procedures and reagents, facilitates the introduction of test results into a court of law, thereby limiting evidentiary challenges that may result from the use of different testing methods or analyses."

Historical and Practical Examples

Technology Advances in Resolving Identification Issues since September 11, 2001

The terrorist attack on the Pentagon on September 11, 2001 using a commercial jetliner and the concurrent loss of American Airlines Flight 77 through terrorist activities proved to be pivotal events in mass fatality organization for the Office of the Armed Forces Medical Examiner, Armed Forces Institute of Pathology (AFIP). The AFIP Forensic Odontology Section's experience during this exercise is discussed and evaluated.

Historical Perspective

The United States Military's Dover Port Mortuary (Carson) has been used as the staging site for military and civilian mass fatality operations since Vietnam. The use of this facility continues presently with a new physical plant. Prior to the September 11th terrorist attacks on the United States the forensic dental section of the Dover Port Mortuary had been experienced in the use of computer applications to assist in rendering potential identification matches on a smaller

scale than required following the events of that day.

The computer program used by this team prior to 2001 was developed by Colonel Lou Lorton and his collaborators and is referred to as CAPMI (Computer Assisted Post Mortem Identification). The CAPMI system is a dedicated dental data base management program in which dental information obtained from an unknown set of remains is rapidly sorted against the antemortem dental data base comprised of the composite antemortem dental records of the multiple fatality incident victims. This program was first employed in 1985 in support of the Arrow Air charter aviation runway accident in Gander, Newfoundland in which United States military personnel returning from Lebanon were killed. (**Figure 3-42**). At that time CAPMI used a DOS based application (**refer to Chapter 6 – Technological Aides in Forensic Odontology**).

Figure 3-42: The basic military dental record was historically input according to the CAPMI protocol for sorting.

Prior to the September 11th incidents radiographs were chemically processed at Port Mortuary. The dental forensic team began developing *evidence based* data; that digital capture would be superior in quality and useful in the field. A Beta test was conducted at the Port Mortuary in which two chemical processors competed with a single digital radiographic capture bay in the processing of radiographs. This exercise was performed during identification of victims of the military aircraft accident in Arizona in April,

2000 involving an Osprey tiltrotor vertical/ short takeoff and landing (VSTOL) multi-mission air-craft. Results indicated that digital capture proved to be far more efficient than chemical means of generating radiographic images. This became the primary mode of dental radiographic storage as the dental identification evolution progressed for the team **(Figure 3-43).**

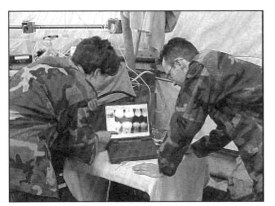

Figure 3-43: The digital capture and storage Of radiographic data.

Observations from the OCONUS (Outside the Continental United States) military missions to Grenada in May, 2000, Serbia in August, 2001 and on site support for the North Carolina Osprey accident in December, 2000 reinforced the premise that the use of a portable radiation capture device in conjunction with a digital sensor was a valuable asset to the forensic dental team **(Figure 3-44).** This proved to be true for large stationary mortuary exercises at the Port Mortuary facility as well as in temporary field morgue environments.

Figure 3-44: The use of portable radiographic equipment for field use.

In light of these experiences a planning team, including dental and medical personnel from the AFIP and Dover Air Force Base (DAFB) laid the ground work to upgrade and strengthen their dental identification infrastructure just months before the events of September 11th **(Figure 3-45).** Needed equipment was ordered to create a 21st century dental identification presence at the mortuary. Coincidentally and eerily some of the equipment to accomplish this task arrived just days before the September 11th attacks.

Figure 3-45: Mortuary computer equipment set-up.

Transition

In light of the experiences described above and with confidence that the AFIP and DAFB dental teams could implement these upgrades *on the fly*, it was elected to transition into a more modern dental identification approach in support of the evolving September 11th mission (Operation Noble Eagle). This decision was made in the early hours of September 13, 2001 just before remains began arriving at the morgue facility. The principal issue encountered was to quickly develop a plan to transition from a traditional antemortem/post mortem dental comparison approach and to restructure team divisions. To accomplish the first goal of transitioning from the traditional comparison protocol whereby single hard copy antemortem records were compared individually with post mortem records arrayed on tables, the following concepts were developed:

- Change from chemically developed radiographs to radiation capture bays using digital sensors

- Reduce the use of hard copy archives by creating a computer network to handle the flow and sorting of information

- Establish a dental identification unit and decide where to set up *shop*.

Accomplishing Transition Goals

The primary concern was to locate a suitable area within an already crowded mortuary where a computer network could be established. An abandoned corner currently being used for temporary storage in a dismantled conventional whole body x-ray suite was chosen for this site. This was quickly gutted and cleared, permitting the installation of tables to house a combined Antemortem/Comparison Computer Center (**Figure 3-46**).

A strike team began unpacking and obtaining hardware needed to activate the nerve center of the dental identification component of Operation Noble Eagle (**Figure 3-47**). This team also laid network cables. Concurrently, additional dental digital radiography sensors were supplied from New Jersey by the Schick Technologies representative. Training on the use of this equipment commenced immediately at the morgue facility.

A core team was also selected to manage the computer center. Impromptu training was implemented for its members with regard to the use of a transparency/film scanner (TPU) for digitizing antemortem radiographs. Training and testing of new WinID 3 sorting software was initiated and a protocol to return the images to the post mortem teams was developed. Issues regarding the seamless merger of antemortem and post mortem information and the development of a *state of the art* forensic dental identification report completed the training of the team.

Figure 3-46: The computer network for antemortem and comparison computers.

Figure 3-47: The strike team of Operation Noble Eagle.

Protocols Developed and Implemented

Post mortem examination teams transcribed their findings to a WinID form and digital radiographs were captured and exported to a CD. That data was transported to the computer center. An immediate hard copy printout of the post mortem radiographs was generated and returned to the Post Mortem Section for quality assurance review and the post mortem clinical examination data was entered into WinID. It was quickly observed that this approach was inefficient and additional laptops were obtained to review the digital films in the Post Mortem Section area. Retrospectively, a wide area network (WAN) should have been used but time constraints did not permit this adjustment (**Refer to Lessons Learned**).

Within the Computer Section each of the workstations could handle a variety of

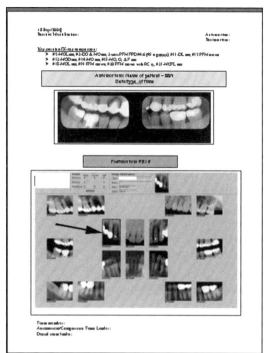

Figure 3-48: A single page comparison report.

different responsibilities including antemortem data entry, post mortem data entry and sorting and report generation. Depending on the immediate needs at that time, priorities shifted. Specifically, if the team was inundated with antemortem records it became the priority to develop composite antemortem records and enter them into the computer data base. This was accomplished by reviewing antemortem hard copy records using traditional methodology to collate and develop a single, composite and current clinical and treatment record for each victim. This task was performed at a workstation in the computer area. The information retrieved was then transcribed onto WinID forms for computer data entry. Selected radiographs were scanned into the computer using a large format TPU scanner. These radiographs were filed in an antemortem directory and later linked with the computer antemortem record.

When a shipment of victim remains arrived, priorities changed and processing this material became the principal task utilizing the same personnel. As the antemortem and post mortem data banks evolved team members

were allocated to commence with the computer sort. Visual computer displays were reviewed to locate potential comparison matches by comparing composite antemortem references with post mortem chartings and radiographs. This replaced the traditional method of pulling paper records and mounted radiographs from a file cabinet for comparison with post mortem records.

The computer comparison techniques developed for Operation Noble Eagle implemented the concept of a single page image embedded forensic dental identification comparison report (**Figure 3-48**). This report contained both text information supporting comparison between antemortem and post mortem evidence and selected embedded radiographic images that facilitated a *visual* comparison. This was the first time this methodology had been employed by the AFIP and DAFB forensic dental units.

During the two month course of this exercise, staffing consisted of a primary core of dental personnel from the AFIP Department of Oral and Maxillofacial Pathology and the Dental Department at DAFB. As Operation Noble Eagle proceeded, additional compliments of support included dentists and ancillary personnel from all branches of the United States military service.

The mortuary units deployed in Operation Noble Eagle processed 184 victims, excluding the terrorists. Sixty-four victims were from American Airlines Flight 77 and 124 from the Pentagon. Of the 184 victims 179 were positively identified. Sixty-five of these identifications (36 percent) were accomplished through by the efforts of the dentists and support personnel of the AFIP and DAFB forensic dental units.

Lessons Learned

Viewing radiographs:

- Transition from viewing mounted radiographs on a view box to analyzing radiographs on a computer monitor is a paradigm shift f o r e m a s t contemporary dental clinicians. Thus, in Operation Noble Eagle the team leaders

163

decided to initially produce a hard copy of the digital radiographs being reviewed.

Data entry – antemortem and post mortem records:

- The issues related to antemortem and post mortem record data entry associated with the victims from the Pentagon and American Airlines Flight 77 made this exercise different from most of the previous cases experienced by the AFIP and DAFB forensic dental units.

- In most typical commercial aviation accidents the dental identification unit would have been presented with a passenger manifest from the beginning of the operation. It took time to develop such a list of the missing among those working at the Pentagon.

- The ability to directly enter data into electronic forms using a hand held device such as a tablet laptop computer provided immediate *electronic* entry of data. This proved more efficient than transcribing information from a handwritten hard copy form.

WAN vs. LAN:

- In a best case scenario a WAN would have been a more suitable network by which to move data between sections than the LAN employed in Operation Noble Eagle.

Workstation components:

- Retrospectively, each work station should have been a complete unit. Rather than having a single large format scanner to be the section workhorse, one should have been provided at each station. This change in protocol would have prevented some of the bottle-necks that occasionally occurred.

Printers:

- It is imperative to have high quality printer capabilities with adequate Random Access Memory (RAM) when generating image

embedded reports. Paper of good quality should also be supplied.

Training and team rotations:

- A training approach was developed that facilitated rotations. After the first week of the exercise the core team trained their replacement through an *on the job training* regimen. In turn, those individuals would repeat the process for their replacements. This provided an opportunity for rest and relaxation (R and R) for personnel and encouraged team members to have a broader exposure and experience in different work stations during the deployment.

Software issues:

- Digital image size of radiographs is critical. Image sizes that are very large result in run time errors because of inherent software *viewing window* constraints.

Small fragments of human remains:

- For isolated small fragments, multiple radiographic views are imperative. This required that the dental teams did have to expose original hard copy radiographs in some cases. Newer digital capture applications, utilized in conjunction with the WinID software, permitted greater menu options in viewing films than experienced by team members prior to September 11th.

Physical plant issues:

Since occasional power lapses can be expected and did indeed occur during Operation Noble Eagle, computer battery backup is required.

The experiences and post mission input from team members supporting Operation Noble Eagle played an important role in providing ideas and concepts regarding the development of current policies, protocols and the state of the art dental identification infrastructure at the AFIP Forensic Odontology Section and the United States Military's Dover Port Mortuary.

Recommended Protocols for Future Deployments of DMORT Dental Personnel Based on Lessons Learned in the Hurricane Katrina Mobilization

Deployment of Dental Personnel for Katrina

Adjust tour length for Dental Team Members to ten days by having them travel Friday, work Saturday - Saturday, travel Sunday. This will reduce the financial impact on practicing dentists and facilitate the retention of qualified dentists for the exercise.

- Saturday overlap will provide time for outgoing team member to orient and train incoming replacements.

- Shorter deployment will encourage and facilitate re-deployment.

- Maintain the current two week rotation for those Dental Team Members who indicate that they prefer that arrangement.

Integrate qualified military dentists with appropriate orders into the rotation following military protocol:

- Armed Forces Institute of Pathology (AFIP) dentists

- Dover Air Force Base Morgue dentists

- Army, Navy, Air Force, Coast Guard, and USPHS dentists

Integrate qualified non-DMORT dentists into the rotation on a volunteer basis. These dentists will provide their own transportation costs but will require housing and meals provided by DMORT. Resources outside DMORT include:

- Faculty of United States Dental Schools screened by DMORT team leaders and /or ABFO diplomates

- ABFO diplomates who are not DMORT members

- UTHSCSA Fellows who are not DMORT

-Private sector dentists screened by DMORT team leaders and /or ABFO diplomates

-Other qualified and trained dentists screened by DMORT team leaders and /or ABFO diplomates

Non-DMORT dentists unfamiliar with digital radiographic procedures and/or computer record management must be provided training in WinID3, Dexis digital radiography, and use of the Aribex Nomad portable X-ray units to integrate them effectively into the morgue operation.

Personnel Requirements

- If the day morgue operation continues at a rate of 50-80 cases per shift, maintain the current level of thirteen post mortem Dental Team Members (12+1 leader)

- If it becomes necessary to work two full shifts per day (day and night), increase the number of Dental Team Members to twenty-six for post mortem operations.

- When and if antemortem operations begin in earnest, the antemortem/ comparison section requires nine Dental Team Members per shift (Antemortem-comparison leader plus 4-two person teams) during the time that the post mortem section is fully engaged. Post mortem Dental Team Members can work in the antemortem-comparison section when time allows.

-Three teams (Six Dental Team Members) to:

Conduct daily interfaces /conferences with the FAC in the procurement of antemortem dental records.

Analyze, translate, and organize antemortem dental records and information.

Enter antemortem data into WinID3 and during down-time in the antemortem section re-auditing of the dental chartings by two member teams should be encouraged. Changes to any records should be authorized by the shift leader and eventually the team leader.

- One team (Two Dental Team Members) to:

Scan radiographs and other images and enter them into Dexis for integration with WinID3. (Other teams may also scan if required and if multiple transparency scanners are available)

If the case flow decreases to 30-50 cases per day (or fewer) and the morgue is open for day operations only, post mortem Dental Team Members can cycle to the antemortem/comparison section for the remainder of their shift - reducing the total number of dentists needed to twenty.

- Ten in post mortem until all cases are completed (leader + 9)

- Nine in antemortem/comparison during morgue ops (leader + 8)

- All Dental Team Members work in antemortem/comparison when morgue operations are suspended.

EDUCATIONAL OUTCOMES

By completing this chapter the reader will:

- Build a foundational knowledge of the organization and planning required for emergency management at international, national, state and local levels.

- Describe the various roles of the forensic odontologist in the formation, training, organization and management of a dental identification team.

- Build a foundational knowledge of the procedures and protocols required to compare antemortem and post mortem dental records in a multiple fatality incident forensic setting.

- Understand the various biological, chemical and physical agents of concern in bioterrorism and weapons of mass destruction incidents.

- Recognize the signs and symptoms associated with exposure to various bioterrorism and chemical weapons agents of multiple fatality incident.

- Critically evaluate relevant forensic, dental, medical and public health scientific literature concerning multiple fatality incident procedures and protocols, identification team organization and bioterrorism and weapons of mass destruction issues based on an understanding of evidence based concepts.

CONTRIBUTORS

Douglas M. Arendt, DDS, DABFO
Robert E. Barsley, DDS, JD, DABFO
Gary M. Berman, DDS, DABFO
Bryan Chrz, DDS, DABFO
J. Curtis Dailey, DDS, ABFO
Thomas J. David, DDS, DABFO
Stacey Davis, FBI/CJIS Management Analyst
Ingrid Gill, JD
Edward. E. Herschaft, DDS, MA, DABFO
L. Thomas Johnson, DDS, DABFO
Jane A. Kaminski, DDS
David K. Ord, DDS
Raymond D. Rawson, DDS, MA, DABFO
David R. Senn, DDS, DABFO
Donald O. Simley, DDS, DABFO
Paul G. Stimson, DDS, MS, DABFO
Allan Warnick DDS, DABFO
Richard A. Weems, DMD MS, DABFO
Edward D, Woolridge, Jr., DDS, DABFO

REFERENCES

Organization and Planning

Colvard MD, Lampiris LN, Cordell GA, James J, Guay A, Lee M, Stokes CM, Scott G (2006). The dental emergency responder: Expanding the scope of dental practice. J Am Dent Assoc 137:468-73.

Glick M (2005). When pigs fly. Confronting the new era of disease transmission. J Am Dent Assoc 136:270, 272, 274.

Katz AR, Nekorchuk DM, Holck PS, Hendrickson LA, Imrie AA, Effler PV (2006). Dentists' preparedness for responding to bioterrorism: A survey of Hawaii dentists. J Am Dent Assoc 137:461-7.

Wood JD, Gould G (2004). Mass fatality incidents: are California dentists ready to respond? J Calif Dent Assoc 32:681-8.

DMORT and DMAT

http://www.dmort.org/DNPages/DMORTPeople.htm. DMORT homepage - People of DMORT.

http://www.dmort.org/DNPages/DMORTHistory.htm. DMORT homwpage - Our History.

http://www.whitehouse.gov/reports/katrina-lessons-learned. The Federal Response to Hurricane Katrina: Lessons Learned.

Katrina/Rita Missing Persons Hotline - Update on calls/cases. http://www.missingkids.com/en_US/documents/KatrinaHotlineUpdate.pdf.

http://www.dhh.louisiana.gov/news.asp?ID=145&Detail=728&Arch=2005. Louisiana Department of Health and Hospitals - Deceased Katrina Victims Released to Families 11-14-2005.

http://oep-ndms.dhhs.gov/dmort.html. National Disaster Medical System - What Is A Disaster Mortuary Operational Response Team (DMORT)?

The White House: Office of Management and Budget. Updates of Statistical Area Definitions and Guidance on Their Uses. http://www.whitehouse.gov/omb/bulletins/fy2006/b06-01.pdf.

http://www.dhs.gov/dhspublic/display?content=4777. U.S. Department of Homeland Security - United States Government Response to the Aftermath of Hurricane Katrina

Vital Statistics of All Bodies at St. Gabriel Morgue 1/18/2006.

Bioterrorism and Weapons of Mass Destruction

Buehler JW, Berkelman RL, Hartley DM, Peters CJ Syndromic Surveillance and Bioterrorism-related Epidemics. Emerging Infectious Diseases www.cdc.gov/ncidod/EID/vol9no10/03-0231.htm.

Butler JC, Cohen ML, Friedman CR, Scripp RM, Watz CG Collaboration Between Public Health and Law Enforcement: New Paradigms and Partnerships for Bioterrorism Planning and Response. Emerging Infectious Diseases http://www.cdc.gov/ncidod/EID/vol8no10/02-0400.htm.

http://www.bt.cdc.gov/surveillance/ears/index.asp. Centers for Disease Control and Prevention. Early Aberration Reporting System.

Eyewitness to History. (2006). US News and World Report:40-45.

Fatah AA, Barrett JA, Arcilesi RD, Ewing KJ, Lattin CH, Moshier (2001). Introduction to Biological Agent Detection Equipment for Emergency First Responders. NIJ Guide 101-00:53

Heffernan R, Mostashari F, Das D, Karpati A, Kulldorff M, Weiss D Syndromic Surveillance in Public Health Practice, New York City. Emerging Infectious Diseases www.cdc.gov/ncidod/EID/vol10no5/03-0646.htm.

Introduction to Biological Agent Detection Equipment for Emergency First Responders. http://www.ncjrs.gov/pdffiles1/nij/190747.pdf.

http://www.leg.state.nv.us/NRS/NRS-631.html#NRS631Sec342. Regulations concerning continuing education.

Rinaggio J, Glick M (2006). The smallpox vaccine: An update for oral health care professionals. J Am Dent Assoc 137:452-60.

Tucker JB Historical Trends Related to Bioterrorism: An Empirical Analysis Emerging Infectious Diseases http://www.cdc.gov./ncidod/eid/vol5no4/tucker.htm.

Historical and Practical Examples

Dailey JC (1987). Computer-assisted identification of Vietnam War dental remains. Mil Med 152:179-92.

Dailey JC, Furue T (1988). A photographic technique for the restoration of damaged radiographs. J Forensic Sci 33:1273-7.

Dailey JC, Webb JE, Jr. (1988). Forensic odontology task force organization. Mil Med 153:133-7.

Eckert B (1977). The Forensic Disaster at Tenerife, the World's Greatest Fatal Aircraft Accident. Journal of the Forensic Science Society 19:236-238.

Gillespie TH, Brannon RB, Grayson FW, Gardner JD (1985). Dental identification of remains from the 23 October 1983 bombing of the U.S. Marine Headquarters, Beirut, Lebanon. Mil Med 150:635-9.

Lorton L, Rethman M, Friedman R (1989). The Computer-Assisted Postmortem Identification (CAPMI) system: sorting algorithm improvements. J Forensic Sci 34:996-1002.

CHAPTER 4

BITE MARK ANALYSIS

His biting is immortal; those that do die of it do seldom or never recover. William Shakespeare, English playwright (1564–1616)

Introduction and History

Bite mark analysis presupposes that there is a biting event that causes an injury or disturbance of some surface and that the effects can be carefully recorded for comparison to the teeth causing the disruption. Thus, a bite mark is a *patterned injury* produced by teeth. From the inception of the scientific study of bite marks it has been assumed that teeth are unique and the comparison of an injury to a specific tooth could be considered similar to tool mark or ballistic analyses.

Subsequent *evidence based* studies have indicated that the human teeth are unique. Thus, the problem for modern forensic odontologists involved in bite mark analysis is based on the interpretive problem of how well the individual features of the dentition can be compared to a patterned mark left on the skin of an individual or on an inanimate object.

Humans are known to have used their dentition as both tools and weapons since the dawn of time. Perhaps the earliest historical documentation of bite mark evidence being introduced in a legal proceeding in America involves the trial of Reverend George Burroughs in 1692. The Reverend was purported to have bitten one of the women accused of witchcraft during the Salem, Massachusetts witch hunt incidents and he paid for this indiscretion on the gallows. The first known publication of a scientific paper discussing a human bite is indicated to have been a case report by a Dr. Skrzeckes in 1874 concerning a *bite infection*.

The first bite mark case in the early twentieth century did not involve an injury of the skin and a tool mark examiner rather than a dentist was prominent as the expert witness in the case. Dr. Irving Sopher, an observer of bite mark injuries in the latter part of the last century, noted that skin was not a very good impression material and he had serious concerns about the accuracy of any comparison between the dentition of a suspect and bite marks on the human body. Later research, however, has demonstrated that skin is capable of reproducing minute detail in a bite mark pattern. Currently, the use of light and scanning electron microscopes as adjuncts in the study of bite marks is being carefully documented (**Figure 4-1**).

Following the first ABFO Bite Mark Workshop in 1984, the Bite Mark Guidelines Committee of the Board was charged with describing the various features that should be identified in bite

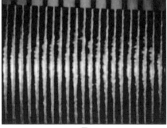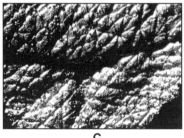

A   B   C

Figure 4-1: **A)** An exhibit derived from the scanning electron microscopic view of an impression in human skin as a result of a die pressed into a specimen. The specific features of the die can be recorded in the human skin sample at a level of 10 microns. **B)** The threaded die used to impress marks for the exhibit in A. **C)** A low power replica of human skin coated with gold-palladium which demonstrates specific incisal edge markings

mark analysis which could facilitate comparison between the teeth and a patterned mark. To date, the work of the committee continues to reevaluate the guidelines and establish common terminology in this discipline to further raise the level of the science practiced regarding bite mark analysis. The current ABFO Bite Mark Guidelines are presented in **Appendix C.**

Dr. Jonathan Taft and other Significant Early Cases

Figure 4-2: Dr. Jonathan Taft (1820-1903) DDS 1850, Ohio College of Dental Surgery, MD (Honorary) 1881, University of Michigan

Dr. Jonathan Taft was the Founding Dean of the University of Michigan College of Dental Surgery and served in that capacity form 1875 to 1903 (**Figure 4-2**). He was instrumental in organizing the National Association of Dental Examiners and was President of the American Dental Association from 1868 to 1869. Dr. Taft made significant contributions that advanced dental education including establishing the four-year curriculum for dental education in 1901. In the late 1800's Dr. Taft was asked to compare a set of teeth to the bite marks on the body of Miss Mary J. Lunsford and it may represent the first documented trial in the United States where bite mark evidence was used.

Three individuals became suspects in the case. However, Ansil L. Robinson was charged and a trial was held. Dr. Taft established a careful

methodology and approach for the study and comparison of the dental evidence in the case and it is important to understand his early contribution to the discipline from a historical and scientific context. He clearly understood the importance of a scientific and reliable evaluation and the principles upon which he based his work serves as a good starting point for any forensic dentist.

It is interesting to note that the issues concerning the bite mark evidence presented during the trial were essentially the same issues encountered today. The pattern wounds were well described by the medical examiner and the dental expert testified regarding the marks, dentition of the suspect and the individuality of human dentition. Dr. Taft noted that when placing the cast of Robinson's teeth upon the marks observed on the body of Mary J. Lunsford that, "…it was a surprising good fit." He described five distinct tooth marks with a specific pattern of missing teeth.

The defense produced a number of physicians who tried to prove that the teeth of the defendant could not be compared to the pattern injury on the victim. Dr. Whitney explained that *he had bitten the deceased* (editor's emphasis) in an effort to see how his own teeth left marks. Dr. Andrew Jackson Howe and Dr. Edmond Osmond cast doubts regarding the accuracy of marks imprinted in the skin. The latter testified, "It is not possible for the human teeth to reprint themselves accurately on the human arm. I think there are cases in which an irregular set of teeth might be detected with a reasonable degree of certainty, but it is not unusual to find five teeth standing in front."

Dr. Bushnell, a physician and surgeon stated, "You can fit the five front teeth of any mouth into the marks of five front teeth of any other mouth." He also expressed concern that any movement or tampering with the arm would have changed the mark such that the perpetrator's teeth would not match the mark.

The remarks and testimony of the experts on both sides in the trial of Ansil L. Robinson should remind contemporary forensic odontologists that there is *nothing new under the sun*. These same arguments are still presented today despite more *evidence based* science and experience of clinicians. The Robinson case never became well known because the defendant was eventually acquitted and the bite mark testimony never entered the body of case law through the appeal process. However, the methods and conclusions of the dental expert are instructive and when considered in a purely scientific sense the jury verdict is immaterial.

7 – Jurisprudence and in **Appendix K - Bite Mark Cases of Note**.

State of the Science

Recognition of Bite Marks

Although bite mark analysis by forensic odontologists has been considered controversial and has been challenged and/or the subject of several law review articles, it is based upon established

ABFO Guidelines of 1986	Terms suggested by Taft in 1870
Gross	
All teeth present in the suspect's mouth	The number of teeth in the mouth
Sizes of the arches	The size of the circle occupied by the teeth
Shape of the arches	The curvature of the circle occupied by the teeth
Tooth position	
Labiolingual position of the teeth	The inward and outward displacement of the teeth
Rotational position of the teeth	The torsion of the teeth
Vertical position of the tooth: Re: the occlusal plane	The relative position of the ends of of the teeth in respect to elongation
Spacing between adjacent marking edges	Spacing between the teeth
Intradental features	
Mesiodistal width of tooth	Teeth broad or narrow
Labiolingual width of tooth	Teeth thick or thin
Distinctive curvature of tooth incisal edges	Variations in the form of the ends or edges of the teeth
Other distinctive features	Teeth uniform or irregular

Table 4-1: A comparison between the terms used by Dr. Taft in the 1870 trial of Ansil L. Robinson and the terms suggested by the American Board of Forensic Odontology in 1986.

It would not be until the 1950s that the first case dealing with bite mark evidence in the United States reached the appellate level - Doyle v State of Texas in 1954. In 1972 Regina v. Boden became the first case in the Canadian judicial system in which bite mark evidence was introduced. The importance of these and other seminal cases, such as People v Marx in California and People v Milone in Illinois, in the latter part of the twentieth century are discussed in more detail in **Chapter**

scientific principles and methods and new techniques and procedures are continually being developed. Their appropriate use in conjunction with older accepted protocols has aided those interested in the analysis of bite mark evidence. The odontologist should use the material presented here as a starting point when undertaking new casework. A review of the bibliography presented with this chapter and the ABFO Bite Mark Guidelines in **Appendix C** provide additional information related to more advanced techniques and procedures employed in the evaluation of bite mark evidence.

Police investigators often seek the advice and help of forensic dental professionals with whom they have previously consulted and trust. Therefore, is important for each experienced forensic odontologist to mentor those less experienced. Consultations requested by police usually involve a request for assistance in resolving a dentally related puzzle presented during a criminal investigation involving additional evidence. The professional expertise and training of the non-police specialist is often essential to clarify technical issues arising from a crime scene examination or to corroborate statements made by witnesses. When faced with a human bite mark case in which key dental evidence must be recovered, examined and analyzed police agencies often request the assistance of dentists with training and experience in forensic odontology.

Based on studies involving the teeth in twins and others evaluating the dentition in large populations the premise that human dentition is unique for each individual is widely accepted. Odontologists attempt to collect, preserve and analyze forensic bite mark evidence based on the assumption that the bite perpetrator may be identified by studying any unique characteristics discovered in the bite mark injury. Living or deceased suspects may be linked to bites in material such as human tissue, foods, or inanimate objects.

The importance of dental treatment as one of the most significant and readily used factors in establishing the positive identification of a deceased individual has been discussed in **Chapter 2 - Human Identification**. The randomness of restorative locations and shapes of dental restorations are unique identifying features which can be verified from preexisting dental records and radiographs. Additionally, these unique features are powerful components of the evidence that may be reflected in a bite wound.

Bite mark analysis depends upon similarities between a pattern injury on a victim or inanimate object and a suspect's dental arch size and shape, tooth size and alignment, missing or damaged teeth and other features including spacing and length of the arch or its teeth. Many bite marks manifest degradation over time which may be associated with inflammatory tissue response and/or post mortem changes. Thus, the diffuse bruising associated with these time dependent changes may allow for numerous sets of teeth to be compared to the pattern injury. Unique features, discrete morphological characteristics and unusual formations are significant in demonstrating specific individual characteristics which may be reflected in the bite mark.

The dental expert may enter a case at any number of different stages. In most instances, the odontologist is called to examine a bite mark when it is first discovered. However, sometimes bite injuries are not discovered at the outset of the case. Occasionally an injury which is originally thought to be from some other cause is subsequently determined to be a bite mark. Therefore, the involvement of the odontologist may be requested long after the initial discovery. The request for input may come from several different sources. If the evidence collection was thorough the comparison may have significant weight. Incomplete evidence collection will result in the importance of any comparison being less significant in most cases.

It is important to recognize the pathology related to bite marks. Ultimately, injuries resulting from bites represent trauma and follow the classical signs of acute inflammation with initial redness, swelling, pain and loss of function of the bitten tissue. There is a cause and effect that permits many of the pathologic events to be described in detail. **Figure 4-3** exhibits escalating degrees of trauma to human skin leading to the resultant visible bite marks and the eventual sequelae related to healing. **Figure 4-4** demonstrates human bite marks left in food. Additionally, bite marks have been recovered from steering wheels, dashboards, stair steps, leather coats, gum, adhesive tape rolls and other inanimate

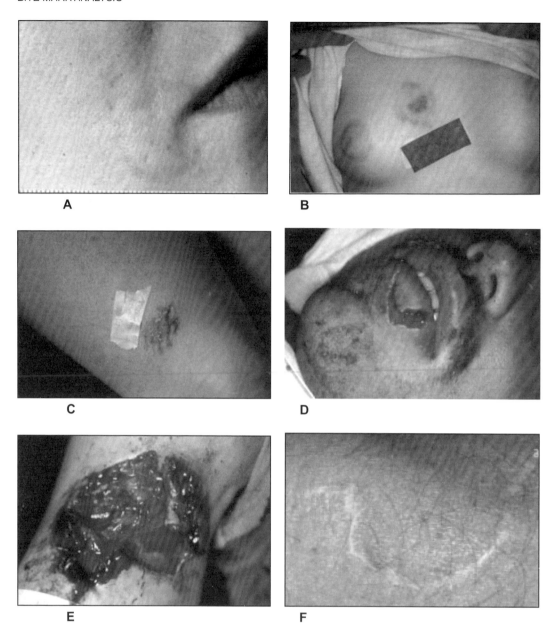

Figure 4-3: Various bite human bite marks on human skin. **A)** A simple erythema. **B)** A contusion caused by biting pressure at the level of conscious acceptance. **C)** An abrasion caused by scraping the teeth over the skin. **D)** Skin laceration caused by biting of the victim during a fight. **E)** An avulsive human bite on the arm of a 14 year old boy. **F)** A scar caused by the healing of a human bite mark laceration.

objects.

Bite marks can be represented by diffuse bruising or very specific indentations and each type of mark presents specific challenges for evidence recovery. Thorough collection

of evidence greatly enhances the ability to reliably compare the mark to the teeth causing the injury.

Many instruments of injury may mimic bite marks and final conclusions should be

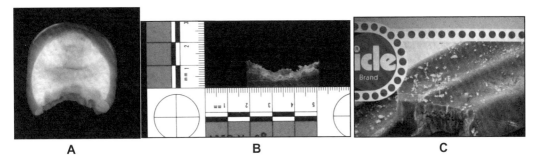

A   B   C

Figure 4-4: A human bite mark left in a green apple, a candy bar and a Popsicle.

carefully made only after thorough analysis. **Figures 4-5** and **4-6** illustrate a non bite mark injury known to be caused by a fall and heal marks from a shoe. It is not reasonable to say that any circular bruise should be considered a bite mark until proven otherwise. It is fair, however, to consider ruling out bite marks when analyzing most surface injuries of the appropriate size of the human dental arches.

If properly preserved and protected, bite mark injury patterns on a victim can provide an important link between the victim and the assailant. The obverse is also true if the suspect has been bitten by the victim in an assault. Law enforcement officers are usually the first to interview a living victim and may examine the body of a decedent in conjunction with a forensic pathologist. It is important for the odontologist to provide instruction to these investigators regarding the proper recognition and handling of bite

mark evidence. Only when the evidence is correctly recovered and preserved will the odontologist have the best opportunity to conduct a meaningful examination and reach significant conclusions.

Knowledge of the etiology, anatomic location, victim demographics and legal disposition of evidence in bite mark cases is be of interest to forensic odontologists as well as medical examiners/coroners, police investigators, criminal profilers, emergency room personnel, psychologists and family service counselors. Bite marks can be found on all anatomic areas of the body and some sites are significantly more likely to be bitten than others. Studies have indicated that the frequency of occurrence of bite injuries at specific locations varies with the type of crime and sex and age of the victim. A survey of 1100 forensic dentists in the United States and abroad conducted in 2004 reviewed 259 bite mark cases that included 778 individual bite marks.

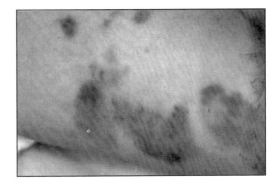

Figure 4-5: A non-bite contusion resembling the gross features of a human bite mark.

Figure 4-6: Heel marks left on the body of a man beaten to death.

The following results were obtained from this project and these are further described in **Tables 4-2** through **4-4** which have been graciously reprinted with the permission of the *Journal of Forensic Sciences*:

- Females were bitten more often than males.

- Perpetrators were male more often than female.

- Most bites occurred on the arm, followed by the breast. Males were bitten on the arm more often than females and females were bitten on the breast more often than males.

- The type of crime and the age of the victim were related to patterns in location distribution and number of bites.

The results of these studies demonstrate that human bite marks can be found at almost every anatomical location, although there is clearly a bias toward certain areas. The likely anatomical location of a bite injury is influenced by the type of crime, age and gender of the subject. Crimes commonly associated with biting are homicide, rape, sexual assault, robbery, assault and intimate partner, child and elder abuse.

Females are almost four times more likely to be bitten than males and the bites are commonly concentrated on the breasts, arms and legs. Female children may suffer numerous bites to many body locations. However, these injuries occur primarily on the face, legs and arms. Males are most frequently bitten on the arms, back and hands. A significant proportion of male bite mark victims are themselves the perpetrators of a violent crime. It is common to find more than one bite mark on a victim and these are often in a different anatomical location from the first injury resulting from a bite.

These data relate to human bite marks and bites from animals will be concentrated in different areas. Odontologists also deal with bites on non-human substrates and these are an important area of practice. Human bite marks inflicted on a victim frequently vary in location, appearance and severity. There are several basic principles which odontologists use when examining any patterned injuries. Investigators should be suspicious of any marks or bruises which have characteristics resembling injuries from teeth. Bite patterns usually appear as oval or circular contusions, bruises or abrasions. Indentations, lacerations

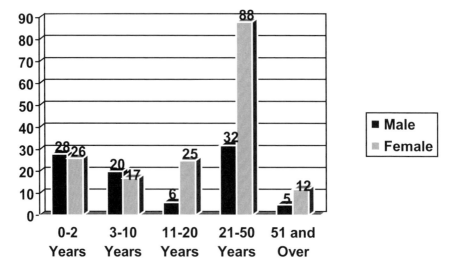

Table 4-2: Victim Distribution by Age and Gender. (Extracted and modified, with permission, from the *Journal of Forensic Sciences*, Vol. 50, No. 6, copyright ASTM International, 100 Barr Harbor Drive, West Conshohocken, PA 19428.)

TOTAL		FEMALE		MALE	
Arm	22.70%	Arm	18.70%	Arm	29.60%
Back	12.10%	Back	16.30%	Legs	14.60%
Legs	11.70%	Breast	14%	Face	11.10%
Face	10.30%	Face	10%	Non-Human	8.70%
Breast	9.20%	Legs	10%	Shoulder	8.40%
Shoulder	7.10%	Shoulder	6.30%	Buttocks	5.20%
Non-Human	5.80%	Buttocks	4.50%	Back	4.90%
Buttocks	4.70%	Neck	4.50%	Genitalia	4.20%
Neck	3.60%	Hand	4.50%	Chest	3.10%
Hand	3.50%	Non-Human	4.10%	Hand	2.80%
Abdomen	2.40%	Abdomen	3.20%	Ear	2.10%
Ear	2.30%	Ear	2.40%	Neck	2.10%
Genitalia	2.20%	Genitalia	1.00%	Breast	1.40%
Chest	1.30%	Head	0.61%	Abdomen	1.00%
Head	0.51%	Chest	0.20%	Head	0.30%
Waist	0.13%	Waist	0	Waist	0.30%

Table 4- 3: Bite Mark Distribution by Gender and Location. (Extracted and modified, with permission, from the *Journal of Forensic Sciences*, Vol. 50, No. 6, copyright ASTM International, 100 Barr Harbor Drive, West Conshohocken, PA 19428.)

or avulsions made by specific teeth may be observed in the skin surface (**Figure 4-7**).

Bite marks may reveal individual tooth marks or may appear as a double arched pattern or a uniform bruise (**Figure 4-8**). Most bite

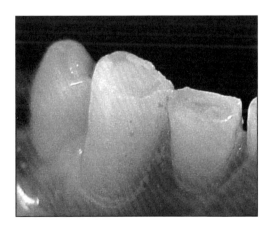
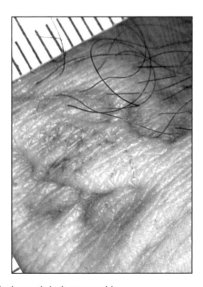

Figure 4-7: Specific teeth and their mark in human skin

TOTAL INCIDENCE		Sexual Crimes		Homicide		Child Abuse	
Arm	22.4%	Breast	18.6%	Arm	24.3%	Arm	28.6%
Legs	12.1%	Arm	15.9%	Legs	14.3%	Legs	18.9%
Breast	16.7%	Face	13.3%	Breast	12.7%	Back	8.5%
Face	10.7%	Legs	9.0%	Face	10.6%	Buttocks	7.3%
Shoulder	8.2%	Shoulder	8.5%	Shoulder	9.1%	Face	7.3%
Back	6.9%	Back	6.9%	Back	6.9%	Shoulder	6.1%
Hand	.7%	Neck	6.9%	Hand	5.3%	Abdomen	5.5%
Buttocks	4.1%	Genitalia	5.3%	Genitalia	3.2%	Ear	4.3%
Neck	4.1%	Hand	4.8%	Abdomen	3.2%	Breast	3.6%
Non Human	3.2%	Buttocks	3.7%	Ear	2.6%	Genitalia	3.0%
Abdomen	3.2%	Abdomen	3.2%	Buttocks	2.1%	Hand	3.0%
Genitalia	3.0%	Ear	1.6%	Chest	2.1%	Chest	1.2%
Ear	2.7%	Head	1.1%	Non Human	1.6%	Neck	1.2%
Chest	1.4%	Non Human	0.5%	Head	1.0%	Head	0.6%
Head	0.7%	Chest	0.5%	Neck	1.0%	Waist	0.6%
Waist	0.2%	Waist	0.0%	Waist	0.5%	Non Human	0.0%

Table 4- 4: Bite Mark Incidence by Anatomical Area and Type of Crime. (Extracted, with permission, from the *Journal of Forensic Sciences*, Vol. 50, No. 6, copyright ASTM International, 100 Barr Harbor Drive, West Conshohocken, PA 19428.)

patterns exhibit markings from several of the six upper and/or six lower front teeth. In some instances, markings from teeth as distal as the molars have been discovered. Occasionally, human bites and, more often, animal bites, result in severe laceration of the skin surface or complete avulsion of sections of skin and tissue (**Figure 4-9**).

Nipples and other areas of the breasts, the abdomen, thighs, back and shoulders, nose, ears and fingers are often targets of human bites (**Figure 4-10**). The extremities including the feet, legs, hands and arms are often bitten in animal attacks. However, large animals will often disfigure the face or strike the neck, body or genitalia. Among animals that attack

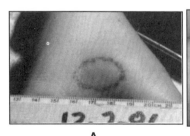 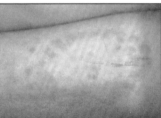 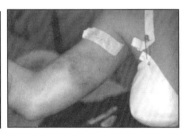

| A | B | C |

Figure 4-8: A) Individual tooth marks. **B)** Double arch. **C)** Bruise marks from a human bite.

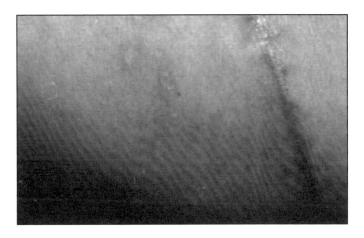

Figure 4-9: The results of a large dog bite on a small child. The injury affected one lung and the spleen. It is well healed now, but leaves a prominent scar.

in packs like feral dogs, the alpha animal will often cause injuries in the upper portions of the body including the neck and facial areas. The other animals will often disable the victim by attacking their legs and lower torso.

Experts have historically thought of bite marks as *tool marks* (**Figure 4-11**). Many of the procedures followed in a bite mark case can be directly compared to the procedures in *tool mark* comparison. A *tool mark* results when a relatively hard object, referred to as a tool contacts a relatively soft object and leaves an impression recorded in the surface of the softer object. This can occur secondary to movement of the tool or while the tool is at rest. In the case of a bite mark a hard tooth leaves its impression as an abrasion, laceration, indentation or other traumatic injury in the soft surface of the skin or inanimate object that is bitten.

Like *tool mark* investigators, odontologists recognize a variety of classifications of the characteristics discovered in these impressions or markings. *Gross characteristics* are used to identify the general source of the tool. By examining the gross features of a footprint impression in sand the evidence may reveal to the *tool mark* evaluator that the mark has *gross characteristics* consistent with a running shoe and not a cowboy boot.

Features such as the overall shape of the mark, including the toe and heel impressions and the pattern of the sole are generally recognizable as originating from a running shoe. Similarly, an odontologist may determine that two approximating semicircular marks found on skin and consisting of several small lacerations with a central area of ecchymosis have the gross characteristics of a human bite mark. This pattern is often distinct from an injury caused by any other source. Thus, care should always be exercised to gain specific information regarding the cause of a pattern injury.

Class characteristics are measurable features of a mark which indicate a restricted origin. When considering tool marks these characteristics result from design factors and are determined prior to manufacture. By comparing the *class characteristics* of the sole pattern to known standards, the footprint examiner can determine that a running shoe is a Reebok and not an Adidas.

Similarly, an odontologist may determine that a bite mark was produced by an adult and not a child by comparing measurements of the size of the teeth and the dimensions, shape and width of the dental arch pattern to known standards in the two populations. It may also be possible to determine that the dimensions of separate bruises, abrasions, or lacerations in the injury are consistent with the *class characteristics* of specific teeth. This may lead the odontologist to conclude that the suspect

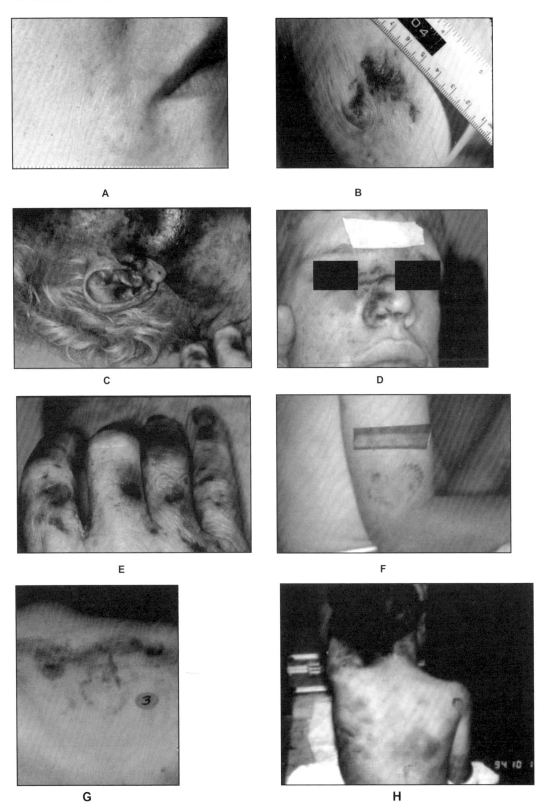

Figure 4-10: Typical areas of occurrence for human bite mark patterns.

cannot be excluded as having caused the bite.

In the evaluation of a mark left by a tool the analyst recognizes *individual characteristics* which are imperfections or irregularities produced accidentally during manufacture or caused by use, misuse, or damage to the tool. Cuts, chips and wear of the sole of the Reebok running shoe may provide sufficient data to allow the footwear expert to positively identify precisely which running shoe made the footprint in the sand. Morphologic or anatomic dental characteristics such as enamel fractures, prominent marginal ridges, curved dental surfaces, talon cusps and missing restorations, among others are recognized as individual dental characteristics which can provide valuable data for the odontologist to associate or relate the teeth of an individual with certain bite mark injury patterns.

If any tooth is examined very closely, it will often demonstrate unique *individual characteristics*. The most useful information for the investigating odontologist is derived from cases in which specific and detailed patterns of the characteristics of individual teeth have been recorded in the injury. If specific individualizing information is available it may be possible to identify the pattern injury as a bite mark. If minimal information is available the type of injury or the tool which caused it may not be identifiable.

The identification of bite mark suspects is usually a criminal matter with organization and funding derived from the police agency having local jurisdiction, Medical Examiner/Coroner,

District Attorney or defense counsel. The process of bite mark identification is complex and requires a high degree of expertise and experience on the part of the odontologist. Although still frequently regarded as new scientific evidence the use of bite mark evaluation has dramatically increased since the introduction of such evidence into the modem justice system.

General Considerations

The examination and analysis of bite mark evidence associated with the commission of a crime is a challenging and stimulating area of forensic dental investigation. It can be a crucial aspect of the criminal investigation since an association between the bite pattern injury and the dentition of the suspect may establish that the suspect was at the crime scene and in violent contact with the victim. Bite mark investigations involve injuries caused by humans and by animals and may involve either deceased or living victims. In most cases, bite marks have been found on victims of violent crimes involving fighting, sexual misconduct, abuse of a child, spouse or elder or other types of violent behavior. Most often, the perpetrator of the crime bites the victim although occasionally the victim bites the perpetrator.

When a bite mark is discovered and an odontologist is called to initially examine the site, law enforcement officers are primarily interested in establishing the forensic significance of the evidence. A preliminary examination of the injury site should focus on the following questions:

 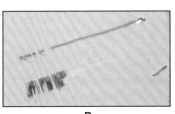 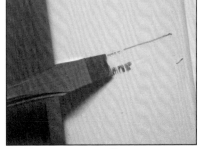

A **B** **C**

Figure 4-11: A flat screwdriver with a defect produced a distinctive tool mark on a painted metal surface.

- Is the injury a bite mark based on an evaluation of its *gross characteristics*?

- If it is a bite, was it caused by human or animal teeth?

- Does the age and appearance of the injury fit the alleged type of crime and its time of occurrence?

- Does the bite reveal unique, *individual characteristics* of the biter's teeth?

- Can these features be compared to the teeth of any suspects which may be apprehended?

The odontologist should carefully analyze the appearance, location, shape, extent and color of any bruises, contusions, or loss of tissue. The amount and severity of the trauma which may have been caused by the teeth of the perpetrator should be considered. The odontologist has a responsibility to estimate the potential value of recovering and analyzing the bite mark. It is important to reach some conclusions about the forensic significance and evidentiary value of the bite mark before attempting to recover any evidence. When making this decision concerning the probative value of evidence related to the bite mark injury or pattern on an inanimate object, the odontologist should consider the following:

- Is it reasonable to assume that accurate exhibits and information with significant evidentiary value can be obtained from the site?

- Can certain features of the teeth of the biter be identified from the shapes, positions and contours recorded in the injury site?

- Is there enough data to establish a high probative value for this evidence and to possibly prove or disprove a physical association with a suspect's teeth?

In some cases a bite mark is found to have little significance. In others, a representation of the teeth of the biter is very clearly recorded in the pattern injury. From the outset of a bite mark case the legal investigators should be informed of the relative value that the odontologist places on the dental evidence. With this information the individual(s) requesting the expertise of the odontologist can determine how much time, effort and financial commitment should be reserved for this aspect of the case. Once the decision to recover the bite mark evidence is reached, every effort should be made to proceed expeditiously.

Bite marks provide both physical and biological evidence. Although the forensic dentist is principally concerned with the visible physical evidence related to the bite pattern the potential presence of invisible biological evidence associated with the bite mark is just as important. If the pattern injury is determined to be a bite mark then an attempt should be made to collect its invisible evidence as well. The mark may be determined to be of little evidentiary value. However, there will never be another occasion to record surface disruption, gather salivary trace evidence or preserve the tissue or specimen for histological and/or histochemical evaluation. Most dental experts concur that more details of the bite mark can be determined with careful study of the material in the laboratory.

The tasks involved in recovery and analysis of bite mark evidence is very similar to the work of investigators in other forensic disciplines in that it is better to gather more evidence than less and to have collected material that is not useful than to have overlooked important factors during the early stages of evidence evaluation. Early recognition and subsequent preservation of a bite mark is critical since the appearance of the injury may begin to change rapidly in a living victim. Additionally, even when bite marks are left on inanimate objects, saliva trace evidence may degrade and be of no value. Thus, it is important to have a recovery protocol established so that a direct and effective procedure can be initiated for its immediate analysis and evaluation for probative value.

The standard protocol for bite mark analysis should include the photographing of the site

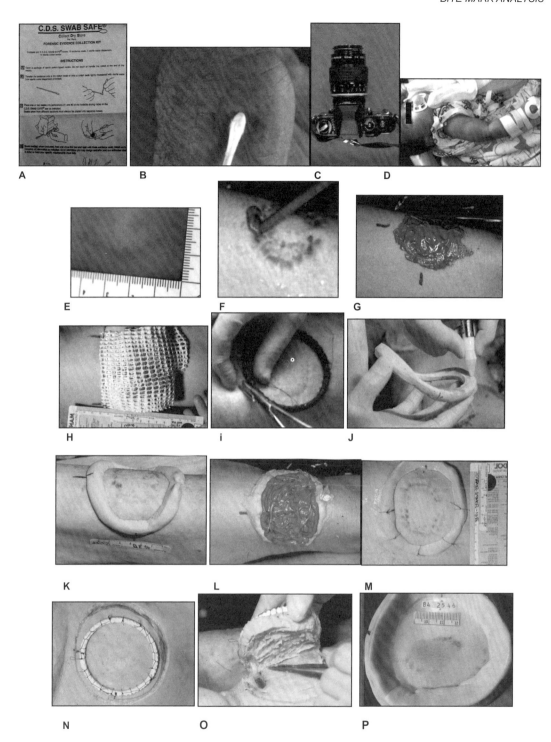

Figure 4-12: An overview of the techniques involved with the swabbing, photography, dental impressions and tissue preservation of bite mark evidence.

before any other procedures are performed that may change or otherwise adversely affect the evidence. After initial photographs are obtained there should be a swabbing of the bite for biological trace evidence. Additional photography of the injury and an impression of the skin to facilitate the production of a cast of its surface can now be obtained. In the case of a deceased victim, the protocol may also include removal of the epidermis and dermis at the bite site for eventual microscopic examination, transillumination studies and long term preservation of the in situ bite mark (**Figure 4-12**).

Victim Examination and Evidence Collection

Non-Invasive Analysis

Two-Dimensional Evidence

Photography

Prior to any other evidence collection a photographic record of the original appearance of the bitten individual or inanimate object should be obtained. These photographs provide for the documentation and numbering of multiple injuries. Additionally, they orient and identify the location of any patterned injuries. These images can also be used for proper identification and orientation of subsequent close-up photographs.

The pattern injury site should be extensively photographed following the Guidelines of the American Board of Forensic Odontology (**Appendix C**) or other scientific standard setting organization. The use of color and black and white film and/or digital storage media is acceptable. Photographic evidence is considered to be among the least expensive components of the evidence recovery protocol and in many cases photographs have been found to be the most significant and useful evidence. Bite marks and bruises change over time in the viable tissue of a living victim. This can also occur in a decedent secondary to decomposition. Thus, it is often helpful to repeat the photographic series at regular

intervals for several days. Twenty-four hour intervals over a period of three to five days have proven effective for recording the bruise maturation phenomenon.

Injuries of approximately two weeks duration can be photographed in color and visible light can be used to recover information about the surface changes in the injury. It is stressed that the opportunity to photograph the bite mark at a specific interval will only present itself once. Therefore, a well planned photographic protocol is essential to forensic bite mark evidence recovery.

General orientation photographs are used to record the location of the bite on the body of the victim. Relationships to known anatomical landmarks should be recorded. Additionally, it is important to be able to identify the individual being photographed. The dentition of the victim should also be photographed to rule out self biting. This is especially important when evaluating bite mark injuries on the forearms of rape or abuse victims who may have put their arms in their mouths to suppress the urge to scream or cry out.

Close-up photographs should be taken with and without the ABFO No. 2 reference scale to record the specific identifying features of the mark or pattern injury. The reference pictures without the scale will preclude eventual challenge to the photographic evidence at trial by showing that the scale was not obstructing the full view of the evidence. A series of photographs using various lighting protocols is also recommended (**Figure 4-13**).

It is important to remove the electronic flash unit from the camera to facilitate aiming the light source at the bite mark from a variety of oblique angles. This technique permits various areas of the injury site to be highlighted. This oblique lighting exposure is especially useful if indentations from the teeth are left in the skin (**Figure 4-14**).

The angle of the photographic lens to the subject is a source of distortion. The variance from the perpendicular can be calculated and any distortion correct as seen in **Figure 4-15**.

CHAPTER 2
HUMAN IDENTIFICATION

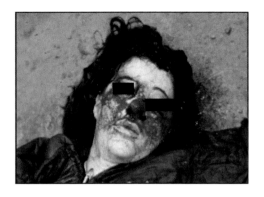

Identification by personal recognition

Identification by personal effects

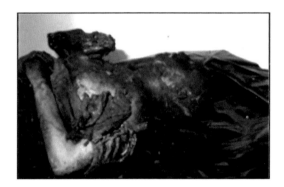

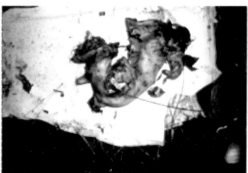

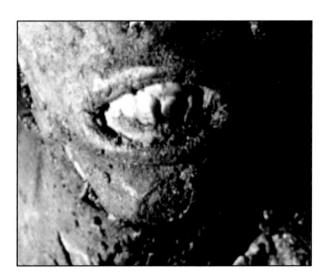

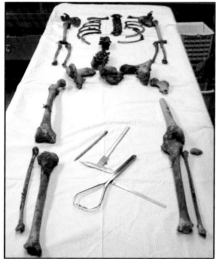

Occasionally, viewing is not possible due to burning, trauma or skeletonization.

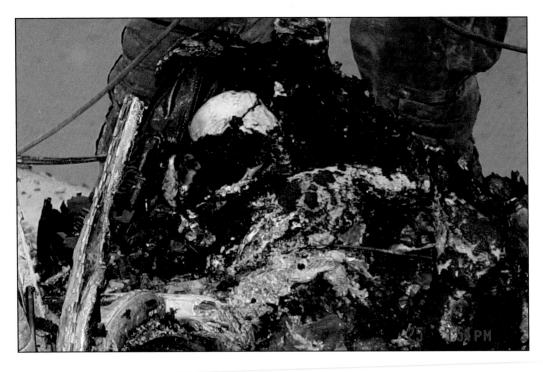

Skull fragments and teeth recovered from a cremated individual 1000 degrees C for 2.5 hours. The skull is clearly identifiable after a typical fire.

Examples of dental *grill* restorations

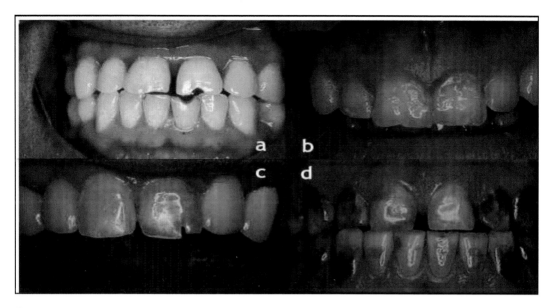

Occupational situations affecting the teeth **(a)** This individual exhibits characteristic notching of the mandibular and maxillary left central incisors associated with electrical wire stripping. The individual has worked as an electrician for many years **(b)** Labial erosion characteristic of the type seen among workers in acidic environments **(c)** A notch caused by the holding of pins between the teeth, this individual was a seamstress **(d)** a severe case of dental fluorosis of the type seen among workers in the superphosphate industries

The composition of a betel quid. (a) leaf of the betel (Piper betel), (b) sliced areca nut, one of the major constituents of betel quid (paan) that can also be chewed on its own, still resulting in the classic stain, (c) sweeteners are added to children's paan (d) once the ingredients have been placed, including lime, the leaf is folded and can be placed for chewingor to suck.

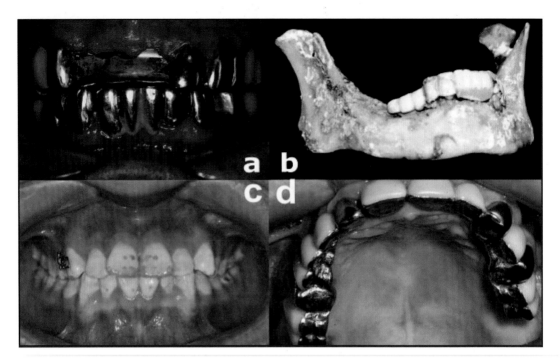

Likely country of residence (a) example of Ukraine dental work (b) example of Chinese dental treatment, (c) individual from China with grade 4 (TF) Fluorosis, (d) example of Russian dental treatment.

CHAPTER 3
MULTIPLE FATALITY INCIDENT, DENTAL IDENTIFICATION AND BIOTERRORISM ISSUES

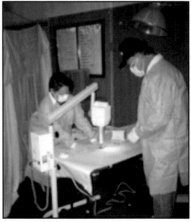

The Nevada Identification Team preparing for National Guard transportation for an exercise.

Radiography of jaw fragments using portable radiographic equipment.

Views of the destruction caused by Hurricane Katrina. All basic infrastructure was damaged, and essential public services were non-existent.

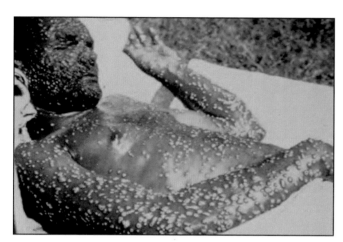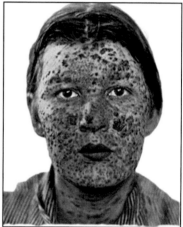

CDC pictures of smallpox in various individuals.

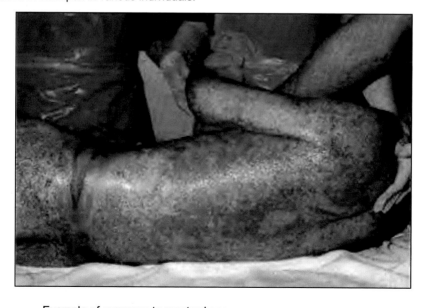

Example of exposure to mustard gas.

CHAPTER 4
BITE MARK ANALYSIS

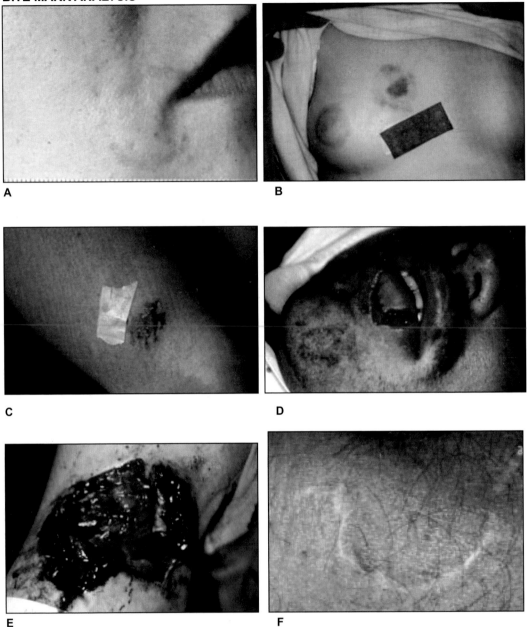

Various bite human bite marks on human skin. **A)** A simple erythema. **B)** A contusion caused by biting pressure at the level of conscious acceptance. **C)** An abrasion caused by scraping the teeth over the skin. **D)** Skin laceration caused by biting of the victim during a fight. **E)** An avulsive human bite on the arm of a 14 year old boy. **F)** A scar caused by the healing of a human bite mark laceration.

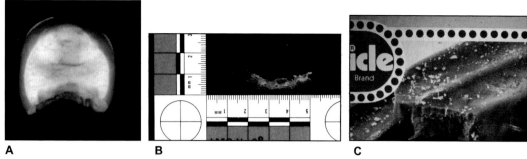

A human bite mark left in a green apple, a candy bar and a popsicle.

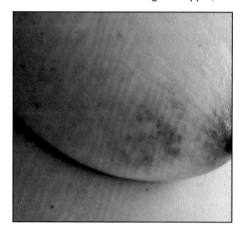

A non-bite contusion resembling the gross features of a human bite mark

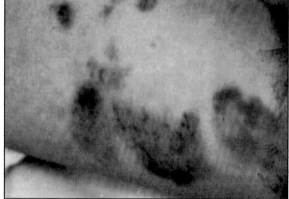

Heel marks left on the body of a man beaten to death

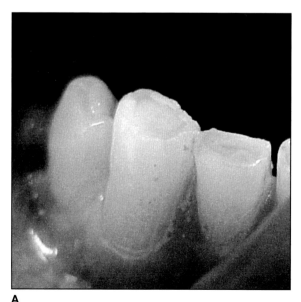

A

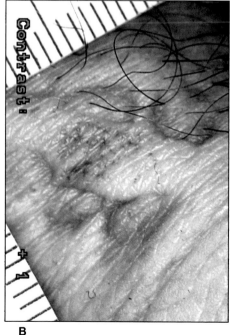

B

Specific teeth and their marks in human skin.

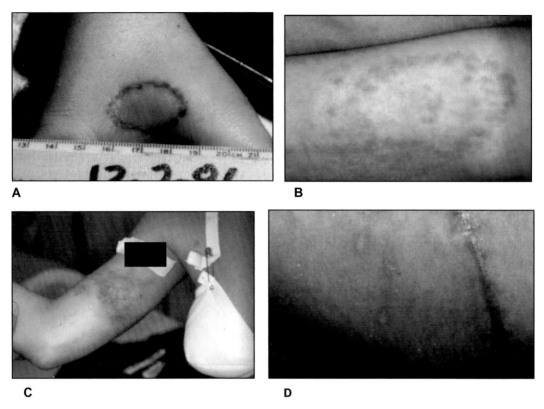

A) Individual human bite marks. **B)** Double arch. **C)** Bruise marks from a human bite. **D)** The results of a large dog bite on a small child, leaving a prominent scar.

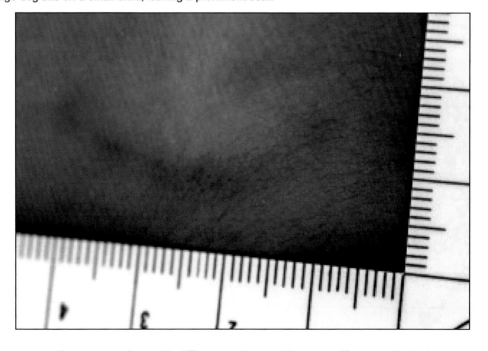

An example of a pattern injury with diffuse markings without significant individual characteristics representing specific teeth.

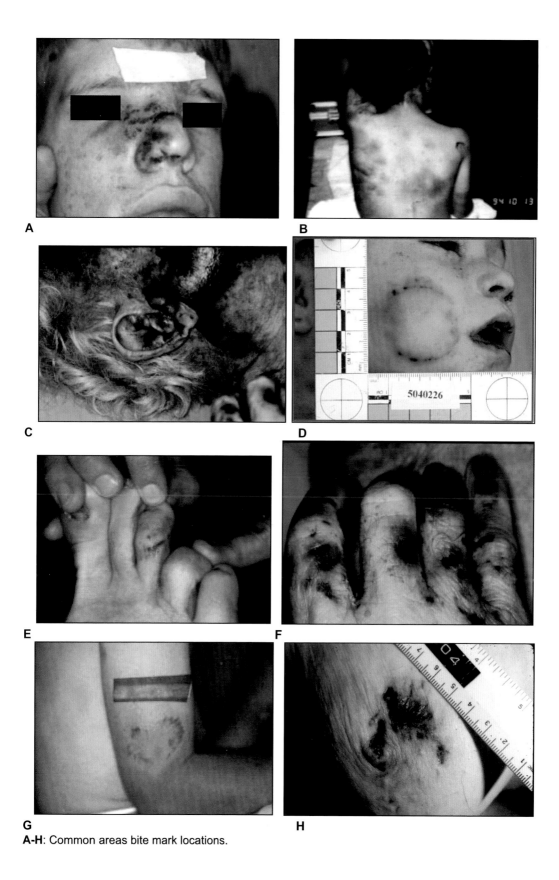

A-H: Common areas bite mark locations.

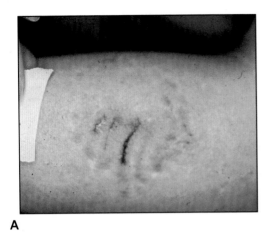 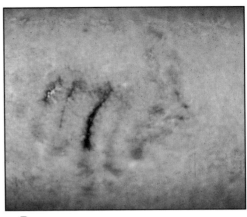

A   B

Examples of an orientation and close-up view of a linear bite mark pattern without scale.

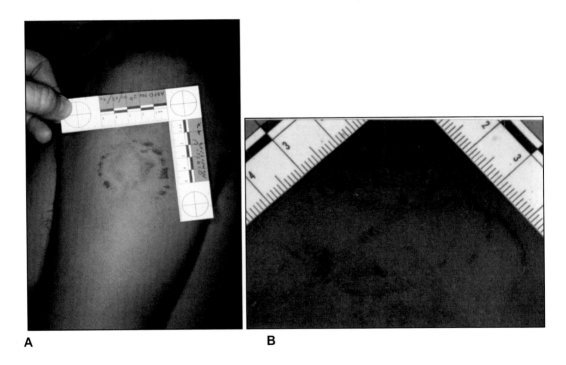

A   B

Examples of an orientation and close-up view of a linear bite mark pattern with ABFO # 2 scale.

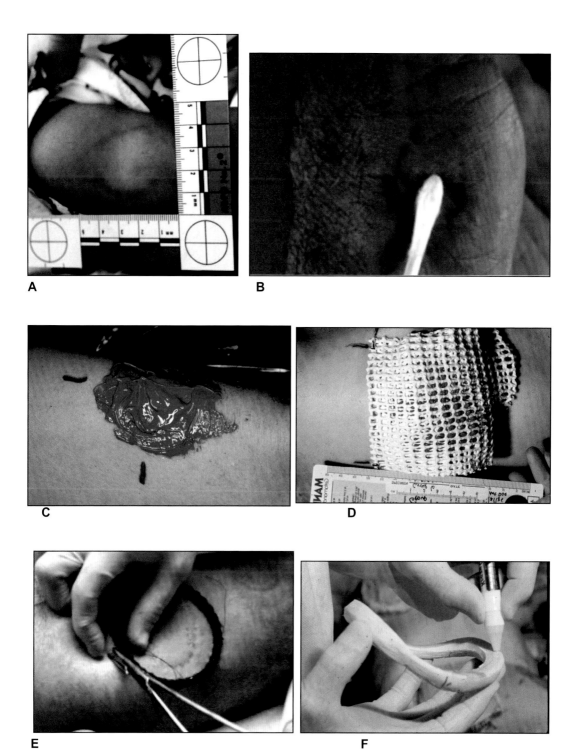

A-F: An overview of the techniques involved with the swabbing, photography, dental impressions and tissue preservation of bite mark evidence.

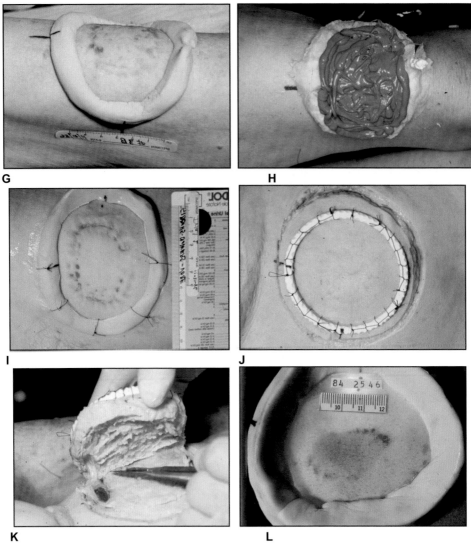

G

H

I

J

K

L

G-L: An overview of the techniques involved with the swabbing, photography, dental impressions and tissue preservation of bite mark evidence (continued).

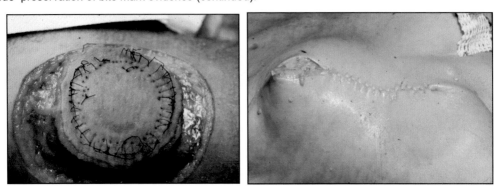

The ring is used to stabilize tissue before removal to avoid the distortion shown in this view.

it is not necessary to leave large excision wound. The tissue can be undermined and sutured for a very acceptable and respectful result.

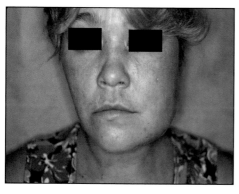 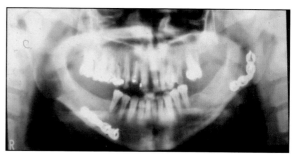

A   **B**

A) Delayed presentation for care approximately 7 days after facial swelling began following inflicted trauma to face of 28 year old Caucasian woman. Note facial asymmetry resulting from mandibular left angle fracture

B) Example of bilateral mandibular fractures previously treated in 29 year old female victim of intimate partner violence shown in previous photo. (Photographs courtesy of John McDowell, DDS)

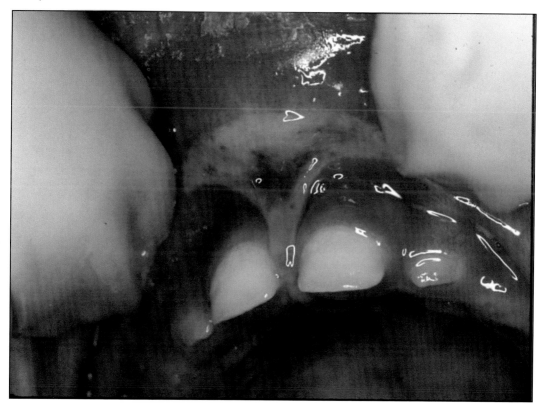

Torn labial frenum in 14 month (Caucasian female) old victim of child abuse (Photographs courtesy of John McDowell, DDS)

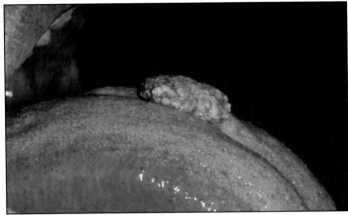

Condyloma on the dorsum of the tongue that could be a sequela of sexual abuse. (Photograph courtesy of Dr. J. Michael Hall)

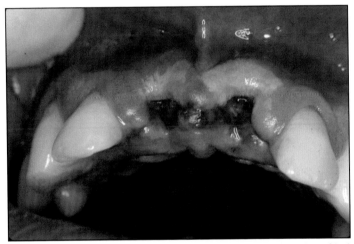

Delayed presentation for care seen in 34 year old Caucasian female victim of intimate partner violence (ITP). Initial presentation for care was approximately four days after most recent assault resulting in avulsion of maxillary central incisors. (Photographs courtesy of John McDowell, DDS)

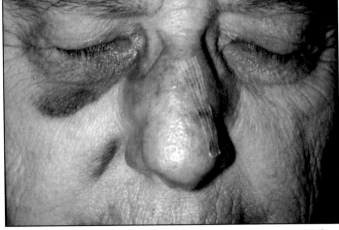

Bilateral periorbital ecchymoses and fractured nasal bone in a 77 year old Caucasian woman. (Photographs courtesy of John McDowell, DDS)

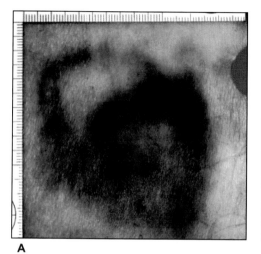
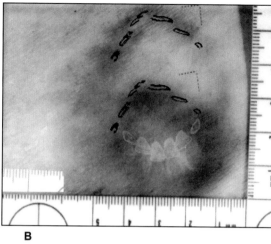

A   B

Typical exhibits prepared for courtroom presentation.

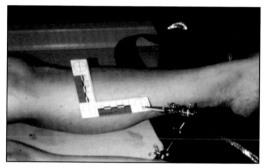

Lower leg photographed under normal light source. Close-up photograph of same area with ALI
(Photograph courtesy of G. Golden, DDS)   showing presence of fluorescing semen.

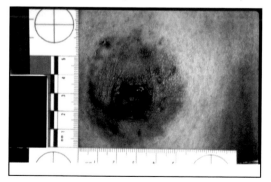

A   B

Bite on breast - full spectrum flash illumination. RUV/UVA Photo of same bite mark. Note individual tooth
pattern visible. (Photograph courtesy of G. Golden, DDS)

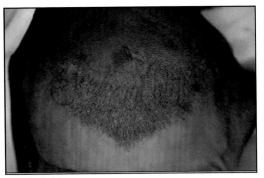

Full spectrum photo - tattoo in scalp.

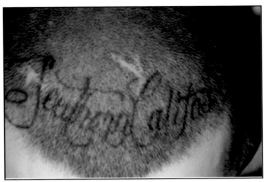

Infrared photo with enhanced tattoo visibility.

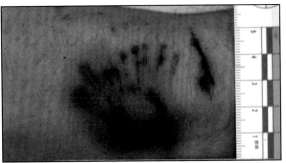

A color photograph of a dog bite.

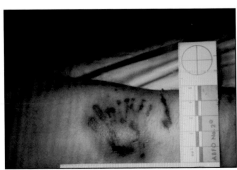

The same bite photographed with ALI.

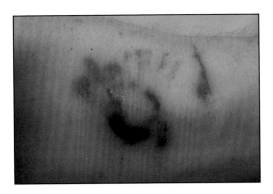

The same photograph with an IR light source.

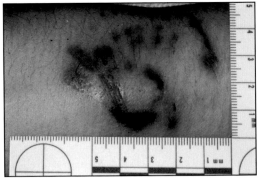

The same photograph with an UV light source.

(Photographs courtesy of G. Golden, DDS)

Photographic documentation of several of the bite mark injuries was accomplished with full spectrum, ALI, IR, and UV photographic techniques. A demonstration of the different photographic results of the same dog bite is provided herein, to show the values and resultant imaging of each of the techniques:

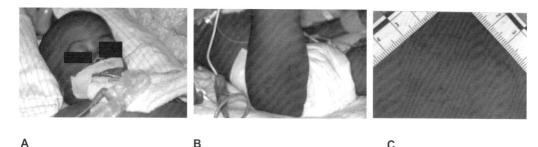

A   B   C

Figure 4-13: Photography starting with a general identification, moving to orientation and then a close-up view.

If the bite mark is discovered on an area of the body with a small radius of curvature such as the edge of the wrist of a child, it may be necessary to photograph the injuries attributed to the maxillary teeth separately from those of the mandibular teeth. The plane of the film should always be kept parallel to the skin surface to avoid perspective distortion. The amount of distortion with a two inch (5.1 cm) diameter of curvature is graphically shown in **Figure 4-16**.

The angle of the film plane of the camera to the injured surface is critical. The principal reason for the development of circles on the ABFO No. 2 reference scale was to verify that the photographic exposure could be rectified to one in which the film plane of the camera was parallel to the image being photographed and thus, not distorted. The following guidelines are helpful when using the ABFO No. 2 reference scale:

- Store the scale on a flat surface in a manner which prevents any warping, curvature, or other damage.

- Position the scale adjacent to the bite mark so the plane of the scale approximates the midpoint between the highest and lowest elevation of the tissue contour at the injury site.

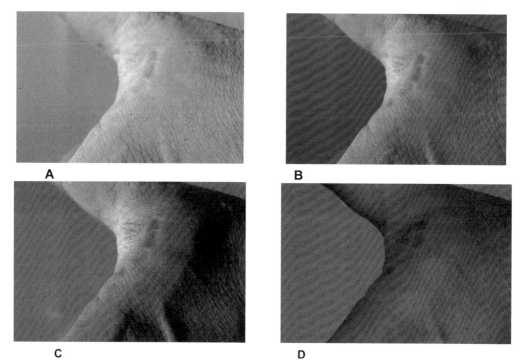

A   B

C   D

Figure 4-14: Lighting of a three dimensional bite mark from different angles.

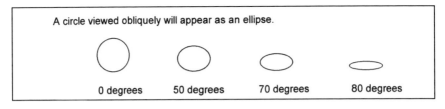

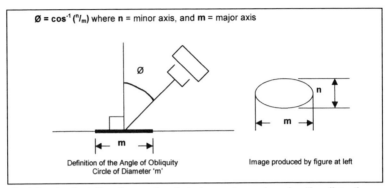

Figure 4-15: The principle of calculating the angle of photography and seeing the distortion produced.

- Record information about the case such as the case number, date and time and investigators' initials directly on the scale or with a label positioned away from the scale markings.

- Stabilize the scale using mechanical support such as an orthodontic soldering jig or Helping Hands device (**Figure 4-17a**). The scale should not be held. Another innovative solution to the problem of stabilization of the camera plane in regard to the bite mark plane is the photographic aid developed by E. Ruth Smith, DDS. This device assures that the camera film or sensor plane is always parallel to the ruler or rulers mounted on special holders (**Figures 4-17 b, c**). Once positioned, the exposure of images is greatly simplified because the photographer only has to concentrate on correctly aligning the ruler before exposing the photograph.

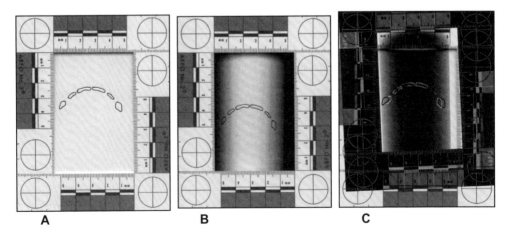

A   **B**   **C**

Figure 4-16: Two photographs taken of the same incisal edge pattern. **A** is on a flat surface and **B** is placed on a two inch (5.1 cm) cylinder. The superimposition of the two in **C** demonstrates the amount of distortion. In this case it is approximately fifteen percent.

- Position the camera over the injury and the scale so the plane of the film is parallel to the plane of the scale. This will save considerable time and effort later in the darkroom or at the computer to rectify any perspective distortion represented by elliptical changes in the circles imprinted on the ABFO No.2 scale.

- Record all of the ABFO No. 2 scale within the photograph. The total length of each arm of the scale, including the circles and cross-hairs at the ends, should be visible through the viewfinder to demonstrate the full advantage of the scale. It is designed for determination of photographic distortion and subsequent rectification.

- Close-up photographs can then be taken of the bite mark injury or pattern which may not include all of the ABFO No. 2 scale.

Chapter 6–Technological Aides in Forensic Dentistry presents detailed information regarding the use of alternative light sources and digital photographic techniques in the acquisition of bite mark evidence.

Salivary Trace Evidence

Serologists estimate that 80-85 percent of the human population secrete agglutinins in their body fluids (saliva, seminal and vaginal fluid, tears and sweat) which can be used to determine the ABH blood group classification of an individual. These ABH blood group tests which analyze A, B and O antigens on the surface of red blood cells are not very discriminating markers and cannot be used to positively identify an individual. Confirmation of salivary amylase on an injury site may indicate that the injury may be a bite mark when this is not readily apparent from the physical appearance of the wound.

More importantly, saliva contains sloughed epithelial cells from the inner surface of the lips and oral mucosa and leukocytes from the gingival fluid and tissues. These cells may provide a source of deoxyribonucleic acid (DNA) evidence. It is unlikely that a bite cannot be inflicted without leaving traces of saliva behind and the analysis of DNA in these samples has become the gold standard for evaluation of salivary trace evidence for identification of a perpetrator.

Photographs of the area to be swabbed should be taken to demonstrate the original

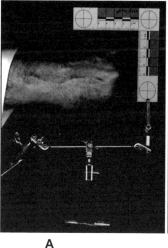

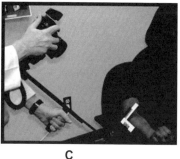

A   B   C

Figure 4-17a-c: **A)** The Helping Hands device used as a stable holder for the scale. **B, C)** The stabilization device developed by E. Ruth Smith, DDS

condition of the wounded area. Following this procedure and before the body of the victim is washed, the bitten area should be gently swabbed using the double swab technique described by Sweet et al and outlined below. Before swabbing, the pathologist should provide the odontologist with information concerning the handling of the body of the victim. This will insure that the injured areas were not washed, touched, or disturbed in any way prior to the attempt to recover the salivary trace evidence.

The odontologist will usually not be the individual who actually recovers the DNA sample. This procedure is routinely performed by other forensic evidence gathering specialists. The only responsibility of the odontologist in this regard may be to ascertain that a DNA sample has been taken from the victim. When the odontologist is involved in the recovery of salivary trace evidence, the following double swab technique should be employed:

- **Materials**:

　-Two sterile cotton swabs

　- 3mL of sterile, distilled water

　- Container for swabs after recovery and air drying (paper envelope, Fitzpak swab box or other commercial product)

- **Method**:

　- Immerse the first swab in the sterile distilled water.

　- Roll the wet swab tip over the surface of the skin or object using moderate pressure and circular motion.

　-Set first swab aside for air drying.

　- Roll the second dry swab over the area using similar pressure and motion to absorb all of the moisture left by the first swab.

- Set the second swab aside for air drying.

- After drying for approximately thirty minutes the swabs can be transferred to the properly labeled storage container (some containers allow drying inside the container).

- Submit swabs immediately to laboratory or store by freezing at -20 degrees C.

When swabbing a putative bite mark for salivary DNA it is not necessary to take a control swab from another area of the skin of the victim. A control DNA sample should be collected in one of the following manners:

　- A whole blood sample

　- A small section of tissue taken at the autopsy of the deceased victim

　- A buccal swab if the subject is living.

Three-Dimensional Evidence

Bite Mark Impressions

In a case involving either a living or a deceased victim of biting an accurate mold of the skin surface can be obtained and accurate casts created using dental impression materials. Impressions of the dentition of the victim are desirable if there is any possibility of a self inflicted bite mark. Low and medium viscosity vinyl polysiloxane (VPS) impression materials have been found to be very accurate and possess good long-term stability. Alginate materials do not provide sufficient detail and accuracy for bite mark analysis and should not be used as an impression material.

Dentists routinely use dispensing systems which provide pressure from a pump to express dental impression material through a mixing nozzle (**Figure 4-19**). These systems have also been useful for taking bite mark impressions since the pre-mixed material is delivered directly onto the injury site. These putty gun systems are mobile, convenient and easy to use and reduce the inclusion of air bubbles in the final impression.

A means of supporting the impression material may provide to reinforce it against dimensional changes and reduce the risk of distortion. Some forensic dentists use heavy body material as a backing for the low or medium viscosity material that is applied directly to the skin. This heavy body material is sufficiently dimensionally stable to allow transportation to the laboratory where plaster or stone bases can be added (**Figure 4-20**). Many different backing materials have been tested in the past. Individual odontologists tend to develop favorite materials for use in their casework.

Rigidity and stability are the criteria for an ideal backing material since these properties of the material maintain the anatomical contour of the impression when it is removed from the skin. Dental laboratory stone, acrylic dental tray material, thermoplastic tray material and thermoplastic orthopedic mesh such as Hexcelite are backing materials that have been widely used by odontologists to stabilize bite mark impressions (**Figure 4-19**). All of these materials appear to satisfy the requirements for rigidity and stability.

Anatomical direction markers should be added to the backing to orient the impression *in situ*

before it is removed from the skin surface (**Figure 4-18**). For example, the number **1** or an **S** can be added to indicate the direction of the impression toward the victim's head (Superior). The number **2** or **M** can be used to indicate its position relative to the midline (Medial). After the impression is poured in dental stone, epoxy, or acrylic, these anatomical indicators can be transferred to the cast so the orientation of the bite mark on the body of the victim can be reestablished

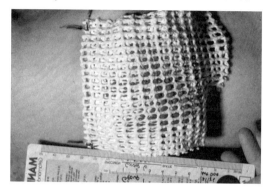

Figure 4-19: The Hexcelite orthopedic material used for tray backing.

The following procedures should be followed when recovering bite mark evidence with impression techniques:

- Hands should be washed and sterile examination gloves placed before contacting the bitten tissue or object. Some impression materials

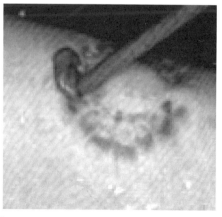

A   B

Figure 4-18: The impression material is carefully expressed onto the injury site until all of the injury and a border are covered. Note the orientation marks placed with a felt tip marker.

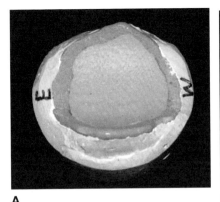 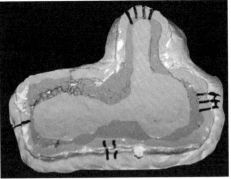

A   B

Figure 4-20: Bases added to bite mark impressions

are inhibited by latex gloves and the use of vinyl or nitrile gloves is recommended.

- Some dental experts prefer to carefully shave or clip excess body hair from the injury site and then gently wash the area with plain water and dry the surface. An alternative approach is to not remove overlying hair but to repeat the impression. It is certainly necessary to have access to the wound pattern if it is in the scalp or pubic hairline.

- The acrylic tray or thermoplastic backing material, when used, is shaped to the anatomical contour of the injury site. A felt or laundry marking pen can be used to record the position of anatomical landmarks on the exposed surface of the material. An appropriate amount of tray adhesive should be painted on the inner surface or retention holes drilled into the backing before the impression is taken.

- The impression material should be expressed onto the injury site with care to avoid the creation of bubbles and to completely cover and record the details of any abrasions, indentations, or lacerations associated with the pattern. The material is gently laid down over the irregularities of the surface. Impression material should

be pushed ahead of the dispensing gun nozzle as it is expressed onto the skin to reduce the incorporation of air bubbles at the interface.

-The impression material should be extended approximately 3-4 cm. beyond the outer edges of the bite mark to ensure that a wide margin of the skin surface is accurately recorded in the impression.

- A thin layer of impression material can be added to the backing material or adhesive on holes in the backing material for mechanical capture. Special care should be exercised to orient the anatomical reference marks correctly.

- A small sample of the VPS material should be expressed onto the skin adjacent to the primary site. This will provide an additional sample which can be checked for completeness of polymerization prior to separating the impression from the bite mark and disturbing the actual exhibit.

- The anatomical reference markers should be clearly visible and if inadvertently covered by impression material, they can be clarified.

- When the material is completely set the exhibit can be removed by carefully raising it by one edge and gently lifting and rolling it away from the bite mark surface.

- The time, date, case details and initials of the odontologist should be clearly recorded on the exhibit according to the guidelines for chain of custody.

Manufacturers of VPS impression materials indicate that the setting time is seven to eight minutes under normal circumstances. This time may be significantly increased if the victim's body has been cooled. In some cases the setting time is increased to 20-30 minutes or longer. The odontologist should not attempt to affect the setting time by altering the manufacturers' recommendations regarding the proportions of impression base to catalyst. Similarly, the use of hair dryers or heat lamps to warm the material and subsequently adjust the setting time is not recommended since the effects of these uncontrolled variables on the accuracy and stability of the impression cannot be predicted.

It is more appropriate to dispense an additional small amount of impression material on the skin beside the subject area when the material is dispensed onto the bite mark. This permits the investigator to check polymerization prior to disturbing the actual impression. The impression should be poured in American Dental Association Type IV dental stone according to the manufacturer's instructions in conjunction with accepted dental laboratory techniques. Following setting of this master cast it should be set aside as a pristine example of the bite mark. Subsequent pours in similar and different materials can be made of the initial impression to produce working casts. These can subsequently be examined, evaluated and analyzed. Each working cast should be consecutively numbered for future reference

The dentition of the bitten individual can be carefully recorded using standard dental impression techniques. The casts generated from this step are important when evaluating possible self inflicted injury and may also prove helpful in cases in which the assailant sustained a bite mark injury initiated by the victim or both parties were bitten during an attack.

Invasive Analyses

Tissue Incision

After all other evidence is collected it may be helpful to investigate the nature of a suspected bite mark by making an incision through the area to attempt to determine if the patterned injury is a surface injury (abrasion or insect activity) or a deeper injury such as a contusion, bruise or bite mark (**Figure 4-21a –d**).

Tissue Excision

Tissue excision is not universally recommended. The value of examination of excised tissue is debated by forensic odontologists. This step should only be considered in certain cases and always with the consent of the medical examiner or coroner for that case. Consideration should be given to the value of the information gained from excision of tissue compared to other evidence collection techniques.

In the case of a deceased person who has been bitten the skin and underlying dermis may be removed and preserved. It is extremely important to attempt to maintain this tissue in its original anatomical shape in an effort to avoid distortion of the bite mark pattern.

A custom fabricated acrylic ring which conforms to the anatomical shape of the body at the bite site is currently the best method to minimize skin shrinkage and distortion.

Stabilizing rings are usually fabricated from self-polymerizing acrylic tray material. The powder and monomer from the tray material can be mixed according to manufacturers' recommendations and formed into a ring before positioning it around the injury site. The rings are then attached to the skin using a combination of cyanoacrylate glue and interrupted sutures. Some odontologists have had success using high quality cyanoacrylate glue alone.

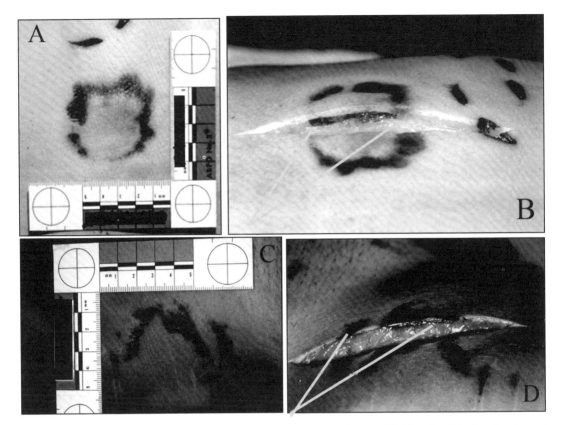

Figure 4-21: (**A** and **B**) Contusions, bruises and bite marks will often exhibit bleeding into the dermis and sub-dermal tissues highlighted by the arrows . (**C** and **D**) Abrasions and surface insect activity will not as highlighted by the arrows.

Since the exhibit is to be removed from the body, it is important to record the anatomical orientation of the ring (and consequently the bite mark) on the victim. Recording a code which indicates the direction toward the head and midline similar to the earlier impression is a good practice. A photograph showing the ring in place with the marks clearly visible is recommended.

When the material is set, the entire structure (ring and skin) can be dissected from the body. The full thickness of the skin through the dermis and underlying fatty tissue is excised and recovered. The materials and procedures required for removal of a tissue specimen containing a bite mark include the following:

Materials:

- Custom-made stabilizing ring of adequate size made from polymethylmethacrylate material

- High quality cyanoacrylate glue

- Sutures on cutting needles

- Scalpel handle and disposable blade

- Suture needle driver and scissors

- Storage container with 10% buffered formalin

- Felt pen

- Sterile examination gloves and PPDs

Procedures:

- Wash hands and use sterile examination gloves.

- Fabricate a stabilizing ring of adequate size. The lower surface of the ring should accurately follow the anatomical curvature of the bite mark site while resting passively on the skin. The diameter of the ring should be such that the inner edge is at least 3-4 cm. from the outer edge of the bite pattern. No substance other than the ring should be in contact with the skin during fixation.

- A layer of cyanoacrylate adhesive is applied to the bottom surface of the ring to glue the ring in position. For additional stability, interrupted sutures may be placed around the circumference of the ring at 2 cm. intervals. Anatomical orientation marks are placed on the ring with a felt pen.

- The skin and ring are removed from the body by cutting completely around the ring with a scalpel approximately 2 cm. from the outside of the ring. It is important not to cut any of the sutures. The tissue specimen is carefully lifted and dissected from the underlying tissues.

- The entire excised specimen should be placed in a container and completely immersed in a buffered 4 percent formaldehyde or 10 percent formalin fixative by volume. Alternately a solution composed of 5 ml of 40 percent formaldehyde, 5 ml of 99.8% glacial acetic acid and 90 ml of 70 percent ethanol for a minimum of ten hours to preserve the skin.

Figures 4-22 a-f illustrate procedures involved in removing and examining tissue. A case involving multiple bite marks is also presented to further demonstrate the steps employed to successfully excise a bite mark tissue sample (**Figures 4-23 a-j**).

Tissue Sampling

Histological Evaluation

The skin is an organ system capable of repair and healing following an injury. The repair process may leave telltale signs at the macroscopic (visual) and microscopic (histological, histochemical and biochemical) levels. In relationship to the life of the organism, this repair process is fleeting. As a result of this rapid loss of evidence in a bite mark injury its collection is important when the causative event is of a criminal nature. Since the collection of visual evidence is noninvasive, relatively simple to execute and easily converted to excellent exemplars for court it is logical to understand the significant effort devoted to this aspect of bite mark evidence collection. The conclusions that the expert bases on the noninvasive evidence recovered from a bite mark becomes the foundation for an opinion that could possibly be offered in court.

On occasion histological evaluation of the pattern injury takes precedence because the weight of the evidence may hinge upon an opinion concerning the age of a bite mark, the age relationship among pattern injuries or concerns related to the age of a bite mark and the time of the assault or death of the victim. The process of aging the bite mark and the validity of any conclusions derived from this process warrant careful scrutiny. If the injury produced by a bite is sufficient and healing is permitted to proceed, a diffuse discolored area, or bruise, may be the result with time.

Bruising has been defined as a superficial injury produced without laceration and an area of soft tissue hemorrhage as a result of rupture of blood vessels secondary to blunt trauma. During the process of healing a bruise will undergo several definitive color changes before fading from visual perception.

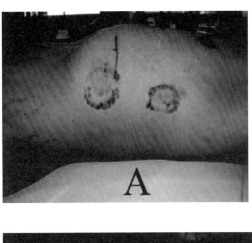
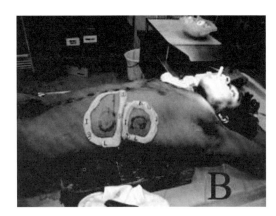

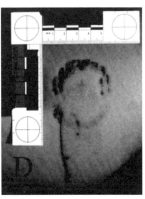
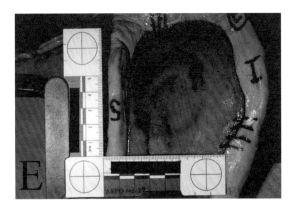

Figure 4-22 a-f: **a)** demonstrates the appearance of the bitten areas before the tissue is harvested. **b)** exhibits the acrylic rings glued to the skin and marked for orientation. **c)** Note the considerable size of the defect left when the skin is removed for two adjacent bite marks. **d** and **e)** The bottom row compares a scaled photograph of the bite mark, a scaled photograph of the excised tissue and **f)** a trans-illuminated view of the excised skin.

The interpretation and application of these *in vivo* color changes to the process of aging a bruise injury is controversial and the scientific literature contains numerous studies attempting to associate certain color changes with the time interval evolved since the injury to the tissue.

The caveat for the forensic odontologist is to tread lightly in this area of bite pattern interpretation. In 2005, an extensive review of the literature by Maguire, et al investigated color changes in bruises *in vivo* and in photographic evidence. Based on their findings, the authors

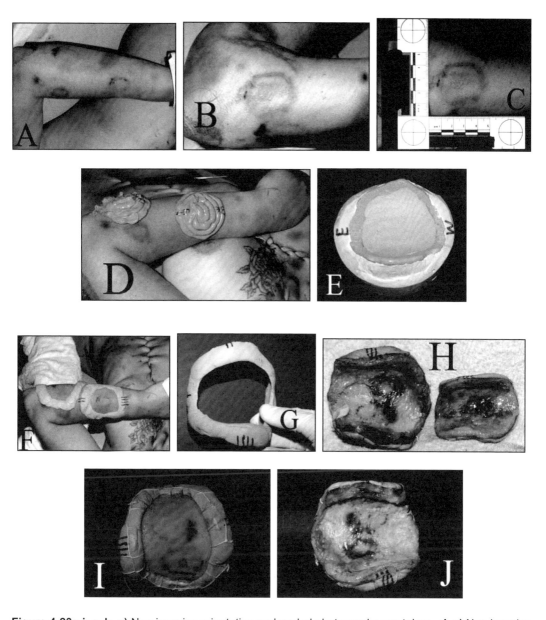

Figure 4-23a-j: a, b, c) Non-invasive orientation and scaled photographs are taken. **d, e)** Non-invasive impressions **f, g, h)** the invasive step of tissue excision **h)** One advantage of tissue excision is the confirmation of the deep tissue injuries **i, j)** The detail from the exterior and interior surfaces of the excised tissue are apparent. Note that suturing as well as cyanoacrylate glue was used for fixation.

determined that "the practice of estimating the age of a bruise from its *in vivo* color has no scientific basis and should be avoided in child protection proceedings." Their conclusions can certainly be extrapolated to situations involving adult and elderly victims.

Prior to giving an opinion regarding the aging of bruises in bite mark injuries most forensic odontologists and researchers currently agree that this evidence… "is not substantive but could be useful correlative data" or a *rough estimate* of the age of the wound." If forensic dental experts offer what appears to be unsubstantiated opinions regarding the age of bite marks the legal community and members of other forensic disciplines will be left with a negative impression of the entire process of bite mark analysis.

Thus, the prudent forensic dental expert who is about to proffer an opinion concerning the age of a bite mark bruise should consider the warning of DiMaio and DiMaio who concluded that, "one would be well advised to simply qualify the age of a bruise as *recent* or *old*.

Transillumination

Transillumination of the excised bite mark specimen is facilitated by using an illuminator with a variable rheostat. The excised specimen can be placed on a glass plate that is supported by a ring. The light is transmitted through the glass plate and the specimen and its intensity is varied by means of the rheostat. Transillumination of the specimen by backlighting the skin and observing the lighter and shadowed areas within the bruise pattern permits examination and analysis of the bite mark which can not be appreciated if the injury remains *in situ*. As stated previously, the forensic value of this type of examination is debated among forensic odontologists.

Suspect Examination and Evidence Collection

When recovering the bite mark evidence from a victim or an object, the odontologist is not usually concerned with issues of informed consent, but should always conduct evidence collection with proper authority. Before recovering bite related evidence from a suspect, however, informed consent must be obtained from that individual. Prior to undertaking any examination of an alleged suspect, a court order, search warrant or written, signed and witnessed voluntary permission from the suspect must be obtained.

Before any attempts are made to recover physical evidence (*exemplars*) from a suspect, the individual must be fully aware of their right to refuse to voluntarily provide such evidence. Informed consent will sustain the medico-legal protections sought by the attending odontologist and will be important to support the eventual admissibility of this evidence at trial. In most cases, the attorneys representing the authority requesting the input of an odontologist will produce the informed consent documentation. However, for the odontologist's knowledge and protection the following details should be included in any written informed consent:

- Date and location of consent

- Printed name and signature of suspect

- Printed name and signature of two witnesses

- Printed name and signature of odontologist or person recovering evidence

- List of specific items of evidence to be obtained (e.g. examination, photographs, dental impressions, bite registrations, buccal saliva swab, blood sample, etc.)

- Statement of understanding that the evidence is being obtained in connection with the investigation.

The time and location assigned for recovering dental exemplars is often determined by the law enforcement personnel who control the pace and flow of the suspect's interrogation. This process may be adversely affected by stopping to acquire the exemplars. When a suspect is in custody and fully cooperative, consider having them transported to the dental office to obtain the dental evidence. Alternatively, if the suspect is to remain incarcerated, the odontologist may have to move the necessary materials and equipment to that location and attempt to acquire the exemplars and conduct an examination.

When examining any patient (and the suspect should be considered a patient while under the care of the odontologist) the odontologist should follow all aspects of the standard of care. A detailed past medical and dental history and physical examination of the suspect should be obtained and appropriately recorded. Proper concern for the patient should be shown and pre-medications provided when necessary. Infection control and asepsis protocols using PPDs such as examination gloves, a mask and safety glasses should be followed. The examination protocol should be explained to the suspect (patient) after obtaining consent to proceed. The suspect should understand that an attempt will be made to work expeditiously and effectively and that their cooperation will aid in the process.

A written record of the date, time, place, and circumstances of the examination and evidence recovery should include the names of those present including deputies, attorneys and dental assistants. The suspect should sign the document. The record should list the instruments and materials used during the examination. This record may be important later as an account of the events which occurred during the examination and the materials used to recover the exemplars. Photographs of the site and setup can help in this documentation.

It is important to inquire if the suspect had any dental treatment concurrent or subsequent to the presumed date of the incident which resulted in the bite mark. The odontologist must observe and record any significant soft or hard tissue factors that may influence the dynamics of the suspect's bite or ability to open the mouth or move the mandible. Such factors as temporomandibular joint status, facial asymmetry and muscle tone and mass may be significant. Measurements of the maximal opening of the mouth should be recorded as well as any deviations and opening or closing and occlusal disharmonies. The presence of facial scars or evidence of previous surgical treatment and the presence of facial hair should also be noted.

Intraorally, the size and function of the tongue should be recorded along with any abnormalities of movement. Periodontal health should be noted with special reference to mobile teeth, areas of inflammation or hypertrophy and missing teeth. Fractured teeth should be recorded accurately with a notation of their condition.

Two-Dimensional Evidence

Photography

A series of photographs of the suspect and the dentition which records the shapes, contours, and positions of the teeth and jaws from a variety of viewpoints is ideal. They should include a photograph of the full face and profile of the suspect. The intraoral photographs should be taken with and without a reference scale included in the field of view. The scale of choice is the ABFO No. 2 reference scale. Lip and cheek retractors will help with close-up lateral, anterior and occlusal views. Photographs of the dentition should include each side with the teeth closed and open. A close-up frontal photograph of the anterior teeth in normal occlusion and another with the teeth slightly apart is desirable (**Figures 4-24** and **4-25**).

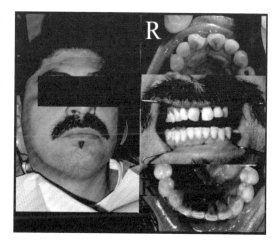

Figure 4-24: Representative photographic views of a suspect.

An occlusal or incisal view of the upper and lower anterior teeth is important for later validation of the dental casts produced by impression. Front surface mirrors are helpful and these procedures are facilitated when they are routinely incorporated into the odontologist's general clinical patient examinations. The forensic dentist should endeavor to use the skills and materials they are most familiar with and those that are used in routine practice.

Buccal Swabs

After initial diagnostic photographs are taken, the odontologist should obtain a biological sample of saliva from the suspect if biological swabs were acquired from the bite mark of the victim or inanimate object. A sterile cotton swab should be used to collect a sample according to the laboratory or directions of the supplier. This is best done by rolling the swab in the vestibule and along the buccal mucosa with enough pressure to pick up saliva and loose epithelial cells. If this is performed properly, the saliva and DNA biological evidence from the suspect can be compared in the laboratory to the results from the victim samples.

Three-Dimensional Evidence

Bite Mark Impressions

Full upper and lower dental impressions should now be obtained using the most accurate and stable impression materials available. Vinyl polysiloxane materials produce extremely accurate models of the teeth of the subject and these materials should be used whenever possible. However, due to the comparatively long setting time of VPS materials, other materials with faster setting times may be chosen. This is especially true if the suspect is uncooperative. For example, alginate impression material sets

quickly so it can be substituted for VPS provided the impressions are handled and poured within the time frame recommended by the alginate manufacturer (**Figure 4-26**).

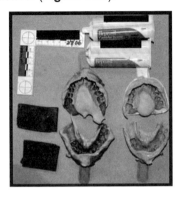

Figure 4-26: Alginate impressions substituted for VPS materials.

Three dental die stone casts should be fabricated. The first study casts will be kept as an untouched record of the suspect's teeth. The second set will be used during bite mark analysis and the third are considered backup exemplars. More than one model can be fabricated from a single VPS impression. Alginate impressions, however, should only be poured once. If this material is chosen, three sets of upper and lower impressions of the suspect's teeth need to be obtained to produce the three sets of study casts (**Figure 4-27**).

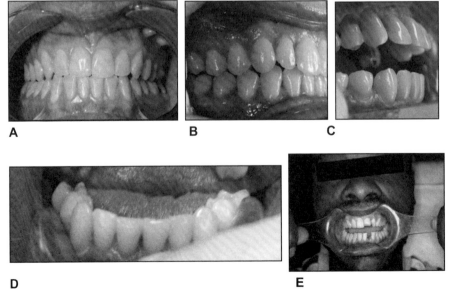

A   B   C

D   E

Figure 4-25: Representative photographic views of a suspect.

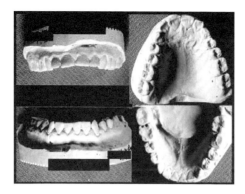

Figure 4-27: Three dental die stone casts of the dentition of the suspect have been fabricated.

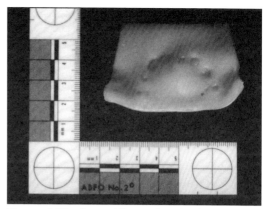

Figure 4-28: A wax bite ready to be filed for later use.

Variation is introduced into the analysis by having different impressions and the most accurate materials should be used whenever possible. Casts may also be constructed from epoxy or cyanoacrylate plastic for specific analytical procedures. All impressions and study casts should be photographed, marked and sealed as exhibits according to the recommendations for chain of custody.

The odontologist should take a wax interocclusal record in centric occlusion using either pink baseplate wax or green sheet wax which has been made pliable with warm water. There are other clinical methods for producing bite registrations with many commercially available products. Most are extremely fast setting addition-cured silicone impression material and they can be applied with self mixing tubes.

The pink wax should be folded in half before use to make a double thickness wafer. The subject should then be instructed to bite down on the warm wax until the teeth are almost touching through it. It is important that the teeth sink deeply enough to completely register all biting surfaces, but not so deeply that they pierce through the wax. If the upper and lower teeth touch, details of the incisal edges will no longer be recorded. In addition to providing information about the occlusal relationship between the upper and lower teeth, many odontologists find the wax record of the pattern of the dental arch and anterior teeth useful in subsequent case analysis (refer to **Bite Mark Analysis and Figure 4-28**).

Immediately after the bite registration is made, the wax wafer or other material should be initialed and dated. Both sides (upper and lower teeth marks) should be photographed with an ABFO No. 2 reference scale. These pictures are important since they preserve the details of positions, rotations, arch form, etc. before any damage or distortion may occur to the wafer. They are often set aside as a simple verification of any imprints that are produced from the hard replica casts of the teeth. The wax should be sealed in a clear exhibit bag and stored in a cool (but not frozen) place. The exhibits should be protected so they remain undisturbed and undistorted.

The previously described procedures are well tolerated by most suspects. Some, however, are uncooperative from the beginning of the examination while others are initially willing to cooperate but change their minds through the process. Every effort should be made to collect as much high quality data and evidence as possible. However, it is recommended that the most significant exemplars, such as photographs, DNA samples and impressions for study casts, be collected early in the examination to preclude the suspect becoming uncooperative.

Organizing the necessary equipment, materials, and instruments close to the site of the examination will facilitate the process by which the odontologist can obtain the best possible evidence. There are two important legal concerns to consider when collecting exemplars from a suspect. Primarily, the rights of the suspect must be protected by not be subjecting the individual to any dental or oral treatment that is not absolutely necessary for the evidence collection. Additionally, the process should not be prolonged beyond the minimum time required which may eventually result in courtroom debate over unnecessary procedures.

The bases of the study casts should be neatly trimmed but cleaning or otherwise disturbing the teeth on the models must be avoided. Wax bites should be handled gently and attention should be directed toward the heat which may be generated by desk lamps during prolonged examinations. Researchers have developed several techniques for preserving the indentations recorded in the wax. For example, some experts advocate gently vibrating dental stone into the wax molds to cast a model of the incisal edges of the teeth which are recorded there.

A similar technique involves painting self-polymerizing dental acrylic into the indentations and allowing the material to set. This can be especially helpful if impressions of the suspect's teeth were not obtained. Others suggest that it is helpful to produce a life-sized image of the biting edges by placing a radiopaque medium in the indentations and exposing a radiograph of the wax bite. Barium sulfate or a mixture of silver amalgam filings and acrylic monomer can be painted into the tooth marks in the bite registration to achieve this effect (**Figure 4-29**).

The indentations from the upper teeth are painted and radiographed separately from the indentations from the lower teeth to avoid overlapping of the radiographic images. After the material solidifies, each wax wafer is placed on a separate occlusal radiographic film and the x-ray beam is directed at 90 degrees to its surface (**Figure 4-30**).

Another method makes use of impression material to record a very accurate impression of the incisal edges of the teeth. Radiopaque material is then vibrated into the impression and subjected to radiographic exposure. The images are very accurate and of high quality (**Figure 4-32**). Additional methods have been devised to record the incisal edges for eventual analysis and comparison with the bite mark.

Whichever method is used, the accuracy should be verified. **Figure 4-31** illustrates the process of verifying the incisal outlines to the actual incisal edges of the suspect. This process is necessary at some point to simply assure the investigator that accurate comparison is being made between the incisal edges of the suspect's teeth and the bite mark injuries.

Analysis and Comparison of the Evidence

Once the dental exhibits from the suspect and

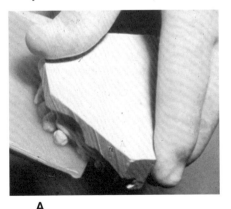

A B

Figure 4-29: The incisal edges of the plaster cast are pressed into wax and the impressions are painted with a radiopaque material.

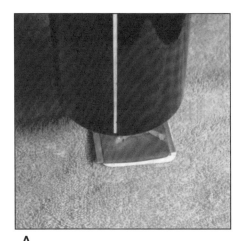

A B

Figure 4-30: The wax bite is placed upon an X-ray film and radiographed and the resultant image is labeled.

the bite mark evidence from the victim or bitten object have been obtained the odontologist should complete a comparative analysis and determine whether a relationship between the evidentiary materials is possible.

Bite mark patterns are examples of physical evidence and as such are analyzed using methods which are similar to those used for comparing other types of patterned physical evidence. Thus, analysis related to physical evidence associated with tool marks, tire and footwear impressions, and fingerprints all involve a detailed comparison of measurements and patterns from the forensic exhibits. Analysis of a bite mark also includes the careful and thorough examination of each aspect of the injury site and a comparison of this pattern with the traits and characteristics of the dental exemplars of the suspect.

The analytical protocol for bite mark comparisons is made up of two broad categories. Initial considerations regard the measurement of specific traits and features and this is referred to as a metric analysis of the evidence. Subsequently, the physical comparison of the configuration and pattern of the injury with the configuration and pattern of the dentition of the suspect is referred to as a *pattern association*.

Description of the Injury

The *metric analysis* and *pattern association* should be components of the final report of the odontologist and should reflect an organized and systematic description which follows the manner in which the evidence was presented to the odontologist. The injury pattern on the victim or alleged bite pattern on an inanimate object should be evaluated initially since copies of the available photographs of the

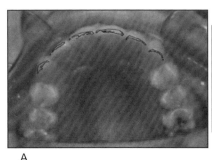

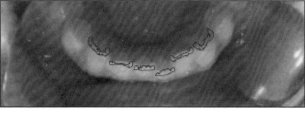

A B

Figure 4-31: These photographs with overlays illustrate the *verification* of incisal outlines by superimposition on photographs of the actual teeth.

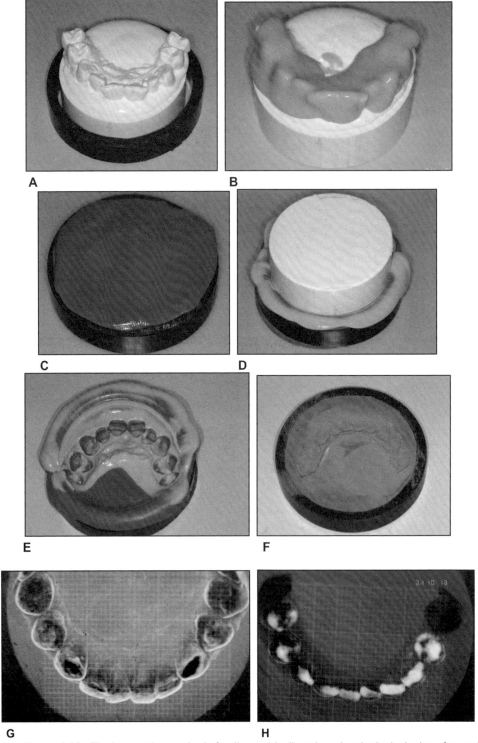

Figure 4-32: The impression method of radiographically enhancing the incisal edges for analysis and comparison purposes. The resulting radiographs demonstrate precise incisal detail.

victim and/or material from the pattern on an object are among the earliest components of the evidence transferred to the forensic dentist. For purposes of illustration an routine case of child abuse in which bite mark evidence is obtained for analysis is presented.

The child was admitted to the local Children's Hospital with breathing difficulties and arrived in a semi-comatose condition. Physical examination of the victim revealed numerous areas of injury patterns suggestive of abuse. Photographic exemplars were used to document several areas of bite mark evidence and all injuries were washed during the first day of hospital admission. **Figure 4-33** shows the general condition of the child with one bite mark visible on the upper right arm, several on the abdomen and additional biting related injuries on the right and left legs.

There are at least twelve marks that are recognizable as human bite marks based on the *gross characteristics* of the pattern injuries (**Figure 4-34**). All of the bite pattern injuries manifest sufficient markings and indentations to indicate that they were inflicted in such a manner that they would probably been painful to a conscious victim. The marks were studied individually and based on *class characteristics* observed in each bite pattern

all appeared to be consistent and inflicted by one biter. Some of the patterns had greater evidentiary value because of the number of individual tooth marks observed in them and the clear delineation of arch size, arch shape and individual morphological characteristics when *metric analyses* were performed.

Description of the Dentition

There were two adults with access to the child concurrent to the time of injury. Although there were similarities in their dentitions, significant differences between them were also noted. The lower arch form and individual position of teeth varied between the two persons of interest in this case and this was a distinguishing and discriminating feature. **Figure 4-35** shows the dentition of the female suspect (Suspect A). This figure also illustrates the reversed incisal images for comparison purposes. The same workup for the male suspect (Suspect B) is presented in **Figure 4-36**.

Comparison of the Dentition to the Injury

Metric Analysis

Each feature or characteristic of the teeth of a

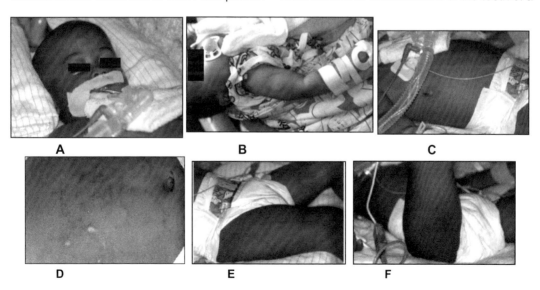

A   B   C

D   E   F

Figure 4-33: The general condition of the child with one bite mark visible on the upper right arm, several on the abdomen, and right and left legs.

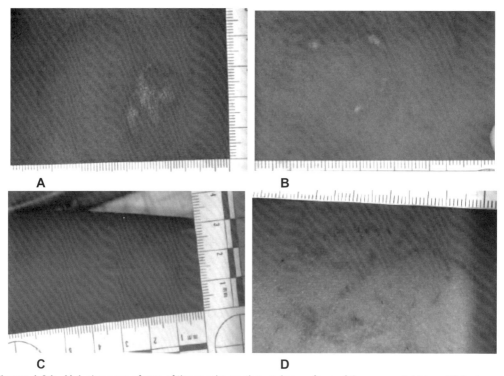

A   B

C   D

Figure 4-34: **A)** A close-up of one of the marks on the under surface of the upper right leg. **B)** A close-up of an abrasive bite mark on the abdomen. **C)** A bite mark on the lower left leg. **D)** Several superimposed bite marks exhibiting some specific dental features.

perpetrator captured in the bite mark should be measured and recorded. The length, width and depth of the markings associated with specific teeth, overall size and shape of the injury site and other dimensions should be calculated. These should include intercuspid (canine) distance, spacing between tooth marks, rotations from normal arch form and indications of malpositioned or missing teeth. The metric lengths of these measurements should be noted.

A similar detailed analysis of the measurements of the comparative points present in the suspect's exemplars can be undertaken. The length, width, and height of specific teeth, the intercuspid dimension, metric width of any diastemas, degree of rotation or malpositioning of individual teeth and any missing teeth can be similarly noted. Comparison of the measurements from the bite pattern exhibits with those from the suspect's exhibits will provide an estimation of the degree of association between the

size and recorded dimensions of the injury discovered on the victim and the dentition of the suspect.

An architect's drawing compass and/or a Boley Gauge can be employed to measure these distances precisely for those forensic dentists who do not have access to computer capabilities to perform these tasks. The former instruments are usually found in stationary or engineering stores marketing high quality technical supplies. It is recommended to purchase an accurate compass which permits the substitution of a second metal point into the position which routinely accommodates the pencil. The distance between the arms of the compass during measurement of regions of a photograph or dental cast should be maintained precisely. To this end, compasses possessing a screw adjustment mechanism (a worm gear with a fine adjustment knob to control the distance between the arms) should be sought. A Boley gauge can be purchased from dental supply companies.

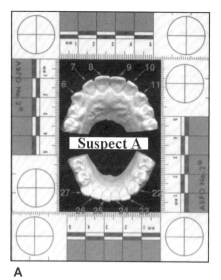
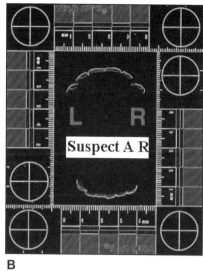

A   B

Figure 4-35: The dental casts for the female adult with the teeth labeled on the left and the incisal outlines on the right.

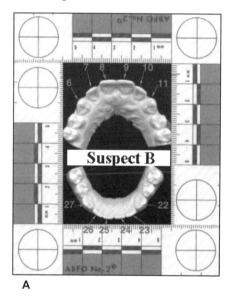
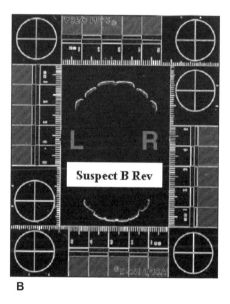

A   B

Figure 4-36: The dental casts for the male adult with the teeth labeled on the left and the incisal outlines on the right.

Overlay Comparison

The overlay method is an additional measurement technique that is precise and accurate when performed correctly. It pictorially demonstrates the areas of similarity among the various points compared between pattern marks and the teeth of the suspect. As previously indicated, hollow outline tracings of the incisal edges of the dentition of the suspect can be transferred by use of a photocopier to clear transparency paper and superimposed over 1:1 images of the bite pattern . Additionally, computer software applications have been developed which enable the odontologist to generate overlays and perform measurements by use of computer. Among these are Adobe Photoshop and Mideo Systems casePACS software. The former is provided with this text as a supplemental disc entitled Digital Analysis of Bite Mark Evidence using Adobe Photoshop by Johansen and Bowers. The latter is discussed in **Chapter 6 – Technological Aides in Forensic Odontology.**

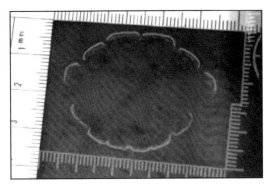

Figure 4-37: The overlay of Suspect B, the male in the household, to one of the bite marks. The comparison demonstrates similar arch form, tooth position and individual characteristics.

In the child abuse case under consideration, **Figure 4-37** illustrates the overlay of Suspect B, the male in the household, to one of the bite marks. The shapes of the arches are similar, the position of the teeth show a high degree of concordance and the individual characteristics of Suspect B's teeth are also observed in the mark.

Figure 4-38 illustrates a similar arch size for the female, Suspect A. Discordance in tooth placement and individual dental characteristics is manifested in this comparison which tends to exculpate Suspect A as the perpetrator.

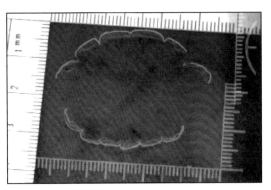

Figure 4-38: The overlay of Suspect A, the female in the household, illustrating discordance, most striking are the marks of the lower central incisors.

Advanced course work and experience in the physical comparison techniques facilitates meaningful bite mark comparisons and helps to develop appropriate conclusions in bite mark analysis cases. It is strongly recommended that even seasoned odontologists seek out appropriate educational opportunities and continuing education courses which offer both didactic instruction in comparison of physical bite mark evidence and hands on practical experience in actual and simulated bite mark cases. A list of some accredited courses can be found in **Appendix B**. Many practitioners involved in this aspect of forensic dental science have also collaborated and networked with experienced experts and these associations provide excellent additional learning opportunities.

Specialized Procedures

There have been numerous adjunctive techniques developed to assist the forensic odontologist in the analysis and evaluation of bite mark evidence. Among these are alternative light source photographic methods, MRI and CT scan radiographic methodologies, videotape, computer software and microscopic procedures. Many of these are discussed in greater detail in **Chapter 6 –Technological Aides in Forensic Odontology**. The following comments are reserved for scanning electron microscopic analysis.

Scanning Electron Microscopy (SEM)

At low power, the scanning electron microscope has been used to produce images of great contrast. It may be useful in documenting unique individual features of the teeth and their impression in skin.

The SEM is an adjunctive instrument that would normally be employed in bite mark evaluation after determination of similar arch form and tooth position between the dentition of the suspect and the pattern injury by more traditional overlay techniques. The SEM focuses on minute internal variations of individual teeth with a theoretical resolving power in the range of twenty nanometers. **Figure 4-39** shows a test bite mark injury on a voluntary subject ten minutes after infliction

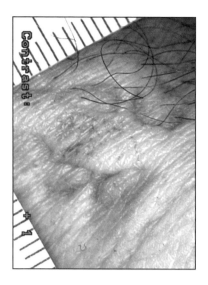

A   **B**

Figure 4-39: The test bite in living human skin and the metal coated cast with an outline of the area of interest.

and is used to exemplify the use of SEM instrumentation. The gold-palladium coated cast of the injury exhibits an outline of the injured area caused by teeth numbers 26 and 27. **Figure 4-40** shows an SEM image fifty power magnification.

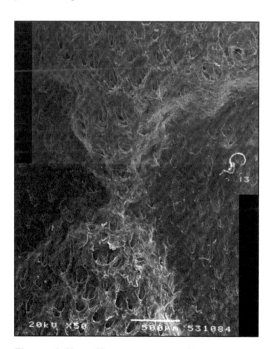

Figure 4-40: The same area of interest as the previous figure with metal coating and viewed at 50X.

Figure 4-41 illustrates a view of the dentition causing the bite mark and **Figure 4-42** illustrates the labeling of the teeth in their normal positions and in a mirror image view which permits the creation of an overlay of the incisal edges for comparison. **Figure 4-43** manifests the mirror image 50X SEM view of teeth numbers twenty-six and twenty-seven. The unique nature of the wear and chipping of the edges is evident.

Figure 4-44 shows a computer generated overlay of the contact point of the teeth with several levels of features displayed. **Figure 4-45** illustrates the overlay on the replicas at 50, 75 and 100X. The overlays demonstrate a very high level of concordance.

The scanning electron microscope is a promising instrument for evaluation of bite mark evidence. The use of this technology in bite mark analysis is discussed in detail in **Chapter 6 – Technological Aides in Forensic Odontology.** As the number of forensic dentists with access to this type of equipment increases the need for guidelines for the use of SEM and other technologies will become clearer. Use of established ABFO protocols and procedural guidelines for analysis of bite mark evidence is recommended.

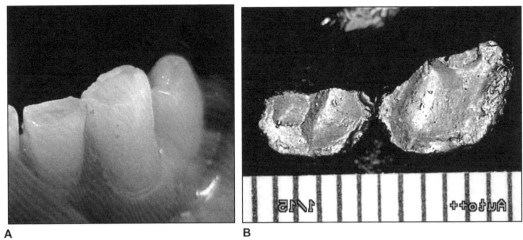

A   B

Figure 4-41: A mirror image photograph of teeth numbers twenty-six and twenty-seven and the metal coated cast illustrating the wear pattern.

Future Directions

With the development of 21st century emerging technologies in photography, radiographic capture and microscopy the forensic odontologist gains a broader armamentarium to analyze and evaluate bite mark patterns. The question of whether these technological advances will resolve the basic issues related to the uniqueness of human or animal bites inflicted in skin remains to be seen. Those involved in this discipline have the responsibility and are encouraged to continue to conduct research concerning bite mark analysis. The results of these efforts must be presented as *evidence based* findings and opinions in peer reviewed articles. This caveat will insure that the *standard of care* regarding bite mark analysis will continue to be validated and remain high.

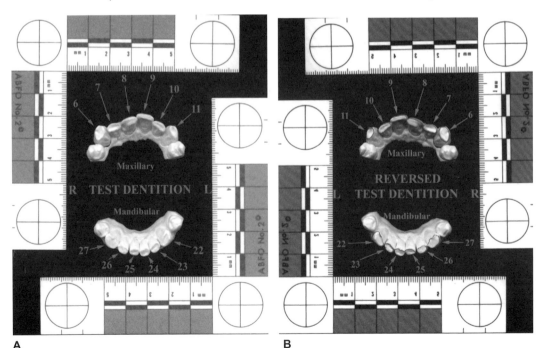

A   B

Figure 4-42: The labeled casts of the anterior teeth on the left and the mirror image and labeled casts on the right.

206

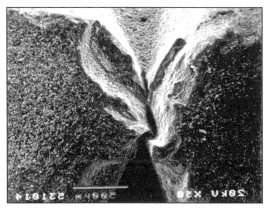

Figure 4-43: The SEM view of the incisal edges of teeth numbers twenty-six and twenty-seven at the contact. They are unique in wear.

Figure 4-44: A computer generated overlay of the contact area of the teeth.

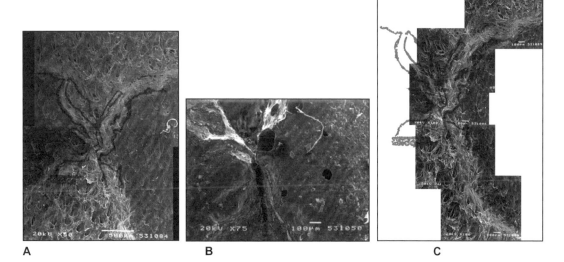

A   B   C

Figure 4-45: The overlay placed on the 50, 75 and 100X views of the bite mark. They demonstrate a high level of concordance.

EDUCATIONAL OUTCOMES

By completing this chapter the reader will:

- Build a foundational knowledge of the history of bite mark analysis and the seminal legal cases associated with this discipline

- Describe the various noninvasive and invasive procedures employed to recover bite mark evidence from a suspect and/or victim or inanimate object.

- Build a foundational knowledge and understanding associated with the procedures and protocols required to compare the dentition of a suspect with a bite pattern injury or bite pattern on an inanimate object.

- Recognize the gross and class characteristics of human bite mark patterns.

- Understand the specialized procedures that are becoming adjuncts in bite mark analysis

207

- Critically evaluate relevant forensic, dental and medical literature concerning incidence of biting injuries, evidence recovery procedures and protocols and technological aides employed in bite mark analysis and comparison based on an understanding of evidence based concepts.

CONTRIBUTORS

Douglas M. Arendt, DDS, MS, DABFO
C. Michael Bowers, DDS, JD, DABFO
J. Curtis Dailey, DDS, DABFO
Robert B. J. Dorion, DDS, DABFO
Adam J. Freeman, DDS
Edward E. Herschaft, DDS, MA, DABFO
Thomas C. Krauss, DDS, Diplomate Emeritus DABFO *
Lawrence J. Pierce, DDS
Iain A. Pretty, BDS (Hons), MSc, PhD, MFDS RCS(Ed)
Bruce R. Rothwell, DMD, MSD
David R. Senn, DDS, DABFO
E. Steven Smith, DDS *
Richard R. Souviron, DDS, DABFO
Norman D. Sperber, DDS, DABFO
Paul G. Stimson, DDS, MS, DABFO
David J. Sweet, DMD, PhD, DABFO
Gerald L. Vale, DDS, MPH, JD, DABFO

Deceased *

REFERENCES

Introduction and History

American Board of Forensic Odontology (1986). Guidelines for bite mark analysis. J Am Dent Assoc 112:383-6.

Clark MA, Sandusky GE, Hawley DA, Pless JE, Fardal PM, Tate LR (1991). Fatal and near-fatal animal bite injuries. J Forensic Sci 36:1256-61.

Manual of Forensic Odontology (1997). 3rd ed. Ontario: Manticore Publishers.

Dr. Jonathan Taft and Other Significant Early Cases

Pierce LJ, Strickland DJ, Smith ES (1990). The case of Ohio v. Robinson. An 1870 bite mark case. Am J Forensic Med Pathol 11:171-177.

Taft J (1870). The Robinson/Lunsford murder case. Dental Register XXIV:457-459.

Recognition of Bite Marks

Davis JE (1958). Introduction to Tool Marks, Firearms and the Striagraph: Charles C Thomas Pub Ltd.

Freeman AJ, Senn DR, Arendt DM (2005). Seven hundred seventy eight bite marks: analysis by anatomic location, victim and biter demographics, type of crime, and legal disposition. J Forensic Sci 50:1436-43.

Harvey W (1976). Dental identification and forensic odontology: Kimpton.

Pretty IA, Sweet D (2000). Anatomical location of bitemarks and associated findings in 101 cases from the United States. J Forensic Sci 45:812-4.

Rawson RD, Koot A, Martin C, Jackson J, Novosel S, Richardson A, Bender T (1984). Incidence of bite marks in a selected juvenile population: a preliminary report. J Forensic Sci 29:254-9.

Rawson RD, Ommen RK, Kinard G, Johnson J, Yfantis A (1984). Statistical evidence for the individuality of the human dentition. J Forensic Sci 29:245-53.

Rothwell BR (1994). Bite Marks in Forensic odontology: Fact or Fiction? In: Controversies in Oral and Maxillofacial Surgery. P Worthington and JR Evans editors. Philadelphia: W B Saunders.

Sperber N (1998). Bite Mark on the Weatherstripping of a Pickup Truck Leads to a Rape Conviction. American Academy of Forensic Sciences, San Francisco.

Vale GL, Noguchi TT (1983). Anatomical distribution of human bite marks in a series of 67 cases. J Forensic Sci 28:61-9.

Wilkinson AP, Gerughty RM (1985). Bite Mark Evidence: Its Admissibility is Hard to Swallow. St. U. L. Rev. 519.

General Considerations

Pretty IA, Sweet D (2001). The scientific basis for human bitemark analyses--a critical review. Sci Justice 41:85-92.

Rawson RD, Brooks S (1984). Classification of human breast morphology important to bite mark investigation. Am J Forensic Med Pathol 5:19-24.

Rothwell BR (1995). Bite marks in forensic dentistry: a review of legal, scientific issues. J Am Dent Assoc 126:223-32.

Noninvasive Analyses

Benson BW, Cottone JA, Bomberg TJ, Sperber ND (1988). Bite mark impressions: a review of techniques and materials. J Forensic Sci 33:1238-43.

Ciesco JN, Malone WF, Sandrik JL, Mazur B (1981). Comparison of elastomeric impression materials used in fixed prosthodontics. J Prosthet Dent 45:89-94.

Dailey JC, Shernoff AF, Gelles JH (1989). An improved technique for bite mark impressions. J Prosthet Dent 61:153-5.

Hyzer WG, Krauss TC (1988). The Bite Mark Standard Reference Scale--ABFO No. 2. J Forensic Sci 33:498-506.

Krauss TC (1984). Photographic techniques of concern in metric bite mark analysis. J Forensic Sci 29:633-8.

Lacy AM, Fukui H, Bellman T, Jendresen MD (1981). Time-dependent accuracy of elastomer impression materials. Part II: Polyether, polysulfides, and polyvinylsiloxane. J Prosthet Dent 45:329-33.

Miller D, Hodges J (2005). Validation of Abacus SALIgAE® Test for the Forensic Identification of Saliva.
Sperber ND (1990). Lingual markings of anterior teeth as seen in human bite marks. J Forensic Sci 35:838-44.

Sweet DJ, Lorente JA, Lorente M, Vlaenquela A, Villanueva E (1997) An improved method to recover saliva from human skin: the double swab technique. J Forensic Sci 42:320-322.

West MH, Barsley RE, Frair J, Seal MD (1990). The use of human skin in the fabrication of a bite mark template: two case reports. J Forensic Sci 35:1477-85.

West MH, Billings JD, Friar J (1987). Ultraviolet photograpghy: bite marks on human skin and suggested techniques for the exposure and development of reflective ultraviolet photography. J Forensic Sci 32:1204-1213.

Invasive Analyses

Bowers CM (1995). The visual aging of bite marks, beyond the pale of forensic odontology. News of the American Board of Forensic Odontology 3:9-12.

Dailey JC, Bowers CM (1997). Aging of bitemarks: a literature review. J Forensic Sci 42:792-5.

DiMaio DJ, DiMaio VJM (1993). Forensic pathology Boca Raton: CRC Press.

Dorion RB (1982). Bite mark evidence. J Can Dent Assoc 48:795-8.

Dorion RB (1984). Preservation and fixation of skin for ulterior scientific evaluation and courtroom presentation. J Can Dent Assoc 50:129-30.

Dorion RB (1987). Transillumination in bite mark evidence. J Forensic Sci 32:690-7.

Dorion RB (2004). Bitemark Evidence: CRC.

Gerrard JM, Duta E, Nosek-Cenkowska B, Singhroy S, Cheang M, Kobrinsky NL (1992). A role for prostacyclin in bruising symptomatology. Pediatrics 90:33-6.

Harvey W (1976). Dental identification and forensic odontology London: Henery Kimpton.

Kibayashi K, Hamada K, Honjyo K, Tsunenari S (1993). Differentiation between bruises and putrefactive discolorations of the skin by immunological analysis of glycophorin A. Forensic Sci Int 61:111-7.

Langlois NE, Gresham GA (1991). The ageing of bruises: a review and study of the colour changes with time. Forensic Sci Int 50:227-38.

Levine LJ (1982). Bite mark evidence. In: Outline of forensic dentistry. JA Cottone and SM Standish editors. Chicago: Year book medical publlishers, pp. 12-27.

Maguire S, Mann MK, Sibert J, Kemp A (2005). Can you age bruises accurately in children? A systematic review. Arch Dis Child 90:187-9.

Millington PF (1974). Histological studies of skin carrying bite marks. J Forensic Sci Soc 14:239-40.

Raekallio J (1972). Determination of the age of wounds by histochemical and biochemical methods. Forensic Sci 1:3-16.

Raekallio J (1973). Estimation of the age of injuries by histochemical and biochemical methods. Z Rechtsmed 73:83-102.

Robertson I, Hodge PR (1972). Histopathology of healing abrasions. Forensic Sci 1:17-25.

Robertson I, Mansfield RA (1957). Antemortem and post-mortem bruises of the skin. J Forensic Medicine 4:2-10.

Robinson E, Wentzel J (1992). Toneline bite mark photography. J Forensic Sci 37:195-207.

Sweet DJ, Bastien RB (1991). Use of an acrylonitrile-butadiene-styrene (ABS) plastic ring as a matrix in the recovery of bite mark evidence. J Forensic Sci 36:1565-71.

Analysis and Comparison of the Evidence

Bowers CM, Johansen RJ (2001). Digital analysis of bite marks and human identification. Dent Clin North Am 45:327-42, ix.

Dailey JC (1991). A practical technique for the fabrication of transparent bite mark overlays. J Forensic Sci 36:565-70.

CHAPTER 5

HUMAN ABUSE AND NEGLECT

*What is evil? Killing is evil, lying is evil, slandering is evil, **abuse** is evil, gossip is evil: envy is evil, hatred is evil, to cling to false doctrine is evil; all these things are evil.*
Hindu Prince Gautama Siddharta, the founder of Buddhism, 563-483 B.C

Overview of Human Abuse

Violent behavior against an individual can occur within or outside of the family unit. Unfortunately, physical or emotional trauma is often directed against those within the nuclear or extended family or multi-generational home who are least able to defend against it. Thus, human abuse can manifes4 itself in several forms and is often defined according to the sub-population affected. Child abuse involves individuals who are less than eighteen years of age who suffer any nonaccidental, physical, mental, emotional or sexual act or trauma that endangers or impairs their physical or emotional health and development. Exploitation or neglect are also components of the problem and the person responsible for committing the abusive act is routinely a caregiver such as a parent, sibling, teacher, religious leader, or other individual acting *in loco parentis* in a position of power or trust.

Elder abuse is similar to that manifested in children except that the victims are geriatric and require care from an adult child or are in an institutional setting. Spousal abuse or intimate partner violence (IPV) is common in western and eastern societies and although it may be cultural in nature it wreaks a tremendous toll on its immediate victims and their children. Abuse of the disabled is also not uncommon and all of these varieties of trauma related abuse can eventually result in significant emotional and physical harm to their victims.

Historically, the lay, medical, dental and forensic literature has included numerous articles concerning abused children and the battered female spouse or intimate partner. However, it is only within the last two decades that significant information has become available describing such equally serious forms of intra-family violence as battery against adult males, elder abuse and violence directed toward dependent individuals including the disabled. Incidence and prevalence data regarding domestic violence varies for reasons that include non-uniform definitions of intra-family violence, the involvement of multiple agencies that may not share information or confer and/ or variable, frequently changing reporting requirements.

Reliable information regarding domestic violence incidence and prevalence usually comes from epidemiologic researchers collecting data from law enforcement agencies, governmental and protective services agencies and information from various *at risk* populations. It is generally accepted that reported incidents of abuse and neglect significantly under represent the actual number of cases that have occurred. One estimate based on the data indicates that almost half of families in the United States have already experienced or are about to experience some form of intra-family violence.

Child abuse is well-recognized as a major health problem, yet reliable estimates indicate that IPV occurs more commonly than does an abuse of children. Abuse in the elderly population is at least as common as child abuse and may actually exceed the number of child abuse incidents. Independent of victim age or gender, a significant number of injuries observed following an abusive situation are found in the head and neck area. Thus, there are common features associated with all forms of human abuse that should increase the suspicion of the dentist examining the patient/victim who has sustained the inflicted trauma. These features include:

- Histories related to the traumatic event are inconsistent with the presenting injury (or injuries).

- Injuries are at various stages of healing (**Figures 5-1 and 5-2**).

- Injuries are bilateral and/or multi-surfaced.

- There is delayed presentation for care following injury.

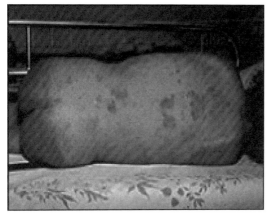

Figure 5-1: Abused 4 year old child with multiple injuries on the back indicating various stages of healing. (Courtesy of Dr. John McDowell)

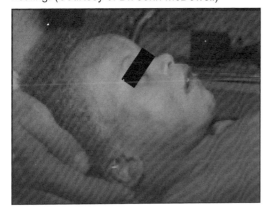

Figure 5-2: Side view of the face of the same child shown in Figure 5-1. (Courtesy of Dr. John McDowell)

These features can increase the dental examiner's index of suspicion of abuse. However, it must be noted that every abusive situation begins with an initial assault or first incident of violence that might not manifest associated evidence of previous trauma.

It is not uncommon to have multiple individuals within the family or intimate relationship at risk for violence. Although this chapter addresses the various forms of human abuse in separate sections, the practicing dentist and forensic odontologist must understand that the victim of IPV may also have a child who is at risk in the relationship. An adult who is abusing an elderly parent may also be abusive to an intimate partner or a child within the dysfunctional relationship. The various forms of human abuse are often separated for reporting purposes, however, when dealing with persons at risk for abuse one form of the problem cannot be separated from the others.

Information Concerning Abusers

The abusive individual commonly presents as one who was them self mistreated as a child and it is commonly recognized that abusive behavior is a learned one. Often an abuser is an over stressed normal parent who just breaks down or is lonely or depressed and lacks support from family or friends. Abusers tend to be emotionally immature and distrustful of others although very few exhibit criminal or psychotic behavior. They come from all socioeconomic and educational classes, ages and both genders (**Chart 5-1**).

When presenting to a dental office with an injured child they are often overly critical of the child and *very reluctant to give information about the child's injuries*. Alternatively, they may fail to bring the child for proper health care, including dental treatment

Child Abuse/Neglect

An additional definition of child abuse includes any non-accidental trauma, neglective act, failure to meet basic needs of the child or abuse inflicted by a caregiver that is beyond the acceptable cultural norm of child care. The history of child abuse and neglect is long and inglorious. In ancient Greece and Rome the law allowed deformed children and unwanted female infants to be exposed and left to die. In 1874 a church group in New York City took a child named Mary Ellen from a home in which she was being abused. Her case went to court and with the help of the Society for

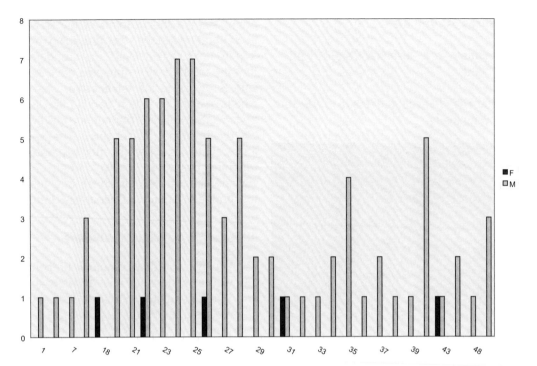

Chart 5-1: Sexual Crimes Suspect Age Distribution by Age and Sex. (Extracted, with permission, from the *Journal of Forensic Sciences*, Vol. 50, No. 6, copyright ASTM International, 100 Barr Harbor Drive, West Conshohocken, PA

the Prevention of Cruelty to Animals (SPCA) the court allowed the child to be removed from the home on the grounds she was a member of the animal kingdom and should be allowed the same protection afforded animals. This case led to the formation of the first Society for the Prevention of Cruelty to Children in the United States.

In 1946, Dr. John Caffey, a pediatric radiologist, documented the common occurrence of spiral bone fractures and subdural hematomas in infants. Although he suspected that this was related to physical abuse by caregivers, he did not publish this opinion until 1965. By 1972, he was also the first to use the term Shaken Baby Syndrome (SBS). Currently, "shaking is considered to be the most frequent cause of permanent disability and death among abused infants." The most vulnerable victims to the effects of shaking are children under two years of age. This is related to the fact that their weak neck muscles are not yet strong enough to fully control their head movements.

SBS results in injuries caused by vigorous shaking of an infant or small child by a frustrated parent or caregiver. These incidents are often triggered by an episode of crying. Since the initial identification of the syndrome many cases of SBS continued to remain undetected. This can be related to minimal external indications of injury on the victim, lack of witnesses to the incidents and refusal of caregivers to admit to shaking the infant. While there is a growing awareness of SBS among medical practitioners, research indicates, however, that over thirty percent of SBS cases are not diagnosed upon the child's initial hospital or pediatric visit.

By 1962, Dr. C. Henry Kempe first used the term Battered Child Syndrome (BCS) to describe the physical signs and symptoms of child abuse. *The Battered Child* by Drs. Kempe and Helfer was published in 1982 and the lay public and members of the health and legal professions began to be aware of and believe that parents and caregivers truly could and did physically abuse their children. Research in the area of child abuse since Dr. Kempe first recognized the signs and symptoms of BCS indicates a strong correlation between physical injuries to the oral, perioral and facial structures and victims of abuse. In abused children injuries associated with the face and mouth have been reported in a range of 58 to 86 percent of victims. Manifestations of oral neglect or sexual abuse can also present to the dental practitioner. Despite these statistics, it is unfortunate that the dental community is responsible for reporting less than one percent of all cases of child abuse.

In the United States, it is mandated in all jurisdictions that health care professionals must report cases of suspected abuse. Licensed dental professionals including dentists and hygienists are mandated reporters under

should be suspicious of abuse if the appointment is associated with the results of facial trauma, rampant caries or other manifestations of dental neglect in a very young child.

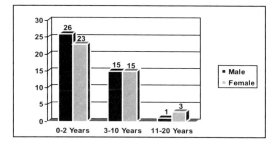

Chart 5-2: Child Abuse Distribution by Age and Gender (Extracted, with permission, from the *Journal of Forensic Sciences*, Vol. 50, No. 6, copyright ASTM International, 100 Barr Harbor Drive, West Conshohocken, PA 19428.)

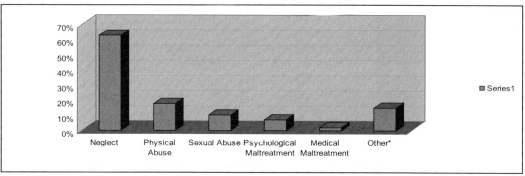

Chart 5-3: Child abuse percentages by type. (Courtesy of Dr. John McDowell)

these laws. As such, they are obligated by their state law or dental practice act to report when they believe a reasonable suspicion of abuse or neglect exists. Regrettably, the statistics clearly show that the dental profession must improve its recognition of the signs and symptoms of this epidemic to effectively participate in curtailing it.

In the dental office, children are frequently seen before they reach school age and this is also the age in which the majority of abuse toward children occurs (**Chart 5-2**). Many general and family dental practitioners treat children at age three and pediatric and oral surgery practices often have patients who are much younger. Although the dental profession encourages parents to bring their children for care at a young age to introduce them to the dental experience through atraumatic procedures, the dentist

Child abuse resulting form non-accidental trauma (NAT) includes the following sub categories:

- Physical abuse and severe corporal punishment

- Sexual abuse

- Exploitation

- Deprivation or failure to thrive

- Emotional abuse

- Neglect - A failure to provide adequate support, supervision, nutrition, medical, dental or surgical care. Neglect is considered an abusive act of omission rather than one of commission.

Each of these often overlapping categories of child abuse has unique characteristics and requires individual approaches to diagnosis and management. A common theme among the various types of abuse is often repeated instances of unexplained injury, inconsistencies in a caregiver's version of the history of the injury that conflicts with the diagnostician's clinical observations and discourse between the victim and the caregiver presenting the child for treatment.

In cases of child abuse the health care professional is often informed by the caregiver that the child is *accident prone* or subject to a rare disease process which is responsible for the injury. The abusing adult may travel great distances with the child victim to obtain care. This ploy is often used to bypass previously contacted professionals or facilities to avoid detection of serial abuse. Health care providers and facilities such as hospital emergency rooms and trauma centers should be on the on alert for this eventuality. A reasonable adult responsible for the welfare of a child would immediately attend to any injury to the minor. Significant delays in seeking treatment on behalf of the child are also common and should be evaluated by the health care provider.

In 2003 the United States Department of Health and Human Services (USDHHS) reported that there were more than 900 thousand children maltreated in this country. This data was confirmed by child protective services and cases representative of maltreatment were identified in the following categories:

- Experienced neglect: 61 percent

- Were physically abused: 19 percent

- Were sexually abused: 10 percent

An estimated 1,500 children died from physical injuries associated with child abuse:

- Deaths from neglect: 36 percent

- Deaths from physical abuse: 28 percent

- Deaths from multiple maltreatment types: 29 percent

In 2004, investigations by child protective service agencies (CPS) in the United States involved an estimated 3.5 million children and 872 thousand were identified as victims of some form of abuse. The percentages of victims who fell into the various categories of abuse are represented in **Chart 5-3**. The 14.5 percent of victims experiencing other types of maltreatment included those who were *abandoned, threatened with harm* and/ or suffered from *congenital drug addiction*.

*Includes abandonment and congenital drug addiction figures reported in some states.

Risk Factors

Multiple factors contribute to an increased risk for child maltreatment. It must be emphasized that the following risk factors are contributory and not direct causes of child abuse. The child may be perceived as being different physically. Although this may be due to a developmental delay or injury, children born prematurely are at three times greater risk of being abused than full term infants. Studies indicate that low birth weight children have a high incidence of being abused.

According to the USDHHS report in 2003, children under four years of age accounted for seventy nine percent of fatalities resulting from maltreatment and infants less than 12 months of age represented forty four percent of the deaths resulting from maltreatment.

Other factors listed by the USDHHS that contribute to increased risk of abuse include:

- Disabilities or mental retardation

- Social isolation of the family

- Parental history of domestic abuse

- Poverty and other socioeconomic disadvantage such as chronic unemployment

- Dysfunctional family unit including disorganization or dissolution of family structure

- History of domestic abuse involving one or more family members especially a history of child maltreatment by an adult in the family

- Substance abuse

- Young, single non-biological parents

- Community violence

- Parental mental health conditions including stress, distress or depression

Abuse may also be triggered by additional crises that are external to the family unit and beyond the control of the caregivers in the family. Some of these may include but are not limited to job loss, death/divorce of a loved one, sickness or other emotional crisis. In these circumstances the caregiver may lash out at the child. Studies indicate that the primary caregiver is most likely to be the suspect, followed by the paramour or partner of the guardian.

Cultural and religious beliefs and practices also influence activities that may result in abusive behavior by a caregiver. Credos based on the philosophies of *spare the rod and spoil the child* and the *values of punishment* are often present in extreme fundamental religious dogmas practiced by cults and nontraditional sects. Overly critical verbal abuse of the child, inappropriate adult/child interaction and unrealistic expectations of the developmental capabilities of the child are often manifested in these situations. The lack of family support for young, often unwed, parents who are unable to develop a supportive extended family network is also contributory to the growing problem of child abuse.

Signs and Symptoms Associated with the Various Types of Child Abuse

It is important to note that although child abuse can be subcategorized into physical, sexual, emotional and neglective domains, these types of abuse are more typically found in combination than independently. A physically abused child, for example, is often emotionally scarred as well and a sexually abused child may also suffer from neglect.

Physical Abuse

The orofacial structures are frequently injured in the maltreated child. Injuries of the neck, head, face and oral cavity represent more than half of the areas of the victim's body that routinely sustain physical trauma in child maltreatment cases. Some of the oral and paraoral signs associated with child maltreatment include:

- **Dental**:

    - Fractured, subluxated or avulsed teeth

- **Intraoral**:

    - Lacerations of the frenula, laceration or contusions of the labial mucosa, buccal mucosa, floor of mouth, oropharynx and soft palate

    - Oropharyngeal ecchymoses associated with oral sex

- **Lips**:

    - Lacerations, contusions, abrasions

- **Nasal tissues**:

    - Fractures, lacerations, contusions

- **Orbital and periorbital areas**:

    - Fractures of orbital bones, soft tissue injuries including trauma to the globe, hyphema and retinal hemorrhages

- **Jaws and appertaining structures**:

    - Fractures - simple and/or complex

- **Head and Skull**:

- Fractures of bony structures, soft tissue injuries including contusions, lacerations, abrasions and subdural hematomas (**Figure 5-3**), traumatic alopecia (**Figure 5-9**)

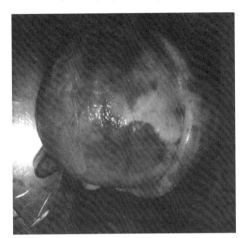

Figure 5-3: Examples of cephalohematoma in a 4 year old Caucasian male homicide victim of child abuse. (Courtesy of Dr. John McDowell)

Subtle signs of physical abuse may include aspects of neglective abuse including poor hygiene, ignoring obvious need for medical or dental care following an injury and failure to insure adequate schooling or nutritional support for the child. Parents may give the child inappropriate food, drink or medications that may be either legal or illicit. Overdressing with inappropriate clothing for the season or climate should raise the examining dentist's suspicion concerning physical abuse. In such cases the dentist should observe the arms and/or legs of the patient/victim to insure that no injuries are masked by such inappropriate clothing.

Abused children will often exhibit a sudden behavior change when approached by a health care provider of the same sex as the abusive parent. Multiple fractures in various stages of healing, greenstick fractures, mandibular and zygomatic fractures of young children (**Figure 5-5**), fractures of the hands and digits or rib cage may be pathognomonic for abuse.

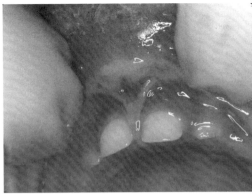

Figure 5-4a: Torn labial frenum in a 14 month old Caucasian female victim of child abuse. (Courtesy of Dr. John McDowell)

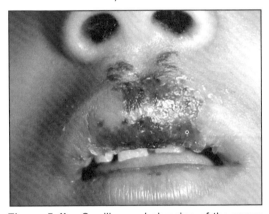

Figure 5-4b: Swelling and abrasion of the upper lip of a child. This injury is secondary to blunt force trauma.

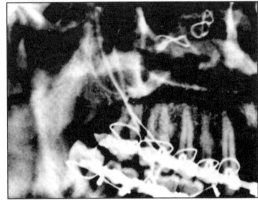

Figure 5-5: Reduced fractured zygoma in a teenage victim of physical abuse.

A torn or lacerated maxillary frenum may be caused by a slap or punch to the face (**Figure 5-4a, b**). Forced feeding, or forcible insertion of a pacifier may result in similar injury to the lingual frenum. An abusive episode must be considered by the examining dentist when a perambulatory child presents with traumatic oral injuries. Once a child begins to walk, however, such injuries may be explainable if other signs and symptoms of child abuse are not discovered.

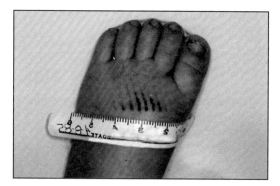

Figure 5-6: Pattern injury made by a comb dragged across the skin surface. Note the neglective abuse associated with the dirty toe nails in this eighteen month old child.

Manifestations of bruising and/or abrasions on the skin of a preambulatory infant are additional signs that should raise the suspicion of abuse for the examiner. In a toddler, or older child such injuries are more likely to occur form mundane incidents like falling from a bicycle or skates. Bruises over bony prominences such as the elbows, knees and extensor surfaces of the forearms are common playground injuries. However, in this same population, injuries to the medial aspects of the thighs or bilateral bruises to the torso should raise abuse suspicions to am examining health care worker. Bruises in multiple stages of healing or patterned injuries should be an additional red flag to the health care provider.

If a specific pattern or shape is present in multiple areas, this may also be indicative of serial abuse. Often it is possible to determine the object responsible for the abusive injury **Figure 5-6** shows an injury made by the teeth of a comb dragged across the dorsal surface of an eighteen month old child's foot. Injuries secondary to slapping will retain the marks of the fingers. These pattern injuries commonly present on the face, upper arms

Water Temperatures Required To Produce Full Thickness Burns

1 seconds	@ 158 ° F
2 seconds	@ 150 ° F
5 seconds	@ 140 ° F
3 0 seconds	@ 130 ° F
1 minute	@.127 ° F
5 minutes	@ 122 ° F

Table 5-1: Estimated time exposures at various temperatures to cause severe burning of the skin.

and buttocks. Such injuries are composed of multiple parallel marks with discernible separations representing the joints of the perpetrator. Injuries sustained by straight objects including rulers, hangers and belts may leave patterns that resemble railroad tracks in their distribution.

Clinical photographs of the injury should follow the principles of proper evidence recovery including placement of a scale such as the ABFO NO.2 scale beside the pattern. This is imperative for evidence gathering and is similar to the evidence recovery techniques described for bite mark pattern injuries. Bite marks are also often observed on the integument of the physically maltreated child. For a more complete discussion of bite mark injury evaluation and documentation of patterned injuries refer to **Chapter 4 – Bite Mark Analysis** in this text.

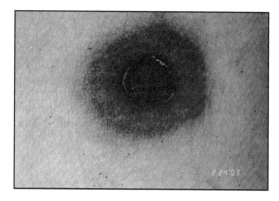

Figure 5-7: Cigarette burn.

Bite mark injury patterns can be found on any anatomic location. When such patterns are detected by the examining dentist during routine diagnostic procedures, it should raise

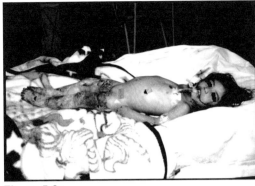

Figure 5-8a

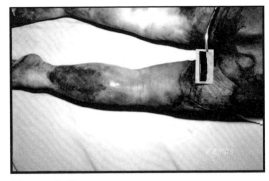

Figure 5-8b

the examiners suspicion that bite marks could potentially be located on the child's body in areas that are covered by clothing. Immediate medical referral and/or contact with law enforcement or child protective services agencies is also appropriate when this occurs and there is the potential for additional bite marks to be located on anatomical areas of the child not normally examined by the dentist.

Burn injuries are also common in child abuse victims. Hot liquids or heated objects are most commonly used. However, chemical burns of the body or oral cavity have been documented. Cigarette burns will present as single or multiple circular ulcerations of 0.5 to 1.0 cm on the skin of the victim (**Figure 5-7**). They are frequently seen on the backs of the hands, soles of the feet, lower back or genital

Evaluation of the Child	Evaluation of the Parent or Adult Caregiver
Has unexplained burns, bites, bruises, broken bones, or black eyes.	Offers conflicting, unconvincing or no explanation for the child's injury.
Has fading bruises or other marks noticeable after an absence from school.	Describes the child as *evil, stupid, retarded, ugly* or uses some other extremely negative descriptor.
Seems frightened of the parents and protests or cries when it is time to go home.	Uses harsh physical discipline with the child.
Shrinks at the approach of adults.	Has a history of abuse or neglect as a child.
Reports injury by a parent or another adult caregiver.	

Table 5-2: Summary of Considerations for the Examining Clinician when Evaluating a Potential Victim of Physical Abuse.

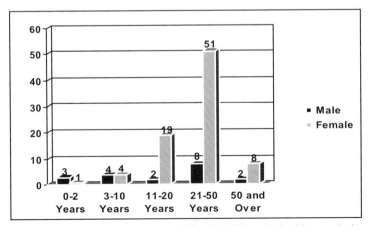

Chart 5-4: Sexual Assaults Distribution by Age and Gender (Extracted, with permission, from the *Journal of Forensic Sciences*, Vol. 50, No. 6, copyright ASTM International, 100 Barr Harbor Drive, West Conshohocken, PA 19428.)

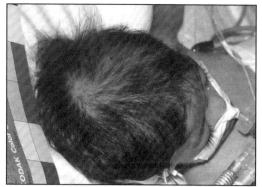

Figure 5-9: Example of traumatic alopecia in 2 year old Hispanic male victim of child abuse. (Courtesy of Dr. Shelly Stromboe)

area. Forced immersion into scalding water will be demonstrated by injuries represented by a symmetrical *high water mark* of burned skin on the victim's hands, feet and/or genital area (**Figure 5- 8a, b**). Splash mark injuries on other portions of the skin surface are lacking (**Table 5-1**).

Hair pulling is frequently seen in abuse cases. Alopecia is a scalp disease that results in hair loss secondary to its loss of root structure. The result of this condition is baldness. In the child abuse setting, when tufts hair have been pulled, broken hair strands and partially denuded patches will be observed (**Figure 5-9**). The victim's eyes should be checked for bilateral periorbital ecchymosis/hematomas. This pattern of injury should be considered non-accidental until proven otherwise. Scleral

hemorrhage or petechiae, ptosis of the eyelid and a deviated gaze may be additional signs of abuse associated with the eyes.

Any dental visit that is prompted by a traumatic event merits close scrutiny by the examining practitioner to rule out the potential for an abusive proximate cause. The following inquiries should be among those considered and included by the clinician during the history gathering process:

- Does the history of the alleged cause of the injury conflict with the injury patterns observe?

- Is the caregiver's explanation of the events leading to the injury inconsistent, contradictory or vague?

- Is there evidence of previous injury such as healing or scarring of older wounds?

- Do the caregivers interact with the child in an appropriate manner?

Table 5-2 is a summary of the principal considerations the examining dentist should review when evaluating a child and the parent or caregiver in a suspected physical abuse situation

Sexual Abuse

Child sexual abuse and exploitation are significant problems in Europe as well as North America. European studies estimate

Evaluation of the Child	Evaluation of the Parent or Adult Caregiver
Has difficulty walking or sitting.	Is unduly protective of the child or severely limits the child's contact with other children, especially of the opposite sex.
Suddenly refuses to change for gym or to participate in physical activities.	IIs unduly protective of the child or severely limits the child's contact with other children, especially of the opposite sex.
Reports nightmares or bed wetting or has sudden onsets of stuttering.	IIs secretive and isolated.
Experiences a sudden change in appetite.	IIs jealous or controlling with family members.
Demonstrates bizarre, sophisticated, or unusual sexual knowledge or behavior.	
Becomes pregnant or contracts a venereal disease, particularly if under age fourteen.	
Becomes a runaway.	
Reports sexual abuse by a parent or another adult caregiver.	

Table 5-3: Summary of Considerations for the Examining Clinician when Evaluating a Potential Victim of Sexual Abuse.

Evaluation of the Child	Evaluation of the Parent or Adult Caregiver
Shows extremes in behavior, such as overly compliant or demanding behavior, extreme passivity, or aggression.	Constantly blames, belittles, or berates the child.
Suddenly refuses to change for gym or to participate in physical activities.	Is unconcerned about the child and refuses to consider offers of help for the child's problems.
Is inappropriately adult in behavior or persona (for example - parenting other children in the household,)	Overtly rejects the child.
Is inappropriately infantile in behavior or persona (for example - frequently rocking or head-banging.	
Is delayed in physical or emotional development.	
Has attempted suicide.	
Reports a lack of attachment to the parent.	

Table 5-4: Summary of Considerations for the Examining Clinician when Evaluating a Potential Victim of Sexual Abuse.

that between ten and twenty percent of the population has suffered some form of sexual assault during childhood. These sexually abusive acts ranged from fondling to rape. An American study concerning the distribution of bite pattern injuries among victims of abuse and sexual trauma indicated the age and gender distribution of victims of sexual assault represented in **Chart 5-4**. Sexual abuse of a child can include incest, prostitution, pornography, date rape, peer sexual violence and institutional sexual abuse.

Sexual abuse has been defined as any sexual activity with a child under the age of eighteen. According to the Victim Advocate Program at Florida State University, this would include, "*oral*, anal, or vaginal penetration by or union with the sexual organ of another or the *oral*, anal, or vaginal penetration of another by any other object." Male children can also be sexually abused through acts of fondling, fellatio and anal sexual activity.

A minor can not be legally consensual in a sexual setting. Thus, in a non-consensual context the following would qualify as sexual abuse when the victim verbally says "NO" and/or is:

- Physically unable to resist (asleep, passed out)

- Threatened of violence to self or others

- Drugged or intoxicated

- Experiencing diminished capacity is mentally challenged or is a *minor*

- Subject to coerced submission (finally agrees to the act)

Silence does not mean consent!

Most sexual offenders are members of the extended family of a victim or are an acquaintance or paramour. Sexual abuse is commonly a progressive activity occurring over a period of time. Forms of this variety of abuse include exhibitionism, masturbation in the presence of the victim, physical molestation including fondling, intercourse (vaginal, *oral* and/or anal) or familial related rape.

Oral signs of sexual abuse may include lesions that are vesicular or exhibit erythema or ulceration. Oral manifestations of sexually transmitted diseases (STDs) including syphilis, gonorrhea and Chlamydia may be seen. Ecchymotic and petechial lesions of the palate or labial frenum associated with fellatio or cunnilingus (**Figure 5-10**) and viral

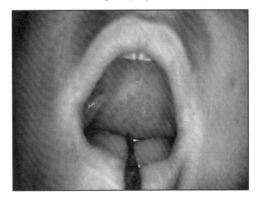

Figure 5-10: Palatal petechiae secondary to fellatio.

Evaluation of the Child	Evaluation of the Parent or Adult Caregiver
Is frequently absent from school.	Appears to be indifferent to the child.
Begs or steals food or money.	Is unconcerned about the child and refuses to consider offers of help for the child's problems.
Lacks needed medical or dental care, immunizations, or glasses.	Overtly rejects the child.
Is consistently dirty and has severe body odor.	Seems apathetic or depressed.
Lacks sufficient clothing for the weather.	Behaves irrationally or in a bizarre manner.
Abuses alcohol or other drugs.	Is abusing alcohol or other drugs.
States that there is no one at home to provide care.	

Table 5-5: Summary of Considerations for the Examining Clinician when Evaluating a Potential Victim of Neglective Abuse.

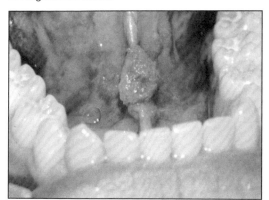

Figure 5-11: A case of oral condyloma accuminata.

infections associated with sexual transmission including condyloma accuminata (**Figure 5-11**) and HIV/AIDS should be ruled out.

Tables **5-3 and** 5-4 are a summary of the principal considerations the examining dentist should review in suspected sexual abuse situations when evaluating a child and the parent or caregiver.

Emotional Maltreatment

Emotional abuse of a child is commonly defined as a pattern of behavior by parents or caregivers that can seriously interfere with a child's cognitive, emotional, psychological, or social development. Emotional abuse of a child is also referred to as psychological maltreatment and can include:

- Ignoring

Either physically or psychologically, the parent or caregiver is not present to respond to the child. He or she may not look at the child, and may not call the child by name.

- Rejecting

This is an active refusal to respond to a child's needs (e.g., refusing to touch a child, denying the needs of a child, ridiculing a child).

- Isolating

The parent or caregiver consistently prevents the child from having normal social interactions with peers, family members, and adults.

- Exploiting or corrupting

In this kind of abuse, a child is taught, encouraged, or forced to develop inappropriate or illegal behaviors. It may involve self-destructive or antisocial acts of the parent or caregiver, such as teaching the child how to steal or forcing a child into prostitution.

- Verbally assaulting

This envolves constantly belittling, shaming, ridiculing, or verbally threatening the child.

- Terrorizing

Here, the parent or caregiver threatens or bullies the child and creates a climate of fear for the child.

- Neglecting the child

This abuse may include medical/dental neglect, where a parent or caregiver denies or ignores a child's need for treatment for medical or dental problems.

Evaluation of the Child	Evaluation of the Parent or Adult Caregiver	Evaluation of the Parent and Child
Shows sudden changes in behavior or school performance.	Shows little concern for the child.	Rarely touch or look at each other.
Has not received help for physical or medical problems brought to the parents' attention.	Denies the existence of—or blames the child for—the child's problems in school or at home.	Consider their relationship entirely negative.
Has learning problems (or difficulty concentrating) that cannot be attributed to specific physical or psychological causes.	Asks teachers or other caregivers to use harsh physical discipline if the child misbehaves.	State that they do not like each other.
Is always watchful, as though preparing for something bad to happen.	Sees the child as entirely bad, worthless, or burdensome.	
Lacks adult supervision. An adult caregiver does not routinely accompany the child to the dental office	Demands a level of physical or academic performance the child cannot achieve.	
Is overly compliant, passive, or withdrawn.	Looks primarily to the child for care, attention, and satisfaction of emotional needs.	
Comes to school or other activities such as the dental office early, stays late, and does not want to return home.		

Table 5-6: Summary of Considerations for the Examining Clinician when Evaluating a Potential Victim of Child Abuse.

Professionals agree that the majority of occasional negative attitudes or actions by parents toward their children are not considered emotional abuse. Even the best of parents have occasions when they have momentarily *lost control* and made hurtful comments to their children, failed to give the child the attention they wanted or unintentionally scared them by their actions.

What is truly harmful, according to James Garbarino of the Family Life Development Center at Cornell University and a national

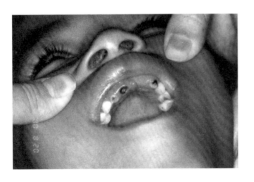

Figure 5-12a: Baby bottle decay observed in a 3 year old child.

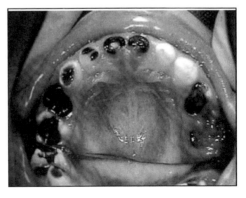

Figure 5-12b: Loss of tooth structure in the maxillary teeth secondary to baby bottle decay.

Summary of Clinical Signs and Symptoms of the Abused Child Adapted from material presented by Dr. Franklin D. Wright, DMD, DABFO www.cincytoothdoc.com	
Lack of eye contact and/or lack of appropriate conversation	Appears distant and overly apprehensive
Fear of touch	Inappropriate behavior or response to unthreatening interaction
Wide mood changes in short periods of time	Oral and injuries that our outside the normal range of childhood bumps and bruises
Signs of injuries in different stages of healing	Slap marks from hands on face, neck or arms
Unusual injuries including cigarette burns, oral abrasions from gags, fracture zygoma	Fractured, discolored or displaced teeth
Untreated rampant caries	Limited jaw opening or deviation when opening
Oral signs of sexually transmitted diseases, bruised palate (forced oral sex)	Teenage or adolescent pregnancy
Overly critical or protective parents	Parents that do not allow the child to answer questions

Table 5-7: Summary of Clinical Signs and Symptoms of the Abused Child of Interest to the Dentist

expert on emotional abuse, is the persistent, chronic pattern that "erodes and corrodes a child." Dr. Arthur Green, director of the Family Center at the Columbia Presbyterian Medical Center in New York City, concurs that emotional abuse is not an isolated incident. According to Dr. Green, "We're talking about the kind of things that a good mother may do ten percent of the time, but a troubled mother does 80 or 90 percent of the time."

Table 5-4 is a summary of the principal considerations the examining dentist should review when evaluating a child and the parent or caregiver in a suspected emotional maltreatment situation.

Neglective Abuse

Table 5-5 is a summary of the principal considerations the examining dentist should review when evaluating a child and the parent or caregiver in a suspected neglective abuse situation.

Neglect in Health Care

Neglective parents or caregivers repeatedly ignore the recommendations of health care providers. This is especially problematic in the presence of treatable chronic disease. By definition, health care neglect exists in this setting. Parents may not acknowledge that a medical emergency exists with their child and refuse to seek appropriate care. Additionally, religious beliefs may contribute to the caregiver's decision to refuse necessary

health care and this may also result in health care neglect. When these issues are resolved through the legal system, it is most often the decision of the court that the right to life and health of the child supersedes the parental constitutional right to religious freedom.

The Ad Hoc Committee on Child Abuse and Neglect of the American Academy of Pediatric Dentistry has defined dental neglect as, "the failure by a parent or guardian to seek treatment for visually untreated caries, oral infections and/or pain, or, failure of the parent or guardian to follow through with treatment once informed that the above condition(s) exists." Nursing or *baby bottle caries* remains a common occurrence in young children who are neglected. This condition is observed in infants and toddlers who are placed to bed with a nursing bottle filled with cariogenic solutions including milk, soft drinks and sweet juices.

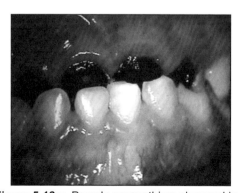

Figure 5-12c: Pseudo prognathism observed in a child with baby bottle decay.

In this situation the mandibular incisors are protected from being bathed in the cariogenic material because of the position of the nipple during sucking. The maxillary incisors, however, are exposed to the sugary solution and take the brunt of the cariogenic effects. The child's dentition manifests severely decayed maxillary anterior dentition causing a pseudo-prognathism or pseudo Class III malocclusion (**Figures 5-12a-c**).

Several siblings in the family may exhibit this pattern of dental decay and once the dentist has diagnosed the condition the cause and treatment options should be explained to the parent. If the parent consents to treatment for the child but then repeatedly fails to keep treatment appointments the dentist should consider reporting the case to the appropriate child protective agency.

Munchausen by Proxy Syndrome (MBPS)

Munchausen by proxy syndrome (MBPS) is also referred to as Factitious Disorder by Proxy. This syndrome is a psychological disorder. It is characterized by a pattern of behavior in which a caregiver, usually a mother, deliberately exaggerates, fabricates and/or induces physical ailments and/or psychological-behavioral-mental health problems in another individual, usually her child. This pattern of behavior constitutes a separate kind of maltreatment of the child.

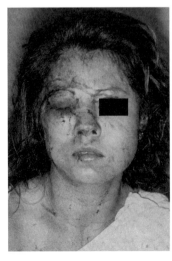

Figure 5-13: Battered woman with fractured nose, mandible and multiple soft tissue injuries of oral/ structures. (Courtesy of Dr. John McDowell)

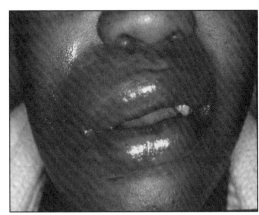

Figure 5-14: Intentionally inflicted trauma to the oral/ region of a 33 year old African-American woman. (Courtesy of Dr. John McDowell)

The mother attempts to gain attention and recognition for herself by putting on the public façade of a dedicated and loving caregiver. When alone with her child, however, she will subject them to physical, sexual, emotional and/or neglective abuse. This is manifested by the mother deliberately attempting to make the child sick, repeatedly bringing them for care and appearing as the heroine for attempting to cure the child of its illness. Thus, the primary purpose of this behavior for the perpetrator is to gain some form of internal gratification, such as attention.

The website *Munchausen by Proxy Survivors Network* offers an extended definition for the disorder: Children who fall victim to a parent suffering from MBPS often require extensive emergency medical care and may undergo several unnecessary medical procedures. These may include being subjected to sophisticated physical tests and/or painful surgeries that are essentially unnecessary. When obtaining a child's health history and chief complaint, health care professionals should be aware of false symptoms provided by the caregiver or parent because MBPS is considered a form of child abuse.

Diagnosis of Child Abuse

Diagnosing child abuse is more involved than recognition of a physical injury in a child. **Tables 5-6 and 5-7 are** a summary of the principal indicators that may signal

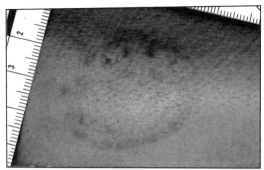

Figure 5-15: Bitemark on forearm of 28 year old Caucasian woman domestic violence victim. (Courtesy of Dr. John McDowell)

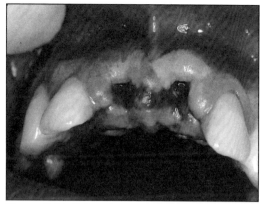

Figure 5-16: Delayed presentation for care seen in a 34 year old Caucasian female victim of IPV. Initial presentation for care was approximately four days after the most recent assault resulting in avulsion of maxillary central incisors. (Courtesy of Dr. John McDowell)

the presence of child abuse or neglect to the examining dentist during his or her evaluation of a child and the parent or caregiver in a suspected abusive situation.

Dental Implications of Child Abuse/ Neglect

Intimate Partner Violence (IPV)

Intimate partner violence (IPV) refers to unwanted aggressive behavior between adults in a variety of living arrangements and social situations. Currently, the historical husband/ wife relationship is only one component of what can be defined as an *intimate partner* relationship. Both heterosexual and homosexual relationships meet the test for inclusion in the definition of an intimate partner union. Health care providers must be cognizant of these relationships as a possible source of physical or emotional injury to their patients. In the 1990s, the American Dental Association enacted a policy to promote the education of dental health professionals in the area of adult abuse and neglect. The United States Department of Justice reported that 85 percent of IPV victims are women; however, individuals in gay, lesbian, bisexual and/or transsexual relationships may also be affected.

In 2003, the website of the Centers for Disease Control and Prevention reported that Intimate Partner Violence (IPV) resulted in nearly two million injuries and approximately 1,300 deaths annually in the United States. In reality, these figures are estimates and it is likely that the figures actually underestimate the true number

of injured or killed individuals. A report released by the United Nations in 2006 compiled global studies concerning horrific forms of violence against women ranging from bride burnings, sex trafficking, mass rape as a weapon of war and female infanticide to beatings, torture and murder. Despite all of these atrocities the report indicated that the most common form of serious abuse against women and girls is violence by intimate partners.

Historically, the battered woman syndrome, now referred to as IPV, has been defined as a sign and symptom complex occurring as a result of abusive actions directed against a woman by her male partner. In these situations the woman has received deliberate, severe and repeated physical abuse by her male partner. The minimal injury reported in these occurrences is severe bruising. Most of the assaults, however, are termed *relatively minor* and involve pushing, shoving, slapping and hitting. It has been reported that some form of violence occurs in approximately twenty percent of relationships and in half of these the abuse takes on more violent forms of assault. These extreme situations often involve punching, kicking, biting, or assault with a weapon.

Most definitions of intimate partner violence emphasize the physical abuse component because of the severe physical injuries that may occur during the battering episode(s)

(**Figure 5-13**). However, the health care provider should be aware that mental abuse and intimidation are integral components of the abuse syndrome.

The sequelae of violence directed against women or men can be severe (**Figure 5-14**). It has been reported that domestic disputes cause approximately one third of all female homicides. Battering episodes have also been reported to lead to more than one-fourth of all suicide attempts among women and men. Additionally, the domestic violence victim can place a significant burden on hospital emergency room, personnel. In some locales approximately thirty percent of emergency department visits are women presenting with physical injuries.

Although IPV incidence and prevalence is high in western society, domestic violence injuries are frequently under recognized by health care providers responsible for either the immediate or delayed care of these victims. The lack of a clear demographic profile of the victim combined with the fact that victims rarely volunteer that they have been abused contributes to the low reporting rate for battered women. Appropriate questioning by health care providers regarding the possibility of non-accidental, intentionally inflicted trauma can result in information gathering that may not otherwise be volunteered by the victim.

In order to achieve the most productive responses the victim of IPV should be interviewed in a private setting. This private, unhurried interview can reduce the potential risk of only acquiring an incomplete, inaccurate or denial history. This is often the result of an interview process in which the abuser tries to remain close to the victim and responding to questions that are directed to the victim. The health professional should be aware that a patient's vague, repeated, subtle, non-specific complaints that are unsubstantiated by the clinician's physical evaluation of the patient can be indicative that the patient is a victim of domestic violence.

The dentist should be particularly aware of the fact that maxillofacial and dental injuries are common in both male and female victims of IPV. Bite marks can also occur when there is direct, violent contact between victim and perpetrator (**Figure 5-15**). Mandibular fractures are routinely observed in victims of domestic violence and some of the most common injuries involve the soft tissues of the face and oral cavity. Lip lacerations, nasal injuries and other soft tissue bruising are also frequently seen in the IPV victim.

Forensic pathologists and forensic odontologists have long known that the same types and locations of physical injury seen in the head and neck region of abused children can also occur in victims of maltreatment by intimate partners and those victimized by elder abuse and maltreatment of the disabled. Health professionals who treat the living are becoming more aware of this fact.

The signs and symptoms observed in victims of domestic violence are interrelated regardless of the subtype. They include the following observations:

- The history conflicts with the physical injury observed by the examining physician or dentist.

- Evasive, contradictory or vague explanations for the injuries are cited.

- References are made to an unusual or rare disease as the explanation for the trauma.

- *Shopping* for care from different physicians, health care facilities and dental practitioners or delay in seeking treatment for traumatic injuries is indicative of a potentially abusive situation (**Figure 5-16**).

Studies indicate that 20-30 percent of women and 7.5 percent of men have been physically and/or sexually abused by an intimate partner in their lifetime. A variety of presenting complaints include neurological problems such as paresthesia, and headaches. Insomnia, diarrhea, generalized anxiety and depression are also common findings.

There are three distinct phases of abuse that are identified in the IPV or domestic violence setting. Initially, over a long duration, tension between the partners escalates. Excessive dependence on alcohol, drug abuse and jealousy lead to hostility. The victim, either male or female, becomes more nurturing or compliant. They avoid recognizing that an interpersonal problem or situation exists by compensating through denial mechanisms. Victims often direct the blame for the problem on themselves.

During the second phase of IPV direct violent behavior begins. The batterer expresses that he, or she only wants to control the partner or "teach them a lesson." Further denial and delay or refusal to seek necessary medical care is common. The victims of domestic violence resist placing additional financial or emotional stresses into the volatile situation. Law enforcement personnel responding to a violent situation are trained to recognize that the victim will often decline to prosecute for fear of later retaliation and/or loss of financial or emotional support from the abuser. The latter concept seems counterintuitive to those not in an abusive, codependent relationship.

The final phase of IPV or domestic violence is often referred to as the *honeymoon phase*. During this period the batterer becomes loving and contrite. This emotional swing is precipitated by the abusive partner's fear that the victim will end the relationship and leave.

In the United States, the Centers for Disease Control initiated a project know as *Safe Dates*. Information gathered from the project indicated that twenty five percent of eighth and ninth graders had experienced some variety of relationship abuse. Twenty five percent of female high school students had been physically or sexually abused by a *dating partner*. These young people often became the victims of domestic violence as they matured because they had learned to accept abusive behavior as normal.

Religious or social beliefs in which women are considered *second class* can contribute to the acceptance of harsh treatment by the abusing spouse or partner. If they are a respected member of the business, political, religious or

ethnic community the victim may additionally fear that attempting to leave the situation will be hopeless. Woman who are illegal aliens are also at greater risk for fear of being reported to the immigration authorities and deported.

Dental Implications of IPV

It has been reported that 94 percent of victims of domestic violence exhibit evidence of trauma in the head and neck region. In 2001, a study described the incidence, etiology and patterns of maxillofacial injury associated with domestic violence injuries among patients admitted to an inner-city hospital over a five year period. Data were collected from a sample of 236 emergency room admissions concerning the type, location and etiology of sustained injuries, alcohol involvement, and treatment approaches.

Eighty-one percent of the victims presented with maxillofacial injuries. Being struck with a fist was described as the source of the injuries in 67 percent of the assaults. The middle third of the face was most commonly involved and injuries were observed in this region in 69 percent of the victims. Left-sided facial injuries were more common than right. This would support the concept that the majority of perpetrators were right-handed. The preponderance of facial injuries indicated in this report reinforces the role of the dental profession and oral and maxillofacial surgery in particular in the care of these IPV victim/patients.

Elder Abuse

Changes in societal demographics in North America and Europe indicated *a graying* of the populations in these areas. This is a result of lower birth rates and health care systems that contribute to longevity of life. Issues related to the interfacing and interaction of the older family member with the rest of the family unit is important when considering the causes of abuse against the elderly. Health care providers and governmental agencies must consider and investigate issues related to numerous etiologic factors that may impact the incidence of elder abuse. Some of these include the cycle of violence within the family unit, the dependence of the older member on others in a family unit for support, mental health issues like dementia (Alzheimer's disease), substance abuse (alcohol, drug or gambling addictions) and personal economics and stress factors affecting the caregivers (*sandwich generation)* in the family.

Currently, the societal problem of elder abuse and its recognition is evolving much as the understanding of child abuse did in the 1970s. Like child abuse, it pervades all social, economic, racial, ethnic and educational subpopulations. Women aged 75 years or older are most frequently targeted primarily because they have physical impairments that may preclude them living independently. However, any older individual can be a victim regardless of health, gender, financial or social status. Those living alone or widowed or who are socially isolated are often controlled or influenced by an abusive caregiver. Victims may have some degree of physical impairment or mental incapacity. Additionally, they may be emotionally distraught. All of these factors should be considered by health care workers and professionals when assessing the older victim.

The profile of an abuser of older individuals indicates that they are often the adult child, spouse or caregiver of the older victim. They may also be strangers who solicit the older person's home to market products or services. Others may pose as police officers, bank investigators, religious leaders or authority figures to the unwitting elderly victim. As with abusers of younger aged individuals, the perpetrator of elder abuse may be an alcoholic, addicted to drugs or have a history of mental illness or emotional problems. Often these individuals are unique because they may be dependent on the older person (victim) for assistance. They may also be resentful of the care giving role.

Senior citizens can be abused/neglected in the following ways:

- **Physical abuse** in the elder population is similar to that found in victims of IPV or child abuse. The head and neck are commonly targeted although the victim may have additional unexplained injuries or a history of *accidents*.

- **Sexual abuse** of the elderly is difficult to comprehend, but, unfortunately is a common occurrence.

- **Passive neglect** is the unintentional failure to fulfill a care giving obligation. Failure to provide adequate food, health care services or other necessities may occur because of the caregiver's own infirmities, inadequate skills or inability to comprehend the importance of such obligations.

- **Active neglect** is an intentional failure to fulfill an obligation to care for an individual. Withholding food, medical services or necessary appliances such as dentures, eye glasses, hearing aids, walkers or wheelchairs constitutes active neglect. Deliberate abandonment can also occur.

- **Self-Neglect** occurs when the older person is not providing for his/her own essential needs. Regardless of the subtype of neglective abuse the victim may appear malnourished, dehydrated, or confused. They may also manifest untreated medical condition(s), an unkempt appearance with inappropriate/dirty clothing and signs of infrequent bathing.

- **Material (financial) abuse** is the illegal or unethical use of an elder's funds/property or other assets for the benefit of the caregiver. Older individuals are targeted for financial abuse because they have access to funds or finances due to retirement incomes and insurance settlements resulting from the death of a spouse. Retention of social security, welfare, retirement or insurance funds by the caregiver are examples of this form of abuse and can be accomplished through theft, fraud, forgery, exploitation and/or the misuse of Powers of Attorney. Indicators of financial abuse can include the fact that the standard of living of the victim is not in keeping with their income or assets. Theft of property, unusual or inappropriate activity in bank accounts and forged signatures on checks and/or documents are also indicative of the problem. An older person may be coerced into signing over legal documents to the abuser. Additionally, the victim may accumulate overdue bills or experience being over-charged for services or products.

- **Psychological abuse** is any action or comment that may cause emotional anguish, fear or diminish the self-esteem or dignity of the older person. Indicators include threats to do harm or institutionalize the victim. Intimidation, humiliation, infantilization or withholding affection or companionship by denying access to grandchildren or other loved ones are also related to this aspect of the elder abuse problem. Harassing phone calls and imposed or sudden isolation or abandonment are additional cofactors. Removal of the victim's decision-making process may be manifested as fear, uneasiness, anxiety, depression, withdrawal, cowering (changes in behavior) reluctance to talk openly and avoidance of contact with the caregiver(s). Additionally, the family/caregiver(s) speak on behalf of the older person or will not allow privacy while making excuses for the older person's inability to answer questions (ill, tired, etc.).

Ironically, when couples/partners have remained together despite a history of IPV the roles of abuser and victim often become reversed. The elderly male, who is now infirm and weak, will often become the target of the mistreatment by the female.

The common pathologic conditions associated with normal aging can often mimic signs and symptoms of physical abuse in the elderly. Therefore, when elder abuse is considered in a differential diagnosis, vascular changes associated with vericosities and vascular stasis, ecchymotic and petechial vascular responses to medication should also be includes. Lupus erythematosis, erythema multiforme, diabetes mellitus and peripheral vascular ulcers or decubitus ulcers are other conditions that can arise from non abusive causes.

IPV among aged partners is not uncommon. A national incidence study was conducted by the United States Administration on Aging in 1996. It indicated that more than 500 thousand persons aged 60 and older experienced abuse, neglect or self-neglect in the twelve months preceding the study. This same report stated that:

- Approximately one in four new cases of elder abuse were actually reported and substantiated by adult protective services agencies.

- Persons over the age of 80 suffered abuse and neglect two to three times more often than those in the 60-79 year age group.

- Known perpetrators of abuse and neglect were family members in 90 percent of cases,

- Sixty-six per cent of abuse perpetrators were adult children or spouses of the abused or neglected individual.

In the last decade, elder abuse and IPV have become recognized as significant public health and medical problems. Unlike the laws that require health care providers to report child abuse to appropriate child protective agencies within the jurisdictions of each of the United States, adult protective services (APS) is not a national program. Although APS was established under Title XX of the Social Security Act of 1975 and is a federally mandated program, little or no funding has been allocated to this program.

Thus, APS programs have developed in accordance with the needs and constructs of each state. While the various state APS programs do have similarities each is tailored to the laws and regulations of the specific state. Each state's ability to respond to survey questions concerning adult protective services is reflective of this fact.

According to a generic definition of APS developed by the National Association of Adult Protective Services (NAAPS), "Adult Protective Services (APS) are those services provided to older people and people with disabilities who are in danger of being mistreated or neglected, are unable to protect themselves, and have no one to assist them." In most states, APS programs are the first responders to reports of abuse, neglect, and exploitation of vulnerable adults. Although states differ in their statutory and regulatory definitions, general definitions concerning the problem of adult abuse are helpful in understanding the reported statistics related to its various subtypes.

Thus, a committee of key members of the National Adult Protective Services Association (NAPSA) defined *abuse* as the:

- Infliction of physical or psychological harm.
- Knowing deprivation of goods or services necessary to avoid physical or psychological harm.

Additionally they defined *neglect* as the:

- Refusal or failure to fulfill any part of a person's obligations or duties to an elder.

- Failure of a person who has fiduciary responsibilities to provide care for an elder.

- Failure on the part of an in-home service provider to provide necessary care.

In 2004 NAAPS substantiated reports that elder abuse had increased by 18 percent compared to 2000. Of the fifteen states

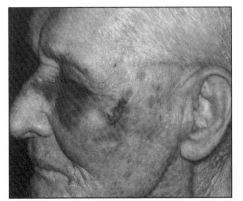

Figure 5-17: Facial trauma (fracture of zygomaticomaxillary complex) in 93 year old Caucasian man. (Courtesy of Dr. John McDowell)

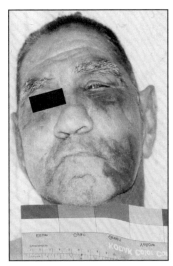

Figure 5-18: 73 year old Hispanic Male victim of inflicted Trauma with multiple Fractures of facial bones. (Courtesy of Dr. John McDowell)

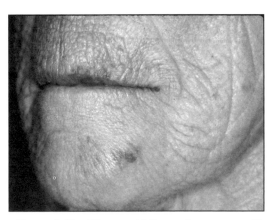

Figure 5-19: 74 year old Caucasian woman with soft tissue trauma (Courtesy of Dr. John McDowell)

reporting, 65.7 percent of the elder abuse victims were female and 42.8 percent were eighty years of age or older. Approximately seventy seven percent of the victims were Caucasian and among those cases of elder abuse reported 89.3 percent occurred in domestic settings.

It has been suggested that in Canada the medical, legal and health care funds or finances professions must consider updating *old* Acts such as the Charter of Rights and Freedoms, Family Law Act, Mental Health Act, Substitute Decision Act, Long Term

Care Act, Nursing Homes Act, Homes for the Aged and Rest Homes Act, Residents Bill of Rights, Professional Codes of Ethics, Tenant Protection Act, and Business Practices Act to better protect the elderly of that country

It is obvious that the problems related to human abuse do not abruptly end at any arbitrary assigned age nor do violent behaviors tend to commence at age sixty five. The years after retirement may be thought of as the *golden years*. However, these decades are not always the safest or most enjoyable for those who manage to reach this plateau. Often,

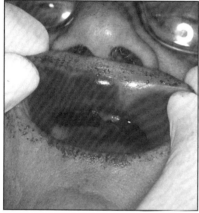

Figure 5-20: Traumatic injury upper lip and edentulous ridge in an 82 year old Caucasian male. (Courtesy of Dr. John McDowell)

Figure 5-21: Lateral radiograph of the facial structures revealing a nasal fracture in a victim of physical elder abuse. (Courtesy of Dr. John McDowell)

the victims of elder abuse fail to report their situation and this is a concern for investigators and health care professionals alike. Reasons for this underreporting are thought to include the following:

- The elder victim is in denial, disbelief or non-recognition of the fact that an abusive incident has occurred.

- They are in fear of reprisal, abandonment, isolation or institutionalization by the abuser.

- They are completely dependent on the abuser for food, shelter, clothing, etc.

- The victim may feel abandoned if the abuser is arrested.

- The victim loves the abuser.

-They are proud and feel shame, embarrassment, guilt, low self-esteem and/ or confusion pertaining to their relationship with the abuser;

- They are unaware of their legal rights because of a lack of understanding of the judicial system.

- They are unaware of available community resources

- Multicultural issues including religious customs and beliefs and language barriers may intercede. These may lead to a feeling that the *sanctity of the family* will be compromised.

- The victim distrusts police or other authorities based on prior interactions in other countries or cultural settings.

- They perceive barriers to protection of confidentiality.

Interdisciplinary teams of physical and emotional health care providers, social services providers and law enforcement personnel should participate in the evaluation of possible elder abuse victims. Whenever

ABUSE AND NEGLECT OF AN OLDER OR VULNERABLE PERSON

(Defined: Any action or inaction by ANY person, which causes harm to the older or vulnerable person.)

If you suspect: Description:	INDICATORS
PHYSICAL ABUSE Any act of violence causing injury or physical discomfort (e.g. slapping, pinching, punching or other rough handling, forcible restraint or intentional over / under medication), including SEXUAL ASSAULT.	**Indicators** - unexplained injuries in areas normally covered (bruises in various stages of healing, burns or bites) alopecia and bleeding scalp from hair pulling, untreated medical problems, history of "accidents", signs of over / under medication, sexual assault, wasting, and dehydration.
PSYCHOLOGICAL ABUSE Any action or comment causing emotional anguish, fear or diminished self-esteem or dignity (e.g. threats to do harm, unwanted institutionalization, harassment, abandonment, imposed isolation, removal of decision making choices).	**Indicators** - fear, anxiety, depression, withdrawal, cowering, reluctance to talk openly, fearful interaction with caregiver, caregiver speaking on behalf of person and not allowing privacy.
FINANCIAL ABUSE Theft or exploitation of a person's money, property or assets (e.g. forgery, misuse of Power of Attorney).	**Indicators** - standard of living not in keeping with income or assets, theft of property noted, unusual / inappropriate activity in bank accounts, forged signatures on checks, forcing a person to sign over a will or property, over-charging for services / products, overdue bills.
NEGLECT Inability to provide basic or personal care needs (e.g. food, water, required medications, shelter, hygiene, clothing, physical aids – hearing aids, eye glasses, dentures, exercise and social interaction, lack of attention, abandonment, undue confinement, inadequate supervision or safety precautions, withholding medical services / treatment). • **ACTIVE NEGLECT** - intentional failure of a caregiver to fulfill their care giving responsibilities • **PASSIVE NEGLECT** - unintentional failure of a caregiver to fulfill their care giving responsibilities because of lack of knowledge, skill, illness, infirmity, or lack of awareness of community supports / resources. • **SELF NEGLECT** - person's inability to provide for their own essential needs because of physical infirmity or inability to make sound choices due to addiction, mental illness and / or cognitive impairment.	**Indicators –** Unkempt appearance, Inappropriate or dirty clothing, Signs of infrequent bathing, Living conditions unhealthy, dangerous and / or in disrepair, Lack of social contact, No regular medical appointments.
INSTITUTIONAL ABUSE Any physical, sexual, psychological, financial abuse or neglect occurring within a care facility involving active victimization, withholding or denial of individual care needs, and / or failure to carry out reasonable requests	

Table 5-8: Summarized Definitions, Signs and Indicators of Elder Abuse

WHAT TO DO	**A**cknowledge Suspicion of abuse may develop over time. Accumulate/document evidence. **B**arriers Fear of retaliation, withdrawal of caregiver support, confidentially. **U**rgency Assess immediate risk of physical harm or if basic necessities of life are provided. **S**creen Assess person's ability to help themselves (i.e. competency). **E**mpower Inform person of their rights, resources and establish a safety plan. **R**efer Seek support or consultation from other professionals.

Table 5-9: ABUSER - Summarized suggestions for decisions related to abuse intervention.

possible, medical, nursing and oral health care providers with training, knowledge and experience in geriatrics/gerontology should be members of the assessment team. Some of the signs and symptoms of diseases and conditions associated with aging might confuse the inexperienced examiner.

Law enforcement or other investigating agencies must remember that elder abuse victims are most likely to be victims of physical violence received from those individuals with

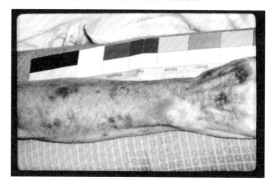

Figure 5-23: Physical signs on the arm of an elderly individual illustrative of purpuretic lesions associated with Coumadin therapy, not physical abuse.

whom they live, most commonly the abused individual's spouse. Forensic odontologists should also be aware of this data as they collect physical evidence from the potential victim of abuse. As with the victims of intimate partner violence, an elderly individual should be interviewed in a quiet, supportive, non-accusatory environment in order to receive the

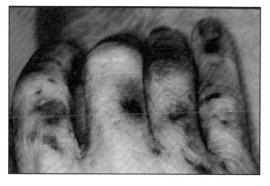

Figures 5-22a: Pattern injuries on the fingers of an elder abuse victim. They were caused by a relative biting the victim.

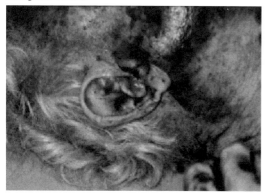

Figures 5-22b: Avulsive bite mark injury on the ear of the same victim

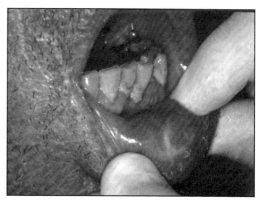

Figure 5-24: Developmentally disabled 51 year old Caucasian male. Scar of lower lip indicating previous injury. Note that there is ecchymosis of the lower lip and left buccal mucosa indicating more recent injuries. (Courtesy of Dr. John McDowell)

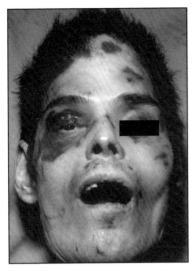

Figure 5-25: 37 year old developmentally disabled Hispanic male victim of homicide. Note the multiple, significant facial injuries. (Courtesy of Dr. John McDowell)

most accurate information from the patient.

Because the aged population in the United States continues to increase, it is not likely that decreasing numbers of elder abuse victims will be encountered in the next generation. Present data from the United States Census Bureau indicates that almost one-fourth of the U.S. population is presently over the age of 65. Census Bureau projections indicate that by the year 2050, the average lifespan of an American-born person will be in excess of 85 years. It is estimated that by the year 2010 nearly 25 percent of the population will be in their seventh decade and older. Many of these persons will live a quality of life unequaled in previous generations.

Although quality of life might improve, most individuals after age 70 will develop chronic diseases and disabilities that limit their activities and ability to be self-sustaining. Many aged individuals will become dependent on the care of others to survive. Unfortunately, some of these elderly persons will be in the care of persons who are incapable, reluctant, unwilling or ill-prepared to deliver the care required. These living conditions can lead to circumstances where the dependent individual can suffer abuse or neglect at the hands of the caregiver. The caregivers can be their spouse, other family members, and employees in a nursing facility or persons employed within the elder's home.

Completely uniform definitions and classifications of elder abuse and neglect are not found in the literature and motivation (intent) is frequently used to separate one form of mistreatment from others. The concept that neglect is less severe than active abuse is frequently not true. Active neglect (intentionally denying or partially withholding care) and passive neglect (unintentionally failing to provide care) can be equally injurious to the elderly. Failing to provide necessary support to a frail elderly person can lead to rapid deterioration and death.

Neglect does not always occur because of the actions of caregivers responsible for the elderly person. Self-neglect is not surprisingly the most frequent form of neglect. When competent and at least partially able to provide their own care, the well-elderly person is ultimately responsible for his/her own well-being and may refuse care even if this refusal may lead to severe health risks. In suspected cases of self-neglect, the dentist should function as an educator, reviewing the possible sequelae of unmet needs.

As with battered women, there is no clear profile of the abused elder. However, there are characteristics that place elders at risk for abuse. Abused elders are more likely than non-abused elders to be in poor health and living with a person at least partially responsible for their care.

Dental Implications of Elder Abuse

As with younger victims of inflicted abusive trauma, the elderly can be victims of physical abuse that involves injuries to the maxillofacial complex (**Figures 5-17 through 5-21**).

Physical evidence of intentional trauma in the elderly may take many forms that can be diagnosed by members of the dental team. Intentional trauma to oral and paraoral structures can include lacerations and contusions of the lip trauma, fractured or subluxated teeth, fractures of the mandible or maxilla, or severe bruising of the edentulous ridges (**Figure 5-20**). In addition to examining the victim for their immediate acute traumatic injuries the dentist should also examine attempt to identify indicators of prior trauma to the orofacial structures. These may include fractures of the zygomaticomaxillary complex, orbital and nasal fractures and bruising of the facial tissues (**Figure 5-21**). Because the injuries associated with elder abuse often involve areas not normally examined by the dentist, when elder abuse is suspected medical referral is also indicated.

Although sexual abuse is not uncommon in the elderly it is less common than other forms of physical injury. Like other forms of assault, sexual abuse may be so severe as to result in death in extreme cases. Oral manifestations of sexually transmissible diseases can be an indicator of sexual abuse of the elderly person. Immediate medical referral to legal, welfare and medical authorities is indicated when the dentist suspects that his/her patient may be a victim of sexual abuse. The possible victim of sexual abuse should be thoroughly examined by medical personnel correlating the systemic physical examination with the oral findings.

Biting activity is not rare in cases of elder abuse (**Figures 5-22a and b**). Forensic odontologists are often consulted to evaluate patterned injuries for possible bite mark evidence in these cases. Not all mucosal or skin lesions that are discolorations are indicators of abuse although they may resemble bite marks of the facial structures. The dentist should be knowledgeable concerning the aging process and geriatric health problems common in the elderly population. Skin lesions that resemble traumatic injuries can be caused by medicines which result in petechial or purpuretic lesions, systemic or dermatologic diseases and fungal, bacterial or viral diseases (**Figure 5-23**). An accurate and thorough history and physical examination is essential in forming a differential diagnosis concerning the etiology of these skin and mucosal lesions.

Abuse of the Disabled

Additional information concerning protocols for evaluating the victim of elder abuse have been developed by a consortium of legal and health care organizations in Hamilton, Ontario, Canada and these can be found in **Appendix J**.

There are both federal and state laws in the United States that deal with abuse and neglect of the physically and/or mentally impaired or disabled. However, incidence and prevalence of abuse and neglect of this population and the location of injuries associated with assaults directed toward the disabled is the abuse topic least documented in the professional and lay literature. Regardless of age, disabled individuals are at higher risk for being targets of abusive or neglective behavior by caregivers than are those without a disability (**Figures 5-24 through 5-26**). Primary caregivers may be abusers simply because they are overwhelmed with the needs of the impaired individual.

Reports indicate that perpetrators of acts of violence against the disabled can include family members, personal home care attendants and institutional health care workers. In institutional settings, other special needs residents can commit acts of violence against co-residents. Neighbors and fellow students can also target vulnerable disabled individuals.

A case in Illinois involved a 23 year old profoundly disabled woman who was sexually assaulted at a long term care facility where she lived. Her subsequent pregnancy resulting from this assault went unnoticed by the supervisory staff. This occurred despite the fact that personnel attending to her immediate needs recorded missed menstrual periods and morning vomiting for several months following the assault. The pregnancy was finally discovered when a staff member of the long term care facility took notice of the movement of the fetus.

Special needs students may be singled out by their class-mates for ridicule that might seem harmless but is in fact terrifying to a disabled person. These individuals are abused and neglected at four times the rate of the general population. Seventy percent of women with developmental disabilities will be sexually assaulted in their lifetime and repeated incidents of abuse appear to be commonly directed toward women with disabilities. These individuals report being abused by a greater number of different perpetrators (assailants) than other women. These same abused women also indicate that the actual assaults last for longer time periods than women without disabilities.

Currently there is a trend toward *mainstreaming* and *deinstitutionalizing* the mentally and physically disabled. These individuals are being placed in group homes within their communities but may also migrate to the ranks of the homeless population. Because of this policy to reintegrate the disabled into the general population it is likely that the dental practitioner will see more of these patients and be exposed to their specific dental problems and needs. The disabled generally have a higher incidence of dentally related issues resulting from their cognitive and/or physical limitations. Such limitations preclude those who are mentally challenged from being aware of the necessity for good oral hygiene. Alternatively, physical limitations may prevent the disabled from performing the tasks required to maintain their own oral hygiene.

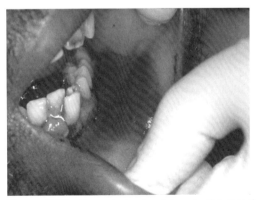

Figure 5-26: Recent abusive injury to the mouth of a 37 year old developmentally disabled African-American male. (Courtesy of Dr. John McDowell)

Unlike the perpetrators of child abuse and IPV, no clear profile of the abuser of the disabled has yet emerged. It does appear, however, that men are more likely than women to be involved in acts of physical violence, sexual violence and emotional or neglective abuse directed toward the elderly.

Examination and Documentation of Suspected Inflicted Trauma Associated With All Forms of Abuse

The following discussion involves the procedures and protocols the dentist should follow when examining and documenting the presence of injuries related to suspected inflicted abusive trauma. These procedures and protocols should be practiced regardless of whether the victim is a child, spouse/partner or elderly individual. Regardless of whether the examination of the victim is performed in a private treatment facility, hospital emergency department, morgue or medical examiner's office, the dentist should follow a specific plan of action if it is suspected that a person is a victim of intentional trauma through abuse.

Whenever practical, the patient should be interviewed and examined by appropriately trained individuals in a private, quiet environment where confidentiality is assured. The patient should be interviewed in a supportive, non-accusatory manner and a female staff member who is familiar with the requirements of patient confidentiality should be present during the interview and examination of all female patients or children. The examiner should record all patient statements regarding the history of abuse in the patient's own words. Any statements that are inconsistent with the physical findings should also be thoroughly documented in the record.

After assessing a child's injuries and determining that child abuse is suspected, documentation of the injuries should take place. A complete and accurate written description of the injuries should be part of the record in all trauma cases. When abuse is suspected, photographs and radiographs of suspicious injuries can be obtained without the consent of the parent in most states. Written informed consent should be obtained from adult victims. This documentation should be placed in the record, clearly stating the purpose of the photographs obtained. The dentist and staff members involved in the examination process should appreciate and understand the fact that shame, embarrassment, blame directed toward self, denial and downplaying of the violent behavior are frequently expressed by the IPV, domestic violence victim.

The health care provider should be especially aware of the presence of multiple bruises of different colors that may present on the victim's skin. These may be suggestive of serial injuries that are both fresh and in various stages of healing. Bilateral injuries including periorbital ecchymoses (black eyes) are also suggestive of intentional trauma. It is appropriate for the dentist to record that it is his/her opinion that the physical findings are inconsistent with the history provided by the victim or caregiver.

Drawing the injuries on an anatomic diagram in the child's chart is recommended. Photographic evidence that accurately represents the injuries of the victim should be obtained and preserved as a part of the record. Ideally, photographs should be taken with a 35mm camera with a macro lens. Color photographs that identify the victim and orient the injuries can be invaluable when prosecution of the offender(s) occurs. Scale photography is essential for a complete analysis in bite mark cases and both close-up and distant orientation photographs should be obtained with a millimeter scale (e.g. ABFO No. 2 scale) included in photographs of the injuries. Identification information may be written on the ABFO No. 2 scale with a permanent marking pen. Additional detailed protocols for photographic evidence gathering are discussed in **Chapter 6 – Technological Aides in Forensic Odontology**.

It is recommended that a second staff member (e.g. dental assistant, office manager) witness and assist in the documentation of evidence. Written records should include the name of the child, their age, sex and address and household phone number as well as the demographic information of the parent or caregiver who accompanied the child. The name of any staff member(s) assisting in the examination should also be entered in the record. The dentist should always have a second or third party present throughout the examination of the abused victim.

Diagnostic images including radiographs, computed tomographic (CT) images or magnetic resonance images (MRIs) are often indicated for purposes of injury analysis. These images are critically important in the diagnosis and treatment of maxillofacial trauma. Evidence of fractures at various stages of healing or evidence of previous surgical procedures (wires, plates, pins, screws, etc) can be evidence of repeated assaults. Fractures might be discovered that are inconsistent with the history given by the patient. As in all forms of human abuse, injuries at variance with the history given should consider strongly suggestive of intentional trauma.

Intervention

The first step in the diagnostic process involves taking the patient history. After analysis of this subjective information including the patient's chief complaint the dentist should evaluate the objective data collected in the context of the physical findings observed. Subsequently a differential diagnosis is established for the cause of the physical injuries observed. This process may involve inquiries into whether the injuries are the result of accidental or non-accidental trauma. Once recognized and documented as being caused by abuse to a child, IPV victim or elder patient the dentist should be prepared to act on behalf of the victim.

All health professionals should be familiar with the mechanism in their state for reporting suspected domestic violence, child and/or elder abuse. As indicated previously, dentists should be aware that reporting laws for adult domestic violence victims are dictated by the individual states and are not presently mandated by federal law as are those related to victims of child abuse. The laws in all states presently require health professionals to report suspected abuse. Since dentists are mandatory reporters of suspected human abuse, a dentist may be held responsible for failing to intervene on behalf of an individual unable to escape the abusive environment.

Dentists should check with their respective state adult protective agencies regarding reporting mechanisms for their adult patients who are suspected to be victims of neglect or abuse. In all jurisdictions, if the mandated reporter's statements concerning suspected abuse are made in good faith, even if eventually proven wrong, the maker of the report is immune from any counter prosecution. Reporting suspected abuse is not an accusation of abuse by the reporter. It is a call for help for the child and for the abuser. Abuse is a problem that requires treatment.

When reporting to a local law enforcement agency, child protection services and/or social services agency, the reporter should have the following available:

- Statement of concern and reasons for suspecting abuse, including any documented evidence,

- The names, addresses and phone numbers of all involved parties.

The immediate and initial report should be made by telephone. The reporter should then provide the agency responsible for evaluating the charges of abuse with a written report as required by the respective state.

Protective Custody Issues

Under most state laws in the United States, if there is reasonable suspicion that a child may come to more serious harm by being returned to the parents, a police officer, physician, hospital or state welfare worker may be able to take the child into protective custody. Usually a hearing must be held in Juvenile Court within 24-72 hours of this occurs.

Resources

The following list of resources concerning the problem of human abuse is presented to provide the reader with an initial set of agencies which can provide further information, incite and assistance when dealing with this problem. It is not meant to be all inclusive.

Center for Disability Resources Library

The library is a collaborative effort between BabyNet/South Carolina Department of Health and Environmental Control, the Center for Disability Resources, the South Carolina Department of Disabilities and Special Needs, and the University of South Carolina School of Medicine Library. The CDR Library consists of books, videos, brochures, and audiotapes covering a variety of disability-related topics. The Center for Disability Resources Library is located within the University of South Carolina School of Medicine Library on Garners Ferry Road.

To check out any of the abuse resources materials listed, contact:

Roz McConnaughy
Phone: 803-733-3310
Email: roz@med.sc.edu
Web site: http://uscm.med.sc.edu/CDR/index.htm

Centers for Disease Control - Injury Prevention Center website

Useful information can be found at the Centers for Disease Control Injury Prevention Center website. (www. cdc. gov)

Crime Stoppers

The local Crime Stoppers telephone number is provided by a civilian organization (Crime Stoppers) which guarantees anonymity for all callers. Available 24-hours a day, the Crime Stoppers office is only interested in acquiring the information that may be pertinent to a crime or suspected crime. All forms of human abuse are crimes and once the avenue for reporting to Crime Stoppers is made available, victims who can remain anonymous are much more willing to call in the information about their situation of those of their colleagues and friends.

Massachusetts Medical Society

As a tool for recognizing and assisting in referral of domestic violence victims, the Massachusetts Medical Society developed the acronym **RADAR** for those responsible for identifying and documenting IPV:

Routine screening:

- Interview patient/victim with no partner/relative present

- Have a female assistant in the room if a male MD, DO or DDS/DMD is the inquiring professional

- Pose simple direct questions

- Have a non-judgmental attitude

Ask direct questions:

- State that because violence is common in women's lives the following are asked routinely:

- Are you in an abusive relationship?

- Have you ever been hit, kicked or punched by your partner?

- I notice you have a number of bruises. Did someone do that to you?

Document the findings:

- Record the statement in patient's own words

- Use assailant name in record if offered

- Record pertinent physical findings

- Prepare a body diagram to document evidence

- Take appropriate photographs if indicated and consent is granted

- Preserve physical evidence

- Document an opinion, i.e. patient's statement is consistent/inconsistent with injuries

Assess the patient's safety:

- Is the victim afraid to go home?

- Has there been an increase in severity/frequency of the abuse?

- Have there been threats of homicide/suicide?

- Have there been threats to the children?

- Is there a firearm in the house?

Review options and referrals:

- If in imminent danger, is there a friend or relative who has safe harbor?

- Is there an immediate need to access a shelter?

- Hotline/resource numbers should be available and these can also be located in the women's restroom.

- Do not force literature on victim since it could become a trigger for further abuse.

- Follow up appointments should be made as necessary.

The National Children's Advocacy Center NCAC)

The National Children's Advocacy Center (NCAC) is a non-profit organization that provides training, prevention, intervention and treatment services to fight child abuse and neglect.
Since being established in 1985, the NCAC has trained more than 54,000 professionals from the United States and 20 countries.

210 Pratt Avenue
Huntsville AL 35801

Phone: 256.533.5437
Fax: 256.534.6883
http://www.nationalcac.org/

The PANDA Program

PANDA is an acronym for Prevent Abuse and Neglect through Dental Awareness. It is the name of an educational program sponsored by Delta Dental of New Jersey through its philanthropic arm, the Delta Dental of New Jersey Foundation, Inc. PANDA is supported by a coalition of public and private organizations and its mission is to help dental office personnel recognize and report suspected cases of child abuse and neglect. The PANDA name was conceived by Delta Dental of Missouri, which began a similar program in 1992 and PANDA programs are available in many states and Canada. In 2003, through a partnership with Blue Shield of California, Blue Shield of California Foundation and Dental Benefit Providers of California, the California Dental Association Foundation was able to expand the PANDA program to incorporate all forms of family violence detection and prevention.

The extremely low abuse and neglect reporting rate by dentists appears to be related to the lack of training dentists receive in this area of practice. Dentists are often unaware of how to recognize and report abuse and neglect. Additionally, many harbor concerns about the ramifications of becoming legally involved in such cases. Since the inception of the PANDA program dental reporting of child abuse has risen sixty percent while reporting of abuse by all professionals has risen only six percent. Studies have indicated that dentists are nearly five times as likely to report suspected abuse if they receive education concerning the problem. The PANDA program addresses these issues so that dental personnel will have the information they need to properly identify, document and report suspected cases of child abuse and neglect.

PANDA Educational Program

The PANDA program consists of a slide presentation and printed materials. Representatives from the PANDA Coalition have formed a speaker's bureau to take the program to their respective audiences. PANDA presentations qualify for continuing dental education credits for re-licensure.

The objectives of the PANDA Coalition are to:

- Educate dental professionals to recognize signs of child abuse and neglect through seminars and written materials.

- Provide dental professionals with information and procedures for reporting child abuse and neglect.

- Promote awareness of child abuse detection within the dental community.

- Provide dental professionals with referral resources for families to help prevent child abuse and neglect.

The PANDA coalition offers educational seminars which provide dental professionals with the following:

- Detailed information on physical and behavioral indicators of child abuse and neglect including printed materials for the dental professional to keep for future reference.

- Information on how to make a formal report and whom to contact.

- A copy of relevant sections of the California Child Abuse and Neglect Reporting Law as they apply to mandated reporters.

- The legal ramifications connected with reporting and not reporting suspected abuse.

- A listing of all pertinent phone numbers and agency contacts.

- Information on how to deal with sensitive issues connected with filing a report.

- Referral resources to help families with child abuse-related problems.

- Information about the Adopt-A-Panda Program. This is a mechanism for dental personnel and individuals to promote public awareness and demonstrate support for child abuse prevention.

- Seminars that provide accredited continuing education (CE).

Additionally, a training videotape is available to lend to individuals who are unable to attend a seminar. The videotape is accompanied by written materials that dental office can retain for reference.

Conclusion

Forensic odontologists must remain keenly aware of the variety of physical, psychological and emotional injuries associated with victims of human abuse and neglect and domestic or intimate partner violence. Competency in this area of forensic odontology demands that the forensic dentist remain educated about the growing epidemic of human abuse and domestic violence and understand his or her obligation to report suspected cases in order to stop the problem and save lives.

EDUCATIONAL OUTCOMES

By completing this chapter the reader will:

- Build a foundational knowledge of the historical and epidemiological information associated with the various forms of human abuse and neglect.

- Describe the role of the forensic odontologist in the recognition, documentation and reporting of physical and neglective abuse.

- Build a foundational knowledge of the procedures and protocols required in the process of reporting abuse.

- Understand the role of the various federal and state, local and support agencies that can intervene in matters of human abuse.

- Recognize the signs and symptoms associated with the dental manifestations of human abuse and neglect.

- Critically evaluate relevant forensic, dental, medical and public health scientific literature concerning human abuse, and intimate partner violence issues based on an understanding of evidence based concepts.

CONTRIBUTORS

Marden E. Alder, DDS, MS, DABFO
Edward. E. Herschaft, DDS, MA, DABFO
John P. Kenney, DDS, MS, DABFO
Elisabeth Latner, Constable (Hamilton, Ontario)
John D. McDowell, DDS, MS, DABFO
David K. Ord, DDS
Raymond D. Rawson, DDS, MA, DABFO
David R. Senn, DDS, DABFO
Frank M. Stechey, DDS
Franklin D. Wright, DMD, DABFO

REFERENCES

Overview of Human Abuse

Goodman PE (2006). The relationship between intimate partner violence and other forms of family and societal violence. Emerg Med Clin North Am 24:889-903.

Halpern LR, Dodson TB (2006). A predictive model to identify women with injuries related to intimate partner violence. J Am Dent Assoc 137:604-9.

Halpern LR, Susarla SM, Dodson TB (2005). Injury location and screening questionnaires as markers for intimate partner violence. J Oral Maxillofac Surg 63:1255-61.

Harley AM (2006). Domestic violence screening: implications for surgical nurses. Plast Surg Nurs 26:24-8.

Herschaft EE (2002). Forensic Dentistry. In: Oral and Maxillofacial Pathology. Bea Neville editor. Philadelphia: W. B. Saunders, pp. 763-783.

Nelson HD, Nygren P, McInerney Y, Klein J (2004). Screening women and elderly adults for family and intimate partner violence: a review of the evidence for the U. S. Preventive Services Task Force. Ann Intern Med 140:387-96.

Thompson RS, Bonomi AE, Anderson M, Reid RJ, Dimer JA, Carrell D, Rivara FP (2006). Intimate partner violence: prevalence, types, and chronicity in adult women. Am J Prev Med 30:447-57.

Tjaden P, Thoennes N (2000). Extent, nature and consequences of intimate partner violence: findings from the National Violence Against Women Survey. http://www.cdc.gov/ncipc/factsheets/ipvfacts.htm.

Waalen J, Goodwin MM, Spitz AM, Petersen R, Saltzman LE (2000). Screening for intimate partner violence by health care providers. Barriers and interventions. Am J Prev Med 19:230-7.

Information Concerning Abusers

http://www.cincytoothdoc.com/. Dr. Frankin D. Wright DMD.

Freeman AJ, Senn DR, Arendt DM (2005). Seven

hundred seventy eight bite marks: analysis by anatomic location, victim and biter demographics, type of crime, and legal disposition. J Forensic Sci 50:1436-43.

Child Abuse/Neglect

Department of Health and Human Services (US) Administration on Children Youth and Families (2005). Child Maltreatment 2003. www.acf.hhs.gov/programs/cb/pubs/cm03/index.htm.

Freeman AJ, Senn DR, Arendt DM (2005). Seven hundred seventy eight bite marks: analysis by anatomic location, victim and biter demographics, type of crime, and legal disposition. J Forensic Sci 50:1436-43.

Kempe CH, Helfer RE (1982). Battered Child: University of Chicago Press.

http://www.masskids.org/sbs/sbscenter_tragedy.htm. Massachusetts SBS Prevention Center, Massachusetts Citizens for Children. Never shake a baby.

Risk Factors

Department of Health and Human Services (US) Administration on Children Youth and Families (2005). Child Maltreatment 2003. www.acf.hhs.gov/programs/cb/pubs/cm03/index.htm.

Klein M, Stern L (1971). Low birth weight and the battered child syndrome. Am J Dis Child 122:15-8.

Signs of Physical Abuse

Jessee SA (1995). Physical manifestations of child abuse to the head, face and mouth: a hospital survey. ASDC J Dent Child 62:245-9.

Needleman HL (1986). Orofacial trauma in child abuse: types, prevalence, management, and the dental profession's involvement. Pediatr Dent 8:71-80.

O'Neill JA, Jr., Meacham WF, Griffin JP, Sawyers JL (1973). Patterns of injury in the battered child syndrome. J Trauma 13:332-9.

Senn DR, McDowell JD, Alder ME (2001). Dentistry's role in the recognition and reporting of domestic violence, abuse, and neglect. Dent Clin North Am 45:343-63, ix.

Sexual Abuse

Freeman AJ, Senn DR, Arendt DM (2005). Seven hundred seventy eight bite marks: analysis by anatomic location, victim and biter demographics, type of crime, and legal disposition. J Forensic Sci 50:1436-43.

www.fsu.edu/~vicad/sexualabuse.html. Florida State University. Victim Advocate Program, Sexual Abuse.

Signs Associated with Types of Abuse

Child Welfare Information Gateway (2006). Recognizing Child Abuse and Neglect: Signs and Symptoms. http://www.childwelfare.gov/pubs/factsheets/signs.cfm.

Signs of Sexual Abuse

May-Chahal C, Herczog M (2003). Child Sexual Abuse in Europe, Council of Europe Publishing.

Intimate Partner Violence (IPV)

American College of Obstetrics and Gynecology (1999). Domestic Violence. Educational Bulletin No. 257. Washington DC.

Coker AL, Smith PH, Bethea L, King MR, McKeown RE (2000). Physical health consequences of physical and psychological intimate partner violence. Arch Fam Med 9:451-7.

Dorian RBJ (2005). Human Bitemarks. In: Bitemark Evidence. R Dorion editor: Marcel Decker Publishers, pp. 323-389.

Ehrensaft MK, Cohen P, Johnson JG (2006). Development of personality disorder symptoms and the risk for partner violence. J Abnorm Psychol 115:474-83.

Marvin DR (1997). The Dynamics of Domestic Abuse. FBI Law Enforcement Bulletin 66:13-18 http://www.fbi.gov/publications/leb/1997/july973.htm.

McDowell JD (2005). Role of Health Professionals in Diagnosing Patterned Injuries from Birth to Death. In: Bitemark Evidence. R Dorion editor: Marcel Decker Publishers, pp. 31-43.

Mehra V (2004). Culturally competent responses for identifying and responding to domestic violence in dental care settings. J Calif Dent Assoc 32:387-95.

Nelson HD, Nygren P, McInerney Y, Klein J (2004). Screening women and elderly adults for family and intimate partner violence: a review of the evidence for the U. S. Preventive Services Task Force. Ann Intern Med 140:387-96.

Newsletter National Center on Elder Abuse. (2001).

Nixon RD, Resick PA, Nishith P (2004). An exploration of comorbid depression among female victims of intimate partner violence with posttraumatic stress disorder. J Affect Disord 82:315-20.

Pittman JF, Buckley RR (2006). Comparing maltreating fathers and mothers in terms of personal distress, interpersonal functioning, and perceptions of family climate. Child Abuse Negl 30:481-96.

Dental Implications

http://www.chooserespect.org/. Centers for Disease Control Injury Prevention Center.

Le BT, Dierks EJ, Ueeck BA, Homer LD, Potter BF (2001). Maxillofacial injuries associated with domestic violence. J Oral Maxillofac Surg 59:1277-83; discussion 1283-4.

Ochs HA, Neuenschwander MC, Dodson TB (1996). Are head, neck and facial injuries markers of domestic violence? J Am Dent Assoc 127:757-61.

Elder Abuse

http://www.aoa.gov/press/fact/alpha/fact_elder_abuse.asp.

http://www.census.gov/population/www/pop-profile/.

Dental Implications of Elder Abuse

Stechy DFM, Personal communication.

Abuse of the Disabled

Glassman P, Miller C, Wozniak T, Jones C (1994). A preventive dentistry training program for caretakers of persons with disabilities residing in community residential facilities. Spec Care Dentist 14:137-43.

Petersillia JR (2001). Crime victims with developmental disabilities: a review essay. Criminal Justice and Behavior 28:655-694.

Sobsey D, Doe T (1991). Patterns of sexual abuse and assault. Sexuality adn Disability 9:243-259.

Sobsey D, Mansell S (1994). An international perspective on patterns of sexual assault and abuse of people with disabilities. International Journal of Adolescent Medicine and Health 7:153-178.

Young ME, Nosek MA, Howland C, Chanpong G, Rintala DH (1997). Prevalence of abuse of women with physical disabilities. Arch Phys Med Rehabil 78:S34-8.

The PANDA Program

Meskin LH (1995). Abusive legislation. J Am Dent Assoc 126:1080, 1082.

CHAPTER 6

TECHNOLOGICAL AIDES IN FORENSIC ODONTOLOGY

"Time changes everything except something within us which is always surprised by change."
Thomas Hardy

Introduction

The beginning of the 21st century has been associated with continuing progress in the development of technologies that can assist those in the forensic disciplines to facilitate their tasks. Hardy's statement, as referenced above, is appropriate for most aspects of forensic investigation. This is especially significant when considering developing technologies in the fields of forensic photography and digital imaging because they are the evidence gathering, storage, retrieval, analysis and transmittal techniques employed by most odontologists.

As technology evolves in photography and new techniques are developed in other areas, it is incumbent upon the forensic scientist practicing evidence based science to embrace the continuously developing state of the science. This is particularly true when considering advances in digital photography and radiography, alternate light source photography, scanning electron microscopy and computer technology. Without remaining abreast of these developments, the forensic dentist may be at a disadvantage by virtue of being unaware of the advances that are occurring. Although expense is often a consideration for the odontologist when acquiring newer more sophisticated equipment, even those not affiliated with a university, government agency, medical examiner's office or large law enforcement agency may certainly work in consultation with those agencies to gain access to these technologies.

In this regard information is presented concerning basic and advanced film-based and digital photographic techniques, the use of alternative light source photography, advances in the use of scanning electron microscopy (SEM) , energy dispersive x-ray spectroscopy

(EDS) and emerging technologies of x-ray fluorescence (XRF) and cone-beam computed tomography. Additionally, updated, most currently available information related to portable radiographic devices and computer software and hardware development are included.

Film Based Photography

Basic Principles

Forensic photographs are taken to accurately document evidence that is of a transient nature, fragile or easily broken and as a record for subsequent analysis or use in any future independent studies. Therefore, It Is the responsibility of the odontologist to properly document all photographic evidentiary material in a case. Further written documentation associated with the photographs should also be maintained. Thorough, complete documentation should include demographic information such as name of victim or suspect, date, time, individuals present during the examination, subject matter and location where the photographs were taken.

Additionally, information concerning the authorizing agency, individual who took the photographs and type of photographic equipment, film, and settings used should also be maintained. Since photographs exposed for forensic dental use are considered to be evidence, the odontologist must adhere to the rules regarding the chain of evidence; all transfer of this material between and among investigators, attorneys, laboratory personnel and odontologists must be documented.

Optical Physics

Lenses accomplish the task of focusing by converging light to a point called the *focal point*. An illuminated object at a distance of infinity has its image formed on the opposite side of the lens at the focal point. The *focal length* of a lens is the distance from the optical center of the lens to the focal point (**Figure 6-1**) and varies with the convexity of the lens. The more convex the lens; the greater light is bent and the shorter the *focal length*.

A *wide angle lens* has a short focal length (40mm or less). This is substantially shorter than the focal length of a normal lens for the image size produced by the camera. This factor is determined by the dimensions of the image frame at the film plane for a film camera and the dimensions of the photosensor for a digital camera. The normal lens should have a focal length approximating the length of the diagonal of the image frame. The wider angle of view described by a wide angle lens is prone to perspective distortion because it tends to be much closer to the subject being photographed (**Figure 6-2**).

which is the location of the film. As the object moves closer to the lens its image comes into focus further and further behind the focal point. Since the film within the camera cannot be moved back the lens must be extended outward (away from the film) to accommodate for the changing position of sharp focus. Most lenses extend enough to focus fully within the frame of object measuring 10 x 15 inches.

A close-up lens, (also called a macro lens) must have the ability to focus on an area at least as small as 24×36 mm. These lenses can fully frame and focus an object as small as 25.4 x 38.1 mm. Since that is the actual size of the film used, the reproduction on film is life-sized. This is expressed as a 1:1 reproduction ratio (RR). When a 50.8 x 76.2 mm object is fully framed on this film its RR is 1:2 or 1:2 life size. A 254 x 381 mm object reduced onto a 25.4 x 38.1 mm film has a 1:10 RR. This represents the close-focusing limits of a conventional lens.

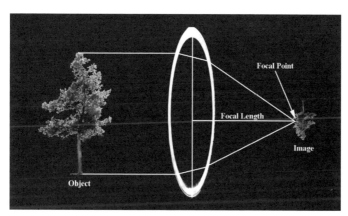

Figure 6-1: Focal Length and Focal Point.

A *telephoto lens* has a long focal length (75 mm or more). It is flatter and barely bends light while capturing it from a narrow angle like a telescope. It excludes much of the scene's periphery that the eye would see it and brings distant objects closer without magnifying them (**Figure 6-2**).

A *zoom lens* includes a range of focal lengths that can be selected at the photographer's discretion to vary the coverage of a scene without the photographer having to move closer or further away. An object at a far distance from the camera is in focus at the focal point –

Lenses can contribute to various types of distortion and image degradation. Some of these problems can be corrected at a price. *Field curvature* is a distortion in which a well focused image is blurred at the periphery. It is due to geometric imperfections at the edges of the lens which cause non-uniform bending of light. Use of smaller apertures helps to alleviate the problem by restricting the lens to the more accurate central area. Close-up lenses and bellow lenses have a *flat-field* correction for field curvature. Refer to Equipment for Forensic Dentistry – Film Based in this chapter for further discussion of the bellow lens.

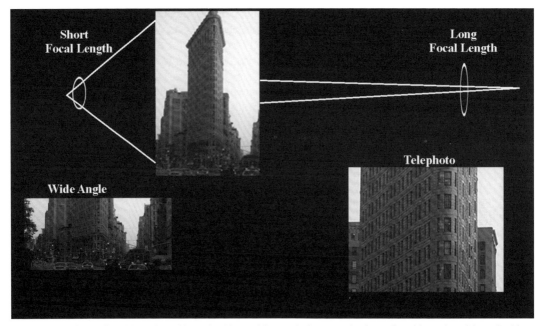

Figure 6-2: Short focal length achieved with a wide angle lens and a long focal length achieved with a telephoto lens.

Diffraction is the capability of a light wave to bend around corners. It is another physical factor that causes loss of image sharpness and primarily occurs when a part of a light wave is cut off by an obstruction. Diffractive effects set an absolute limit on the quality of an image observed through an optical instrument such as a camera. This diffractive limit occurs because the camera lens is of finite size. Thus, the lens diffracts light because part of the light wave is cut off as it moves through the components of the lens.

Incoming light is regulated through the lens by a variable opening termed the aperture The smaller the an aperture the greater the percentage of incoming light waves that will hit the iris periphery and be deflected outward instead of being focused. The use of wider apertures overcomes loss of resolution resulting from diffraction. In most lenses, the aperture size which produces the sharpest image and best resolution is about two f stop positions below its widest aperture. This balances the effects of both diffraction and field curvature which are accentuated at opposite ends of the *aperture range.*

A lens cannot focus all portions of a three dimensional scene or object on film. Recall that any information in front of a sharply focused area comes into focus behind the film while information further away will come into focus in front of the film. Thus, only a narrow plane will be in focus while sharpness progressively deteriorates for portions of the subject in front of and behind the focused plane. This can be overcome by a law of optical physics that predicts that the smaller the lens aperture, the larger will be the zone of sharpness in front of and behind the focused plane of a three dimensional object. Therefore, this so-called *depth of field* increases as the aperture decreases.

Perspective distortion is not a true distortion but a relative difference in the way the eye and the lens records an image. In optics perspective refers to the apparent size difference in equally sized objects viewed from different distances. Obviously, a 3 meter tall column viewed from a distance of 6 meters looks larger than a 3 meter column 33 meters away. The eye, as a lens/camera, objectively records this disparity but our brain interprets this as dimensionality rather than a size difference.

Even if one's stereoscopic vision failed because of loss of one eye, one would still perceive dimension through perspective. When the camera lens duplicates the perspective of the eye, size relationships are properly interpreted in terms of distance on the two dimensional photograph. However, when a three dimensional object is photographed closer than the usual viewing distance, or at a peculiar angle, perspective is exaggerated and spatial relationships as they appear on film may be misinterpreted by the eye.

Wide angle lenses are incorrectly described as causing perspective distortion yet these lenses simply have to get closer to the subject than do other lenses in order to fill their frame. Therefore, the lens is not inherently distorted

the focal length of the lens. Working distance should be comfortable. Thus, it should not be so far that the photographer cannot easily manipulate or illuminate the subject and not so close that perspective distortion is created. Working distance (WD) is expressed by the simple formula:

Working distance = Focal length [1/ magnification + 1]

Thus, for a 1/10 magnification (portrait) a 50 mm lens requires a working distance of 550 mm. A 100 mm lens requires twice the WD - almost 1.21 meters. Making a portrait at 1.21 meters affords a more comfortable distance and natural perspective than one made at 0.61 meters. Therefore, the 100 mm lens

Figure 6-3. Wide angle lens used in close quarters for a full body picture.

nor is the final photograph. It merely records a perspective that is different and unusual relative to common visual experience. A 90-100 mm focal length lens renders perspective similar to that seen by the eye. Such a lens should be used to photograph close-ups of all three dimensional objects.

The *working distance*, or distance between the lens and the subject is a function of the desired magnification (reproduction ratio) and

is preferred. A 1:1 (life sized) magnification made with a 50 mm lens requires a WD of 101.6 mm. The 100 mm lens, however, would permit a comfortable 203.2 mm WD while improving perspective control.

Conversely, it is desirable to shorten WD for larger subjects by using shorter focal lengths. A 1.8 meter subject calls for a WD of 6 meters with a 100 mm lens. Such a distance might place the photographer out of the room or behind an obstruction. Selecting a 50 mm lens would reduce the camera-subject distance to 3 meters. In a fire disaster requiring the photographing of burned human remains, a 24 mm lens was necessary to obtain wide angle views in close quarters (**Figure 6-3**).

Exposure

A photographic image is obtained when the proper amount of light is focused by a lens on film. Most modern cameras provide meters and automatic functions to indicate and help select correct exposure. Exposure is determined by four factors under control of the photographer:

- Duration of light striking the film (shutter speed)

- Size of the lens opening (aperture)

- Sensitivity of the film (International Organization for Standardization – ISO rating This is related to the film speed which is the measure of a photographic film's sensitivity to light. Film with a lower sensitivity (lower ISO speed rating) requires a longer exposure and is thus referred to as slow film. Higher sensitivity (higher ISO speed rating) film can be exposed at shorter times.

- Intensity of light

Under low-light or natural conditions, particularly close-up photography, without the assistance of flash or strobe lighting texposure times must be extremely short to eliminate the image blur caused by camera or subject movement. The focal length of the lens, proximity to the subject and subject movement all factor into the correct shutter speed necessary to *freeze* motion. A 1/30 of a second may suffice when photographing a still scene with a wide angle lens while 1/1000 of a second may be necessary for a life-sized close-up with a telephoto lens.

Utilizing a tripod mounted camera one can overcome blur caused by camera movement. An electronic flash limits duration of light to 1/1000 of a second or faster. This effectively freezes all motion for the needs of the forensic dental photographer. When using an electronic flash the camera's shutter speed must be set to synchronize with the flash according to the manufacturer's directions.

Lens apertures are expressed in *f* stops and the aperture range varies with the particular lens. Standard lenses typically have the following apertures for selection: 2, 2.8, 4, 5.6, 8, 11 and 16. The smallest number represents the widest aperture. The numbers appear arbitrary but each represents a multiple of two. Thus, each opening doubles or halves the amount of light of the adjacent aperture. Certain lenses extend the aperture range allowing openings as small as f/22, f/32 or even f/45. These openings are advantageous when great depth of field is needed. Large openings bring maximal light to the film and are an advantage in low light situations. Depth of field is a priority in close-up photography of three dimensional objects. Lenses that offer at least f/22 must be selected in this situation. Apertures smaller than f/22 are discouraged in extreme close-up photography because the negative effects of diffraction outweigh the improvements in depth of field.

The third component of exposure is film sensitivity. Given the compromises already imposed on light getting to the film (short duration and small apertures) it would be beneficial to use a highly light sensitive film. This, however, is not a viable option since such faster film produces grainy, granular images which are not desirable in scientific photography. Fortunately, the last determinant of exposure, light intensity, can be used to compensate for the other variables by using a powerful electronic flash.

Equipment for Forensic Dentistry – Film Based

Camera Body

The 35 mm single lens reflex (SLR) camera has been the workhorse in forensic dentistry. It allows interchange of lenses and through-the-lens (TTL) viewing which permits the operator

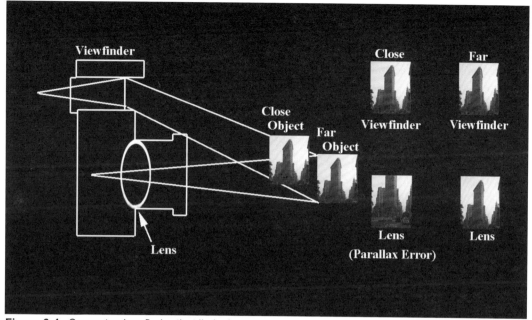

Figure 6-4. Separate view-finder that limits lens selection and causes parallax error.

to see exactly what the lens is seeing. Less expensive cameras feature a separate view-finder window that approximates the lens coverage. This limits lens selection and causes parallax error which magnifies the difference between the lens' and viewer's viewpoint at close distances (**Figure 6-4**). Parallax error is a result of the apparent shift of an object against a background due to a change in observer position created by viewing the object from the separate view-finder window.

Most mid-priced modern day 35mm SLR camera bodies are acceptable. All are equipped with light meters and most have automatic exposure with manual override. Because of the specialized needs of forensic dentists the more expensive models usually ensure the needed latitude of features. Some options worth considering are listed below:

- *TTL Film Plane Flash Metering* – useful option which automatically turns off a dedicated flash once proper exposure has been determined by a sensor located at the film plane. Calibrations of proper light intensity for close-ups can be cumbersome or guesswork without this option.

- *DX Coding* - permits camera to automatically read and set film speed once the film is loaded into the camera body, thereby eliminating the need to do this manually.

- *Auto-Film Advance* - a convenience permitting the film to be automatically advanced to the next frame after the shutter is pressed.

- *Data Back* - option which allows the electronic imprinting of time, dates, or case numbers in one corner of the film.

- *Auto Focusing* – generally is a welcome feature for portrait and landscape photography however in close-up photography can become problematic.

Lenses

The principal lens used in forensic dentistry should be a good quality macro lens. Most major camera manufacturers make such lenses for their respective camera bodies. Ironically, most standard lenses supplied by the manufacturer lack the specifications needed for forensic dentistry. Characteristics of an ideal lens for forensic dentistry (or intraoral photography) include the following:

- *90,100, or 105 mm Focal Length* – This focal length allows the optimum working distance between camera and subject for most views in forensic dentistry and renders minimum perspective distortion of curved objects.

- *Aperture Range of f/2.8 – f/22 or f/32* – The small apertures (f/22/32) provide the lens needed depth of field while the largest aperture (f/2.8), though not generally used for close-up photography admits ample light for composing and focusing objects.

- *Focusing From Infinity to Life-Sized Images* - Lenses that require an adaptor to achieve this range are judged inconvenient. Lenses with continuous focusing to RR 1:1 and do not use an adaptor are preferred.

- *Macro zoom lenses* that offer close-focusing should be carefully reviewed before purchase. Most cannot focus beyond a 1/4 reproduction (4 x 6 inch view).

- *Bellows lenses* - As an alternative to macro-lenses, close focusing bellows lenses, which have been advocated in the past, are still available and have their disciples. These are optically excellent lenses that are separated from the camera body by a movable cloth bellows that allows lens extension. These cumbersome systems have been made obsolete by the less bulky, computer designed, optically perfected macro lenses discussed previously.

Electronic Flash

Portable, powerful electronic flash units illuminate subjects at small apertures and freeze motion. Integrated systems are available from Lester Dine, Adolf Gasser, Washington Scientific and Trojan Camera. Specifications of attributes to consider are listed below:

- *Guide Number of 10-45* for the least sensitive film you expect to use. – The Guide Number is a measure of the maximum intensity of a flash factored to film sensitivity. A less powerful flash would require faster film or wider aperture than recommended. If the flash is too powerful, it will be bulky and may overexpose some views.

- *Dedicated to Camera for TTL Film Plane Metering* - If this option was selected on the camera body, a compatible flash is needed. A dedicated flash electronically communicates with the electronic light metering system inside the camera body enabling the photographer to choose a preferred aperture and automatically obtain the correct flash intensity.

- *Battery Powered* with Optional AC Cord is preferred.

- *Warning light or beep* to indicate incorrect exposure.

- *Point Flash* - gives directional lighting to render shadow detail, texture and dimensionality. It must be positioned adjacent to the lens surface (not on camera body) so that it will be correctly aimed at close subjects. This requires a special mount allowing the flash to rotate around the lens.

- *Ring Flash* - the flash tube encircles the lens like a donut and is always correctly aimed at the subject. However, it renders flat, shadowless images with circular reflections on shiny objects. For most forensic cases requiring close-up photography, the ring flash is less desirable than a point flash.

- *Ring/Point Combinations* – photographer chooses either ring or point light with a toggle switch. Because of the variable light source this is preferred.

Film

Photographic film is a celluloid acetate strip containing grains of light-sensitive silver halide. The size of the halide salt grains determines its light sensitivity/speed (ISO). In general, slow films require more light but produce the best resolution due to the small, uniform grain particles. ISO ratings of 25 to 160 are recommended for films used in forensic photography and include:

Kodachrome 25 & 64
Kodachrome 64 color transparency film
Ektachrome 100
Ektachrome 160 tungsten
Ektar 25 color print film
Kodacolor 100
Panatomic X (ASA 36)
Plus X (ASA 125) black/white print film
T-Max 100 (ASA 100)

Film selection depends on the photographer's needs, flash power, color compatibility with the flash and lens, and processing time. For example, the recommended auto-exposure flash distributed by Lester Dine, Inc. is powerful enough to enable the use of *Kodachrome 25* but gives poor color balance with *Kodachrome 64*. Flash attachments distributed or manufactured by the Adolf Gasser and Trojan companies lack the power to make best use of *Kodachrome 25*. *Kodachrome* transparencies have excellent archival life, retaining their color dyes for 100 years. The color dyes in *Ektachrome*, however, are stable for only 20-25 years.

*Kodachrome slides (*unlike the transparencies) are vulnerable to severe color degradation within months if exposed to continual room light. The turnaround time for Ektachrome processing is rapid and can be performed by neighborhood commercial laboratories. Kodachrome, on the other hand, must be processed by Kodak laboratories and this can require a week or more.

Other Desirable Accessories

Other desirable accessories that the forensic odontologist should consider when establishing his or her photographic armamentarium include, but are not limited to, the following:

- *Copy Stand* - to duplicate radiographs, printed material and specimens.

- *50 or 55 mm Macro Lens* - For use with copy stand to reduce the camera/subject with large objects. This can also be used for scene photography and full body views.

- *35-70 Zoom Lens* - ideal for scene photography or full body views in confined spaces. Variable focal length simplifies and expedites framing for best comparison.

- *Sturdy Tripod* (with good range of motion) required in infrared and ultraviolet bite mark photography and low ambient light scene photography.

- *Second 35 mm SLR Camera Body* – to hold different films.

- *Camera Bag*

- *Extra Batteries*

- *Extra Film*

- *Green and Yellow Filters* - for improved contrast of red and blue contusions respectively in black and white photography. These can be lens mounted or flash mounted filters.

- *UV Filter* - kept on each lens for protection. It is important to remember that these filters must be removed prior to taking ultraviolet photographs.

- *18A W Filter* - for taking ultraviolet photographs

- *Non-glare, Accurate, Rigid Rules* – An ideal type of rule to use is the ABFO No. 2 Scale.

- *ID Tags, Scotch Tape, Marking Pens*

- *Background Material* - non-glare, medium hued, matte cardboard or felt to render non-distracting backdrops for specimens.

- *Mirrors and Cheek Retractors* – For intraoral views on live patients.

- *Point and Shoot 35 mm Range Finder*

Auto-focus Camera with Built-in Flash

- These light, quick, convenient cameras are useful at scenes and mass fatalities where larger camera systems are too cumbersome. They are no substitute for an SLR camera with a macro lens as a primary camera.

- *Polaroid Camera* - for occasions when instant prints are necessary. Not to be used as a primary camera.

Digital Based Photography

The best advice that can be given the reader who wants to create a digital imaging system is to seek professional help from experienced system builder/providers. Let these experts assemble the components of the imaging system that is appropriate for the needs of the forensic dental photographer. Do not accept the recommendations of the retail computer store clerk without getting several other independent opinions when organizing a forensic dental digital photography kit. It is preferable to find a supplier that will assemble the hardware, load the appropriate image management software on the computer, direct the forensic investigator to a proper camera, provide a certain amount of training, and be available when technical help is requested.

No matter what is written about the current state of digital photographic technology it is likely that by the time a textbook publication has reached the public domain many new innovations will have been developed and introduced for commercial use. Competition among camera manufacturers and computer companies insures that the best affordable imaging system at any given moment will be practically obsolete within months of its release. Unfortunately, most people who are considering purchasing a digital imaging system focus their initial attention to purchasing the camera with little or no regard or forethought to image management

Each person who ventures into digital imaging must decide beyond which camera to purchase while concentrating on what their individual needs and requirements are and what they plan to do with the images generated. Is the system to be strictly dedicated to forensic use or will the technology be used for the other image gathering needs of the photographer. Using a low-to-medium priced digital camera to take images at family vacation sites is certainly different form creating professional images during forensic investigation. If the images are expected to be printed, the print size and resolution (sharpness) determine how big a computer file one needs for durable storage of each image. Many current mid-priced digital cameras have the capability of producing from three megabyte up to fifteen megabyte file-sized images in both RAW and JPG file formats.

RAW is a file type containing minimally processed data from the image sensor of a digital camera or image scanner. The image sensor in a digital camera is the equivalent of the photographic film in a standard camera. RAW files derive their name from the fact that they are not yet processed. Therefore, they are not ready to be used by a bitmap graphics editor, printed, or displayed by a typical web browser. The JPG (J-Peg) format is employed for those photo images which must require small files such as web sites or emails. The JPG format is frequently the default mode for saving images on digital camera memory cards and the file is often compressed to only 1/10 of the size of the original data. This compression efficiency comes with a price, however, because some image quality is lost when the JPG data is compressed and saved. With each successive opening and closing of the file, some resolution is lost. Unfortunately, this quality can never be recovered.

The larger the image file, the bigger the print that can be created from it. However, large files tend to generate storage problems. Thus, the photographer must determine how many images he/she anticipates storing, on what type of media and for what length of time. Additionally, consideration for the speed of the computer processor and amount of resident memory during the handling of large graphics files must be taken into consideration. Larger images require more time for the computer to process and print.

When considering purchasing a digital camera, simplification and versatility at a reasonable price are the primary goals for most manufacturers. Each company has its own list of models that fulfill the demands of the photographer. Advances in Charge-Coupled Device (CCD) and Complementary Metal-Oxide Semiconductor (CMOS) technology are continuously being made. Researchers at Bell Laboratories invented the CCD in the late 1960s and it was originally conceived as a new form of computer memory circuit. In addition to its original use the CCD has many other applications including signal processing and imaging. The photoactive region of the CCD is, generally, an interface between a thin film of ionic phosphorus and a substrate layer of polycrystalline silicon. This region defines the channel in which the photogenerated charge packets will travel. The CCD sensor in a digital camera is the primary image capture mechanism and is the camera's electronic eye. The CCD collects light and converts it to a charge and eventually emits the signal that creates the digital image.

CMOS has become the predominant technology in digital integrated circuits. CMOS chips include microprocessor, microcontroller, static RAM, and other digital logic circuits. This is the principal semiconductor technology for microprocessors, memories and application specific integrated circuits (ASICs). By the beginning of the 21st century CMOS technology had also been used for a wide variety of analog circuits such as image sensors, data converters, and highly integrated transceivers for many types of communication.

CMOS models have advantages over other technologies because they have much smaller power dissipation. These devices do not produce as much heat as other forms of logic and they allow a high density of logic functions on a chip. CMOS logic on a CMOS process dissipates less energy and is denser than other implementations of the same functionality. With each new version CCD and CMOS released the photographer is able to

capture larger file sized images at a faster rate. The forensic investigator should find a vendor with the knowledge and expertise necessary to assist in the purchase of state of the art equipment that will serve their needs for several years before being completely outdated.

Basic Digital Protocol

The basic digital camera requirements for the forensic odontologist include a TTL light metering SLR 35 millimeter format digital camera body with interchangeable lenses. There should be adequate storage capacity on a removable flash memory card. Flash memory technology is a form of non-volatile computer memory that can be electrically erased and reprogrammed. Flash memory has become the dominant technology wherever a significant amount of non-volatile, solid-state storage is required. Examples of applications include digital audio players, digital cameras and mobile phones. It is also employed in USB flash drives (thumb drives, handy drive) which are used for general storage and transfer of data between computers

The photographer should have the ability to program and set camera functions according to the situation and type of photography required. Some of these features include:

- An adjustable ISO
- Manual mode
- Auto and manual focus
- Time delay
- Aperture and shutter priority modes
- LCD display
- Built-in flash
- Automatic metering system.
- Data embedding to multiple formats of files

A *professional/consumer* class digital camera will typically be adequate enough to capture images in full spectrum and ALI photographic applications. Once the digital system is assembled, it is the responsibility of the investigator to understand the limitations and parameters regarding digital imaging within the judicial system of his local jurisdiction. An

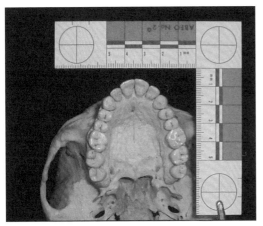
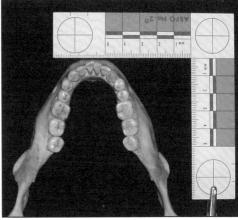

Figure 6-5: Occlusal View of the maxilla and mandible with scale at the occlusal plane.

excellent guide to digital image acquisition and management can be found in the Scientific Working Group on Imaging Technology's (SWGIT) imaging guidelines.

The SWGIT guidelines are valuable tools that every investigator should use in order to be in compliance with the accepted standards established. Forensic odontologists should be familiar with the SWGIT guidelines if using photographic evidence and displays when called upon to testify concerning his or her findings and opinions in a case. One important recommendation found in the guidelines advises the odontologist to keep a running history of which keystrokes and modifications were used during any image manipulation. This gives others the ability to take the RAW originally stored image and reach the same end modifications in alternately saved formats.

The ABFO has adopted many similar guidelines for image management that are published on its website at www.ABFO.org. For a more in-depth explanation of digital components and specific details about digital photography refer to Chapter Seven in the Forensic Science Series publication *Bite mark Evidence* edited by Robert B. J. Dorion. This material provides detailed information on the workings of digital cameras and explains how they acquire images and perform their other functions.

Forensic photography is not only challenging but extremely rewarding when results are successful. Documentation of bite marks and other forensic evidence with accurate photographs is the best avenue the

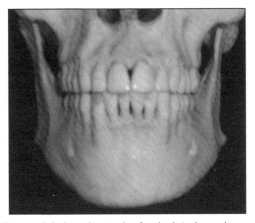

Figure 6-6: Anterior teeth of articulated specimen.

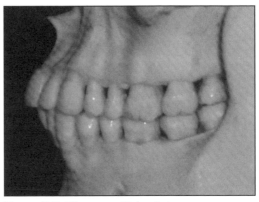

Figure 6-7: Close-up of lateral view.

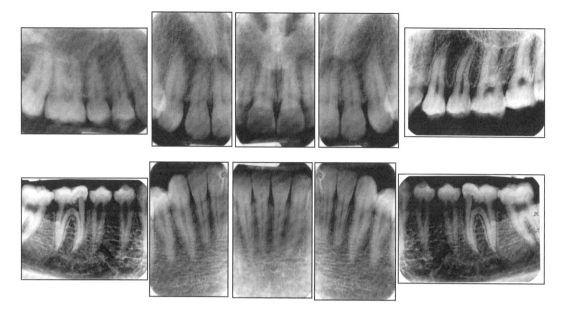

Figure 6-8: Photographs of representative radiographs.

odontologist has for demonstrating this type of evidence in court and determining the conclusions from its analysis. The competent odontologist should not on

Standard Photography Views

Identification Cases

Regardless of whether or not film based or digital formats are used, at least two sets of photographic records should be made for all views. It would be reasonable and prudent to copy all digital or photographic images before providing the originals to the court since material seized for courtroom exhibits and /or evidence may be lost to the dentist. All views should have a case number in an unobtrusive location. The following views are suggested:

- View of facial area as first seen by the odontologist. This serves to document the case and illustrate the need for a dental identification by showing the initial preservation/destruction. In viewable bodies, this photo my serve for visual identification if a putative victim is proffered.

- Initial close-up of anterior dentition. This may serve to assist in identification if a photograph

of the victim smiling is located. It also captures photographically a true and accurate image of the dentition prior to manipulation the maximal preservation of carbonized teeth which may be destroyed during jaw resection or other manipulation.

If the jaws are removed, they should be cleaned of blood and attached decomposing or otherwise offensive extraneous soft tissue. If this is not accomplished resulting photographs may be deemed unsuitable for courtroom presentation because of their inflammatory or prejudicial nature. The following views are suggested:

Occlusal Views of all the dental evidence:

- Views should be from directly overhead with arches aligned on a straight plane, using modeling clay, if necessary (**Figure 6-5**).

- Full frame close-up of occlusal aspect of maxilla.

- Full frame close-up of occlusal aspect of mandible.

Anterior and Lateral Views:

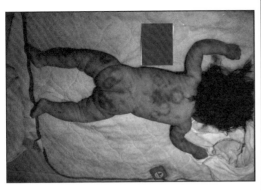

Figure 6-9: Orientation Photograph. (Photograph courtesy of G. Golden DDS)

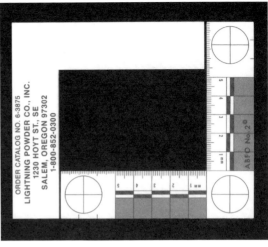

Figure 6-10: Both sides of the ABFO No. 2. Scale for forensic photography.

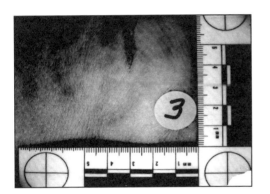

Figure 6-11: ABFO No. 2 scale and a common coin in same plane as bite mark.

- Full frame close-up of anterior teeth of articulated specimen in centric occlusion. The occlusal plane should be parallel to the film plane, f/16 or f/22 used, and the plane of sharpest focus should be the distal of the upper lateral incisors to maximize the depth of field (**Figure 6-6**).

- Full frame close-up of right and left lateral views in centric occlusion (f/16 or f/22 is best) (**Figure 6-7**).

Special views of noteworthy findings:

- Photographs of antemortem and post mortem radiographs and comparisons for courtroom presentation, teaching or documentation (**Figure 6-8**).

Bite Mark Cases

Bite mark injuries and those resulting from intimate partner violence, child abuse, elder abuse, sexual assault and criminal physical assault are situations in which physical evidence may be transitory and require processing on an emergency basis. There is urgency to record the bite mark at the most opportune time after initial observation/recognition. However, it is appreciated that changing patterns of bite marks can occur in both living victims and decedents over a period of several days. In some cases, detail within a bite mark may improve. Thus, bite marks should be observed for several days after the earliest photographs are made. Then additional photographs should be obtained if indicated.

Color photographs should be recorded from positions that include orientation and correct angulation views of the bite mark. Working close-ups can be recorded in digital format, or panchromatic (black and white) and color print film. All film-based photographs should be exposed in duplicate and properly labeled as they are recorded, using markers in the area being photographed. Varying lighting positions should be used and. Bracketing exposures is recommended as a safeguard against miscalculations leading to highly overexposed or underexposed films. Digitally captured images usually have the advantage over photographic film of immediate viewing of the acquired image via liquid crystal display (LCD).

Bite Mark Photographs

Initial Photographs

These photographs precede all other investigations and represent the pristine bite mark evidence which appeared to the photographer before it was altered by touching, moving, impressing, swabbing or cleansing. A case identification number should be placed in an unobtrusive location. An argument can be made for making the first exposure without a

case number to assure that nothing has been concealed. If dirt, blood, hair or other distracters partly conceal the mark they are left in place for this photograph. After the initial photographic.

Orientation Photographs

These views show the location(s) of the bite mark(s) on the body and must include sufficient anatomy to accurately reconstruct the location of the marks (**Figure 6-9**). The initial photographs may serve as orientation if the bite mark is shown to advantage. Since these the initial orientation photographs do not constitute working photographs, the bite mark may appear small in the photo in favor of demonstrating its relationship to surrounding anatomy. Digital format or color film is preferred for this view.

Close-Up Working Photographs

These views are eventually used for direct size and shape comparison with any potential suspect's teeth. Fastidious technique is necessary to ensure accuracy, resolution, focus, depth of field, perspective control and size reproducibility. A rigid ruler like the ABFO No. 2 scale (**Figure 6-10**) is placed in an unobtrusive manner adjacent to the bite mark.

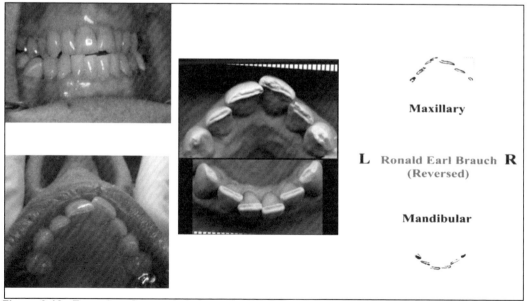

Figure 6-12: Examples of suspect photographs, models and the hollow volume overlays

The scale is placed on the same plane as the bite mark and photographed with the film plane parallel to the bite mark/rule assembly (**Figure 6-11**). Strict adherence to this composition is required to assure size accuracy in the final print and to minimize perspective distortion which occurs when objects are photographed at varying angles.

Further protection against perspective distortion can be obtained by placing a circular scale in the same orientation plane as the bite mark. If an ABFO # 2 scale is not employed, a coin placed in the field can help to accomplish the same task (**Figure 6-11**). In this manner, photogrametric perspective can be checked and corrected in the final image.

far away view cannot achieve the resolution of detail obtained in a close-up exposure. Following accepted protocols for trace salivary evidence collection, extraneous dirt, blood, and hair should be removed taking care not to introduce other skin injury. Good depth of field is necessary in these close-up views and smaller apertures of f/11-f/22 are within the preferred range, although f/8 is acceptable for flat or barely contoured marks.

Lighting should be positioned from various directions because glare from a flash is unpredictable and often washes out detail on skin surfaces and in rulers and scales. Indentations left by tooth marks can be illustrated by oblique lighting which renders textured detail through shading. The flash

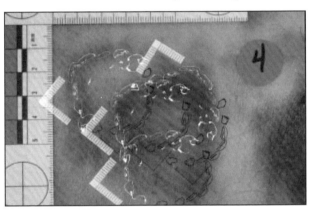

Figure 6-13: Typical exhibits prepared for courtroom presentation.

Objects of known size within the photograph (including rulers) cannot be used to size the bite mark unless they are in the same plane as the bite mark. According to Johansen and Bowers in *Digital Analysis of Bite Mark Evidence Using Adobe Photoshop,* certain types of photographic distortion are not correctable. Additionally, thought should be given to control any internal distortion of the bite mark itself. When known, the bitten area should be photographed in the position in which the bite occurred. If the position is not known the bitten area should be photographed in its full range of possible positions.

Sharp detail is required in this photograph. Thus, in the close-up photograph the bite mark and rule should nearly fill the frame, usually at RR 1:4 or 1:3. Simple enlargement of a

should be detached from the camera to achieve these low angles.

The recording of wound patterns by means other than visible light photography has gained increased acceptance by forensic photographers. The most recent ABFO Bite Mark Guidelines make note of both reflective ultraviolet photography and alternate light imaging (**Appendix C - ABFO Bite Mark Guidelines**). The techniques involved and the various non-visible wavelengths used in these techniques are discussed further in this chapter.

Photographic Documentation of Persons of Interest

These images can be captured with the same protocol as those used when photographing

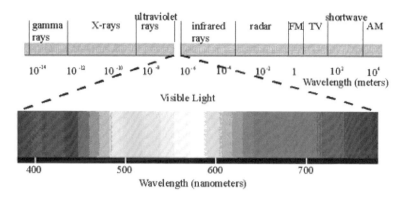

Figure 6-14: The electromagnetic spectrum (Photograph courtesy of http://www.safespectrum.com/light.html)

the bite mark. After obtaining proper informed consent or court order, photographs of any suspected bites should be collected. The views of the dentition of the purported suspect(s) duplicate the previous views discussed when photographing the dentition of decedents, adhering to clinical intra-oral protoco*l*.

Photographs for Analysis

If study casts are obtained, they should be photographed or digitally scanned in a manner similar to the close-up view (ruler or scale placed in the same plane as the teeth and with the camera positioned with the film plane parallel to the occlusal plane). The life-sized image allows direct comparison either digitally or with cellophane tracings that can be superimposed over the life-sized print of the bite mark for comparison (**Figure 6-12**).

Life-sized prints of the bite mark and casts can be made for easier drawing and illustration to jurors. An overlay is a representation of only the incisal, biting edges of the anterior teeth in a two-dimensional plane. It can either be created manually on clear acetate or digitally. When properly superimposed over a bite mark bruise a comparison can be made by the observer as to the relative likelihood of the person of interest having created the bite mark pattern.

Trial Aids

When presenting evidence in court, admissibility of photographic evidence will vary among jurisdictions according to what the judge will allow. There are no strict standards for courtroom presentation. However, there are certain suggestions and guidelines in this regard.   Some forensic dental experts prefer to use projected slides or PowerPoint presentations to illustrate findings in courtrooms that have adequate facilities (projector, screen and recessed lighting and computer capabilities).   In this manner, with the authorization of the judge, findings can be explained in a controlled, narrative, and educational manner to all jurors simultaneously.   Additionally, photographic comparison exemplars demonstrating an opinion by superimposition of transparent hollow volume overlays on life-sized prints can be very effective for presentation to the trier of fact. (**Figure 6-13**).

Photographing Printed Material

Duplicating printed material and radiographs is best performed with a copy stand, light box or scanner. Refer to the website http://www.linear-systems.com/products/ilighting.htm for further information concerning these aides. When photographing material printed on white paper a white background placed under the paper intensifies the whiteness and blocks out patterns or color of the underlying copy stand base. If, however, the white paper photographed has double-sided printing it should rest on a black background to obscure the printing on the reverse side.

Black paper fitted around the lens barrel can be used to shield metallic parts of the camera

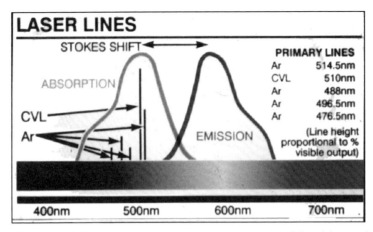

Figure 6 -15: Stokes Shift in fluorescence. (Image courtesy of Omnichrome Inc.)

from being reflected back into the image when glass is used to flatten the subject. Reflections can also reduced by eliminating stray sources of ambient room light. Exposure is indicated by the camera's light meter. Because the meter is calibrated to scenes of medium reflectance it will be fooled by the white paper and indicate too small an aperture. Thus, the aperture should be manually adjusted to 1 to 1-1/2 stops wider than the aperture indicated by the meter.

Alternatively, accurate exposure indications can be obtained by metering off of an 18 percent grey card which provides *average reflectance*. When color film is used it should be color-balanced for the type of light. If this can not be accomplished proper filters must be employed. The appropriate color correcting filter is determined by the source of the light, whether it be tungsten, sunlight, fluorescent bulb, or strobe flash.

Photographing Radiographs

Reproducing radiographs photographically is best accomplished with transilluminated light from a light box. The authors recommend using either black and white film or grayscale digital mode for reproducing radiographs from fluorescent light sources. When daylight balanced color film is used the fluorescent light will cause a green discoloration of the final photograph. An FL-D filter helps correct this problem.. An equally effective method for radiograph reproduction and storage is by

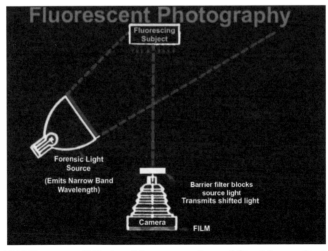

Figure 6 -16: Typical ALI (fluorescent) Protocol.(Image courtesy of Omnichrome Inc.)

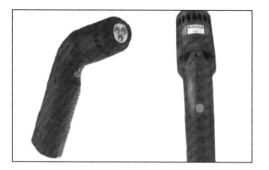

Figure 6 -17: The Ultra Lite and Accessories. (Photos supplied by manufacturer)

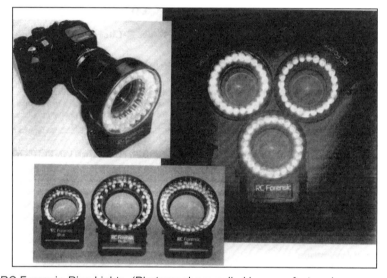

Figure 6 -18: RC Forensic Ring Lights (Photographs supplied by manufacturer)

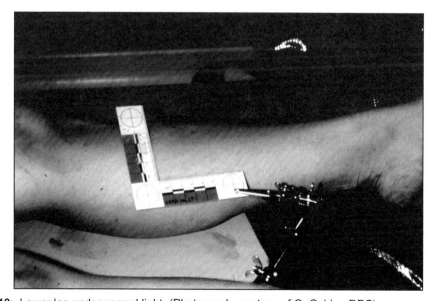

Figure 6-19: Lower leg under normal light. (Photograph courtesy of G. Golden DDS)

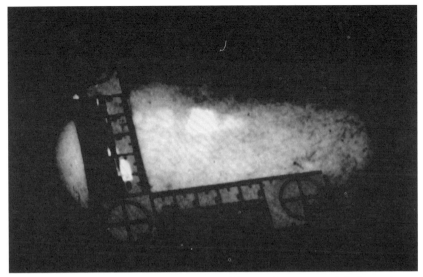

Figure 6-20: Leg close-up with ALI showing presence of fluorescing semen. (Photograph courtesy of G. Golden DDS)

flatbed scanner. However, the scanner must have the equivalent of a light box behind the film so that the reading sensor will record the image. The digital file created by the scanner may be stored indefinitely, or transmitted electronically to a different location for comparison for identification.

Advanced Photographic Techniques

Forensic photographic techniques are continually evolving. This is especially true for those using the opposite ends of the non-visible light spectrum. New equipment is always being introduced that makes capturing these images easier and more reliable

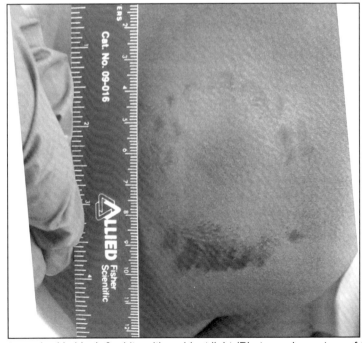

Figure 6-21: Photographed in black & white with ambient light (Photograph courtesy of G. Morales)

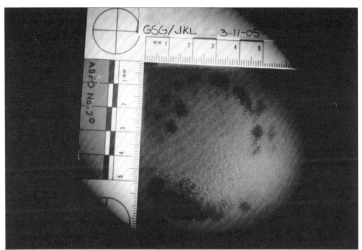

Figure 6-22: Same bite pattern taken with ALI. Canon EOS 10D Digital camera, 55mm macro lens, # 15 Tiffen filter, Omnichrome OP 1 ALS at 450 nm, liquid light guide, ¼ sec exposure at f-5.6. (Photograph courtesy of G. Golden, DDS).

for the crime scene photographer and the odontologist.

The Electromagnetic Spectrum and Photography

Visible light encompasses a very narrow portion of the electromagnetic spectrum (**Figure 6-14**). As a result, most film and digital cameras are manufactured and designed to capture light energy that ranges in the visible light spectrum between 400 and 700 nanometers. When functioning as forensic photographers, odontologists consequently spend most of their time and efforts utilizing that visible area of the spectrum to document cases. Thus, the resultant photographic end product is limited to what can actually be seen with the unassisted eye. Forensic photography becomes challenging when the forensic dentist dentist steps outside of the of the visible spectrum parameters. The following is a description of three advanced photographic protocols for capturing what the unassisted eyes cannot see.

Alternate Light Imaging (ALI / Fluorescent Photography)

The energy from a powerful forensic light source striking a subject creates an excitation at the molecular level. As the molecules return to a normal energy state they leave behind a faint visible glow known as fluorescence.

This phenomenon lasts for about 100 ns (10-7 seconds). A special technique called Alternate Light Imaging (ALI) is required for the eye to see and camera to record this type of fluorescence. The technique is valuable to forensic investigators in that it becomes useful in locating and documenting latent fingerprints, serological fluids, (blood, semen, saliva), illicit drugs, gun shot residue and residual fiber. Most importantly to the odontologist, it potentially enhances the bruise pattern of bite marks on human skin.

The technique of ALI is founded upon the Stokes Shift phenomenon. This is named for Professor G.G. Stokes who reported in 1853 that the remitted wavelength of a predominant color of light is of a different frequency than the illuminating source (**Figure 6-15**). Part of the energy of light at a particular frequency (measured in nanometers) is absorbed by the subject matter it strikes. Once that energy is absorbed in the form of electrons, it creates a molecular excitation that seeks to return to its unexcited state. The return of the electrons to their resting state releases that energy as fluorescence. The remitted fluorescent light is of a higher frequency, lower intensity, and usually cannot be seen unless viewed through certain colored filters that pass the remitted light and block the incident light. These are called band pass filters.

Figure 6-23: Forensic Photo Frame (Photograph courtesy of the manufacturer)

The equipment requirements for ALI are similar to most normal forms of macro-photography with the exception that one must employ the forensic light source for the incident light and the band pass filter over the lens to capture the fluorescent image. A tripod-mounted 35mm SLR film-based or digital camera and macro-lens are part of the standard armamentarium (**Figure 6-16**).

There are many companies that manufacture alternate light sources (ALS). Most recently, the trend is for these devices to be user-friendly, easy to transport and require minimal storage. Manufacturers have generated numerous personal light sources. Examples of some personal light sources follow. Most of these are battery powered and come in one of two configurations:

- Those in the shape of a hand-held flashlight such as the Ultra Light (**Figure 6-17**). This has light emitting diodes for illumination.

- Those that are attached directly to the lens of the camera such as the RC Forensics ring light (**Figure 6-18**).

These light sources provide the advantages of reasonable cost, portability, and reduced size. Just like the larger power-driven units, *personal lights* are either pre-tuned or can be filtered to produce discreet wavelengths of incident light ranging from white light, near UV, blue light (450nm) and/or infrared (IR).

Colored plexiglas goggles provided by the

manufacturer of the ALS and similar to the band pass camera filters are required for the observer to detect or observe latent evidence and view enhanced fluorescing objects. Choosing the proper color frequency of source-light and shade of goggles depends upon the subject matter being illuminated and photographed. Different materials acquire peak fluorescence at different wavelengths. **Figure 6-19** is a pre-autopsy color photograph of the lower leg of a homicide victim taken with a strobe flash. **Figure 6-20** is a close-up of the same leg taken with 450nm blue light and filtered with a Tiffen #15 yellow filter over the lens. A previously undetected semen stain is fluorescing in the central area of the photo.

Illuminating human and animal epithelial, cutaneous and subcutaneous tissues with the ALI technique provides a distinct advantage when photographing bruises, pattern injuries, and bite marks by creating a net overall effect that enhances the visibility of the injury. **Figure 6-21** is a digital image of a bite mark on the left shoulder of a young, black female homicide victim, taken with ambient (room) light. The same bite mark is depicted in **Figure 6-22** with ALI revealing the enhanced features of the dentition of both dental arches. ALI is most useful in situations where there is minimal bruise pattern information present on the surface of the tissue while below the epidermis there exists significant bruising.

ALI Protocol

ALI must be accomplished in total darkness with the exception of the alternate light

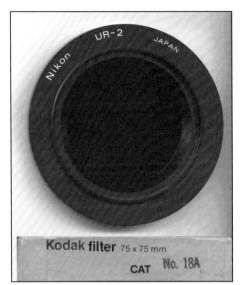

Figure 6 - 24: Kodak Wratten 18A glass filter in Nikon UR-2 filter holder. Photo courtesy F. Wright, DDS (Photograph courtesy F. Wright, DDS)

Figure 6-26: Nikkor UV 105 quartz lens (Photograph courtesy of G. Golden, DDS)

source illuminating the subject. Routinely, the photographer should be able to capture an adequate image with a minimum of 100 ISO film or the equivalent digital setting. Exposure times can vary depending on several factors such as skin pigmentation and brightness of the source illumination. With 100 ISO film and digital equivalents typical exposures range between ¼ sec. to 2 seconds at f-stop settings of f/4 to f/5.6 apertures. The light source and camera should ideally be placed at distances of 12 to 18 inches from the subject.

Some digital cameras have the capability to reach ISO settings of 1200 and higher. The higher the ISO, the more light sensitivity, the lower the exposure time required for image capture. A very high ISO may allow the photographer to capture ALI at exposure times that negate the necessity of a tripod, depending on the strength of the alternate light source (ALS).

Using normal bite mark photography protocol, the camera should be positioned with the lens at a 90-degree angle to both the plane of the injury and the ABFO No. 2 scale. An excellent tool that can help prevent operator induced photographic distortion is the Forensic Photo Frame. This provides an adjustable distance to target and rigid, pre-set correct camera angulation for many types of forensic photo-documentation applications (**Figure 6-23**).

It is advisable to prepare the field of view and focus prior to turning out the overhead lights. The subject is then illuminated with only the alternate light source and no other ambient lighting is used. The light meter readings are then taken through the lens with the filter in place. Multiple images should be collected by bracketing with varied exposure times. Whenever possible, exposure factors should be recorded for future reference as described below.

Figure 6-25: Recommended RUV/UVA equipment. (Photograph courtesy of G. Golden, DDS)

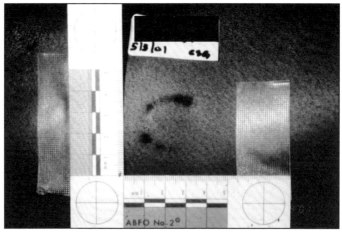

Figure 6-27: Bite on back, normall lash. (Photograph courtesy of G. Golden, DDS)

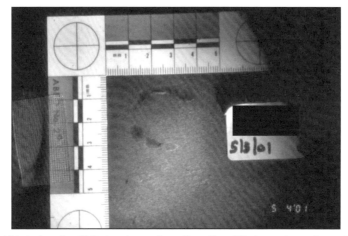

Figure 6-28: Near UV photo using ALS showing surface disruption. (Photograph courtesy of G. Golden, DDS)

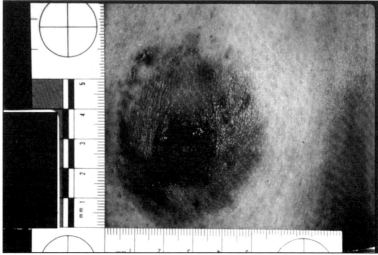

Figure 6-29: Bite on the right breast of a homicide victim - full spectrum flash illumination. (Photograph courtesy of G. Golden, DDS)

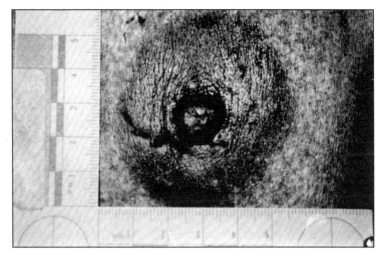

Figure 6-30: RUV/UVA Photo of the same bite mark. Arrows indicate individual tooth positions below the nipple. (Photograph courtesy of G. Golden, DDS)

Slightly underexposed images may contain more information than normal or overexposed images. Automatic TTL light meters frequently misread the intensity of illumination of monochromatic light and allow a larger aperture or longer exposure time than is necessary for an accurate exposure. This problem can be corrected by changing the aperture setting and/or the exposure time for one-to-two f-stops under what the light meter reads as *normal.*

In general, photographers attempting fluorescent photography should become familiar with their camera equipment, its capabilities, and the appropriate exposure settings prior to actual casework. Pre-testing equipment under controlled conditions is highly recommended and when film with ALI images is processed the f-stop and shutter speed of each exposure should be noted. Optimal settings will vary for each combination of camera and *ALS.*

Reflective (Long Wavelength) Ultraviolet Photography (UVA)

The fundamental principles of employing reflective (UVA) ultraviolet photography as applied to bite mark documentation have in general remained the same since 1985 when Krauss and Warlen pioneered the protocol

Figure 6-31: Suspect's maxillary dental cast oriented over the bitepattern. (Photograph courtesy of G. Vale, DDS)

described previously. Subsequently, there have been considerable contributions to the literature confirming this technique in applications which use black and white film. It is encouraging to find that there have been some advances in the development of digital camera sensors and chips that are capable of capturing the ultraviolet part of the non-visible light spectrum.

Currently, most UV capable digital imaging systems are comprised of a video camcorder connected to a Personal Computer (PC), or laptop computer. This system becomes almost impractical for photographic use because of the cumbersome accessory equipment required to position the camera. The space requirements for tethering the camera to the computer are a further limiting factor. Digital camera companies currently developing UV-capable chip technology are Fuji, Nikon, Canon, and to a lesser degree, Kodak. Fujifilm North America was the first company to release a digital camera designed specifically for ultraviolet and infrared photography. The S3 Pro UVIR and S9000 IR models have been beta tested and production was started in the summer of 2006. Sales of the S3 began in the fall of that year.

Unlike ALI which demonstrates the sub-epidermal bruise pattern and distribution of blood components underneath the surface of the skin, UVA instead shows the observer the damaged tissue and surface disruption of the upper layers of the epidermis. Traditional Reflective UVA photography captures these subtle differences on film emulsion that cannot be seen with the unaided human eye.

Ultraviolet Photography Protocol

UVA photography requires specific photographic equipment and techniques. The armamentaria for film-based UV photography includes the following:

- -35mm SLR camera body with a lens that transmits UV light

- -UV light source

- -UV specific band pass filter (Kodak Wratten 18A or OX1 glass UV filter) (**Figure 6-24**)

- -Film or digital electronics sensitive to UV light

Best results can be achieved with panchromatic films such as Kodak T-Max and Plus X in ISO speeds 64 to 400.

As with all advanced photographic techniques, it is highly recommended that the photographer become familiar with the UV process before an actual bite mark case is attempted. An ideal film based UV photography setup has been offered from Nikon Corporation (**Figure 6-25**). It includes the Nikon SB 140 full spectrum flash unit and the Nikkor UV105 quartz lens. The Nikkor UV 105 quartz lens is currently out of production (**Figure 6-26**). There are, however, quartz lenses for purchase from other sources. The quartz lens permits 75 percent transmission of ultraviolet and infrared light and eliminates the need for shifting the focal length for UV photography. Most ground glass lenses normally transmit very little UV energy due to fluorite coatings placed onto them during manufacture.

As noted in the ALI technique, with the UV protocol the camera must be mounted on a stable tripod and pre-set to manual mode. This permits the photographer to control both the aperture and exposure time. The camera's built-in metering feature will become inoperable once the 18A UV filter is placed in front of the lens since this filter blocks all visible light. Once accurate focus has been achieved without the filter in place, the UV filter can be repositioned over the lens being careful not to disturb the lens focus. Bracketing exposures is recommended by varying f–stops from the most open to the smallest available aperture.

The exposure time can remain standard at 1/60th to 1/90th of a second and the flash

Figure 6-32: The Fuji FinePix S3Pro UV/IR Digital SLR Camera (Photograph by Fuji Inc.)

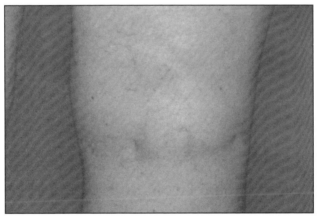

Figure 6-33: Normal flash image of leg. Live subject (Photograph courtesy of G. Golden, DDS)

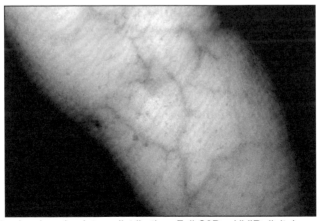

Figure 6-34: IR photo showing circulatory distribution. Fuji S3Pro UVIR digital camera, 55mm lens, full flash, # 87 filter, 1/60th at f-8, ISO 200. (Photograph courtesy of G. Golden, DDS)

output should be set to manual for maximum brightness. By aperture bracketing the photographer is more likely to capture a range of photographic evidence that includes the best UV available and a maximum depth of field. An example of ultraviolet effects can be seen by observing the differences in **Figures 6-27** through **6-31**.

Figures 6-29 and **6-30** are of the right breast of a homicide victim. After steadfast denial of his implication in the case, the primary suspect admitted to having been with the victim on the eve of her death once confronted with the comparison of his teeth to the UV photo (**Figure 6-31**). This is the first case in California where probative evidence was substantiated with salivary DNA corroboration obtained from the victim's bite injury. The suspect was convicted for the murder of the female victim.

Infrared (IR) Photography

At the opposite end of the visible spectrum from ultraviolet light is the infrared zone. Ranging from about 700 to 1350 nanometers, this non-visible part of the spectrum has several applications to forensic photography. Detection by infrared has long been utilized in military applications for night vision, aviation, and weapons guidance technology. In law enforcement and security, infrared videography has been a key tool used in surveillance. Questioned document examiners use IR photography primarily for revealing the different chemical and reflective agents in ink. Other applications for IR photography include documentation of gunshot residue, penetrative wound tracking, and vascular mapping primarily in tumor detection. . IR photographic technology has also been employed in numerous non-forensic settings including fine art photographic techniques.

As a result of an increase in focal depth, IR photographs of skin and bite marks appear differently than ultraviolet (UV) and alternate light images (ULI). The focal plane in infrared photography is up to three millimeters below the surface of the skin. While not very useful for visualizing individual tooth characteristics in bite marks, the IR technique does have an advantage in visualizing faded or occluded tattoos on normal and decomposing tissue. It can also reveal wound damage under a blood stain before the surface of the skin is washed. Other applications to forensic odontology will undoubtedly become popular as more research emerges and more is learned about this fascinating area of the light spectrum.

Infrared Protocol

Film based IR photography requires the standard photographic equipment previously listed except for the types of filters and films used. The Nikon SB 140 flash that was previously recommended for UV photography can also be filtered for use with IR photography with the IR band pass filter placed over the lens of the flash. Infrared light emitting diode LED light sources are also available. Similarly, a No. 87 IR pass filter is required to be placed over the camera lens. Most commercially coated lenses block the IR zone of the spectrum from passing through the lens. However, the same Nikkor 105 macro-lens or equivalent quartz lens will readily pass both UV and IR wavelengths of light and it eliminates the focal shift required for non-quartz lenses.

When using a film-based camera, Kodak high-speed black-and-white infrared film is the emulsion of choice. There is no preset ISO for this film, however, results have shown an optimum camera ISO set at 25 for best exposures. During the developing phase of film processing, IR films can be pushed several f-stops to increase contrast. The term pushing refers to developing the film for longer than normal time intervals. This type of film must be handled in total darkness due to its extreme light sensitivity.

As previously discussed, Fujifilm North America has recently developed a prototype UV/IR digital camera designed specifically to capture both the UV and IR zones of the non-visible spectrum. The FinePix S3 Professional UV/IR camera has several advantages over infrared film-based cameras (**Figure 6-32**). It provides preview LCD imaging and immediate image feedback of the exposure for the photographer rather than the delay associated with having to wait for film developing and processing to occur. Using LCD imaging permits the photographer to immediately observe each exposure.

The digital format also saves considerable time and money in film and processing expenses. The ISO is flexible and can be set at speeds up to 1600 for low-light conditions requiring non-flash photography, as in surveillance.

Some IR images taken with the Fuji UV/IR prototype camera are demonstrated and described in the following text and **Figure 6-33** through **Figure 6-40**. **Figures 6-33** and **Figure 6-34** demonstrate the ability of IR photography to reveal the vasculature of human skin in live subjects. Under normal lighting conditions (**Figure 6-33**) the venous detail of this leg is not as revealed as it is in **Figure 6-34**.

Figure 6-35 is a normal flash photo of the scalp of a homicide victim. There is a tattoo inside the hairline that is visible but very difficult to decipher under full-spectrum photography. The IR photograph reads the ink of the tattoo at a level below the surface of the skin and reduces intensity of the hair so that the tattoo becomes enhanced and more easily visualized (**Figure 6-36**).

Figures 6-37 and 6-38 are images of the same leather wallet. Figure **6-37** was exposed using normal flash photography with an orange filter placed over the lens to attempt to facilitate visibility of the ink writing. Figure **6-38** is the same wallet taken with Kodak hi speed infrared film and a # 87 filter over the lens. Note the increased visibility of the ink.

In the area of gunshot residue, IR photography becomes extremely helpful. Figure **6-39** is a color photo of a blue shirt with a bullet hole in the center. The shirt was also blood-stained. The digital infrared image shows the gun powder residue pattern on the shirt through the blood stain (**Figure 6-40**).

It is recommended that reflective UV, ALI, and infrared images be taken whenever possible. It is often particularly important that a series of images be gathered over as long a time span as practical. This is especially important in the living subject. In many cases, both UV and ALI photographic techniques permit visualization of relatively fresh wounds as well as those that are undergoing healing or have healed. This can be of extreme value in documenting cases of suspected abuse in which a history of violent injury may well prove to be an important element of the case. Although conventional photography remains the standard in bite mark and patterned injury cases, the most complete photographic documentation of a wound pattern should also include the adjunctive methods photographic techniques. An illustrative case presentation involving a homicide resulting form a dog attack is presented in **Appendix K**.

Radiology

Digital Radiology

The use of digital radiography (DR) in forensic dental situations has been a debated subject

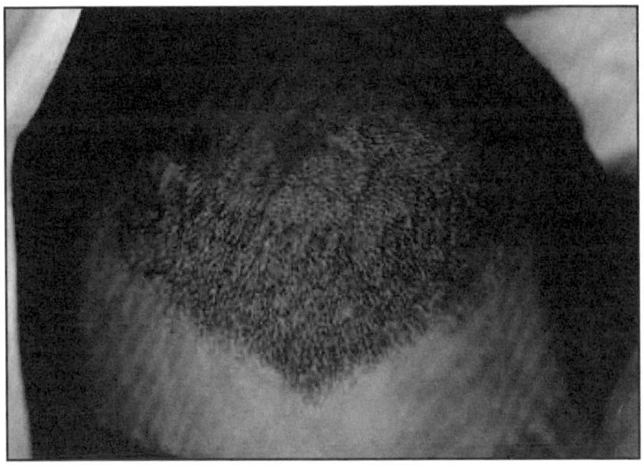

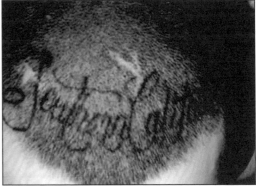

Figure 6-35: Full spectrum photo - tattoo in scalp. (Photograph courtesy of G. Golden, DDS)

Figure 6-36: Infrared photo with enhanced tattoo visibility. Fuji S3 Pro UVIR digital camera, 55mm lens, full flash, # 87 filter, 1/60th at f-5.6, ISO 200. (Photograph courtesy of by G. Golden, DDS)

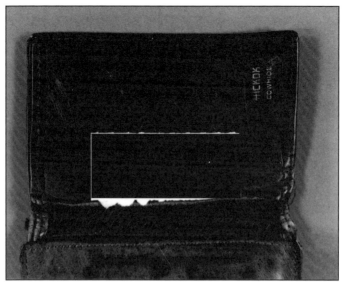

Figure 6-37: Brown leather wallet with writing. Photo taken through an orange filter using normal light. (Photograph courtesy of M. Robitaille, Corona, CA Police)

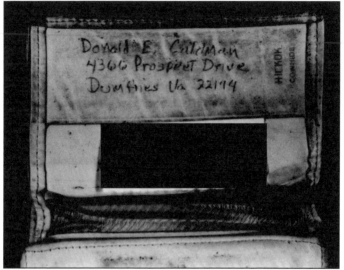

Figure 6-38: Same wallet with Kodak hi speed IR film and #87 filter. Note legible writing. (Photograph courtesy of M. Robitaille, Corona, CA Police Dept)

since the introduction of this technology in the mid 1990s. The objective of this discussion is to define basic terminology associated with electronic imaging, describe how the technology works, present the legal ramifications of the science, compare DR technology to radiographic film protocols and relate the application of DR to forensic dental identification. The information presented is derived from a review of the literature and clinical experience using both film based and digital radiographic technologies in dental practice and during the dental identification efforts following the TWA Flight 800 accident in July, 1996, the World Trade Center disaster in September, 2001 and Hurricane Katrina in August, 2005.

Basic Terminology Associated with Electronic Imaging

DR requires the use of a conventional x-ray source such as a 70 KvP x-ray machine capable of 1/100 second exposure. Long

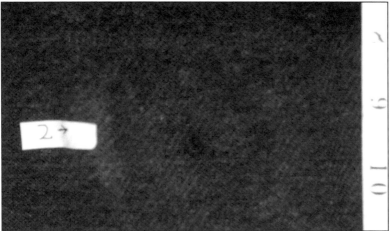

Figure 6-39: Blue polo shirt with gunshot and blood stain. Photograph courtesy of P. Mahoney, San Bernardino, CA Police Department)

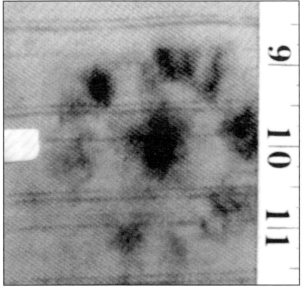

Figure 6-40: Same shirt photographed in digital IR. Note powder resdue pattern. (Photograph courtesy of P. Mahoney, San Bernardino, CA Police Department)

or short cone and bisecting or paralleling exposure techniques are the same as those employed with radiographic film. Three types of DR are recognized including:

- Digitizing After (film) Development (DAD) this methodology requires normal film exposure and scanning of the processed film into a computer.

- Phosphor Dental Radiography (PDR) this methodology uses a phosphor substrate that is shaped and used like radiographic film. It is placed in the patient's mouth,

exposed and then scanned into the computer by a special proprietary device.

-Direct Digital X-Ray (DDR) the methodology employs a sensor sized and shaped like a radiographic film. It made of a scintillation screen and a CCD or CMOS. When the screen is energized by radiation it emits energy that is received by the pixels on a charge coupled device (CCD) or a complementary metal oxide semiconductor (CMOS). The image is then sent through a wire or wirelessly directly to a computer. This technology is recommended for clinical and forensic work because it is the only one among the three that saves time. . Although radiation load is not a problem for deceased victims, those individuals exposing the radiographs are subject to scatter radiation. Digital radiographic procedures reduce exposure times to ten percent of those for film-based radiography. Therein lies an additional advantage in employing this technology.

The term Digital describes electronic technology that generates, stores and processes data in either of the following two states: positive (1) and non-positive (0). Definitions of other terms important to the understanding of electronic image generation include:

- *Bit* - (binary digit) Electronic information is described in finite information storage units, the smallest being the *bit*. It is either 1 or 0 (on or off). Digital radiography requires that a continuous entity (intensity of light) be grouped in finite quantities. Stringing *bits* together allows for a wide range of values.

- *Byte* - A *byte* equals 8 *bits* and can represent 2 or 256 different states.

- *Pixel* – Is a contraction of the terms *picture element*. It is the basic, smallest unit from which a video or computer picture is made and is a dot with a given color and brightness value. If there are more *pixels* that make up the image the resolution of the picture will be higher. *Pixels* are square in computers and rectangular in video.

- *Mega Pixel* - The imaging term for an image sensor of one million pixels or more. The higher geometric pixel resolution of these sensors produces higher quality digital photographic or radiographic images.

Each *pixel* can exhibit approximately 512 shades of gray (9 bits). *Sensors* are composed of a maximum of 1.85 mega pixels. Image size is determined by the number of *pixels* (resolution) multiplied by the number of *bits* used to determine shades of gray. A 1.85 *mega pixel* CCD with 9 *bits* is equivalent to 16.65 million *bits* or 2.33 *megabytes* per image.

The quality of either a radiographic film based or sensor based image collector is objectively measured and assessed by evaluating resolution, contrast and sensitivity. Resolution is measured by the number of lines produced per millimeter. Radiographic film can produce 24 to 48 lines per mm and a sensor generates 14 to 44 lines per mm. It is important to note that the unaided human eye can only differentiate up to a maximum of nine lines per millimeter.

Contrast is essentially the number of shades of gray that can be perceived in an image. The digital image has 512 shades of gray and there are 256 shades of gray in the film image. The lay individual, untrained in analyzing film or digital images can identify approximately 64 shades of gray. Although not all those trained in radiography can recognize 256 separate shades of gray there are systems that can differentiate between these shades.

Sensitivity is the measure of the resolution of the image which can be obtained on a radiograph. Sensitivity is affected by exposure parameters (voltage, amperage, time and source-film distance), subject sharpness image contrast/ film density, film quality and processing technique.

Advantages of DR Technology

The sensitivity of the digital sensor is one of its most advantageous properties. Digital sensors require approximately 90 percent less radiation to expose an image than Type D film and about half that of Type E film. Reducing radiation exposure is extremely beneficial when exposing radiographs on the living individual.

There is an additional ergonomic advantage to using DDR technology. This translates into ease and comfort of use of the system. By decreasing the time required to take radiographs and increasing productivity digital radiography is an important adjunct during mass fatality dental identification. The advantages of DR include: instant imaging, automation of the x-ray template, facilitation of retakes, staff acceptance, higher system usage and elimination of the costs and complications associated with film processing and duplicating equipment, toxic developing and fixing reagents and radiographic film and mounts. DR also eliminates the environmental impact of the wastes that film processing produces. There is no need to scan radiographic films and radiographic information can be uploaded easily into WinID.

In a multipe fatalty incident setting the greatest advantage of DR is associated with the saving of time. This helps to alleviate the principal causes of inadequate radiographs in these scenarios. After a set of conventional radiographs are exposed, developed and mounted they are then reviewed and retakes generated until an adequate set of radiographs is produced for comparison with antemortem records. The time pressure of a mass fatality incident is always present

Although it should be avoided, this pressure may result in a philosophy among members of an odontology team to accept the non-diagnostic radiographs as being just good enough. With digital radiography the exposure of an image takes 6 to 10 seconds. If the quality of the image is unacceptable the equipment can be reoriented and a new image exposed. If the image is slightly under or overexposed the program corrects the image. Thus, pre-programmed system compensatory mechanisms reduce the possibility of generating a less than perfect set of radiographs.

Enhanced diagnostic capability is another benefit that more than makes up for differences in resolution between DR and film based protocols. Brightness and contrast of the DR image can be computer enhanced to a limited degree. Images that are slightly too dark or light can be enhanced to an ideal contrast. Magnifying the DR image by adjusting computer settings improves the diagnostic value of the image and is an excellent technique when comparing dental morphology of antemortem and post mortem images.

Adding computer generated color to the DR image enables its further subjective interpretation. By assigning colors to each shade of gray the computer can improve the diagnostic value of the image by permitting it to be viewed in a colored medium. Additionally, it is easier for the untrained eye to differentiate structures of different densities. An image can also be viewed as a negative to visualize further diagnostic information.

The computer's ability to store and transmit images electronically also increases the value of the image. The images can be stored on a variety of mediums including hard disc, tape and compact disc. Permanent archiving of images can also be achieved by storage on a write once read many (WORM) optical disc. When required, it is easy to rapidly copy digital radiographic images. Electronic storage and transmittal of images is not without potential problems and hard discs, tapes and compact discs can be damaged or mishandled in a number of different ways including crushing and exposure to corrosive substances.

Even under ideal situations film-based radiographic images may be underdeveloped, or overdeveloped or improperly fixed. Unlike chemically developed radiographs properly archived DR images are static and do not change over time. The image can easily be sent electronically to other facilities or to experts for consultation as DR systems are becoming Digital Imaging and Communications in Medicine, Version 3 (DICOM-3) compliant. Thus, digital images are highly secure and can be freely viewed by anyone authorized to access them without the necessity for proprietary software.

Disadvantages of DR Technology

Despite the advantages listed previously for using DR technology there are some disadvantages attendant to it. The principal problem of this technology is often associated with user *interpretation* of the digital image. The diagnostician must adapt from looking at a transparency that is illuminated from behind to one that is presented as a video image on a monitor or as a printed image. The clinician initially viewing DR images perceives them as transparencies and interprets them as such. A short learning curve is required for the operator to adapt to the new type of image presentation.

Legal Ramifications of DR Technology

Some believe that digital radiographs are more prone to fraud than conventional films. Currently, it is easy to scan a radiographic film into a computer. A computer aided design (CAD) program can then be employed to change the image and transfer it back onto film. As with film, if a CAD program imports a digital image, it too can change the image and export it back to its original source or onto paper or film. Therefore, both methods of are equally susceptible to fraud.

To prevent fraud and provide for chain of evidence of a DR image, the original image should be stored and maintained in an unaltered state. This includes maintaining original digital images in their native file formats. Duplicates or copies should be used for working images when applicable. The following media are recommended for the preservation of original images because of their quality, durability, permanence, reliability, and ease with which copies may be generated:

- Write-Once Compact Disk Recordable (CDR)

- Digital Versatile Disk Recordable (DVD-R)

Some programs use secure tagged block file extensions, which cannot be changed. To modify the image, it is saved as a different file extension while the original is preserved. The steps of manipulation can then be repeated during a trial or other legal setting to document that no fraudulent changes were performed. Often, it can be more difficult for an expert witness to prove that an original film purported to be original and unaltered is authentic during testimony than to document the preservation of a DR image.

Precedent setting case law for the introduction of digital evidence in the courts of the United States is based on the following cases: the State of California vs. Phillip Lee Jackson and the State of Washington vs. Eric Hayden. In both of these cases, digital enhancement of fingerprint images was accepted as evidence by the court.

The U.S. Department of Justice and the FBI initiated a scientific working group for imaging technologies in 1999. This group established *Definitions and Guidelines for Use of Imaging Technologies in the Criminal Justice System* addressing the issues of image integrity, quality assurance, training and qualifications and proficiency of image generating technicians and experts.

Standard operating procedures established in these guidelines call for the following protocols for generating and retaining electronically derived images:

-Images should be recorded in an unalterable, archival form soon after the records are created.

-Images should include information related to their creation or generation (e.g., setting, exposure time).

-The agency generating the images must maintain control and custody of the images at all times.

Digital Technology / Radiographic Film Comparison

Storage media longevity is a significant issue when comparing radiograhic film based images and DR images. With less than 40 percent relative humidity the image on a radiographic film will survive for fifty years at 70 degrees F and an estimated one thousand years at 30 degrees F. Magnetic media such as recording tape has a half life of less than five years and under archival conditions may last for twenty years. A CD-ROM or DVD has an estimated archival life of seventy to two hundred years.

Electronic image transfer within a local area network allows the immediate access of information between the morgue and the dental comparison unit of a mass fatality team. Thus, immediate use of data for faster comparison of antemortem and post mortem radiographs is achieved. Through a secure internet connection immediate identifications can be possible because a post mortem identification team will no longer have to wait for antemortem films to arrive by mail or courier.

Application of DR in Forensic Dental Identification Cases

TWA Flight 800 – July 17, 1996

On the evening of July 17, 1996 a Boeing 747-131 jetliner, TWA flight 800, took off from JFK airport en route to Paris, France. Following an explosion on the airplane at an altitude of 13,700 feet, the airplane disintegrated and dove into the sea at approximately eleven minutes into the flight. The incident occurred over the Atlantic Ocean just south of Long Island, New York. There were no survivors among the 230 souls on board.

The identification exercise following the crash of TWA Flight 800 was the first time that DR technology was employed in a mass fatality situation. Soon after the incident, the bodies and body parts of numerous victims began arriving at the morgue. It quickly became apparent that the generation of post mortem dental radiographs was a slow and tedious bottleneck in the body processing protocol. A member of the team deployed to identify the victims of the TWA 800 incident asked the team leader, Dr. B.K. Friedman, if DR technology could be introduced to facilitate the post mortem radiographic process.

It was agreed that a DR unit would be provided for morgue use under the condition that routine dental radiographic films of each victim were to be concurrently obtained. Initially, all team members were resistant and reluctant to using the DR technology. Eventually, however, they recognized that the image quality and generation speed of the DR process could not be matched by conventional radiographic film technology. At that juncture, DR became the sole method of recording and storing dental radiographs.

A second DR system was obtained and this unit operated concurrently. The result of this innovation in the generation of post mortem radiographs resulted in the efficient and high quality production of post mortem dental comparative evidence facilitating the identification of the decedents of the TWA 800 tragedy. All information was stored on tape several times daily. Additionally, all data was retained by producing archival quality prints that were immediately filed in the respective victim's chart. All files were subsequently stored on CDs for the permanent record.

The World Trade Center – September 11, 2001

Although it occurred over five years after the TWA 800 accident, during the identification exercise following the World Trade Center terrorist incident digital radiographic technology was not permitted to be used.

Conventional radiographic film images were generated and then developed in a Peri-Pro automatic film processor and an automatic solution replenishing film processor. Since radiographic film was used exclusively in this exercise, procedures that guaranteed the integrity of the radiographic films produced were adhered to, including:

- A qualified individual was assigned the responsibility for processor oversight.

- Proper infection control techniques were followed,

- Each case's film was adequately separated from the others.

- Standards for tracking films during processing were maintained.

- Water and developing and fixing chemicals were properly maintained.

- Redundant copies of radiographs were made and easily produced using double film packets.

Using the DAD protocol preciously described, all radiographic films were subsequently scanned into a computer for storage and future retrieval.

Hurricane Katrina – August, 2005

The dental identification procedure used after Hurricane Katrina was an example of the full potential of digital radiography in mass fatality identification. The DR protocol developed by Drs. David Senn. Richard Weems and Bryan Chrz employed a portable radiation source with compatible computer technology and software designed specifically for forensic purposes. This permitted a highly efficient and accurate identification process. A review of the deployment and lessons learned from the exercise was undertaken immediately after the incident. This important action insured that the next disaster response requiring the use of DR technology would be managed at an even higher standard

The Future Role of DR Technology in Dental Identification Settings

The following suggestions are provided to establish guidelines for the use of DR technology and acceptance of this technology by the forensic dental community for use in future mass casualty incidents:

- Develop a protocol for the use of DR creating guidelines for the equipment, methods, storage of information and printing of results. A chain of custody must be developed to insure that when the images are manipulated, it can be established that the essential evidentiary quality of the image has not been changed. A protocol must be developed for alignment of antemortem radiographic images with post mortem fragmentary jaw specimens for proper comparison.

- Compatibility of dental identification programs and DR software must be developed to permit the direct interfacing of DR into these programs. This has already been accomplished with the implementation of the DICOM-3 standard.

- On-site post mortem DR technology will facilitate the identification process. Portable computers and radiation sources would allow for immediate dental identification at the accident site, with the body, if possible, still in place. This is especially advantageous when the body has been burned or otherwise rendered susceptible to damage during transit. Secure satellite communication would permit electronic images to be relayed to the command center.

- Forwarding of antemortem records (charts, photographs and radiographs) can be accomplished by scanning and transmitting by a secure Internet connection. This will eliminate antemortem record procurement as the number one roadblock in making positive identifications. Hard copies can be sent by the postal service or courier.

- Annual training of personnel in DR technology by local mass fatality dental identification teams and DMORT.

- A registry of qualified and experienced personnel should be developed and disseminated to appropriate authorities to insure the proper use of DR technology internationally.

- Equipment need not be purchased and stored in the mobile morgue. Hardware and software are evolving too quickly to justify the expense. An agreement should be reached with major manufacturers of DR equipment to provide the necessary equipment wherever the morgue is established.

With every new technology it is important to develop a standard format for communication. Digital radiographic technology has evolved to a level in which its use by forensic specialists is accepted. Thus, there are no technical or legal reasons why DR technology should not be the standard method of producing dental radiographs for victim identification in the future.

Hand Held Portable X-Ray Generators

Following the 2004 multinational tsunami disaster which devastated the coasts of countries bordering the Indian Ocean, Dr. Irena Dawidson, Chief Forensic Odontologist of the Swedish Identification Commission, was deployed to the Thai Tsunami Disaster Victim Identification command center in Phuket, Thailand. While there, Dr. Dawidson was the forensic odontologist in charge of the dental identification section responsible for matching antemortem and post mortem dental records of victims from over thirty nations. Among the problems encountered in this task, she described how the conventional portable radiographic units that were deployed to mortuary sites had failed following this massive natural disaster. This was due to a lack of electricity and damage caused by constant line fluctuations even when power could be generated.

These issues relate to the inability of a dental identification team to maintain the flow of its output to that of other disciplines in the autopsy and identification process when using conventional radiographic armamentarium. The significance of the problem cannot be overstated since the majority of successful identifications in mass fatality situations are often principally based on dental record comparison. DNA comparison in these disasters is less effective initially and is associated with increased expense and prolonged time requirements for comparisons to be effected. Thus, repatriation of victims relies on efficient and reliable work products of the dental identification teams.

Figure 6-41: Aribex Nomad Investigator cordless, hand-held, 60 kVp x-ray generator

The problems outlined above were mitigated with the arrival of a cordless, hand-held, 60 kVp x-ray generator at the identification command center in Phuket, Thailand. The unit employed was an Aribex Nomad Investigator (**Figure 6-41**). According to Dr. Dawidson, "…it revolutionized our ability to take x-rays quickly and effortlessly (*since*) it could be carried to the body on a gurney and we didn't have to take the power problems into consideration."

Concurrent to Dr Dawidson's experience following the tsunami, in the United States Drs. Brian Chrz, James McGivney, David Senn and Richard Weems had worked to develop a digital radiography standard operating procedure (SOP) for DMORT. This employed a Dexis digital sensor and the Dexis software bridged to WinID. Their protocol, however, still required the deployment of cumbersome and heavy conventional x-ray heads to generate radiographs. Fortunately, prior to the Hurricane Katrina disaster, Dr. Chrz had been testing an Aribex Nomad Investigator and in conjunction with a Dexis digital sensor established exposure levels required for different applications of the unit.

These tests were conducted on living patients and skeletal remains using a Dexis CCD sensor to convert the x-ray energy into transferable digital information. The Dexis sensor was connected by cable to a PCMCIA capture board. PCMCIA is an acronym for the Personal Computer Memory Card International Association. Founded in 1989, this international standards body and trade association establishes standards for Integrated Circuit cards and promotes interchangeability among mobile computers where ruggedness, low power, and small size are critical. PCMCIA has changed as the needs of mobile computer users have changed.

The capture board was inserted into the PCMCIA slot of a Toshiba Satellite laptop with 15 inch LCD screen. The computer was then loaded with Dexis version 7 and used to view and enhance images created by the sensor and the software package. During testing, the portable unit's fully charged 14.4 volt battery could be used for five days with no further

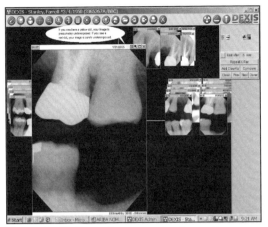

Figure 6- 42: Properly exposed radiograph.

charging and its one second per minute duty cycle limit was never approached at testing exposure times of 0.01 to 0.08 seconds. The latter setting was deemed to consistently provide images of non-skeletonized subjects that were clear, diagnostic and detected by the Dexis software to be properly exposed (**Figure 6-42**). On skeletonized specimens the Dexis software recognized radiographs taken at 0.02 seconds as well exposed images (**Figure 6-43**).

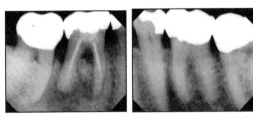

Figure 6-43: A skeletal radiograph exposed at .02 sec.

The problems associated with standard x-ray machines on tripod legs and reliance on unreliable electrical supplies at temporary morgues could have been repeated during the aftermath of Hurricane Katrina. However, the DMORT teams deployed with NOMAD units (affectionately known as *Baby Rays*) which were used in conjunction with the Dexis sensors and WinID software. When required, the dental identification section could run the laptops and NOMAD units on battery power. Thus, even if generator power was inoperable the radiographic and comparison capability of the dental identification team was functional. It

is recommended that in mass fatality settings with their requirements for very demanding rates of radiographic film exposure that an extra charged battery be available and ready for use if necessary. At the exposure times indicated above for eighteen film full series the expected battery life should exceed 300 exposures.

The *NOMAD units (Baby Rays)* were found to be durable, easy to manipulate and they greatly improved the ability of the teams to produce ideal radiographs beyond those of traditional arm-mounted tube-heads. Proper projection geometry was very easy to attain regardless of whether the body was intact or if the maxilla and mandible were resected. The extremely accurate exposure timer was perfect for the highly sensitive digital x-ray sensors now used in the DMORT morgues and the battery life permitted several hundred exposures to be taken before recharging was necessary. These units are safe for the operator and reliable and there does not appear to be a problem for clinicians to switch from a conventional x-ray head to the portable hand-held device. There is no difference in the quality of radiographs produced using hand-held versus conventional x-ray generators.

There are additional uses for portable, hand-held radiographic devises in dental practice besides the obvious need to employ anecdotal reports to support this new radiographic technology in mass fatality settings. A portable x-ray generator coupled with a digital sensor can facilitate identification of individual cases in a coroner/medical examiner morgue setting. These units can be carried to the facility, set up and established as a fully functional x-ray station in minutes. Additionally, they can be used in the dental office for exposing bitewing radiographs, production of radiographs for emergency examinations, endodontic cases and in situations where a patient is sedated.

Hospital dental care is facilitated as well as dental radiographic requirements in the treatment of nursing home patients by permitting easy access and correct angulation of tube head to sensor in the supine patient.

Figure 6-44: MinXray HF70D Ultra Light Portable Dental X-Ray Unit being hand held. (Photograph courtesy of the manufacturer)

Thus, dental care can now be provided for the patient who is unable to ambulate to the dental office. Portable x-ray generators might become integral equipment in the dental office, forensic dental practice and for the treatment of invalid patients. When packaged with a digital sensor system these devices have a small footprint and can be easily transported and stored.

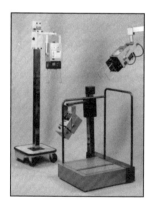

Figure 6-45: The unit attached to various stands. (Photograph courtesy of the manufacturer)

Besides the Aribex Nomad Investigator several other hand held portable x-ray generators are currently available for use in dental practice and forensic dental identification settings. These include three products made by MinX-

ray, Inc. an independent corporation founded in 1967 that is dedicated to providing compact portable x-ray equipment for use where larger units would be impractical, inaccessible or too costly. Currently available from this company are the HF70D, P200D and the HF8015+ fitted with a dental cone specifically for forensic dental use.

- MinXray HF70D Ultra Light Portable Dental X-Ray Unit - chosen by the US Armed Forces (**Figure 6- 44**). This is a self-contained (monobloc) portable dental unit that passed very stringent standards for minimal radiation leakage, making it acceptable to the Armed Forces for use while hand-holding, or affixed to a stand (**Figure 6-45**). The device is powerful and capable of kVDC settings of 60, 65 and 70, while producing 10 mA at all settings. It is fully compatible with the latest in digital imaging systems and features an advanced high frequency design operating at 70 kHz. The unit weighs ten pounds and has a high radiographic output power-per-pound resulting in extremely short exposure times. The unit comes equipped with a back scatter shield which can be attached to the cone and is shipped in a military-specification hard carrying case (**Figure 6-46**).

Figure 6-46: The military case for transportation. (Photograph courtesy of the manufacturer)

Figure 6- 47: The MinXray HF8015+ in the middle. For complete details and specifications, contact: MinXray, Inc by phone @ 800-221-2245 or 847-564-0323; or by Email @ info@minxray.com. (Photograph courtesy of the manufacturer)

- MinXray P200D - a device that has been in the field for many years and is widely used by forensic odontologists. Its radiographic output is produced by electronic circuitry resulting in self-rectification control of the x-ray tube (**Figure 6-48**). Weighing 18 lbs eighteen pounds, the unit operates at a fixed setting of 63kVp, 12mA. Although the unit displays minimal radiation leakage it is usually used with either a tripod stand (**Figure 6-47**) or the stand shown in **Figure 6-45**. It comes packed in a sturdy commercial carrying case (**Figure 6-46**).

- MinXray HF8015+ - this is most recent addition to the MinXray armamentarium for forensic odontology and is fitted with a dental cone (**Figure 6-49**). This unit, also features an advanced high frequency electronic design and was developed for all forensic subspecialties needing variable size digital X-ray capture. When used primarily for odontology, the dental cone remains in place. With the dental cone removed, the unit, with variable kVDCs ranging from 50 to 80, features a light beam collimator and is capable of capturing radiographs of large skeletal fragments (hands, feet, jaws, skull), when used with a larger format imaging system.

Cone-Beam Computed Tomography (CBCT)

Cone-Beam Computed Tomography (CBCT) is a relatively new three-dimensional imaging modality that has been developed over the past five to seven years for oral and maxillofacial imaging that also has potential as a new imaging modality for use in forensic dentistry. Using a low energy x-ray generator with a cone-shaped x-ray beam, images are made in a single 360 degree arc around the patient's head. This process is similar to what occurs when exposing radiographs in a panoramic machine. The object of CBCT is to collect a complete maxillo-mandibular-facial anatomical volume of data which the computer then reconstructs into the visible image. The reconstructed image can subsequently be subjected to numerous computer analyses for diagnostic interpretation and treatment planning purposes

Initially used for dental implant and orthodontic imaging, the technology is now being utilized for various surgical assessments including those associated with impacted teeth, pathologic jaw conditions, TMJ evaluations, and other applications where 3D visualization is vital to treatment planning and outcome.

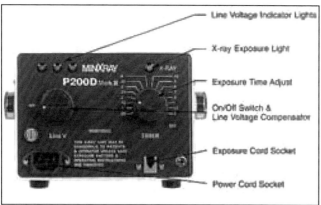

Figure 6-48: The self-rectified power source and control for the P200D. (Photograph courtesy of the manufacturer)

Currently, there are five machines available. One is a patient supine unit similar to medical devices. The others use a seated-patient panoramic configuration. Depending upon the machine, exposure times range from approximately 10-40 seconds. Image field of view (FOV) can be varied depending upon the area of interest and by machine. FOV can range from a regional 3.0x4.0 cm to a 17x17 cm full volume. Image voxel size also varies with the FOV and reportedly ranges from 0.1 to 0.4 mm^3. Data volumes are rendered for viewing by generally using, 12 bit gray-scale level systems while newer devices are upgrading to 14 bit systems. This gray scale increase offers potentially greater interpretive yield of both hard and soft tissues.

CBCT Role in Forensic Odontology

The craniofacial/dental complex is an important component of forensic science investigations. Numerous variations of these structures by natural development, disease and acts of human intervention can produce identifying markers specific to select individuals. Use of dental analysis is common and usually involves visual examination, assessment of radiographs, bite mark analysis and the evaluation of impression-derived stone casts of forensic subjects.

Each of these methods has disadvantages since the resultant data are only a portion of the complete specimen. Also, obtaining the information may be compromised by the condition of the specimen. Traditionally, panoramic radiography has been utilized to overcome intraoral access problems with some specimens. Although helpful, this radiographic procedure produces only a two-dimensional image and thus limited resultant data. It would be more desirable to create three-dimensional visualization and an efficient method for deriving such information.

Developing indications and methods for using CBCT in forensic investigations will be the next progressive step in data collection and interpretation. Multi-planar sectioning of the acquired image volume allows investigators to perform infinite virtual dissections of the specimen without additional physical damage. Data analyses that can separate tissues and objects could vastly increase the understanding, interpretation and the detection of conditions associated with death as well as victim identification. Efficiency is enhanced because a head/neck jaw specimen would need only an adequate infection control/contamination protocol and supportive platform to be imaged in a CBCT device. Once imaged, the computer analyses would complete the examination. If desired, computer generated acrylic models can be derived from the volume data.

Such current 3D imaging technology and the potential for future enhancements is certain to broaden and facilitate investigative procedures. Studies to develop protocols and utilization standards are necessary to best determine the appropriate application and value of this new investigative modality.

Scanning Electron Microscopy with Energy Dispersive X-ray Spectroscopy (SEM/EDS) Imaging

Introduction

SEM/EDS is a well established combination of instrumental techniques which gives information about the microstructure and inorganic elemental composition of a sample. The techniques have been used in the identification of dental materials and tooth material as trace evidence. The use of SEM imaging has also been proposed as an adjunctive method in bite mark analysis. The following discussion assesses the techniques and protocols involved in the use of SEM/EDS.

The information derived from SEM/EDS is potentially important in identification of human remains, verification of restorative procedures as stated in dental records and proof of brands and classes of materials used in those procedures. The techniques are applicable to both non-incinerated and incinerated remains. In the latter case SEM/EDS might offer the forensic odontologist a last line of approach to acquire evidence. The ability to analyze microscopic evidence by SEM/EDS permits the forensic dentist to obtain results from trace amounts of evidence (**Figure 6-50**).

Figure 6-50: Drs. Bush and Miller operating a Field Emission SEM.

SEM Imaging Concepts

In the SEM, an energetic electron beam (typically 15-25 keV) is scanned on the sample surface in the vacuum chamber of the instrument. Emissions occur as a result of interaction of the beam with the sample and as the beam scans, these emissions may be collected and used to create an image of the sample surface. With the advent of Field Emission SEMs, magnifications in excess of 300,000 times life size can be achieved. Since the SEM may be used as a metrology tool, the magnification is marked on each SEM image. There is also a scale bar with a legend indicating the length of the scale in metric units. While the ultimate magnification of a given image depends on its final print or display size, the scale bar will always indicate the size of objects in the image correctly.

Most SEM images in the published literature are secondary electron images. Secondary electrons are emitted from a thin surface layer and the image that results from collection of these electrons contains high resolution surface shape or morphology information. Secondary electron images also have a much greater depth of field than optical images. This permits large areas of a sample to remain in focus during imaging.

Another type of electron image is the backscattered electron image. Backscattered electrons are reflected from atoms in the sample surface. The number or yield of backscattered electrons emitted depends on the atomic number of the atoms in the sample. As the beam scans across the sample higher atomic number elements produce a greater number of emitted electrons. Thus, areas of brightness in the resulting image represent regions of higher average atomic number. The relative brightness in the image, therefore, reveals areas of different composition in the sample. These images are analogous to a radiograph in which high atomic number regions are bright (radiopaque).

Figure 6-51: Vacuum coating units. Left, gold sputter coater, right, carbon evaporator.

Energy Dispersive X-Ray Spectroscopy (EDS)

X-rays are also generated by interaction of the beam with atoms in the sample. The x-rays have characteristic energies that are related to the specific element and atomic shell of that element. The energies of the x-rays can be measured and displayed as a spectrum and this forms the basis of the analytical technique EDS. The detection limit in this technique is relatively high (approximately 1 percent for most elements). The technique therefore is considered appropriate for major and minor elemental content (>0.1 percent wt) rather then trace element content (1 to 1000 parts per million). EDS is rapid and very small areas of sample can be analyzed. A recognizable spectrum can be collected in < 10 seconds from areas as small as 1 micron. The presence or absence of an x-ray peak positively confirms the presence or absence of major elements in the sample. A limitation of EDS is that depending on the type of x-ray detector, elements of lower atomic number than sodium or carbon in the periodic table may not be detectable.

Sample Preparation for SEM

Samples must be small for insertion into the vacuum chamber. Depending on the model of the SEM, sample size could range from a single tooth to a mandible, although accommodating the latter is rare. If the sample is electrically non-conductive (such as a tooth) then it must be coated with a thin layer of metal or carbon. This enables the production of a reasonable electron image without interference from buildup of a charge cloud (analogous to static electricity). Equipment for coating samples is standard in SEM laboratories (Figure 6-51). If only elemental analysis is required, coating is not necessary.

The SEM laboratory will have an assortment of small vises, platforms and sample mounts to which the sample is attached using conductive double-sided tape or glue. If necessary, the sample is then coated with carbon or metal and introduced to the vacuum chamber of the SEM for analysis.

If the original sample is large and cannot be cut, coated or otherwise altered, replication techniques can be used in which an impression and cast of the surface are made. Extremely accurate surface detail can be replicated by this means. A standard protocol would involve the use of light body polyvinyl siloxane (PVS) impression materials to take the impression and then creation of an epoxy model as described later in this chapter.

Distinguishing Tooth Structure from Bone and Other Materials

All electron images shown in the following sections are secondary electron images unless otherwise specified. Evidence taken from a scene may include fragments of material that are questionable as to their nature. These may include suspected bone or tooth structure. The outer surface of undamaged enamel is often smooth under microscopic examination. Teeth may exhibit rounded dimples that reflect the enamel prism structure but these may not be seen over the entire tooth surface (**Figure 6-52**).

Light chemical etching of enamel with phosphoric acid reveals the prism structure allowing positive identification of the material as enamel (**Figure 6-53**). In fractured enamel, the fracture often takes place along the axes of the enamel rods, resulting in a unique fracture surface.

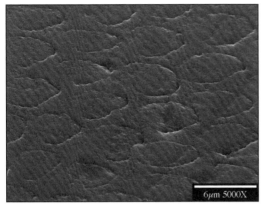

Figure 6-52: Surface of unetched enamel showing evidence of the prism structure.

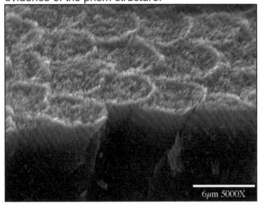

Figure 6-53: Surface of enamel etched with phosphoric acid (37 percent) for 15 seconds. The prism structure and microstructure of the apatite crystals is revealed.

The outer surface of dentin on dental roots is covered with an amorphous layer of cementum making it difficult to distinguish from other materials by structure alone. However, the internal structure of dentin is distinctive with dentinal tubules approximately 2µm in diameter (**Figure 6-54**). Thus, fractured or etched dentin will exhibit a unique and recognizable structure by SEM imaging.

The elemental composition of enamel and dentin (calcium phosphate) as determined by EDS is indistinguishable from bone, with

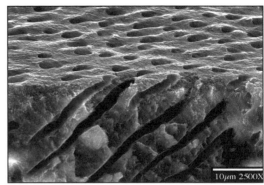

Figure 6-54: View of fresh dentin showing fracture surface (lower half) and etched top surface with open tubules. The dentin tubules are an unmistakable characteristic feature. Tubule diameter in fresh dentin is around 2 microns

the Ca/P ratio being the same for all three materials. The presence of these elements in the correct ratio suggests the presence of biological mineralized tissue, but will not necessarily distinguish human material from animal. A naturally occurring mineral, apatite, also contains Ca and P in the same ratio, but the structural characteristics of the biological tissues allow distinction. In a field of mixed debris fragments, SEM/EDS can rapidly distinguish suspected tooth and bone from other materials such as ceramics, minerals, metals or organic particles. Many EDS systems allow automated analysis and classification of fields of particles.

Both enamel and dentin undergo microstructural changes on exposure to extreme temperatures. The nanometer-scale acicular hydroxyapatite crystallites that make up the mineral phase of teeth recrystallize to form a globular structure. This recrystallization together with the loss of organics results in significant shrinkage of the tissues. In enamel, the prism structure is still evident (**Figure 6-55**). In dentin, the tubular structure is preserved, with densification of the peritubular dentin (**Figure 6-56**). Bone also undergoes recrystallization, but has a larger globular microstructure (**Figure 6-57**). The structure of each is still unique, and recognizable by microstructural features, even after exposure to high cremation temperatures. The magnifications of the three images (**Figures 6-55, 56, 57**) are the same.

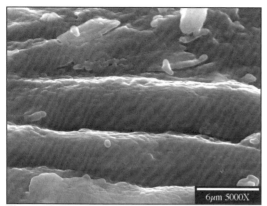

Figure 6-55: Detail of enamel fractured after exposure to 1000 degrees C for 1 hour. What were formerly nano-scale apatite crystals have now fused to form globular grains on the order of a micron.

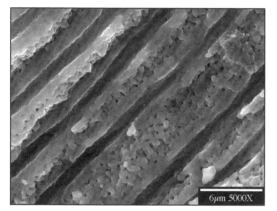

Figure 6-56: Dentin fracture surface after exposure to 1000 degrees C for 1 hour. The dentin tubule structure is preserved and the peritubular dentin has become dense. The tubule diameter is now around 1-1.5 microns.

Evidence of Restorative Procedures

Marks left as a result of restorative procedures can be recognized microscopically. Ridges left by the use of a bur in cutting a preparation may be seen readily by SEM imaging. Visualization of such artifacts by optical microscopy is difficult due to the lower resolution, poor depth of field and inherent contrast problems. Thus, only SEM can reveal the microstructural evidence of restorative procedures.

Written documentation in a dental chart of a restorative procedure such as etch and bond technique and verification of that procedure could potentially help identify recovered remains. Resin tags in dentin formed by the use of the etch and bond technique can be

Figure 6-57: Cremated bone microstructure (1010 degrees C, 2.5 hrs). The apatite has again undergone recrystallization, but is less dense than enamel. The bone has a larger globular structure.

revealed. In the etch and bond technique, an acid, typically phosphoric acid, is used to remove the smear layer resulting from preparation with a high speed instrument. A low viscosity resin is then placed and light cured. Resin tags are formed in the tubules as a result of penetration of the low viscosity dentin bonding agent. Dentin may either be fractured to show the tags or the preparation base may be etched to reveal the presence of tags. **Figure 6-58** shows a fractured edge of fresh dentin, following placement of a restorative resin using etch and bond technique.

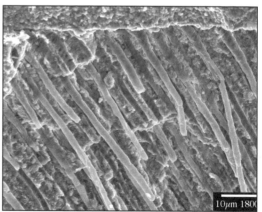

Figure 6-58: Fracture through resin bond in fresh dentin. Resin tags can be seen infiltrating the tubules, clearly showing that the tooth has received an etch and bond technique.

Even after cremation, evidence of etch and bond technique can be revealed. **Figure 6-59** shows a mandible segment with two teeth recovered from a cremated individual.

The enamel has fragmented from the teeth, but inspection showed the possibility of a preparation base still evident in the coronal dentin of tooth #19. Low magnification SEM revealed the rotary tool marks clearly (**Figure 6-60**). High magnification shows a dramatic difference in appearance of the dentin in the preparation base (**Figure 6-61**) as compared to the fractured dentin outside the preparation (**Figure 6-62**). In the base area the dentin tubules are demineralized and widely patent, while those in the fractured dentin are shrunken and become dense. This is clear evidence of the use of etch and bond technique and this evidence remarkably survived cremation. Dental records in this case confirmed the use of the acid etch technique in tooth #19.

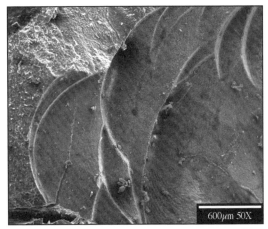

Figure 6-60: SEM image of same preparation. The semicircular marks left by the cutting bur are clearly seen and it can be demonstrated that there had been a restorative procedure performed on this tooth.

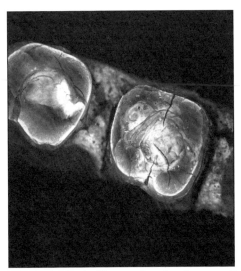

Figure 6-59: Optical image of occlusal preparation in cremated tooth #19. All of the enamel has splintered from the tooth. Even with the aid of stereomicroscope, it is difficult to demonstrate that a restoration was placed in this tooth.

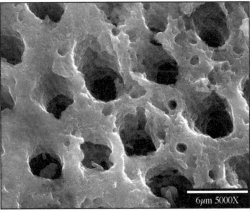

Figure 6-61: Detail of dentin from base of preparation. The tubules are open and have a demineralized appearance. This is due to the effect of the acid etching agent. This evidence remains even after the tooth experienced cremation temperatures.

Analysis of Restorative Materials

There has been an increase in product development of restorative materials in recent years. Almost every class of dental material including restorative resins, bonding adhesives, cements, sealers, posts and crowns and endodontic materials has undergone generational changes in material composition. In many of these products, manufacturers have added radiopacifiers and other components that make the products elementally or structurally distinct from one another. Even within a single manufacturer's products, there may be sufficient differences to distinguish brand.

The complexity of these materials is an advantage to the forensic odontologist, in that analysis may establish use of a specific material. This places an added responsibility on the clinician, for detailed dental records will be required in order to use this information for victim identification. As an example, in a 1999 murder case, *Blom v Minnesota*, a recorded use of cement that uniquely contained zirconium followed by SEM/EDS analysis of

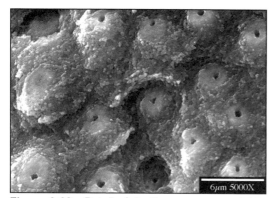

Figure 6-62: Detail of dentin on an area outside of the preparation which had not been etched. The dentin is distinctly different, with peritubular densification and shrunken tubules. Note the same magnifications in these two images.

the recovered tooth aided in identification of the victim and conviction of the suspect.

Tooth colored resins used in restorative procedures present the widest variation of all dental materials in terms of microstructure and composition. There are over 50 resin products on the market at time of writing. These are organic resin mixtures that contain inorganic filler particles. This broad description encompasses a variety of product types including hybrids, microhybrids, microfills, nanofills, packables and flowables. The analytical methods discussed are useful in distinguishing brand or brand group of material based on the microstructure and inorganic filler elemental composition. It is also this elemental composition that determines the radiopacity of a given product.

In **Figures 6-63** through **6-65,** the dramatic differences in microstructure between resin brands can be seen. These images are backscattered electron images in which the brightness is related to atomic number. Figure **6-63** shows the resin Quixx (Dentsply, Milford, DE) with inset EDS spectrum. In **Figure 6-64** the resin Gradia Direct (GC America, Alsip, IL) and its elemental constituents are presented. Similarly, **Figure 6-65** shows the resin Tetric Ceram (Ivoclar, Amherst, NY). Hence for the product Tetric Ceram, the bright regions in the image correspond to particles of Yb glass, a heavy rare earth element. Likewise, the large particles in the Quixx resin are high in Sr content.

Figure 6-63: Polished surface of Quixx Posterior restorative resin. Backscattered electron image showing bright particles which are strontium-rich (high atomic number). Note the relatively large particle size. Inset is an EDS spectrum showing the unique presence of strontium, silicon and aluminum.

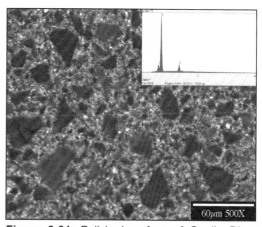

Figure 6-64: Polished surface of Gradia Direct resin. The large dark particles are pre-polymerized silica-filled particles. Backscattered electron image. The EDS spectrum shows the presence of aluminum, silicon and potassium. There are no high atomic number elements, and thus a radiograph of this material would show low radiopacity.

Figure 6-66 is an image of Tetric Ceram resin on tooth surface after cremation. The EDS spectrum shows that although the resin has fused, disrupting the resin microstructure, the elemental composition has not changed. This holds true for all filled resins studied to date. It is the inorganic filler particles that remain after exposure to heat.

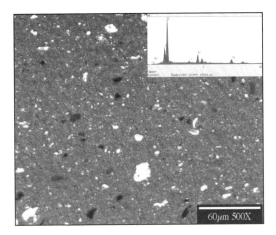

Figure 6-65: : Polished surface of Tetric Ceram resin. Backscattered electron image showing very bright particles which are ytterbium glass. The EDS spectrum shows barium and ytterbium in addition to aluminum and silicon.

Figure 6-67: Gutta percha in canal after cremation, backscattered image. The canal contents show bright due to the presence of zinc and barium which survived the high temperature

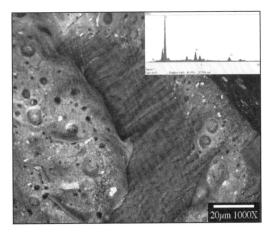

crown shape is slumped and distorted due to the heat of cremation and contact with tooth or bone. The calcium in the tissue acted as a fluxing agent, allowing partial melting of the refractory porcelain. The metal shape, however, is not altered and could still be matched to the antemortem radiographs.

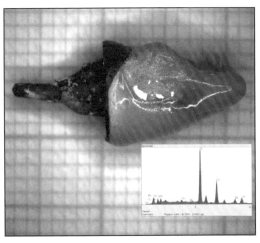

Figure 6-66: Fused Tetric resin (at left) on tooth surface after cremation, backscattered electron image. The elemental content is the same as before cremation, allowing positive recognition of this material even after exposure to high temperatures.

Figure 6-67 is a backscattered image of a cremated root interior in which the gutta percha did contain zinc and barium. In both of these examples, simple analysis added another piece of information for forensic identification.

Figure 6-68 is an optical image of a cast post recovered from cremated remains. EDS analysis confirmed the composition of the metal to be cobalt chrome alloy. The porcelain

Figure 6-68: Cast post found in cremated remains. The porcelain crown has partially melted, but EDX analysis of the custom post demonstrates the post composition to be a cobalt chrome alloy, which is resistant to melting.

Figure 6-69 is an antemortem radiograph of tooth #8 in which radiolucency was noted in the post space. The optical image of the post and crown as recovered from the cremains shows the core to be fibrous in nature (**Figure 6-70**). EDS analysis showed the fibers to be carbon, which explained the radiolucency of the core (**Figure 6-71**). There are relatively few carbon fiber post manufacturers and the use of this specific material should be recorded. Armed with this knowledge and detailed dental records an additional point of concordance could be gained.

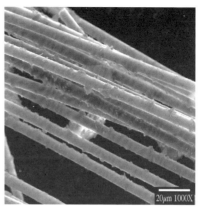

Figure 6-71: SEM image shows individual fibers from the post and EDX analysis showed the fiber to be carbon. This explained the radiolucency in the radiograph.

Figure 6-72: Silver point extending from the apex of a molar in a cremated maxilla.

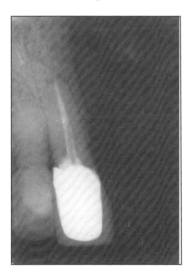

Figure 6-69: Antemortem radiograph of tooth #8. The post is radiolucent.

Figure 6-70: The post and crown are seen as found in the cremains. The post is clearly a fibrous material but the nature of the fiber was not determined from visual inspection.

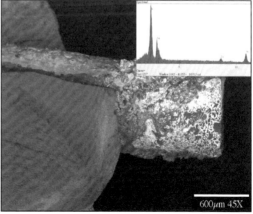

Figure 6-73: Backscattered electron image of silver point and EDX analysis. This particular brand of point had high bismuth content, allowing a further possible identification point.

In **Figure 6-72**, a maxilla from a cremated individual is demonstrated. A silver point can be seen extending from the root apex. EDS analysis showed the point to have a high bismuth content which could be used as a possible factor in identification (**Figure 6-73**). In the case of sealants, their presence may be difficult to determine clinically. Indeed, some manufacturers have incorporated fluorescent dyes so that they may be detected by the clinician. SEM, however, can readily show their presence due to their amorphous surface structure that contrasts with the underlying etched enamel structure (**Figure 6-74**).

Figure 6-75. Amalgam after cremation. During exposure to high temperatures the amalgam undergoes partial melting and phase separation. The crystalline and smooth structures seen here have different ratios of tin, silver and copper. The mercury originally present in the amalgam has evolved.

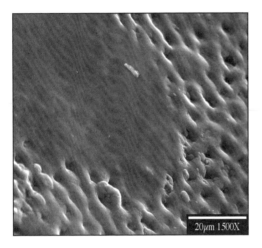

Figure 6-74: Etched enamel surface with sealant covering most of the surface. The etched prism structure can be seen in areas not obscured by the sealant. Sealants are difficult to detect visually and SEM can readily show their presence.

Figure 6-75 shows the surface of an amalgam restoration after incineration. The amalgam has undergone partial melting, phase separation and subsequent recrystallization, forming the microstructures visible in this image. The complete loss of mercury from the EDS spectrum shows that the amalgam attained sustained temperatures of over 500 dregree C, the temperature at which mercury evaporates from amalgam.

The persistence and existence of restorative materials has been demonstrated after the cremation process. Commercial cremation is a two step procedure. Even after the extreme step of comminution in a mortuary processor (grinder) particles of these materials can be found. **Figure 6-76** shows amalgam particles in field of processed cremains. The usefulness of this type of analysis is demonstrated in that backscattered imaging reveals the location of the high atomic number amalgam particles. EDS analysis can then be performed on each particle at high magnification to confirm composition.

Figure 6-76: Amalgam particles in field of processed cremains, backscattered electron image. Each bright particle is amalgam. This illustrates the usefulness of this type of imaging. Following location based on brightness, the composition of each particle can be verified by EDS analysis.

The variety and complexity of the new generation of dental materials demands that we keep pace in our knowledge of their composition and structure. The presence and detection of distinct classes of materials in the dentition potentially adds to the certainty of odontological identification when their use is included in the dental record. The rationale for accurate descriptive record keeping in dental charts is emphasized by the increasingly diverse and possibly unique combinations of restorative materials. For these analyses to be effective as evidence, it is paramount that the use of specific materials be recorded. It becomes our duty as forensic odontologists, therefore, to be educators and advocates for careful descriptive charting.

Every forensic case is unique and the approach necessary to retrieve evidence and determine its significance is determined by the situation encountered. The situations and accompanying images shown in this chapter are presented as examples of the use of SEM/EDS in forensic odontology. The combination of microstructure and elemental composition can be powerful evidence. SEM facilities are increasingly accessible today and they provide an excellent resource when traditional methods are exhausted.

Bite Mark Analysis and Evidence from Skin Using SEM

The use of SEM has been demonstrated to have potential as a valuable supplemental technique in bite mark analysis. SEM can visualize the presence of three dimensional characteristics that are sometimes produced in the tissues or other substances associated with biting activity. This type of analysis is designed to highlight individual as opposed to class characteristics. If individual characteristics are seen in both a bite mark and the dentition of a suspect they should be evaluated for potential consistencies. However, SEM analysis is not intended to replace the traditional methods of bite mark analysis.

The use of acetate overlays, digital photographic analysis and image enhancement are still considered essential methods in bite mark analysis for the forensic odontologist. Nevertheless, these methods yield only a two dimensional representation of three dimensional tissues – skin and teeth. Comparison of patterned injuries (such as bite marks with teeth) involves pattern recognition which usually consists of evaluation of various class characteristics. In some instances, however, class characteristics alone may not enable the odontologist to separate multiple suspects.

Relatively common class characteristics such as inter-cuspid arch width or size and shape of incisor markings may have limited value and not be specific enough to discriminate among various individual suspects. These situations necessitate collection and analysis of additional data to allow a more detailed comparison. This is the essential role that SEM can play in bite mark analysis. The presence of individual characteristics in a bite mark may not be readily apparent. The good spatial resolution of the SEM can potentially distinguish an individual characteristic that increases the strength of an odontologist's

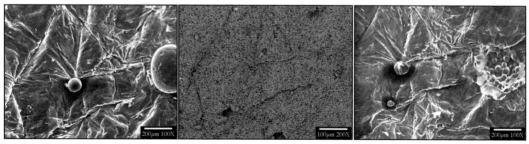

Figure 6-77: shows the relative detail obtained from epoxy (left), acrylic (middle) and dental stone (right). The casts were made from the same impression, and the area of view is identical. Note the polymer beads in the area of acrylic where it failed to penetrate mold detail.

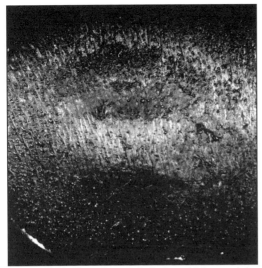
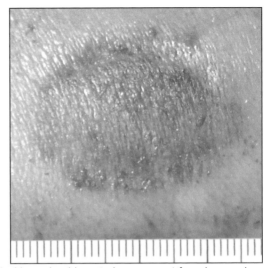

Figure 6-78: Experimentally induced bite mark in pigskin and gold coated epoxy cast from impression. Some topographic features can be recognized in the cast. (Courtesy of Dr. R Dorion)

opinion in a bite mark analysis by potentially linking a suspect to a bite mark through that individual characteristic.

Materials & Methods

Non-invasive evidence gathering procedures involving the victim's skin including photography and DNA collection should be completed prior to taking impressions of the skin. Impression from both the dentition of the suspect and the skin of the victim should be obtained using light body polyvinylsiloxane (PVS) as the material

of choice. A backing may be applied to the PVS to provide rigidity as described in **Chapter 4 - Bite Mark Analysis**. The impressions are cleaned by gentle brushing with isopropanol. The impression is then boxed and a low viscosity epoxy resin used to pour the cast. To obtain the highest level of detail a low shrinkage, slow cure resin like those used for metallographic embedding is recommended. Application of vacuum after pouring the cast aids in producing detail in the cast and eliminates air bubbles. The vacuum must be released prior to onset of polymerization. **Figure 6-77** illustrates the

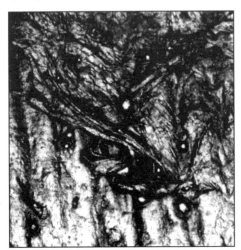
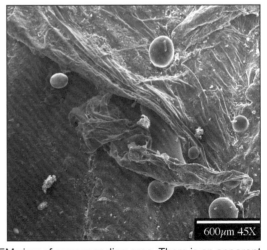

Figure 6-79: Detail of gold coated epoxy cast, and SEM view of corresponding area. There is an apparent peeling and folding of the stratum corneum due to abrasion. Note the superior resolution of the SEM image. . (Courtesy of Dr. R Dorion)

relative levels of detail obtained from epoxy, acrylic and dental stone.

After curing is complete, the cast is removed and trimmed to fit the SEM stage. A conductive coating is then applied to the surface by vacuum sputter coating or evaporation (**Figures 6-78 and 6-79**). Pieces of a conductive material such as copper tape or wire may be applied to provide a reference point to locate features of interest when the surface is magnified in the SEM.

Exemplar Analyses

Examination and documentation of the coated casts by stereomicroscopy or macrophotography may first be performed. The resulting images are also useful for navigation during SEM examination. The magnification range of a typical stereomicroscope overlaps that of the low end of SEM magnification. In addition, the three-dimensional view afforded by the stereomicroscope is exceptionally useful in location of features of interest. Unfortunately, this quality does not transfer to images taken by a camera mounted on such a microscope.

Figure 6-81 illustrates a cast from an impression taken from an area of shaved forearm. The detail of the shaved hairs is retained, and the normal wrinkles and creases of the skin are evident.

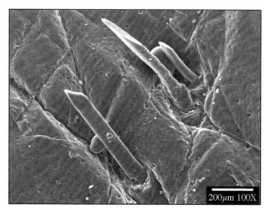

Figure 6-80: An epoxy cast of human skin on the forearm. Detail of shaved hairs are evident, along with the normal appearance of skin with patterns of creases. Impression courtesy Dr. R. Miller.

In bite marks and indentation wounds, tears in the stratum corneum or deeper structures are sometimes evident in areas adjacent to the contact region. They appear as lines of striations perpendicular to the stretching direction of the epidermis. **Figure 6-81** shows an example of stratum corneum tears on the lingual contact area of an incisor bite.

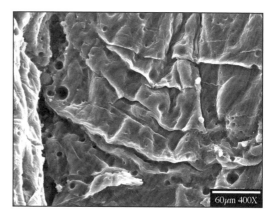

Figure 6-81: Parallel tear marks in the stratum corneum of the epidermis, indicating the presence of an indentation wound. The stretching direction of the epidermis is toward the top of the picture. This exceptional detail is retained in the epoxy cast. Impression courtesy Dr. Mary Bush.

Impressions of clothing in skin can also be revealed by this method. **Figures 6-82A** and **6-82B** show the structure of nylon stockings and a weave pattern of the same stocking in the skin, secondary to a human bite. The detail and pattern of the fiber weave is transferred to the skin and is clearly visualized when viewed at magnifications higher that 50x in the SEM. This detail is not readily visible by visual inspection of the skin or the impression.

Interpretation of Analyses

A series of test bites were produced to illustrate the unique nature of the individual characteristics and the ability to distinguish these features utilizing the SEM. **Figure 6-84** shows the bite mark within minutes after production and the subsequent photographic and SEM observation in **Figure 6-85**.

Comparison of three dimensional details of the bite mark to incisal edge details of the

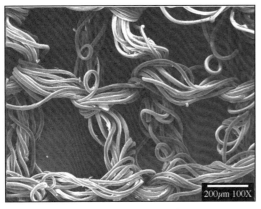
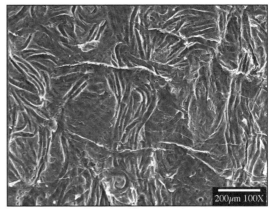

Figure 6-82 A and B: Nylon stocking structure and the resultant pattern in skin secondary to a human bite. The weave pattern is transferred and readily recognizable in the bitten area. Outlines of individual fibers can be clearly distinguished in the epoxy cast on the right. (Impression courtesy of Dr. R. Miller)

teeth should help to illustrate any individual characteristics that are common to both (**Figure 6-87** and **6-88**).

The simple overlay in **Figure 6-89** is helpful in determining similarities but the final comparison of individual characteristics is definitive.

The strength of an opinion in bite mark analysis is dependent on the degree of correlation between class and individual characteristics seen when comparing bite mark and dental exemplars. Although both characteristics are important, specific attention should be focused on distinguishing one from the other. In addition, corresponding individual characteristics between bite mark and dental exemplars should be noted. Special significance is given to characteristics that correspond with respect to shape and sequence as indicated in **Figures 6-84** and **6-85**. The presence of specific individual characteristics that correspond not only in configuration but sequence is strongly suggestive of a common origin.

Conclusion

SEM analysis can be a useful adjunct when conventional means of bite mark analysis fail to reveal sufficient evidence to permit inclusion or exclusion of all potential suspects. SEM provides additional evidence to further narrow the field of suspects. If three-dimensional features exist in a bite mark pattern, their presence may be revealed by taking an impression and performing optical and electron microscopy. Examination and documentation of these features can provide additional evidence linking the dentition of the suspect to a particular bite mark pattern.

X-Ray Fluorescence (XRF)

The technique of X-Ray Fluorescence (XRF) is well established and represents another non-destructive inorganic elemental analysis method. Characteristic x-rays are excited by either gamma radiation from a radioactive source or by x-rays from an x-ray generator. As in EDS, the characteristic x-rays are detected and displayed as peaks on an energy scale. The major difference between the techniques is the type of radiation used to excite the characteristic x-rays.

This difference further determines the background intensity in the spectra. Because the background is low for XRF small peaks can be seen in the spectra. Thus, the detection limit for elements analyzed by XRF is very low and ranges in parts per million. Thus XRF may be considered a trace element analysis technique as well as a major element technique. An example of this may be analysis of bone or teeth, in which trace amounts of strontium (100-600 ppm) are readily detectable by XRF but not by SEM/EDS. In addition, with XRF, quantification of elemental content is relatively easy.

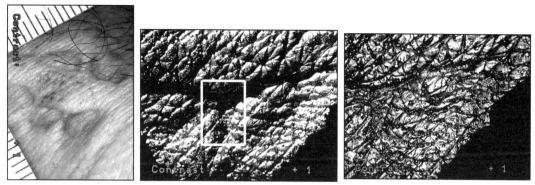

Figure 6-84: Macrophotographs of a test bite inflicted on the right wrist and after coating of the impression. Courtesy Dr. Thomas David.

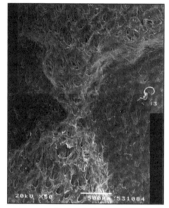

Figure 6-85: A 50x SEM vie w of the bite mark model as outlined in Figure 6-84. The contact area is between teeth numbers 26 and 27.

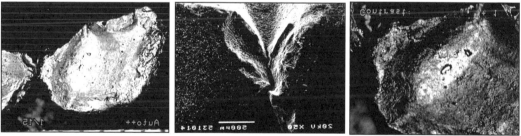

Figure 6-86: Optical and SEM images of the incisal view of the contact area of teeth numbers 26 and 27 at three different magnifications to illustrate the unique individual characteristics.

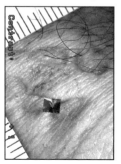 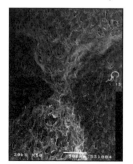 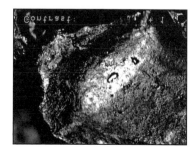

Figure 6-87: An overlay image of the contact area for orientation and a comparison of individual characteristics of the bite mark. The contact area between teeth numbers 26 and 27 is on the right.

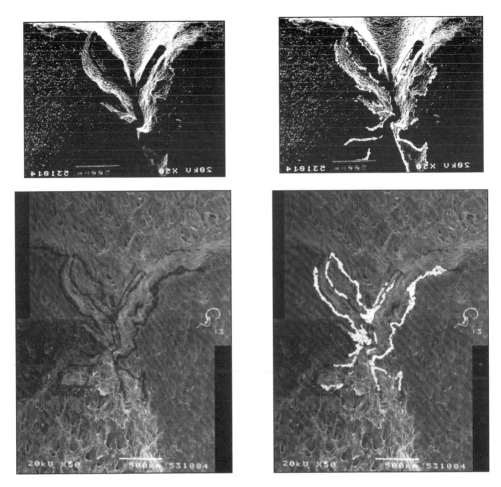

Figure 6-88: Overlay outlines from the tooth contact area to the bite mark showing a high degree of concordance.

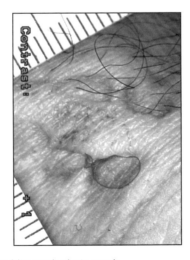

Figure 6-89: Overlay of outline on bite mark photograph.

There is great variability in the construction of XRF instruments and most are laboratory-based devices. These may have multiple radiation sources and detectors to maximize detection of all elements. The instrument of most interest to the forensic odontologist, however, is the portable XRF. Technological advances in miniaturization have resulted in the construction of small x-ray sources which when combined with a small detector and computer make portable XRF instrumentation very sophisticated.

Previously, portable XRF units used radioactive material as the excitation source. Instruments so designed created concomitant concerns including those associated with cross-border transportability, disposal and replacement. These concerns have been eliminated with the use of a miniaturized x-ray tube in newer devices. The advantages of portable XRF are therefore:

Figure 6-91: Portable XRF mounted in a test stand. Samples may be placed inside the protective cover for analysis.

- Excellent detection limits for most elements

- Accurate quantitation of major and trace element compositions

- Rapid analysis

- Portability for use in the field

- Non-destructive analysis.

Figure 6-90: The Innov-X Systems Alpha 2000 portable unit. In portable mode the unit is controlled by a palm-type computer.

These portable units are small, lightweight and easily transportable. A typical instrument weighs about three pounds and is comparable in size to a hair dryer (**Figure. 6-90**). It can be used handheld in the field or placed in a test stand simulating a mobile laboratory unit (**Figure. 6-91**). Such an instrument is ideal for use in established morgue laboratories and temporary mortuaries created by disaster recovery teams. Its rapid data acquisition capabilities are useful in situations where high volume processing is necessary such as mass fatalities. The unit is capable of wireless data transmission, allowing immediate transfer of data into applications such as WinID.

Use of the instrument is relatively simple. The analyzer head must be placed no further than 2mm from the object being analyzed. Once placed, the trigger is squeezed and a characteristic x-ray spectrum will appear on the palm type computer in six to ten seconds (**Figure 6-90**). When the unit is placed in the test stand, it can be controlled by a laptop computer instead of the internal palm computer. The software is equipped with a periodic table tool that aids in distinguishing elements. If the concentrations of the elements of interest

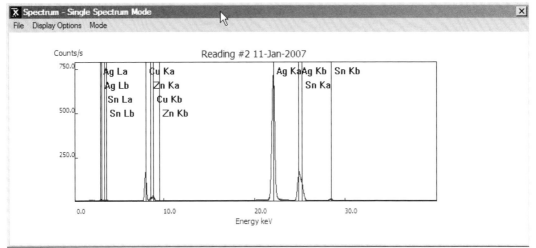

Figure 6-92: XRF spectrum of amalgam recovered from an incinerated individual. The spectrum shows the presence of copper, silver, tin and zinc, consistent with burned amalgam

Figure 6-93: Amalgam recovered from an incinerated individual. The material resembles a small round pebble. The material is placed on 1mm size graph paper. XRF analysis showed the presence of copper, silver, tin and zinc, consistent with burned amalgam.

are low, the analysis can run for extended time. This longer running time provides more precise data. The software will also return quantitative analytical results of elemental content in parts per million (ppm). Spectral libraries can easily be generated that can be used to match field unknowns with standard samples.

The principal application of XRF for the forensic odontologist is its ability to detect and identify information from trace amounts of evidence. Thus, it can provide rapid detection and identification of restorative materials and can be a useful adjunctive tool in the identification of individuals when all traditional means have been exhausted. Thus, in situations when human remains are found and these remains are fragmented or incinerated even to the point of cremation, XRF technology can help rapidly distinguish restorative materials, suspected prosthesis, and even aid in separating tooth and bone from other materials.

In the field, restorative materials and prosthesis can be missed due to their resemblance to other objects. Amalgam recovered from an incineration scene can look like a small pebble, but XRF can rapidly identify the elemental content (**Figure 6-92**). Gold crowns can turn black due to oxidation of the copper content (**Figure 6-93**).

Restorative resins, which maintain their

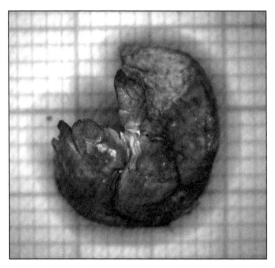

Figure 6-94a: Restorative resins, which maintain their inorganic elemental content even after incineration, can be recovered and analyzed.

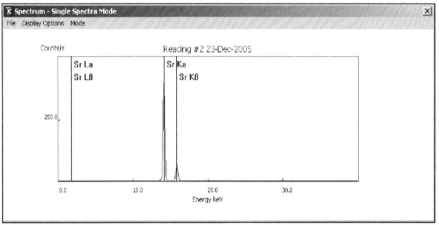

Figure 6-94b Spectrum from a particle recovered from a cremation retort. The spectrum makes this a perfect match for the restorative resin Quixx (Dentsply, Milford, DE). The resin material has retained its shape even after cremation.

inorganic elemental content even after incineration, can be recovered and analyzed **(Figure 6-94a and b)**. One of the limitations of the portable XRF is the inability to detect elements lower than phosphorus on the periodic table. Thus, the element silicon will not be seen. If a resin only has silicon glass (silica) as its filler this analysis will not return useful information. There was a period during early development of restorative resins in which silica was the only filler added. Today, however, most manufacturers add heavy elements as radiopacifiers in restorative materials. These elements will readily be detected by XRF.

The XRF will also identify elemental composition in amalgams. Co/Cr castings, porcelain fused to metal (PFM) crowns, posts, and other various restorative materials. In addition to dental materials, the XRF will correctly identify the composition of personal effects such as jewelry. It can distinguish between materials with similar appearance such as nickel, silver, white gold or platinum and diamond versus cubic zirconia **(Figures 6-95** and **6-96)**. An individual may be known to family members as wearing certain specific jewelry types and the data produced by the XRF could easily be added to the victim information in WinID. Thus, the overall goal in using this technique is to obtain the maximum information in every given circumstance that might aid in identification.

New analytical tools will be increasingly used in victim identification, as well as other areas of forensic science. The portable XRF is one such tool and already has found utility in forensic geology, trace evidence analysis of automotive paints, detection of gunshot residue and detection of chemicals used in methamphetamine laboratories.

Forensic odontology can be aided by a technique such as XRF, especially when traditional means of identification yield few clues. It is therefore important to be aware of resources available for appropriate situations. Familiarity with emerging technology allows the forensic odontologist to extract information from situations that might otherwise seem beyond reach.

Computer Software and Hardware

Digital forensics has existed for as long as computers have stored data that could be used as evidence. The use of computer technology in the creation and retrieval of dental information for identification in missing and unidentified cases and mass fatality cases is well documented. Their use permits the speedup and automation of the once time consuming task of comparing individual dental records in the mass fatality scenario. In past mass fatality incidents, antemortem dental records had to be spread out over a series of long tables for review. An examiner walked along the table with a post mortem record stopping at each antemortem record to compare the dental data and radiographs. This technique could often require several hours of comparison time.

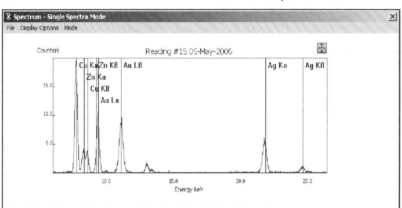

Figure 6-95: XRF spectrum of a 10 carat gold ring. 10 carat gold is approximately 41 percent gold. The balance is copper and silver. Silver and copper peaks are present.

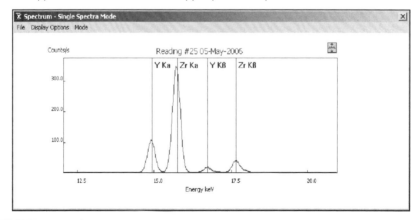

Figure 6-96: Spectrum of cubic zirconia gemstone. Cubic zirconia typically has added yttrium (Y), and peaks for both zirconia and yttrium are present.

Historical Programs

Starting in the mid 1970s several dental computer software programs were developed that attempted to incorporate this technology into mass fatality identification efforts. Sperber reports to have used a computer program in a 1978 airline crash of a PSA plane in San Diego. The crash in Gander, Newfoundland in 1985 involving a charter plane bringing US servicemen home from Lebanon for Christmas led to the US Military developing a computer dental matching program known as Computer Assisted Post Mortem Identification (CAPMI). CAPMI was developed by Colonel Lewis Lorton at the US Army Institute of Dental Research. Unfortunately, the source code for these early programs has been lost and they can not be updated.

Ident.exe is a disc operating system (DOS) based program developed in 1988. The DOS operating systems were dominant for the personal computer (PC) compatible platform in the 1980s. These systems were replaced on most desktop computers by various versions of the Windows operating system by 2000. Ident.exe was written in the programming language known as Basic and employed a simple flat data file. Flat data files contain records and are best exemplified by database lists consisting of a small, fixed number of fields: Name, Address, and Phone Number or web page HyperText Markup Language (HTML) tables, consisting of rows and columns. Ident.exe attempted to individualize mass fatality victims on the basis of significant teeth. A significant tooth is defined in this program as any tooth that is not virgin. Examples of significant teeth include: an extracted tooth, one with an MOD amalgam restoration and a tooth with a large carious lesion.

Toothpics was a program developed in the mid 1980s following the MGM Fire in Las Vegas, Nevada. It was a very easy program to use with an odontogram for input and simple search capabilities for matching antemortem and post mortem records. It was very useful in the identification of victims of the United

Flight 191 crash at Sioux City, Iowa in 1991. Although originally developed for the Apple computer it was later updated for MS Dos, but is no longer supported and is not generally available.

The programming language Microsoft Visual Basic (VB) was first released in 1991. VB allowed programmers to add the many features of Microsoft Windows to their programs including such important features as pointing, clicking and dragging with the mouse; improved graphics; scroll bars and drop down lists among others.

WinID

The first version of WinID was written in VB and used a flat data file. WinID2 utilized Microsoft Access as its database. WinID3 was released in 2001 during the World Trade Center identification effort in New York City. WinID3 incorporated Microsoft ActiveX Data Objects (ADO) for accessing data sources. ADO offers data management tools and increased graphics capabilities. Currently, WinID3 has been linked to the Dexis Digital Radiographic Software. WinID3 was used in a paperless mode at the hurricane Katrina identification effort by DMORT personnel. In the paperless mode all data, radiographs and graphics were stored and manipulated on the computer.

Antemortem and post mortem data can be entered into WinID3. The antemortem data is collected in the form of a dental record from the victim's dentist of record. A new antemortem dental record is added to the database. Dental information obtained from the dental record and radiographs is placed into the new record using WinID coding. Common dental restorative patterns are entered as primary and secondary codes. Unusual finding can also be entered in the comments section in text format. The antemortem radiographs are scanned, formed into a single graphic and then linked to the new record. WinID3 builds a graphic representation of the dental data known as an odontogram. When the new antemortem record is displayed, written demographic information such as age, height, eye color and blood type can be entered.

Post mortem information is collected at the dental post mortem examination of the victim. The teeth are charted and entered into the program as WinID codes (**Table 6-1**). Digital radiographs are exposed and linked to the new post mortem record. WinID3 permits comparisons between antemortem and post mortem records. The database can be filtered to return only records that meet a certain criterion. If a gold crown is found on a post mortem case, only those antemortem records that have a crown on the corresponding tooth can be viewed. WinID3 then allows antemortem odontogram or digital image of the radiograph to be compared to the post mortem record. If the comparison does not look promising, the next antemortem record is then displayed.

Table 6-1: WinID3 Codes

Primary Codes	
M	mesial surface of tooth is restored.
O	occlusal surface of posterior tooth is restored.
D	distal surface of tooth is restored.
F	facial surface of tooth is restored.
L	lingual surface of tooth is restored.
I	incisal edge of anterior tooth is restored.
U	tooth is unerupted
V	non-restored tooth - virgin
X	tooth is missing- extracted
J	tooth is missing post mortem or the clinical crown of the tooth is not present for examination. Also used for avulsed tooth. The root or an open socket is present, but no other information is available.
/	no information about tooth is available.

Secondary Codes	
A	an anomaly is associated with this tooth. Specifics of the anomaly may be detailed in the comments section.
B	tooth is deciduous
C	crown
E	resin filling material.
G	gold restoration.
H	porcelain.
N	non-precious filling or crown material. Includes stainless steel.
P	pontic. Primary code must be **X** to indicate missing tooth.
R	root canal filled.
S	silver amalgam.
T	denture tooth. Primary code must be **X** to indicate missing tooth.
Z	temporary filling material. Also indicates gross caries (used sparingly).

WinID3 also employs an algorithm to facilitate the matching of antemortem to post mortem records. The teeth on the selected post mortem record are looked at one tooth at a time. The post mortem tooth is compared to each corresponding antemortem tooth. The comparison can yield one of four outcomes:

- **A Hit**: the restorative pattern on the two teeth can match exactly, exemplified by an occlusal restoration matching an occlusal restoration.

- **A Miss**: the restorative patterns on the two teeth do not match. An example of a miss is an occlusal restoration post mortem compared to an extracted tooth antemortem.

- **A Possible**: the restorative pattern present on the post mortem tooth could have arisen from the antemortem restorative pattern. An example of a possible occurs when a post mortem crown is compared to an occlusal amalgam restoration.

- **No Information**: this situation occurs whenever a tooth with no information is compared to any other tooth.

As the post mortem record is compared tooth-by-tooth to all the antemortem records, a running tally is kept for each of the four possible comparison outcomes for each of the antemortem records. The sum of each record's four tallies will equal 32 (resulting from the 32 tooth comparisons for each antemortem record with each comparison resulting in one of four outcomes).

Ranked lists of the *best-matches* can be generated once all the antemortem records have been compared. The ranked lists can be formed using different criteria to rank the tallies of each antemortem record. WinID3 generates a ranked list where the antemortem records are listed in decreasing order of the number of hits. A record with the most hits will be at the top, while the record with the least hits is at the bottom. WinID3 also generates lists ranked by the following criteria:

- Least mismatches

- Most hits attributable to restored surfaces

- The number of identified hits. An identifier hit is a match of non-dental data such as height, weight and hair color.

The WinID3 user can select an antemortem record from any of the ranked lists by double-clicking on the list item. This action brings up one of three comparison screens:

- **The odontogram comparison screen**: The antemortem dental coding and odontogram are at the top half of the screen. The post mortem dental coding and odontogram occupy the bottom half. The two odontograms can be readily compared. If the comparison is not favorable, the *next record button* can be pressed. Pressing the *next record button* causes the next lower antemortem record from the ranked list to be displayed while keeping the post mortem odontogram constant. This allows very rapid screen comparisons of many records.

- **The graphic comparison screen**: Functions in the same manner as the odontogram comparison screen except the odontogram is replaced with the linked graphic.

- **The identifier comparison screen**: Permits rapid comparison of identifier (non-dental) information.

When WinID3 software is used at a mass fatality morgue many computers can be loaded with the WinID3 program and they can all draw their data from a single database on a server computer. This allows many computers to be networked permitting numerous antemortem and post mortem records to be entered, edited and compared simultaneously.

Backing-up WinID3 data is a simple process. The Microsoft Access database containing the WinID3 data for situations involving mass fatalities is copied from the server to the back-up medium. Back-up media include CD and DVD disks and a thumb drive. It is good computer practice to store one copy of the back-up data off site, in case of a calamity at the worksite.

In incidents involving mass fatalities, computers can also assist the dental team in obtaining antemortem data. Email attachments can carry entire dental records and digital copies of antemortem radiographs. The internet can be searched to find contact information for dentists of record. Scientific articles such a standard tables for the eruption of teeth can also be queried and obtained online. Additionally, WinID3 and the Access database allow comparison reports to be easily written and such reports can contain the dental coding and graphics used to establish a positive identification.

Other Software Programs

As constant advances in technology provide investigators with the tools to gather and share more data, an efficient forensic laboratory environment becomes increasingly dependent on technologies that support information management, security, comparison and sharing of data. The information obtained by an odontologist in identification and pattern injury cases needs to be accurately gathered, well documented for storage and easily retrieved and communicated to legal agencies and officers of the court.

It is not unusual for an odontologist to perform numerous tasks in the retrieval of evidence in a bite mark case. Often, the evaluation and comparison of this evidence reaches far beyond a straight forward hollow volume comparison of the dentition of the suspect and the bite pattern injury. Thus, the technology used in evaluation of bite mark and identification evidence has also evolved to meet the scientific demands of the odontologist. This is reflected in the ABFO Guidelines which have been updated to include emerging technological advances in photography, radiology and computer software which facilitates comparison in cases involving dental identification and/or bite mark evidence.

Adobe Photoshop

Many forensic laboratories and odontologists who routinely analysis images are using products such as Adobe Photoshop to apply light filters, rotate, size and prepare the reports of such analyses. Drs. Raymond J. Johansen and C. Michael Bowers have graciously provided an electronic version of their text, *Digital Analysis of Bite Mark Evidence Using Adobe Photoshop* as a supplement to the *ASFO Manual of Forensic Odontology*, 4th edition. Comments related to the use of the Adobe Photoshop 5.0 program for visual comparison of two and three dimensional physical evidence obtained from forensic investigations can be found in the disc which supplements this text.

Mideo Systems CASEWORKS

Mideo Systems CASEWORKS is a newly developed software application that securely facilitates the analysis, optimization, communication and output of digital images in

dental identification and/or bite mark cases. The use of CASEWORKS in dental identification cases at the Clark County Coroner's Office has reduced the odontologist's analysis and reporting time by 75 percent in some cases.

This system answers security concerns that often arise during information exchanges across labs or between odontologists. CASEWORKS achieves this by immediately archiving the originally acquired or imported images, producing copies for users to optimize or manipulate. CASEWORKS provides a detailed chain of custody and image history for each object in its database.

The CASEWORKS software is user friendly. It incorporates commonly used filters and optimizing tools from other popular imaging programs, but with a simplified point and click, drag and drop functionality. Further, the software automatically places associated case and image data into customizable report templates and maintains a secure digital asset management system. Its state-of-the-art acquisition tools permit CASEWORKS to import images directly into a secure environment that immediately begins tracking its history and chain-of-custody. This type of technology will continue to help odontologists perform their work securely, accurately and efficiently.

CASEWORKS stores all digital assets as objects, thus, metadata of any sort can be attached to them. Metadata is structured, encoded data that describe characteristics of information-bearing entities to aid in the identification, discovery, assessment, and management of the described entities. It is of special interest in various fields of computer science, including information retrieval and the semantic web. Metadata is used to speed up and enrich searching for resources. In general, search queries using metadata can save users from performing more complex filter operations manually; it helps to bridge the semantic gap. By telling a computer how data are related and how these relations can be evaluated, it is possible to efficiently perform complex filter and search operations. The quantity of data associated with an entire

Figure 6-96: Mideo Systems CASEWORKS folder with custom fields.

forensic dental case or single image in a case file often increases exponentially as the case wears on. For example, in a bite mark case the data that parallels a pattern injury image may include information regarding extra-oral and intraoral examination of the suspect's hard and soft tissues that may reflect on the biting dynamics of the suspect. Measurement of maximal opening of the mouth, notation of deviations in opening or closing and recording of significant occlusal disharmonies also become components of the acquired data in the case. The presence of facial scars or evidence of surgery may be significant in addition to the presence of facial hair. The CASEWORKS system attaches this information and other customized data fields directly to the corresponding image or case file.

When performing identification of post mortem remains, the initial step of the identification process is often image management and importation. The CASEWORKS program permits the user to keep all digital assets within its secure database structure. Storage of these images in a standard windows environment does not provide the level of security obtained in the CASEWORKS system, nor allow the flexibility and configurability as within this program. This permits analysis, the ability to search, data-mining and instant report generation beyond the capabilities provided by a Window based operating system. **Figure 6-96** is an example of a case folder given

custom fields regarding location, victim age, sex, race, etc. of the questioned remains in a post mortem identification case.

When images of each tooth are brought into the folder the user is prompted to enter information about its location in the dental structure, any significant markings and several other customized fields specific to the investigation. The program permits an odontologist to keep this information organized and attached to the relevant image and additionally provides the ability to search within or across cases for particular notes, markings, or placement of teeth for analysis.

Additionally and significantly, when images are imported into a workspace and selected for print, a customized print template automatically retrieves associated case (folder) and image information from each selected image and displays it in the report (**Figure 6-97**). Thus, formatting and information gathering for the report are completed as images are imported.

Beyond the database other tools permit a user to perform modifications to a still photograph or living image. These additional assets include a measurement tool, 1:1 imaging tool, scalability and opacity and rotation tools. Images can be streamed in real time from a microscope, imported from a camera card or driver or acquired directly into the system. The CASEWORKS program enables an

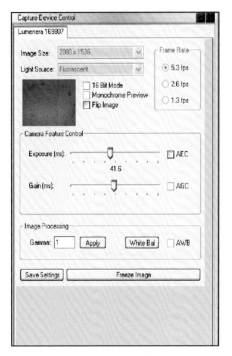

Figure 6-97: The importation of photographs and their corresponding sources.

operator to scale a live digital video stream to 1:1, adjust opacity and overlay a live video of post mortem remains onto an existing photograph of antemortem remains at a 1:1 scale. All of these tasks can be accomplished while maintaining the live digital video feed.

Using conventional tools, a medical examiner often needs to take dozens of photographs to successfully replicate the angle of an antemortem picture in a post mortem

comparative photograph. Scalable live video projected through opacity settings and other comparison filters permits an examiner to overlay the live video stream on top of an existing photograph, determine the correct angle and distance from the remains and lock the camera in place at the correct setting. Beyond a more efficient methodology that eliminates the need for multiple photographs – the CASEWORKS program permits a precise comparison to be achieved without digitally skewing or otherwise altering an antemortem or post mortem image. Thus, the comparative capability of this software is limitless, as the user can import as many images or digital information sources into a single workspace as desired.

CASEWORKS and Bite Mark Identification

The ability to associate data directly with a case file or a particular image facilitates report generation and image comparison. However, under standard protocols, much work must be completed before a report is ready to be filed. A key feature of the CASEWORKS system is that it can be used for advanced comparison and sizing techniques as well as be employed in data organization, management, security and finally output.

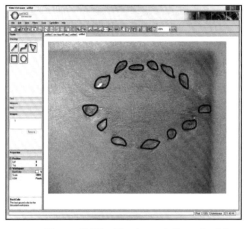

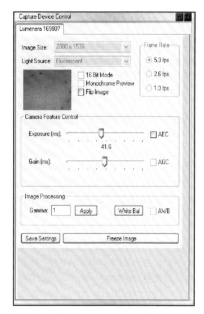

Figure 6-98: The importation of a bite mark photograph and the superimposition of the hollow volume overlay for comparison purposes.

Hollow volume analysis with image overlay (**Figure 6-98** and **6-99**) is a common technique used to associate or disqualify a suspect as the alleged bite mark perpetrator. However, prior to performing an overlay or 1:1 sizing, images must first be shown to be either orthographic or photographed from the same angle.

A common method of demonstrating an orthographic angle is by overlaying a perfect circle on the circle found on either end of a standard forensic measure such as the ABFO No.2 Reference Scale. Because CASEWORKS uses vector graphics, the resolution of the circle is sharp regardless of the level of image enlargement or reduction. Once an image is resized or scaled any annotations (including text, arrows, etc) maintain the same proportion to the image without pixilation or distortion.

Once two images are determined to be taken from the same camera position, CASEWORKS offers numerous tools for annotating and adjusting the image properties. Vector line tools permit an operator to trace the edge of a bite wound or inanimate sample for a clearer assessment of the comparison (**Figure 6-100**). The various filters discussed previously can also be applied to an entire image or portions of it providing the odontologist with maximum flexibility in their analyses of the material.

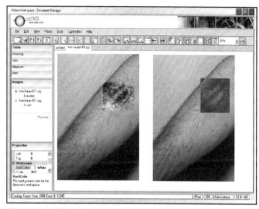

Figure 6-99: The superimposition of incisal models over the injury.

New Output Technology

One of the most notable features of the architecture of the CASEWORKS software is its ability to quickly print high-resolution, professional reports and posters for files or court display. This time saving aspect of the program is in addition to that associated with data organization and comparison tasks. The print engine of the CASEWORKS software generates material more rapidly than comparable programs. When CASEWORKS is used with proprietary printing technology the odontologist can print portions of the workspace in various size formats and at any output. This includes generation of poster-size

Figure 6-100: The use of vector line tools to point out features.

images, annotated display or customizable report templates.

Meta-data attached to any given image can also be easily placed and displayed within the print. Available parameters can be specifically selected and placed for a given printing. Additionally, a report template imports specified data when each printing is requested. The CASEWORKS program prints material based on overlays or rectangular objects which represent a single page of print instead of print area being determined by visible region. Thus, the same workspace used for analysis can produce a professional print without removing private case notes and/or annotations. This can be performed by simply dragging the annotations outside of the print overlay box.

Conclusion

As emerging photographic, radiographic, electron microscopic and computer technologies continue to provide the forensic scientist with newer and more intense informational resources the forensic odontologist must remain aware of these tools and continue to keep abreast of the exponential growth in knowledge in their applications to forensic odontology. The future of forensic dental practice will continue to evolve into a team effort between those who can provide technological laboratory support and the forensic odontologist in the field.

Educational Outcomes

By completing this chapter the reader will:

-Build a foundational knowledge of the advances in photographic, radiographic, scanning electron micrographic and computer technologies that assist forensic dentists in their tasks.

-Understand the principles of photographic, radiographic and scanning electron micrographic technology in the resolution of forensic dental identification problems.

-Understand the principles of photographic, radiographic and scanning electron micrographic technology in the resolution of problems of bite mark analysis.

-Build a foundational knowledge of the procedures and protocols required to use the technologies discussed in this chapter in a forensic setting.

-Describe the methods used in a forensic setting to employ the technologies discussed in this chapter.

-Critically evaluate relevant forensic dental scientific literature founded on an understanding of evidence based concepts concerning technological advances in the areas discussed in this chapter.

CONTRIBUTORS

Robert E. Barsley, DDS, JD, DABFO
Mark L. Bernstein, DDS, DABFO
Ashley Bradford, BA, MAR
Mary A. Bush, DDS
Peter J. Bush, BS
Bryan Chrz, DDS, DABFO
J. Curtis Dailey, DDS, DABFO
Robert A. Danforth, DDS
Thomas J. David, DDS, DABFO
Scott R. Firestone, DDS
Arnold Hermanson, DDS
Edward E. Herschaft, DDS, MA, DABFO
James McGivney, DMD, DABFO
Thomas Krauss,DDS, Diplomate Emeritus ABFO *
John D. McDowell, DDS, MS, DABFO
Raymond Miller DDS
Gene L. Mrava, BSME, MS
David K. Ord, DDS
D. Clark Turner, PhD.
Richard A. Weems, DMD, MS, DABFO
Michael H. West, DDS

Deceased *

REFERENCES

Photography

Bernstein ML (1983). The application of photography in forensic dentistry. Dent Clin North Am 27:151-70.

DeVore DT (1977). Radiology and photography in forensic dentistry. Dent Clin North Am 21:69-83.

Eastman Kodak Company (1976). Biomedical photography: A Kodak seminar in print.

Eastman Kodak Company (1989). Using Photography to Preserve Evidence Saunders Photographic Inc.

Freehe CL (1983). Photography in dentistry: equipment and technique. Dent Clin North Am 27:3-73.

Guidelines for bite mark analysis. American Board of Forensic Odontology, Inc. (1986). J Am Dent Assoc 112:383-6.

Hyzer WG, Krauss TC (1988). The Bite Mark Standard Reference Scale--ABFO No. 2. J Forensic Sci 33:498-506.

Luntz LL, Luntz P (1973). Handbook for dental identification; techniques in forensic dentistry, by Lester L. Luntz and Phyllys Luntz Philadelphia: Lippincott.

McNamee R, Sweet D (2003). Adherence of forensic odontologists to the ABFO guidelines for victim evidence collection. J Forensic Sci 48:382.

Sherrill C (1976). Professional techniques in dental photography: Topics in biomedical photography: Eastman Kodak Co.

Standish SM, Cottone JA (1982). Outline of forensic dentistry Chicago: Year Book Medical Publishers.
Stokes GG (1853). On the staging refrangibility of light. Philosophical Transactions of the Royal Society of London:385-396.

Wright FD (1998). Photography in the bite mark and patterned injury documentation. Part I. J Forensic Sci 43:877-879.

Reflective Ultraviolet Photography

Ando Y, Yokoki Y, Kadota K (1987). Ultraviolet-photographical and ultrastructural observations on swine ovarian haemangioma. Nippon Juigaku Zasshi 49:547-50.

Bachem A, Reed CI (1931). The Penetration of Light Through Human Skin. American Journal of Physiology 97:86-91.

Baker AA (1976). Field photography: Beginning and advanced techniques San Francisco: W. H. Freeman

Barsley RE, West MH, Fair JA (1990). Forensic photography. Ultraviolet imaging of wounds on skin. Am J Forensic Med Pathol 11:300-8.

Breit R, Kleber H, Will W (1982). Measurement of erythemal response to ultraviolet radiation by "monochromatic" photography. Arch Dermatol Res 272:93-6.

Edwards EA, Finklestein NA, Duntley SQ (1951). Spectrophotometry of living human skin in the ultraviolet range. J Invest Dermatol 16:311-21.

Hempling SM (1981). The applications of ultraviolet photography in clinical forensic medicine. Med Sci Law 21:215-22.

Hyzer WG (1992). Photography and the Purkinje Shift. Photo Electric Imaging:8-9.

Hyzer WG, Krauss TC (1988). The Bite Mark Standard Reference Scale--ABFO No. 2. J Forensic Sci 33:498-506.

Jacquez JA, Kuppenheim HF, Dimitroff JM, McKeehan W, Huss J (1955). Spectral reflectance of human skin in the region 235-700 mu. J Appl Physiol 8:212-4.

Kikuchi I, Idemori M, Uchimura H, Inoue S (1979). Reflection ultraviolet photography in dermatology. Part 2: photography of skin lesions. J Dermatol 6:87-93.

Kikuchi I, Inoue S, Idemori M, Uchimura H (1983). Reflection ultraviolet photography as surface photography of the skin. J Dermatol 10:551-9.

Krauss TC, Warlen SC (1985). The forensic science use of reflective ultraviolet photography. J Forensic Sci 30:262-8.

Lunnon RJ (1959). Direct ultra-violet photography of the skin. Med Biol Illus 9:150-4.

Lunnon RJ (1961). Some observations on the photography of the diseased skin. Med Biol Illus 11:98-103.

Lunnon RJ (1968). Clinical ultraviolet photography. J Biol Photogr Assoc 36:72-8.

Lunnon RJ (1976). Reflected ultraviolet photography of human tissues. Med Biol Illus 26:139-44.

Marshall RJ (1976). Infrared and ultraviolet photography in a study of the selective absorption of radiation by pigmented lesions of skin. Med Biol Illus 26:71-84.

Marshall RJ (1981). Ultraviolet photography in detecting latent halos of pigmented lesions. J Audiov Media Med 4:127-9.

Mustakallio KK, Korhonen P (1966). Monochromatic ultraviolet-photography in dermatology. J Invest Dermatol 47:351-6.

Salthouse TN (1958). Photography of the Negro skin. Med Biol Illus 8:150-9.

West M, Barsley R, Frair J, Stuart W (1990). Reflective ultraviolet imaging systems (RUVIS) and the detection of trace evidence and wounds on human skin. Journal of Forensic Identification 50:249-55.

West M, Barsley RE, Frair J, Stewart W (1992). Ultraviolet radiation and its role in wound pattern documentation. J Forensic Sci 37:1466-79.

West MH, Barsley RE, Hall JE, Hayne S, Cimrmancic M (1992). The detection and documentation of trace wound patterns by use of an alternative light source. J Forensic Sci 37:1480-8.

West MH, Billings JD, Frair J (1987). Ultraviolet Photography: Bite Marks on Human Skin and Suggested Technique for the Exposure and Development of Reflective Ultraviolet Photography. Journal of Forensic Sciences 32:1204-13.

Radiology

Bidgood WD, AlSafadi Y, Tucker M, Prior F, Hagan G, Mattison JE (1998). The role of digital imaging and communications in medicine in an evolving healthcare computing environment: the model is the message. J Digit Imaging 11:1-9.

http://www.opensourceforensics.org/. Carrier B. Open source digital forensic tools: the legal argument.

http://dicom.nema.org/. Digital Imaging and Communication in Medicine.

Firestone SR (2004). Digital Dental Radiography. Journal of Homeland Security and Emergency Management 1.

National Institute of Justice - Mass Fatality Incidents: A Guide for Human Forensic Identification. http://www.ncjrs.gov/pdffiles1/nij/199758.pdf.

Page D (2005). Digital Radiography in Forensic Odontology. Forensic Magazine.

Parks ET, Williamson GF (2002). Digital radiography: an overview. J Contemp Dent Pract 3:23-39.

Scientific Working Group on Imaging Technologies (SWGIT) (1999). Definitions and Guidelines for the Use of Imaging Technologies in the Criminal Justice System. Forensic Science Communications
http://www.fbi.gov/hq/lab/fsc/backissu/oct1999/swgit1.htm.

Scientific Working Group on Imaging Technologies (SWGIT) (2001). Definitions and Guidelines for the Use of Imaging Technologies in the Criminal Justice System. Forensic Science Communications 3.

Singh RP, Madhava Rao E, Singh T Crucial Factor Affecting Film Radiography. http://www.ndt.net/article/wcndt00/papers/idn071/idn071.htm.

Tsang A, Sweet D, Wood RE (1999). Potential for fraudulent use of digital radiography. J Am Dent Assoc 130:1325-9.

Hand-held Radiographic Devices

http://aribex.com/pressreleases.htm. Chrz B. Clinical and Field Use of Aribex NOMAD Hand-help Portable X-Ray.

Danforth RA, Dus I, Mah J (2003). 3-D volume imaging for dentistry: a new dimension. J Calif Dent Assoc 31:817-23.

Goren A, Bonvento M, Biernacki J (2006). Dose measurements and use of the NOMAD portable x-ray system. American Academy of Oral and Maxillofacial Radioology, Kansas City, MO. 41

Hatcher DC, Dial C, Mayorga C (2003). Cone beam CT for pre-surgical assessment of implant sites. J Calif Dent Assoc 31:825-33.

SEM

Beckstead JW, Rawson RD, Giles WS (1979). Review of bite mark evidence. J Am Dent Assoc 99:69-74.

Bush MA, Bush PJ, Miller RG (2006). Detection and classification of composite resins in incinerated teeth for forensic purposes. J Forensic Sci 51:636-42.

Carr RF, Barsley RE, Davenport WD, Jr. (1986). Postmortem examination of incinerated teeth with the scanning electron microscope. J Forensic Sci 31:307-11.

Chesne AD, Benthaus S, Brinkmann B (1999). [Forensic identification value of roentgen images in determining tooth-colored dental filling materials]. Arch Kriminol 203:86-90.

Cottone J (1982). Outline of Forensic Dentistry: Year Book Medical Pub

David TJ (1986). The Use of Scanning Electron Microscopy in Bite Mark Analysis. In: Electron Microscopy in Forensic, Occupational and Environmental Health Sciences. New York: Plenum Press, pp. 85-95.

David TJ (1986). Adjunctive Use of Scanning Electron Microscopy in Bite Marks Analysis: A Three-Dimensional Study. Journal of Forensic Sciences 30:1126-34.

Dorion RBJ (2005). Bitemark evidence New York: Marcel Dekker.

Fairgrieve SI (1994). SEM analysis of incinerated teeth as an aid to positive identification. J Forensic Sci 39:557-65.

Harsanyi L (1975). Scanning electron microscopic investigation of thermal damage of the teeth. Acta Morphol Acad Sci Hung 23:271-81.

Jakobsen J, Holmen L, Fredebo L, Sejrsen B (1995). Scanning electron microscopy, a useful tool in forensic dental work. J Forensic Odontostomatol 13:36-40.

Merlati G, Danesino P, Savio C, Fassina G, Osculati A, Menghini P (2002). Observations on dental prostheses and restorations subjected to high temperatures: experimental studies to aid identification processes. J Forensic Odontostomatol 20:17-24.

Merlati G, Savlo C, Danesino P, Fassina G, Menghini P (2004). Further study of restored and un-restored teeth subjected to high temperatures. J Forensic Odontostomatol 22:34-9.

Muller M, Berytrand MF, Quatrehomme G, Bolla M, Rocca JP (1998). Macroscopic and microscopic aspects of incinerated teeth. J Forensic Odontostomatol 16:1-7.

Pretty IA, Smith PW, Edgar WM, Higham SM (2002). The use of quantitative light-induced fluorescence (QLF) to identify composite restorations in forensic examinations. J Forensic Sci 47:831-6.

Rawson RB, Starich GH, Rawson RD (2000). Scanning electron microscopic analysis of skin resolution as an aid in identifying trauma in forensic investigations. J Forensic Sci 45:1023-7.

Robinson FG, Rueggeberg FA, Lockwood PE (1998). Thermal stability of direct dental esthetic restorative materials at elevated temperatures. J Forensic Sci 43:1163-7.

Rossouw RJ, Grobler SR, Phillips VM, van WKTJ (1999). The effects of extreme temperatures on composite, compomer and ionomer restorations. J Forensic Odontostomatol 17:1-4.

Smith BC (1990). A preliminary report: proximal facet analysis and the recovery of trace restorative materials from unrestored teeth. J Forensic Sci 35:873-80.

Sognnaes RF (1975). Forensic identifications aided by scanning electron microscopy of silicone-epoxy microreplicas of calcified and cornified structures Annual Meeting of the Electron Society of America, Las Vegas.

Sognnaes RF (1979). Forensic bite-mark measurements. Dent Surv 55:34, 37-8, 43-7.

Sognnaes RF, Rawson RD, Gratt BM, Nguyen NB (1982). Computer comparison of bitemark patterns in identical twins. J Am Dent Assoc 105:449-51.

State of Minnesota v Donald Blom. 682 N.W. 2d 578

Suzuki K, Hanaoka Y, Minaguchi K, Inoue M, Suzuki H (1991). [Positive identification of dental porcelain in a case of murder]. Nihon Hoigaku Zasshi 45:330-40.

Ubelaker DH, Ward DC, Braz VS, Stewart J (2002). The use of SEM/EDX analysis to distinguish dental and osseus tissue from other materials. J Forensic Sci 47:940-3.

USAF (2005). Synopsis of Restorative Resin Composite Systems. Dental Evaluation and Consultation Service https://decs.nhgl.med.navy.mil/3QTR05/PRODUCTEVALUATIONS/compositesynopsis.htm.

Vale GL, Sognnaes RF, Felando GN, Noguchi TT (1976). Unusual three-dimensional bite mark evidence in a homicide case. J Forensic Sci 21:642-52.

Ward DC (2000). Use of an X-Ray Spectral Database in Forensic Science. Forensic Science Communications 2.

Wilson DF, Massey W (1987). Scanning electron microscopy of incinerated teeth. Am J Forensic Med Pathol 8:32-8.

Wilson GS, Cruickshanks-Boyd DW (1982). Analysis of dental materials as an aid to identification in aircraft accidents. Aviat Space Environ Med 53:326-31.

XRF

http://www.abfo.org/. ABFO. Bite Mark Guidelines. Figure 6-94: The superimposition of incisal models over the injury.

Benthaus S, DuChesne A, Brinkmann B (1998). A new technique for the postmortem detection of tooth-coloured dental restorations. Int J Legal Med 111:157-9.

Bush MA, Miller RG, Prutsman-Pfeiffer J, Bush PJ (2007). Identification through x-ray fluorescence analysis of dental restorative resin materials: a comprehensive study of noncremated, cremated, and processed-cremated individuals. J Forensic Sci 52:157-65.

Chesne AD, Benthaus S, Brinkmann B (1999). [Forensic identification value of roentgen images in determining tooth-colored dental filling materials]. Arch Kriminol 203:86-90.

Clark DH, Ruddick RF (1985). Post mortem detection of tooth coloured dental restorations by ultra violet radiation. Acta Med Leg Soc (Liege) 35:278-84.

Durell WR (1985). Data Administration: A Practical Guide to Successful Data Management McGraw-Hill Companies.

Miller M (2004). Composite resin fluorescence. J Esthet Restor Dent 16:335.

Miller MB (2003). The elusive nature of fluorescence. Pract Proced Aesthet Dent 15:84.

Monsenego G, Burdairon G, Clerjaud B (1993). Fluorescence of dental porcelain. J Prosthet Dent 69:106-13.

Panzeri H, Fernandes LT, Minelli CJ (1977). Spectral fluorescence of direct anterior restorative materials. Aust Dent J 22:458-61.

Schweitzer JS, Trombka JI, Floyd S, Selavka C, Zeosky G, Gahn N, McClanahan T, Burbine T (2005). Portable generator-based XRF instrument for non-destructive analysis at crime scenes. Nuclear Instruments and Methods in Physics Research Section B 241:816-9.

Trombka JI, Schweitzer J, Selavka C, Dale M, Gahn N, Floyd S, Marie J, Hobson M, Zeosky J, Martin K, McClannahan T, Solomon P, Gottschang E (2002). Crime scene investigations using portable, non-destructive space exploration technology. Forensic Sci Int 129:1-9.

Uo M, Okamoto M, Watari F, Tani K, Morita M, Shintani A (2005). Rare earth oxide-containing fluorescent glass filler for composite resin. Dent Mater J 24:49-52.

CHAPTER 7

DENTAL JURISPRUDENCE

"Laws control the lesser man... Right conduct controls the greater one."
Mark Twain, American humorist, writer and lecturer (1835-1910)

The intent of the following discussion is to provide the reader with an overview of the legal system regarding the participation of dentists as experts in medico-legal investigations and court proceedings. It is imperative that dentists providing forensic odontology services be fully aware of legal principles regarding Rules of Evidence and expert witness testimony. Additionally, the practice of forensic odontology requires an understanding of the judicial system in both the criminal and civil law domains. Both arenas accept dental testimony in the resolution of questions that are in controversy and under debate in the legal proceedings.

In criminal cases, dentists typically render opinions concerning dental identification of a decedent, identification of a suspect's dentition from tooth marks within a pattern injury or recognition of pattern injuries related to human abuse. Civil cases may also involve the presentation of opinions based on the identification of victims in mass disasters, the acceptable quality the care rendered by dentists or some aspect of the relationship between the patient and a defendant dentist.

The Admissibility of Scientific and Non-Scientific Evidence in Court

The power of scientific evidence flows from a fundamental characteristic science shares with judicial proceedings: both are mechanisms employed to seek truth. Science, however, is the accumulation of past experiences of those seeking truth and not itself truth. It evolves and changes as knowledge is broadened by systematic evaluation of the universe and its components. Using the scientific method investigators develop explanatory principles which can be repeatedly tested by independent observers for verification. Although the goal of science is to approach true explanations as closely as possible, its practitioners can claim no final or permanent explanatory truths.

Attorneys attempting to establish where truth lies within the law often call upon science for assistance. This may be associated with an attempt by counsel to proffer a conclusion in a case by offering scientific evidence in support of his or her argument before the finder of fact (jury or judge). Scientific testimony in the courtroom establishes the fact that others, evaluating circumstances similar to those in the case derived parallel, corroborating, circumstantial evidence. This testimony guides the fact finder to where truth is more likely to be found in the case. However, Sir Karl R. Popper stated in The Logic of Scientific Discovery that, "if science were truth, no harm would be done by such juror acquiescence. It is not truth, however, but only a collection of tested hypotheses and observations based on those tests."

In the last thirty years, the United States judiciary has seen a tremendous increase in the use of expert witnesses in court. The principal concern during the last decade of the 20th century was that this proliferation of experts was associated with disciplines that did not or could not substantiate their efforts based on the highest levels of scientific evidence. Forensic opinions regarding bite mark identification, for instance, became acceptable at both the federal and state judiciary levels in the United States during the 1950s following the first case dealing with bite mark evidence to reach the appellate level - *Doyle v State of Texas in 1954*. It would be another twenty years until significant bite mark cases including *People v Marx* in California and *People v Milone* in Illinois began the increase leading to the hundreds of cases that have followed into case law (**Appendix L- Pitluck's Bite Mark list**).

It is interesting to note, however, that the

area of dental evidence dealing with bite marks only became a formalized discipline during to this period with the incorporation of the ABFO in 1976. The subsequent cases have often been accepted judicially without substantial evidence based scientific research in the areas of anatomic skin distortion during biting, error rates among dentists examining and comparing bite marks or the ability of dentists to reliably examine bite marks for common dental characteristics and individual (distinctive) dental characteristics.

As new technologies and methodologies are developed and refined by the scientific communities involved in the resolution of forensic issues their acceptance and validity in court is often challenged. The safeguards available to opposing parties involved in trial or certain administrative law proceedings includes the right to prevent the admission by the opposing party of specific types of evidence into trial deliberations. Should a court admit testimony based on the use of alternative light imaging? Should a dentist with no specific training in tool mark analysis be permitted to testify as to whether a particular tool caused an injury on the victim's body? While controversy swirls on issues such as these, American courts have been in the process of reevaluating the standards to be followed when determining the admissibility of evolving technologies as scientific evidence.

The arguments to prevent admission of specific types of evidence are made outside the presence of the jury in the form of hearings or petitions to the court to exclude specific evidence. There are various legal strategies for these procedures however the essence of these maneuverings is to protest testimony offered by an opponent due to its flawed nature. The subject of this mechanism may be witness testimony, specific documentary evidence and/or expert testimony. These court decisions may have a significant impact on all forensic sciences regarding the types of evidence that will be permitted to be introduced into court.

The following discussion is a brief overview of this subject oriented to the needs of the forensic odontologist. For an in-depth review of the admissibility of scientific evidence the reader is referred to the bibliography at the conclusion of each section and to the references in the articles listed. Beginning in the fourteenth century courts based on English Common Law have limited the admission of hearsay evidence. This is particularly true when opinion testimony is considered. The exception to this general practice concerns the admissibility of opinion testimony when the evidence is "outside the realm of common knowledge and the evidence was based on the testimony of a witness qualified as an expert by virtue of training, knowledge, skill or experience in the pertinent subject area."

Rules of Evidence

The United States federal judicial system has numerous rules and views on the accuracy and credibility of experts and the opinions they provide in court. As part of legal education attorneys are provided in-depth study of the Rules of Evidence at federal and state levels; rules that many times determine the outcome of trials. Knowledge of these rules is the principal strategic weapon in the armamentarium of successful trial lawyers to prevail in their cases.

Prior to 1993 in the United States two cases set the validity standards for scientific evidence: *Frye v. United States* and *United States v. Downing*. Both the federal courts and courts in forty-five states historically followed the Frye general acceptance in the scientific community rule in deciding whether or not to admit scientific evidence. Frye requires that when a new technique is introduced as evidence, there must be general acceptance of the underlying scientific principle or discovery in the field to which it belongs. In essence, the Frye Rule permits the scientific community (to which the new technique belongs; not the judges or attorneys) to determine whether the technique is scientifically sound.

Critics of the general acceptance test noted that novelty was not synonymous with unreliability, especially since every scientific technique is new at some point in time. The

Frye test was used to prevent various types of expert testimony beginning with lie detectors and later including hypnotically induced testimony, psychological stress evaluations, and voiceprints. The Frye test is considered old law in some, but not all states and rules of evidence based on a subsequent case (*Kelly v State*) established additional factors for the judicial acceptance of scientific opinion. The three parameters that satisfy *Kelly v State* include that the underlying scientific theory is valid, the technique applying the theory is valid, and the technique was properly applied on the occasion in question.

In 1993 the United States Supreme Court changed the basis for admitting scientific evidence in federal cases by its decision in the *Daubert v. Merrell Dow Pharmaceuticals* case. The Court established that the Federal Rules of Evidence (FRE) supersede Kelly/Frye and that under Federal Rule 702 scientific testimony "must be derived by the scientific method." The admissibility test under Daubert requires an independent judicial assessment of scientific validity. The clear majority of informed legal opinions following the Daubert decision seemed to favor applying a Daubert-like standard to all expert opinion testimony whether derived from clearly identified scientific principles or technical or other specialized knowledge.

The Supreme Court clarified its Daubert opinion in the case of *Kumho Tire Co. v. Carmichael* by mandating that the trial judge has the duty to act as the gatekeeper charged with insuring that only reliable expert opinion evidence be admitted and this standard should apply to all forms of expert testimony Thus, the trial judge, not the scientific community, is the gatekeeper determining whether the testimony's reasoning or methodology is scientifically valid and whether that reasoning or methodology can properly be applied to the issue at hand.

Further refinements to the Federal Rule 702 in the post-Daubert courts are based on *General Electric v. Joiner*. The original Daubert decision was explicit in stating that the trial judge's focus in determining reliability was to be directed solely toward examining the "principles and methodology employed by the expert, not on the conclusions they generate." In *General Electric v. Joiner* the Court stepped back from this position and recognized that "conclusions and methodology are not entirely distinct from one another." A restated Federal Rule 702 directs a trial court to determine not only whether the methods used by an expert and the principles upon which their analysis rests have been determined to be reliable, but also whether "the witness has applied the principles and methods reliably" to the facts that are at issue in the particular case.

The contemporary debate on the varied methods used by the courts to evaluate the reliability of an expert's opinion at trial is contained in voluminous records of trial cases and legal commentaries. The scientific method has recently been included as a tool used by the courts to interpret an expert's validity of methods and the reliability of results. The application of these new standards was intended to end the current state of affairs associated with the battle of the experts.

Under Daubert the task of the expert witness is not to prove that the method is generally accepted but to prove to the court that it is scientifically valid. The Supreme Court's ruling stated that, "...the trial judge must ensure that any and all scientific testimony or evidence admitted is not only relevant, but reliable." One of the thorny problems raised by the Supreme Court's Daubert decision is the need for the trial judge, often with limited scientific expertise, to determine whether or not to exclude an expert's opinion because of flaws in the scientific reasoning or methodology.

Daubert requires the court to examine the following when experts attempt to prove to trial judges that their methods and techniques are scientifically valid:

- Can the methodology be tested and has actually been tested. If it is not testable and tested it is not considered scientific knowledge.

- Peer review and publication are persuasive, but not essential.

- Consideration is given to whether there is known error rate and standards for applying the method.

- General acceptance by the scientific community is a consideration under Daubert but is merely one of the factors to be considered rather than the sole determinant.

Subordinate issues considered under Daubert are the expert's qualifications and stature in the scientific community, ability of other experts to replicate results and the ability to explain the technique and its results with sufficient clarity and simplicity so that the court and the trier of fact can understand its implications in the case at hand. These are all independent findings by the court. They are not mutually exclusive and all need not be considered in a particular case.

The advent of the new science of DNA profiling in criminal identification and debates among judicial pundits following the Daubert decision has prodded the judiciary at all levels to attempt to redefine the nature of scientific proof versus personal opinion. Since the Daubert ruling rests on an interpretation of the Federal Rules of Evidence based on a decision in a statutory, rather than constitutional, case; state courts are not required to adopt or follow the FRE and are therefore not required to consider the Daubert guidelines since the Daubert ruling rests on an interpretation of the FRE based on a decision in a statutory, rather than constitutional, case,. However, many courts of appeals in their interpretation of applicable law are ordering remands or new evidentiary hearings because trial courts failed to conduct a Daubert hearing, There is wide variability among the states as to how these hearings are conducted. The states are free to choose from three discretionary options in regard to evidence admissibility rules including:

- Adopting the FRE and Daubert guidelines (generally requiring state legislative action).

- Following a general acceptance or Kelly/Frye rule.

- Developing and implementing some other admissibility rules.

It has been stated that, "Whatever the specific admissibility rule, all trial court judges in the civil, criminal, juvenile and family court systems and at both federal and state levels are being put in the position of deciding the relevancy, utility, and probative value of proffered scientific evidence whether using a Kelly/Frye standard, a Daubert standard, or some other standard." As jurisdictional and jurisprudential issues evolve relative to the use of the Daubert admissibility standard the various states will continue to exhibit variability in how they choose to use it.

California follows the Kelly/Frye rule and decided not to use the Daubert criteria in 1994. In People v. Leahy, the California Supreme Court stated that, "Although the Frye test may be difficult to apply and at times excludes relevant evidence, it has proven its value for over 60 years." The Court further stated that Frye "... has helped to assure that determinations of guilt or innocence are not influenced by the vagaries of pseudo-science.'"

There are differing views on the effect that Daubert will have regarding the introduction of new methods. On one hand, the introduction of new methods may be facilitated, because it is no longer essential that the scientific community generally accepts the method. If the new method is based on sound scientific procedure it should be admissible no matter how novel or controversial it may be. Thus, it would seem possible to introduce novel scientific theories once barred by Frye.

On the other hand, the new methodology may conceivably be subjected to more rigorous examination. It is no longer sufficient for the expert to merely testify that the overwhelming majority of experts in the field agree with the new proposition. Under Daubert, the expert must be prepared to describe the scientific methodology used to verify the hypothesis, e.g. the tests conducted, the standards used, and the error rate. The method may not be accepted if, for example, it has not been adequately tested. In addition, as pointed out by Imwinkelried, some generally accepted techniques that are now in widespread use may be vulnerable to attack if they do not have an adequate scientific basis.

The Daubert court is quoted as follows: "Once it is posited that general acceptance is not the exclusive test for admissibility, conventional scientific evidence is no longer immune from attack." Forensic dental experts who have been involved in the introduction of new evidence in several states believe that the difficulty of introducing new evidence in the immediate future will depend, not so much on the rules, but on the manner in which they are applied by the courts. "Arguments continue to this day as to whether the Daubert standard is more stringent than Frye, less stringent than Frye or more or less the same. The answer, based on emerging federal and state case law on the admissibility of expert testimony continues to be 'it depends'"

Indeed, by making the trial judge the gatekeeper in determining scientific validity, Daubert gives the judge greater latitude in determining what evidence is admissible. This increased judicial latitude appears to have been the reason some prosecutors seeking admissibility of DNA evidence have strongly favored the Daubert decision.

These events have generated heated and lively conversation and debate among members of the forensic identification disciplines (ballistics, tool mark analysis, DNA analysis, fingerprint analysis, odontology and anthropology) concerning the real basis of their testimonial expert opinion and what the future holds for continued admissibility of expert testimony in their disciplines. To date there has not been sufficient pressure to bear to make the opinions of experts in these disciplines invalid in court.

Whether using the FRE or other standards, admission of evidence can be prevented under certain circumstances. Primarily, proffered

evidence must be relevant and germane to the prevailing case. This implies that the material must have a direct relationship to an issue at trial. Presenting photographs of an unrelated case is an example of evidence that may not be admissible unless it can answer a foundational question concerning the current case. Relevancy of photographs and other exhibits has to be proven at trial.

The probative value of the evidence or exhibit is always a major consideration in the decision by a judge to admit or exclude evidence. Probative value is related to the material's ability to prove or disprove a fact at issue or under review by the court. If the evidence does not help in this regard it is not probative. Additional objections can be made based on the material not being best evidence or on it being unverifiable. The potential prejudicial effect that some evidence, such as grisly autopsy or crime scene photographs, may cause by disturbing or inflaming the jury must also be considered during admissibility decisions.

In bite mark and other cases in which injury patterns are disturbing or offensive, evidentiary materials must focus on the immediate site of the alleged injury patterns. Although the use of a photograph which orients the injury on the victim's body is important, this view should be kept separate from the other exhibits and it should be reviewed by counsel before being displayed in the courtroom.

The Odontologist's Role as an Expert Witness

"Gentlemen of the jury, there are three kinds of liars: the common liar, the damned liar, and the scientific expert." W. L. Foster, 1897

An expert witness is an individual who possesses relevant knowledge in a given field or fields in greater depth than the public at large. The knowledge may be acquired by education, experience or training. Following the Daubert decision, Rule 702 of the FRE was amended in 2002. It currently states that, "If scientific, technical or other specialized knowledge will assist the trier of fact (editor's note - judge or jury depending on the circumstances of the trial) in issue, a witness qualified as an expert by knowledge, skill, experience, training or education, may testify thereto in the form of an opinion {emphasis added} or otherwise, if the:

- Testimony is based upon sufficient facts or data,

- Testimony is the product of reliable principles and methods,

- Witness has applied the principles and methods reliably to the facts of the case."

The importance of the impact of expert testimony on the proceedings cannot be understated. In essence, the expert witness is permitted to render an opinion on matters that occurred outside of his or her presence. This differs from the testimony of a fact witness who may only testify to an event or thing that actually occurred in his or her presence. In the United States, experts are retained by either side in the adversarial system – not by the court. Thus, the presence of an expert or several experts can affect the legal arguments in a positive and/or negative manner since each expert testifies for only one side during the proceedings. Because of the specialized subject matter presented, the opposing attorney may also acquire the services of an expert to rebut an unfavorable opinion proffered by their opponent. This provides the adversarial attorney the needed expertise to vigorously attack the import and value of their opposing expert during cross-examination and may provide a different interpretation of the evidence to the judge and jury.

In this setting, the fundamental role and duty of an expert in the judicial system must remain to assist the trier of fact in understanding complicated subjects/issues beyond their usual knowledge in their search for truth. Despite the fact that an expert is retained by only one of the adversaries, it is the responsibility and duty of the forensic dental expert to provide an impartial opinion, independent of the interests held by the employer. The responsibility is to present the facts, making them understandable to the jury and/or judge and expressing an opinion that is sound, logical and well-grounded in science. The forensic dental expert witness should be prepared to comment on facts and opinions of the opposing expert(s) and be able to define the standard (omit the word professional) of care in the profession.

The expert witness has a special privilege by being able to proffer an opinion and must educate the jury in the technical matters at hand. In this regard, an expert is not unlike an undergraduate professor convincing students (jurors) that they understand the technical issues presented in a class (court). Achieving a perception of understanding, the expert can convince the jurors that they are making independent decisions concerning the correctness of the expert's testimony.

The testimony of expert witnesses is inevitably theater and jurors have no alternative but to judge that testimony on the personal credibility of the witness. This credibility is most often influenced by the academic degrees, specialty board certification, and publications of the witness. Additional factors influencing a jury's perception of the expert's credibility may be more subjective and include physical appearance, race, gender, command of the English language and personality.

The role of the expert is clearly different from that of the attorney. The attorney is an advocate, whose role is to advance the cause of the client. On the contrary, the expert's views should be independent and objective and they should not be an advocate for either adversary. If the expert cannot reach conclusions and opinions that support the case theory, this should be made clear to the attorney. A forensic expert who feels compelled to testify in every case may be substituting personal gain for objectivity.

Once an impartial, objective opinion has been formed, the expert has the right, duty and obligation to strongly defend that opinion. It is important, however, for the expert to understand the difference between advocating an objective, scientific conclusion as opposed to being an advocate for guilt or innocence of the defendant. Admitting a witness as a qualified expert does not create an obligation to accept the views of that expert; rather the judge or jury is free to accept or reject the expert's views, even in the absence of contrary evidence or expert opinion.

The forensic dental specialist should strive to be an outstanding expert. This can be accomplished by diligently addressing the following guidelines:

- Insure that one's credentials match or exceed the expert for the opposition. The expert should provide the attorney with an outline (curriculum vitae) of his or her training and experience. This will be helpful in qualifying the witness as an expert in court. *(Editor's note – Ideally, this is a situation that all forensic dental experts would like to occur. The fact remains that forensic dental experts do not get to choose the opposing expert and therefore ultimately have no control over whether their credentials match or exceed those of the expert retained by the opposition.)*

- Develop a strong well-founded background in forensic dental science and apply sound and reasoned judgment in the analysis of evidentiary material.

- Exhibit a confident demeanor and attitude and act professionally in all respects by keeping emotion in check and under control.

- Have good communication skills and be believable.

- Present a professional appearance in court by dressing in good taste and appearing dignified.

- Possess a good measure of common sense by being able to translate complicated technical information into simple and practical concepts that a lay juror can comprehend as understandable truths.

- Be ethical by not committing any of the following expert witness abuses:

- Selling a report or work product to the opposing side if a decision is made not to use the expert's services

- Withholding information

- Switching sides in a case

- Falsifying credentials

- Submitting an untrue opinion or report

- Being argumentative

- Providing lengthy preambles to every answer

- Failing to keep and maintain confidentiality

- Destroying evidence in testing

- Using only one's vast experience without documentation of scientific, technical or professional testing.

Pre-Trial Preparation

Preparation for the trial begins the day the forensic odontologist is first contacted about the case. By the time the forensic dental expert takes the witness stand their job should be 90-95% complete. The following should be addressed when considering involvement as an expert:

- Record the date and time of initial contact. Similarly, each time the expert works on the case they should record what was done so this information will be available.

- Determine the terms and agreements between the expert and the agency or attorney requesting their services. This includes establishment of an understanding with the agency or attorney of the forensic dental expert's fee schedule prior to offering an initial opinion in the case. This should be accomplished by submitting a contractual letter including an hourly rate, consideration for normal expenses and time out of the office expenses. Additional consideration for out of pocket expenses for trial exhibit preparation, airline fares, hotel accommodations, etc. should be included. The attorney or agency should be billed as the odontologist completes the various phases of pretrial preparation since an actual trial may be an event in the distant future or may never occur.

- Determine who the opponents are in the case and their methods and style of testimonial presentation.

- Gain a clear understanding of the role that the forensic odontologist is expected to play in the case. This may change through the case, but must be clear at the beginning. For example, is bite mark evidence the only substantive evidence in the case?

- Establish the leeway to decide whether to accept or refuse the case after an initial review of the evidence, associated facts and case material and background research.

- Do not accept a case in which the dental expert's training or special expertise is not documented. For example, an oral surgeon should not serve as an expert witness in a banded orthodontic case.

- Present the attorney or agency requesting the expert's services a letter of acceptance with terms so there will be no misunderstanding of the dentist's role.

- Remain in contact with the attorney or agency requesting the forensic dentist's services since communication is critical.

Evidence Management

The usefulness of physical evidence is determined by its probative value in verifying the issues in the case, identifying the victim and/or perpetrator and exonerating all other individuals under suspicion. To accomplish these tasks and insure that the evidence is not tainted or corrupted, it must be properly handled and managed to maintain the chain of custody. All who are involved in possessing, testing, transporting or evaluating the physical evidence in a case must maintain a written and signed log concerning its management. This would include police authorities, crime laboratory and coroner/medical examiner personnel, forensic dental experts, other forensic specialists and the attorneys in the case.

When physical evidence is first received it should be initialed and dated in a manner that does not compromise its probative value. At trial, perhaps months later, this evidence can be examined and identified by the appropriate markings. If the evidence is modified as a result of the expert's examination or is transferred to another individual authorized to possess it, this information should be carefully recorded. It is important to preserve the best evidence for use in court. To satisfy the legal requirements concerning physical evidence, the expert witness must be able to:

- Identify each piece of evidence, even months\years after its collection

- Describe the exact location and the conditions at the time of its collection

- Prove that from its collection until its presentation at trial the evidence was maintained in a proper chain of custody

- Describe alterations or changes that may have occurred in the evidence between the time of its collection and its introduction as evidence in court.

The expert witness' notes provide the best record of events related to evidence collection and management. They are the personal property of the expert and the most readily available record of their involvement in the case. Additionally, good notes are an asset when developing the raw material for the final written report of the case. This formal report will ultimately be presented to the attorney of record and may not require the level of detail or items of information that arose in the evidence analysis process. The recorded detail in one's notes should anticipate both the information to be placed on the final written report and the possibility of the doctor being questioned on a given point in the record by the attorneys or the court.

Thus, it is not uncommon for a forensic dental expert to rely on their memory of associated events to give cryptic or individual items in the notes a comprehensive interpretation. Others rely on more detailed notes and this reflects a personal choice. However, the objective in either case is to establish a record of events that will remain meaningful to the expert for months or years. They should, of course, be supplemented by photographs, diagrams, radiographs, etc., as applicable.

The following are essential items but are not intended to represent all categories of data you may wish to record:

- Date, time, location, authorization

- Detailed examination or charting

- Camera type and film used for photographs

- Discovery of significant items of evidence

- Failure to locate items (Missing denture)

- Detailed description of victim or suspect in terms of the expert's area of expertise.

It is recommended that the forensic dental expert maintain a different notebook or file for each case. This may also be achieved by using a loose leaf notebook to maintain case notes and/or records. These methods of record management preclude admixing of case information and the potential for unauthorized disclosure concerning matters not related to the case at hand. As with other information in dental practice, the forensic dental expert's notes and records should be kept permanently and securely. Proper maintenance of this material will prove valuable even if the case results in a conviction. There

is always the possibility of an appeal or some other civil action that will require the doctor's reappearance in court.

Original records, radiographs, photographs, charts, casts, etc. should be presented as evidence whenever possible. If duplicates are offered, the evidence may be challenged on the ground that the other party is being denied the opportunity to examine the best evidence.

Prepare the written report carefully, since the expert must be ready to defend every word in court. Depending on circumstances, the report may be brief or rather detailed. It should describe the nature of the study, the conclusions and the basis for the conclusions. Either the report or the working notes should be sufficiently detailed so relevant information is available for a trial that may be many months in the future. The expert's report to the attorney should be formulated with a goal of identifying key issues of the case and educating the attorney about the field of forensic dental expertise.

Since this material is usually discoverable it should be written in non-technical language so that its simplicity and clarity make it understandable to anyone who has the occasion to read it. The report should be presented to the attorney in a timely manner so that it can be discussed and issues resolved well in advance of trial. Remember that reports can always be amended, or a supplemental report can be filed, prior to closure of discovery.

If the findings are considered significant, the expert may be asked to testify at a deposition, preliminary hearing, grand jury hearing or trial. However, it is no disgrace not to be asked to testify. Indeed, a major reason there are numerous contested bite mark cases is the absolutely erroneous belief that the expert has an obligation to provide testimony favorable to the side that contacted them. The continual parade of bite mark cases with teams of experts arguing on both sides raises important questions about:

- The reliability of bite mark evidence and/ or
- The motives of the experts.

A meeting with the attorney is essential prior to the expert's testimony. If the attorney is too busy to meet, it is unlikely that the expert's testimony will be presented effectively. The attorney will usually welcome the opportunity to be educated by the expert and will appreciate receiving literature on the subject at hand. The expert should be informed and educated about the legal considerations of the case as well. Thus, both individuals will become more cognizant of the other's role in the process. Neither the attorney not the expert should be surprised at trial by not being provided with enough material and information about the case. When appropriate, the expert should inquire about the feasibility of examining the scene or scene photographs, seeing the patient, evaluating histological slides and other laboratory evidence appropriate for review, etc. This extra attention to the details of the case can enhance the expert's credibility and professionalism.

It is extremely important that the discussion with the attorney describes the strengths and weaknesses of the evidence. Additionally, the attorney should be informed in advance concerning the level to which the expert is willing to state the strengths of his or her opinion in their testimony. Remember, it is the expert and not the attorney who decides what testimony will be given.

The intervals between meetings, report writing and trial should be spent in productive preparation for court. Through the discovery process the expert should be provided with the opposing expert's findings and credentials. Additional time should be spent collecting, reviewing and cataloging supporting and conflicting scientific literature apropos to the case. Prior to trial, the expert should develop the visual aids and exhibits that will be most useful in helping the judge or jury to understand and accept the relevant information. This may include professionally developed poster displays, charts, slides, videotapes, models or casts, radiographs, PowerPoint presentations, etc.

Trial exhibits should succinctly and directly demonstrate and support the expert's verbal opinion in a given case. Although these exemplars may be used by the expert to supplement their verbal testimony they should also be designed for the jury to reference and assess during its deliberative process. As with their verbal testimony, the expert should design supplemental visual trial aides that are objective, unbiased, non-inflammatory and truthful in their presentation. A variety of potential trial exhibits are listed and issues regarding their preparation and presentation are discussed:

Television Video Tapes

Case law supporting admission of this type of evidence is based on the first case in which this occurred (U.S. v. Martin). Video tapes permit the expert to demonstrate comparisons and observations that were made during trial preparation. The court may still require the expert to produce the casts, photographs and other analytical materials depicted on the videos. The methods used for comparison or the particular technique employed in the video may also have to be demonstrated by the expert before the jury or judge.

Enhanced Photographs

Procedures exist that can alter the photographic or computer generated color of a bite mark pattern to intensify specific points for effect. Other techniques are available to create an image of a radiograph that transposes and highlights dark and light areas. How is such material introduced as evidence to insure that it has not been adulterated in such a manner that it is no longer considered probative? Because this is often a point of contention this material is often subjected to intense questioning by the legal adversary. The expert employing these techniques must be certain that they can explain how these special procedures were accomplished and what effect if any they may have on the value of the evidence.

Easel Displays

Not all forensic dental experts have access to sophisticated audiovisual aides for the presentation of evidence at trial. Nor do all forensic dental experts possess the computer skills required to prepare this type of courtroom presentation. Thus, the use of easel displays in which photographs or diagrams are attached to poster boards or display frames is also considered an acceptable venue in the presentation of evidence. These displays may vary in size and are often designed to be folded. A caveat concerning this type of evidence relates to the fact that it can be cumbersome and by necessity large.

If the trial is to be in a local community it may be transported in one's automobile. If however, travel plans for trial involve flying or other means of transportation this type of display may require special arrangements for transporting, storage and safety. It is advisable to display trial information on frames measuring no greater than 36 inches by 24 inches. These displays can be stored in an airplane's overhead luggage compartment or if properly packaged, processed as checked baggage. One or more of these displays can be utilized to illustrate the expert's points at trial.

When creating easel displays in identification cases, radiographs may be utilized as negatives to produce substantial photographic enlargements which are then mounted on display boards. By employing rubber cement to attach the images surface blemishes or blisters are eliminated. The antemortem photograph is then placed above the post mortem photograph and self adhering narrow tapes are used to indicate comparable details. All of these materials are obtainable from graphic art supply stores.

An alternative method of comparing details is accomplished by appending numbers to the visual displays. This method is a little more complex to create but is just as easy for members of the jury to follow. Number labeling is easily accomplished by obtaining self-adhering figures from a graphic art supply outlet. Inexpensive tape printing devices are also a convenient tool employed to generate numbers and letters for display.

In bite mark cases exhibits may include the actual casts, tracings and bite mark photographs, impressions of dental incisal edges of the casts, SEM photomicrographs and photographs of the casts. Determination to use any or all of these techniques or others ultimately rests with the forensic dental expert. Exhibits may be constructed with the dental casts, a variety of test bites and the bite mark photographs. Other variations may include photographs of the alleged biter's teeth related to test bites in various materials and to the bite mark itself.

Slide and/or PowerPoint Presentations

Although these can be highly effective, the difficulty with this type of demonstration is associated with its use by the jury during its deliberation. Jurors involved in the deliberative phase of the decision process do not have the benefit of an attending expert to re-explain the details of the presentation during their review of the evidence. This problem can be circumvented by creating slide and PowerPoint presentations that are titled, well documented and can easily be understood by a lay jury. The PowerPoint program also permits the inclusion of lines, arrows and text boxes to facilitate the identification of comparable details to the untrained juror's eye.

Overhead Projection Presentations

Presentation of overhead projections is associated with some of the same difficulties as slide and PowerPoint projections because the expert is unavailable for further demonstrations during jury deliberations.

Bite Mark Demonstrations

Occasionally, the courts will allow the expert or court officers to demonstrate the position of the alleged biter to the victim or object bitten. Such demonstrations can also be illustrated through the use of cameras or camcorders prior to trial.

The expert should discuss with their attorney the courtroom aids that have been prepared and determine what will be used in court. Such conferences may clarify issues concerning what the court may accept or rule to be inadmissible evidence. Some exhibits may be excluded upon objection by the opposing attorney after the motion is sustained by the presiding judge. Despite all pre-trial preparation the expert must be prepared to accept such setbacks.

While only the expert can determine a conclusion, the attorney is in charge of running the case. Show and tell presentation is very effective testimony and is easily remembered by the jury. Therefore, in addition to determining how the physical evidence will be presented, the expert should learn how the attorney intends to elicit the expert's views. Attorneys will occasionally ask an expert to describe the case in its entirety, and will want the expert to testify in narrative form. In this case, the bulk of the pretrial preparation falls to the expert. More commonly, the attorney intends to elicit the information in question-answer format. With the question-answer format it becomes even more important to educate the attorney about the expert's findings, so that appropriate questions will be asked.

The expert must be thoroughly familiar with all relevant facts of the case including any important dates such as the dates of the murder and discovery of the body, etc. Familiarity with any relevant autopsy findings is mandatory and would include information such as whether a bite mark injury showed inflammatory changes, whether the pathologist's measurement of the bite mark differs from the measurement made by the odontologist, etc. The expert should be thoroughly familiar with their own studies in the case so this material can be presented in an organized and convincing manner.

In a complex case, it is desirable to outline the above material for ready reference in the courtroom. However, care should be taken that any notes brought into the courtroom are accurate, as opposing counsel may request the right to examine and copy these notes. The expert may be contacted by the attorney for the adverse side. There is no legal obligation to speak or meet. However, a refusal to meet might be brought up in trial and used to portray the expert as a biased partisan, rather than an impartial expert. Consequently, it may be wise to agree to meet with the opposing attorney under controlled circumstances. This should include the presence of a witness, to assure that any statements made will not be misquoted later.

The Trial

Once the trial date arrives the expert witness should be well rested and have reviewed all materials and reports. An excellent report is worthless if court appearance and delivery are mediocre or poor. Whether it is the first trial for the forensic dental expert or they are a seasoned veteran expert witness, they should remember that they enter the court as a highly trained professional with a defined task to perform in the judicial process. They will have more knowledge about the subject at hand than others in the courtroom and this awareness should prepare them for the thought provoking questions anticipated from the opposition attorneys in the case. In general, with attention to the previously discussed proper pre-trial preparation the process of testifying as an expert should not be difficult and should be viewed as a challenge, not an obstacle. However, even with appropriate pre-trial preparation, testimony may at times still be difficult and is dependant on the experience level of the expert and opposing counsel as well as the complexity of the case.

Qualifying the Expert Witness

The expert will be called and asked to step forward when the court is ready for testimony. Before taking the witness stand they will be asked to raise their right hand and swear that they will tell the truth in the matter before the court. After saying, "I do," the expert will be seated in the witness stand and asked to state and spell their name. The attorney calling the witness then begins to qualify them as an expert by following certain legal formalisms before their testimony is accepted by the court.

Primarily, they must establish to the judge's satisfaction that the witness has the proper forensic dental qualifications to be considered an expert in this field.

The first question usually asked is, "What is your occupation?" This is generally followed by a series of questions concerning the witness' education, training related to forensic odontology and experience in this discipline. The attorney may also inquire about the witness' teaching experience and scientific articles written. Previous experiences in being qualified to testify as an expert witness in various jurisdictions will also be brought forth. The attorney may elicit this information by asking the witness to provide a narrative description of training and experience or may bring out the information through a series of questions.

The opposing counsel may request to stipulate that the witness is qualified. This is done when the witness is "clearly qualified and opposing counsel would prefer that the jury not dwell on the witness' background and experience." If the opposing attorney does not stipulate to their qualifications the expert witness must describe his or her background, practice, or academic experience and any other training or experience that is relevant to the case. After hearing the witness' qualifications the opposing attorney may also elect to challenge the witness' right to testify as an expert. The odontologist should not be rattled if their credentials are challenged. If the expert lacks experience they must admit this if questioned. However, they may also emphasize the amount and quality of training they have received.

The opposing attorney in the case will have vetted the dental expert as part of their pretrial preparation by conducting a thorough background check. Information obtained may reveal sensitive issues related to the forensic dental expert's personal and/or professional life which could be used to discredit them. If the attorney who has hired the expert is made aware of these skeletons they can preempt any damage by direct questioning that will permit the expert to explain each sensitive issue to the jury. These may include, but are not limited to the following:

-How did you get involved in this case?

-Do you advertise your services and fees in legal journals looking to make huge sums of money?

-How much are you being paid for your testimony? Remember, that the expert is not paid for testimony. As a professional they are remunerated for their time to evaluate and assess the evidence presented and for the assistance and knowledge they bring to the case.

-Are there any potential trouble spots in your background? These may include the disclosure of failing grades in undergraduate or dental school, failed state board licensure examinations, student loan collection problems, divorce, failure to make child support payments, DUI or other convictions, etc.?

General Comments Regarding Testimony

For an expert witness, the foremost qualifications are effective presentation and teaching ability.

The expert witness' attitude should be to help the jury in its search for truth. The expert witness' demeanor should display integrity, dignity, and politeness. To this end, the expert would do well to dress conservatively, to use the terms Sir. Madam or the attorney's name when addressing attorneys for both sides and to say thank you for any small courtesies extended in the courtroom. The expert should be friendly, confident and poised, not arrogant, supercilious, or condescending. In presenting testimony, the expert should use effective body language and speak clearly using non-technical language while avoiding slang and jargon.

The expert is not in court to display erudition but to be understood. The witness should present an opinion fully and accurately without becoming an advocate for either side. Their role is that of a scientist, not a lawyer.

The expert witness should speak to the jury in a distinct, moderately-paced voice that is loud enough to be heard. Racing through the responses may create the embarrassment of having the court reporter request that the witness slow down. Additionally, responding to a question too quickly may not permit the expert's attorney to object to the question if he or she desires. Thus, the expert should develop a response rate time interval that indicates to the jury that they have carefully considered the question and are contemplating an answer. If the response rate is too long it may be perceived that the expert is hiding information, being deceptive or just does not know the answer.

The expert should be conscious of the fact that each word is being recorded and may be resurrected for referral later in the course of the trial, or, in a future trial. As a matter of public record, what the expert says under oath on a witness stand will be obtainable by anyone and perjury is an issue to be avoided at all costs. Because of the serious nature of the work done by forensic odontologists, the expert witness in this discipline must be thoughtful, conscientious and consider all reasonable possibilities in reaching his or her conclusion on a forensic matter in issue.

Having done so, the expert has both the right and the obligation to effectively and persuasively present their conclusion and opinions to the trier of fact in written documents and courtroom testimony. If the opinion of the expert rises to the level of reasonable dental or scientific certainty, the expert should be prepared to define these terms and to vigorously and persuasively present his or her justification for reaching this level of certainty.

When appropriate, the use of equivocal or ambiguous terms such as perhaps, could be, possible, might be, similar to or probably is, should be avoided. These terms do not convey very useful information and may suggest significant uncertainty in the mind of the expert. While this is a true as a general statement, on cross examination experts are often asked intentionally ambiguous questions to elicit apparent confusion or contradiction on their part before the trier of fact. Therefore, this technique of questioning during cross examination should be noted by the expert and responded to accordingly. Unfortunately, the forensic dental expert witness does not have the opportunity to ask questions at trial – they just get to provide the answers.

The expert should not refer to themselves in the third person (we) when describing what they did as an individual. The witness cannot testify regarding the observations of another since this is considered hearsay. If there were coworkers, these individuals must testify as to their own conclusions. If the expert worked with others, they can simply describe their own experiences and speak in the singular.

The witness should respect courtroom protocol. They are not free to leave the witness stand at will. The witness should, for example, address the judge with the request, "May I step down from the witness stand to operate the projector?" Whenever it is graceful to do so, the expert witness should establish eye contact with the jurors and address remarks to them. This may seem awkward because one is normally expected to address the person who asked the question -- the attorney. This problem can be overcome by asking the attorney in advance to phrase key questions by saying something such as "Doctor, would you please tell the jury why you reached that conclusion?"

Direct Examination

Direct examination is the first examination of the witness on the actual merits of the case, as distinguished from the preliminary examination or voir dire, which may occur if the witness' qualifications are challenged. Direct examination is conducted by the attorney for the party that called the witness. As a consequence, it is friendly questioning. The general comments stated previously regarding testimony are applicable. The witness may use appropriate exhibits, as previously arranged with the attorney who called them. However, the opposing attorney will usually examine the exhibits in advance and may object to their use. In this case the judge will decide what the jury will be permitted to see.

On direct examination, unless precluded by state law, the witness should always state their opinions first followed by any relevant explanations. This technique avoids having the expert's opinions excluded on the basis of objections to explanations. Invariably, explanations on direct examination are relatively easy to present after the fact. Without opinions on direct testimony the opposition may be able to move for a directed verdict. The argument for this move would be that the opposing party failed to meet their evidentiary burden of proof.

On cross examination, however, explanations should be stated before opinions. This precludes opposing counsel from terminating the explanations of the expert after getting a favorable answer to an opinion question and erroneously giving the trier of fact the wrong impression concerning the response of the witness. In either event, the expert should be prepared to describe the procedures followed from the receipt of the evidence to completion of work on the case in a step by step fashion providing any dates that are significant.

The expert witness may be called upon to answer the so-called hypothetical question. In this situation the expert must assume that certain facts are true. The expert is then asked to draw a conclusion based on those facts. The expert witness must learn to be sensitive to the reaction of the jury. This is especially true when the expert is giving testimony in narrative form. The expert must particularly sense whether the jury is attentive and seems sympathetic and must be guided accordingly. This is helpful in order to develop the best possible rapport with the trier of fact. In addressing a jury the testimony should be presented in an interesting manner and be informative as well.

Cross Examination

A statement attributed to the eminent forensic anthropologist Dr. William R. Maples is that "the courtroom is not a classroom." In the classroom the instructor never anticipates a

difficult cross examination from their students. Cross examination is the examination of a witness by the party opposed to the side that originally called the witness. Black's Law Dictionary says that a witness is cross examined on the evidence that he has given "...to test its truth, to further develop it or for other purposes." It has also been noted that the objectives of cross examination are to bring out information not elicited on direct examination that is favorable to the other party. Cross examination can also be structured to attempt to destroy the effectiveness of the witness' testimony given on direct examination.

The cross examiner sometimes also attempts to destroy the witness personally. This is done by attempting to show bias, error or incompetence, thereby diminishing or destroying the witness' credibility. Additionally, the cross examining attorney may deliberately try to provoke the witness to anger or otherwise upset their composure. Remember the caveat that an angry witness is a careless witness.

It is crucial for the expert witness to remember that the trial is an adversarial procedure, and that the cross-examining attorney is merely doing a job by representing the client as vigorously as possible. The expert witness must remain calm and composed under any circumstances. In preparation for cross-examination, the expert witness should practice being cross examined and should think about what questions could discredit their direct testimony. This not only helps to prepare for possible questions, it also helps to put the concept of cross examination in its true perspective.

When being questioned, it is always important for the witness to listen carefully and concentrate intently on the question. This is particularly important on cross-examination, since the questioning is likely to be deliberately devious in nature. If the witness did not hear the question, they need to say so, and ask that it be repeated. This also pertains to questions that are not understood by the witness. Not infrequently, the judge may comment that he/she, too, did not understand the question. The expert should be cautious when presented with conflicting testimony that they have provided in previous trials. Remember that the selected words are probably taken out of context. Therefore, the expert witness should not hesitate having a question read if they are not clear about its intent or requesting that an exact statement be presented so there is no misunderstanding about what was actually said. The expert can also state that their opinion has changed since the original testimony because the science has evolved through further evidence based research and case work.

If the witness does not know the answer to a question, they should so state. Guessing is not only unproductive in terms of the search for the truth it is also likely to cause trouble for the witness. By guessing or not having the fortitude to say "no" or "I do not know," the witness may have to defend a position for which there is no firm basis. Even Nobel Prize laureates do not know everything in their field.

On cross-examination the witness is defending their direct testimony. The expert should be very cordial, but firm. Opposing counsel may attempt to misstate or distort the views. The task of the expert witness is to be sure that the true views are made clear without being unnecessarily argumentative. On occasion, the witness may have to wait to be rehabilitated on redirect examination.

The expert witness should be prepared for questions inferring bias, such as, "Isn't it true that you always testify for the prosecution?" If this is not true they should respond accordingly. If true, the expert might wish to point out that although their testimonial record appears to be prosecutorial, they are available to give truthful and impartial testimony for whichever side happens to request their services. Compensation questions might be responded to by stating, "Yes, sir (or madam), and I believe that most of us are compensated for our time." Keep answers to questions brief and to the point, but try to give explanations when necessary to clarify the answers.

Not infrequently on cross examination, the examiner will attempt to get the expert witness to give a simple yes or no answer because an explanation will destroy the point they wish to make. The forensic dental expert should politely stand their ground when the opposing attorney attempts to elicit this type of response to a question. This genre of questions usually can not be answered with either response without qualifying remarks. The opposing attorney can request the judge to instruct the expert witness to, "Answer the question, doctor," Prior to complying the forensic dental expert should state to the judge that, "The question cannot be answered with a yes or no response without some qualifications."

This point is illustrated by the following example. The expert has given the opinion that a particular bite mark was made by the defendant's teeth. The opposing counsel inquires, "Could anyone else have made the bite?" The expert might reply, "Yes, that is possible, but the tooth alignment in this case is so very unusual that such a possibility would be very remote." The attorney may object on the ground that the expert is volunteering information and insists on a yes or no answer. The witness may reply that, "The question has been phrased in such a way that a yes or no would be inaccurate or misleading." Alternatively, the expert may explain that, "I cannot truthfully answer that question yes or no," or "I can only answer that question with an explanation." The judge may permit an explanation. However, if he rules that the question can be answered yes or no, the witness must comply.

In addition to retaining composure if provoked, the expert witness must retain the confidence of the jury by demonstrating that they are secure in that their test results are correct. The expert may be questioned as to whether other tests could have been performed and other conclusions reached. In such cases it would be best to agree that this is possible. However, they should continue by stressing that the tests conducted were appropriate for this problem and their results strongly support the conclusion derived.

Opposing counsel may also suggest the

possibility of error. When pressed, the witness must admit that error is always possible. However, they should continue to show that there is no reason to believe that there is error in the case at hand because several different trials led to the same conclusion. Alternatively, counsel may suggest that the continued testing and trials, (perhaps even after a preliminary conclusion was reached) suggests uncertainty or possibility of error. In this scenario the expert should indicate that, "On the contrary, the scientific method provides for continued checking and rechecking of results to greatly reduce or eliminate the possibility of error."

When asked if the witness is familiar with a particular expert's contributions to the scientific literature in the field, he or she can assume that an effort will be made to show that it contradicts their position. This method of questioning is referred to as the textbook ploy. If the expert is familiar with the work they should reply cautiously. For example, "Yes, although I am generally familiar with the text (or article) I am not necessarily aware of every statement made by the author." When asked if the witness considers the author an expert in the field, they should leave some room to explain their possible disagreement with the challenging expert's views. An appropriate response might be, "Yes, they are one of a rather large number of individuals active in this field." This helps to clarify that the other expert's views are not gospel.

After opposing counsel reads the statement that is intended to destroy the witness' testimony, it is almost always advisable for the expert to request to see the book or article being read. This gives the witness additional time to think and provides the opportunity to improve their understanding of the text's statement. This will also permit the expert to discover the date of the challenging reference since the expert may have subsequently changed their views or the information may be outdated. Importantly, by reading the material in context, the witness may realize that the supporting text upholds the position that their opinion and views are not in opposition to the written material as the cross-examiner espouses. It may show that the author was referring to a different type of situation that is simply not applicable to the matter at hand.

If the expert witness agrees that a particular textbook or article is authoritative, they may have to accept everything the author has included in the text even if it is in opposition to the experts position. In this situation the expert should state that, "Although the text is good, nevertheless, I differ with certain areas which I am prepared to discuss." This tack projects the testifying expert witness to the jury as having knowledge equal to or better than the text in question. Potential problems associated with the textbook ploy could be resolved or circumvented with adequate pretrial preparation, alerting the expert to the fact that their viewpoint may be in disagreement with published authority. They will then have ample time to prepare an explanation for the apparent difference of opinion. No matter their number or their content, the expert witness should not rush through any documents provided for examination while testifying. The individual providing these materials for expert review may ask specific question concerning the documents and the expert should provide an answer that is carefully considered and applicable to the situation.

In summary, the forensic odontologist testifying as an expert witness should be well prepared, professional in appearance and manner, alert but composed, and above all, should remember that the task at hand is to assist the judge or jury in their search for the truth. Finally, to maintain a professional demeanor throughout the process, the expert should not outwardly jump for joy when the judge states, "Doctor, you are excused!"

Malpractice: Professional Liability Issues

Dental malpractice cases have become a major concern for all practicing dentists whether they are in general or specialty practice. Often forensic dentists are called upon to review malpractice cases by defense and plaintiff attorneys because of their experience in evaluating evidence and providing expert testimony in deposition and courtroom settings important to the civil trial attorney. A dental expert reviewing a malpractice case should be well versed in the scientific literature related to the issue at hand. Medical and dental texts, professional and scientific journals and the respective state's Dental Practice Act are research resources for dental experts retained by both defense and plaintiff attorneys.

Legal Background

The law is acknowledged as a set of rules of conduct established and enforced by a sovereign authority. It can be divided into the following subdivisions:

- Criminal Law is the law of crimes and their punishment. The citizens in a society (the public) bring suits in criminal court through a district attorney (in South Carolina a solicitor.)

- Civil Law is the law of the private rights of citizens. It is also the law established by a nation or state for its own jurisdiction. Suits in civil court are brought by individual entities (citizens, corporations) through private attorneys. Tort and contract law are the two divisions of civil law. Dental malpractice claims are civil cases under tort law.

- A tort: is a wrongful act or injury with or without force that one person may do to another individual or their property for which a civil action may be imposed. A tort does not involve a breach of contract. To support a tort claim the following must be met:

- A legal duty is owed by someone to another

- The duty has been breached by the accused

- There was damage or harm (not necessarily a physical injury) to the accuser which was caused proximately by the accused individual's breach of duty.

In matters of confidentiality, the patient's right to privacy is breached by a dentist who unreasonably and seriously interferes with the patient's interest in not having their affairs known to others or their likeness exhibited to the public Therefore, the dentist would be liable to the patient in situations in which confidentiality is compromised (refer to HIPAA in this chapter) .

In order to meet the proximate cause test an injury must occur in a natural continuous sequence, unbroken by any efficient intervening cause, producing an injury. Thus, without the proximate cause the injury would not have occurred. Legal liability does not result solely from a negligent or otherwise wrongful act. The negligent or wrongful act must have been the proximate cause of the injury for which the plaintiff seeks redress by the way of damages. Negligence and proximate cause are issues of fact which must be proven to the trier of fact by the plaintiff's side.

The proximate cause of the injury can best be determined by reviewing the patient's history, records, radiographs, diagnostic casts and photographs and performing a literature review of similar cases. Although the treatment rendered by the dentist may indeed be the proximate cause of the injury to the patient, in certain situations it does not necessarily imply that the test for proving negligence has been satisfied. For instance, a mandibular third molar extraction resulting in a trigeminal nerve, Division 3 paresthesia may be an expected result if it were a difficult extraction. If the patient were so advised under informed consent, no accusations of negligence on the part of the dentist could be brought by the patient.

There is a special consideration under tort law in which a situation or phenomenon is so probative on the issue of negligence that its occurrence is held to present a prima facie case of negligence. The occurrence tells its own tale in this case or, "The thing speaks for itself." The legal term for this situation is res ipsa loquitor, referring to situations in which it is assumed that a person's (patient's) injury was caused by the negligent action of another party (dentist) because the accident was the sort that would not occur unless someone was negligent. Unless counter evidence is produced by the defendant tending to show the absence of negligence the trier of fact is justified in finding the defendant guilty of negligence. Thus, the burden of proof is shifted from the plaintiff to the defendant in a res ipsa loquitor setting.

A component of the legal duty owed by the dentist to the patient is the concept of practicing and providing services within the standard of care established for the profession. The legal definition of standard of care may best be described by the quote from Supreme Court Justice Oliver Wendell Holmes, "What is usually done may be evidence of what ought to be done, but what ought to be done is fixed by a standard of reasonable prudence whether it usually is complied with or not." Therefore, proper use of materials, knowledge of the subject and adequate documentation in the record with radiographs, casts, photographs, etc., are required to defend a case involving the standard of care in dental practice.

A physician or dentist is not an insurer of health. He or she undertakes only for the standard of skill possessed generally by others practicing in the field and for the care which they would give in similar circumstances. This is presumed to be the care of administered by a similar, reasonable, prudent, practitioner under the same or similar circumstances. Thus, when a general dentist performs a specialty procedure (i.e. endodontics, periodontics, orthodontics), they are held to the standard of care of a specialist in that particular field. The health care practitioner must have latitude for reasonable variability in diagnostic, treatment planning and technical skills. Judgments concerning not too obvious or gross errors should be determined according to the prevailing practice of their craft.

At trial, the standard of care for the procedure in question is generally described and presented by expert witnesses and so must the departure from it. Currently in the United States there is a universal standard of care for the nation. Although for practical purposes the standard of care can be considered a national one and the locality rule regarding regional standards of practice no longer applies, in certain states the expert is expected to acquiesce to the legal powers within that state. In North Carolina & Tennessee, for example, there are specific elements that must be met in order to qualify as a standard of care expert according to local or community standards within those states. These specific elements have come about as a result of State Supreme Court decisions and require familiarity with certain demographic statistical data and dental practice norms concerning related areas of practice in those states.

There is a misconception among the public and plaintiff attorneys in particular that the treating dentist is omnipotent and their treatments must always produce good results. Obviously, this is not true or even possible. The dentist is held to only a reasonable standard of care and failure to please the patient is not malpractice. If proper procedures have been performed, but the result is not what was anticipated, that in and of itself is not negligence. For instance, if a third molar is removed with due care and the patient develops a temporomandibular joint disorder, this is not malpractice. If the oral surgeon, however, ignores the problem and does nothing to recommend treatment for the patient or does not institute any treatment for the temporomandibular problem himself, this would be considered below the standard of care.

If a general practitioner performs an endodontic procedure using a rubber dam with proper instrumentation of the canal, proper radiographic documentation and proper filling of the canal with approved materials and failure develops in the tooth, this in and of itself is not malpractice. The plaintiff attorney, when evaluating the case will want to know not only what the proximate cause was, but whether the act in and of itself was negligent or below the standard of care. Then he will want to know what are the damages that occurred to the patient and what are the future costs involved in its correction. With this in mind, a treating dentist should be cognizant of these facts when performing irreversible procedures.

Standard of Care Issues

Periodontics

Failure to diagnose periodontal disease is the leading reason that malpractice suits are brought against practicing general dentists. According to the dental scientific literature and guidelines proposed by the American Academy of Periodontology, periodontal disease is appropriately diagnosed by obtaining a proper patient history and evaluating among other factors, the patient's nutritional status, results of clinical examination, radiographs, sulcus depth probings, occlusal analysis and tooth mobility testing. All test results should be documented in the treating doctor's charts and records.

If a defendant dentist does not perform the proper tests to diagnose periodontal disease, the deviation from the standard of care and resultant misdiagnosis will lead to the dentist's failure to prevail in a malpractice case. The fact that a defendant dentist may state that certain tests were performed but not recorded will also fail to meet the standard of care parameters established by the dental profession.

Endodontics

The placement of a rubber dam is required for all endodontic procedures in which files are placed into the pulp chambers of a tooth. Although this is the standard of care relative to this procedure, it is not universally employed by general dental practitioners performing endodontic therapy. Unfortunately, this is true despite the required use of rubber dam material in dental schools throughout the United States and for procedures indicating competency in clinical endodontics on state licensing examinations. In cases in which a dentist performed an endodontic procedure without a rubber dam and the patient swallowed an instrument, it is extremely difficult to defend the dentist in a malpractice action.

Additionally, in endodontic cases treatment radiographs in which working lengths are determined may not be retained by the dentist. This practice is discouraged although in and of itself it does not constitute malpractice. By not retaining working radiographs in the patient's record, the dentist is certainly more vulnerable to claims of negligence and less defensible than if the working measurement radiographs were retained.

In the United States, the use of a material or technique should be avoided if it does not comply with the standard of care approved by the American Dental Association (ADA) and/or the American Academy of Endodontics (AAE) in performing endodontic therapy. This is especially true of the N2 or Sargenti technique. Although used by approximately one third of the general dental community this technique is not within the endodontic standard of care boundaries and is an invitation for malpractice disaster. Paraformaldehyde is used within the dental pulp chamber and canals in this technique. This is a non-approved substance by the ADA and is considered a toxic chemical and carcinogen. By statute in the State of Florida and other jurisdictions the use of the N2 material in performing endodontics falls below the standard of care.

Oral and Maxillofacial Surgery

Malpractice cases involving oral and maxillofacial surgical miss-events are documented in the dental and legal literature. Publications by the American Association of Oral and Maxillofacial Surgeons (AAOMS) and the ADA are excellent sources for reviewing exodontia, temporomandibular joint dysfunction and fracture reduction cases that have resulted in malpractice litigation. Failure to diagnose and/or misdiagnosis associated with cancer of oral hard and soft tissues is also well documented and can result in inappropriate observation or treatment that can seriously effect the patient's long term prognosis. Early detection of oral and paraoral lesions, regardless of whether they are malignant, should be documented in the record and the patient so advised.

Chronic complaints of swelling, sores that do not heal or irritation areas should not be overlooked by the general dentist or specialist. Regardless of the patient's presenting symptoms or chief complaint a full mouth examination of every patient is warranted to preclude the misadventure of failing to diagnose a cancer or other significant lesion. If a diagnosis is not obvious, the patient should be referred for a second opinion with a specialist in oral and maxillofacial pathology, oral medicine and/or oral and maxillofacial surgery. Copies of all correspondence including biopsy reports and results of clinical laboratory and radiographic studies performed by the specialist should be retained in the general dentist's record for that patient.

Some general dentists and many surgical and pediatric dental specialists perform their services while administering general anesthesia to the patient. Although the general dentist or specialist is not an anesthesiologist general anesthesia performed in a dental office exposes the practitioner to the same standard of care requirements provided by the anesthesiologist in a hospital.

Temporomandibular Joint Dysfunction

Resources for information concerning temporomandibular joint disorders may be found through the ADA, the American Equilibration Society, the American Society of Cranio-Mandibular Disorders and the International College of Cranio-Mandibular Orthopedics. An act of iatrogenic negligence or the result of a personal injury to the patient culminating in temporomandibular joint dysfunction must be documented completely by the reviewing expert. Certain questions are relevant in the review of TMJ disorders. These may include but are not limited to the following:

- What is the relationship of the injury to the complaints of the patient? Did the injury result in the complaints of the patient?

- Was the injury (automobile accident, sports injury, altercation) the proximate cause of the plaintiff's complaint?

- Was the treatment performed by the defendant dentist the proximate cause of the plaintiff's complaint?

Malpractice

Breaches of the previous principles concerning tort law result in dental malpractice cases. Unfortunately, the increase in this type of litigation has become a major concern for all dentists whether they are in general or specialty practice. Because of their experience in evaluating evidence and providing expert testimony in deposition and in courtroom settings, forensic dentists are often called upon to review malpractice cases by civil trial attorneys representing defendants or plaintiffs. A forensic dentist usually has expertise in the preparation of visual aids and courtroom displays that will assist the attorney as well as the trier of fact in understanding the technical evidence in the case. Dental malpractice cases can be challenging and as in those forensic cases which involve personal injury, bite mark or identification evidence; professionalism, honesty and truth are paramount components of the forensic expert's testimony.

Due diligence should be followed in evaluating evidence in dental malpractice cases. Evidence review of the defendant dentist's correspondence (including letters, messages), records, charts, radiographs, casts, laboratory and drug prescriptions, hospital records and responses to interrogatories and depositions are crucial to the proper evaluation of the case. Statements made by subsequent treating dentists and specialists related to the patient's care by the defendant dentist are vital to the overall outcome of an alleged malpractice case. The more data provided to the expert witness the better they will be able to develop the interrelationships among the components of the evidentiary materials and render an accurate and truthful opinion.

Radiographs are especially important components of the objective evidence concerning the maintenance of standard of care procedures and thus, the competence of the practitioner. Failure to take and/or maintain radiographs prior to the removal of a third molar or other oral surgical or periodontal surgical procedure may prove to be the key to the plaintiff's success in bringing a malpractice claim upon a defendant dentist.

Radiographs that inadequately provide proper landmarks for the placement of implants are also grounds for a successful malpractice verdict on the plaintiff's behalf.

Well maintained, accurate dental records are legal documents and among the most important aspects of the dental practice. Other factors related to good dental practice that are of equal importance to properly documented and maintained records would certainly include technical competence, good doctor/patient communication, ethical practice and integrity. The patient records of a dental practice are the property of the dentist or practice if it is incorporated (LLC, Ltd., PC). Although these principles are well established there are instances where a defendant dentist has altered their records in an attempt to provide a better defense for their position in a malpractice case. Such self-serving altered records can prove to be extremely damaging to the defendant dentist when discovered through review of the evidence in the case. Altered records are considered fraud in the courts and will negate the statute of limitations of the case. The defendant dentist may also be put at risk for punitive as well as compensatory damages when records are fraudulently altered.

Additionally, fraudulent dental records may result in termination of the defendant dentist's malpractice insurance coverage and place them at risk for criminal charges if statements given in deposition under oath are based on the altered records. The altering of one's dental records ultimately exposes the dentist to criminal actions for perjury beyond the original civil malpractice action.

Malpractice insurance carriers will not defend a dentist in a case resulting from the dentist's perjured testimony. Therefore, it is often the responsibility of the examining forensic dental expert to review the evidence properly and advise the defense or plaintiff attorney concerning the expert's opinion relative to the authenticity of the records. Access to original records is most import when attempting to assess and evaluate their authenticity. Although the forensic dentist is not a forensic document expert, access to such experts and referral of any questionable records for proper evaluation is highly recommended.

The lost record may be just as damaging to the defendant dentist's position as the altered record. Information that is missing from a patient's record is presumed to never have occurred and if "it never happened" this may raise doubts concerning the integrity and professionalism of the defendant dentist. The burden of proof indicating that a negligence situation has occurred rests with the plaintiff (patient). If crucial records are not in the defendant dentist's files then the position or charge of the plaintiff is assumed to be true. Civil case law is replete with examples of the damage inflicted upon a defendant dentist's position at trial because they could not produce a record in question.

For example, the proof of a properly endodontically filled root canal must be supported radiographically. Radiographs can objectively document the overextension of a file, failure to use a rubber dam, and/or perforation of a canal. The plaintiff may allege that a rubber dam was not placed during the endodontic procedure or there was an iatrogenic overextension of a file. If the defendant dentist's supporting radiographic evidence, indicating that a rubber dam was employed or no overextension of a file was documented, is lost or missing from the record it will be assumed that the plaintiff's charge is true. Thus, no rubber dam was used or the overextended file was the proximate cause of the plaintiff's chronic sinusitis.

Similarly, the patient's informed consent signed and recorded prior to a surgical procedure that cannot be located by the defendant dentist forces the court to unfortunately assume that the patient was never properly informed of the risks and/or alternatives to the surgical procedure. Additional arguments in this regard can be made relative to documenting and maintaining diagnostic casts, treatment plans, photographs, radiographs, etc., since any and all may be crucial to the defense of a malpractice case.

Plaintiff Review

When reviewing a case on behalf of a plaintiff the dental expert should provide the plaintiff's attorney with a disclaimer statement. This should indicate the following information, "My opinion in this case is based upon my review and analysis of the following:

- The records provided to me by (plaintiff's attorney's name)

- The history statement of (plaintiff name)

- My clinical examination of (plaintiff name).

This opinion is subject to modification or change should further records or information be made available."

The expert witness' evaluation of the evidence in a malpractice case will initially be provided to the retaining attorney as a verbal opinion regarding the merits of the case. If the opinion is in favor of the defendant doctor and the dental expert is retained by the attorney representing the defendant, the defendant's malpractice insurance adjuster or defense attorney will require the submission of an opinion letter concerning the expert's findings. This letter should be drafted very carefully because it may be discoverable and used later in the process of the suit.

If, however, the dental expert is retained by the plaintiff's attorney and his or her opinion is favorable for that side, the expert may be asked to provide an opinion letter. This letter should be very brief. It should not contain extraneous details nor be drafted as a narrative report. In some states the opinion letter is forwarded to the insurance company. In this situation the plaintiff's attorney will often request that the opinion letter contain extensively detailed information concerning damages, proximate cause and future costs of correction of the injury. In other scenarios involving cases to be litigated the plaintiff's attorney will request that a notarized affidavit containing the expert's opinion be submitted. The affidavit provides the attorney, whether a defense or plaintiff

with a sworn statement by the expert witness concerning their opinion in the case.

The opinion letter or affidavit basically states the following:

- Name of the reviewing doctor

- Credentials of the reviewing doctor

- Material that was reviewed and germane to the case

- The defendant's name

- Opinion of the expert concerning what procedures were performed below the standard of care.

The opinion letter generated by the plaintiff's expert is discoverable and can be reviewed by the defendant, their attorney and expert witness. The defendant dentist, in turn, will be queried by the plaintiff's attorney. These questions are referred to as interrogatories and responses to them in many cases, requires legal opinion. Most interrogatories are answered by the defendant's attorney in a very nonspecific manner. Response to interrogatories may be used in later court testimony for impeachment of the defendant dentist. It is highly recommended that a consultation be held with the defendant dentist, the defendant's expert witness and the defense attorney in order to properly answer the interrogatories.

Often, when an opinion letter provided by a plaintiff's attorney is not favorable to the plaintiff's case it is considered a work product of that attorney and is not discoverable. Additionally, when a dental expert retained by a plaintiff's attorney has an opinion that is unfavorable to the plaintiff's case and reveals this information to the defendant's dental expert it is considered unethical and a violation of patient/attorney privilege. The expert witness under these circumstances may be liable for damages by the plaintiff.

There are two principles under which expert witnesses, fact witnesses, treating doctors, relatives, etc. are deposed. By taking a witness' deposition an attorney has the opportunity to reveal facts and opinions that will be at issue during the trial prior to the time of trial. Additionally, statements made during a deposition can be used for future impeachment of a witness. The process of impeachment involves the disputation, disparagement, denial or contradiction of the testimony provided during the deposition with the intent of casting doubt upon the witness' statements.

The discovery, deposition and impeachment process involving the dental expert witness in a malpractice case is crucial to both defendant and plaintiff. It cannot be emphasized enough that preparation by the expert witness prior to being deposed is crucial. Having knowledge of the facts in the case, (delete –having) well organized records and documents and reviewing and abstracting previous depositions are important preparatory considerations that will insure the accuracy of the dental expert's testimony.

In the interest to all parties concerned in a malpractice civil litigation, the expert witness' testimony and opinions which are elicited under oath in the deposition can only be accurate when the witness has full knowledge of the facts in the case. As in criminal cases, the adversarial attorneys in civil malpractice case are interested in exposing conflicting statements identified in the various experts' opinion letters, interrogatories and dental records at the time of the deposition. The deposition is considered sworn testimony and if inaccurate or fraudulent, the testimony exposes the respondent to criminal perjury charges. Thus, depositions are excellent devices for attorneys to use at trial to discredit opposing witnesses.. The deposition is usually taken months, even years, prior to trial testimony and then will be referred to in detail during cross examination of the expert witness.

An expert witness who provides forthright, truthful testimony at a deposition will not have a problem with conflicting testimony during cross examination at trial even if this occurs

months or years after the deposition. Most dental malpractice cases are dismissed with a summary judgment prior to trial or are settled through mediation or other means. Settlements occur mainly if the evidence is overwhelmingly in favor of the plaintiff. Summary judgments are issued by the judge when the plaintiff is unable to produce an expert witness or if the facts of the case are overwhelmingly in favor of the defendant dentist.

Additionally, settlements may be handled through mediation in which both parties present their cases to each other and to a mediator. Expert witnesses are not routinely called upon to testify at mediation hearings. Mediation is handled through the respective attorneys in the case and an (delete – compromise) agreement may be reached through compromise. This prevents trial testimony and the possibility of a jury attempting to resolve the issues at hand that is considered aberrant by either of the adversaries. Additionally, mediation saves considerable sums in attorney and expert witness fees.

Personal Injury Cases

There has been a decline in personal injuries involving the face, mouth and oral structures since the enactment of automobile seat belt legislation in many states. Despite this positive trend, other traumatic situations involving facial, oral and paraoral structures continue to occur. These may be associated with sports related injuries, motorcycle accidents, workplace or school yard incidents, intoxication and road rage or gang related incidents.

Dentists untrained in forensic odontology may not provide the requesting attorney with a personal injury report that satisfies their requirements for assessment of oral and paraoral problems associated with the proximate causative trauma. The attorney and eventually the trier of fact must be provided with information that will permit them to understand the nature and severity of the client's injuries. Following are several concerns that an attorney may request a dentist to address prior to initiating negotiations for a settlement in a personal injury case or a motion to file a personal injury claim in a court of law:

- Is there evidence of permanent damage to the teeth or oral structures?

- Will the victim suffer a disability from the traumatic event such as temporomandibular joint dysfunction (TMD), ankylosis or permanent scarring?

- Was there pain, swelling and/or facial discoloration following the injury?

- What medicines were prescribed for pain and/or infection? Is the patient still taking these or other drugs and what is their potential need to be medicated indefinitely?

- Will the teeth involved require immediate restoration as well as future restoration?

- What is the life expectancy of the needed dental restorations? Insurance companies will usually allow replacements of most fixed prostheses and removable partial or full dentures at least every five to ten years. The number of replacements needed during the patient's life time is a vital calculation that insurance companies determine from actuarial data.

- What were the results of the initial pulp tests following the injuries? How long has it been since the teeth were last tested? Were there any differences in the results?

If the reporting dentist is not the dentist of record they must obtain copies of the treating dentist's pre-trauma radiographs and compare them with those taken since the traumatic event. This will help to establish the status of the injured patient's teeth prior to the accident. The report should include statements concerning the patient's periodontal health, history of compliance through recall appointments and quality of personal oral hygiene maintenance prior to the traumatic incident. Treatment performed subsequent to the injury must be documented as well as identification of loose teeth and bony fractures. Resulting stabilization and potential requirement for surgical procedures should be listed. Information in the report should also include long term treatment plan concepts for endodontics, orthodontics, dental prosthetic reconstruction, physical therapy and TMJ and/or orthopedic therapy. Cosmetic procedures needed to reconstruct the patient's appearance must be documented and supported by photographs taken before and after the traumatic event.

Thus, it is important to include all services required for the patient's future care. The following hypothetical example is a plan for a twelve year old female who suffered dental trauma (fracture) to the maxillary central incisors after sustaining injuries in an automobile/pedestrian accident while walking home from school.

- Triage and assessment with pulp testing and radiographs

- Stabilization of mobile teeth

- Pulp capping

- Temporary crowns

- Recall visits and reevaluation with further testing and radiographs until age 18-20

- Permanent esthetic crowns or porcelain restorations.

The personal injury report should include cost estimates for all anticipated future dental care. This should take into consideration that the final permanent restorations may have to be replaced during the patient's actuarial life expectancy of 73 years. It is likely that the requesting attorney may request a second opinion and the patient may be referred accordingly. Insurance companies generally expect that when the reporting dentist is the doctor of record this relationship with the patient will likely result in a higher estimate of dollar damages. Whenever possible the reporting dentist should provide at least three alternative treatment plans appropriate for the patient's life expectancy. Include estimates for each plan based on current prevailing fee schedules. It should be noted in the report that these fees and estimates are not adjusted for inflation.

Color photographs should be obtained when indicated. Pictures taken soon after the time of the accident will always be appreciated by the patient's attorney. As in other photographic evidence, close up and orientation exposures and those with and without scales should be considered. The report should be neatly typed, free of spelling and grammatical errors and presented on the (delete –doctor's) letterhead stationery of the doctor. Mounted copies of all radiographs and photographs should me labeled with the patient's demographic information, doctor's name and demographic information and date of exposure. The final report should be dated and signed.

A detailed time sheet outlining the nature and extent of the reporting dentist's efforts should be included with the report. For billing purposes, an hour is generally subdivided into tenths. The fee for service statement should be included on a separate page. The reporting dentists may have gotten a written agreement with the patient's attorney that includes their remuneration in the case being given a lien status, payable from the (delete -patient's) damage award to the patient. In this situation the dentist should remind the attorney to protect their claim at the end of litigation or settlement. Ideally, this sort of fee arrangement should be avoided because any indication that the compensation of the expert is contingent on an award to the plaintiff in a legal proceeding smacks of a conflict of interest and should be discouraged at all costs. This type of arrangement could be perceived as a conflict of interest and is unwise from a strategic point of view regardless of any ethical considerations.

Ethical Considerations

Ethical actions involve or express societal or religious moral approval or disapproval and are also related to conformation with accepted professional standards of conduct or duties associated with precepts of moral conduct, motive or character. The professional literature is sparse concerning the field of expert witness ethics and professionalism. It is common, however, in modern litigation to call individuals from a vast array of professions to testify as expert witnesses. A survey of California civil jury trials revealed that at least one expert testified in eighty-six percent of all cases involving his area of expertise. Additionally, two opposing experts testified in fifty-seven percent of the trials in this discipline. The question which arises in these situations concerns the ethical actions of the experts who appeared to be professional experts rather than experts who are professionals.

Professional Ethics

When considering the obligations of the expert witness it is necessary to address the interrelated concepts of professional ethics and professionalism. The former typically refers to the distinct, mandatory responsibilities undertaken by individuals in the course of practicing a trade or calling. Breaches of professional ethics may result in discipline by a governing association of the profession, fee forfeiture or other adverse consequences. In contrast, the latter term is often used to identify admirable, model, or ideal conduct that is generally expected within a given profession although not absolutely required.

Professional ethics compel a physician or dentist to maintain a patient's confidences. Violating confidences may result in censure. A sense of professionalism by these healthcare providers implies they are courteous, communicate clearly and are punctual among others. Abandoning these standards may result in a loss of patient confidence or respect. The two concepts are not wholly distinct since both are aspirational and most professionals certainly do not adhere to ethical standards simply as a means of avoiding discipline or liability.

Many professional obligations are identical to those associated with personal ethics or moral standards. Perjury, for example, would commonly be understood as both a moral fault and a violation of professional standards. In many situations, however, professional standards and professional ethics may be quite different from those related to personal ethics. While most citizens believe in their duty to report crimes, attorneys usually must maintain confidences even when their clients have revealed serious criminal behavior. Conversely, physicians, dentists and social workers, among others, are expected to contact authorities in cases of suspected human abuse. The juxtaposition of personal and professional ethics is sometimes referred to as role differentiation because ethical requirements vary according to the role one has assumed.

All expert witnesses are governed by personal ethics, and all must obey the rules of the court in which they appear. There is no single source providing definitive standards for the expert witness' professional ethics. A few organizations have attempted to draft codes of conduct for expert witnesses although none of these guidelines have achieved broad acceptance.

There are certainly ethical actions that should be considered for experts in litigation. Before accepting employment the expert should always ensure that no conflict of interest exists. An expert must obtain instructions from the attorney retaining their services concerning confidentiality and other client concerns. When potential conflicts are identified permission should be sought in writing to consult with prior confidants. There are penalties for consulting or acting as an expert in a conflict of interest situation. These may result in the expert's disqualification from testifying. Additionally, the attorney and expert may be completely disqualified from the case.

The oath that the expert takes prior to testifying is his or her affirmation that their work in the case and their ensuing testimony are based on ethical principles. Other governing ethical guidelines include standards of care in the expert's field, the attorney's canon of ethics and state licensure and professional codes. Legal ethical principles are indirectly applicable to the expert since the latter is an agent of

the retaining attorney. Although breaches of ethical standards by experts may not result in their punishment for infractions, the attorney may be vulnerable in this regard.

Experts may be drawn from virtually any field or calling from aviation to zoology. Their own profession will often have a well developed code of ethics. This is true among such diverse professions as accounting, medicine, law, and dentistry among others. Experts in these disciplines must certainly adhere to the standards of their own respective profession concerning matters such as confidentiality and conflicts of interest. They may even be subject to professional regulation or discipline for their conduct as witnesses.

Other professions are unlicensed or unregulated. A musician or composer may be an expert witness in a copyright infringement case and economists may testify in antitrust or contract law disputes. However, neither profession has promulgated a code of ethics. Thus, there are no generally recognized standards governing the conduct of experts in these disciplines in forensic matters. The same is true for experts in the humanities and social sciences such as demographers, political scientists, penologists, journalists and other who are frequently requested to testify in court. However, the absence of an exacted code of conduct should not imply an absence of content-related professional standards. Academic and industrial scientists, for example, are expected to adhere to strict requirements of objectivity and to follow precise methods of investigation.

The single most important obligation of an expert witness is to approach every question with independence and objectivity. Recall that expert testimony is allowed only if the expert's "specialized knowledge will assist the trier of fact to understand the evidence." This is precisely Rule 702, Federal Rules of Evidence. The expert's opinion, in turn, cannot assist the fact finder's understanding unless that opinion is candidly and frankly based upon the witness' own investigation, research, and understanding. An objective expert views the facts and data dispassionately, without regard to the consequences for the client. An independent expert is not affected by the goals of the party for which they were retained and is not reticent to arrive at an opinion that fails to support the client's legal position.

One of the most important aspects of this concept concerns thee situation in which a treating dentist acts concurrently as an expert for his or her patient who is also a plaintiff in a law suit. As a treating dentist, one's obligation is to act as an advocate for their patients' well being. However, as an expert the obligation of the dentist is to act with independence relative to the truth relative to the facts in a case. These different obligations create at least the appearance of a conflict of interest. Therefore, a treating dentist should not act as an expert in cases involving legal actions on behalf of their patients.

The Attorney's Ethics in Dealing with Experts

Attorneys' ethical obligations are contained in each state's Rules of Professional Conduct or Code of Professional Responsibility. While no specific rule deals directly with attorneys and expert witnesses, some of the American Bar Association Model Rules of Professional Conduct are applicable. By 1993, the Model Rules had been adopted by thirty seven states, the District of Columbia and the Virgin Islands. There are provisions of the model rules which impact upon an attorney's use of expert witnesses. These include:

- Candor Toward the Tribunal

- Special Responsibilities of a Prosecutor

- Responsibilities Regarding Non-lawyer Assistants

- Reporting Professional Misconduct

- Misconduct.

In addition to the above, an attorney is also obligated to follow the following ethical guidelines:

- They shall not fabricate evidence or counsel or assist a witness to testify falsely.

- They shall not offer an inducement to a witness that is prohibited by law.

- They shall not make frivolous discovery requests or intentionally fail to comply with a legally proper discovery request.

- They shall not make false statements of material fact or law to a third person, such as an expert witness.

- They may not promise an expert a fee contingent on the outcome of the case.

- They may not share fees with an expert.

An attorney has been held to have an ethical obligation to pay an expert's fees unless he or she gives an express disclaimer of responsibility. Attorneys have been sanctioned by the bar for abusing an expert witness on cross- examination. A prosecutor was suspended from the practice of law for thirty days for improperly eliciting irrelevant testimony from the defense's expert psychiatric witness. The prosecutor insulted the witness, ignored the court's sustained rulings on defense objections and inserted his personal opinions on psychiatry and the insanity defense into his questioning.

The Expert's Ethical Obligations

Besides the attorney's ethical standards in dealing with experts there are ethical constraints which direct the expert's behavior in court. One must become aware of the expert's ethical obligations under the codes established by certifying bodies or professional associations. For example, members of the AAFS and ABFO are prohibited from making material misrepresentations of their education or of the data upon which their professional opinions are based. If an AAFS member or ABFO diplomate is found to have violated these ethical standards, ethics committees in these organizations may impose sanctions including censure, suspension, or expulsion from the organization.

Some courts have sanctioned experts for their unethical behavior. In Schmidt v. Ford Motor Co. the court banned the plaintiff's accident reconstruction expert from testifying in federal court in Colorado because he had conveyed intentionally misleading information in depositions and informal conversations with a defense expert. The expert also concealed his knowledge from the defendant that one of the plaintiffs had tampered with the evidence.

Because of an expert's important role in successful litigation in the current litigious environment, attorneys actively shop for those experts willing to support their cause even if the expert must be retained based on an exorbitant fee schedule. Today, criticism of expert witnesses is widespread throughout the legal community. One can find and hire an expert to testify on virtually any topic and even simple lawsuits often involve the testimony of an expert witness. As a result, questions regarding the impartiality of expert testimony and concerns about the potential for ethical misconduct often arise.

Absolute Immunity – The Rationale

The concept of witness immunity stemmed from the Old English common law to encourage witnesses to participate in litigation without fear of retaliating lawsuits from unhappy participants. In the case of Briscoe v. Laffue the United States Supreme Court held that trial witnesses are entitled to absolute immunity for their trial testimony. The Court noted that ignoring liability for testimony in a judicial proceeding could have the effect of inducing two types of self-censorship:

"…witnesses might be reluctant to come forward to testify'. And once a witness is on the stand, his testimony might be distorted by the fear of subsequent liability…. A witness who knows that he might be forced to defend a subsequent lawsuit, and perhaps, to pay damages, might be inclined to shade his testimony in favor of the potential plaintiff, to magnify uncertainties, and thus to deprive the finder of fact of candid, objective and undistorted evidence."

Witness immunity has also been held to extend to pretrial statements and opinions offered in deposition testimony and advisory reports prepared in the course of litigation. This is a logical extension to include those items the witness has to prepare leading up to his or her testimony.

Expert witnesses have enjoyed almost universal immunity from liability as a result of their court testimony. Within the last few years, however, this immunity is being eroded to the point that experts should be cautious and dutifully careful in their preparation yet confident when expressing their opinions. As recently as 2000, courts in only eight states had addressed the issue of expert witness immunity. Up to that time, no court had allowed an expert witness to be sued by an adversarial party over testimony proffered. However, lawsuits against friendly experts are increasing.

Expert Witness Immunity Relative to Dental Testimony

A decision by a State Court of Appeals in 2000 upheld the granting of summary disposition to a forensic odontologist retained by a county medical examiner's office who was the defendant in a civil case brought by a plaintiff who had been convicted of rape and murder based on bite mark evidence proffered by the odontologist that was overturned during a second trial. The plaintiff sued the defendant alleging gross negligence on the part of the odontologist in the presentation of the bite mark evidence and the opinion derived from it.

The defendant odontologist had "moved for summary disposition arguing that he was entitled to absolute witness immunity; that, pursuant to the public-duty doctrine, he owed no duty to plaintiff and that plaintiff's claim was barred by the statute of limitations. The circuit court granted the motion, concluding that the public-duty doctrine was applicable and the defendant, therefore, owed plaintiff no duty of care." In arriving at its decision the court reasoned that, "as a government employee, the odontologist was immune from tort liability while engaged in governmental functions if he was acting, or reasonably believed he was acting, within the scope of his authority, unless his conduct amounted to gross negligence that was the proximate cause of the plaintiff's injury or damage."

The Court stated that "the statute specifically authorizes county medical examiners to employ non-licensed physicians to assist in the investigation of deaths if the medical examiner determines that persons with specialized qualifications and knowledge are needed to assist in that investigation. Considering this legislative scheme, we see no reason to limit the analysis... simply to the appointed county medical examiner. To the contrary, the logic.., would apply to any person duly authorized by the examiner to assist in an investigation authorized and, in fact, required by the statute. ... We conclude that the protection afforded a county medical examiner extends to persons employed by the medical examiner to assist in the investigation of a death. The county medical examiner here employed defendant, an odontologist, to assist in the investigation of a crime where the victim had bite marks that might have helped establish identity of the assailant.

Having been authorized by the medical examiner to assist in the investigation because of the special knowledge and experience he brought to the case, the defendant's only duty was to the medical examiner and to the state, and the defendant fulfilled that duty by providing his expert opinion and testimony to aid in the investigation of the offense. Thus, under the medical examiner's statute, defendant owed no duty to plaintiff'."

The Court further stated that no duty was owed to plaintiff for a separate and independent reason as well. "Defendant's role in the investigation was plainly adversarial to plaintiff's interests and defendant's duty as a witness at the preliminary examination was owed to the court, not to plaintiff. We conclude that defendant would have owed plaintiff no duty even if the medical examiner's statute was inapplicable."

Although the Appellate Court affirmed the dismissal of the plaintiff's case it recognized and accepted as true the allegations that the defendant odontologist had crossed the line between prosecution and persecution in the presentation of his testimony and performed his tasks in an incompetent manner. The court sympathized with the plaintiff but concluded that regardless of how badly the defendant performed his investigation and the harm that resulted, the plaintiff's claims were so clearly unenforceable as a matter of law that they could not go to a jury.

The case discussed above concerns expert opinions and testimony expressed on behalf of a government agency. However, other situations may arise where an expert opinion may be provided on behalf of some other entity than a government agency. In this scenario, including civil cases involving malpractice, there may be no existing protection from litigation arising from negligence on the part of the dental expert in their presentation of evidence and the opinion derived from it. Thus, in these types of cases an expert may not have any safeguard from subsequent civil litigation based on their expert testimony.

Principally, the dental malpractice insurance carrier of the expert witness may not provide coverage in the case of litigation arising from a claim related to forensic odontology. Some malpractice carriers consider forensic odontology outside the scope of the clinical practice of dentistry and do not cover the practitioner under the terms of the policy that is issued. Therefore, if a dentist's forensic odontology practice is not specified as being covered when the dentist is retained as a government agent in a criminal case, the dentist should contact the legal agency that has retained them and verify that immunity from litigation is in effect.

Additionally, the dentist who practices forensic odontology should query their malpractice carrier and verify in writing that the malpractice policy covers the clinician when acting as a forensic expert outside the scope of routine clinical practice. Without this written acknowledgement from the malpractice insurer the dental expert may need to purchase a separate policy that does cover issues arising from forensic dental practice.

Thus, the caveat to all who present themselves as experts in the forensic dental discipline is to be cognizant of the former cases and similar situations which have recently arisen. The forensic dental expert must realize that there is the growing potential for legal vulnerability for the odontologist who falls short of complying with ethical and professional standards in the practice of this profession.

A Perspective

There is little doubt that scientific testimony will impress a jury and it is most compelling when ethically and articulately presented by an individual viewed as an expert in his or her discipline. It has been said that "many trials are but a battle among experts." This concept may impart a greater role or credit to the expert witness than they deserve, although some judicial scholars are concerned about the ethics or advocacy displayed by some experts. It has been argued that the only experts who should be permitted the opportunity to testify are those who are called by the court. Indeed, this is the procedure by which experts serve the courts in many European nations. All other individuals placed on the witness stand by either side at trial should be considered advocates or consultants.

Currently, there is substantial disagreement among legal pundits regarding the value of experts. Much of this concern is focused on expert witness' attempts to advocate, present biased evidence or indulge in behaviors that are less than impeccably ethical. The various forensic professional organizations have established ethical rules that influence and act as guideposts for expert witnesses. None, however, have succeeded in eliminating biased testimony among some witnesses or preventing the use of "jukebox experts who sing the tunes for which they are paid." As a result, verdicts and settlements which should be based on the merits of cases are often won by the parties with the ability to create a formable expert witness team.

HIPAA Regulations – Applications to Forensic Odontology

The National Transportation Safety Board (NTSB) Academy in Washington, DC presented a program in 2006 entitled, Mass Fatality Incidents for the Medicolegal Professionals. While all aspects of mass fatality incidents were considered the question of how HIPAA regulations relate to the forensic dentists ability to obtain antemortem dental records for forensic purposes was stressed. Although the HIPAA regulations provide for this necessity most forensic dentists have not actually studied and interpreted the law as it applies to the release of medical and dental records to law enforcement personnel, medical examiners and coroners.

On April 14, 2003, pursuant to the federal Health Improvement, Portability and Accountability Act (HIPAA) of 1986, a set of regulations entitled Standards for Privacy of Individually Identifiable Health Information (the Privacy Rule) became effective in the United States. The regulations are found at 45 CFR Parts 160 and 164 and are listed for review and discussed in the following section.

104th Congress
PUBLIC LAW 104-191
AUG. 21, 1996
HEALTH INSURANCE PORTABILITY AND ACCOUNTABILITY ACT OF 1996 (HIPAA)
http://www.hhs.gov!ocr/regtext.html

Code of Federal Regulations (CFR) 45

Subpart C - Compliance and Enforcement

§164.512 Uses and disclosures for which consent, an authorization, or opportunity to agree or object is not required.

45 CFR 164.512 (g) HIPAA Exception for Law Enforcement

    (f) Standard: Disclosures for law enforcement purposes.

(3) A covered entity may disclose protected health information in response to a law enforcement official's request for such information about an individual who is or is suspected to be a victim of a crime

45 CFR 164.512(g) HIPAA Exemption for Medical Examiners and Coroners

(g) Standard: Uses and disclosures about decedents.

(1) Coroners and medical examiners. A covered entity may disclose protected health information to a coroner or medical examiner for the purpose of identifying a deceased person, determining a cause of death, or other duties as authorized by law. A covered entity that also performs the duties of a coroner or medical examiner may use protected health information for the purposes described in this paragraph.

As a result of the Privacy Rule the use and disclosure of medical information became primarily governed by federal, as opposed to state law. This marked a significant departure from historical practice. Except for a limited set of regulations governing the use and disclosure of information regarding alcohol and drug abuse patients, the federal government had not previously regulated medical information confidentiality; leaving the area almost entirely to state governments.

This section is not intended as a primer or general exposition of the Privacy Rule. Most dental service providers should already have a good working knowledge of the Privacy Rule's application to dental practice. Rather, this discussion specifically addresses the Privacy Rule's applicability to forensic odontologists. It focuses on those provisions of the Rule that govern most of the use and disclosure situations commonly encountered in a forensic odontology practice.

A caution is in order. While the Privacy Rule is comprehensive, it did not sweep away state law.

Rather, the medical information confidentiality laws of the various states continue to apply to the use and disclosure of certain types of medical information. For example, the laws of Nevada impose significantly greater burdens on the use and disclosure of certain types of information than does the Privacy Rule. These include disclosure of information regarding communicable disease, sexually transmitted disease and DNA-testing information. This section does not address or consider specific state laws and forensic odontologists are encouraged to seek additional information concerning their own state's law from local resources.

The pertinent, although perhaps not-so-obvious, entry level questions for the forensic odontologist are, "Does the Privacy Rule apply to forensic odontology practice and is a forensic odontologist a covered entity?" The Privacy Rule applies only to the use and disclosure of protected health information by covered entities. The Rule applies indirectly to the business associates of covered entities. There are three types of covered entities as noted in Section 160.102 of the Rule:

§ 160.102 Applicability.

Except as otherwise provided, the standards, requirements, and implementation specifications adopted under this subchapter apply to the following entities:

- A health plan

- A health care clearinghouse

- A health care provider who transmits any health information in electronic form in connection with a transaction covered by this subchapter

If a forensic odontologist is a covered entity it will be by virtue of the fact that they are a health care provider as defined in the Privacy Rule as:

- Health care provider means a provider of services (as defined in section 1861(u) of the Act, 42 U.S.C. 1395x(u)), a provider of medical or health services (as defined in section 1861(s) of the Act, 42 U.S.C. 1395x(s)), and any other person or organization who furnishes, bills, or is paid for health care in the normal course of business.

The Rule defines health care as follows:

- Health care means care, services, or supplies related to the health of an individual. Health care includes, but is not limited to the following:

  - Preventive, diagnostic, therapeutic, rehabilitative, maintenance or palliative care

  - Counseling, service, assessment, or procedure with respect to the physical or mental condition or functional status of an individual or that affects the structure or function of the body

  - Sale or dispensing of a drug, device, equipment, or other item in accordance with a prescription.

The work of a forensic odontologist covers the following types of tasks:

- Identification of unknown human remains through dental records and assisting at the scene of a mass disaster.

- Age estimations of both living and deceased persons including neo-natal remains.

- Analysis of bite marks found on victims of attack.

- Identification of bite marks in other substances such as wood, leather and foodstuffs.

- Analysis of weapon marks using the principles of bite mark analysis.

- Presentation of bite and weapon mark evidence in court as an expert witness.

- Assistance in building up a picture of lifestyle and diet at an archeological site.

- Assessment of cases of abuse (child, spousal, elder).

- Civil cases involving malpractice.

None of these undertakings appear to comprise "care or services... related to the health of an individual." Forensic odontology does not appear to involve the following:

- Delivery of preventive, diagnostic, therapeutic, rehabilitative, maintenance, or palliative care

- Counseling or provision of a service, assessment, or procedure with respect to the physical or mental condition, or functional status, of an individual or that affects the structure or function of the body.

Thus, it would appear that a forensic odontologist is not a person "who furnishes, bills, or is paid for health care in the normal course of business." Therefore, the forensic odontologist is not a health care provider under the definition used by HIPAA.

Even in the case of a contrary interpretation (i.e., that a forensic odontologist is a health care provider under HIPAA) it does not follow that the forensic odontologist would be a covered entity. This is because a health care provider is only a covered entity when the provider "transmits any health information in electronic form in connection with a HIPAA Transaction. Transaction means the transmission of information between two parties to carry out financial or administrative activities related to health care. The term includes the following types of information transmissions:

- Health care claims or equivalent encounter information

- Health care payment and remittance advice

- Coordination of benefits

- Health care claim status

- Enrollment and un-enrollment in a health plan

- Eligibility for a health plan

- Health plan premium payments

- Referral certification and authorization

- First report of injury

- Health claims attachments.

Transactions under HIPAA refer to those between providers and third party payers in order to obtain payment for health care services. The work of forensic odontology does not lead to such transactions. Therefore, except in unusual circumstances, it is unlikely that HIPAA will apply directly to forensic odontologists.

When a forensic odontologist also conducts an active dental practice, the conduct of that practice will make the odontologist a covered entity under HIPAA. However, if the dental practitioner's forensic odontology practice is sufficiently separated from his or her dental practice the forensic odontology practice could still remain out of the ambit of the Privacy Rule. Preferably, this is accomplished by conducting the operations of the dental practice and the forensic practice out of separate business entities The Privacy Rule allows for other means of separation; notably the Rule's provisions as to hybrid entities and covered components. A forensic odontologist who also conducts an active dental practice should consult counsel and work to maintain Privacy Rule separation between the practices.

Voluntary Observance of the Privacy Rule

Even though a carefully separated forensic odontology practice should not be considered a covered entity subject to the Privacy Rule, forensic odontologists are still well advised to comply with the Privacy Rule's provisions. Most states have enacted laws which grant medical information privacy protection and

confidential status. As noted above, the Privacy Rule did not pre-empt these state laws. They continue to apply to medical information held by health care professionals. Most of these state statutes are not so finely drawn as the Privacy Rule and could be interpreted to apply to medical information held by a forensic odontologist.

Since most health care providers are covered entities, most comply with the Privacy Rule. As a result, the Privacy Rule now establishes the standard of care for the conduct of health care providers with respect to ensuring the confidentiality of medical information. Where a case is brought under a state medical information confidentiality statute against a forensic odontologist alleging the improper use or disclosure of medical information, it is likely that the reviewing court will consider the Privacy Rule's provisions in determining the appropriateness of the odontologist's actions. Thus, uses and disclosures which run afoul of the Privacy Rule could limit the use of the evidence produced by the forensic odontologists or even expose the forensic odontologist to liability.

The Privacy Rule - Key Terms

While this discussion assumes a good working knowledge of the Privacy Rule's application to dental practice, a review of key terms is in order. The Privacy Rule governs the use and disclosure or protected health information (PHI). Generally stated, PHI is any information that is "created or received by a health care provider" which relates to:

- The past, present or future physical or mental health or condition of the subject

- The provision of health care to the subject

- The past, present or future payment for the provision of health care provided to the subject

- Any demographic information, where such information identifies the subject.

Where uses or disclosures of protected health information are permitted, the Privacy Rule requires compliance with the so-called minimum necessary rule. The minimum necessary rule provides for the following application:

- When using or disclosing protected health information or when requesting protected health information from another covered entity a covered entity must make reasonable efforts to limit protected health information to the minimum necessary to accomplish the intended purpose of the use, disclosure, or request.

Application of the minimum necessary rule is not warranted in situations involving use or disclosure required by law. Examples would include response to a court order or disclosure specifically required under a statute (e.g., child abuse reporting).

Coroners and Medical Examiners

With respect to providing PHI to coroners, the Privacy Rule is simple and straight forward. A covered entity may disclose protected health information to a coroner or medical examiner for the purpose of identifying a deceased person, determining a cause of death, or other duties as authorized by law. Thus, PHI may be disclosed to a coroner for the purposes of assisting the coroner in making any investigation or discharging any duty that the coroner is authorized by law or make or discharge.

Law Enforcement Officials

Law enforcement officials may seek information through the use of legal process through subpoenas or court orders. Such requests would be handled as provided below under those headings. Where a request from law enforcement is not accompanied by legal process, PHI may be disclosed only for specific purposes. In all cases, disclosures must be made in compliance with the minimum necessary rule, as well as any other specific limitations noted below:

- Identification or location of a suspect, fugitive, missing person or material witness. For identification and location disclosures, the Privacy Rule limits the PHI that may be disclosed. The information that may be provided to law enforcement for this purpose is the subject's:

- Name and address

- Date and place of birth

- Social Security number

- ABO blood type

- Type of injury

- Date and time of treatment

- Date and time of death

- Distinguishing physical characteristics.

The provider may not disclose PHI relating to DNA, dental records, or typing, samples or analysis of body fluids or tissue.

- Information about a person who is suspected to be a victim of a crime, Any PHI can be disclosed where the subject agrees. Where the subject of the information cannot agree due to incapacity or emergency, PHI may be disclosed to law enforcement if law enforcement represents that:

- Such information is needed to determine whether another person committed a crime and the information will not be used against the subject

- The law enforcement activity would be materially and adversely affected by waiting until the subject is able to agree.

- Information about a deceased subject. PHI can be disclosed if the covered entity suspects the death may have occurred from criminal activity.

- Information necessary to report a crime. Where the crime occurred on the covered entity's premises, PHI may be disclosed. However, if the crime did not occur on the covered entity's premises, PHI may be disclosed only if necessary to alert law enforcement to the:

- Commission and nature of a crime

- Identity, description and location of the perpetrator.

Court Order, Subpoena and Summons

A covered entity may disclose protected health information in compliance with and as limited by the relevant requirements of a:

- Court order or court-ordered warrant

- Subpoena or summons issued by a judicial officer

- Grand jury subpoena.

Where PHI is sought though an administrative request, including an administrative subpoena or summons, a civil or an authorized investigative demand, or similar process, PHI can only be disclosed where the:

- Information sought is relevant and material to a legitimate law enforcement inquiry

- Request is specific and limited in scope to the extent reasonably practicable in light of the purpose for which the information is sought

- De-identified information could not reasonably be used.

Subpoenas from Private Attorneys

A covered entity may disclose PHI "in the course of any judicial or administrative proceeding" in compliance with a court order or a subpoena. Where a court order is received for the release of PHI, HIPAA requires only that the covered entity limit disclosure to information "expressly authorized by such order." However, where a subpoena is not accompanied by "an order of the court or administrative tribunal" PHI may

only be released in thee circumstances:

- Option One/ Notice Given - The covered entity must receive satisfactory assurance from the party seeking the PHI that "reasonable efforts have been made to ensure that [the subject] has been given notice" of the subpoena. In such a case a satisfactory assurance is a written statement from the seeking party and accompanying documentation demonstrating that the:

- Seeking party has made a good faith attempt to provide written notice of the subpoena to the subject (or if the subject's location is unknown, has mailed a notice to the last known address.)

- Notice included sufficient information about the litigation or proceeding to permit the subject to raise an objection to the court or tribunal

- Time to raise objections to the court or administrative tribunal has elapsed, and either;

- No objections were filed

- All objections filed have been resolved by the court or tribunal and the disclosures being sought are consistent with such resolution.

- Option Two/ Qualified Protective Order - The covered entity must receive satisfactory assurance from the party seeking the PHI that "reasonable efforts have been made to secure a qualified protective order". A satisfactory assurance means a written statement from the seeking party and accompanying documentation that demonstrate that:

- The parties to the dispute have agreed to a qualified protective order and have presented it to the court or tribunal

- The seeking party has requested a qualified protective order. A qualified protective order means an order of the court or a stipulation by the parties that:

- Prohibits the parties from using or disclosing the PHI for any purpose other than the litigation or proceeding for which the PHI was subpoenaed

- Requires that the PHI (and all copies made) be returned to the covered entity or destroyed at the end of the litigation or proceeding.

- Option Three/ Covered Entity's Initiative.

- A covered entity may disclose PHI pursuant to a subpoena if the covered entity makes reasonable efforts to provide notice to the subject and allows the subject time sufficient to seek a qualified protective order, as detailed above.

Public Health Agencies

In some cases, the provision of information to public health agencies is required by law (e.g., abuse reporting). The Privacy Rule permits such reporting.

A covered entity may disclose protected health information for the public health activities and purposes described in this paragraph to a public health authority that is authorized by law to collect or receive such information for the purpose of preventing or controlling disease, injury, or disability. This includes, but not limited to, the reporting of disease, injury, vital events such as birth or death and the conduct of public health surveillance, public health investigations, and public health interventions. At the direction of a public health authority, protected health information may also be disclosed to an official of a foreign government agency that is acting in collaboration with a public health authority.

Although it is not a defined term, the government agency responsible for administering the Privacy Rule interprets the phrase authorized by law to mean that a legal basis exists for the activity being conducted by the agency for which the PHI is sought. This is a very broad interpretation. An agency is not required to point to a specific disease or to condition-specific laws to demonstrate authorization for the collection of information.

Disaster Assistance

Covered entities are permitted to use or disclose protected health information to a "public or private entity authorized by law or by its charter to assist in disaster relief efforts." Such agencies would include FEMA and the Red Cross. The intent of allowing such disclosure is to facilitate coordination with these agencies in the notification of an individual's family member, a personal representative of the individual or another person responsible for the care of the individual concerning the individual's location, general condition, or death. Such notification could include identification of the individual's remains.

Educational Outcomes

By completing this chapter the reader will:

- Build a foundational knowledge of the federal and state rules and regulations governing the admissibility of evidence in the courts of the United States.

- Describe the forensic odontologist's role and responsibilities as an expert witness during pre-trial and trial phases of a case.

- Know the procedures involved in expert witness qualification, direct testimony and cross examination.

- Understand the special considerations to consider in tort cases involving personal injury or malpractice.

- Describe the professional ethical considerations that must be considered by the forensic dental expert and retaining attorney when preparing a case for trial.

- Build a foundational knowledge of the procedures and protocols required to secure patient information in a forensic setting while complying with HIPAA regulations.

- Critically evaluate relevant forensic dental, scientific, legal and legislative literature dealing with significant malpractice, personal injury, bite mark and dental identification cases at trial.

CONTRIBUTORS

C. Michael Bowers DDS, JD, DABFO
Thomas J. David, DDS, DABFO
Edward E. Herschaft, DDS, MA, DABFO
Jeremy A. Herschaft, JD, LLM
Philip J. Levine, DDS, MA, MS, MSM, DABFO
Curtis A. Mertz DDS, DABFO *
Kelly Testolin, JD
Richard A. Rawson, JD
Norman D. Sperber DDS, DABFO
Richard Souviron, DDS, DABFO
Paul G. Stimson DDS, DABFO
Gerald L. Vale, DDS, MDS, JD, DABFO

Deceased *

REFERENCES

The Admissibility of Scientific and Non-Scientific Evidence in Court

Black's Law Dictionary. 8th edition, St. Paul: West. Publishing Co., 2004.

Bowers CM, Introduction to Forensic Odontology. In: Bowers CM and Bell GL (eds): Manual of Forensic Odontology, 3rd ed, Ontario, Canada: Manticore Publishers, 1997: Chapter 4, pp 113-115

Bowers CM, Jurisprudence issues in forensic odontology, in Fixot, ed. The Dental Clinics of North America: Forensic Odontology, Vol. 45:2, April 2001, WB Saunders Company. Philadelphia, pp 399-415

Brief of the Carnegie Commission on Science, Technology, and Government as Amicus Curiae in Support of Neither Party, Daubert v. Merrell Dow Pharmaceuticals, Inc., 113 S. Ct. 2786 (1993) (No. 92-102) citing National Academy of Sciences, Science and Creationism: A View from the National Academy of Sciences 8 (1984)).

Gianelli, P.C., and Imwinkelried, E.J. (1993). Scientific Evidence, Vols. I and II. Michie.

Jasanoff, S. (1995). Science at the Bar: Law, Science and Technology in America. A Twentieth Century Fund Book

Kay, DH, Proof in Law and Science, 32 Jurimetrics J. 313, 315 (1992). See also Thomas S. Kuhn, The Structure of Scientific Revolutions 23 (1970).

Kuhn, TS, The Structure of Scientific Revolutions 23 (1970).
Popper, KR , The Logic of Scientific Discovery, 39-40 (1965).

Mattco Forge, Inc. v. Arthur Young & Co., 5 Cal.App 4th 392, 6 Cal. Rptr.2d 781,(1992).
Id., at 789.

Moenssens, A, Starrs, JE, Henderson, C.E., Inbau, F.E. (1995). Scientific Evidence in Civil and Criminal Cases, page 98, 4th Ed., The Foundation Press, Westbury, N.Y. 1995. Referring to Bruce v. Byrne-Stevens & Assoc. Engineers, Inc., 113 Was.2d 123, 776 P.2d 666 (1989).

Id., Moenssens, AA., et al, pp 91-93.

Id., Moennssens, AA, et al, 95.

Id., Moennssens, AA et al, 95. Referring to (1) Fricker, "Pathologist's Pleads to Turmoil," American Bar association Journal, Mar. 1993, at 24 and (2) Fricker, "Reasonable Doubts," American Bar association Journal, Dec. 1993, 38 and (3)

Moenssens, AA, "Novel Scientific Evidence in Criminal Cases: Some Words of Caution," 84 J.Crim.L. & Criminology 801 (1993).

Monnett CG and Jordan, KM. Scientific Evidence Following Daubert Vs. Merrill Dow: Are Pet Scans Admissible To Establish Traumatic Brain Injury? 2000 www.carolinalaw.com/CM/Articles/article-scientific-evidence.asp

Nesmith, J. (1999) Science on Trial. Atlanta J. Const, June 13, 1999, at D4.

Out of the Blue, American Bar Association Journal, February 1996.

Rules of Evidence

Black, B., Ayala, F.J., and Saffran-Brinks, C. (1994). "Science and Law in the Wake of Daubert: A New Search for Scientific Knowledge." Texas Law Review, Vol. 72, pgs. 715-803.

Brief of the Carnegie Commission on Science, Technology, and Government as Amicus Curiae in Support of Neither Party, Daubert v. Merrell Dow Pharmaceuticals, Inc., 113 S. Ct. 2786 (1993) (No. 92-102) citing National Academy of Sciences, Science and Creationism: A View from the National Academy of Sciences 8 (1984)).

Briscoe v. Laffue,460 US 325, 103 S.Ct 1108,page 333 (March 7, 1984),

Brown, El. Judge. 1999. Eight Gates for Expert Witnesses. 36 Hous. L Rev. 743, 779.

Daubert v. Merrell Dow, (1993) 125 L Ed 2d 469. Reference Manual on Scientrfic Evidence, Federal Judicial Center. Shepards, McGraw Hill, 1994, p. 69.

Daubert v. Merrell Dow Pharmaceuticals, 509 U.S. 579, 113 S.Ct. 2786, 125 L.Ed.2d 469 (1993).

Dobbin SA, and Gatowski SI. A Judge's Deskbook on the Basic Philosophies and Methods of Science, The Judicial Role in Evidentiary Decision-Making, Chapter 2 http://www.unr.edu/bench/chap02.htm

Doyle v. Texas, 159 Tex.Crim 310, 263 S.W.2d 779 (App.1954).

Faigman, D.L. (1995). "The Evidentiary Status of Social Science under Daubert: Is it 'Scientific,' 'Technical,' or 'Other' Knowledge." Psychology, Public Policy, and Law, Vol. 1(4), pgs. 960-979.

Faigman, D.L., Kaye, D.H., Saks, M.J., and Sanders, J. (1997). Modern Scientific Evidence: The Law and Science of Expert Testimony, Vols. I and II. Minnesota: West.

Faigman, D.L., Porter, E., and Saks, M. (1994). "Check Your Crystal Ball at the Courthouse Door Please: Exploring the Past, Understanding the Present, and Worrying About the Future of Scientific Evidence." Cardozo Law Review, Vol. 15, pgs. 1799-1835.

Federal Judicial Center. (1994). Reference Manual on Scientific Evidence. Washington: Government Printing Office. http://www.fjc.gov/EVIDENCE/science/sc_ev_sec.html

Federal Rules of Evidence 702. Testimony by Experts

Fenner, G.M. (1996). "The Daubert Handbook: The Case, Its Essential Dilemma, and Its Progeny." Creighton Law Review, Vol. 29, pg. 939.
Federal Rules of Evidence 702

Frye vs. United States, 293 F. 10 13 (D.C. Cir. 1923).

General Electric Co. et al. v. Joiner 78 F. 3d 524 (11th Cir. 1996), 118 S. Ct. 512 (1997). http://supct.law.cornell.edu/supct/html/96-188.zx.html

Imwinkelried EJ, "The Daubert Decision," Trial, Sept., 1993, pp. 60-65. Los Angeles Daily Journal, Aug. 5, 1994, p. 1.

Imwinkelried EJ, Presentation to American Board of Forensic Odontology, February 12, 1995.

Keierleber, JA and Bohan, TL. Ten years after Daubert: The Status of the States. J Forensic Sci, Sep.2005, Vol 50, No.5
http://judiciary.house.gov/media/pdfs/printers/109th/evid2005.pdf

Kelly v State 824 S.W.2d 568.

McCarthy, LS, Maine Law Review, Volume 46, Number 2, 1994, Life After Daubert v. Merrell Dow: Maine As A Case Law Laboratory for Evidence Rule 702 Without Frye http://www.rudman-winchell.com/mlr46-2.htm

Mealey's Daubert Report: Reviewing the Law and Admissibility of Expert Witness Testimony. http://www.mealeys.com/daubert.html

Monnett CG and Jordan, KM. Scientific Evidence Following Daubert Vs. Merrill Dow: Are Pet Scans Admissible To Establish Traumatic Brain Injury? 2000 www.carolinalaw.com/CM/Articles/article-scientific-evidence.asp

People v. Jordan, 448 N.E.2nd.237 (Ill.App.1983).

People v. Leahy, S03520, quoted in the Los Angeles Daily Journal, Oct. 28, 1994, p. 1.

United States v. Downing, 753 F. 2d 1224 (3d Cir. 1985).

Walker, L. and Monahan, J. (1996). "Daubert and the Reference Manual: An Essay on the Future of Science in Law." Virginia Law Review, Vol. 82, pg. 837.

The Odontologist's Role as an Expert Witness

Foster, W.L. 1897. Expert Testimony: Prevalent Complaints and Proposed Remedies.
11 HA.RVL. REV. 169, 169. Retrieved November 15, 2004, from http://www.lawforensic. com/ethic_and_experts.htm.

Kolczynski, P.J. 1997. How To Be A Successful Expert Witness. Phillip J. Kolczynski Law Corporation. Retrieved November 15, 2004, from http://www.aviationlawcorp.com/content/sussessfulexpert.html

Lubet, J. 1998. Expert Testimony: A Guide for Expert Witnesses and the Lawyers Who Examine Them Chicago: MTA. pp. 169-189.

Starrs, J, "In the Land of Agog, An Allegory for the expert witness," Journal of Forensic Sciences, Vol 30, page 301, 1985.

Vale GL, Introduction to Forensic Odontology. In: Bowers CM and Bell GL (eds): Manual of Forensic Odontology, 3rd ed, Ontario, Canada: Manticore Publishers, 1997: Chapter 4, pp 106-112

Pre-Trial Preparation

United .States v. Martin, 9 M.J. 73 1 (NCMR) 1979

Malpractice: Professional Liability Issues

Medical Experts & Establish Standards of Care in Malpractice Cases excerpted, modified or otherwise prepared by the 'Lectric Law Library from a work by The Medical & Public Health Law Site at http://plague.law.umkc.edu

Personal Injury Cases

Souviron, R, . In: Bowers CM and Bell GL (eds): Manual of Forensic Odontology, 3rd ed, Ontario, Canada: Manticore Publishers, 1997: Chapter 4, pp

Bite Mark Cases

Bowers, C.M., "The Visual Aging of Bite marks, Beyond the Pale of Forensic Odontology," News of the American Board of Forensic Odontology l995;3(1):9- 12.

Daily JC, Bowers CM, Aging of Bite marks: A Literature Review, Manual of Forensic Odontology, 3rd Ed., ASFO, 1995.

Devore, DT, Bite marks for identification? A preliminary report, Med Sci Law, 11(3): 144-5.

DiMaio, D.J., DiMaio, V.J.M., Forensic Pathology. Boca Raton: CRC Press, 1993.

Dorion, R.B.J. 2005. Bitemark Evidence. In B.M. Pitluck, (Ed.), Le2al Liability of an Expert Witness (pp 521, 524- 525). New York: Marcel Dekker.

Dorland 's Illustrated Medical Dictionary, 1 51 27th ed. Philadelphia: Saunders, 1988.

Langlois, N.E.I., Gresham, G.A., "The Ageing of Bruises: A Review and Study of the Colour Changes with Time," Forensic Science International 1991;50:227-38.s

Levine, L.J., "Bite Mark Evidence," In: Cottone, J.A., Standish, S.M., Editors. Outline of Forensic Dentistry. Chicago: Year Book Medical Publishers, 1982; 1 12- 27.

Millington, P.F., "Histological Studies of Skin Carrying Bite Marks," J Forensic Science Society 1974; 14:239-40.

Raekallio, J., "Determination of the Age of Wounds by Histochemical and Biochemical Methods," Forensic Science 1972; 1 :3- 16.

Robertson, I., Hodge, PR., "Histopathology of Healing Abrasions," Forensic Science 1972;1:17-25.

Millington, P.F., "Histological Studies of Skin Carrying Bite Marks," J Forensic Science Society 1974; 14:239-40.

Robertson, I., Mansfield, R.A., Antemortem and Post-mortem Bruises of the Skin," J Forensic Medicine 1957;4(1):2-10.

Sognnaes, R, et al, Computer comparison of bite mark patterns in identical twins, JADA Vol. 105, September 1982, pp449-451.

Spillsbury, B., "The Medicolegal Significance of Bruises," Medico-Legal Criminal Review 1939;7:215-27. 1161

Robertson, I., Hodge, PR., "Histopathology of Healing Abrasions," Forensic Science 1972;1:17-25.

Ethical Considerations

Black, B.C. 1990. Black's Law Dictionary. St. Paul: West.

Briscoe v. Laffue,460 US 325, 103 S.Ct 1108,page 333 (March 7, 1984),

Brown, El. Judge. 1999. Eight Gates for Expert Witnesses. 36 Hous. L Rev. 743, 779.

Dorion, R.B.J. 2005. Bitemark Evidence. In B.M. Pitluck, (Ed.), Le2al Liability of an Expert Witness (pp 521, 524-525). New York: Marcel Dekker.

Foster, W.L. 1897. Expert Testimony: Prevalent Complaints and Proposed Remedies.
11 HA.RVL. REV. 169, 169. Retrieved November 15, 2004, from http://www.lawforensic. com/ethic_and_experts.htm.

Fry v. United States, 293 F. 1013 (D.C. Cir. 1923)

General Electric v. Joiner, 522 U.S. 136 (1997)

Graham, M.A. (1986). Expert Witness Testimony and the Federal Rule of Evidence: Insuring Adequate Assurance of Trustworthiness. U. ILL. L. REV. 43, 45.

Hansen, M, American Bar Association Journal, November, 2000

Hollien, B. (1990). The Expert Witness: Ethics and Responsibilities. Journal of Forensic Sciences. pp 1414, 1422.

Kolczynski, P.J. 1997. Bow To Be A Successful Expert Witness. Phillip J. Kolczynski Law Corporation. Retrieved November 15, 2004, from http://www.aviationlawcorp. com/content/sussessfulexpert.html

Kumho Tire Co. v. Carmichael, 119 S.Ct. 1167 (1999)

Lubet, 5. 1998. Expert Testimony: A Guide for Expert Witnesses and the Lawyers Who Examine Them Chicago: MTA. pp. 169-189.

Lubet, J. 1999. Expert Witnesses: Ethics and Professionalism. Georgetown Journal of Legal Ethics. Retrieved November 15, 2004, from http:l/www. law. gmu/edu/innofcourtlpubs/expert. html.

Moenssens, A.A., Starrs, J.E., Henderson, C.E., Inbau, F.E. (1995). Scientific Evidence in Civil and Criminal Cases. Westbury, NY: The Foundation Press, Inc., pp 91-93.

Murphy, J.P. 2000. Expert Witnesses At Trial: Where Are The Ethics. Georgetown Journal of Legal Ethics. Retrieved November, 15, 2004, from, http://www.lawforensic.com/ethic_and_experts.htm

Nesmith, J. (1999) Science on Trial. Atlanta J. Const, June 13, 1999, at D4.

United States v. Downing, 753 F. 2d 1224 (3d Cir. 1985).

HIPAA Regulations – Applications to Forensic Odontology

45 CFR Parts 160 and 164

Appendix A

The Scientific Method and Forensic Odontology

Introduction

The participant in the practice of forensic odontology is exposed to a rewarding field of forensic science in which their assistance can lead to the resolution of numerous forensic problems or issues including among others:

- Identification of individual human remains not identifiable through other means can be positively identified through the comparison of antemortem and post mortem analysis of the dentition.

- Identification of mass fatality incident victims through the use of similar comparison techniques, DNA (deoxyribonucleic acid) analysis of dental structures to establish individuality and gender and comparative computer software programs developed by forensic dental colleagues.

- Assessment of injuries to the dentition and/or the facial hard and soft tissues can be to determine whether the injuries are the result of intentionally inflicted trauma (physical abuse) or are the result of an accidental incident.

- Assessment of age estimations through analysis of the anatomical development of the dental structures or the alteration in chemical amino acid composition in the dental hard tissues. These chemical changes are also associated with aging.

- Analysis of patterned bite mark injuries caused by a unique human or animal dentition may be useful in determining or exculpating an alleged biter. Additionally, trace salivary evidence can be analyzed for DNA or other identifying markers or for indicators of disease.

Independent of the problem or concern that the forensic odontologist is requested to resolve, the procedures used in their resolution should employ and be based upon the scientific method.

The Scientific Method

In general terms, science is a means by which the natural world is described or interpreted. Isaac Newton described science as a system of gathering observable, empirical, measurable evidence, subject to the principles of reasoning. Additionally, it has been defined as a set of logical and empirical methods which provide for the systematic observation of empirical phenomena in order to understand those phenomena.

Further refinement of the definition of science considers it an objective, observational system that can be used for gaining new knowledge by using information that is both accurate and reproducible. The accomplishments or discoveries claimed or cited by one scientist should be able to be replicated by others. When a previously described observation or experiment cannot be duplicated or confirmed in additional attempts that employ the same parameters, either the original or repeated experimental model has been flawed in design, methodology, observation, calculation or calibration.

Once new information is confirmed as reliable and accurate, it can be employed to correct previous errors in the body of scientific knowledge. Although the earth was considered to be flat prior to the age of exploration in the late fifteenth century, Columbus, Magellan and others proved this theory to be incorrect. As a result of the reproducible, measurable, independent observations of sixteenth century astronomers including Copernicus, Tycho Brahe and Kepler the prevailing Ptolemaic astronomical theory which placed the earth at the center of the solar system was replaced with a model in which the planets orbit the sun.

Other theories describing events in the physical world have been proven or discarded through observation, study and experimentation. Medical practitioners in the eighteenth century believed that bloodletting was a cure for a broad range of diseases and injuries before this concept was proven through observation to do more harm than good. Prior to the scientific community's knowledge of microbes it was theorized that disease was attributable to smelling bad air (malaria). Even within the last 100 years, mental illness was still attributed to supernatural forces and not the result of emotional or biochemical pathology which is now the prevailing concept based on scientific evidence.

Valid, reliable, reproducible information has contributed to the advancement of all fields of science and forensic science is no exception as it continues to evolve. The goal forensic scientists to present this same valid, reliable and reproducible information has consistently been of great benefit to the legal system as well. For example, sensitive and specific DNA analysis has been used to overturn convictions that may have been based on less reliable evidence such as eyewitness testimony.

As defined by the American Academy of Forensic Sciences (AAFS), "Forensic science is the application of scientific principles and technological practices to the purposes of justice in the study and resolution of criminal, civil and regulatory issues." Simply stated, forensic science is the application of one or more scientific disciplines to the law. Since it is axiomatic that scientists would use the scientific method as they practice their specialty, competent forensic odontologists should be performing procedures that follow protocols or guidelines that have developed using the scientific method.

The scientific method is a general set of rules or a body of techniques employed for investigating, explaining and understanding physical, chemical and biological phenomena. It can also be used to create and test a hypothesis and acquire new knowledge or correct and integrate previous knowledge into other areas or disciplines that may not have been previously considered relevant.

The process of the scientific method usually incorporates the following:

- Initial recognition, observation and description of a phenomenon (or phenomena), problem or unknown using data that is relevant, reliable and replicable.

- Development of a preliminary hypothesis to explain the problem, phenomenon (or phenomena) or unknown state. A hypothesis is a tentative supposition, assumption or explanation for an unknown, an observation or phenomenon that can be investigated or analytically tested through comparison to that which is already known or through experimental investigation or discovery of facts not previously known and suggested by the hypothesis.

- Use of the preliminary hypothesis to predict future phenomena or describe present or past events or phenomena.

- Performance of tests used to assess the value of the hypothesis. Systematic experimentation by other independent scientists to validate, corroborate (or reject) or modify the hypothesis.

Ultimately, by using the scientific method the scientist is precluded from risking the intrusion of their personal, cultural, economic or religious beliefs or values into the investigation. Such an intrusion could create bias or prejudice while a hypothesis or theory is being tested or an opinion developed.

Bias and Scientific Peer Review

Bias is usually described as a flaw in experimental design or data measurement that leads to results that are inaccurate or skewed. It can also indicate prejudice or personal preference that influences one's decision making process. The process of peer review reduces the risk of biased reports becoming accepted as valid. This is accomplished by having multiple members of the scientific community review the reports and findings of other scientists. Through testing and retesting the methods and results of the published reports, those reports can be verified as accurate. Bias must be avoided if evaluators are to remain neutral, impartial and objective and the resulting science based on sound evidence.

Scientific peer review is the process by which a researcher or clinician's disseminated information, in the form of observational and experimental scholarly activity, is evaluated by recognized and respected experts working in that same field of study. It may include pre-publication critique and review of the scholar's case reports and technical notes and/or evaluation and prioritization of grant proposals submitted to funding agencies. Although peer review is often initiated at the time of pre-publication evaluation, it does not end when the scholarly work has been selected for publication.

All of those who read the published research article, literature review or case report have access to the author's materials and methods, raw data, data analysis and conclusions. Thus, ultimately the entire scientific community can and must evaluate the published material for reproducibility, validity and accuracy. Readers are encouraged to critique the published material for experimental design, usefulness and relevancy. This is routinely accomplished through the letters to the editor section of the journal in which the material has been published.

Presentation of an independent evaluation by another individual practicing in the field (second opinion) is an additional form of peer review. It is often useful and commonly employed in medical and dental science and forensic odontology. Diagnoses can be confirmed, modified or even rejected through objective assessment and testing by another individual working independently of the first evaluator or diagnostician. Although not mandatory, it is often prudent for one forensic odontologist to have others independently evaluate the same evidence and the validity of the conclusions drawn from that evidence.

Junk Science and Pseudoscience

Junk science has been defined as "...work presented as valid science that falls outside the rigors of the scientific method and the peer review process. It can take the form of presentation of selective results, politically motivated distortions of scientifically sound research or the publication of material in quasi-scientific non-reviewed journals." Five practices have been described that are often associated with questionable, inadequate, unreliable or unacceptable scientific activity that compromises the validity of the claims made:

- Lack of appropriate credentials: the scientific findings presented are the result of efforts by one or more persons lacking appropriate background or training.

- Lack of peer review: the scientific findings have not been subjected to peer review or were used despite being found to be invalid during the peer review process.

- Lack of publication: the scientific findings have not been published in a recognized, authoritative peer-reviewed journal or presented in an appropriate venue.

- Weak bibliographic lineage: the scientific finding should be dismissed or treated with caution when not based on the previous body of knowledge or research.

- Fraud: data or findings should be dismissed because researchers have been shown to have manipulated their approach or falsified findings.

The Internet has compounded and amplified the problems associated with junk or pseudoscience because in many cases the Internet lacks peer review. It has been noted that "...anybody can publish anything, truth or fiction, that will in turn become available to people throughout the world." The prudent reader should use the previously listed criteria when evaluating information that is available on the Internet.

It has been suggested that the following steps be followed when evaluating a website:

- What does the website represent and where does its funding come from?

- Who are the website's members or officers and what is their interest in the subject?

- Are the materials and articles supporting the website's position unbiased and free from personal interests?

- Is the information presented balanced, presenting the facts rather than taking one side of the issue when there is potentially more than one valid opinion regarding the topic?

- If possible, determine what reputable individuals or scientific professional organizations have to say about the website. Study the credentials of authors or contributors. Is the author truly an authority on the subject matter? Check for significant articles by the same author or authors on a similar topic. Check to see if the writer is cited positively by other authors writing on the same topic.

Pseudoscience is generally defined as "…any body of knowledge purporting to be factual and scientific, but which has failed to be validated in accordance with the scientific method." Examples of activities or fields of knowledge that have been described as falling under the rubric of pseudoscience include psychic surgery, phrenology, astrology, telekinesis, numerology, dowsing, channeling, recovered memories and precognition. Although there might be individuals who purport to be experts in these areas, they clearly should not be allowed to serve as expert witnesses in the courtroom unless testifying to the lack of scientific rigor associated with these fields.

The Daubert v. Merrell Dow Pharmaceuticals, 509 U.S. 579 (1993) ruling by the United States Supreme Court held that when evidence based upon scientific knowledge is offered at trial, the judge should act as a gatekeeper and therefore determine whether the proffered evidence is scientifically valid and reliable, upon proper motion by a litigant who challenges the admissibility of evidence,

The Amended Language of Federal Rules of Evidence Rule (FRE) 702 emphasizes that there is a non-exclusive check list useful in judging whether expert witness testimony meets the Daubert criteria of reliability and follow the scientific method. This topic is discussed in detail in Chapter 7 – Dental Jurisprudence.

Dr. Satiani describes suggested minimal qualifications for an expert witness to be allowed to testify at the state court level. It is suggested that these include:

- Disclosure of information materially related to the reliability of expert testimony in the issue before the court.

- Filing a Daubert brief which is a summary of the opinion of the plaintiff's expert along with a resume outlining his/her knowledge, skill, experience, training and education, reputation in the field relevant to the litigation and complete details of the methodology used by the expert.

- Filing an oath or declaration that acknowledges the duty to disclose all information known to the person to be material to the reliability of the expert witness.

Although perhaps not practical in all cases, the recommendations of Dr. Santiani seem to follow the scientific method and might be an area for consideration and potential implementation by forensic odontologists serving as expert witnesses.

Evidence-Based Practice of Forensic Odontology

Forensic scientists in each area of expertise agree that they should utilize the best scientific evidence available in the fulfillment of their duties. However, many forensic scientists would also agree that there are examples of cases which demonstrate how the best evidence may not always be presented in the litigation process. Unfortunately, junk science and pseudoscience and fraud posing as science have too often found their way into the courtroom.

Sound data and reliable information to support a decision or opinion can be drawn from multiple sources. In clinical medicine and dentistry, the strength of evidence or hierarchy of evidence can range from weak data to strong supportive evidence. The former is often drawn from limited personal experience, case reports involving few samples and anecdotal reports. The latter is developed through more structured studies based on the scientific method. These same standards regarding strength of evidence can be applied to forensic odontology. The source of the evidence used in the procedures performed by forensic dentists should be as scientifically viable as possible.

There are instances when new tests, procedures or techniques are being investigated using the scientific method, but, have not yet risen to standard of criteria required to be termed evidence based. Evidence-based forensic odontology procedures involve the use of those tests, procedures and analytical techniques that have met the established standards for good quality research. Odontologists should only perform procedures or utilize those techniques that have been proven reliable and have demonstrated to be highly sensitive and specific. Sensitive and specific tests can significantly reduce the risk of false positive and/or false negative investigative results.

Sensitivity indicates the ability of a test to identify true positive outcomes. A comparison of antemortem and post mortem radiographic evidence is a highly sensitive test. With adequate, diagnostic images this like to like comparison technique permits the examiner to eventually state that the post mortem remains are those of a certain individual. Additionally, there are evidence based testing criteria that allow the physician or dentist to state with reasonable certainty that injuries being evaluated are the result of intentionally inflicted trauma and are not the result of an accident. Tests that are specific reveal the true negative event. DNA from post mortem remains that does not match the DNA of an individual purported to be the decedent indicates the two DNA samples analyzed are not from the same individual and this would be considered a specific test.

Forensic odontologists will be practicing within the parameters acceptable to their peers and to the courts by employing procedures that have been validated through the scientific method and are evidence based, Junk science and pseudoscience have no place in the unbiased, competent practice of forensic odontology. During all phases of evidence collection and analysis forensic odontologists would be well-advised to follow the principles of the scientific method.

CONTRIBUTOR

John D. McDowell, DDS, MS, DABFO

REFERENCES

Evidence-Based Practice of Forensic Odontology

Evidence-based medicine. A new approach to teaching the practice of medicine. Evidence-Based Medicine Working Group. (1992). JAMA 268:2420-5.

Evidence based medicine overviews, bulletins, guidelines and the new consensus. (2000). Postgraduate Medical Journal 76:383-389.

Murlow CD (1995). Rationale for systematic reviews. In: Systematic Reviews. Chalmers I, Altman DG editors. London: BMJ Publishing.

Junk Science and Pseudoscience

Barbalace RC (2006). Sorting out Science from Junk Science: Is it really science? http://environmentalchemistry.com/yogi/environmental/200608junkscience.html.

Daly HE (2001). Globalization and Its Discontents. Philosophy & Public Policy Quarterly 21:12-13.

Satiani B (2006). Expert witness testimony: rules of engagement. Vasc Endovascular Surg 40:223-7.

The Scientific Method

Carroll RT (2003). The Skeptic's Dictionary: A Collection of Strange Beliefs, Amusing Deceptions, and Dangerous Delusions. 1 ed.: Wiley.

McGraw-Hill Encyclopedia of Science and Technology (2002). 9 ed.: McGraw-Hill Professional.

Newton, I (1726). Rules for the study of natural philosophy, Philosophiae Naturalis Principa Mathmatica, book three. The system of the world. Cohen B and Whitman A translators. University of California Press.

Summary

Huber PW (1003). Galileo's Revenge: Junk Science in the Courtroom: Basic Books.

Appendix B: Representative Acceptable Courses in Forensic Odontology

Armed Forces Institute of Pathology (AFIP) Course on Forensic Dentistry

Mailing Address:
Armed Forces Institute of Pathology
6825 16th Street NW
Washington, DC 20306-6000

http://www.afip.org/Departments/edu/upcoming.htm
http://www.afip.org/Departments/edu/coursehtm/07fordent.htm#anchor11625 Bottom of Form

Southwest Symposium on Forensic Dentistry

Contact UTHSCSA, Continuing Dental Education, (210) 567-3177 for Symposium information.
Contact David Senn for course content information senn@uthscsa.edu
Information and links also at www.utforensic.org
Follow the Summer Courses links at http://smile.uthscsa.edu for information and online registration after January, 2008

McGill University Forensic Odontology Course

http://www.mcgill.ca/dentistry/conted/
Director: Dr. Robert B. J. Dorion
Registration contact for all courses:

Nikoo Taghavi
Continuing Dental Education
Faculty of Dentistry
3460 University Street
Montreal, QC H3A 2B2
Tel.: 514-398-7203, ext 00061
Fax: 514-398-8900

Forensic Odontology in a Medical Examiner's Office

http://dental.udmercy.edu/continuing_education/schedule.php

Advanced training for dentists
Wayne County Medical Examiners' Office, Detroit, MI.

Miami-Dade County - Medical Examiner Forensic Course

Miami-Dade County Medical Examiner Department - Forensic Odontology
F.D.O. - Forensic Dentistry Online ...
www.miamidade.gov/medexam/odontology.asp

UNLV School of Dental Medicine Bite Mark Course

Bite Mark Management and Case Review
Contact Dr. David Ord
david.ord@unlv.edu

Appendix C: ABFO Guidelines

ABFO BODY IDENTIFICATION GUIDELINES

The American Board of Forensic Odontology has developed a series of Guidelines, Standards and Policies. They can be accessed through the web site of the Board at: **http://abfo.org/.**

> A *guideline* may state the optimum or ideal situation. It would outline the most desirable approach but, if not followed may be excusable.

> A *standard* might be less comprehensive but would state the minimal requirements of acceptability.

> A *policy* would not necessarily have anything to do with correctness but would carry the maximum imperative to comply and is not appropriate for scientific investigation.

Guidelines Available:

- Development of a Dental ID Team

- Human Identification

- Bite Marks

- Missing Person and Unidentified Body Cases

Appendix D: Charts on Facial Tissue Depth for Reconstruction

Tables of facial tissue depth according to age, race, and sex.

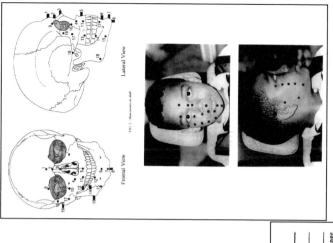

Frontal View   Lateral View

TABLE 2—Tissue depth means (mm) for black children of normal weight ages 3–18 years.

Point Numbers & Descriptions	3–8 Years						9–13 Years						14–18 Years					
	Female (N = 52)			Male (N = 37)			Female (N = 59)			Male (N = 62)			Female (N = 25)			Male (N = 12)		
	Mean	SD	Range	Mean	SD	Range	Mean	SD	Range	Mean	SD	Range	Mean	SD	Range	Mean	SD	Range
1 Glabella	4.0	0.91	2–6	4.1	0.74	3–6	4.3	0.83	3–6	4.5	0.97	3–7	4.7	1.14	3–7	5.3	0.78	4–7
2 Nasion	4.9	0.96	3–8	5.4	0.96	3–7	5.4	1.00	3–7	5.4	0.98	3–8	5.3	1.11	4–8	6.1	0.51	5–7
3 End of nasals	1.7	0.61	1–3	1.8	0.48	1–3	1.7	0.56	1–3	1.9	0.46	1–3	1.7	0.54	1–3	2.1	0.51	1–3
4 Lateral nostril	7.0	1.48	5–11	7.3	1.68	5–11	7.6*	1.58	5–12	7.4	1.91	4–13	8.1	2.14	5–12	7.9	1.98	5–10
5 Mid-philtrum	8.9	1.57	6–14	9.0	1.18	6–14	9.6	1.56	7–13	10.0	1.69	7–18	9.9	2.20	7–16	12.1	1.73	10–15
6 Chin lip fold	8.2	2.05	3–15	8.6	1.44	6–12	10.3	1.77	7–15	9.8	1.84	6–13	10.1	1.79	7–13	12.6	1.93	10–16
7 Mental eminence	8.3	2.16	4–14	8.3	1.59	6–11	10.0	2.60	5–16	9.9	3.03	5–18	10.0	2.65	4–15	9.5	2.78	5–13
8 Beneath chin	4.8	1.61	2–10	4.5	1.12	2–6	5.8	2.15	2–12	5.5	2.09	2–11	5.6	1.93	2–10	6.3	1.86	4–10
9 Supraorbital	4.5	1.02	3–7	4.5	0.65	3–6	5.3	1.03	3–8	5.2	1.12	3–9	5.7	1.46	2–10	5.8	0.94	4–7
10 Suborbital	5.6	1.14	3–9	5.6	1.07	3–8	6.1	1.12	4–10	5.8	1.19	3–9	6.4	1.50	4–11	6.0	0.74	5–7
11 Supracanine	8.8	1.59	5–14	8.9	1.86	6–15	10.0	1.79	7–16	10.7	2.74	7–27	10.6	1.50	8–13	12.3	2.05	9–17
12 Subcanine	9.0	2.20	5–15	8.5	1.24	6–11	10.2	2.16	6–17	11.0	3.02	7–24	11.0	2.25	7–16	12.8	2.67	8–17
13 Posterior maxilla†	23.0	3.39	15–32	22.1	2.47	17–27	24.5	3.72	18–34	23.6	4.35	12–33	27.6	3.52	22–37	26.0	2.89	21–30
14 Sup mid mandible‡	18.0	3.26	10–26	17.4	2.68	10–25	20.0	3.58	10–26	20.1	4.18	11–28	23.2	3.99	18–33	21.9	4.91	12–29
15 Inf mid mandible‡	9.8	3.16	5–20	8.7	2.03	5–14	10.8	2.99	6–18	10.3	3.85	4–20	12.0	3.16	7–20	11.2	3.93	7–20
16 Lateral eye orbit	3.9	0.89	2–6	4.1	0.85	2–6	4.4	1.24	2–10	4.4	0.89	3–7	4.6	1.08	3–8	4.4	0.67	3–5
17 Anterior zygoma§	8.3	2.23	4–15	7.8	1.55	5–12	8.9	2.22	6–14	8.3	2.66	4–15	9.2	1.68	6–13	7.3	2.05	3–5
18 Gonion	13.5	2.87	8–21	12.8	2.02	10–17	14.6	3.41	3–23	14.7	3.06	9–22	16.2	3.36	10–23	17.9	3.63	11–24
19 Root of zygoma	4.7	1.21	3–8	4.2	0.98	3–6	4.8*	1.55	3–8	5.0†	1.73	2–12	6.2	2.30	3–11	6.0	2.37	3–11

* Indicates N = 58.
† Indicates N = 61.
‡ Parallel to zygoma marker (bases of 13, 14, and 17 line up vertically in the Frankfort plane).
§ Marker placed just below bony ridge of eye orbit (see Fig. 1).

TABLE 4—*Tissue depth means (mm) for Hispanic children of normal weight ages 3–18 years.*

| | 3–8 Years | | | | | | 9–13 Years | | | | | | 14–18 Years | | | | | |
| | Female (N = 6) | | | Male (N = 3) | | | Female (N = 9) | | | Male (N = 8) | | | Female (N = 1) | | | Male (= 4) | | |
Point Numbers & Descriptions	Mean	SD	Range	Mean	SD	Range	Mean	SD	Range	Mean	SD	Range	Mean	SD	Range	Mean	SD	Range
1 Glabella	4.2	0.75	3–5	4.7	0.58	4–5	3.8	0.83	3–5	4.1	0.83	3–5	7.0	–	–	4.5	1.00	4–6
2 Nasion	5.0	1.10	3–6	6.3	1.15	5–7	5.3	0.87	4–6	4.9	1.25	3–7	5.0	–	–	4.8	0.50	4–5
3 End of nasals	1.7	0.52	1–2	1.7	0.58	1–2	1.6	0.53	1–2	1.6	0.52	1–2	1.0	–	–	1.5	0.58	1–2
4 Lateral nostril	6.3	1.03	5–8	6.3	1.53	5–8	5.7	1.12	5–8	7.9	2.23	5–12	9.0	–	–	5.0	0.82	4–6
5 Mid-philtrum	8.0	1.55	7–10	7.3	0.58	7–8	9.2	1.20	8–11	9.3	1.75	5–10	8.0	–	–	11.5	1.29	10–13
6 Chin lip fold	8.7	2.07	6–11	7.0	2.00	5–9	9.2	1.48	7–12	10.0	1.85	6–12	11.0	–	–	11.3	2.06	9–14
7 Mental eminence	8.0	2.00	5–10	6.0	1.00	5–7	8.4	1.59	6–11	8.4	2.77	5–13	15.0		–	10.3	0.96	9–11
8 Beneath chin	4.2	1.72	2–6	4.7	1.53	3–6	5.1	1.36	3–7	5.1	0.99	4–6	9.0		–	5.8	0.96	5–7
9 Supraorbital	4.2	0.75	3–5	4.3	0.58	4–5	4.9	0.93	3–6	4.9	0.99	4–6	7.0		–	5.5	1.29	4–7
10 Suborbital	5.5	1.87	3–8	5.0	2.00	3–7	5.0	1.12	3–6	6.4	1.41	4–9	10.0		–	5.8	0.96	5–7
11 Supracanine	9.3	2.66	7–14	8.0	1.00	7–9	10.3	1.66	9–13	10.0	2.33	6–13	11.0		–	12.0	0.82	11–13
12 Subcanine	8.2	2.32	6–11	6.7	0.58	6–7	8.3	1.32	6–10	10.8	2.12	8–14	10.0		–	10.0	3.16	6–13
13 Posterior maxilla*	24.8	3.37	20–28	19.7	3.51	16–23	24.6	4.13	16–29	24.4	2.33	21–28	32.0		–	25.3	4.27	19–28
14 Sup mid mandible*	20.8	6.15	10–28	14.7	4.73	11–20	20.0	5.12	9–26	21.4	2.83	18–27	24.0		–	21.0	1.41	20–23
15 Inf mid mandible*	11.5	3.94	5–16	7.3	4.04	5–12	11.3	2.78	6–15	10.8	3.11	5–14	18.0		–	10.3	4.57	5–15
16 Lateral eye orbit	4.3	0.82	3–5	3.0	0.00	3–3	3.8	0.44	3–4	4.6	0.52	4–5	5.0		–	4.3	0.96	3–5
17 Anterior zygoma†	8.5	2.66	5–13	6.3	2.08	4–8	7.4	1.13	6–9	8.4	1.69	6–11	14.0		–	7.8	1.89	5–9
18 Gonion	14.0	3.41	8–18	13.7	5.03	9–19	14.6	3.05	10–19	15.4	4.63	7–21	24.0		–	15.3	4.86	9–20
19 Root of zygoma	4.3	0.82	3–5	4.3	2.31	3–7	4.6	1.33	3–6	6.3	1.28	5–8	8.0		–	4.8	1.50	3–6

* Parallel to zygoma marker (bases of 13, 14, and 17 line up vertically in the Frankfort plane).
† Marker placed just below bony ridge of eye orbit (see Fig. 1).

TABLE 5—*Pearson's correlations (r) between tissue thickness and age for children (ages 3–18).*

Point Numbers & Descriptions	White (N = 237)	Black (N = 247)	Hispanic (N = 31)
1 Glabella	0.350†*	0.330†	0.131
2 Nasion	0.191†*	0.180†	0.057
3 End of nasals	0.119	0.057	−0.154
4 Lateral nostril	0.177†	0.171†§	−0.011
5 Mid-philtrum	0.351†	0.350†	0.404‡
6 Chin lip fold	0.511†	0.497†	0.614†
7 Mental eminence	0.191†	0.264†	0.498†
8 Beneath chin	0.350†	0.243†	0.372‡
9 Supraorbital	0.441†	0.416†	0.551†
10 Suborbital	0.065	0.208†	0.261
11 Supracanine	0.336†	0.423†	0.557†
12 Subcanine	0.395†	0.412†	0.469†
13 Posterior maxilla	0.427†	0.380†	0.275
14 Sup mid mandible	0.369†	0.444†	0.284
15 Inf mid mandible	0.304†	0.237†	0.203
16 Lateral eye orbit	0.128‡	0.228†	0.248
17 Anterior zygoma	0.078	0.082	0.161
18 Gonion	0.446†	0.399†	0.360‡
19 Root of zygoma	0.415†	0.320†	0.286

* N = 236.
† p < .01.
‡ p< .05.
§ N= 246.

TABLE 6—*Summary of ANOVA (Duncan) showing significant variation among Black, White, and Hispanic children (3–18 years).*

| Groups | Measurement Sites | | | | | | | | | | | | | | | | | | |
	1	2	3	4	5	6	7	8	9	10	11	12	13	14	15	16	17	18	19
White females (A)	–	B	D	E	B,D	B,C,D	C,D	–	–	–	B,D	C,D	D	D	C,D	–	D	–	D
White males (B)	C	A,C,D,E,F	–	E	A,C,E	A	–	–	–	C	A	D	D	C,D	C,D	–	D	C,D	D
Black females (C)	B	B,D	D	E	B,D	A	A	–	–	B	–	A,E	D	B	A,B	–	D	B	D
Black males (D)	–	B,C	A,C	E	A,C,E	A	A	–	–	–	–	A,B,E	A,B,C	B	A,B	–	A,C	B	A,B
Hispanic females (E)	–	B	–	A,B,C,D	B,D	–	–	–	–	–	–	C,D	–	–	–	–	–	–	–
Hispanic males (F)	–	B	–	–	–	–	–	–	–	–	–	–	–	–	–	–	–	–	–

NOTE: Letters indicate the groups between which the differences in tissue thickness are significant. (p < .05).

TABLE 7—*Tissue depth means (mm) for Black adults of normal weight.*

| Point Numbers & Descriptions | 19–34 Years | | | | | | 35–45 Years | | | | | | 45–55 Years | | |
| | Female (N = 18) | | | Male (N = 19) | | | Female (N = 21) | | | Male (N = 3) | | | Female (N = 5) | | |
	Mean	SD	Range	Mean	SD	Range	Mean	SD	Range	Mean	SD	Range	Mean	SD	Range
1 Glabella	4.6	0.70	4–6	5.2	1.12	3–7	4.5	0.93	3–7	5.3	1.53	4–7	4.8	0.84	4–6
2 Nasion	6.0	0.91	4–8	6.6	0.84	5–8	5.2	1.25	4–8	5.7	2.08	4–8	6.0	1.00	5–7
3 End of nasals	1.7	0.46	1–2	2.2	0.42	2–3	1.5	0.51	1–2	1.7	0.58	1–2	2.0	0.71	1–3
4 Lateral nostril	8.4	1.98	6–12	9.2	2.82	6–15	8.4	2.01	5–13	10.3	2.52	8–13	8.4	1.52	6–10
5 Mid-philtrum	9.2	1.82	6–13	13.0	2.20	10–18	8.8	1.92	6–13	11.0	1.73	9–12	8.2	2.49	6–13
6 Chin lip fold	11.8	2.20	7–15	12.7	2.05	10–17	11.7	2.42	10–17	12.7	1.15	12–14	10.0	3.11	6–13
7 Mental eminence	10.8	2.68	5–15	12.1	2.90	7–18	11.2	2.25	7–15	12.3	4.51	8–17	10.8	3.11	8–16
8 Beneath chin	6.7	2.02	3–10	8.8	1.89	6–13	6.4	2.65	3–12	7.0	2.00	5–9	7.2	1.92	4–9
9 Supraorbital	6.1	0.83	5–7	6.4	1.30	4–9	6.0	1.22	3–9	6.3	0.58	6–7	5.8	0.84	5–7
10 Suborbital	6.2	1.17	5–9	5.8	1.26	3–8	6.9	1.96	4–13	7.0	1.00	6–8	5.8	1.30	5–8
11 Supracanine	10.0	2.28	6–15	12.8	1.86	10–16	9.6	2.75	6–15	10.3	1.53	9–12	9.0	2.45	7–13
12 Subcanine	10.9	2.44	6–15	14.4	2.89	9–21	11.5	1.60	9–15	10.7	0.58	10–11	12.4	3.91	7–17
13 Posterior maxilla*	26.6	4.36	18–34	28.2	3.46	23–38	26.8	4.47	19–38	27.3	4.51	23–32	26.8	4.09	22–31
14 Sup mid mandible*	21.7	3.99	13–29	24.5	4.05	17–33	22.5	3.93	15–31	23.7	4.04	20–28	21.2	5.89	11–26
15 Int mid mandible*	12.6	2.85	8–19	14.1	4.21	8–23	13.1	4.17	6–22	13.3	2.31	12–16	13.4	4.04	9–19
16 Lateral eye orbit	5.0	0.84	4–7	4.8	0.76	4–7	4.9	1.18	3–7	3.7	0.58	3–4	4.8	0.84	4–6
17 Anterior zygoma†	10.2	2.28	6–15	8.4	2.22	5–13	9.8	2.38	5–15	6.3	0.58	6–7	9.8	3.27	6–15
18 Gonion	17.0	4.23	9–27	21.1	3.24	17–29	16.2	3.64	11–24	20.7	2.89	19–24	14.8	2.86	11–18
19 Root of zygoma	6.4	2.25	3–11	7.4	1.77	5–12	5.6	2.22	3–10	5.7	1.15	5–7	6.0	2.24	5–10

NOTE: There are no males over 45 years of age, and no females over 55.
* Parallel to zygoma marker (bases of 13, 14, and 17 line up vertically in the Frankfort plane).
† Marker placed just below bony ridge of eye orbit see Fig. 1).

TABLE 8—*Tissue depth means (mm) for White adults of normal weight.*

| Points | 19–34 Years | | | | | | 35–45 Years | | | | | | 46–55 Years | | | | | | >56 Years | | | | | |
| | Female (N = 52) | | | Male (N = 28) | | | Female (N = 15) | | | Male (N = 10) | | | Female (N = 6) | | | Male (N = 5) | | | Female (N = 9) | | | Male (N = 5) | | |
	Mean	SD	Range	Mean	SD	Range	Mean	SD	Range	Mean	SD	Range	Mean	SD	Range	Mean	SD	Range	Mean	SD	Range	Mean	SD	Range
1	4.8	0.95	4–6	5.0	0.67	4–6	4.7	1.03	4–7	5.5	1.27	4–7	4.8	1.17	4–8	6.0	1.41	4–8	5.2	0.97	4–7	5.6	1.52	4–8
2	5.5	1.16	3–8	6.0	1.12	4–9	5.3	1.39	3–8	6.4	1.43	4–8	6.2	0.75	5–7	7.2	1.64	5–7	6.0	1.22	4–8	6.6	1.52	5–8
3	1.8	0.63	1–4	1.9	0.45	1–3	1.6	0.51	1–2	2.4	0.97	1–4	1.8	0.41	1–2	1.8	0.45	1–2	1.8	0.67	1–3	2.0‡	3.03	1–3
4	8.6	1.99	4–13	7.5	1.9	5–12	8.0	1.73	6–12	9.8	1.81	7–12	10.8	1.94	9–14	10.4	2.51	8–14	9.8	2.22	6–13	10.8	1.52	7–13
5	9.1	1.69	6–13	9.1	2.24	7–17	7.4	1.30	5–10	10.6	1.43	8–13	8.0	1.41	6–10	11.6	1.67	6–10	11.4	2.65	5–12	9.4	3.03	5–13
6	10.3	1.55	6–13	11.1*	1.85	7–15	9.6	1.50	5–12	13.1	1.52	9–13	9.8	2.32	6–12	12.3	1.79	6–12	11.7	1.42	5–13	12.2	1.52	10–14
7	9.9	1.45	6–14	11.1	1.73	6–13	9.2	1.33	2–9	8.0	1.05	10–15	9.8	2.80	6–8	11.6	1.79	8–12	9.4	1.87	5–13	11.8	1.79	10–15
8	6.0	1.04	3–9	7.2	1.25	3–7	5.5	1.19	3–8	6.2	0.88	4–7	6.3	0.84	6–8	8.0†	1.79	5–9	8.0	1.00	5–8	12.2	2.05	10–15
9	5.7	1.04	4–10	5.3	1.58	3–11	5.7	1.33	4–9	6.9	1.87	5–9	6.5	4.08	6–8	10.7	1.67	7–9	6.3	1.87	5–8	5.6	0.89	5–7
10	6.1	1.05	4–8	5.8	1.58	4–10	5.7	1.37	3–8	6.9	2.13	4–11	6.7	2.84	6–8	6.8	1.67	6–8	6.3	1.00	5–8	5.0	1.14	4–7
11	9.3	1.74	5–14	5.3	1.58	4–10	7.8	1.33	4–9	10.1	2.13	5–10	7.7	2.84	6–8	6.8	2.00	6–8	7.0	1.87	5–12	5.0	1.14	5–12
12	9.4	1.56	5–12	11.9*	2.65	5–14	8.7	1.37	5–10	10.2	1.32	4–12	7.7	1.86	6–10	10.0	2.00	6–10	8.0	2.50	5–14	9.2	2.0	5–12
13	26.3	4.94	9–31	28.5	4.69	5–12	25.1	2.23	4–12	24.6	2.13	4–11	27.2	1.86	6–12	10.0	2.35	8–12	9.7	2.00	6–11	11.8	2.30	6–11
14	21.1	4.53	18–35	14.2	4.15	9–31	20.1	6.74	21–39	13.0	6.45	12–32	18.0	2.97	6–12	10.0†	3.85	20–35	29.4	3.39	5–14	11.8	3.39	5–14
15	13.7	3.25	7–22	4.2	4.48	18–35	8.7	5.15	18–35	15.6	6.69	6–23	13.0	6.11	20–35	28.2	7.53	17–35	17.4	4.82	20–36	20.6	8.11	20–36
16	4.7	0.88	3–6	4.2	0.79	7–22	4.3	4.21	6–22	4.3	4.81	3–5	4.5	4.29	2–7	5.4	3.85	5–6	4.9	5.28	3–5	13.4	3.65	13–33
17	9.3	1.70	6–12	7.8	2.38	3–6	8.7	0.90	3–6	8.2	0.82	3–5	10.2	1.87	2–7	5.4	0.55	2–7	8.0	1.76	2–7	6.4	0.45	2–7
18	17.4	3.70	7–27	20.0	4.27	6–12	15.3	2.74	4–16	19.6	2.20	4–16	14.7	1.60	9–13	19.0	2.05	6–12	16.9	2.45	7–15	14.0	4.95	8–20
19	7.4	2.07	4–13	7.8	2.29	7–27	4.9	4.50	9–25	6.6	5.87	9–25	6.0	4.68	7–20	5.4	4.69	15–25	7.4	3.39	11–21	5.2	1.10	4–6

* Indicate: N = 27 (number excludes men with beards and mustaches).
† Indicate: N = 3 (number excludes men with beards and mustaches).
‡ Indicate: N = 4 (number excludes men with beards and mustaches).

TABLE 9—*Pearson's correlations (r) between tissue thickness and age for adults (ages 19–55).*

Point Numbers & Descriptions	White (N=130)	Black (N=66)
1 Glabella	0.197‖	−0.019
2 Nasion	0.157	−0.238
3 End of nasals	−0.036*	−0.273‖
4 Lateral nostril	0.363§	−0.020
5 Mid-philtrum	−0.355§†	−0.460§
6 Chin lip fold	0.109*	−0.170
7 Mental eminence	0.330§	−0.022
8 Beneath chin	0.090*	−0.236
9 Supraorbital	0.282§	−0.142
10 Suborbital	0.095	0.186
11 Supracanine	−0.334§‡	−0.460§
12 Subcanine	−0.125	−0.136
13 Posterior maxilla	−0.046	0.017
14 Sup mid mandible	−0.123	−0.037
15 Inf mid mandible	0.020	0.086
16 Lateral eye orbit	0.141	−0.017
17 Anterior zygoma	0.082	0.203
18 Gonion	−0.243§	−0.343§
19 Root of zygoma	−0.269§	−0.343§

* $N = 129$.
† $N = 128$.
‡ $N = 127$.
§ $p < .01$.
‖ $p < .05$.

TABLE 11—*Comparison of tissue depth measurements for white males (19–55 years) between LSU, His (1895)†, and Kollmann-Büchly (1898)*.

Point Numbers & Descriptions				LSU (N=43)	His (N=24)	K–B (N=21)
LSU	His	K–B				
1	2	st₂	Glabella	5.23	5.10	4.29
2	3	nw	Nasion	6.23	5.55	4.31
3		ns	End of nasals	1.98		2.12
5	6	lg	Mid philtrum	11.27*	9.51	9.46
6	7	lf	Chin lip fold	11.64*	10.26	9.84
7	8	kw	Mental eminence	10.56	11.43	9.02
8	9	k₃	Beneath chin	7.38*	6.18	5.98
9	10	abr	Superior eye orbit	5.72	5.89	5.41
10	11	ua	Inferior eye orbit	5.98	5.08	3.51
17		wb	Zygomaric	7.93		6.62
19		jb₂	Root of zygoma	7.21		7.42

* $N=38$.
† (as modified by Krogman and İşcan, 1986).

TABLE 12—*Adult (19–55 Years) tissue depth means for normal weight comparison between FACES and Rhine's* measurements.*

Point Numbers		LSU Descriptions	Black Adults						White Adults					
			Male			Female			Male			Female		
FACE	Rhine		FACES (N=28)	Rhine	Diff	FACES (N=44)	Rhine	Diff	FACES (N=43)	Rhine (N=37)	Diff	FACES (N=73)	Rhine (N=19)	Diff
1	2	Glabella	5.18	6.25	−1.07	4.57	6.00	−1.43	5.23	5.25	−0.02	4.79	4.75	0.04
2	3	Nasion	6.45	6.00	0.45	5.61	5.25	0.34	6.23	6.50	−0.27	5.52	5.50	0.02
3	4	End of nasals	2.14	3.75	−1.61	1.66	3.75	−2.09	1.98	3.00	−1.02	1.77	2.75	−0.98
5	5	Mid philtrum	12.68	12.25	0.43	8.86	11.25	−2.39	11.27†	10.00	1.27	8.64	8.50	0.14
6	8	Chin lip fold	12.73	11.75	−0.98	11.55	12.25	−0.07	11.64†	10.75	0.89	10.12	9.50	0.62
7	9	Mental eminence	12.09	11.50	0.59	11.00	12.50	−1.50	10.56	11.25	−0.69	9.30	10.00	−0.70
8	10	Beneath chin	8.59	8.25	0.34	6.61	8.00	−1.39	7.38†	7.25	0.13	5.90	5.75	0.15
9	12	Supraorbital	6.36	8.50	−2.14	6.02	8.00	−1.98	5.72	8.25	−2.53	5.74	7.00	−1.26
10	13	Suborbital	6.00	7.75	−1.75	6.48	8.25	−1.77	5.98	5.75	0.23	6.12	6.00	0.12
13	19	Posterior maxilla	28.09	22.00	6.09	26.70	20.25	6.45	27.56	19.50	8.06	26.14	19.25	6.89
14	21	Sup. mid mandible	24.36	16.50	7.86	22.00	17.00	5.00	23.77	16.00	7.77	22.59	15.50	7.09
17	15	Anterior zygomatic	8.14	13.25	−5.11	9.95	13.00	−3.05	7.93	10.00	2.07	9.23	10.75	1.52
18	18	Gonion	21.00	13.00	8.00	16.36	13.50	2.86	19.79	11.50	8.29	16.77	12.00	4.77

* Adapted from Rhine and Moore, 1982; revised 1984.
† N=38.

TABLE 10—*Summary of ANOVA (Duncan) showing significant variation among black and white adults (19–55 years).*

Groups	Measurement Sites																		
	1	2	3	4	5	6	7	8	9	10	11	12	13	14	15	16	17	18	19
White females (A)	B	B,D	D	–	B,D	B,C,D	B,C,D	B,C,D	D	–	B,D	B,C,D	–	–	B	–	B,D	B,D	–
White males (B)	A,C	A,C	C	–	A,C,D	A,D	A,D	A,D	–	–	A,C,D	A,D	–	–	A,C	C	A,C	A,C	C
Black females (C)	B,D	B,D	B,D	–	B,D	A,D	A	A,D	–	–	B,D	A,D	–	–	B	B	B,D	B,D	B
Black males (D)	C	A,C	A,C	–	B,C,D	B,C,D	A,B	B,C,D	A	–	B,C,D	B,C,D	–	–	–	–	A,C	A,C	–

Letters indicate the groups between which the differences in tissue thickness are significant. (p < .05).

Appendix E: Resources of Agencies or Individuals to Assist in Forensic Identification and Mass Fatality Incident Information Retrieval

Local and State Agencies:

Hospitals and other health care facilities
Dental Schools
Health Care Providers
Employer Dental Insurance Carrier
Public Aid Insurance Administrator
Component Dental Associations
American Board of Forensic Odontology

Federal Agencies:

NCIC
FBI Building
10th & Pennsylvania, N. W.
Washington, D.C. 20535
(202) 324-5049

Council on Dental Affairs and the Federal Dental Service
1111 14th Avenue, N.W. # 1200
Washington, D.C. 20005

Military Records Depository
900 Paige Blvd.
St. Louis, MO

Insurance Carriers:

Council on Dental Care Programs
American Dental Association
2 11 E. Chicago Avenue
Chicago, IL 60601

Other Resources:

Family/Friends/Co-Workers
Medical Records
Prior Military Service
Prior Judicial Detention in County
State or Federal Institutions
Prior Hospitalizations (chest films, skull films)
Oral Surgeons in the Area
Veteran's Administration Hospitals
Any Previous Areas of Residence
Chiropractic radiographs
Orthodontists in the area if under treatment

References for Trained Odontologists:

American Board of Forensic Odontology
American Society of Forensic Odontology
American Academy of Forensic Sciences
P.O. Box 669
Colorado Springs, CO 8090 1-0669
(719) 636-1 100 (719) 636-1993 fax

U.S. Department of Justice
Federal Bureau of Investigation
Washington, D. C. 20535-0001

American Dental Association

Han SZ, Alfano MC, Pstoter WJ, Rekow ED (2003). Bioterrorism and catastrophe response: a quick reference guide to resources. *JADA* 134:745-752.

Law Enforcement Online (LEO)

Instructions for the National Dental Image Repository (NDIR)

What is LEO?

Law Enforcement Online (LEO) provides the law enforcement, criminal justice and public safety communities a secure *anytime* and *anywhere* national and international method of electronic communication, education, and information sharing. The LEO system provides a state-of-the-art, secure, common communications link to all levels of law enforcement, criminal justice, and public safety by supporting broad, immediate dissemination and exchange of information.

LEO is accessed through the Internet using a dial-up connection like America Online (AOL), Microsoft Network (MSN), or any other Internet service provider, DSL, Cable Modem, or LAN connection with Internet access. The Law Enforcement Online (LEO) network system is only available to persons duly employed by a law enforcement, criminal justice, or public safety agency/department and whose position requires secure communication with other agencies.

How do you get access to LEO?

Complete and return the application provided. You will receive your LEO user name and password in approximately three weeks.

How do I access the LEO website once I receive my LEO user name and password?

Open a browser window. (i.e., Internet Explorer, Netscape)

Navigate to the URL: **http://cgate.leo.gov.**

Click **Yes** on the Security Alert dialogue box. If additional prompts appear, click **Yes.**

Enter your current LEO user name and password and click **Sign In**.

Click **Yes** to close the browser window.

The Launchpad will appear indicating you are securely connected to LEO via the clientless VPN. The Launchpad displays easy access to links. Please note: In order to access links on the LEO secure site directly, you will need to type the URL into the Launchpad. You cannot access LEO links by typing them directly into the browser's address line.

How do I access the NDIR Area on LEO from the Launchpad?

Click on **Home-LEO** in the Launchpad.

Enter your LEO Username and password. Click **Log In**.

Click on **LEOSIGS**. (Found to the left of the Screen.)

Click on **Public SIGS.**
Click on **CJIS.**

Click on **Programs.**

Click on **National Crime Information Center.**

Click on **National Dental Image Repository.**

How do I access my LEO E-mail?

LEO provides a secure e-mail called webmail that is accessible from the Internet. There is no set-up required. Mailboxes have a 100MB storage capacity. You access your LEO Webmail from the Launchpad.

Open a browser window. (Internet Explorer, Netscape)

Navigate to the URL: **http://cgate.leo.gov.**

Click **Yes** on the Security Alert dialogue box. If additional prompts appear, click **Yes.**

Enter your current LEO user name and password and click **Sign In.**

Click **OK** to close the browser window.

The Launchpad will appear indicating you are securely connected to LEO via the clientless VPN.

Click on **LEO Webmail**.

Enter your LEO Username and Password.

If you experience difficulty or have questions regarding how to use LEO Webmail, contact the **LEO Helpdesk, available 24 hours a day/7 days a week at 1-888-334-4536.**

The National Dental Image Repository (NDIR) on the Law Enforcement Online (LEO)

The NDIR is now available on the Law Enforcement Online (LEO) website and provides an image repository for law enforcement agencies who wish to post supplemental dental images related to National Crime Information Center (NCIC) Missing, Unidentified, and Wanted Person records in a web environment. This allows for easier access and retrieval of the information by qualified individuals performing dental comparisons.

Participation is voluntary. The NDIR is purely an additional tool for agencies to use in attempting to more easily identify missing, unidentified, and wanted persons. The NDIR is not intended to supplant any of the procedures in your state. Please check with your CJIS Systems Officer (CSO) to ensure there are no policies within your state that would prevent or apply to your agency submitting supplemental dental images to the NDIR. If you serve as the CSO, please disseminate this information to agencies within your state and advise them of any state policy that may apply to their participation in the NDIR.

The NDIR website on LEO provides specific technical instructions for scanning and submitting images to the NDIR. Please note: LEO is easier to access now that special software is no longer required. Step-by-step instructions on how to effectively use the new LEO access and locate the NDIR can be found at the following web site. To obtain a LEO account, please e-mail your request to **AGMU@leo.gov**.

The CJIS Division is anxious for agencies to submit information to the NDIR and is actively looking for agencies willing to participate. More information regarding the NDIR can be obtained by contacting: **Mrs. Stacey C. Davis, FBICJIS Division, at (304) 625-2618.**

Medical examiners, coroners, *forensic dentists* and anthropologists who work in conjunction with law enforcement agencies will also have an interest in the web site. Please disseminate this information to those individuals as well as other law enforcement agencies within your jurisdiction where possible.

Protocol and Technical Requirements for Submitting *Missing and Wanted Person* Information to the National Dental Image Repository (NDIR)

Agencies must submit all of the required documents in a digital format package via e-mail to **NDIR@leo.gov**. Law Enforcement Online (LEO) has a limit of 10 megabit (MB) for the transmission of any e-mail attachments. The detailed and specific instructions for submission can be found at the NDIR website. The NIC number should appear on all documents and images.

Required documents include the following digitized scans or copies:

- Supplemental dental records

- *Missing and Wanted Person* Submission Form

- NCIC Record

- Dental Condition Worksheet

- NCIC Person Dental Report Form

- Treating dentist's treatment records with image(s) labeled with *right* and *left* designators to ensure all films in the image are oriented the same way. Only treatment notes and odontograms indicating completed treatment should be submitted.

- All available radiographs

- Any miscellaneous material relevant to the case including, but not limited to: intraoral/extraoral photographs showing teeth, digital photographs of dental models, cephalometric radiographs or other medical radiographs of the head and neck region

Protocol and Technical Requirements for Submitting *Unidentified Person* Information to the National Dental Image Repository (NDIR)

Agencies must submit all of the required documents in a digital format package via e-mail to **NDIR@leo.gov**. Law Enforcement Online (LEO) has a limit of 10 megabit (MB) for the transmission of any e-mail attachments. The detailed and specific instructions for submission can be found at the NDIR website. The NIC number should appear on all documents and images.

Required documents include the following digitized copies:

- Supplemental dental records

- *Unidentified Person* Submission Form

- NCIC Record

- Completed Dental Condition Worksheet

- NCIC Person Dental Report Form.

- NCIC Missing Person Dental Report

- All available radiographs. Image(s) should be labeled with right and left designators to ensure all films in the image are oriented the same way. They should be clearly marked as to the year they were taken.

- Any miscellaneous material relevant to the case including, but not limited to: intraoral/extraoral photographs showing teeth, digital photographs of dental models, cephalometric radiographs or other medical radiographs of the head and neck region

Appendix F: Tooth Conversion Tables

Chapter 2 - Dental Identification

TABLE 2-1. Dental Nomenclature Conversion Table: Deciduous Teeth.
Compiled by Robert Dorion, DDS, DABFO

Upper Right   Upper Left

	2M	1M	C	I2	I1	I1	I2	C	1M	2M
Universal	A	B	C	D	E	F	G	H	I	J
Palmer	E+	D+	C+	B+	A+	+A	+B	+C	+D	+E
FDI	55	54	53	52	51	61	62	63	64	65
Hareup	05+	04+	03+	02+	01+	+01	+02	+03	+04	+05
Other	V	IV	III	II	I	I	II	III	IV	V
Other	5D	4D	3D	2D	1D	1D	2D	3D	4D	5D
Other	d5	d4	d3	d2	d1	d1	d2	d3	d4	d5
Other	5m	4m	3m	2m	1m	1m	2m	3m	4m	5m
Other	A	B	C	D	E	E	D	C	B	A
Other	dm2	dm1	dc	di2	di1	di1	di2	dc	dm1	dm2
FDI Modified	55	54	53	52	51	61	62	63	64	65

Lower Right   Lower Left

	2M	1M	C	I2	I1	I1	I2	C	1M	2M
Universal	T	S	R	Q	P	O	N	M	L	K
Palmer	E-	D-	C-	B-	A-	-A	-B	-C	-D	-E
FDI	85	84	83	82	81	71	72	73	74	75
Hareup	05-	04-	03-	02-	01-	-01	-02	-03	-04	-05
Other	V	IV	III	II	I	I	II	III	IV	V
Other	5D	4D	3D	2D	1D	1D	2D	3D	4D	5D
Other	d5	d4	d3	d2	d1	d1	d2	d3	d4	d5
Other	5m	4m	3m	2m	1m	1m	2m	3m	4m	5m
Other	A	B	C	D	E	E	D	C	B	A
Other	dm2	dm1	dc	di2	di1	di1	di2	dc	dm1	dm2
FDI Modified	75	74	73	72	71	81	82	83	84	85

27

Manual of Forensic Odontology

Table 2-2a. Dental Nomenclature Conversion Table: Permanent Teeth. Compiled by Robert Dorion, DDS, DABFO

	Upper Right								Upper Left							
	3M	2M	1M	2P	1P	C	I2	I1	I1	I2	C	1P	2P	1M	2M	3M
Other	UR8	UR7	UR6	UR5	UR4	UR3	UR2	UR1	UL1	UL2	UL3	UL4	UL5	UL6	UL7	UL8
Hareup	8+	7+	6+	5+	4+	3+	2+	1+	+1	+2	+3	+4	+5	+6	+7	+8
Palmer	8⌐	7⌐	6⌐	5⌐	4⌐	3⌐	2⌐	1⌐	⌐1	⌐2	⌐3	⌐4	⌐5	⌐6	⌐7	⌐8
Universal	1	2	3	4	5	6	7	8	9	10	11	12	13	14	15	16
FDI	18	17	16	15	14	13	12	11	21	22	23	24	25	26	27	28
Bosworth	8	7	6	5	4	3	2	1	1	2	3	4	5	6	7	8
Lowlands	M3	M2	M1	P2	P1	C	I2	I1	I1	I2	C	P1	P2	M1	M2	M3
Europe	D8	D7	D6	D5	D4	D3	D2	D1	G1	G2	G3	G4	G5	G6	G7	G8
Holland	sdM3	sdM2	sdM1	sdP2	sdP1	sdC	sdI2	sdI1	sgI1	sgI2	sgC	sgP1	sgP2	sgM1	sgM2	sgM3
FDI Modified	18	17	16	15	14	13	12	11	21	22	23	24	25	26	27	28
Other	16	15	14	13	12	11	10	9	8	7	6	5	4	3	2	1

28

Chapter 2 - Dental Identification

TABLE 2-2B. Dental Nomenclature Conversion Table: Permanent Teeth. Compiled by Robert Dorion, DDS, DABFO

	Lower Left								Lower Right							
	3M	2M	1M	2P	1P	C	I2	I1	I1	I2	C	1P	2P	1M	2M	3M
Other	LL8	LL7	LL6	LL5	LL4	LL3	LL2	LL1	LR1	LR2	LR3	LR4	LR5	LR6	LR7	LR8
Hareup	-8	-7	-6	-5	-4	-3	-2	-1	1-	2-	3-	4-	5-	6-	7-	8-
Palmer	|8	|7	|6	|5	|4	|3	|2	|1	1|	2|	3|	4|	5|	6|	7|	8|
Universal	17	18	19	20	21	22	23	24	25	26	27	28	29	30	31	32
FDI	38	37	36	35	34	33	32	31	41	42	43	44	45	46	47	48
Bosworth	H	G	F	E	D	C	B	A	A	B	C	D	E	F	G	H
Lowlands	M3	M2	M1	P2	P1	C	I2	I1	I1	I2	C	P1	P2	M1	M2	M3
Europe	g8	g7	g6	g5	g4	g3	g2	g1	d1	d2	d3	d4	d5	d6	d7	d8
Holland	giM3	giM2	giM1	giP2	giP1	giC	giI2	giI1	diI1	diI2	diC	diP1	diP2	diM3	diM2	diM3
FDI Modified	48	47	46	45	44	43	42	41	31	32	33	34	35	36	37	38
Other	17	18	19	20	21	22	23	24	25	26	27	28	29	30	31	32

29

Appendix G: Information for DMORT Membership

To join a DMORT or for more information, contact the Team Leader in your region.

DMORT Regional Team Leaders

REGION I (ME, NH, VT, MA, CT, RI)
Michael Oneil

REGION II (NY, NJ, PR, VI)
John C. Oldfield 212-362-6160

REGION III (PA, MD, DC, DE, VA, WV)
Patricia Kauffman 610-828-8973

REGION IV (AL, KY, TN, NC, SC, GA, MS, FL)
Cotton Howell 803-329-7270S

REGION V (MN, WI, IL, IN, MI, OH)
Frank Saul 419-382-2070

REGION VI (NM, TX, OK, AR, LA)
Todd Ellis 806-272-4574

REGION VII (NE, IA, KS, MO)
William Young

Dean Snow 816-776-2255

REGION VIII (MT, ND, SD, WY, UT, CO)
Lance Peterson 801-778-6682

REGION IX (AZ, NV, CA, HI)
John Linstrom 760-497-6255

REGION X (WA, AK, OR, ID)
Duane Bigoni 503-248-3746

Appendix H: Tasks Related to WIN ID Comparison Procedures

Protocols developed from Katrina.

All of the tasks described in Appendix G were performed to acquire data that permitted dental team members using WinID3 software to compare post mortem and antemortem information in an effort to determine identity of the victim. The WinID User Manual gives basic instructions for using the software. Becoming proficient with comparisons requires practice and experience and DMORT dental team members received primary training including a PowerPoint presentation that illustrated step-by-step WinID instruction. Excerpts from that presentation are included here.

DMORT Dental Autopsy and WinID3/Dexis Protocol
Established – Katrina Deployment - Louisiana

Post Mortem Teams

Personnel:

- Post Mortem Leader
- Personnel for Stations 1-3:

- #1 (Cutter) - Performs Dental Autopsy
- #2 (Shooter) - Assists #1 and operates Aribex Nomad X-ray generator
- #3 (Geek) - Enters data into computer and controls pace of examination after:
- Opening WinID3 (*by Post Mortem Section Leader only on initial startup*)
- Clicking on the **WinID3.4.5** Icon
- Choosing the network shortcut **WinID Katrina Baton Rouge.mdb**

- Photographer – Acquires and manages all images for all stations
- Rover – Monitors stations supplies and equipment. Substitutes for any position as needed.
- IT expert

Team Tasks

- Receive gurney from the tracker

- #3 (The Geek):
- Clicks on **Add New** and chooses **Post Mortem** - a RED Bordered Screen will open
- Enters the victim's body number and the full name of the team member entering the record.
- Verifies the number (by voice confirmation) by repeating it to the tracker. Once number confirmation is obtained, clicks **OK** and the **Unique Case Number** appears automatically.
- Enters the **Post Mortem Condition** field in the **Name** tab, clicks on ` the **Identifiers** tab and fills in the **Sex** field (if determinable)

- Enters the following in the *P1* and *P2* fields:
    P1 - the name of the photographer
    P2 - the words *per protocol.* When the photographer has completed the photographs he/she will report the number of pictures taken.
- Enters number of pictures taken in front of the *per protocol.*

- While #3 performs the tasks listed above:
    - #1 (The Cutter) and #2 (The Shooter) clean the mouth and ready the oral cavity for charting and radiographs.
    - Any post mortem exfoliated teeth are replaced if possible. #1 and 2 must agree and #3 must confirm this procedure radiographically

- The Photographer takes the following pictures once the area is cleaned:
    - Body label under the chin for the facial photo.
    - Anterior edge of teeth (slightly open to reveal the Maxillary and Mandibular incisal edges.
    - Maxillary occlusal view.
    - Mandibular occlusal view.
    - Any additional photos that will aid in the identification.

- #3 (The Geek):
    - After the photographs are completed post mortem radiographs are recorded by:
        - Clicking on the *Graphics* tab and then on the *DEXIS* button. The *DEXIS* window opens over top of the *WinID* window. *DEXIS* will create the new *DEXIS* file with the same body number.
        - Insuring that the *tooth icon* is highlighted if a full mouth series is to

        be taken

        - Clicking on the *x-ray icon* . A dialog box appears
        - Clicking the *DONE* button.
        - Clicking the *full mouth* button begins an 18-film series sequence automatically prompting the area of mouth to be exposed next:
            - For this operation the sequence is:

1. Max R Molar		10. Mand R Molar
2. Max R Premolar		11. Mand R Premolar
3. Max R Bitewing Projection		12 Mand R Bitewing Projection
4. Mand L Molar		13. Max R Canine
5. Mand L Premolar		14. Max Centrals
6. Mand L Bitewing Projection		15. Max L. Canine
7. Max L Molar		16. Mand L. Canine
8. Max L. Premolar		17. Mand Centrals
9. Max L Bitewing Projection		18. Mand R Canine

- Telling #1 where to place the sensor using the highlighted *Orange Colored Odontogram* as a guide. Green bars indicate *DEXIS* is *ready.*

- #1 places the sensor and #2 triggers the radiograph.

- #3 notes when the green bars turn red, indicating the sensor is fully exposed. When this occurs #3:

- Shouts **RADIATION** informing #1 and #2 that the sensor is exposed. The radiograph appears in the area between the green / red bars.

  - Decides whether to accept of retake the radiograph and informs #1 of the decision.

  (A **persistent yellow dot** means that the radiation level (number of pulses) needs to be increased. A **persistent red dot** means that the radiation level (number of pulses) needs to be decreased. The shift supervisor will advise concerning adjustment for *waffling* of images.)

- Continues to follow the changing odontogram until the series is completed.

- Presses the back button to allow a retake while the sensor is still placed in the same area of the mouth. If a retake is required, it should be done immediately to avoid unnecessary changes in equipment and positioning.

- Verifies that all images are optimal (retake if necessary) and arranged with no overlapping images. The **Home ICON** is used to view the final positioning of the radiographs. (After clicking on **Export All to WinID** the operator can not come back to this step)

- Click on a radiograph enlarging it. Brightness and contrast can be adjusted by placing the cursor in the radiographic image, holding down the left mouse button and dragging the cursor.

1. Once you are satisfied with your adjustments, have the #1 and #2 review and if they accept, verify that all images are optimal and arranged with no overlapping images you are ready to save and export. Use the **Home ICON** to get rid of overlap.
2. Click on the 'Export file' icon.
3. On the pop-up window that appears, click on the **Export All** button. Make sure that all the checkboxes have a checkmark in them.
4. Click on the **Export All to WinID**.
5. When this pop-up window disappears, the x-rays have been exported.
6. Minimize **DEXIS**. You should see the **WinID** post mortem form.
7. Click on the **Name** tab. Then click on the **Add Graphic** button.
   a. A dialog box will open that has all the files of the x-rays that will be linked to WinID. Navigate to the file where the name matches the Patient ID number. For instance, if your patient is 10-101010, then the x-ray file to link to WinID post mortem is '10-101010.jpg'.
   b. Select the proper jpg file and then click the **Open** button.
   c. The path to this file will appear in the textbox next to the **Add Graphic** button.
8. Click on the **Graphic** tab and you should see the x-rays on the screen in WinID.
9. Click on the **Dental** tab.
10. In the record banner at bottom of post mortem window move one record back or forward

to assure that changes are saved.
11. Prepare for next case… go to step 1.

Modified for DMORT- Katrina- Louisiana

Protocol Example 2.

DMORT Dental Photography Protocol
DMORT Katrina Louisiana

Beginning of day procedures:

1. Turn on the Dental Morgue Photography Computer & bring up the desktop.
2. Create a new folder on the desktop for today's photo session entitled "MM.DD.YY photos" (where MM is the month, DD the day and YY the last digits of the year).
3. Set up the camera equipment.
4. Check the number of available exposures remaining on the Compact Flash Card by looking at the "Top Control Panel" to make sure you have enough memory for the days work.
5. Take a sample photo & check the camera settings for optimal operation.
6. Delete the sample photo.

Photography protocol:

1. When the Tracker brings a new case to the Dental Section, prepare a label with case number.
2. 1st photo: close up of the label with case number.
3. 2nd photo: Full-face photo with case number label visible in the field. (before dental autopsy)
4. Allow the dental autopsy team to clean the teeth & any removable appliances.
5. 3rd photo: Anterior teeth close-up. (maxillary and mandibular incisal edges visible)
6. 4th photo: Maxillary arch photo.
7. 5th photo: Mandibular arch photo.
8. Supplemental photos as needed (i.e. unique restorations, removable appliances, malocclusions, etc.)
9. Final photo: close up of the label with case number.
10. Count number of photos taken (include label photos in the count).
11. Initial & sign the tracker's paperwork for Dental Photography & fill in the space for number of photos taken (includes label photos in the count).
12. Give total photo count to the person operating the dental post mortem computer.

Photographic file management:

1. Transfer photo files from the camera to the photo computer.
2. Import images into Dexis.
3. Backup files onto the dedicated Dental Photography USB Drive.

End of day procedures:

1. Prior to unplugging the camera or USB Drive from the computer use the "unplug or eject hardware" icon/function on the lower right side of the launch bar. (for Windows 2000 computers)

2. The Dental Photographer clips the USB Drive back onto their lanyard for safekeeping.
3. The Dental Photographer keeps the USB Drive in his/her possession at all times.
4. Shut Down the photo computer.
5. Turn off the flash unit & camera, remove the camera battery & place in the charger, and store the camera & flash back in the photo bag.

Modified for DMORT-Katrina- Louisiana

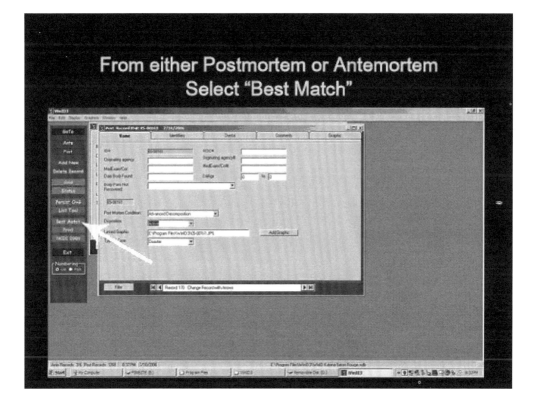

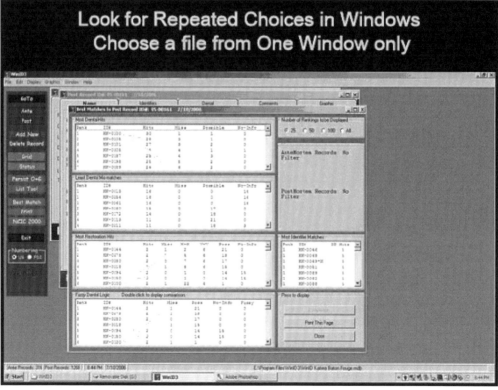

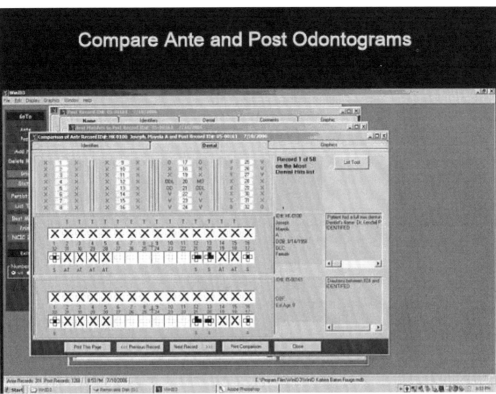

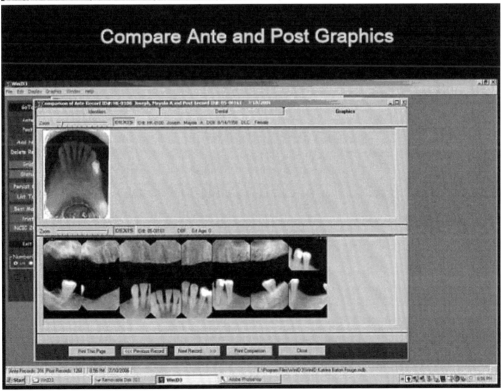

Compare Ante and Post Odontograms

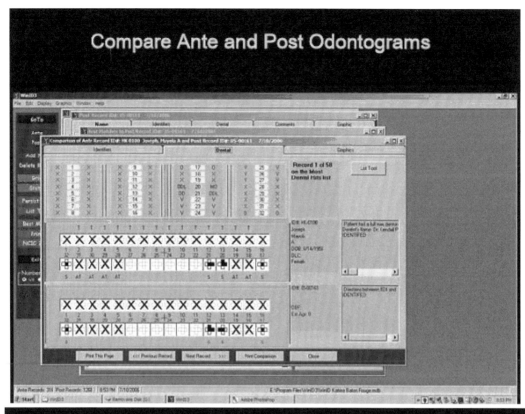

Next Graphic or Odontogram will be Displayed
Continue until all are viewed or match is made

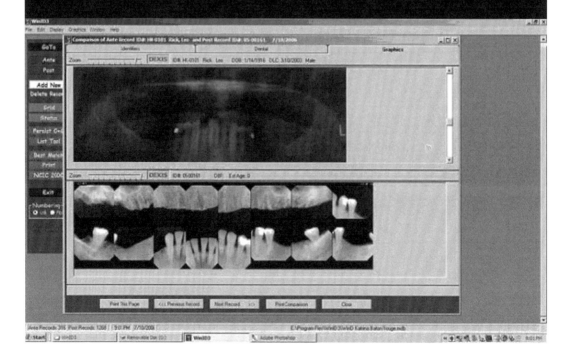

Appendix I: Court Rulings of 1st and 4th Amendments and the Patriots Act.

Court rulings concerning Constitutional violations of the First, Fourth Amendment have been handed down since the inception of the Patriot Act of 2001. These challenges primarily relate to issues concerning the balancing of the rights of the accused against National security. Principal decisions are listed here.

Legal Decisions - Patriot Act of 2001

Compulsory, secret, and un-reviewable production of information required by FBI's application of 18 U.S.C. Sec. 2709 violated the Fourth Amendment, and

Non disclosure provision violates the First Amendment
–   John Doe v. John Ashcroft, 334 F.Supp. 2d 471 (Patriot Act Provision Sec. 505 modifying 18 U.S.C. Sec. 2709 concerning national security letters served on recipients with permanent non disclosure provisions violates First Amendment and prevents access to courts in violation of the Fourth Amendment)

On commenting on the President's reach in combating terrorism, the Supreme Court has declared, "We have …long made clear that a state of war is not a blank check for the President when it comes to the rights of the nation's citizens." Hamidi v. Rumsfeld, 542 U.S. 507, 159 L.Ed. 578, 124 S.Ct. 2633, 2650 (2004)

Judge Victor Marrero wrote "that even the war power does not remove constitutional limitations safeguarding essential liberties."

–   John Doe v. John Ashcroft, 334 F.Supp. 2d 471 (Patriot Act Provision Sec. 505 modifying 18 U.S.C. Sec. 2709 violates First Amendment and Fourth Amendment)

"It is under the pressing exigencies of crisis that there is the greatest temptation to dispense with fundamental constitutional guarantees which, it is feared, will inhibit governmental action."
–   John Doe v. John Ashcroft, 334 F.Supp. 2d 471 (Patriot Act Provision Sec. 505 modifying 18 U.S.C. Sec. 2709 violates First Amendment and Fourth Amendment)

"It is precisely such times that demand heightened vigilance, especially by the judiciary, to ensure that, as a people and as a nation, America steers a principled course faithful and true to its still honored founding values."- John Doe v. John Ashcroft, 334 F.Supp. 2d 471 (Patriot Act Provision Sec. 505 modifying 18 U.S.C. Sec. 2709 violates First Amendment and Fourth Amendment)

"The high stakes pressing the scales thus compel a court to strike the most sensitive judicial balance, calibrating by delicate increments toward a result that adequately protects national security without unduly sacrificing individual freedoms, that endeavors to do what is just for one and just for all."
–   John Doe v. John Ashcroft, 334 F.Supp. 2d 471 (Patriot Act Provision Sec. 505 modifying 18 U.S.C. Sec. 2709 violates First Amendment and Fourth Amendment)

"In short, the September 11 cases will challenge the judiciary to do September 11 justice, to rise to the moment with wisdom equal to the task, its judgments worthy of the large dimensions that define the best September 11 brought out of the rest of American society."
–   John Doe v. John Ashcroft, 334 F.Supp. 2d 471 (Patriot Act Provision Sec. 505 modifying 18 U.S.C. Sec. 2709 violates First Amendment and Fourth Amendment

Appendix J: Abuse and Neglect Protocols

ST. JOSEPH'S HEALTHCARE • HAMILTON HEALTH SCIENCES • ST. PETER'S HOSPITAL • COUNCIL AGAINST ABUSE OF OLDER PERSONS • HAMILTON POLICE SERVICE • McMASTER CENTRE FOR GERONTOLOGICAL STUDIES • HAMILTON ACADEMY OF MEDICINE • HAMILTON ACADEMY OF DENTISTRY •

ABUSE AND NEGLECT OF AN OLDER OR VULNERABLE PERSON

Any action or inaction by ANY person, which causes harm to the older or vulnerable person.

WHAT TO DO AND WHAT TO CHECK FOR:

Acknowledge Suspicion of abuse may develop over time. Accumulate/document evidence.

Barriers Fear of retaliation, withdrawal of caregiver support, confidentially.

Urgency Assess immediate risk of physical harm or if basic necessities of life are provided.

Screen Assess person's ability to help themselves (i.e. competency).

Empower Inform person of their rights, resources and establish a safety plan.

Refer Seek support or consultation from other professionals.

PHYSICAL ABUSE

Any act of violence causing injury or physical discomfort (e.g. slapping, pinching, and punching
or other rough handling, forcible restraint or intentional over / under medication), including

SEXUAL ASSAULT.

Indicators - unexplained injuries in areas normally covered (bruises in various stages of healing, burns or bites) alopecia and bleeding scalp from hair pulling, untreated medical problems, history of "accidents", signs of over / under medication, sexual assault, wasting, and dehydration.

PSYCHOLOGICAL ABUSE

Any action or comment causing emotional anguish, fear or diminished self-esteem or dignity (e.g. threats to do harm, unwanted institutionalization, harassment, abandonment, imposed isolation, removal of decision making choices).

> **Indicators -** fear, anxiety, depression, withdrawal, cowering, reluctance to talk openly, fearful interaction with caregiver, caregiver speaking on behalf of person and not allowing privacy.

FINANCIAL ABUSE

Theft or exploitation of a person's money, property or assets (e.g. forgery, misuse of Power of Attorney).

Indicators - standard of living not in keeping with income or assets, theft of property noted, unusual /inappropriate activity in bank accounts, forged signatures on checks, forcing a person to sign over a will or property, over-charging for services /products, overdue bills.

NEGLECT

Inability to provide basic or personal care needs (e.g. food, water, required medications, shelter, hygiene, clothing, physical aids – hearing aids, eye glasses, dentures, exercise and social interaction, lack of attention, abandonment, undue confinement, inadequate supervision or
safety precautions, withholding medical services / treatment).

• **ACTIVE NEGLECT** - intentional failure of a caregiver to fulfill their care giving responsibilities.

• **PASSIVE NEGLECT** - unintentional failure of a caregiver to fulfill their care giving responsibilities because of lack of knowledge, skill, illness, infirmity, or lack of awareness of community supports / resources.

• **SELF NEGLECT** - person's inability to provide for their own essential needs because of physical infirmity or inability to make sound choices due to addiction, mental illness and / or cognitive impairment.

Indicators - Unkempt appearance, inappropriate or dirty clothing, signs of infrequent bathing, living conditions unhealthy, dangerous and / or in disrepair, lack of social contact, no regular medical appointments.

INSTITUTIONAL ABUSE

Any physical, sexual, psychological, financial abuse or neglect occurring within a care facility involving active victimization, withholding or denial of individual care needs, and / or failure to carry out reasonable requests.

DOMESTIC VIOLENCE

Actual or threatened physical, sexual, financial or psychological abuse of a person by someone with whom they have an intimate, familial or romantic relationship which aims to instill fear and / or to coercively control an individual whether it be a female, male or intimate partner.

INTERVIEW STRATEGY

1. Develop trust and be sensitive to person's culture, religion, comfort level and timing in obtaining disclosure - Interview alone, listen, be patient, non-threatening, non-judgmental,
validate feelings, offer emotional support, and avoid premature assumptions and suggestions.

2. Note suspicious histories - Explanation vague, bizarre or incongruent with type or degree of injury, denial of obvious injury, long delay between injury and treatment, history of "doctor hopping".
3. Be alert to person's wishes, ability to understand.

Assess competency, capability and capacity.

4. Identify what information is missing - Frequency, duration, urgency, need for physical examination.

5. Be aware of interdependent relationships / power differences
Use of Substitute Decision Maker, be cautious of involvement of abuser, note conflicting histories, where appropriate interview family members. Some cultures may require a family member to be present during the interview or it may be necessary to negotiate in order to interview someone alone.

POSSIBLE INTERVENTIONS

Consider impact on person, their wishes, their willingness to change and their ability to recognize abuse. Note their capability and understanding of the consequences of their decisions. Your role could be singular or part of a team of service providers that could support the person to be healthy and safe. Be aware of appropriate resources or know how to link with the broader community.

A. EDUCATION

Provide information and support according to the interests expressed by the person. Be aware of services outside the health care system which are specific to the needs of older or vulnerable persons who are being victimized or are at risk.

B. SAFETY PLAN

The plan may include a change to an element of their environment or their relationship which could result in the elimination of the role of the abuser or context of the abuse. Consider:

• Home visits, telephone contact, contact with other family and friends, regular appointments.

• Secure assets e.g. Hide emergency money (coins for pay phone) somewhere outside home.

• Give copies of important documents and keys to trusted friends or family members.

• Plan escape by packing a bag of extra clothing, medicine & personal aids (e.g. glasses, hearing aids).

• Keep phone numbers of friends, relatives, shelters or other trusted individuals handy.

POSSIBLE INTERVIEW QUESTIONS
• Is there something that you would like to share with me?

• Are you afraid of anyone at home?

• Has anyone at home ever hurt you?

• Has anyone ever forced you to do things you didn't want to do?

• Has anyone ever failed to help you take care of yourself when you needed help?

• Have you ever signed any documents that you didn't understand?

• Who makes decisions about your life, like how or where you should live?

• Would you like some help with…?

• It must be hard for you to look after…?

Appendix K: Case Presentation of a Dog Bite Homicide

A twenty-seven year old male individual was attacked and killed by a total of eight pit bull terriers. Photographic documentation of several of the bite mark injuries was accomplished with full spectrum, ALI, IR, and UV photographic techniques. A demonstration of the different photographic results of the same dog bite is provided herein, to show the values and resultant imaging of each of the techniques:

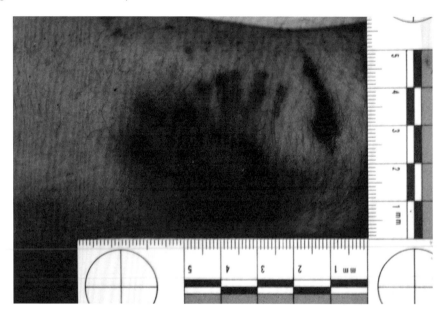

Full Spectrum color flash photo: Canon 10D digital camera, 50mm compact macro lens, ring light

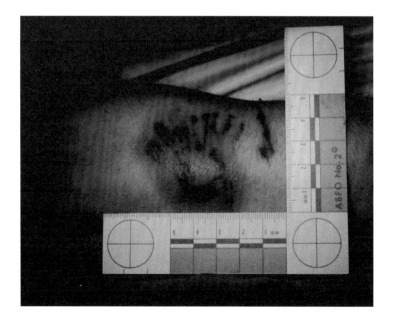

ALI photo: Canon 10D digital camera, 50mm compact macro lens, Tomar 460nm Light Source, #15 yellow lens filter

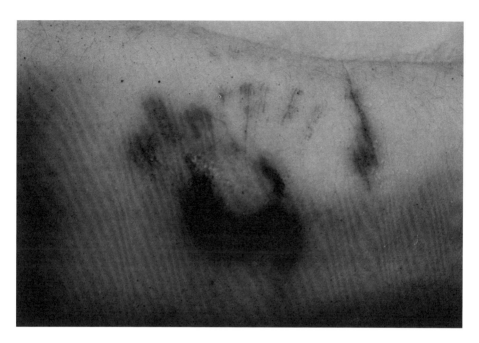

IR photo: Fuji FinePix S3Pro UVIR Digital Camera, Sigma 55mm non-quartz macro lens, #87 IR filter, no flash. Note: focal depth is below superficial levels of bruise pattern.

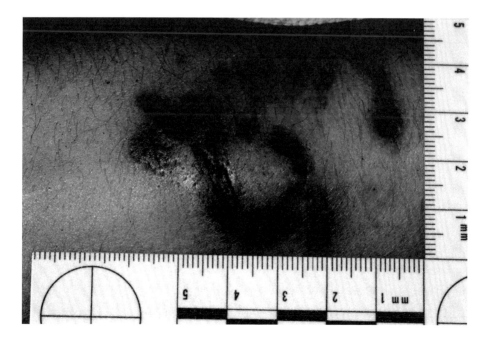

UVA Photo: Fuji FinePix S3Pro UVIR Digital Camera, Nikkor UV 105 macro lens, 18A filter, SB 140 Flash w/ UV filter. Note: surface detail is enhanced.

Appendix L: Bite Mark Cases of Note

BITE MARK CITATIONS

PREPARED BY: HASKELL M. PITLUCK

"BITE MARK CASE MANAGEMENT AND LEGAL CONSIDERATIONS UPDATE 1999"

November 18 - 20, 1999

Las Vegas, Nevada

1. Doyle v. State. 159 Tex. C.R.310, 263 S.W.2d 779 (Jan. 20, 1954)

2. People v. Johnson. 8 Ill.App.3d 457, 289 N.E.2d 722 (Nov. 16, 1972)

3. Patterson v. State. 509 S.W.2d 857 (Tex. Crim 1974) (Mar. 13, 1974)

4. People v. Allah. 84 Misc.2d 500, 376 N.Y.S.2d 399 (Nov. 20, 1975)

5. People v. Marx. 54 Cal.App.3d 100, 126 Cat. Rptr. 350 (Dec. 29, 1975)

6. People v. Johnson. 37 Ill.App.3d 328, 345 N.E.2d 531 (Apr. 7, 1976)

7. People v. Milone. 43 IU.App.3d 385, 356 N.E.2d 1350 (Nov. 12, 1976)

8. Niehaus v. State. 265 Ind. 655, 359 N.E.2d 513 (Jan. 25, 1977)

9. State v. Routh. 30 Or .App. 901, 568 P.2d 704 (Sep. 12, 1977)

10. People v. Watson. 75 Cal.App.3d 384, 142 Cal. Rptr. 134 (Nov. 28, 1977)

11. State v. Kendrick. 31 Or .App. 1195, 572 P.2d 354 (Dec. 12, 1977)

12. People v. Slone. 76 Cal.App.3d 611, 143 Cal. Rptr. 61 (Jan. 6, 1978)

13. State v. Howe. 136 Vt. 53, 386 A2d 1125 (Mar. 15, 1978)

14. State v. Garrison. 120 Ariz. 255, 585 P.2d 563 (Sept. 20, 1978)

15. State v. Bridges. 123 Ariz. 452, 600 P.2d 756 (Aug. 2, 1979)

16. U.S. v. Martin. 9 M. J. 731 (NCMR 1979) (Aug. 7, 1979)

17. State v. Jones. 273 S.C. 723, 259 S.E.2d 120 (Oct 11, 1979)

18. Deutscher v. State. 95 Nev. 669, 601 P.2d 407 (Oct. 18, 1979)

19. State v. Peoples. 227 Kan. 127, 605 P.2d 135 (Jan. 19, 1980)

20. State v. Sager. 600 S.W.2d 541 (Mo. App.) (May 5, 1980)

21. People v. Middleton. 428 N.Y.S. 2d 688, 76 A.D.2d 762 (June 10, 1980)

22. State v. Klevpas. 602 S.W.2d 863 (Mo. App.) (July 10, 1980)

23. Exparte Sue Dolvin. 391 So.2d 677 (Alabama Sup. Ct.) (Sep. 12, 1980)

24. State v. Temple. 302 N.C.I, 273 S.E.2d 273 (Jan. 6, 1981)

25. People v. Smith. 443 N.Y.S.2d 551, 110 Misc.2d 118 (July 24, 1981)

26. State v. Geer. 624 S.W.2d 143 (Mo. App.) (Sep. 22, 1981)

27. People v. Middleton. 54 N.Y.2d 42, 429 N.E.2d 100 (Oct. 27, 1981)

28. Aguilar v. State. 98 Nev. 18, 639 P.2d 533 (Jan. 28, 1982)

29. Kennedy v. State. 640 P.2d 971 (Oklahoma) (Feb. 3, 1982)

30. State v. Turner. 633 S.W.2d 421 (Mo. App.) (Mar. 2, 1982)

31. U.S. v. Martin. 13 M.J. 66 (CMA 1982) (Apr. 19, 1982)

32. State v. Green. 305 N.C. 463, 290 S.E.2d 625 (May 4, 1982)

33. Bludsworth v. State. 98 Nev. 289, 646 P.2d 558 (June 18, 1982)

34. People v. Queen. 108 Ill.App.3d 1088, 440 N.E.2d 126 (July 13, 1982)

35. Commonwealth v. Maltais. 387 Mass.79, 438 N.E.2d 847 (Aug. 4, 1982)

36. Commonwealth v. Graves. 456 A.2d 561 (Pa. Super 1983) (Feb. 4, 1983)

37. State of Kansas v. Galloway, unpublished opinion filed March 26, 1983

38. People v. Jordan. 114 Ill.App.3d 16, 448 N.E.2d 237 (Apr. 14, 1983)

39. Miller v. State. 448 N.E.2d 293 (Ind. 1983) (May 6, 1983)

40. State v. Stokes. 433 So.2d 96 (La. 1983) (May 23, 1983)

41. People v. Dixon. 191 Cal. Rptr. 917 (Cal.App. 4th Dist. 1983) (June 7, 1983)

42. People v. Columbo. 118 Ill.App.3d 882, 455 N.E.2d 733 (June 24, 1983)

43. State v. Sapsford. 22 Ohio App.3d 1 (Nov. 9, 1983)

44. Chase v. State. 678 P.2d 1347 (Alaska App.) (Mar. 9, 1984)

45. Marblev v. State. 461 N.E.2d 1102 (Ind. 1984) (Apr. 19, 1984)

46. State v. Welker. 683 P.2d 1110 (Wash.App. 1984) (May 21, 1984)

47. Bundy v. State. 455 So.2d 330 (Florida Sup.Ct.) (June 21, 1984)

48. People v. Smith. 63 N.Y.2d 41, 468 N.E.2d 879 (July 2, 1984)

49. State v. Asherman. 193 Conn. 695, 478 A.2d 227 (July 17, 1984)

50. People v. Schuning. 125 Ill.App.3d 808, 466 N.E.2d 673 (July 19, 1984)

51. State v. Adams. 481 A.2d 718 (R.L 1981) (Aug. 21, 1984)

52. Southard v. State. Slip opinion, Court of Appeals of Arkansas (Aug. 29, 1984)

53. Graves v. State. Slip opinion, 1st Court of Appeals, Houston (Aug. 30, 1984)

54. Mavnard v. State. 455 So.2d 632 (Florida App.) (Sep. 13, 1984)

55. People v. Jordan. 103 IU.2d 192, 469 N.E.2d 569 (IU.Sup.Ct.) (Sep. 20, 1984)

56. People v. Williams. 128 Ill.App.3d 384, 470 N.E.2d 1140 (Oct. 22, 1984)

57. State v. Perea. 142 Ariz. 352, 690 P.2d 71 (Nov. 1, 1984)

58. State v. Bullard. 312 N.C. 129, 322 S.E.2d 370 (Nov. 6, 1984)

59. Smith v. State. 253 Ga. 536, 322 S.E.2d 492 (Nov. 16, 1984)

60. People v. McDonald. 37 Cal.3d 351, 690 P.2d 709 (Nov. 21, 1984)

61. State v. Thomton. 253 Ga. 524, 322 S.E.2d 711 (GA 1984) (Nov. 21, 1984)

62. Bradford v. State. 460 So.2d 926 (Fla.App. 2d Dist. 1984) (Nov. 30, 1984)

63. Tuggle v. Commonwealth. 228 Va 493, 323 S.E.2d 539 (Nov. 30, 1984)

64. People v. Bethune. 484 N.Y.S.2d 577, 105 A.D.2d 262 (Dec. 31, 1984)

65. People v. Queen. 130 Ill.App.3d 523, 474 N.E.2d 786 (Jan. 11, 1985)

66. Southard v. State. Slip opinion. Supreme Court of Arkansas (Apr. 1, 1985)

67. State v. Dickson. 691 S.W.2d 334 (Mo.App. 1985) (Apr. 2, 1985)

68. State v. Carter. 74 N.C.App. 437, 328 S.E.2d 607 (May 7, 1985)

69. Clemons v. State. 470 So.2d 653 (Miss. 1985) (May 29, 1985)

70. Standridge v. State. 701 P.2d 761 (Okl. Cr. 1985) (June 6, 1985)

71. Tuggle v. Commonwealth. 230 Va. 99, 334 S.E.2d 838 (Sept. 6, 1985)

72. State v. Ortiz. 198 Conn. 220, 502 A.2d 400 (Dec. 31, 1985)

73. People v. Walkey. 177 Cal.App.3d 268, 223 Cal. Rptr. 132 (Cal.App.4th Dist) (Jan.23, 1986)

74. Thomton v. State. 255 Ga. 434, 339 S.E.2d 240 (Feb. 13, 1986)

75. Wade v. State. 490 N.E.2d 1097 (Ind., 1986) (April 3, 1986)

76. People v. Vigil. 718 P.2d 496 (Colo. 1986) (April 14, 1986)

77. Commonwealth v. Cifizzari. 397 Mass. 560, 492 N.E.2d 357 (May 14, 1986)

78. State v. Bingham. 105 Wash.2d 820, 719 P.2d 109 (Wash. 1986) (May 15, 1986)

79. Rogers v. State. 256 Ga. 140, 344 S.E.2d 644 (Ga. 1986) (June 25, 1986)

80. State v. Johnson. 317 N.C. 343, 346 S.E.2d 596 (Aug. 12, 1986)

81. People v. Prante. 147 Ill.App.3d 1039, 498 N.E.2d 889 (Oct. 3, 1986)

82. Smith v. State. Unpublished opinion, Texas Ct. of Appeals (Oct. 9, 1986)

83. State v. Johnson. 721 S.W.2d 23 (Mo. App.) (Oct. 14, 1986)

84. State v. Stinson. 134 Wis.2d 224, 397 N.W.2d 136 (Oct. 28, 1986)

85. In Re The Marriage of Rimer. 395 N.W.2d 390 (Minn. App.) (Nov. 4, 1986)

86. McCrory v. State. 505 So.2d 1272 (Ala. Cr. App.) (Dec. 9, 1986)

87. Marquez v. State. 725 S.W.2d 217 (Tex. Cr. App.) (Jan. 14, 1987)

88. Bundv. Wainwright. 808 F.2d 1410 (llth Cir.) (Jan. 15, 1987)

89. DuBoise v State. Slip opinion. Supreme Court of Florida (Feb. 19, 1987)

    (Superseded by Case #110 below)

90. People v. Davis. 189 Cal.App.3d 1177, 234 Cal. Rptr. 859 (Feb. 26, 1987)

91. People v. Dace. 153 Ill.App.3d 891, 506 N.E.2d 332 (Mar. 23, 1987)

92. People v. Drake. 129 A.D.2d 963, 514 N.Y.S.2d 280 (Apr. 3 1987)

93. State v. Vital. 505 So.2d 1006 (La. App.) (Apr. 9, 1987)

94. State v. Kendrick. 47 Wash.App. 620, 736 P.2d 1079 (May 11, 1987)

95. Ngoc Van Le v. State. 733 S.W.2d 280 (Tex. App.) (May 14, 1987)

96. People v. Wachal. 156 Ill.App.3d 331, 509 N.E.2d 648 (May 29, 1987)

97. State v. Moen. 86 Or.App.87, 738 P.2d 228 (June 24, 1987)

98. Handley v. State. 515 So.2d 121, Court of Criminal Appeal of Alabama (June 30, 1987)

99. Jackson v. State. 511 So.2d 1047 (Fla. App.) (Aug. 7, 1987)

100. State v. Crump. Slip opinion, Ohio Court of Appeals (Aug. 11, 1987)

101. People v. Perez. 194 Cal.App.3d 525, 239 Cal. Rptr. 569 (Aug. 26, 1987)

102. Strickland v. State. 184 Ga.App. 185, 361 S.E.2d 207 (Sept. 11, 1987)

103. State v. McDaniel. 515 So.2d 572 (La. App. 1 Cir) (Oct. 14, 1987)

104. Inman v. State. 515 So. 2d 1150 (Miss. Sup. Ct.) (Nov. 18, 1987)

105. People v. Watson. 521 N.Y.S.2d 548, 134 A.D.2d 729 (Nov. 19, 1987)

106. People v. Hampton. 746 P.2d 947 (Colo. Sup. Ct.) (Nov. 30, 1987)

107. Busby v. State. 741 S.W.2d 109 (Mo. App.) (Dec. 8, 1987)

108. State v. Hasan. 205 Conn. 485, 534 A.2d 877 (Dec. 15, 1987)

109. Harward v. Commonwealth. 5 Va.App. 468, 364 S.E.2d 511 (Jan. 19, 1988)

110. DuBoise v. State. 520 So.2d 260 (Fla. Sup. Ct.) (Feb. 4, 1988)

    (Supersedes #89 above)

111. State v. Pierce. Slip opinion not designated for publication. Supreme Court of Kansas (Feb. 19, 1988)

112. Valenti v. Akron Police Dept.. et al. Slip opinion, Court of Appeals of Ohio, 9thApp.Dist. (Mar. 2, 1988)

113. People v. Howard. 529 N.Y.S.2d 51, 139 A.2d 927 (Apr. 8, 1988)

114. State v. Armstrong. 369 S.E.2d 870 (W.Va.) (Apr. 22, 1988)

115. Mitchell v. State. 527 So.2d 179 (Fla. Sup. Ct.) (May 19, 1988)

116. State v. Jamison. Slip opinion, not designated for publication, Supreme Court of Kansas (June 3, 1988)

117. People v. Ferguson. 172 Ill.App.3d 1, 526 N.E.2d 525 (June 30, 1988)

118. People v. Rich. 755 P.2d 960 (Cal. Sup. Ct.) (June 30, 1988)

119. People v. Randt. 530 N.Y.S.2d 266, 142 A.2d 611 (July 5, 1988)

120. State v. Kirsch. Unpublished opinion, Wis. Ct. of App. (July 20, 1988)

121. Commonwealth v. Jones. 403 Mass. 279, 526 N.E.2d 1288 (Aug. 18, 1988)

122. Andrews v. State. 533 So.2d 841 (Fla.App.5 Dist) (Oct. 20, 1988)

123. People v. Hemandez. 253 Cal.Rptr. 199, 763 P.2d 1289 (Nov. 28, 1988)

124. State v. Combs. 1988 Ohio App. Slip opinion, (Dec. 2, 1988)

125. Commonwealth v. Edwards. 521 Pa. 134, 555 A.2d 818 (Mar. 6, 1989)

126. State v. Turner. Slip opinion, Term. Cr. App. (Mar. 20, 1989)

127. People v. Marsh. 441 N.W.2d 33 (Mich.App. 1989) (May 15, 1989)

128. Commonwealth v. Thomas. 561 A.2d 699 (Pa. 1989) (June 27, 1989)

129. Bromley v. State. 380 S.E.2d 694 (Ga. 1989) (June 30, 1989)

130. Chaney v. State. 775 S.W.2d 722 (Texas App. - Dallas) (July 5, 1989)

131. Green v. State. 542 N.E.2d 977 (Ind. 1989) (Aug. 30, 1989)

132. Fox v. State. 779 P.2d 562 (Okl. Crim. App.) (Aug. 30, 1989)

133. State v. Mebane. 19 Conn. App. 618, 563 A.2d 1026 (Sept. 9, 1989)

134. State v. Hill. Slip Opinion, Ohio App. (Nov. 27, 1989)

135. Cox v. State. 555 So.2d 352 (Sup.Ct. of Florida) (Dec. 21, 1989)

136. Commonwealth v. Henry. 524 Pa. 135, 569 A.2d 929 (Feb. 8, 1990)

137. Litaker v. State. 784 S.W.2d 739 (Tex. App.) (Feb. 21, 1990)

138. People v. Bass. 553 N.Y.S.2d 794, 160 A.D.2d 715 (April 2, 1990)

139. Bouie v. State. 559 So.2d 1113 (Sup. Ct. of Florida) (April 5, 1990)

140. Monk v. Zeiez. 901 F.2d 885 (10th Cir.) (April 25, 1990)
     (Monk is also known as Martin of case #'s 16 and 31)

141. State v. Ford. 301 S.C. 485, 392 S.E.2d 781 (May 7, 1990)

142. People v. Calabro. 555 N.Y.S.2d 321, 161 A.D.2d 375 (May 15, 1990)

143. Williams v. State. 790 S.W.2d 643 (Tex. Crim. App.) (June 6, 1990)

144. Spence v. State. 795 S.W.2d 743 (Tex. Crim. App.) (June 13, 1990)

145. State v. Richards. 166 Ariz. 576, 804 P.2d 109 (Aug. 7, 1990)

146. Howard v. Kellv. Slip opinion, (US Dist. Ct. W.D. New York) (Sept. 18, 1990)
(Same Defendant/Same incident as in Case #113)

147. Baker v. State. 797 S.W.2d 406 (Tex. App.) (Oct. 19, 1990)

148. State v. Gardner. Slip opinion, (Tenn. Crim. App.) (Oct. 25, 1990)

149. State v. Jackson. 570 So.2d 227 (La. App. 5 Cir.) (Nov. 14, 1990)

150. Mallory v. State. 563 N.E.2d 640 (Ind. App. 1 Dist.) (Dec. 10, 1990)

151. Salazar v. State. Slip opinion, (Tex. App.-Houston) (Jan. 10, 1991)

152. People v. Cardenas. 209 Ill.App.3d 217, 568 N.E.2d 102 (Jan. 16, 1991)

153. Harris v. State. 260 Ga. 860, 401 S.E.2d 263 (Feb. 28, 1991)

154. State v. Wimberly. 467 N.W.2d 499, (Sup. Ct. of So. Dakota)(March 20,1991)

155. Wilhoit v. State. 809 P.2d 1322 (Ct. of Crim. App. ofOkla.) (April 16, 1991)
816 P.2d 545 (same opinion with appendix)

156. Williams v. State. 815 S.W.2d 743 (Tex. App.-Waco) (May 30, 1991)

157. People v. Perkins. 216 Ill.App.3d 389, 576 N.E.2d 355, (June 28, 1991)

158. State v. Edwards. Slip opinion, (Ohio App.) (July 3, 1991)

159. Adams v. Peterson. 939 F.2d 1369 (9th Cir.) (July 30, 1991)
     (Opinion withdrawn March 27, 1992)

160. People v. Case. 218 Ill.App.3d 146, 577 N.E.2d 1291 (July 30, 1991)

161. State v. Thomas. 329 N.C. 423, 407 S.E.2d 141 (Aug. 14, 1991)
     (same defendant/same case as #238)

162. Deutscher v. Whitlev. 946 F.2d 1443 (9th Cir.) (Oct. 15, 1991)
     (Same Defendant/Same Incident as Case #18)

163. Washington v. State. 822 S.W.2d 110 (Tex App-Waco) (Nov. 20, 1991)
     (Co-Defendant of #156)

164. State v. Correia. 600 A.2d 279 (Sup. Ct. of Rhode Island) (Dec. 5, 1991)

165. People v. Stanciel. 225 I1L App. 3d 1082, 589 N.E. 2d 557 (Dec. 11, 1991)

166. State v. Ukofia. unpublished opinion, Minn. Ct. of App. (Dec. 17, 1991)

167. State v. Pearson. 479 N.W.2d 401, Minn. Ct. of App. (Dec. 31, 1991)

168. Davasher v. State. 308 Ark 154, 823 S.W. 2d 863 (Jan. 27, 1992)

169. Mitchell v. State. 595 So. 2d 938, Florida Supreme Court, (Feb. 6, 1992)
     (Another appeal of Case #115)

170. State v. Joubert. 603 A. 2d 861, Maine Supreme Court, (Feb. 21, 1992)

171. Williams v. State. 829 S.W. 2d 216, (Tex. Crim. App-En Bane) (April 15, 1992)
(Same Defendant/Same incident as case's #143 & 156)

172. State v. Williams. 80 Ohio App. 3d 648, 610 N.E. 2d 545 (May 20, 1992)

173. Adams v. Peterson. 968 F.2d 835 (9th Cir) (June 24, 1992)
(Same Defendant/Same incident as case #159)

174. State v. Hill. 64 Ohio St. 3d 313, 595 N.E. 2d 884 (Aug. 12, 1992)
(Same Defendant/Same incident as case #134)

175. People v. Dunsworth. 233 IU. App. 3d 258, 599 N.E. 2d 29 (Aug. 19, 1992)

176. People v. Holmes. 234 IU. App. 3d 931, 601 N.E. 2d 985 (Sept. 8, 1992)

177. Freeman v. State. Slip opinion (Alabama Crim. App.) (Sept. 18, 1992)

178. U.S. ex rel. Milone v. Camp. Slip opinion (U.S. Dist. Court, N.D. IL.) (Sept. 29, 1992) (Same defendant/same incident as case #7and #204)

179. Williams v. State. 838 S.W. 2d 952, (Tex. App.- Waco) (Oct. 14, 1992)
(Same defendant/same incident as case #143, 156, 8s 171)

180. Harris v. State. Slip opinion, (Arkansas App.) (Nov. 18, 1992)

181. People v. Stanciel. 153 IU. 2d 218, 606 N.E. 2d 1201 (Nov. 19, 1992)
(Same defendant/same incident as case #165)

182. People v. Blommaert. 237 IU. App. 3d 811, 604 N.E. 2d 1054 (Nov. 30, 1992)

183. State v. Jones. 83 Ohio App. 3d 723, 615 N.E. 2d 713 (Dec. 2, 1992)

184. Davis v. State. 611 So. 2d 906 (Miss. Sup. Ct.) (Dec. 17, 1992)

185. People v. Noguera. 4 Cal. 4th 599, 842 P. 2d 1160 (Dec. 28, 1992)

186. R.M. v. Dept. of Health & Rehabilitation Services. 617 So. 2d 810 (Fla. App.) (April 30, 1993)

187. State v. Bennett. 503 N.W. 2d 42, (Iowa. App.) (May 4, 1993)

188. State v. Schaefer. 855 S.W. 2d 504 (Mo. App.) (June 22, 1993)

189. Spindle v. Berrong. 996 F. 2d 311 (Table) Unpublished Disposition (U.S. Court of Appeals,   10th Circuit - Kan.) (June 24, 1993)

190. U.S. v. Dia. 826 F. Supp. 1237 (U.S. Dist. Ct. Ariz) (July 8, 1993)

191. Murphy v. State. Slip opinion, not designated for publication, (Tex. App.-Dallas) (July 20, 1993)

192. State v. DonnelL 826 S.W. 2d 445 (Mo. App.) (Sept. 21, 1993)

193. State v. Williams. 865 S.W. 2d 794 (Mo. App.) (Oct. 13, 1993)

194. Rodoussakis v. Hosey. 8 F. 3d 820 (U.S. Ct. of Appeals 4th Cir. W.Va) (Oct. 20, 1993)

195. State v. Lyons. 124 Or.App. 598, 863 P.2d 1303 (Nov. 17, 1993)

196. State v. Welbum. Slip Opinion (Ohio App.) (Nov. 17, 1993)

197. Verdict v. State. 315 Ark 436, 868 S.W.2d 443 (Dec. 20, 1993)

198. Kinney v. State. 315 Ark. 481, 868 S.W.2d 463 (Jan. 10, 1994)

199. State v. Hodgson. 512 N.W.2d 95 (Minn.Sup.Ct.) (Feb. 11, 1994)

200. State v. Cazes. 875 S.W.2d 253 (Tenn.Sup.Ct.) (Feb. 14, 1994)

201. Mobley v. State. 212 Ga.App. 293, 441 S.E.2d 780 (Feb. 16, 1994)

202. People v. Gallo. 260 IU.App.3d 1032, 632 N.E.2d 99 (Mar. 18, 1994)

203. Harrison v. State. 635 So.2d 894 (Miss.Sup.Ct.) (Apr. 14, 1994)

204. Milone v. Camp. 22 F.3d 693 (7th Cir.) (Apr. 21, 1994)

(Same defendant/same incident as cases #7 and #178)

205. Morgan v. State. 639 So.2d 6 (Flor.Sup.Ct.) (June 2, 1994)

206. Commonwealth v. Alvarado. 36 Mass.App.Ct. 604, 634 N.E.2d 132 (June 3, 1994)

207. State v. Hummert. Slip Opinion, (Ariz.App.Div.I) (July 26, 1994)

208. People v. Brown. 162 Misc.2d 555, 618 N.Y.S.2d 188 (N.Y.Co.Ct.) (Oct. 6, 1994)

209. State v. Martin. 645 So.2d 190, (La.Sup.Ct.) (Oct. 18, 1994)

210. U.S. ex rel Dace v. Welbom. Memorandum opinion, US Dist. Court, N.D. IL
(Same defendant/same incident as case #91) (Oct. 25, 1994)

211. State v. Carpentier. unpublished opinion, Minn. Ct. of Appeals (Dec. 6, 1994)

212. People v.Tripp. 271 Ill.App.3d 194, 648 N.E.2d 241 (March 10, 1995)

213. Brim v. State. 654 So.2d 184 (Flor. App.2d Dist.) (April 12, 1995)

214. State vs. Wamess 77 Wash.App. 636, 893 P.2d 665 (May I, 1995)

215. Chaplin vs. McGrath 85 Donohue. 626 N.Y.S.2d 294 (May 4, 1995)

216. Bass v. Scully. Memorandum Order, U.S. Dist. Court, Eastern Dist. N.Y.
(Same defendant/same incident as case #138) (May 25, 1995)

217. People v. Rush. 630 N.Y.S.2d 631 (N.Y.- Sup. Ct. Kings Co.) (June 7, 1995)

218. State v. Mann. Slip opinion (Ohio App. 8th Dist.) (June 15, 1995)

219. Purser v. State. 902 S.W.2d 641 (Texas App.-El Paso) (June 15, 1995)

220. State v. Krone. 182 Ariz. 319, 897 P.2d 621 (Ariz.Sup.Ct.) (June 22, 1995)

221. Tuggle v. Thompson. 57 F.3d 1356 (U.S.Ct of Appeals - 4th Circuit-Virginia)
(Same defendant/same incident as case #63 and #71) (June 29, 1995)

222. State v. Boles. Slip opinion, (Ariz. Ct. of Appeals) (Aug.3, 1995)

223. State v. Teasley. Slip opinion (Ohio App. 8th Dist.) (Aug. 17, 1995)

224. People v. Cumbee. Unpublished, not precedential, opinion, (Ill.App.Ct. 2nd Dist.) (Nov. 15, 1995)

225. Franks v. State. 666 So.2d 763, (Mississippi Sup. Ct) (Nov. 30, 1995)

226. Hodgson v. State. 540 N.W.2d 515, (Minnesota Sup. Ct.) (Dec. 15, 1995)
(same defendant/same incident as case #199)

227. Jackson v. Day. Slip Opinion, (U.S. Dist. Ct. E.D. Louisiana, Jan. 9, 1996)
(Jackson is same defendant/same incident as case #149 and #231)

228. People v. Shaw. 278 Ill.App.3d 939, 664 N.E.2d 97 (March 26, 1996)

229. Spence v. Johnson. 80 F.3d 989, U.S. Ct. of Appeals 5th Circuit Texas
(Same defendant/same incident as in case #144) (March 29, 1996)

230. Tuggle v. Netherland. 79 F.3d 1386, U.S. Ct of Appeals 4th Circuit, Virginia
(Same defendant/same incident as case #63, #71 and #221) (April 3, 1996)

231. Jackson v. Day. Slip opinion, U.S. Dist. Ct, E.D. Louisiana
(Jackson is same defendant/same incident as case #149 and #227) (May 2, 1996)

232. People v. Payne. 282 Ill.App. 3d 307, 667 N.E. 2d 643 (June 19, 1996)

233. State v. Wilkinson. 344 N.C. 198, 474 S.E.2d 375, (Sept. 6, 1996)

234. Government of The Virgin Islands v. Byers. Slip opinion, Dist. Ct. Virgin Islands. (Oct. 11, 1996)

235. State v. Lyons. 324 Or. 256, 294 P 2d. 802, (Oct. 11, 1996)

236. State v. Hamilton. Slip opinion. Court of Appeals of Ohio, 2nd Dist. not designated for publication (Oct. 25, 1996)

237. Johnson v. State. 326 Ark. 430, 934 S.W.2d 179 (Oct. 28, 1996)

238. State v. Thomas. 344 N.C. 639, 477 S.E.2d 450 (Nov. 8, 1996)
      (same defendant/same case as #161)

239. Al-Mosawi v. State. 929 P.2d 270 (Okla. Crim. App) (Nov. 21, 1996)

240. McGrew v. State. 673 N.E. 2d 787 (Ind.App.) (Nov. 27, 1996)

241. Brown v. State. 690 So.2d 276, (Miss. Sup. Ct.) (Dec. 12, 1996)

242. Move v. State. Slip opinion, (Tex. App. - Dallas) (April 16, 1997)
      Not designated for publication

243. Howard v. State. 697 So.2d 415, (Miss. Sup. Ct.) (June 26, 1997)

244. Brown v. Commonwealth. 25 Va.App. 171, 487 S.E.2d 248, (July 8, 1997)

245. Marquez v. State. Slip opinion, (Tex.App. - Dallas) (July 15, 1997)
      Not designated for publication

246. State v. Kiser. 87 Wash. App. 126, 940 P. 2d 308, (July 28, 1997)

247. Rios v. State. Slip opinion (Tex. App. - San Antonio) (Oct. 31, 1997)
Not designated for publication

248. Banks v. State. Slip opinion, (Miss. Sup. Ct.) (December 8, 1997)

249. Commonwealth v. Henry. 706 A.2d 313 (Pa. 1997) (December 23, 1997)
      (Same defendant/same incident as case #136)

250. People v. Daniels. 73 Cal.Rptr. 2d 399, (Cal. App.) (March 12, 1998)

251. People v. Steward. 295 IU. App. 3d 735, 693 N.E.2d 436 (March 31, 1998)

252. State v. Butler. Slip Opinion (Mo.App.) (March 31, 1998)

253. State v. Landers. 969 S.W.2d 808 (Mo. App.) (May 26, 1998)

254. Brewer v. State. 725 So.2d 106 (Miss. Sup. Ct) (July 23, 1998)

255. Walters v. State. 720 So.2d 856 (Miss. Sup. Ct.) (Aug. 20, 1998)

256. Middleton v. State. 114 Nev. 1089, 968 P.2d 296, Nov. 25, 1998

257. Waltman v. State. 734 So.2d 324 (Miss.App) Feb. 23, 1999

258. State v. Fortin. 318 N.J.Super.577, 724 A.2d. 818, March 1, 1999

259. State v. Mataya. unpublished opinion (Wisc.App) Mar 17, 1999

260. State v. Anderson. 350 N.C. 153, 513 S.E.2d 296, April 9, 1999

261. State v. Davidson. 267 Kan. 667, _____ P.2d ___, July 9, 1999

262. Brooks v. State. (Miss. Sup.Ct.) Oct. 7, 1999

LAW REVIEW ARTICLES

11 Santa Clara Computer 85 High Tech L.J. 269 (July 1995)
2 Health Matrix, Journal of Law-Medicine 303Case Western Reserve University School of Law Summer, 1992
24 American Criminal Law Review 983 (1987)
37 Florida Law Review 889 (1985)

16 Cumberland Law Review 127 (1985-86)

12 Western State University Law Review 519 (Spring, 1985)

61 North Carolina Law Review at 1149 (1983)

4 Campbell Law Review 179 (Fall, 1981)

32 So. Car. Law Review 119 (October, 1980)

51 So. Cal. Law Review 309 (1978)

77 ALR 3d 1108 (1977 8s 1999 supp.)

Articles

"Bite Mark Evidence: Making an impression in court" by Captain D. Ben Tesdahl in The Army Lawyer, July, 1989

"Bite Mark Evidence: Its Worth in the Eyes of the Expert" by Pamela Zarkowski in Journal of Law and Ethics in Dentistry, Vol. 1, No. 1, 1988

1999 Haskell M. Pitluck

Index

A

ABFO 360
Abnormalities of Tooth formation and Eruption xiv
Abuse xiii, 19, 223, 240
Abuse and Neglect xiii, 19, 223, 240
Abuse of the Disabled xvi, 235
ADA approved 41
Addictions xiv, 67
Adobe Photoshop xvii, 306
Advanced Photographic Techniques xvi, 262
Advantages of DR Technology xvi, 274
Age xiii, 53, 55, 64
Age Estimation xiii, 53, 55, 64
ALI Protocol xvi, 264
Allele 80
Alternate Light Imaging (ALI/Fluorescent Photography) xvi
Amalgam 35, 47, 125, 292, 300
American Academy of Forensic Sciences AAFS iii, xi, 2, 97, 101, 114, 208, 355, 367
American Society of Forensic Dentistry ASFO 1
AmpFLP 85, 86
Analysis of Restorative Materials xvii
Antemortem xiii, 26
Antemortem Considerations xiii, 26
Antemortem Section xiv, 117, 119, 145
Anthropology xiv, 5, 62
aperture 11, 246, 248, 250, 260, 267, 268, 269
Aperture Range 250
A tort 331
Autopsy xiii, 32
Autoradiograph 80

B

Biochemical xiv, 57
Biochemical Changes xiv, 57
Biological Agents xv, 155, 159
Biological Weapons xv, 154
Bioterrorism xiii, xiv, xv, 9, 19, 29, 153, 154, 158, 159
Bioterrorism and Weapons of Mass Destruction xv, 153
Bite Mark xv, xvii, 26, 217, 293
Bite Mark Analysis xv, xvii, 26, 217, 293

Bite Mark Cases xvi, 256, 353
BITE MARK CITATIONS 392
Bitewing 51
Burning Process xiii, 45

C

Camera Body 248, 251
CASEWORKS 306, 307, 308, 309, 310
casts 30, 33, 41, 51, 72, 283, 293, 295, 322, 323, 324, 331, 332, 334, 335
CBCT Role in Forensic Odontology xvii, 283
CCD 24, 144, 253, 273, 274, 279
CE Type 1 125, 126
CE Type 2 125, 126
CE Type 3 125, 126
CE Type 4 125
CE Type 5 125
chain of evidence 31, 41, 143, 244, 276
Charting xiii, 27
Charting, Retention of Records and Data Bases xiii, 27
Chemical Composition of DNA xiv
Child Abuse xvi, 211, 225
Child Abuse/Neglect xvi, 211, 225
Child Neglect xvi, 211, 225
Child protective service 3
Children xiii, 8, 14, 32, 33, 64, 212, 224, 239
Chromosome 80
Class characteristics 177
Clinical xiii, 29
Clinical Record xiii, 29
Communication xiv, 109, 112
Comparison xiii, xiv, xvi, 17, 23, 51, 74, 79, 80, 117, 127, 148, 162, 276, 295
Comparison Section xiv, 117, 127, 148
Compensation xiv, 111, 129, 152, 329
Computer Hardware xvii
Computer Software xvii, 144
Computer System xiv, 128
Cone-Beam Computed Tomography (CBCT) xvii, 282
Criminal Justice Information Services 16
Criminal Justice Information Services (CJIS) Division. 16
Criminal Law 331, 399
Critical Errors 125, 126
Cross Examination xvii, 328

D

Data Bases xiii, 27
Daubert 316, 317, 318, 351, 352, 357
Deceased xiv, 60
Deceased Individuals xiv, 60
Decomposition xiii, 38
Degradation of DNA 80
Dental xiii, 47
Dental Age Estimation xiii, 55, 64
Dental Evidence xiii, 47
Dental Identification xiii, xiv, xvii, 8, 16, 19,
    29, 112, 113, 115, 123, 277, 278
Dental Identification Team xiv, 19, 112, 113,
    115
Dental Jurisprudence xvii, 357
dental pulp 58, 72, 73, 87, 88, 333
Dental Testimony xvii, 342
Diffraction 246
Digital Based Photography xvi, 252
Digital Radiology
  DR xvi
Direct Examination xvii, 327
Disadvantages of DR Technology xvi, 275
District attorneys 3
DMAT xiv, xv, 108, 130, 136, 137, 152, 153
DMORT vii, viii, xiii, xiv, xv, 19, 108, 113,
    126, 130, 131, 132, 133, 135, 136,
    137, 138, 139, 140, 141, 145, 146,
    147, 148, 149, 150, 151, 152, 165,
    278, 279, 280
DNA xiv, 74
DNA from Oral Tissues xiv, 87
Dog Bite xviii, 390
Doyle v State of Texas 170, 314
Duplicated Radiographs 23

E

EDUCATIONAL OUTCOMES 6, 90, 166,
    207, 241
Educational Outcomes 310, 350
Elder Abuse xvi, 227, 232, 234
Electromagnetic xvi, 263
Electromagnetic Spectrum and Photography
    xvi, 263
Electronic Flash 250
Electronic Imaging xvi, 272
Electrophoretic gel 81
Emergency Medical Care xiii
Emotional Maltreatment xvi, 221
Endodontics 333
Energy Dispersive X-Ray Spectroscopy xvii,
    285
Equipment for Forensic Dentistry – Film
    Based xvi, 248
Ethical Considerations xvii, 339, 353
Ethnicity xiv, 64
Evidence xiii, xiv, 47, 87
Evidence-Based 357, 358
Evidence Management xvii, 321
Examination xv, xvi, xvii, 64, 182, 194, 236,
    295, 296, 327, 328
Exclusion 53
Exemplar Analyses xvii, 295
Expert Witness xvii, 318, 325, 342, 352, 353
Exploiting or corrupting 221
Exposure xvi, 21, 23, 94, 158, 248, 260,
    265, 311
Extraoral Incisions 43

F

Facial Reconstruction xiii, 12
Facial Superimposition xiii, 9
FBI iv, 16, 26, 107, 108, 109, 120, 139, 154,
    159, 160, 166, 276
Fifth Degree Burns or cremated remains 45
Film xvi, 11, 23, 50, 93, 244, 245, 248, 249,
    250, 251, 268, 270, 276, 312
Film Based Photography
  Film
    Photography xvi, 244
Film Processing 23
Fingerprinting xiii
First Degree Burns 44
Forensic Dentist xiii, 6
Forensic Imaging Techniques xiii, 20
Forensic Odontology i, ii, iii, vii, viii, x, xi, xii,
    xiii, xvi, xvii, xviii, 4, 5, 8, 16, 17, 18,
    20, 26, 103, 114, 160, 164, 237, 283,
    306, 344, 351, 352, 353, 354, 357
Fourth Degree Burns 44
FRE 316, 317, 318, 357

G

Gene iv, 81, 91, 310
Genetic (DNA) Comparison xiv, 74
Gross characteristics 177
Guidelines 360

H

Habits xiv, 67
Habits and Addictions xiv, 67

Hand Held Portable X-Ray xvii, 278
HIPAA viii, xvii, 31, 331, 344, 345, 346, 347,
    349, 351, 353
Histological xiii, 57
Histological Changes xiii, 57
Historical Programs xvii, 303
Homicide xviii, 176, 390
HUMAN ABUSE xvi, 210
HUMAN ABUSE AND NEGLECT xvi, 210
Human Identification xiii
HUMAN NEGLECT xvi, 210
Hurricane Katrina viii, xv, 135, 136, 141,
    145, 148, 165, 278, 279, 280

I

Identification xiii, xiv, xv, xvi, xvii, 8, 9, 16,
    18, 19, 29, 32, 39, 48, 53, 103, 106,
    112, 113, 115, 116, 123, 128, 135, 155,
    158, 160, 237, 255, 277, 278, 303,
    308, 346, 348, 354
Identification Cases xvi, xvii, 255, 277
Ignoring 221
Image Comparison 23
Imaging Techniques xiii, 20
Immunity xvii, 342
Incident Command System (ICS) xiv, 109,
    137
Incineration xiii, 44
individual characteristics 171, 179, 180, 204,
    293, 295, 296
Infrared Photography
    IR xvi
Infrared Protocol xvi, 270
Injury xv, xvii, 96, 199, 201, 238, 241, 242,
    337, 351, 352
Innov-X 299
Interpretation of Analyses xvii, 295
Intimate Partner Violence
    IPV xvi, 225
Invasive Analyses xv, 189, 209
Isolating 221

J

Jaw artiulation 40
Jaw Resection 43
Junk Science and Pseudoscience 356
JURISPRUDENCE 314

K

Katrina viii, xv, 126, 133, 134, 135, 136, 137,

    138, 139, 141, 142, 144, 145, 146,
    148, 149, 150, 151, 152, 165, 167,
    272, 278, 279, 280, 303, 375, 378,
    379, 383
Kelly/Frye 316, 317

L

Laboratory xiv, xv, 4, 31, 48, 86, 352
Lateral jaw 51
Lateral skull 51
Length specific typing 81
Lenses 244, 245, 248, 249, 250
LEO 106, 107, 367, 368, 369
light 25, 40, 47, 49, 50, 71, 72, 77, 80, 87,
    89, 92, 110, 112, 161, 168, 182, 185,
    194, 204, 244, 245, 246, 248, 249,
    250, 251, 252, 253, 258, 259, 260,
    261, 262, 263, 264, 265, 267, 268,
    270, 271, 272, 274, 275, 282, 285,
    287, 294, 306, 311, 312, 315, 323,
    349, 390
Living Individuals xiv, 58
Locus 81
Louisiana 379

M

Macro zoom 250
Malpractice xvii, 330, 333, 334, 335, 352
Management of the Evidence xiv, 87
Maples' Aging Method xiv
Medical Conditions and Treatments xiv, 66
Medical Conditions with Oral Hard Tissue
    Manifestations xiv
medical examiners 16, 115, 129, 132, 343,
    344, 345
Methods of DNA Analysis xiv, 84
ME Type 2 125
ME Type I 125
ME Type I - 125
Microsatellite 82, 85
Minisatellite 82
Minor Errors 125
Mitochondrial DNA (mtDNA) xiv, 77
MNR Type 1 125
MNR Type 2 126
Moderate Errors 125, 126
Multiple Fatality Incident xiv, 8, 103, 106
Munchausen by Proxy Syndrome
    MBPS xvi, 224

N

National Dental Image Repository (NDIR) xiv, 8, 106
National Incident Management System xiv, 109, 137
National Response Plan xiv, 108, 109, 112, 136
NCIC 8, 26, 29, 105, 106, 107, 366, 368, 369, 370
NDIR xiv, 8, 106, 367, 368, 369
Neglect xiii, 19, 223, 240
Neglecting the child 221
Neglective Abuse xvi, 221, 223
NIMS Integration Center (NIC) xiv, 109, 112
NOMAD 280, 312
Notification of Team Existence xiv, 115
NRP Maintenance xiv, 109, 112

O

occlusal analysis 40
Occupation xiv, 64, 65
Odontologist iii, xiv, xvii, 86, 318, 352
Odontology i, ii, iii, vii, viii, x, xi, xii, xiii, xvi, xvii, xviii, 3, 4, 5, 6, 8, 16, 17, 18, 20, 26, 91, 92, 93, 94, 97, 103, 114, 160, 164, 170, 182, 204, 205, 208, 209, 237, 283, 306, 310, 312, 344, 351, 352, 353, 354, 357, 358, 359, 360, 366, 367
Oligonucleotides 82
Optical Physics xvi, 244
Oral and Maxillofacial Surgery 333
Oral Autopsy xiii, 32
Oral Hard Tissue Manifestations xiv, 66
Organization xiv, 117
Organization and Planning for Emergency Management xiv, 108

P

PAGE 82, 85
PANDA xvi, 240
Partial Decomposition xiii, 38
Partial Remains xiii, 48
PCR 72, 80, 83, 84, 85, 86, 87
Peer Review 355
Periapical 22, 35, 51
Periodontics 333
Personal Effects xiii, 9
Personal Injury Cases xvii, 337, 352
Personal Recognition xiii, 9
Photographs 20, 40, 119, 126, 185, 195, 255, 256, 257, 259, 261, 323

Photography xiii, xiv, xvi, 20, 117, 118, 244, 252, 255, 263, 267, 268, 270
Physical Abuse xvi, 215, 218
Place of Residence xiv, 70
Plaintiff Review xvii, 336
Point Flash 250
Polymorphism 83
Portable X-Ray Generators xvii, 279
Possible Identification - 53
posterior teeth 44, 47, 48, 53
Post Mortem xiii, xiv, 32, 117, 118, 128, 140, 146, 160, 162, 303
Post Mortem Section xiv, 117, 140, 146, 162
Pre-Trial Preparation xvii, 320, 352
Preparedness xiv, 109, 112
Privacy xvii, 344, 345, 347, 348, 350
Professional Ethics xvii, 339
Professional Liability Issues xvii, 330, 352
Progressive Changes in Developing Teeth xiii, 56
Protocols for Use in Future Multiple Fatality Incidents xv
Pseudoscience 356, 357, 358
Purification of DNA 83

Q

Quality of DNA 83
Quantity of DNA 83

R

Radiography xiii, xiv, 8, 20, 24, 117, 118, 119, 144, 273
Radiography and Photography Section xiv, 118
Radioisotope 83
Radiology xvi, 271
Record xiii, 29
Records xiii, 17, 27, 30, 31, 120, 121, 125, 126
Records Availability xiii, 17
Reference specimen 83
Reflective xvi, 267
Regina v. Boden 170
Rejecting 221
Residence xiv, 70
resins 48, 92, 94, 288, 289, 300, 301, 312
Resources xvi, xviii, 109, 141, 165, 238, 334, 366, 383
Responsibilities of the Odontologist xiv, 86
Restriction enzymes 83
Retention of Records xiii, 27

RFLP 83, 84, 85, 86, 87
Ring Flash 250
Rules of Evidence xvii, 314, 315, 316, 317,
    340, 351, 352, 357

S

Salivary DNA Recovered From Human Bite
    Marks xiv, 89
Salivary Trace Evidence 185
Scanning Electron Microscopy xiii, xvii, 25,
    284
Scientific Method 354
Second Degree Burns 44
SEM xvii, 25, 26, 284, 285, 288, 291, 292,
    293, 294, 295, 324
SEM/EDS xvii, 25, 26, 284, 288, 293
SEM Imaging Concepts xvii, 284
Sequence-specific typing 84
Sex xiv, 72
Sex Determination xiv, 72
Sexual Abuse xvi, 219, 220
Sinus 41
Skeletonized xiii, 22, 40, 48
Skeletonized Remains 40
Software xvii, 144, 164, 302, 303, 305
Software Programs xvii, 305
Standard of Care xvii, 333
Standard Photography Views xvi, 255
State Identification Teams xiii, 19
Stryker Saw 43
Suspect Examination xv, 194

T

Team Administration xiv, 115
Team Organization xiv, 117
Temporomandibular joint 51
Temporomandibular joint (TMJ) 51
Terrorizing 221
Testimony xvii, 96, 319, 326, 342, 352, 353
Third Degree Burns 44
Three-Dimensional Evidence xv, 186, 196
Tissue Depth for Reconstruction 361
Tissue Excision xv, 189
tool mark 168, 177, 179, 315, 318
Tooth Conversion Tables xviii, 371
Tooth Mineralization 61
Transillumination xv, 194, 209
Trauma xiii, xvi, 37, 38, 230, 236
TTL Film Plane Flash Metering 249
Two-Dimensional Evidence xv, 182, 195

U

Ultraviolet Photography xvi, 267, 268
Ultraviolet Photography Protocol xvi, 268
Undocumented Individuals xiii, 32

V

Verbally assaulting 221
Video Tapes 323
VNTR 80, 84, 85

W

Weapons Agents xv, 155
WIN ID xviii, 375
WIN ID Comparison Procedures xviii, 375
working distance 247, 250

X

X-Ray Fluorescence xvii, 296
X-ray Spectroscopy xiii, xvii, 25, 284